T0214112

Communications
in Computer and Information Science 1386

More information about this series at http://www.springer.com/series/7899

Minh Nguyen · Wei Qi Yan ·
Harvey Ho (Eds.)

Geometry and Vision

First International Symposium, ISGV 2021
Auckland, New Zealand, January 28–29, 2021
Revised Selected Papers

Springer

Editors
Minh Nguyen 🆔
Auckland University of Technology
Auckland, New Zealand

Wei Qi Yan 🆔
Auckland University of Technology
Auckland, New Zealand

Harvey Ho 🆔
Auckland Bioengineering House
Auckland, New Zealand

ISSN 1865-0929   ISSN 1865-0937   (electronic)
Communications in Computer and Information Science
ISBN 978-3-030-72072-8   ISBN 978-3-030-72073-5   (eBook)
https://doi.org/10.1007/978-3-030-72073-5

This Springer imprint is published by the registered company Springer Nature Switzerland AG
The registered company address is: Gewerbestrasse 11, 6330 Cham, Switzerland

Preface

The International Symposium on Geometry and Vision (ISGV 2021) took place on 28 and 29 January 2021 in Auckland, New Zealand. This was an international conference that brought together academics and researchers working in the areas of digital geometry, graphics, image and video technologies, computer vision, and multimedia technologies. ISVG 2021 was brought to you by the Centre for Robotics & Vision (CeRV), Auckland University of Technology (AUT), in collaboration with the University of Auckland. The best papers of this international symposium were awarded the Reinhard Klette Award to memorialize Professor Reinhard Klette, the founding Director of CeRV. Professor Reinhard Klette (1950–2020) was a Fellow of the Royal Society of New Zealand (RSNZ), a Helmholtz International Fellow (Germany), a Friendship Ambassador of Shandong province (Shandong, China), and a winner of the Quancheng Friendship Award (Jinan, China).

We invited submissions aiming either at highlighting relationships between adjacent topics within the listed areas or contributing to a particular topic within one area which is of fairly general interest. In the context of the listed areas, the submissions addressed the basics or applications under a geometric viewpoint in:

- Computer Vision,
- Robot Vision,
- Pattern Recognition and Machine Learning,
- Signal Processing,
- Multimedia Processing and Interaction,
- Medical Image Processing,
- Stereovision,
- HCI, AR, VR,
- Autonomous Vehicles,
- Others.

The conference was planned to take place at the end of 2020 (with the acronym of ISGV 2020). However, due to COVID-19 lockdowns the conference was put back for two months, to 28 and 29 January 2021 (with the acronym of ISGV 2021). This conference used double-blind review, which means both that the authors were concealed from the reviewers, and vice versa, throughout the review process. By the end, we had 50 full papers submitted to the EasyChair conference system. We received 136 reviews in total. The average number of reviews per paper was 2.72; on average, each reviewer was assigned approx. three papers to assess. After the double-blind reviewing process, 29 papers were accepted for presentation at the conference. This resulted in a 58% acceptance rate.

We, therefore, had 29 oral presentations, grouped in four sessions during the two days of the conference. From the selected papers, we chose three papers for the best paper awards (Reinhard Klette awards).

Additionally, we successfully invited three renowned keynote speakers:

- Professor Nikola Kasabov (Fellow IEEE, Fellow RSNZ, Fellow INNS College of Fellows) Professor at SECMS and Founding Director KEDRI, Auckland University of Technology, Auckland, New Zealand.
- Professor Richard Green (IEEE) Professor of Computer Science, Department of Computer Science and Software Engineering, College of Engineering, University of Canterbury, New Zealand.
- Professor Dacheng Tao (ARC Laureate Fellow, FACM, FIEEE, FAA) Professor of Computer Science, School of Computer Science, The University of Sydney, Australia.

February 2021

Minh Nguyen
Wei Qi Yan
Harvey Ho

Organization

General Chairs

Wei Qi Yan   Auckland University of Technology, New Zealand
Harvey Ho   University of Auckland, New Zealand

Program Committee Chairs

Minh Nguyen   Auckland University of Technology, New Zealand
Zhixun Su   Dalian University of Technology, China

Organization Chairs

Robert Yang   Auckland University of Technology, New Zealand
Gisela Klette   Auckland University of Technology, New Zealand
Yanqiang Li   Shandong Academy of Sciences, China

Steering Committee

Wei Qi Yan   Auckland University of Technology, New Zealand
Mariano Meraz   Centro de Investigación, Mexico
Atsushi Imiya   Chiba University, Japan
Domingo Mery   Pontificia Universidad Católica de Chile, Chile
Nicolai Petkov   University of Groningen, The Netherlands
Harvey Ho   University of Auckland, New Zealand
Jiande Sun   Shandong Normal University, China
Ryszard Kozera   Warsaw University of Life Sciences, Poland
Ralf Reulke   Humboldt University Berlin, Germany
Fay Huang   National Ilan University, Taiwan
Yanqiang Li   SDAS, China
Loulin Huang   Auckland University of Technology, New Zealand
Xiaoyi Jiang   University of Münster, Germany
Anko Börner   German Aerospace Center, Germany
Martin Stommel   Auckland University of Technology, New Zealand
Hsiang-Jen Chien   Auckland Transport, New Zealand
Derek Zhang   Auckland Transport, New Zealand
Zhixun Su   Dalian University of Technology, China
Akihiro Sugimoto   National Institute of Informatics, Japan
Minh Nguyen   Auckland University of Technology, New Zealand

Program Committee

Ahmed Al-Jumaily	Auckland University of Technology, New Zealand
Akihiro Sugimoto	National Institute of Informatics, Japan
Akila Pemasiri	Queensland University of Technology, Australia
Alfred M. Bruckstein	Technion - Israel Institute of Technology, Israel
Ali Reza Alaei	Southern Cross University, Australia
Amita Dhiman	Air New Zealand, New Zealand
Andrew Gilman	PlantTech Research Institute Limited, New Zealand
Andrew Lowe	Auckland University of Technology, New Zealand
Andy Nguyen	University of Oulu, Finland
Anko Börner	German Aerospace Center, Germany
Anthony Griffin	Auckland University of Technology, New Zealand
Atsushi Imiya	Chiba University, Japan
Brendon J. Woodford	University of Otago, New Zealand
Chris Rapson	Auckland Transport, New Zealand
Clinton Fookes	Queensland University of Technology, Australia
Cunjian Chen	Michigan State University, USA
Daisuke Miyazaki	Hiroshima City University, Japan
Daniel Lopresti	Lehigh University, USA
Derek Zhang	Auckland Transport, New Zealand
Domingo Mery	Pontificia Universidad Católica de Chile, Chile
Du Huynh	The University of Western Australia, Australia
Gunilla Borgefors	Uppsala University, Sweden
Fatih Kurugollu	University of Derby, UK
Fay Huang	National Ilan University, Taiwan
George Azzopardi	University of Groningen, The Netherlands
Haokun Geng	University of Auckland, New Zealand
Harvey Ho	University of Auckland, New Zealand
Hongmou Zhang	German Aerospace Center, Germany
Hsiang-Jen Chien	Auckland Transport, New Zealand
Ikuhisa Mitsugami	Hiroshima City University, Japan
Jean-Bernard Hayet	Centro de Investigación en Matemáticas, México
Jiande Sun	Shandong Normal University, China
Jules-Raymond Tapamo	University of KwaZulu-Natal, South Africa
Kar-Ann Toh	Yonsei University, South Korea
Kaushik Roy	West Bengal State University, India
Kazunori Okada	San Francisco State University, USA
Kien Nguyen Thanh	Queensland University of Technology, Australia
Loulin Huang	Auckland University of Technology, New Zealand
Lucio Marcenaro	University of Genoa, Italy
Mariano Meraz	Centro de Investigación en Matemáticas, Mexico
Mark Beckerleg	Auckland University of Technology, New Zealand
Mark Nixon	University of Southampton, UK
Martin Stommel	Auckland University of Technology, New Zealand
Michael Werman	The Hebrew University of Jerusalem, Israel

Minh Nguyen	Auckland University of Technology, New Zealand
Mohammad Norouzifard	Auckland University of Technology, New Zealand
Nicola Strisciuglio	University of Twente, The Netherlands
Nicolai Petkov	University of Groningen, The Netherlands
Noor Saleem	Auckland University of Technology, New Zealand
Parma Nand	Auckland University of Technology, New Zealand
Patrice Delmas	The University of Auckland, New Zealand
Ralf Reulke	Humboldt University Berlin, Germany
Robert Le	Auckland University of Technology, New Zealand
Ryszard Kozera	Warsaw University of Life Sciences, Poland
Samaneh Madanian	Auckland University of Technology, New Zealand
Sandino Morales	aescape, Mexico
Syeda Fouzia	Auckland University of Technology, New Zealand
Shmuel Peleg	The Hebrew University of Jerusalem, Israel
Titas De	AlignHD, India
Tom Moir	Auckland University of Technology, New Zealand
Trevor Gee	The University of Auckland, New Zealand
Wannes van der Mark	The University of Auckland, New Zealand
Wei Qi Yan	Auckland University of Technology, New Zealand
Xiaoyi Jiang	University of Münster, Germany
Xinguo Yu	Central China Normal University, China
Yanqiang Li	SDAS, China
Zahra Moayed	Auckland Transport, New Zealand
Zhixun Su	Dalian University of Technology, China

Additional Reviewers

Farah Sarwar	Mridul Ghosh
Henry Pham	Payel Rakshit
Huy Tran	Ramit Kr. Roy
Jia Lu	Sabeeha Mehtab
Jing Ma	Soumen Mukherjee
Ke Liu	Tung Nguyen
Kunal Das	Wenbo Wan
Liming Zou	Xiaoxu Liu

Sponsors

AUT - Electrical and Electronic Engineering Department
AUT - Computer Science Department
AUT - Information Technology and Software Engineering Department
Centre for Artificial Intelligence Research (CAIR) @ AUT
Centre for Robotics and Vision (CeRV) @ AUT
N3T.KIWI

Contents

A New Noise Generating Method Based on Gaussian Sampling for Privacy Preservation

Bo Ma[1]([⊠]), Wei Qi Yan[1], Edmund Lai[1], and Jingsong Wu[2,3]

[1] School of Engineering, Computer and Mathematical Sciences,
Auckland University of Technology, Auckland 1010, New Zealand
{bo.ma,weiqi.yan,edmund.lai}@aut.ac.nz
[2] Department of Electrical Engineering, Universidad de Chile, Santiago, Chile
jswu@ieee.org
[3] Department of Artificial Intelligence, Guilin University of Electronic Technology,
Guilin, China
http://www.aut.ac.nz

Abstract. Centralised machine learning brings in side effect pertaining to privacy preservation, most of machine learning methods prone to using the frameworks without privacy protection, as current methods for privacy preservation will slow down model training and testing. In order to resolve this problem, we develop a new noise generating method based on information entropy by using differential privacy for betterment the privacy protection which owns the architecture of federated machine learning. Our experiments unveil that this solution effectively preserves privacy in the vein of centralized federated learning. The gained accuracy is promising which has a room to be uplifted.

Keywords: Differential privacy · Noise generating · Gaussian subsampling

1 Introduction

Privacy leakage is defined in [16] as "the accidental or unintentional distribution of private or sensitive data to an unauthorized entity". The methods for tackling the private sensitive data include:

- randomization [23];
- k-anonymity [18] and l-diversity [13];
- distributed privacy preservation [12];
- downgrading the effectiveness of data mining [3]

Randomization by deliberately introducing noises into a datasets, is a simple and effective way to provide differential privacy (DP). It has been applied to adaptive boosting (AdaBoost) [14], principal component analysis (PCA) [21],

© Springer Nature Switzerland AG 2021
M. Nguyen et al. (Eds.): ISGV 2021, CCIS 1386, pp. 1–12, 2021.
https://doi.org/10.1007/978-3-030-72073-5_1

linear and logistic regression [8], support vector machines (SVM) [5], risk mini-mization [19], and continuous data processing [22]. A general mechanism to control the amount of added Gaussian noises was introduced in [6], in conjunction with the idea of ε-differential privacy, it provides the same amount of privacy to individuals so that the statistical results based on the dataset are roughly independent on the data of any individuals.

In this paper, we explore and exploit an image-based privacy preserving algorithm in the dataset where the noises of the data are identified. It is true that data sampling process is able to assist to identify information from the sensitive attributes. Furthermore, data sampling is a key determinant in measuring the quality of privacy preservation because the excellent methods for privacy preservation offer users to provenance their original data. The challenges are how to retrieve and connect those links together as evidences, so as to identify the levels of a user's privacy leakage, and trace unspecific users with a high accuracy. In this paper, we address the problem of data provenance from the viewpoint of collaborative learning for privacy preservation.

Our contribution in this paper is to present noise generating methods with a machine learning framework which outperforms the existing solutions. The remaining parts of this paper will be organized as follows. We present the existing methods for privacy preservation in Sect. 2.1, our proposed methods for privacy presentation will be explicated in Sect. 3. We will demonstrate our resultant evaluations in Sect. 4, our conclusion will be drawn in Sect. 5.

2 Related Work

2.1 Gaussian Noise Generating

Noise sampling and generating are the vital methods for protecting privacy in differential privacy. An approach by using Gaussian noise sampling $\{\phi_n\}$ was proffered [15] for privacy preservation. This approach applies probability density function (PDF) with noisy samples as $p_\phi(\phi_n)$ having zero mean, if the standard deviation and mean are denoted as σ and μ respectively, the PDF is

$$p_\phi(\phi_n) = \frac{1}{\sigma\sqrt{2\pi}} e^{-\frac{(\phi_n-\mu)^2}{2\sigma^2}}. \tag{1}$$

In Eq. (1), the Gaussian PDF is obtained from

$$\phi = \frac{1}{\sigma\sqrt{2\pi}} \int_{-\infty}^{\infty} e^{j\phi_n - (\frac{\mu^2}{2\sigma^2})\phi_n^2} d\phi_n \tag{2}$$

The Gaussian noise is generated from the PDF of samples,

$$E\{z\} = A^2[\Sigma_{n=1}^{N}|a_n|^2 + \frac{1}{\sigma\sqrt{2\pi}} e^{-\frac{(z-\mu)^2}{2\sigma^2}}] \tag{3}$$

where A^2 is the power of samples, $|a_n|^2$ is the deterministic weights, z is the discrete Fourier transform of the given samples.

However, this method relies on the PDF of input samples, the deviation of weighting coefficients $\{a_n\}$ depends on the PDF, the deviation of noises can not be employed to protect the privacy efficiency.

2.2 Whittle's Noise Estimator

In 1954, Whittle [20] proposed a method to estimate the noise level. In this method, it is assumed that x_t is the sample of $\mathbf{X} = \{x_t, t = 1, 2, \cdots, n\}$ in the self-fitting process. For this process, all other parameters except the variable $var(\mathbf{X})$ and the parameter H are known. Let $S(A : H)$ denote the power spectrum of $\mathbf{X}$ if it is normalized to the variance 1.0, let $I(A)$ denote the power spectrum of x_t, and the power spectrum is estimated by using Fourier transform. In order to estimate H, we need to find the minimum of H

$$g(\hat{H}) = \int_{-\pi}^{\pi} \frac{I(\lambda)}{f(\lambda : \hat{H})} d\lambda. \tag{4}$$

If the length of $\mathbf{X} = \{x_t, t = 1, 2, \cdots, n\}$ is n, then under the frequencies, the number is converted into a discrete summation

$$\lambda = \frac{2\pi}{n}, \frac{4\pi}{n}, \ldots, \frac{2(n-1)\pi}{n}. \tag{5}$$

This estimator reflects the truth that $I(A)$ is independent, the mean is subject to the distribution $f(A; H)$ as an exponential function, the variance of the estimator is

$$\sigma_H^2 = 4\pi \left[\int_{-\pi}^{\pi} \left(\frac{\log f(\omega)}{\log H} \right)^e d\omega \right]^{-1} \tag{6}$$

By examining the sample paths, Whittle's estimator is applied to compare with σ_H^2, which determines whether $\hat{H}$ is within the acceptable range of H. The Whittle's estimator is not a test regarding whether a sample is consistent with long-range dependence. Rather than, it is an estimator of H, given the assumption that the power spectrum of the underlying process corresponds to $f(\lambda : H)$.

2.3 The Method Based on Fourier Transform

A method [10] is proposed for synthesizing fractional Gaussian noises by using discrete time Fourier transform (DTFT), where $f(\lambda : H)$ is known as a variance, the fractional Gaussian noises have been generated via power spectrum. In addition, it constructs a sequence of complex numbers z which is akin to power spectrum, Besides, z_i is the sampling path for frequency-domain and an inverse discrete time Fourier transform is employed to find the best output of x_i related to z_i. Because x_i is generated from power spectrum of fractional Gaussian noises(FGN), FGN is automatically corrected via the power spectrum by utilizing the Fourier pair, hence, x_i is guaranteed to enable the automatic correction, this is also the salient attribute of FGN process.

However, this approach has a problem, because $f(\lambda : H)$ must be accurately computed, z_i is connected to the power spectrum of FGN. Hence, z_i is independent and $f(\lambda : H)$ may not be so accurate due to the changes of z_i.

Because DTFT and its inverse are rapidly computed by using fast Fourier transform (FFT), we prefer to using our method as an FFT method for synthesizing the fractional Gaussian noises. We will not prove that the method results in true FGN due to various approximations whilst the method is being developed. But we will assert that the method effectively produces FGN noises. By the way, the sample paths generated by using this method are indistinguishable with the current FGN tests for the purposes such as simulations, the sample paths are with a high degree of confidence.

2.4   Distributed SGD for Differential Privacy

Stochastic gradient descent (SGD) provides an effectively iterative solution to minimize a function so as to reach the local minimum, which has been applied to artificial neural networks, Bayesian networks, genetic algorithms, and simulated annealing. A SGD method for privacy preservation was proffered in 2016 [1]. In 2018, an efficient approach was developed and improved for privacy-preservation [2] so as to approach the local minimum. Thus, through a mapping $M : X \rightarrow O$, the privacy cost is defined as

$$Pr(M(f(D_1)) \in S) \leq e^\varepsilon Pr(M(f(D_2)) \in S) + \delta \qquad (7)$$

where $f(D)$ is an iteration for SGD, the probability δ means ε -differential privacy is breached, especially, the noises are generated by using [1].

$$M(f(D)) \triangleq f(D) + \mathcal{N}(0, S_f^2 \cdot \sigma^2) \qquad (8)$$

where $\mathcal{N}(0, S_f^2 \cdot \sigma^2)$ is the distribution of samples and S_f^2 is sensitivity of $f(\cdot)$.

To avoid the deviation problem in Eq. (3), we put forward a privacy preservation method to refrain this issue, set forth a privacy measurement to detect the deviation between training samples and added noises, the latter can be added during the training process. We compared the existing method in Eq. (8), the test result will be given in evolution phase.

3   Our Methods

3.1   Contribution

Our contribution in this paper is to present noise generating methods fit into the exists machine learning framework which outperforms the existing solutions. The remaining parts of this paper will be organized as follows. We present the existing methods for privacy preservation in Sect. 2.1, our proposed methods for privacy presentation will be explicated in Sect. 3. We will demonstrate our resultant evaluations in Sect. 4, our conclusion will be drawn in Sect. 5.

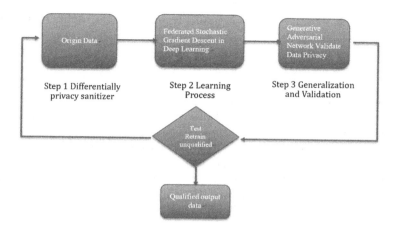

Fig. 1. The process for privacy preserving with Gaussian noise sampling

3.2 The Process of Our Methods

In order to protect the privacy, in this paper, we develop the method based on noise analysis [15] and link the existing approach with differential privacy [2]. Figure 1 shows the process to tackle the problem of privacy preservation by using federated machine learning. The first step is to run a sanitizer [4] for differential privacy. The sanitizer usually is denoted as an algorithm to protect ε-differential privacy. In privacy preservation, the dataset does not affect the sanitizer, the data entropy is measured by using estimators, the effective noisy pattern is identified.

The second step is a machine learning stage. In this step, the noises generated in the first step are injected into the data by using SGD in federated machine learning. The final step is related to generalization. The function is assigned for model validation which is related to privacy of the output data. In this step, generative adversarial network (GAN) is taken into account to detect data leakage. The last step is to generate similar data from the original input data so as to measure its privacy.

The fake data is employed to reproduce the privacy if the proposed privacy preserving method fails to protect privacy. The step 1, 2, and 3 are formed as a dynamic process, the noises need to be rechecked so as to ensure the original data is safe enough to defence privacy leakage.

3.3 Noise Variant in Stochastic Gradient Descent

For privacy preservation, we assume the distance between two datasets is $d(\mathbf{D}, \mathbf{D}') = \|\mathbf{D} - \mathbf{D}'\|$, an attacker is expected to infer whether the dataset is $\mathbf{D}$ or $\mathbf{D}'$, according to the distance between local sensitivity $f(\mathbf{D})$ and the output in local differential privacy or ε-differential privacy [7].

In order to protect the privacy in model training, recent results divulge that the variant of stochastic gradient descent achieves optimal error for minimizing Lipschitz convex functions over 2-bounded sets, the randomized 'dropout' is applied to prevent overfitting, which also strengthens the privacy and guaranteed to find the solution.

In previous work, this problem [17] is identified through collaborative deep learning under multiple participants. However, the existing algorithms [17] cannot be executed in complex environment, because most of data are stored in the cloud. The new challenge of collaborative deep learning is how to cooperate with the cloud and local terminals. Thus, the second problem is how to preserve the privacy during and after the model training process, how to balance the costs of privacy preservation and the utility of data output or training efficiency.

In order to balance the privacy cost and the utility of the resultant estimations in statistics, the boundary of mutual information has to be found and the noise subsampling has to be determined. These two steps will influence the amount of privacy preserved. The subsampling based on Gaussian distribution will be presented in the next section.

3.4   Gaussian Distribution for Subsampling

In the proposed solution, we mingle (Gaussian) distribution estimator for differential privacy, and machine learning algorithms together. We create this solution to speed up the model training process for privacy preservation, we also provide feedback mechanism to test results, and amend the generated noises in preparing stage. Our new approach leverages the impact between privacy and training. In addition, we use GAN-based generation method to measure and adjust the privacy level of output data so as to give feedback to the process of noise generating. In addition, differential privacy sanitizer is synthesized with traditional statistical methods like support vector machine or multilayer perceptron. Moreover, the kernel for pattern classification has been analysed via the sanitizer, the input data and generated noisy data are hashed in the learning process. In order to estimate the probability of privacy leakage from training output, the existing approach needs to test samples through our entropy analysis model. The entropy analysis is associated with data privacy protection.

We present the randomized method as $M : \mathbf{G} \rightarrow \mathbf{R}$ with Gaussian distribution $\mathbf{G}$ and range $\mathbf{R}$ which satisfies (ε, δ)-differential privacy. We assume the adjacent inputs as $i \in \mathbf{G}$, the random noise is $n' \in \mathbf{G}$ for any subset of outputs $D \subseteq \mathbf{R}$ and it has $Pr[M(d) \in \mathbf{R}] \leq Pr[M(d') \in P]$. The output of ε-differential privacy is obtained according to $\delta \leq \frac{\Delta p_2 \log \frac{1.25}{\delta}}{\varepsilon}$. We apply the noise generating model to sample the subset $D_t \leq K(x, y)$. The noise generating model n_t updates itself by using $\Delta n^k = n^k - n_t$, where n^k is the generated noise sample, n_t is the noise n at time t. We expand the Gaussian distribution-based noise generating model as

$$n_{t+1} \leftarrow n_t + \frac{1}{m} \left(\Sigma_{k=0}^{m_t} \frac{\Delta n^k}{max(<\Phi(x), \Phi(y)>, \frac{\|\Delta n^k\|_2}{P})} + \mathcal{N}(0, \varepsilon^2 P^2) \right) \quad (9)$$

Equation (9) suits for input noisy data, we update the noises by using n_{t+1}, $\sum_{k=0}^{m_t} \frac{\Delta n^k}{max(1, \frac{\|\Delta n^k\|_2}{P})} + \mathcal{N}(0, \varepsilon^2 P^2)$ is the sum of the updated noises, the sum of updated noises is denoted as $\sum_{k=0}^{m_t} \frac{\Delta n^k}{max(<\Phi(x), \Phi(y)>, \frac{\|\Delta n^k\|_2}{P})}$, $<\Phi(x), \Phi(y)> = K(x, y)$, $N(\mathcal{N}, \varepsilon^2 P^2)$ is the noise scaled to P.

Based on the sanitizer, we tackle the problem of privacy preservation by using the RKHS smoothing, RKHS means the reproducing kernel Hilbert spaces.

$$\mathcal{H}(x, y) = exp\{\frac{-|x - y|^2}{\delta}\} \tag{10}$$

$$X_i(t) = \mu(t) + \sum_{j=1}^{m} j^{-\frac{2}{p}} U_{ij} v_j(t) \tag{11}$$

In Eq. (10) and Eq. (11), x and y represent input dataset in the Hilbert space $\mathcal{H}$, δ means the risk is fixed by choosing ε in the definition of differential privacy. All comparisons encompass privacy restrictions ε and other factors occurring on a grid of equal distances, in the RKHS kernel, $\delta = 0.1$. The parameter of Kernel $\mathcal{H}$ is used to define $\rho = 0.001$ and the parameter $x_i(t)$ is set at $p = 4$. The parameters of median function, sample size, and differential privacy are set to $\mu(t) = 0.1 sin(\pi t)$, $N = 25$, $\varepsilon = 1.0$, $\delta = 0.1$, respectively.

Algorithm 1 shows the procedure of our solution. The inputs include the size of sample data, loss function, and other parameters, such as learning rate, noise scale, and gradient bound. The process is split into three parts: From line 1 to line 7, the task of this part is for sampling input data and generating noises. The second part is for conducting SGD, the local minimum is attained and the noises are added during the time of seeking the local minimum by using the gradient descent. The last part is the process for outputting the results. The evaluation of the proposed solution is presented at the end of this algorithm.

4   Evaluations

The effectiveness of the noise generating method presented in Sect. 3 is evaluated through using the CIFAR-10 and CIFAR-100 datasets [9]. CIFAR-10 consists of a total of 60,000 small images with the size of 32×32 pixels distributed in 10 classes. Each class contains 5,000 training and 1,000 test images. CIFAR-100 has the same size of images as CIFAR-10, the images are allocated in 100 classes, with 600 images belonging to each class. Therefore, there are 500 training and 100 test images per class.

In order to compare the new approach with SGD, we compare the learning rate with multiple training epochs. In the experiment, we take use of CNN with 60D PCA algorithm and CIFAR-10 dataset, 1,000 hidden units. The noise levels (ε, δ) for (ε, δ)-differential privacy in the neural network for PCA projection is set as $(4, 7)$.

Algorithm 1. Gaussian Noise generating algorithm under the federated SGD

Input: Data source $D_1, D_2, \ldots D_N$ and data size N, the parameters are: Loss function $L(\Theta) = \frac{1}{N} \Sigma_i \mathcal{L}(\theta, d_n)$, learning rate η, noise scale τ and gradient bound G.

Output: Training data Θ, privacy cost (ρ, ω)

1: **procedure** GENERATE NOISE(Obtain stochastic sample D_n and parameter group $P_{new}(\eta, \tau, G)$ and replace previous parameters $P_{prev}(\eta, \tau, S, G)$)
2:    **for** $n \in [\mathcal{N}]$ **do**
3:        Obtain parameter group $P_{global}(\eta, \tau, G)$ from P_{prev}
4:        Replace previous parameters and generate $P_n(\eta, \tau, G)$
5:        Fetch stochastic sample D_n and probability $\frac{D}{N}$
6:        Test distribution of sample D_n
7:        Generate noise samples with the same distribution D_n
8:        **for each** $i \in L_t$ compute $g_t(d_i) \leftarrow \vartheta_{\Theta_t} \mathcal{L}(\Theta_t, d_n)$ **do**
9:            Clip gradients
10:            $\dot{g}_t(d_i) \leftarrow \frac{g_t(d_i)}{max(1, \frac{\|g_t(d_i)\|_2}{G})}$
11:            Add Gaussian Noises
12:            $\dot{g}_t \leftarrow \frac{1}{N}(\Sigma_i g_t(d_i) + \mathcal{N}(0, \eta^2 G^2 I))$
13:            Descent and output $\dot{g}_t$
14:            $\Theta_{t+1} \leftarrow \Theta_t - \eta_t \dot{g}_t$
15:        **end for**
16:    **end for**
17:    Sort gradients in $\dot{g}_t(d_i)$ and output largest Θ_{t+1}
18:    Choose gradient sample D_{n+1} inferior to the bound G
19: **end procedure**

4.1   Our Experiments for Comparing Learning Rates

Figure 2 (a) shows the comparison of accuracy rates, the x-axis indicates Root Mean Square Error (RMSE) and the y-axis represents accuracy rate. Compared with our proposed approach: Federated privacy-preserving SGD, the original SGD has better learning rate, but the advantage is not obvious, which reveals that the learning rate with the new federated SGD method is able to approach the original SGD if the number of training epochs grows, the approach asserts that the learning performance is acceptable. It also spots that the new approach is able to leverage the balance between privacy and learning, the deviation between our new approach and the original method is acceptable.

Figure 2(b) shows the experimental results related to learning rate during model training, we take use of the same environment, i.e., under CelebA [11] dataset and parameter setting. We compare the accuracy and learning rates from 0.05 to 0.14. In Fig. 2(b), x-axis shows learning rate and y-axis represents accuracy rate, the accuracy meets the peak point if the learning rate reaches 0.06. The trend declines smoothly.

Besides, the proposed privacy-preserving noise generating scheme with federated SGD (PPNGFSGD) tends to have better accuracy with original non-privacy

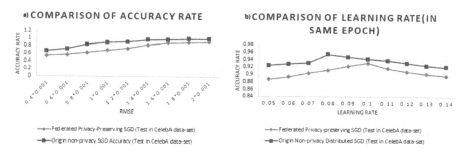

Fig. 2. The comparisons of accuracy rate and learning rate with different approaches

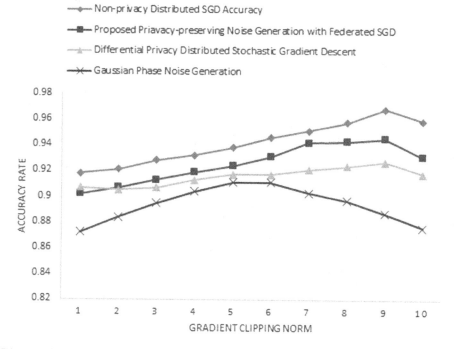

Fig. 3. The comparison of privacy-preserving approaches with different gradient clipping norms

SGD approach if the learning rate is between 0.06 and 0.1. If the learning rate gets up to 0.1, the accuracy rate by using the new approach slashes faster than original SGD approach. All two drops are out of 0.9 if the learning rate is up to 0.14. The experiment shows the learning rate between 0.05 to 0.07 is the best one for our proposed approach. Compared with original SGD, the gap between the

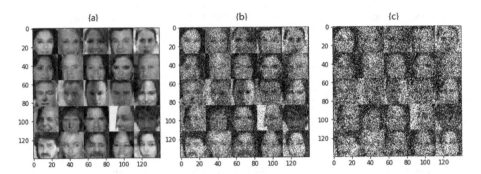

Fig. 4. The comparisons of different noise sampling approaches with CelebA [11] dataset

new and former federated SGD is not clear. The new approach replaces original one and the deviation is controlled under an acceptable way.

In next experiment, we take use of CNN having 60D PCA projection and 5,000 hidden units with CelebA [11] dataset, which was trained by using the size 2,400 and clipping threshold 8.

4.2 Experiments for Gradient Clipping and Noise Levels

In Fig. 3, we have compared two noise generating models and observe the variation of accuracy rates by using the CelebA [9] dataset. The bottom model, named as Gaussian phase noise generating (GPNG) scheme was proposed by [15]. The second model, namely, differential privacy-preserving distributed stochastic gradient descent(DPDSGD) was developed by Abadi [1]. The privacy-preserving noise generating model with federated SGD(PPNGFSGD) is proposed in this paper. The last one is the distributed SGD without any process in privacy protection. As y-axis in Fig. 3, the clipping gradient means when the training data increases, the more noises will be added into the set, the training accuracy in x-axis will be changed correspondingly.

The clipping gradient degrades the integrity of the estimate as shown in this test, if the clipping parameters are too low, the average clipped pattern may appear in different directions based on the true pattern. On the other hand, raising the normal forces the gradients to add less noise as we did. In practice, a good way to select a value is to replace a mediator of the non-clipped gradient terms for the training, the training accuracy in x-axis will be altered correspondingly.

In Fig. 3, by adding less noises, each privacy deficit is proportionally smaller, thus, we have more on the accumulated privacy budget, which means how many noises will be added into the data, what distribution of the data is subjected by adding noises to the original data. The selection thus has a significant impact on accuracy.

For instance, if the normal increase, the less noises will affect on the methods PPNGFSGD and DPDSGD. As controlled, the accuracy will be increased by using non-privacy SGD, whilst the clipping norm is climbing. But for GPNG, due to this method without control via noise level, the accuracy is lower than others.

In nutshell, if gradient clipping norm has less training data and less noises, the gap between original non-privacy SGDs will be less. While gradient clipping norm is being increased, the accuracy rates from our proposed method and non-noise-added SGD method are better than those of PPNGFSGD and GPNG having different gradient clipping norms. The average distance with original non-privacy SGD is the smallest one of our solution among the three privacy-preserving methods.

In Fig. 3, x-axis means noise level and y-axis is accuracy rate. At the low noise level, it shows the accuracy grows smoothly, on the high noise level, it drops very fast. Without privacy, the SGD approach tends to have a better accuracy than the new approach, but the distance between the two is not obvious. The experimental results show that the levels of inaccuracy privacy-preserving methods are acceptable, the deviation is acceptable under control.

Figure 4 reflects the results of noises added into the dataset [9]. Figure 4{a} is the original dataset without adding noises. Figure 4{b} was generated from our proposed method PPNGFSGD and Fig. 4{b} was from GPNG. As shown in Fig. 4{c}, the CPNG is hard to find any information, but we still are able to view the shapes of human faces from the images 4{b}, it is the reason why the results in Fig. 2 and Fig. 3 show higher accuracy rates than that of GPNG.

5   Conclusions

Our framework is applied to adaptive control based on well-trained weights and parameters, such as the lot size, the gradient norm boundary, and the noise level. Our experiments with multiple noise levels in model training show a trend of improvement compared with GPNG, it is interesting to consider more sophisticated schemes for aptly choosing these parameters. In the near future, our project will continue focusing on sampling approach so as to uplift the training efficiency.

References

1. Abadi, M., Chu, A., Goodfellow, I., McMahan, H.B., Mironov, I., Talwar, K., Zhang, L.: Deep learning with differential privacy. In: Proceedings of ACM SIGSAC Conference on Computer and Communications Security, pp. 308–318 (2016)
2. Agarwal, N., Suresh, A.T., Yu, F.X.X., Kumar, S., McMahan, B.: CPSGD: communication-efficient and differentially-private distributed SGD. In: Advances in Neural Information Processing Systems, pp. 7564–7575 (2018)
3. Aggarwal, C.C., Yu, P.S.: A general survey of privacy-preserving data mining models and algorithms. In: Aggarwal, C.C., Yu, P.S. (eds.) Privacy-Preserving Data Mining. Advances in Database Systems, vol. 34, pp. 11–52. Springer, Boston (2008). https://doi.org/10.1007/978-0-387-70992-5_2

4. Chaudhuri, K., Monteleoni, C.: Privacy-preserving logistic regression. In: Advances in Neural Information Processing Systems, pp. 289–296 (2009)
5. De Brabanter, J., De Moor, B., Suykens, J.A., Van Gestel, T., Vandewalle, J.P.: Least Squares Support Vector Machines. World Scientific, Singapore (2002)
6. Dwork, C., McSherry, F., Nissim, K., Smith, A.: Calibrating noise to sensitivity in private data analysis. In: Halevi, S., Rabin, T. (eds.) TCC 2006. LNCS, vol. 3876, pp. 265–284. Springer, Heidelberg (2006). https://doi.org/10.1007/11681878_14
7. Dwork, C.: Differential privacy: a survey of results. In: Agrawal, M., Du, D., Duan, Z., Li, A. (eds.) TAMC 2008. LNCS, vol. 4978, pp. 1–19. Springer, Heidelberg (2008). https://doi.org/10.1007/978-3-540-79228-4_1
8. Hsieh, F.Y., Bloch, D.A., Larsen, M.D.: A simple method of sample size calculation for linear and logistic regression. Stat. Med. 17(14), 1623–1634 (1998)
9. Krizhevsky, A., Nair, V., Hinton, G.: The CIFAR-10 Dataset, vol. 55 (2014). http://www.cs.toronto.edu/kriz/cifar.html
10. Lee, S., Rao, R., Narasimha, R.: Characterization of self-similarity properties of discrete-time linear scale-invariant systems. In: IEEE International Conference on Acoustics, Speech, and Signal Processing. Proceedings (Cat. No. 01CH37221), vol. 6, pp. 3969–3972. IEEE (2001)
11. Liu, Z., Luo, P., Wang, X., Tang, X.: Deep learning face attributes in the wild. In: Proceedings of International Conference on Computer Vision (ICCV) (2015)
12. Lou, Y., Yu, L., Wang, S., Yi, P.: Privacy preservation in distributed subgradient optimization algorithms. IEEE Trans. Cybern. 48(7), 2154–2165 (2017)
13. Machanavajjhala, A., Kifer, D., Gehrke, J., Venkitasubramaniam, M.: l-diversity: privacy beyond k-anonymity. ACM Trans. Knowl. Discov. Data (TKDD) 1(1), 3-es (2007)
14. Margineantu, D.D., Dietterich, T.G.: Pruning adaptive boosting. In: International Conference on Machine Learning, vol. 97, pp. 211–218. ICML (1997)
15. Richards, M.A.: Coherent integration loss due to white Gaussian phase noise. IEEE Sig. Process. Lett. 10(7), 208–210 (2003)
16. Shabtai, A., Elovici, Y., Rokach, L.: A Survey of Data Leakage Detection and Prevention Solutions. Springer, Boston (2012). https://doi.org/10.1007/978-1-4614-2053-8
17. Shokri, R., Shmatikov, V.: Privacy-preserving deep learning. In: Proceedings of the 22nd ACM SIGSAC Conference on Computer and Communications Security, pp. 1310–1321 (2015)
18. Sweeney, L.: k-anonymity: a model for protecting privacy. Int. J. Uncertain. Fuzziness Knowl.-Based Syst. 10(05), 557–570 (2002)
19. Vapnik, V.: Principles of risk minimization for learning theory. In: Advances in Neural Information Processing Systems, pp. 831–838 (1992)
20. Whittle, P.: Estimation and information in stationary time series. Arkiv för matematik 2(5), 423–434 (1953)
21. Wold, S., Esbensen, K., Geladi, P.: Principal component analysis. Chemom. Intell. Lab. Syst. 2(1–3), 37–52 (1987)
22. Wombacher, A.: Data workflow-a workflow model for continuous data processing. Data Process. (2010)
23. Zhu, Y., Liu, L.: Optimal randomization for privacy preserving data mining. In: Proceedings of the Tenth ACM SIGKDD, pp. 761–766 (2004)

Traffic-Sign Recognition Using Deep Learning

Zhongbing Qin$^{(\boxtimes)}$ and Wei Qi Yan$^{(\boxtimes)}$

Auckland University of Technology, Auckland, New Zealand
{xyp1014,wyan}@aut.ac.nz

Abstract. Traffic-sign recognition (TSR) has been an essential part of driver-assistance systems, which is able to assist drivers in avoiding a vast number of potential hazards and improve the experience of driving. However, the TSR is a realistic task that is full of constraints, such as visual environment, physical damages, and partial occasions, etc. In order to deal with the constrains, convolutional neural networks (CNN) are accommodated to extract visual features of traffic signs and classify them into corresponding classes. In this project, we initially created a benchmark (NZ-Traffic-Sign 3K) for the traffic-sign recognition in New Zealand. In order to determine which deep learning models are the most suitable one for the TSR, we choose two kinds of models to conduct deep learning computations: Faster R-CNN and YOLOv5. According to the scores of various metrics, we summarized the pros and cons of the picked models for the TSR task.

Keywords: Traffic signs · Faster R-CNN · YOLOv5 · CNN · NZ-Traffic-Sign 3K

1 Introduction

Traffic scene understanding is an important topic in the field of computer vision and intelligent systems [20, 21]. Traffic signs effectively assist drivers in the process of driving and keep them driving much safely by informing drivers of road status and potential hazards [1]. TSR as one of the important parts of driver-assistance systems has become much valuable and a lot of relevant research work emerged recently.

Generally, there are two steps in a typical TSR. The first one is to locate and get the information of traffic signs in natural scene images, which is known as traffic sign detection. The second step is to categorize detected traffic signs into the corresponding subclasses, which is known as traffic sign classification, the step is generally completed manually. Although TSR has gained a plethora of popularity in driver assistant systems, there are still numerous difficulties for identifying real-world traffic signs by using computer algorithms due to various sizes of visual objects [2, 18, 19], color deteriorations, and partial occlusions [3].

In order to deal with these obstacles, many approaches and algorithms have been proposed. In the past, TSR mainly relies on traditional algorithms for object detection, the pipeline of traffic sign detection normally utilized hand-crafted features to extract region proposals, and combined classifiers to filter out the negatives. Recently, deep learning methods are emerging, various cutting-edge approaches have been widely applied to

© Springer Nature Switzerland AG 2021
M. Nguyen et al. (Eds.): ISGV 2021, CCIS 1386, pp. 13–25, 2021.
https://doi.org/10.1007/978-3-030-72073-5_2

this area, such as deep convolutional networks (CNNs). CNNs have brought possibility of learning features from an amount of data without preprocessing, which avoids the process of designing hand-crafted features and absorbs generalized features [4]. Besides, CNN has been already set forth as an object classifier in machine learning which has been leveraged on traffic sign classification.

In the development of traffic sign recognition, German traffic-sign detection and classification benchmarks brought in a vast majority of benefits for evaluation across various algorithms, which were not comparable until the release of the benchmarks. German Traffic Sign Detection Benchmark (GTSDB) [5] and German Traffic Sign Recognition Benchmark (GTSRB) [6] presented two public extensive and available datasets, there are a few methods that have achieved high accuracy rate based on these datasets. Besides, other datasets are also available in public recent years, such as LISA traffic sign dataset (LISATSD) [1], Swedish Traffic Signs Dataset (STSD) [7], and Chinese Traffic Sign Dataset (CTSD) [3]. The GTSRB and GTSDB datasets are the most popular ones for recognizing traffic signs, a great deal of methods have been successful. The contributions of this paper are shown as follows:

- In order to effectively recognize New Zealand's traffic signs, we have created a new and realistic traffic-sign benchmark, which contains partial traffic sign because of physical and time limitations. The benchmark is composed of seven classes of traffic signs, various sizes of real-world signs were captured. The distinction of this benchmark is that it covers numerous small-size objects, which cannot be identified in off-the-shelf datasets. We call this benchmark as NZ-Traffic-Sign 3K.
- We conducted an experiment for traffic sign recognition based on the latest deep learning model (YOLOV5) and accomplish a comparison across the proposed algorithms. The evaluation results illustrated the robustness.

Overall, the ultimate goal of this paper is to complete the customized traffic-sign recognition and figure out which state-of-art neural networks are better fit into this project.

2 Literature Review

Traffic sign recognition (TSR) has benefited a large number of realistic applications, such as driver assistance system, autonomous vehicles, and intelligent mobile robots since they have delivered the current state of traffic signs into various systems. However, there are a few difficulties for computers to recognize traffic signs on the roads, which are mainly from two aspects: One is related to the complex traffic scene [8], the other is about unbalanced class frequencies in the datasets [5].

As for the difficulty of real-world traffic scenes, traffic signs are always well designed for drivers to easily read and recognize the signs during the driving time, including vivid colors, strong and bolded words, as well as various specific and simplified shapes, it is a tricky task to design the features combined with contaminated conditions [9]. For example, the conditions are with weak illumination, small-size signs in scenes, partial occlusions, rotations and physical damages. All of these factors will have a huge impact on the performance of computer algorithms to recognize traffic signs.

In terms of the characteristics of benchmarks, there is usually an uneven distribution of data categories. As we known, traffic signs have various types. For instance, the GTSRB includes 43 classes with the lowest frequency rate of 0.5% and the highest frequency rate of near 6% across all classes [10].

YOLO is a refreshingly straightforward and effective model for visual object detection. Firstly, YOLO as a simple convolutional neural network simultaneously predicts multiple bounding boxes and class probabilities. It initially is trained based on full images and the performance is optimized [11]. Secondly, YOLO is extremely fast which can achieve more than twice of the mean average precision (mAP) of other real-time systems [12].

However, YOLO still lags behind advanced detection architectures in accuracy. For example, it has a poor performance in accuracy compared to one of the top detection methods, Faster R-CNN [13]. In 2020, three YOLO versions had been released, including YOLOv4, YOLOv5, and PP-YOLO. While YOLOv4 was released, it was considered as the fastest and most accurate real-time detection model. It inherits the DarkNet and has obtained a distinct AP value (43.5%) on COCO dataset while achieved a fast detection speed on Tesla V100. Compared with YOLOv3, the AP and FPS have been effectively improved. After the release of YOLOv4, YOLOv5 emerged with the implementation process, rather than the use of original DarkNet. YOLOv5 has achieved 140 FPS compared with YOLOv4 under the same Ultralytics PyTorch library.

3 Methodology

TSR is considered with both object detection and classification. It is a real-world application that computer vision techniques are aligned to develop driver assistant system. In practice, the implementation of this task usually confronts with uncertain issues, such as color fading, disorientation, and variations in size and shape. Recently, there is a lot of research work which is available to deal with these problems and provide solutions to boost the performance of TSR.

Traffic signs mainly are categorized into three groups: Regulatory (i.e., general, parking and road user restrictions), Warning (i.e., temporary and permanent), Advisory (i.e., guide and route signs, e.g., street name, community facilities, tourist signs, service signs and general information signs). Although the design of traffic signs followed the dominant trends and international standards, the traffic signs have various shapes and functions. Thus, it is necessary to take the customized dataset into consideration for effectively recognizing traffic signs.

3.1 Data Collection

In this project, we used a 12-megapixel wide-angle camera of iPhone 11 to capture the realistic traffic sign images in Auckland. Due to lower frequent appearance of traffic signs to pedestrians and vehicles, we directly took traffic signs using digital cameras instead of recording videos. The pixels of the images are stored in JPEG format with the resolution 1080×1440. Our dataset (NZ-Traffic-Sign 3K) consists of 3,436 images and 3,545 instances in total: Stop (236 samples), Keep Left (536 samples), Road Diverges

(505 samples), Road Bump (619 samples), Crosswalk Ahead (636 samples), Give Way at Roundabout (533 samples), and Roundabout Ahead (480 samples) as shown in Fig. 1.

Fig. 1. The examples of seven classes of traffic signs in our dataset

In order to avoid overfitting during training the chosen models, we utilize data augmentation to expand our dataset. The basic manipulations for data augmentation include flipping, rotating, shearing, and adding noises as well as blurring images. In this case, we merely applied two augmentation operations, including adding noises and blurring images, based on our original dataset because these methods could deal with the distorted objects, which could impact the quality of our dataset and even degrade the accuracy of our training models. The manipulations were implemented by importing a Python library, named Skimage.

3.2   Research Design for Training Faster R-CNN

In this experiment, we chose Faster R-CNN to conduct recognition of traffic signs with on our own dataset. Faster R-CNN needs a traditional CNN as the basic convolutional layers for feature extraction. A pretrained VGG16 model was employed to assist us in exporting the feature map.

In order to successfully implement Faster R-CNN, our dataset follows the structure of PASCAL VOC. The dataset structure is split into five parts, namely, Annotations, ImageSets, JPEGImages, and SegmentationClass as well as SegmentationObject.

Table 1. The parameters for training Faster R-CNN

Parameters	Setting
Momentum	0.9
Learning rate	0.01
Max epochs	200
Batch size	24
Weight decay	0.0005

Due to the implementation based on Python, the dependencies should be prein-stalled to setup the experimental environment. *Caffe* must be built with the support of Python layers. The Python packages are needed, including Cython, Python-OpenCV and EasyDict, etc. In order to train Faster R-CNN with VGG16, the CUDA device with Tesla V100-SXM2-16GB are necessitated. Amid training the Faster R-CNN, critical parameters are preliminarily set, and the details are shown in Table 1.

3.3 Research Design for Training Faster YOLOv5

The second model in this project is YOLOv5, which was less than 50 days later than the release of YOLOv4. Although the appearance has gained a lot of attentions and debates in the community, it was indeed published with a number of improvements and distinctions. The improvements are mainly reflected in two aspects: Improved the accessibility for detecting real-time objects and the performance of prediction based on either training speed or accuracy.

In order to train YOLOv5 model, the first step is to label the images in our dataset. A graphical image annotation tool (*LabelImg*) was employed to label the images in our dataset. After generated the label files based on our dataset, the next step is to organize directories which save the training and validation images and labels. The model structure of YOLOv5 is as same as the single-stage object detector. It has three main parts: Model backbone, model neck, and model head.

The choice of activation functions is vital in deep neural network. Recently, there are a lot of activation functions available like Leaky ReLU (LReLU) [14], mish, etc. The chosen activation functions in YOLOv5 are LReLU and sigmoid. Specifically, the LReLU is added into the middle/hidden layers, the sigmoid function is added into the final detection layer. In terms of ReLU, it was proposed to alleviate potential problems caused by zero gradient, which allows a small and non-zero gradient if the unit is not active [14],

$$h^{(i)} = \max\left(w^{(i)T}x, 0\right) = \begin{cases} w^{(i)T}x & w^{(i)T}x > 0 \\ 0.01w^{(i)T}x \ else \end{cases} \tag{1}$$

where $w^{(i)}$ represents the weight vector of the ith middle layer and x is the input. For the optimization function in YOLOv5, we have two options, including Stochastic Gradient Descent (SGD) and ADAM. The default optimizer is SGD, which is transferred to ADAM by using the parameter option "-- adam".

In YOLOv5, the loss is computed based on three values: Objectiveness score, class probabilities, and the regression score of bounding box. YOLOv5 imports the Binary Cross-Entropy with Logits Loss (BCELoss) from PyTorch for calculating the compound loss. This method combines a sigmoid layer with the BCELoss in one single class, which is more numerically stable than adding the BCELoss after a sigmoid layer. The unreduced loss is described as:

$$l(x, y) = L = \{l_1, \ldots, l_N\}^T \tag{2}$$

$$l_n = -W_n\left[y_n \cdot \log \sigma(x_n) + (1 - y_n) \cdot \log(1 - \sigma(x_n))\right] \tag{3}$$

where N is the batch size. If the reduction is not zero, the error of a reconstruction is measured by using

$$l(x, y) = \begin{cases} mean(L), & reduction = {'}mean{'} \\ sum(L), & reduction = {'}sum{'} \end{cases} \tag{4}$$

Whilst predicting the multilabel classification, the loss is expressed as follows, which achieves by adding weights into positive instances.

$$l_c(x, y) = L_c = \{l_{1,c}, \ldots, l_{N,c}\}^T \tag{5}$$

$$l_{n,c} = -W_{n,c}\big[p_c y_{n,c} \cdot log\,\sigma\,(x_{n,c}) + (1 - y_{n,c}) \cdot log(1 - \sigma\,(x_{n,c}))\big] \tag{6}$$

where c is the class number. For example, $c = 1$ refers to the single label classification and n is the number of the instances in the batch as well as p_c is the weight of positive instances for the class c.

Table 2. The installed dependencies for YOLOv5

Package name	Version
Cython	---
matplotlib	$\geq 3.2.2$
numpy	$\geq 1.18.5$
Opencv-python	$\geq 4.1.2$
Pillow	---
PyYAML	≥ 5.3
Scipy	$\geq 1.4.1$
Tensorboard	≥ 2.2
Torch	$\geq 1.6.0$
Torchvision	$\geq 0.7.0$
tqdm	$\geq 4.41.0$

Table 3. The parameters for training YOLOv5

Parameters	Setting
Momentum	0.95
Learning rate	0.00128
Max epochs	200
Batch size	16
Weight decay	0.000201
giou	1.2
cls	15.7
cls_pw	3.67
obj	20
obj_pw	1.36

In this section, we introduce how we set up the experimental environment and explicit the parameters of training YOLOv5. Firstly, YOLOv5 was developed. The details of requirements for this project are shown in Table 2. Furthermore, this experiment was conducted based on *Colab* using Tesla *V100-SXM2-16GB*.

In order to comprehensively evaluate the performance of YOLOv5 and Faster R-CNN, six metrics were considered in this TSR, namely, Generalized Intersection over Union (GIoU), the predicted probability of Objectness, Classification, Precision and Recall as well as mean Average Precisions with multiple IoU (Table 3).

4   Results

4.1   Experiment Results of Faster R-CNN

In this experiment, we used Faster R-CNN as the detector and VGG16 as the classifier to perform the TSR. The experimental results are provided in Table 4. We evaluate the performance of Faster R-CNN with VGG16 by mainly using three measures, namely, precision, recall, and mean average precision with IoU 0.5. Fortunately, the accuracy of predictions is relatively high across seven classes (Table 5).

In order to evaluate the performance of our proposed model based on smaller traffic signs, we conducted another experiment and justified the results from this perspective. The same measures are applied to estimate the prediction results.

After trained 200 epochs, a trend of convergence is shown in the process of training and validation for the losses of GIoU, Objectness, and classification. In terms of GIoU loss, the final score converges to less than 0.02. Incorporating the GIoU loss improved the model performance based on our datasets [15]. The objectiveness loss is 0.005 during the training and reaches to zero while validating the model. Classification loss almost

Table 4. Experimental results for Faster R-CNN across seven classes

Classes	Precision	Recall	mAP@0.5
Roundabout ahead	0.957	0.952	0.961
Stop	0.970	0.959	0.972
Keep left	0.899	0.903	0.900
Road bump	0.925	0.930	0.933
Crosswalk ahead	0.937	0.939	0.943
Road diverges	0.929	0.930	0.932
Give way at roundabout	0.964	0.958	0.962

Table 5. Prediction results of various sizes of the traffic signs based on Faster R-CNN

Pixel size	Precision	Recall	mAP@0.5
≤ 200	0.907	0.914	0.915
[200, 400]	0.977	0.973	0.979
≥ 400	0.945	0.947	0.950

reaches zero both in the processes of training and validation. The results are shown in Fig. 2 and Fig. 3.

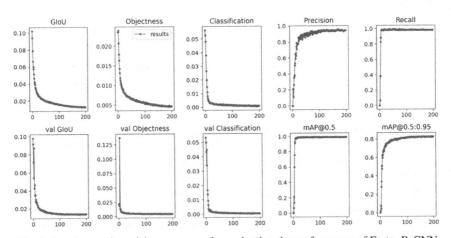

Fig. 2. The loss and precision measures for evaluating the performance of Faster R-CNN

Fig. 3. The test images with class indexes and confidence scores

4.2 Experiment Results of YOLOv5

In this experiment, we chose YOLOv5, a newly released end-to-end network, which is different from the Faster R-CNN. Similarity, we conducted the model training based on the seven classes of our dataset (NZ-traffic-sign 3K). The experimental results are provided in Table 6.

An overall performance of YOLOv5 was justified in this case. The distribution of training and validation sets are invariant, 80% for training and 20% for validation. The evaluation is conducted according to the same measures as the Faster R-CNN, including different losses, precision and recall as well as the mAP with multiple IoU. At the end of the experiment, we test the overall performance of the YOLOv5. The details are shown in Fig. 4 (Table 7).

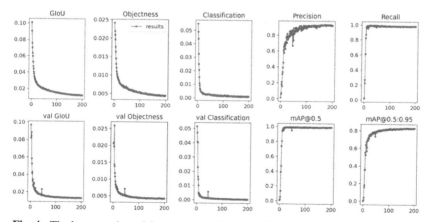

Fig. 4. The losses and precision measures for evaluating the performance of YOLOv5

Table 6. Experimental results for YOLOv5 across seven classes

Classes	Precision	Recall	mAP@0.5
Roundabout ahead	0.949	0.951	0.954
Stop	0.952	0.956	0.959
Keep left	0.901	0.912	0.923
Road bump	0.922	0.927	0.929
Crosswalk ahead	0.933	0.938	0.941
Road diverges	0.934	0.930	0.936
Give way at roundabout	0.955	0.957	0.960

Table 7. Prediction results of various sizes of the traffic signs based on YOLOv5

Pixel size	Precision	Recall	mAP@0.5
≤ 200	0.883	0.892	0.890
[200, 400]	0.976	0.971	0.974
≥ 400	0.931	0.939	0.939

5   Analysis

After comparing the results of two models, we concluded that the Faster R-CNN has achieved a higher accuracy rate than YOLOv5 for recognizing the traffic signs in NZ. The Faster R-CNN has achieved lower loss while gaining higher precision, such as the consistent trend of precision and recall as well as mAP.

However, in the testing phase, we noticed that the end-to-end model YOLOv5 is much efficient while it was applied to deal with the data of inference. The test video in the inference is composed of 2,074 frames. The processing time for per frame of the YOLOv5 is only around 0.011 s but the time consumption for Faster R-CNN (37 s) is much longer than YOLOv5. From the perspective of time consumption, YOLOv5 is a much reasonable option for performing the recognition.

In summary, Faster R-CNN is an accurate model for recognizing traffic signs without considering the time consumption. YOLOv5 is a better one if the data processing time is taken into consideration (Fig. 5).

Fig. 5. The test images with class indexes and confidence scores

6 Conclusion and Future Work

One of the objectives of this paper is to propose a customized benchmark for recognizing traffic signs because there is no benchmark that can fit into TSR. Our dataset consists of 3,436 images in total and contains seven classes of traffic signs. The distribution of these classes is more even compared to the most popular benchmark GTSRB, which is an improvement directly contributed to the distinct performance of the two chosen models. Most importantly, we trained CNN models to recognize small traffic signs, thus there are sufficient instances of smaller signs in our dataset. The results of two models based on our dataset are promising and impressive.

Another objective of this paper is to evaluate the neural networks for TSR. We evaluated the performance of a one-stage model (YOLOv5) and a two-stage model (Faster R-CNN with VGG16). According to the comparison between the two models, we see that Faster R-CNN is a better option for TSR without considering the time consumption as the higher-level accuracy. YOLOv5 is much sufficient and important, there is a slightly degrade of accuracy compared to Faster R-CNN.

In future, we will complete our benchmark by covering more types of the traffic signs in NZ so that we can make this project much instructional in this field [16, 17, 27–29]. On the other hand, more object recognition techniques will be employed to TSR [22–26]. For example, recognizing visual objects utilizes heatmaps methods. Finally, more evaluation measures also should be applied to estimate the performance of various models.

References

1. Mogelmose, A., Trivedi, M., Moeslund, T.B.: Vision-based traffic sign detection and analysis for intelligent driver assistance systems: perspectives and survey. IEEE Trans. Intell. Transp. Syst. **13**(4), 1484–1497 (2012)
2. Zhu, Y., Zhang, C., Zhou, D., Wang, X., Bai, X., Liu, W.: Traffic sign detection and recognition using fully convolutional network guided proposals. Neurocomputing **214**, 758–766 (2016)

3. Yang, Y., Luo, H., Xu, H., Wu, F.: Towards real-time traffic sign detection and classification. IEEE Trans. Intell. Transp. Syst. **17**(7), 2022–2031 (2015)
4. Zhang, J., Huang, M., Jin, X., Li, X.: A real-time Chinese traffic sign detection algorithm based on modified YOLOv2. Algorithms **10**(4), 127 (2017)
5. Stallkamp, J., Schlipsing, M., Salmen, J., Igel, C.: Man vs. computer: benchmarking machine learning algorithms for traffic sign recognition. Neural Netw. **32**, 323–332 (2012). https://doi.org/10.1016/j.neunet.2012.02.016
6. Stallkamp, J., Schlipsing, M., Salmen, J., Igel, C.: The German traffic sign recognition benchmark: a multi-class classification competition. In: International Joint Conference on Neural Networks (2011)
7. Larsson, F., Felsberg, M.: Using Fourier descriptors and spatial models for traffic sign recognition. In: Heyden, A., Kahl, F. (eds.) SCIA 2011. LNCS, vol. 6688, pp. 238–249. Springer, Heidelberg (2011). https://doi.org/10.1007/978-3-642-21227-7_23
8. Wang, G., Ren, G., Quan, T.: A traffic sign detection method with high accuracy and efficiency. In: International Conference on Computer Science and Electronics Engineering (2013)
9. Sermanet, P., LeCun, Y.: Traffic sign recognition with multi-scale convolutional networks. In: International Joint Conference on Neural Networks (2011)
10. Mao, X., Hijazi, S., Casas, R., Kaul, P., Kumar, R., Rowen, C.: Hierarchical CNN for traffic sign recognition. In: IEEE Intelligent Vehicles Symposium (IV) (2016)
11. Redmon, J., Divvala, S., Girshick, R., Farhadi, A.: You only look once: unified, real-time object detection. In: IEEE CVPR, pp. 779–788 (2016)
12. Redmon, J., Farhadi, A.: YOLO9000: better, faster, stronger. In: IEEE CVPR, pp. 7263–7271 (2017)
13. Girshick, R.: Fast R-CNN. In: IEEE ICCV, pp. 1440–1448 (2015)
14. Maas, A.L., Hannun, A.Y., Ng, A.Y.: Rectifier nonlinearities improve neural network acoustic models. In: ICML (2013)
15. Rezatofighi, H., Tsoi, N., Gwak, J., Sadeghian, A., Reid, I., Savarese, S.: Generalized intersection over union: a metric and a loss for bounding box regression. In: IEEE Conference on Computer Vision and Pattern Recognition (2019)
16. Yan, W.Q.: Computational Methods for Deep Learning - Theoretic. Practice and Applications. Springer, Heidelberg (2021). https://doi.org/10.1007/978-3-030-61081-4
17. Yan, W.Q.: Introduction to Intelligent Surveillance - Surveillance Data Capture, Transmission, and Analytics, 3rd edn. Springer, Heidelberg (2019). https://doi.org/10.1007/978-3-319-602 28-8
18. Pan, C., Yan, W.Q.: Object detection based on saturation of visual perception. Multimed. Tools Appl. **79**(27–28), 19925–19944 (2020). https://doi.org/10.1007/s11042-020-08866-x
19. Pan, C., Li, X., Yan, W.: A learning-based positive feedback approach in salient object detection. In: IEEE IVCNZ (2018)
20. Liu, X., Yan, W., Kasabov, N.: Vehicle-related scene segmentation using CapsNets. In: IEEE IVCNZ (2020)
21. Liu, X., Neuyen, M., Yan, W.: Vehicle-related scene understanding using deep learning. In: Cree, M., Huang, F., Yuan, J., Yan, W.Q. (eds.) ACPR 2019. CCIS, vol. 1180, pp. 61–73. Springer, Singapore (2020). https://doi.org/10.1007/978-981-15-3651-9_7
22. Wang, J., Bacic, B., Yan, W.Q.: An effective method for plate number recognition. Multimed. Tools Appl. **77**(2), 1679–1692 (2017). https://doi.org/10.1007/s11042-017-4356-z
23. Zheng, K., Yan, W., Nand, P.: Video dynamics detection using deep neural networks. IEEE Trans. Emerg. Top. Comput. Intell. **2**(3), 224–234 (2018)
24. Shen, Y., Yan, W.: Blind spot monitoring using deep learning. In: IEEE IVCNZ (2018)
25. Qin, G., Yang, J., Yan, W., Li, Y., Klette, R.: Local fast R-CNN flow for object-centric event recognition in complex traffic scenes. In: Satoh, S. (ed.) PSIVT 2017. LNCS, vol. 10799, pp. 439–452. Springer, Cham (2018). https://doi.org/10.1007/978-3-319-92753-4_34

26. Wang, J., Yan, W.: BP-neural network for plate number recognition. Int. J. Digit. Crime Forensics **8**(3), 34–45 (2016)
27. An, N., Yan, W.: Multitarget tracking using Siamese neural networks. ACM TOMM (2021)
28. Liu, X., Yan, W.: Traffic-light sign recognition using Capsule network. MTAP (2021)
29. Xing, J., Yan, W.: Traffic sign recognition using guided image filtering. In: ISGV (2021)

Tree Leaves Detection Based on Deep Learning

Lei Wang[✉] and Wei Qi Yan[✉]

Auckland University of Technology, Auckland 1010, New Zealand

Abstract. In this paper, digital images related to five kinds of leaves which are available at New Zealand are collected as our dataset, two deep learning models, namely, Faster R-CNN and YOLOv5, representing two-stage and one-stage algorithms, are employed to conduct tree leaves detection. Our results show that YOLOv5 model obviously outperforms to the Faster R-CNN in the speed of both model training and object detection. The difference between these two methods is not significant in the comparison of mAPs. We conclude that YOLOv5, as the representative of one-stage algorithm, is obviously better than Faster R-CNN, as the representative of two-stage algorithms, especially, its advantage in speed makes sure it a bright prospect in deep learning applications.

Keywords: YOLOv5 · Faster R-CNN · Leaf detection · Deep learning

1 Introduction

1.1 Background and Motivation

New Zealand is one of the well-known scenic countries in the world. The forest resources are quite abundant. There are a variety of tree species growing everywhere, many of them are unique worldwide [1]. The research work for leaf classification has been conducted for decades, plant recognition via digital images has become an interdisciplinary subject in the field of plant taxonomy and computer vision [2]. The research work of plant automatic taxonomy has made great progress, but with the continuous expansion of its applications, it is still hard to fully meet the needs of reality [3].

Object detection is an important branch of image processing and computer vision [20, 21]. In deep learning, object detection algorithms have been explored rapidly. However, visual objects often have distinctive poses and are often blocked. Taken into consideration of the complexity and diversity of scenes, this is still a challenging topic, there are rooms to be improved.

Visual object detection is roughly grouped into two categories. The first one is R-CNN family algorithms based on regional proposals, whose representative network is R-CNN, Fast R-CNN, SPPNet, Faster R-CNN, FPN, Mask R-CNN, etc. They are characterized by using two-stage methods, which require the algorithms to generate the candidate boxes of an object, namely, position of the object, and conduct the classification and regression of the candidate boxes.

One-stage algorithms, which do not need the region proposals, directly generate the class probability and position coordinates of the object. Its representative network is

© Springer Nature Switzerland AG 2021
M. Nguyen et al. (Eds.): ISGV 2021, CCIS 1386, pp. 26–38, 2021.
https://doi.org/10.1007/978-3-030-72073-5_3

YOLO series, like YOLO, YOLOv2, YOLOv3, YOLOv4, YOLOv5, SSD, RetinaNet, etc.

There have been a lot of research work for tree leaves classification. Compared with traditional image classification, visual object detection is obviously in line with practical needs. In reality, it is often impossible to have only one visual object in a scene. The requirements for visual object detection are much complicated, required algorithms not only verify what an object is, but also determine where the object is in the image. There is relatively little research work on leaf detection, but more focus on automatic driving, video monitoring, mechanical processing, intelligent robot, and other fields. Therefore, in this paper, we endeavor to explore the performance of deep learning algorithms for tree leaves detection.

Pertaining to object detection algorithms over the past decades [23–30, 31], this project adopts two representative algorithms based on deep learning for visual object detection, namely, YOLOv5 based on one-stage algorithms and Faster R-CNN based on two-stage algorithms. Generally, the detectors based on two-stage algorithms have high positioning and recognition accuracy, while one-stage detectors have the advantage of speed. The difference between them is that the two-stage detectors have a step of generating region proposals, while the one-stage detectors directly regress and classify the prediction boxes. In this paper, our two algorithms are applied to the leaf dataset collected locally in New Zealand.

1.2 Contribution

There has been a great deal of literature on leaf classification for decades. However, with the emergence of various new models in deep learning, computer vision has gradually shifted from image classification to object detection, object tracking, semantic segmentation, and instance segmentation. In view of 3D shape of leaves in object detection, leaf images observed from different angles of view may be completely different, object detection is more difficult than image classification. In addition, different from traditional leaf classification, this project is not only to identify and classify single leaf on digital images, but also to realize the recognition of multiple types of leaves in videos.

Pertaining to object detection, there are three issues that make object detection more difficult: (1) Multiple objects with different classes and the number of objects, (2) multiple scales, for example, visual objects with different sizes, (3) external environment interference, such as the changes of illumination, the existence of occlusion, and the quality of images.

In this project, we trained two different models representing one-stage and two-stage algorithms respectively. At the same time, local leaves of New Zealand were collected as datasets. Experimental results of two models were compared and analyzed through the detection of actual leaves in our videos.

2 Literature Review

There is literature regarding leaf classification, the research work on object detection is also very ample and full in recent years. However, the research work on leaf detection is relatively limited.

In 2012, deep convolutional neural network showed excellent performance in ILSVRC-2012 large-scale image classification task. The model received training of more than one million images, the error rates of the top 5 in the 1000 classes are reduced to 15.3% which almost halves the error rate of the best competing methods. This success led to a revolution in computer vision [4].

In 2017, three deep learning networks GoogLeNet, AlexNet, and VGGNet were used to identify plant species on LifeCLEF 2015 dataset [5], with an overall accuracy 80% for the best model [6].

In essence, object detection is also an image classification technique. In addition to object classification, the algorithms identify the locations of object instances from numerous predefined classes of natural images. Object detection is one of the most basic and challenging tasks in computer vision [7].

After CNN achieved great success in the 2012 ImageNet classification task [8], Girshick firstly proposed the region-based convolutional neural networks (R-CNN) in 2014, its algorithmic structure became the classical one of two-stage algorithms. Since then, object detection algorithms have been developed at an unprecedented speed [9].

At present, deep learning methods for object detection are mainly grouped into two directions: Two-stage algorithms and one-stage algorithms. The former refers to the algorithm generating a series of candidate frames as samples and classifying the samples through CNN; the latter does not need to generate candidate frames, but directly transforms the problem of object border locating into a regression problem. The performance of the two methods is also different. Generally, the former is superior in the accuracy of object detection and positioning, while the latter outperforms in algorithmic speed.

Fast R-CNN algorithm was proposed in 2015 [10], which designs a pooling layer structure for ROI and effectively solves the problem that R-CNN algorithm must crop and scale the image to the same size. The idea of multi-task loss function is also proposed. Gradient is transmitted directly through ROI Pooling layer. But it still does not get rid of the limitations of generating positive and negative candidate boxes in the selective search algorithm.

In order to solve the defects of Fast R-CNN algorithm, Faster R-CNN algorithm was proposed in 2015 [11]. Region Proposal Network (RPN) was designed, its advantage is that the whole network process can share the feature information extracted by CNN, which saves the computational costs, solves the problem that Fast R-CNN algorithm is slow in generating positive and negative candidate boxes, and avoids the decrease of algorithmic accuracy due to too much extraction of candidate boxes. RPN network can generate multi-size candidate boxes in the convolution feature map of fixed size, resulting in the inconsistency between the size of the variable object and the fixed receptive field. This is a shortcoming of the Faster R-CNN model.

In view of the existence of RPN structure, the two-stage methods are represented by R-CNN algorithms, though the detection accuracy is getting higher and higher, its speed of detection reaches a plateau, which makes it difficult to meet the real-time requirement. Therefore, one-stage algorithm is represented by YOLO based on regression method. The one-stage algorithm can classify the class and location information directly through the trunk network without using RPN network. It's faster, but initially less accurate.

In 2015, YOLO algorithm inherits the idea of overfeating, its speed of detection reaches 45 frames per second. P-ReLU activation function is adopted during model training. However, it has problems such as the accuracy of positioning and recall rate are dissatisfied. Besides, the detection for very small object is ineffective. At last, generalization ability is relatively weak [12].

YOLOv2 [13] and YOLOv3 [14] algorithms were proposed on CVPR 2017, focusing on solving the poor recall rate and positioning accuracy. It uses DarkNet-19 as the feature extraction network and adds batch normalization as the pretreatment. The original YOLO uses the full connection layer to directly predict the coordinates of the bounding box, while YOLOv2 refers to the idea of Faster R-CNN, introduces anchor mechanism, and calculates a better anchor template in the training set.

The operation of anchor boxes is applied to the convolutional layer so as to improve the prediction of the bounding boxes. Meanwhile, the positioning method with strong constraints is adopted to greatly improve the recall rate of the algorithm. Combined with the fine-grained features, the shallow feature and the deep feature are connected, which is helpful to the detection of small-size objects.

In 2020, YOLOv4 was released [15], which is a significant update to the YOLO family, with an increase in AP and FPS of 10% and 12% based on COCO datasets, respectively. On June 25, 2020, Ultralytics released YOLOv5 on Github, which performs excellently, especially the frame rate 140FPS of YOLO v5s model is amazing.

3   Methodology

YOLO and Faster R-CNN, namely, two-stage algorithms, were taken into account in this project to detect local leaves, compare and analyze the differences between them. The reason why these two algorithms are chosen is that they are the most representative ones of single-stage and two-stage algorithms, respectively.

3.1   Working Principle and Structure Analysis of YOLO

The bounding boxes and class labels of Pascal-VOC and Kaggle datasets are saved in.xml file. However, this format of annotation cannot be imported directly into MATLAB. We wrote a program for converting XML format files to MATLAB files.

In YOLOv5, four versions of object detection network are given, namely, YOLOv5s, YOLOv5m, YOLOv5l, and YOLOv5x. YOLOv5s model was used in this project. YOLOv5s is the network with the minimum depth and the minimum width in YOLOv5 series. The YOLOv5s is the fastest one, but the AP is relatively less accurate. However, this model is also a good choice if the focus of object detection is on larger targets and less complex scenarios, which are speed oriented. The other three networks of YOLOv5 series are based on YOLOv5s to continuously deepen and widen the network, the AP is also continuously improved, but the speed will become slower.

The structure of YOLOv5 is very similar to that of YOLOv4, both use CSPDarkNet53 (i.e., Cross Stage Partial Network) as the Backbone net. PANET (i.e., Path Aggregation Network) and SPP (i.e., Space Pyramid Pooling) were employed as the Neck net.

The input of YOLOv5 adopts the same way of mosaic data enhancement as YOLOv4. Mosaic refers to the method of CutMix data enhancement [16]. However, CutMix only takes use of two images for splicing, while mosaic data enhancement utilizes four images, which are randomly scaled, cropped, and resized. In addition, YOLOv5 is also optimized in terms of adaptive image scaling.

The function of backbone is to aggregate and combine different fine-grained images to form a convolutional neural network. The backbone of YOLOv5s adopts CSPNet, which takes use of gradient information in other CNN frameworks.

Neck is a series of network layers that mix and combine image features and transfer them to the prediction layer, also known as Head. The Neck part of YOLOv5s adopts PANET [17]. Generating feature pyramids is the main function of the Neck. The feature pyramid enhances the detection of visual objects with multiple scales, thus it recognizes the same object with various sizes and scales.

The Head of the model is mainly employed for final judgment. In YOLOv5 model, the model Head is as same as the previous versions of YOLOv3 and YOLOv4. Each Head has (80 classes + 1 probability + 4 coordinates) × 3 anchor frames, 255 channels in total.

The loss function for object detection is generally composed of classification loss and recurrence loss of bounding boxes. GIOU is used as the loss function of bounding boxes in YOLOv5. In the postprocessing of object detection, NMS operation is usually needed for filtering visual objects. In YOLOv5, weighted NMS is accommodated.

The selection of activation function is very important for deep neural networks. In YOLOv5, Leaky ReLU is used in the middle/hidden layer, sigmoid function is applied to the final detection layer.

YOLOv5 provided us with two optimization functions Adam and SGD. The default one is SGD. If we train a smaller dataset, Adam is a better choice. Adam is offered in this project.

3.2 Analysis of the Working Principle of Faster R-CNN

After the accumulation of R-CNN and Fast R-CNN, Faster R-CNN algorithm was proposed in 2016. Faster R-CNN integrates feature extraction, proposal extraction, bounding box regression, and classification into one network, which greatly uplifts the overall performance, especially the detection speed. The main implementation steps of Faster R-CNN are as follows.

The first step is to extract features. Faster R-CNN firstly extracts feature map of the candidate image. The feature map is shared for subsequent RPN (Region Proposal Network) layer and fully connected layer.

The second step is to enter RPN (i.e., Region Proposal Network), which is used to generate regional image blocks. This layer determines through "softmax" that anchors belong to the foreground or background and take use of bounding box regression to get precise proposals.

The third step is ROI pooling. This layer collects the input feature map and candidate object regions. The feature map of the object region is extracted and sent to the following fully connected layer to determine the object class.

The fourth step is classification. The feature map of object region is used to classify the class of the visual object, the regression of boundary boxes is used to obtain the final precise location of the box.

Therefore, we see that the highlight of Faster R-CNN is that it proposes an effective method to locate the object area, which greatly reduces the time consumption of convolution operation, the speed has been greatly accelerate.

3.3 Environmental Deployment

Since model training and validation need a lot of computing power, we employ Google Colab platform for the computations. Google Colab is a free cloud-based deep learning platform based on Jupiter notebook, which provides a free Tesla P100 GPU for deep learning users. In this project, the requirement of computational power needed to make and annotate datasets is relatively weak, we only utilize local computing power to complete it. The dataset is imported into the Colab platform for model training and validation. In the local environment, we use LabelMe software to label the collected images.

3.4 Data Set Preparation

The basic dataset encapsulates five types of tree leaves which were collected from a park at Auckland, New Zealand: (1) Magnolia grandiflora, (2) Boehmeria nivea, (3) Clausena lansium, (4) Euphoria longan, (5) Hibiscus. Firstly, we collected these five kinds of leaves from the park, we took pictures as the collected visual data, including various distances, view angles, and so on. The shooting background includes wood floor and white paper. The shooting includes single leaves and the combination of multiple leaves. A total of eight groups of video footages were captured as the samples, the video durations are various from 30 s to 80 s, the frame rate was 60 FPS. An example of a screenshot taken with a white paper background and a wood floor background is shown in Fig. 1.

Fig. 1. Leaf images collected

We extracted frames from the video to obtain 419 images. We used software LabelMe, a data annotation software, to label the obtained images. In the process of labeling, leaf abbreviations are combined with numbers and initials of leaf names. 1 –"m.g." stands for Magnolia Grandiflora, 2 –"b. n." refers to Boehmeria nivea, 3 –"c. l." means Clausena Lansium, 4 –"e.l." shows Euphoria longan, and 5 –'h.' represents for Hibiscus. Given the relatively small number of overall datasets, data augmentation is necessary. The specific operations include flipping, zooming in, zooming out, clipping, and combining. The 419 images were expanded four times to 1676 images. The data is split into training set and validation set according to the ratio of 8:2. The final training set has 1,340 images and 336 images in the validation set. The final test was conducted by using a 37 s video shot having a mixture of leaves against a wood floor background.

3.5 Evaluation Methods

AP means average precision, which is the area under the precision-recall curve. mAP is the mean average precision, which is the average AP value of multiple categories of AP. The size of mAP must be in the interval [0, 1.0], the larger the better. This index is a key index to measure the detection accuracy in object detection. The loss function of object detection consists of two parts: Classification loss and regeneration loss of bounding boxes. The loss of classification is mainly based on cross-entropy loss function, which has not been changed much in recent years. IOU and GIOU are representative methods in the development of regression of bounding boxes. YOLO v5 adopts the more advanced GIOU.

RPN network is introduced into Faster R-CNN network. At the same time, the loss function of RPN network is also used as the loss function of Faster R-CNN algorithm whilst training RPN network. In addition to mAP, another important performance of object detection algorithm is speed. A measure of speed is FPS (frame per second), the number of images that can be processed per second.

4 Analysis and Discussions

4.1 Comparison of Object Detection Results

In order to compare the differences between the two models accurately, it is necessary to be tested in multiple scenarios, including model testing in single leaf scene, in a small number of mixed leaves, and in complex scenarios with multiple leaves.

In the single-leaf scenario, we see that YOLOv5 accurately identified visual objects, the selection of bounding boxes is much appropriate. Meanwhile, Faster R-CNN identifies the majority of objects accurately. Based on the "E.L." leaf, two results were

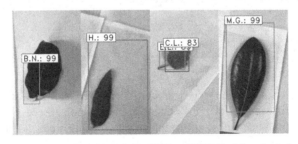

Fig. 2. The results of Faster R-CNN and YOLOv5 for single leaf

exported. In addition, when the model Faster R-CNN identifies the "B.N." leaf, it only recognizes a part of the leaf, the bounding box is too large when it identifies the 'H' leaf (Fig. 2).

In the scenario of model testing with a small number of mixed leaves, we see that Faster R-CNN model accurately identifies most of visual objects, but it also missed a few of individual leaves. At the same time, there are few cases where the box is too large or too small (Fig. 3).

For YOLOv5, even if a partial leaf is able to be recognized, the box size is appropriate. But one of them was wrongly identified, the 'H' leaf was wrongly identified as the "BN leaf".

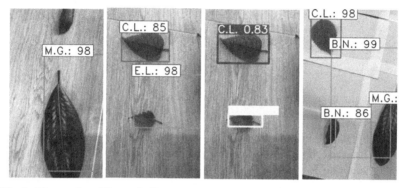

Fig. 3. The results of Faster R-CNN and YOLOv5 in a small number of mixed leaves

In the complex scene where all the five kinds of leaves are contained, YOLOv5 model identified almost all the leaves accurately. However, the toy wheel in the lower left corner of the first set of pictures is mistakenly identified as a leaf. The Faster R-CNN model can only identify part of the leaves in this scene, and the box selection is not very accurate. But it also doesn't recognize the toy wheel in the lower left corner of the first set of images as a leaf (Fig. 4).

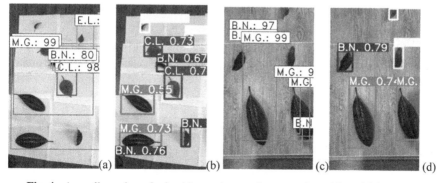

Fig. 4. A small number of mixed leaves in complex scenarios with multiple leaves

4.2 Comparative Analysis of the Two Proposed Models

In Fig. 5, in terms of classification task, both algorithms decline steadily, but the training loss of YOLOv5 fells faster.

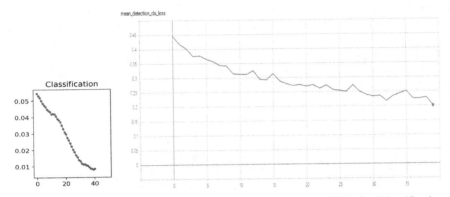

Fig. 5. The training loss curve of YOLOv5 and Faster R-CNN model for leaf classification

In Fig. 6, the two algorithms maintain the trend decline for regression loss. YOLOv5 started with a brief rise, but tends to be stable in the later stage, the whole process presents a bit amplitude. Faster R-CNN drops much steadily and has a small amplitude of shock.

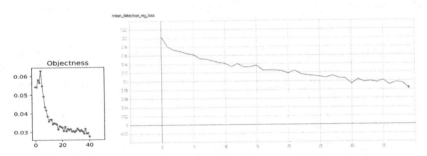

Fig. 6. The training loss curve of YOLOv5 and Faster R-CNN model for regression

For the total loss curve, YOLOv5 decreases faster in the early stage and then tends to slow down, while Faster R-CNN also decreases slowly and steadily in the whole process as shown in Fig. 7.

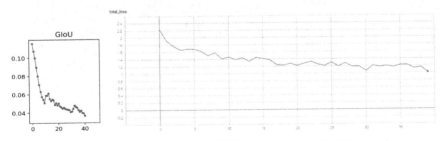

Fig. 7. The training loss curve of YOLOv5 and Faster R-CNN model

The network structure of the model determines the training speed and execution speed of the model as well as the memory usage. The training speed, execution speed and memory usage of the two models are shown in Table 1. YOLOv5 has obvious advantages in speed and memory consumption. Compared with Faster R-CNN, YOLOv5 is nearly 32 times faster in training speed, nearly 39 times faster in execution speed, and nearly 8 times smaller in memory occupancy.

Table 1. Comparisons of speed and memory consumption of the two models

Types	YOLOv5	Faster R-CNN
Training speed	26 ms/step	814ms/step
Execution speed	0.011	0.432s
Memory usage	14MB	109MB

Based on the IoU threshold value of 0.5, the mAP results obtained by using the two models are shown in Fig. 8. Both methods kept the accuracy increasing gradually, but YOLOv5 increased from 0, while Faster R-CNN grew from 0.80, which indicates that it increases much slowly. The primary reason why the initial accuracy of Faster R-CNN is so high is that the model is a two-stage algorithm. In the training for RPN candidate boxes in the first stage, there are many candidate boxes in each column, the boxes that have not objects are classified as negative classes, resulting in a high accuracy even if all the results are negative.

After the model training, we selected the one with the lowest loss as the optimal model and carried out validation. Finally, we calculated that the mAP of YOLOv5 was 0.932 and the mAP of Faster R-CNN was 0.918.

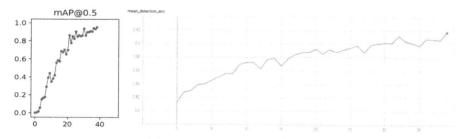

Fig. 8. The training curve of YOLOv5 model and Faster R-CNN model

4.3 Discussions

From the experimental results of this project, the YOLOv5 model representing the one-stage algorithms is superior to the Faster R-CNN model on behalf of the two-stage algorithms in most indicators. The differences between them in training speed, execution speed, model size, accuracy, and others are shown in Table 2. YOLOv5 model also performs better in rectangular box regression. In addition, YOLOv5 takes up less memory and executes faster, so it is able to be adapted to more devices and scenarios.

Table 2. Comparisons of experimental results between YOLOv5 model and Faster R-CNN model

Type	YOLOv5	Faster R-CNN
Training speed	26 ms/step	814 ms/step
Execution speed	0.011 s	0.432 s
Memory usage	14 MB	109 MB
mAP	0.932	0.918
Total loss	0.032	1.028

To sum up, YOLOv5 has made various optimizations in data augmentation, feature extraction, loss function, and other aspects, which shows its excellence in both accuracy and speed and is suitable for more complex and diverse applications.

5 Conclusion and Future Work

In this paper, YOLOv5 model and Faster R-CNN model were employed to implement object detection of leaves collected locally in New Zealand. Experimental results show that YOLOv5 algorithm is superior in almost all indicators. Especially, YOLOv5 algorithm is superior to Faster R-CNN algorithm in terms of speed, memory occupancy, and accuracy of object position prediction. From the viewpoint of loss functions, YOLOv5 model is better.

In this project, the number and species of leaves as datasets are relatively small. In order to ensure the outperformance experimentally, the shapes of leaves are significantly different. However, in practical applications, the kinds of leaves with very similar shapes may appear, the difficulty of leaf identification will be greatly increased. Therefore, it is necessary to train the model with more numbers and types of tree leaves in future.

The background of this experiment is relatively simple, but in practical application, the background of leaves is often very complex. How to implement object detection with high recognition rate under complex background is our future work [18, 19].

References

1. McGlone, M., Buitenwerf, R., Richardson, S.: The formation of the oceanic temperate forests of New Zealand. NZ J. Bot. **54**(2), 128–155 (2016)

2. Sun, Y., Liu, Y., Wang, G., Zhang, H.: Deep learning for plant identification in natural environment. Comput. Intell. Neurosci. (2017)
3. Goëau, H., Bonnet, P., Joly, A.: Plant identification in an open-world. Lifeclef (2016)
4. Krizhevsky, A., Sutskever, I., Hinton, G.E.: ImageNet classification with deep convolutional neural networks. In: Advances in Neural Information Processing Systems, pp. 1097–1105 (2012)
5. Joly, A., et al.: LifeCLEF 2015: multimedia life species identification challenges. In: Mothe, J., et al. (eds.) CLEF 2015. LNCS, vol. 9283, pp. 462–483. Springer, Cham (2015). https://doi.org/10.1007/978-3-319-24027-5_46
6. Ghazi, M.M., Yanikoglu, B., Aptoula, E.: Plant identification using deep neural networks via optimization of transfer learning parameters. Neurocomputing **235**, 228–235 (2017)
7. Zou, Z., Shi, Z., Guo, Y., Ye, J.: Object detection in 20 years: a survey. arXiv preprint arXiv: 1905.05055 (2019)
8. Hinton, G.E., Krizhevsky, A., Sutskever, I.: ImageNet classification with deep convolutional neural networks. In: Advances in Neural Information Processing Systems, vol. 25, pp. 1106–1114 (2012)
9. Girshick, R., Donahue, J., Darrell, T., Malik, J.: Rich feature hierarchies for accurate object detection and semantic segmentation. In: IEEE Conference on Computer Vision and Pattern Recognition, pp. 580–587 (2014)
10. Girshick, R.: Fast R-CNN. In: IEEE International Conference on Computer Vision, pp. 1440–1448 (2015)
11. Ren, S., He, K., Girshick, R., Sun, J.: Faster R-CNN: towards real-time object detection with region proposal networks. In: Advances in Neural Information Processing Systems, pp. 91–99 (2015)
12. Redmon, J., Divvala, S., Girshick, R., Farhadi, A.: You only look once: unified, real-time object detection. In: IEEE Conference on Computer Vision and Pattern Recognition, pp. 779–788 (2016)
13. Redmon, J., Farhadi, A.: YOLO9000: better, faster, stronger. In: IEEE Conference on Computer Vision and Pattern Recognition, pp. 7263–7271 (2017)
14. Redmon, J., Farhadi, A.: YOLOv3: an incremental improvement. arXiv preprint arXiv:1804. 02767 (2018)
15. Bochkovskiy, A., Wang, C.Y., Liao, H.Y.M.: YOLOv4: optimal speed and accuracy of object detection. arXiv preprint arXiv:2004.10934 (2020)
16. Yun, S., Han, D., Oh, S.J., Chun, S., Choe, J., Yoo, Y.: CutMix: regularization strategy to train strong classifiers with localizable features. In: IEEE International Conference on Computer Vision, pp. 6023–6032 (2019)
17. Wang, K., Liew, J.H., Zou, Y., Zhou, D., Feng, J.: PANet: few-shot image semantic segmentation with prototype alignment. In: IEEE International Conference on Computer Vision, pp. 9197–9206 (2019)
18. Yan, W.Q.: Computational Methods for Deep Learning - Theoretic. Practice and Applications. Springer, Heidelberg (2021). https://doi.org/10.1007/978-3-030-61081-4
19. Yan, W.Q.: Introduction to Intelligent Surveillance - Surveillance Data Capture, Transmission, and Analytics, 3rd edn. Springer, Heidelberg (2019). https://doi.org/10.1007/978-3-319-602 28-8
20. Pan, C., Yan, W.Q.: Object detection based on saturation of visual perception. Multimed. Tools Appl. **79**(27–28), 19925–19944 (2020). https://doi.org/10.1007/s11042-020-08866-x
21. Pan, C., Li, X., Yan, W.: A learning-based positive feedback approach in salient object detection. IEEE IVCNZ (2018)
22. Liu, Z., Yan, W., Yang, B.: Image denoising based on a CNN model. In: ICCAR, pp. 389–393 (2018)

23. Zheng, K., Yan, W., Nand, P.: Video dynamics detection using deep neural networks. IEEE Trans. Emerg. Top. Comput. Intell. **2**(3), 224–234 (2018)
24. Xiao, B., Nguyen, M., Yan, W.: Apple ripeness identification using deep learning models. ISGV (2021)
25. Zhao, K., Yan, W.: Fruit detection from digital images using CenterNet. ISGV (2021)
26. Al-Sarayreha, M., Reis, M., Yan, W., Klette, R.: Potential of deep learning and snapshot hyperspectral imaging for classification of species in meat. Food Control (2020)
27. Al-Sarayreh, M., Reis, M.M., Yan, W.Q., Klette, R.: A sequential CNN approach for foreign object detection in hyperspectral images. In: Vento, M., Percannella, G. (eds.) CAIP 2019. LNCS, vol. 11678, pp. 271–283. Springer, Cham (2019). https://doi.org/10.1007/978-3-030-29888-3_22
28. Al-Sarayreh, M., Reis, M., Yan, W., Klette, R.: Detection of red-meat adulteration by deep spectral–spatial features in hyperspectral images. J. Imaging **4**(5), 63 (2018)
29. Al-Sarayreh, M., Reis, M.M., Yan, W.Q., Klette, R.: Detection of adulteration in red meat species using hyperspectral imaging. In: Paul, M., Hitoshi, C., Huang, Q. (eds.) PSIVT 2017. LNCS, vol. 10749, pp. 182–196. Springer, Cham (2018). https://doi.org/10.1007/978-3-319-75786-5_16
30. An, N., Yan, W.: Multitarget tracking using Siamese neural networks. ACM TOMM (2021)

Deep Learning in Medical Applications: Lesion Segmentation in Skin Cancer Images Using Modified and Improved Encoder-Decoder Architecture

Ranpreet Kaur[(⊠)] ⓘ, Hamid GholamHosseini ⓘ, and Roopak Sinha ⓘ

ECMS, Auckland University of Technology, Auckland 1010, New Zealand
ranpreet.kaur@aut.ac.nz

Abstract. The rise of deep learning techniques, such as a convolutional neural network (CNN) in solving medical image problems, offered fascinating results that motivated researchers to design automatic diagnostic systems. Image segmentation is one of the crucial and challenging steps in the design of a computer-aided diagnosis system owing to the presence of low contrast between skin lesion and background, noise artifacts, color variations, and irregular lesion boundaries. In this paper, we propose a modified and improved encoder-decoder architecture with a smaller network depth and a smaller number of kernels to enhance the segmentation process. The network performs segmentation for skin cancer images to obtain information about the infected area. The proposed model utilizes the power of the VGG19 network's weight layers for calculating rich features. The deconvolutional layers were designed to regain spatial information of the image. In addition to this, optimized training parameters were adopted to further improve the network's performance. The designed network was evaluated for two publicly available benchmarked datasets ISIC, and PH^2 consists of dermoscopic skin cancer images. The experimental observations proved that the proposed network achieved the higher average values of segmentation accuracy 95.67%, IoU 96.70%, and BF-score of 89.20% on ISIC 2017 and accuracy 98.50%, IoU 93.25%, and BF-score 84.08% on PH^2 datasets as compared to other state-of-the-art algorithms on the same datasets.

Keywords: Image segmentation · Medical image analysis · Skin cancer · Deep learning

1 Introduction

Medical image analysis is the process of analyzing image information generated in clinical settings. The primary target behind image analysis is to obtain relevant information for diagnosis. The recent developments in computer vision techniques have made medical image analysis one of the exciting research areas. Deep learning is one of the popular choices of researchers to use in solving medical problems, such as lung cancer [1], breast tissue detection [2], glaucoma eye diagnosis [3], and blood pressure monitoring [4]. Our

© Springer Nature Switzerland AG 2021
M. Nguyen et al. (Eds.): ISGV 2021, CCIS 1386, pp. 39–52, 2021.
https://doi.org/10.1007/978-3-030-72073-5_4

research focuses on the extraction of lesion areas from skin cancer images that would further analyze the type of cancer, such as benign and malignant. Skin cancer is the most commonly found problem around the world that occurs due to overexposure to ultraviolet sun rays. The incidence of skin cancer has been overgrowing, and it is the 19th most common cancer worldwide [5], thus become an issue of great concern in the healthcare community.

Skin cancer is the excessive growth of abnormal cells in the outermost skin layer known as the epidermis. The cancerous cells overgrow into the body and damage surrounding tissues to form a malignant tumor. The main type of skin cancer is squamous cell carcinoma, basal cell carcinoma, and melanoma [8], as shown in Fig. 1. Melanoma is rare but the deadliest form of other skin cancer types because the cancerous cells multiply unexpectedly. The risk factors that contribute towards the formation of melanoma include fair complexion, overexposure to sun rays, sunburn, genetic history, and weak immune system [6, 7].

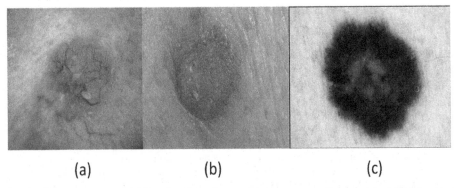

(a)   (b)   (c)

Fig. 1. Skin cancer types: (a) Basal cell carcinoma (b) Squamous cell carcinoma (c) Melanoma.

Researchers are on track to develop an efficient and cost-effective software tool to detect cancer at an early stage, which can significantly reduce the mortality rate. Deep learning approaches are widely applied in image analysis applications. For the accurate diagnosis of medical problems, it is pertinent to understand image patterns that are possible through the image segmentation process. Segmentation is one of the crucial steps of image analysis to differentiate object descriptions from their background [9]. Manual skin image segmentation is a tedious and time-consuming task in a clinical environment to identify each patient's skin patterns. Thus, there is a tremendous need for developing an automatic segmentation approach which is the primary aim of the current research. To design an automated classification system, a precise and efficient lesion segmentation approach is one of the key requirements.

We introduced three contributions in this paper, firstly four blocks of down-sampling layers consisted of convolutional, batch normalization, leaky ReLU, and pooling layers were designed as encoder block to extract spatial information of the image and to store max-pooling indices. Corresponding to each down-sampling layer, the decoder section was designed to perform up-sampling. The indices computed by down-sampling layers were used by up-sampling layers in the decoder section to regain the spatial resolution. Secondly, a leaky ReLU layer was used instead of the ReLU layer to add more balance and faster learning. At last, the proposed framework was effectively evaluated for a large database to make it more general for other applications.

2 Related Study

Many attempts have been made to extract lesions using traditional image processing techniques, machine learning algorithms, and the latest deep learning approaches. There is no standard method of segmenting images because the area of interest and object description varies from application to application. Hence selection of segmentation technique depends upon the type of images given in the input. Segmentation of lesions is a challenging task due to the large variations in terms of color, size, shape, location, and texture. The approaches that have been applied in the field of lesion segmentation are categorized into six groups, edge-based methods [10, 11], thresholding-based methods [12–16], clustering methods [17, 18], active contour methods [19–21], and supervised algorithms [22–24]. These old image processing methods have become indispensable in solving very complex and challenging image segmentation problems. In 2013, an initial attempt was made to employ a deep learning approach for the segmentation of X-ray images [25]. They applied patch-wise classification on raw images to identify bone tissues and selected only rib regions to reduce training time. A similar approach was applied to fundus images for the segmentation of blood vessels proposed by Melinscak et al. in 2015 [26]. They used a deep convolutional neural network that made use of max-pooling layers instead of subsampling or downsampling layers and achieved an average accuracy of 94%.

In 2015, Long et al. proposed the first end-to-end pixel-wise segmentation technique, a fully convolutional neural network (FCN) [27]. They adapted AlexNet, VGGNet, and GoogleNet classification models for semantic segmentation by replacing convolutional layers with fully connected layers to generate segmentation maps. In 2015, Hong et al. proposed a semi-supervised learning approach, deconvolution networks (DeconvNet), as an extension of FCN networks [28]. This architecture decoupled classification and segmentation tasks by adding bridging layers to construct class-oriented feature maps that reduce training and inferencing time. The main problem with FCN was pooling layers, that increased field of view and discarded the actual information. In 2017, an idea of encoder-decoder-based architecture was presented by Badrinarayanan et al. [29] that has a network layout similar to VGG16. In this network, the encoder section reduces spatial dimensionality with pooling layers and the decoder gradually regains the object information and spatial details. U-Net is another famous network inspired by encoder-decoder architecture which is successfully applied for the segmentation of medical images [30]. More details of these networks are given in review papers [31, 32]. Some research work studied the impact of changing network architecture using a transfer learning approach in terms of layer structure [33–35], optimizing training parameters [36–39], aiming to reach an optimal solution that reduces computation time, power and increase network accuracy.

Motivated by the recent developments in deep learning algorithms, we aimed to propose a modified encoder-decoder framework to perform segmentation. Instead of applying any pre-processing or post-processing approach to improve segmentation accuracy, we focused on designing an end-to-end learning network that can process raw images contaminated with different noise levels and can accurately extract a region of interest. In this paper, we explored the VGG19 network [40], which was originally designed for the ImageNet classification task. The network applied convolutional and pooling operation over an entire image to extract features. A cross-entropy loss function was used to predict the pixel-wise labels. The lesion occupies a small portion of the whole image that tends loss function to be biased towards background information. Thus, a weighted cross-entropy loss function was used to improve segmentation results. The designed framework was evaluated on two publicly available datasets, ISIC, and PH^2.

3   Materials and Methods

3.1   Encoder-Decoder Framework

The proposed model was inspired by VGG19 [40] deep neural network, whose layers were modified and improved to design deep encoder-decoder architecture for lesion segmentation. The CNN architecture designed for skin cancer segmentation is shown in Fig. 2. The idea of an encoder-decoder network was originally designed for doing semantic segmentation of road scene applications. The proposed network was designed by changing network depth, layer configuration, and optimizing hyperparameters. The first half of the architecture called the encoder section having four blocks that further consists of multiple convolutional, batch normalization, leaky ReLU, and max-pooling layers. In contrast, the lower half was the decoder section having deconvolutional layers, batch normalization, leaky ReLU layer, and max-unpooling layers corresponding to each layer in the encoder section, followed by a cross-entropy loss function-based segmentation layer. In this network, the pooling indices computed by the max-pooling layers of the encoder section were used to perform up-sampling in the decoder section. The fully connected layers in the previous networks were removed, which made the encoder section smaller and reduced the number of learnable parameters.

In the encoder section, a convolutional operation was performed with a set of kernels to generate feature maps. These were then batch normalized and the negative values were set to any fixed value by applying element-wise leaky rectified linear units (PReLU). Following this, a max-pooling operation was implemented with a 2×2 window size, a stride of 2, and padding 0. The max pooling was used to reduce the size of feature maps while preserving significant characteristics. It is often placed between two convolutional layers and is responsible for decreasing the number of parameters and calculations in the network. Pooling operation can be applied using the equation as:

$$FM\left[x, y\right] = f_p \times I_{x,y} \tag{1}$$

$FM\left[x, y\right]$ shows the output feature map, f_p is the pooling function, $I_{x,y}$ is the input feature map from the previous layer. Max pooling calculates a maximum value from the portion overlapped by the kernel. The repetitive use of max-pooling and striding at consecutive layers reduces the spatial resolution of the output feature map. Some architectures such as fully convolutional networks used a 'transposed convolutional layer' but it results in more time and memory. In the original VGG19 network, there was the successive use of several convolutional layers to achieve high translation invariance for more robust classification. However, there was a loss of spatial resolution which is not suitable for segmentation. Therefore, it is significant to preserve boundary information after sub-sampling layers. To achieve this, max-pooling indices were stored, i.e. the location of maximum features was memorized and used in the decoder section to perform upsampling that regains spatial resolution. The high dimensional feature maps were fed to a multi-class softmax pixel-wise classifier that generates K-channel probabilities for each pixel, K is the number of classes. We add here, Deconvnet, SegNet and U-Net shares similar kind of architecture, but have some differences in terms of layer organization, hyperparameters, and training. Deconvnet is hard to train end-to-end due to the presence of fully connected layers, SegNet is very time consuming and U-Net does not reuse pooling indices.

3.2   Network Architecture Details

The network consists of 60 layers designed from scratch broadly divided into encoder and decoder sections, as shown in Fig. 2. The layers of the encoder block follow the VGG19 layout with some additional layers, whereas the corresponding decoder block is our contribution. The first section has 29 layers that extract object details by downsampling the feature maps and the second section has respective deconvolutional layers to upsample the image information. The network consists of a total of 60 layers, 134 layer connections, and generates an output feature map of different sizes after each layer, and the network details are demonstrated in Table 1.

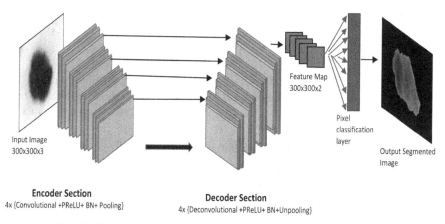

Fig. 2. The proposed CNN architecture for skin cancer segmentation

Encoder Section. This is the first half of the section responsible for down-sampling of feature maps and extracts features of input images using the following layers.

Convolutional Layer: This layer in the encoder section generates a feature map by sliding a kernel over an entire image and determines the product between the kernel and underlying region of an image using the formula:

$$FM[x, y] = \sum_{i=1}^{l} \sum_{j=1}^{l} [I_{x-i,y-j}] \times K[i,j] \qquad (2)$$

$FM[x, y]$ represents the output feature map, $[x, y]$ shows the pixel positions in the spatial domain, l is the kernel size, I is the input image, and K is the kernel or template. The other parameters used in this layer are kernel size, number of kernels, stride, and padding. The kernel size chosen for the current network is 3×3, as this size is suitable for images and covers all pixels positions of an image. Moreover, the larger kernel size leads to more time and memory consumption. Each encoder performs a convolutional operation with multiple kernels to produce a feature map. The higher number of kernels helps extract very fine details of the image, but it also takes a longer execution time. We chose the number of kernels as 64 kernels; however, in original VGG19 networks, the number of kernels at each convolutional layer varies from 64 to 512. Then, the stride value is taken as '1' that defines the step size of the kernel when sliding over an image. The last parameter is padding selected as '1' which adds extra ones at the end of the image border to prevent cropping.

Batch Normalization Layer: The outputs of the convolutional layer, i.e. output feature map are fed to batch normalization. This layer does not reduce the size of the feature map. It allows each layer to learn on a more stable distribution of inputs, i.e. rescales inputs between 0 and 1 and accelerate the training of the network.

PReLU Layer: It applied the threshold function to each element in the input and multiplied all negative values by a fixed scalar. This layer passes the output element as the input to the next layer directly if it is positive; otherwise, its output to value multiplied by a fixed scalar using the following activation function:

$$PReLU(x) = \begin{cases} scalar * x, & x < 0 \\ x, & x \geq 0 \end{cases} \qquad (3)$$

Max-pooling Layer: This layer reduces the spatial size of the network by decreasing the number of parameters and computation, also called down-sampling. Max-pooling layer in the current network used window size '2×2', padding [0 0 0 0] and stride value [2 2]. The stride value in the max-pooling layer denotes the number of shifts over the input matrix and padding inserts extra zeros so that the filter exactly fits the input image.

Decoder Section. The decoder in the second half of the network performs the reverse operation of pooling and reconstructs the original image resolution. The deconvolutional layers used the same number of kernels with the same size, stride, and padding value to obtain an activation map through up-sampling layers that swap forward and backward pass of a convolution. As a result, a dense feature map is produced that represents high image resolution. Then batch normalization and PReLU layers are placed in the same pattern as in the encoder section. After that, the max-pooling indices applied that were calculated during the first section to obtain the same image resolution. In this way, the network learns from global information and fine details to perform segmentation.

Table 1. Architecture and parameter details of the proposed network.

Encoder-section			Decoder-section		
Layer	Filter	Output size	Layer	Filter	Output size
Conv1_1	3 × 3	300 × 300 × 64	UnPool4	2 × 2	37 × 37 × 64
Conv1_2	3 × 3	300 × 300 × 64	De_Conv4_2	3 × 3	37 × 37 × 64
Pool1	2 × 2	150 × 150 × 64	De_Conv4_1	3 × 3	37 × 37 × 64
Conv2_1	3 × 3	150 × 150 × 64	UnPool3	2 × 2	75 × 75 × 64
Conv2_2	3 × 3	150 × 150 × 64	De_Conv3_2	3 × 3	75 × 75 × 64
Pool2	2 × 2	75 × 75 × 64	De_Conv3_1	3 × 3	75 × 75 × 64
Conv3_1	3 × 3	75 × 75 × 64	UnPool2	2 × 2	150 × 150 × 64
Conv3_2	3 × 3	75 × 75 × 64	De_Conv2_2	3 × 3	150 × 150 × 64
Pool3	2 × 2	37 × 37 × 64	De_Conv2_1	3 × 3	150 × 150 × 64
Conv4_1	3 × 3	37 × 37 × 64	UnPool1	2 × 2	300 × 300 × 64
Conv4_2	3 × 3	37 × 37 × 64	De_Conv1_2	3 × 3	300 × 300 × 64
Pool4	2 × 2	18 × 18 × 64	De_Conv1_1	3 × 3	300 × 300 × 2

Pixel Classification Layer and Weighted Cross-Entropy Loss Function. The output of the decoder blocks given to the pixel classification layer that generates each pixel's posterior probability using weighted cross-entropy loss [41]. This loss function measures the error between prediction scores P and targets T. The weighted cross-entropy loss between P and T can be calculated as:

$$Loss = \frac{1}{N} \sum_{i=1}^{K} \sum_{n=1}^{N} w_i T_{ni} \log(P_{ni}) \tag{4}$$

Here, N is the number of observations, K is the number of classes, and w is a vector of weights determined by the network for each class. The entropy loss is mostly used to evaluate the performance of medical image segmentation in comparison to the ground truth images.

Network Training Algorithm. Training a deep neural network for 5694 images with different lesion shapes was a challenging task. As explained in the previous section, the network consists of 60 layers where 8 convolutional and 4 pooling layers perform encoding function and corresponding 8 deconvolutional and 4 unpooling layers to regain the original information. In the end, the classification layer classifies each pixel into 2 classes, i.e. lesion or background, and generated a posterior probability map for each pixel. Few parameters were fine-tuned for the proposed network to execute effective training.

Adaptive Moment Estimation (ADAM) Optimizer: This optimization algorithm emerged from gradient descent and momentum to update the network training parameters, weights, and bias aiming to minimize loss value. It computes the adaptive learning rate for each parameter of the network, unlike stochastic gradient descent that calculates a single learning rate for all weights updates. The original gradient descent for updating the network in the direction of the negative value of loss function given as:

$$\theta_{i+1} = \theta_i - \alpha \nabla L(\theta_i) \tag{5}$$

Here, i denotes the iterations, $\alpha > 0$ is the learning rate taken as 0.01, θ is the parameter vector and $L(\theta)$ is the loss function. In the standard stochastic gradient method, the gradient of the loss function, $\nabla L(\theta)$ is evaluated for the entire training dataset. In contrast, the ADAM optimizer adds a term called 'momentum' to do an element-wise average of parameter gradients and their squared values. The above equation can be rewritten as:

$$m_i = \beta_1 m_{i-1} + (1 - \beta_1)\nabla L(\theta_i)$$
$$v_i = \beta_2 v_{i-1} + (1 - \beta_2)[\nabla L(\theta_i)]^2 \tag{6}$$

The optimizer used moving average to update the network as:

$$\theta_{i+1} = \theta_i - \frac{\alpha m_i}{\sqrt{v_i} + \epsilon} \tag{7}$$

β_1 and β_2 are gradient decay factor set as '0.95' and squared gradient decay factor set as '0.99' respectively and the learning rate α was specified as 0.03.

4 Simulations and Results Discussion

4.1 Dataset Preparation

Data collected from the ISIC 2018 archive repository [42], was nearly 5694 images of BCC, Melanoma, Squamous, and Nevus skin cancer types. Approximately 3100 images from ISIC 2017 challenge were used for testing purposes. Another dataset used for testing was PH^2 [43], which consists of almost 200 images, including ground truth images. Ground truth images are necessary for evaluating segmentation results to predict whether the approach correctly classified all the pixels into the foreground and background. The original images had dimensions $1022 \times 767 \times 3$ which is too large to process and can slow down the processing of the system. Thus images were downsized to $300 \times 300 \times 3$. Different image size was taken into consideration, such as 224×224, 227×227, and 256×297, but the 300×300 had given optimal performance. To prepare datasets for training and validation, the whole dataset is split into the ratio of 80%, and 20% respectively (Fig. 3).

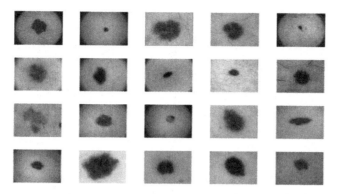

Fig. 3. Skin cancer images dataset [42, 43].

4.2 Quality Metrics

The performance evaluation metrics used in our experiments are accuracy, intersection over union (IoU), and BF score. The values of these parameters are expected to be high for efficient segmentation and these are calculated on the testing dataset. The parameters TP, TN, FP, FN denotes the true positives, true negatives, false positives, and false negatives.

Accuracy is the number of corrected pixels identified over the total number of pixels.

$$Accuracy = \frac{TP + TN}{TP + TN + FP + FN} \tag{8}$$

Intersection Over Union (IoU) is the ratio of correctly classified pixels to the total number of pixels that are assigned a class by the ground truth and the predictor.

$$IoU = \frac{TP}{TP + FP + FN} \tag{9}$$

BF Score computes the Boundary F1 contour matching score between the predicted segmentation in prediction and the true segmentation in the ground truth.

$$BF \ Score = \frac{2*precision*recall}{Precision + recall} \tag{10}$$

4.3 Comparison with Other State-of-the-Art Methods

To evaluate the effectiveness of the network, it is compared with other state-of-the-art methods from the last four years (2016–2019) and it is observed that the designed network outperformed as compare to others. The qualitative segmentation results using the proposed network are displayed for the input images (see Fig. 4). It showed that the lesion region was extracted accurately, however, some irrelevant background object information exists for a few highly noisy images.

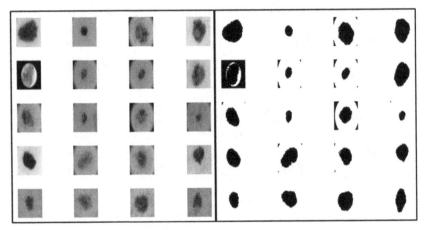

Fig. 4. Segmented output Images corresponding to original images using the proposed network.

The proposed network was trained for 5694 RGB images and tested for 3300 images different from the training set to measure the performance parameters. The comparative analysis with other similar research studies based on these metrics on the ISIC dataset is illustrated in Table 2. It clearly shows the higher performance of the proposed approach as compared to others in terms of accuracy and IoU also called a Jaccard index which should be expected higher for better segmentation results. The literature studies chosen for the comparison are based on the same dataset, i.e., ISIC 2017 and PH^2. Our network achieved a high value of this parameter with a difference of 0.43% as compared to other mentioned studies. Moreover, it gained almost higher accuracy and BF score except given in [39] but it outperformed other studies with the highest Jaccard score of 96.7% and accuracy of 95.6%.

Table 2. Performance-based on the ISIC 2017 dataset and compared to other similar studies.

Method	Accuracy%	BF%	Iou%
Proposed Approach	**0.956**	**0.892**	**0.967**
FCRN [39]	0.947	**0.927**	0.962
VGG16 [39]	0.903	0.794	0.707
GoogleNet [39]	0.911	0.848	0.776
Modified SegNet [44]	–	0.853	0.771
Supervised Saliency Detection [45]	0.930	0.839	0.749
Jeremy Kawahara [34]	0.930	0.837	0.752
FCN with Jaccard loss function [46]	0.934	0.849	0.765
DCI-PSL [47]	0.940	0.856	0.777

Table 3 Illustrates parameters on the PH^2 dataset, and it shows a higher performance of the proposed network over other approaches from the years 2016–2019 in terms of accuracy and IoU. Our model is gaining higher accuracy and overlapping index (IoU) as compared to other state-of-the-art methods which show the network is efficient in segmenting lesions from dermoscopic images on the PH^2 dataset.

Table 3. Performance analysis based on the PH^2 dataset and compared to other similar studies.

Method	Accuracy%	BF%	IoU%
The proposed approach	**0.985**	0.840	**0.932**
Supervised Saliency Detection [45]	0.979	**0.952**	0.923
DCL-PSI [47]	0.953	0.921	0.859
MFCN [48]	0.940	0.906	0.839

The impact of choosing the different depths of encoder-decoder architecture is illustrated in Table 4. It shows that architectural depth below 4 given a lower performance in terms of segmentation accuracy, whereas, depth higher than 4 given little increase but leads to higher execution time. Thus, '4' was selected as an optimal network depth for the proposed model.

Table 4. Performance of the network by the varying depth of the architecture and evaluated on the ISIC 2017 dataset.

Encoder-Decoder Depth	Accuracy %	Execution Time in hours (approximately)
2	63.56	3
3	79.23	5.5
4	**95.67**	**6**
5	**96.08**	11

5   Discussion and Conclusion

In this paper, we presented a modified deep learning framework to meet the challenges of automatic lesion segmentation on dermoscopic images. The new network leverages the increased segmentation accuracy despite highly noisy data and varying lesion shapes. The design of a new network is inspired by the VGG19 classification network and encoder-decoder models. The layers of the encoder section are organized taking the VGG19 framework as a base with some additional layers such as leaky ReLU in each block. To boost the network's performance, a leaky ReLU layer, fine-tuned training parameters such as kernel size, number of filters, learning rate, momentum, and batch size, and the weighted cross-entropy loss function was used. The network was trained for ISIC 2018 dataset and performance was evaluated for two datasets, ISIC 2017 and PH^2. It was concluded that the proposed network yields better performance as compared to the other state-of-the-art methods. It is illustrated in Tables 2 and 3 that our proposed model outperformed previous studies by gaining higher values of accuracy, and IoU index. The proposed network can be efficiently applied in clinical settings to understand lesion patterns for the early diagnosis of the type of skin cancer. In some instances, there is a lack of properly segmented region due to the presence of intense hairlines, asymmetrical shapes, and color variations. Therefore, there is room for further improvement in segmentation results by applying any pre-processing techniques and improving network configuration. Moreover, in the future, our research will focus on the design of a more optimal segmentation network having low execution time and high accuracy.

References

1. Skourt, B.A., El Hassani, A., Majda, A.: Lung CT image segmentation using deep neural networks. Procedia Comput. Sci. **127**, 109–113 (2018)
2. Zhang, Y., et al.: Automatic breast and fibroglandular tissue segmentation in breast MRI using deep learning by a fully-convolutional residual neural network U-net. Acad. Radiol. **26**(11), 1526–1535 (2019)
3. Yu, S., Xiao, D., Frost, S., Kanagasingam, Y.: Robust optic disc and cup segmentation with deep learning for glaucoma detection. Comput. Med. Imaging Graph. **74**, 61–71 (2019)
4. Wu, D., Xu, L., Zhang, R., Zhang, H., Ren, L., Zhang, Y.-T.: Continuous cuff-less blood pressure estimation based on combined information using deep learning approach. J. Med. Imaging Health Inform. **8**(6), 1290–1299 (2018)
5. Skin Cancer-Index (2018). https://www.isic-archive.com. Accessed 2019
6. What is Melanoma Skin Cancer? https://www.cancer.org/cancer/melanoma-skin-cancer/about/what-is-melanoma.html. Accessed 2019
7. Bogo, F., Peruch, F., Fortina, A.B., Peserico, E.: Where's the lesion?: Variability in human and automated segmentation of dermoscopy images of melanocytic skin lesions. In: Dermoscopy Image Analysis, pp. 82–110. CRC Press (2015)
8. Types of Skin Cancer. https://www.everydayhealth.com/skin-cancer/types. Accessed 2020
9. Sridevi, M., Mala, C.: A survey on monochrome image segmentation methods. Procedia Technol. **6**, 548–555 (2012)
10. Barcelos, C.A.Z., Pires, V.: An automatic based nonlinear diffusion equations scheme for skin lesion segmentation. Appl. Math. Comput. **215**(1), 251–261 (2009)
11. de Souza Ganzeli, H., Bottesini, J.G., de Oliveira Paz, L., Ribeiro, M.F.S.: Skan: Skin scanner-system for skin cancer detection using adaptive techniques. IEEE Latin Am. Trans. **9**(2), 206–212 (2011)
12. Norton, K.A., et al.: Three-phase general border detection method for dermoscopy images using non-uniform illumination correction. Skin Res. Technol. **18**(3), 290–300 (2012)
13. Qaisar Abbas, M., Celebi, E., Fondón, I.: Computer-aided pattern classification system for dermoscopy images. Skin Res. Technol. **18**(3), 278–289 (2012)
14. Garnavi, R., Aldeen, M., Celebi, M.E., Varigos, G., Finch, S.: Border detection in dermoscopy images using hybrid thresholding on optimized color channels. Comput. Med. Imaging Graph. **35**(2), 105–115 (2011)
15. Ma, Z., Tavares, J.M.R.: A novel approach to segment skin lesions in dermoscopic images based on a deformable model. IEEE J. Biomed. Health Inform. **20**(2), 615–623 (2015)

16. Cavalcanti, P.G., Scharcanski, J.: A coarse-to-fine approach for segmenting melanocytic skin lesions in standard camera images. Comput. Methods Programs Biomed. **112**(3), 684–693 (2013)
17. Shan, P.: Image segmentation method based on K-mean algorithm. EURASIP J. Image Video Process. **2018**(1), 1–9 (2018). https://doi.org/10.1186/s13640-018-0322-6
18. Choudhry, M.S., Kapoor, R.: Performance analysis of fuzzy C-means clustering methods for MRI image segmentation. Procedia Comput. Sci. **89**, 749–758 (2016)
19. Kasmi, R., Mokrani, K.: Classification of malignant melanoma and benign skin lesions: implementation of automatic ABCD rule. IET Image Proc. **10**(6), 448–455 (2016)
20. Vasconcelos, F., Medeiros, A., Peixoto, S., Filho, P.: Automatic skin lesions segmentation based on a new morphological approach via geodesic active contour. Cognit. Syst. Res. **55**, 44–59 (2019)
21. Bayraktar, M., Kockara, S., Halic, T., Mete, M., Wong, H.K., Iqbal, K.: Local edge-enhanced active contour for accurate skin lesion border detection. BMC Bioinform. **20**(2), 91 (2019). https://doi.org/10.1186/s12859-019-2625-8
22. Manjón, J.V., et al.: MRI white matter lesion segmentation using an ensemble of neural networks and overcomplete patch-based voting. Comput. Med. Imaging Graph. **69**, 43–51 (2018)
23. Tan, T.Y., Zhang, L., Lim, C.P., Fielding, B., Yu, Y., Anderson, E.: Evolving ensemble models for image segmentation using enhanced particle swarm optimization. IEEE Access **7**, 34004–34019 (2019)
24. Alshayeji, M.H., Al-Rousan, M.A., Ellethy, H., Abed, S.: An efficient multiple sclerosis segmentation and detection system using neural networks. Comput. Electr. Eng. **71**, 191–205 (2018)
25. Cernazanu-Glavan, C., Holban, S.: Segmentation of bone structure in X-ray images using convolutional neural network. Adv. Electr. Comput. Eng **13**(1), 87–94 (2013)
26. Melinščak, M., Prentašić, P., Lončarić, S.: Retinal vessel segmentation using deep neural networks. In: 10th International Conference on Computer Vision Theory and Applications (VISAPP 2015) (2015)
27. Long, J., Shelhamer, E., Darrell, T.: Fully convolutional networks for semantic segmentation. In: Proceedings of the IEEE Conference on Computer Vision and Pattern Recognition, pp. 3431–3440 (2015)
28. Hong, S., Noh, H., Han, B.: Decoupled deep neural network for semi-supervised semantic segmentation. In: Advances in Neural Information Processing Systems, pp. 1495–1503 (2015)
29. Badrinarayanan, V., Kendall, A., Cipolla, R.: Segnet: a deep convolutional encoder-decoder architecture for image segmentation. IEEE Trans. Pattern Anal. Mach. Intell. **39**(12), 2481–2495 (2017)
30. Ronneberger, O., Fischer, P., Brox, T.: U-net: convolutional networks for biomedical image segmentation. In: Navab, N., Hornegger, J., Wells, W.M., Frangi, A.F. (eds.) MICCAI 2015. LNCS, vol. 9351, pp. 234–241. Springer, Cham (2015). https://doi.org/10.1007/978-3-319-24574-4_28
31. Okur, E., Turkan, M.: A survey on automated melanoma detection. Eng. Appl. Artif. Intell. **73**, 50–67 (2018)
32. Hesamian, M.H., Jia, W., He, X., Kennedy, P.: Deep learning techniques for medical image segmentation: achievements and challenges. J. Digit. Imaging **32**(4), 582–596 (2019). https://doi.org/10.1007/s10278-019-00227-x
33. Yang, X., Zeng, Z., Yeo, S.Y., Tan, C., Tey, H.L., Su, Y.: A novel multi-task deep learning model for skin lesion segmentation and classification. arXiv preprint arXiv:1703.01025 (2017)
34. Kawahara, J., BenTaieb, A., Hamarneh, G.: Deep features to classify skin lesions. In: 2016 IEEE 13th International Symposium on Biomedical Imaging (ISBI), pp. 1397–1400. IEEE (2016)

35. Nida, N., Irtaza, A., Javed, A., Yousaf, M.H., Mahmood, M.T.: Melanoma lesion detection and segmentation using deep region based convolutional neural network and fuzzy C-means clustering. Int. J. Med. Inform. **124**, 37–48 (2019)
36. Nasr-Esfahani, E., et al.: Dense fully convolutional network for skin lesion segmentation arXiv preprint arXiv:1712.10207 (2017)
37. Vesal, S., Ravikumar, N., Maier, A.: SkinNet: a deep learning framework for skin lesion segmentation arXiv preprint arXiv:1806.09522 (2018)
38. Zhang, X.: Melanoma segmentation based on deep learning. Comput. Assist. Surg. **22**(s1), 267–277 (2017)
39. Yu, L., Chen, H., Dou, Q., Qin, J., Heng, P.-A.: Automated melanoma recognition in dermoscopy images via very deep residual networks. IEEE Trans. Med. Imaging **36**(4), 994–1004 (2016)
40. Simonyan, K., Zisserman, A.: Very deep convolutional networks for large-scale image recognition arXiv preprint arXiv:1409.1556 (2014)
41. Bishop, C.M.: Pattern Recognition and Machine Learning. Springer, New York (2006)
42. The International Skin Imaging Collaboration. www.isic-archive.com. Accessed 2019
43. Dermofit Image Library. https://licensing.edinburgh-innovations.ed.ac.uk/. Accessed 2019
44. Ninh, Q.C., Tran, T.-T., Tran, T.T., Tran, T.A.X., Pham, V.-T.: Skin lesion segmentation based on modification of SegNet neural networks. In: 2019 6th NAFOSTED Conference on Information and Computer Science (NICS), pp. 575–578. IEEE (2019)
45. Jahanifar, M., Tajeddin, N.Z., Asl, B.M., Gooya, A.: Supervised saliency map driven segmentation of lesions in dermoscopic images. IEEE J. Biomed. Health Inform. **23**(2), 509–518 (2018)
46. Yuan, Y., Chao, M., Lo, Y.-C.: Automatic skin lesion segmentation using deep fully convolutional networks with Jaccard distance. IEEE Trans. Med. Imaging **36**(9), 1876–1886 (2017)
47. Bi, L., Kim, J., Ahn, E., Kumar, A., Feng, D., Fulham, M.: Step-wise integration of deep class-specific learning for dermoscopic image segmentation. Pattern Recogn. **85**, 78–89 (2019)
48. Bi, L., Kim, J., Ahn, E., Kumar, A., Fulham, M., Feng, D.: Dermoscopic image segmentation via multi-stage fully convolutional networks. IEEE Trans. Biomed. Eng. **64**, 2065–2074 (2017)

Apple Ripeness Identification Using Deep Learning

Bingjie Xiao[✉], Minh Nguyen[✉], and Wei Qi Yan[✉]

Auckland University of Technology, Auckland 1010, New Zealand
vty0884@autuni.ac.nz, {mnguyen,wyan}@aut.ac.nz

Abstract. Deep learning models assist us in fruit classification, which allow us to use digital images from cameras to classify a fruit and find its class of ripeness automatically. Apple ripeness classification is a problem in computer vision and deep learning for pattern classification. In this paper, the ripeness of apples in digital images will be classified by using convolutional neural networks (CNN or ConvNets) in deep learning. The goal of this project is to verify the capability of deep learning models for fruit classification so as to lessen our human labor. Our experiments consist of four parts, namely, image preprocessing, apple detection, ripeness classification, and resultant evaluations. The contribution of this paper is that the classifiers are able to achieve the best result, i.e., the ripeness class of an apple from a given digital image is able to be precisely predicted. We have optimized the deep learning models and trained the classifiers so as to achieve the best outcome.

Keywords: Ground truth · Apple ripeness classification · YOLO

1 Introduction

Deep learning is a vital method for modern computer vision [24, 34, 38, 53]. Deep learning, namely, deep neural networks classify semantic objects and export the output of pattern classification [15, 19, 27–29, 51, 58, 59], which has shown its super capability to outperform than our human visual system.

There are existing software products for fruit classification which achieve very fast speed and high accuracy. Different from the existing classifiers, in our experiments, our attention is paid to the classification of a single fruit. However, the purpose of this paper is to identify the ripeness of apples. Apples are basically grouped into three categories, i.e., unripeness, ripeness, and overripeness. The key of this project is to detect visual objects and figure out the best methods for apple classification. Based on the requirement of this research question, the corresponding experiment firstly needs to locate the apples in an image, then classify them and label them.

The motivation of this project lies in the classification of fruit ripeness based on deep neural networks [1, 3, 9, 12, 66, 67]. A myriad of computational models has been exploited to classify the class of fruit ripeness [37]. The trends of fruit ripeness classification have been surveyed. Based on the obtained knowledge, a method with the

© Springer Nature Switzerland AG 2021
M. Nguyen et al. (Eds.): ISGV 2021, CCIS 1386, pp. 53–67, 2021.
https://doi.org/10.1007/978-3-030-72073-5_5

capability of classifying fruits owing to an effective neural network has been proffered. Non-maximum suppression is propounded to achieve object detection [2, 55]. All the detected bounding boxes were sorted by using scores. A predefined threshold was taken to suppress the overlapping with the detected boundary box that achieves the maximum score. The process is based on a regression for all bounding boxes.

In this project, a soft-NMS continuous function is adopted for calculating the scores of all visual objects. The soft-NMS function enhances the mean average precision (mAP) by modifying the NMS algorithm, no parameters is required to be adjusted.

In this paper, digital images captured by using mobile phones are primarily labelled in three classes (unripeness, ripeness, and overripeness). The core work of this project is to classify the visual objects and develop optimal methods. Given the requirement analysis, the corresponding implementations should be designed for the purposes of locating the apples in an image, extracting visual features, classifying the apple ripeness using the labelled data.

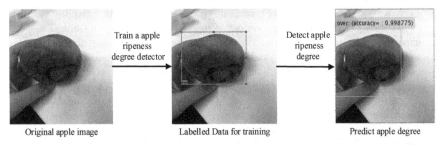

Fig. 1. Apple ripeness classification using supervised learning.

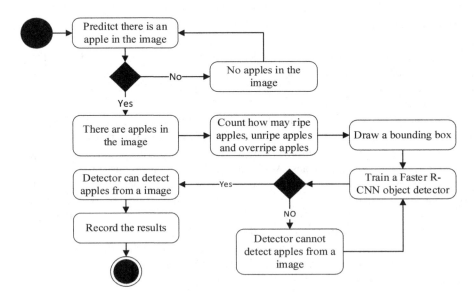

Fig. 2. The workflow of apple ripeness classification.

In Fig. 1, we detect an apple in a given image successfully, we thus draw a rectangle as the bounding box around it. This often involves two operations: (1) Predicting a class of apple ripeness (ripeness, unripeness, or overripeness); (2) Drawing a bounding box around the detected apple. After all apples are detected [46], we are use of a neural network as the classifier for apple classification.

The procedure is shown in Fig. 2. In Fig. 2, we manually label the location and ripeness class of the apples in each image as the labels and import the labelled data into the selected deep learning models for training. Then, we obtain a well-trained classifier associated with parameters (e.g., weights, network layout, etc.) that is able to classify the ripeness of the given apples [47].

The remaining parts of this paper are organized as follows. In Sect. 2, we review the literature. In Sect. 3, we elucidate our methodology. In Sect. 4, we explicit our experimental results. Our conclusion is drawn in Sect. 5, meanwhile the future work will be envisioned.

2 Related Work

A rich assortment of methods has been applied to apple classification. The first method was employed to find the edges, corners, colors, these visual features were extracted from digital images to classify visual objects. Although our human brain is proficient in classifying visual objects through our eyes, how the visual features take effect in the classification is still remaining unclear. Conventional machine learning methods have often been fulfilled directly by applying a broad spectrum of visual features from digital images [20, 25, 26, 30, 31, 41, 48, 49, 62, 64]. In fact, through long-time observations, experiments and evolutions, machine learning algorithms are subsequently employed to classify visual objects in the given images based on these visual features.

Feature extraction is the fundamental problem of pattern classification. Visual features usually encapsulate color, histogram, texture, edge, corners, motif, parts, etc. [10, 43, 50, 54, 62, 64, 65]. The extracted visual features will assist apple ripeness classification by exploiting deep neural networks [23, 65].

Besides feature extraction, artificial neural networks, especially deep neural networks, are trained by using the labelled images. A deep neural network has multiple layers of neurons in the end-to-end paradigm, in which each layer is connected to the next layer. The deep learning models are trained, tested, and validated by using the visual features extracted from the input images.

The existing work for visual object classification falls into CNN models and other machine learning methods [52, 62, 64, 65]. Deep learning methods are categorized into two groups: CNNs and RNNs [4, 5, 11, 13, 16, 20, 42]. In our surveys, R-CNN and Fast R-CNN are slower than YOLO and SSD in training, while the latter is proved to be with lower accuracy [6–8, 21, 22, 32, 33, 39, 40, 56]. Hence, training a classifier based on Faster R-CNN to conduct apple ripeness classification is regarded as an optimal method.

Based on Faster R-CNN, a hybrid detector was explicated for partially occluded object detection [21, 22]. The work emphasized on network depth. However, even if a network with the depth from sixteen to thirty is employed, the accuracy would not be further uplifted. Exploding gradient problem hampers the convergence at the beginning of the training processing. Normalization can assist the convergence of deep neural networks by using stochastic gradient descent (SGD) for backpropagation. With the depth growth of the neural network, degradation problem occurs, the accuracy is down-regulated. Trimming the network layers cannot dramatically affect the accuracy of deep learning models. In contrast, excessive network layers lead to accuracy saturation.

A method using Fruits-360 dataset has been propounded for fruit recognition [18]. By taking advantage of the depth of convolution neural networks, the cost of computations is diminished, while the robustness is enhanced, the performance of deep learning models is prone to be better.

The low-quality depth map with multilevel features is originated from RGB images [61]. Color images may enclose abundant appearance information. A novel RGBD saliency model based on bottom-up module explores the color images and depth information. Taken the abundant information into consideration, the module embeds attention models associated with salient objects.

The collection of visual data and deep learning models are key parts of our experiments. In this paper, we choose ResNet-50 and GoogLeNet as our models for apple detection, Faster-RCNN for apple ripeness classification. We also apply YOLO, one of DarkNet models, to compare the accuracy and training time.

ResNet-50 is a residual neural network, which has 50 layers. There are four groups of blocks in ResNet-50, three convolutional layers in each block. Ideally, the accuracy raises with the growth of the number of the network layers.

GoogLeNet is a 22-layer network with the structure of inception network, average pooling layer replaces the fully connected layers in the end of the network. To avoid the gradient vanishing, the network additionally adds two auxiliary softmax layers for the forward gradient. The model is better for parallel computing.

GoogLeNet takes use of Inception model. Inception v3 model has two branches, each branch generates one output. We harness a branch of the Inception v3 model to calculate convolution features.

Faster R-CNN refers to region-based CNN model which exhibits high efficiency and accuracy [35]. Fast R-CNN associated with feature maps by using selective search method for object detection. The loss function exploits regression during the training process and then optimizes the gained results. Faster R-CNN method inherits the attributes of Fast R-CNN. The critical change is the mechanism of object position prediction because the selective search method of Fast R-CNN has too much computational redundancy.

Visual data collected from real world could be blurry, rotated, or jitter with noises [33, 68]. Noises and invalid data may affect the result of object detection. In this project, we create an image degradation model based on YOLO. A mathematical model is established to generate degraded images which are dominantly applied to train YOLO object detector.

Compared to R-CNN model, YOLO networks have lower accuracy for identifying the position of a visual object. The prediction of bounding boxes in each grid cuts down the times of the object detection. The region proposal method has curbed overlapping. Furthermore, YOLO model adjusts the network structure, employs multiscale features for object detection, and replaces softmax function with logistic function for object classification. In terms of visual feature extraction, YOLO net harnesses a network structure DarkNet-53 (i.e., 53 convolutional layers), which is better than the residual networks.

With competitive accuracy rates, YOLOv3 is faster than other models. Furthermore, YOLOv4 has the attainment in both speed and accuracy of computations.

3 Our Approaches

Different from the existing approaches, in this project, we will work for apple ripeness classification using deep learning. The workflow is shown in Fig. 3. Our work is different from the existing one, we implement YOLO models for the purpose of comparisons. The reason is that the focus of our experiments is on practical applications. Fig.3 intuitively assists us to understand the experimental process using Faster R-CNN. As one of object detection methods, Faster R-CNN firstly harnesses a set of basic layers including convolutional layers, revolution layers, and pooling layers to extract image feature maps. The feature maps are shared for the subsequent RPN layer and fully connected layer. The RPN network is used to generate region proposals. This layer judges that the anchors belong to the foreground or background through softmax layers, then takes use of regression algorithms to correct the anchor boxes so as to obtain the accurate proposals. This layer collects the input feature maps and proposals, extracts the proposal feature maps after integrating the information, and sends them to the subsequent fully connected layer to classify the target category. We take use of proposal feature maps to calculate the category of apples, bounding box regression to obtain the final precise position of the detected object.

In this project, we not only determine whether there is an apple in an image, but also mark the location of this apple. Locating an apple implies to determine the specific location of the apple in an image. There are three types of bounding boxes in Fig. 4, ground truth box (blue), anchor box (green), and predicted box (yellow) which represent the labelled location, the detected location, and the predicted location, respectively [57].

The ground truth boxes are labelled manually, which reveal the real locations of apples in the given image. Naturally, the images in the training dataset all have been labelled. An anchor box is the sliding window which traverses through the image. The anchor box describes how Faster R-CNN model extracts features from the given images [6, 7]. An image cell may belong to multiple anchor boxes. The input is the whole image and the output is the labels.

Usually, anchor box in an image is not generated by a training dataset, which usually is distributed across the image. The essence of this kind of anchor boxes is the sliding window which traverses the image. A cell will correspond to multiple anchor boxes. The quantity of anchor box is set at the initialization stage. For instance, if we cut an image into 3×3 grids and set 2 anchor boxes, those two boxes will go through all the grids and make predications.

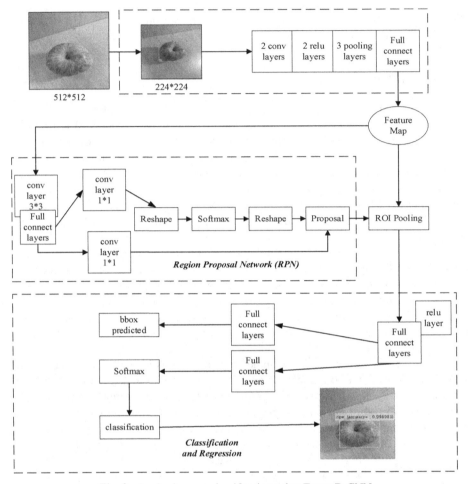

Fig. 3. Apple ripeness classification using Faster R-CNN

In our experiment, c_1, c_2, and c_3 represent three classes of apple ripeness. The bounding box is located by using four corner points. We donate the width of the bounding box as w, the height is h. In Fig. 5, i, j, and k represent the subscripts of bounding boxes, respectively. The vector $\mathbf{T}$ is

$$\mathbf{T} = (x, y, z, w, h, c_1, c_2, c_3). \tag{1}$$

The proposed model is to calculate the regression of bounding boxes $R_i(\cdot)$ that approaches to the ground truth $R_g(\cdot)$ iteratively,

$$R_1(A_1, B_1, C_1, D_1) \rightarrow \cdots \rightarrow R_i(A_i, B_i, C_i, D_i) \rightarrow \cdots \rightarrow R_g\left(A_g, B_g, C_g, D_g\right), i = 1, 2, \tag{2}$$

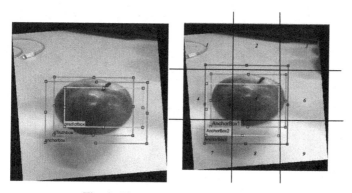

Fig. 4. The sample of bounding boxes.

The predicted bounding boxes are generated based on the regression of anchor boxes. Non-maximum suppression (NMS) allows each box to retain only one predicted bounding box and export all the probabilities from the highest to the lowest one. Each box only has the one with the maximum probability, the offsets are set as

$$\Delta x = (x_i - x_k)/w_k \tag{3}$$

$$\Delta y = (y_i - y_k)/h_k \tag{4}$$

$$\Delta w = \log(w_i/w_k) \tag{5}$$

$$\Delta h = \log(h_i/h_k) \tag{6}$$

where (x_k, y_k) denotes the center point of the predicted bounding box, h_k and w_k are the width and height, respectively. Δx, Δy, Δw, and Δh are the scaling or zooming factors of the bounding boxes calculated by using the region proposal regression.

In Fig. 5, A_1, B_1, C_1 and D_1 are applied to represent the predicted anchor box. x_k and y_k stand for the midpoint of the predicted apple location, h_k refers to the number of vertically divided anchors, w_k indicates the number of horizontally divided anchors, x_i, y_i, w_i and h_i refer to the coordinates, Δx, Δy, Δw and Δh should be the required values calculated by using region proposal. Actually, w_i and h_i may be larger or smaller than w_j and h_j. The loss function makes Δx, Δy, Δw and Δh get the minimum. In Fig. 5, the yellow boxes mark the actual apple position, the blue one is the position predicted.

In this paper, we design our experiments to compare the accuracy of apple classifications by using Faster R-CNN and YOLO models. ResNet-50 and GoogLeNet are chosen as training networks [14, 17]. In order to gain the best apple ripeness classification [6, 7, 9, 57, 61], mini-batch size, learning rate, epoch, quantity of data and quality of data are chosen as the optional parameters.

We train ResNet-50 model by using Dataset I. The mini-batch size was set as 1.000 in apple ripeness classification. Setting the learning rate as 0.001 is appropriate because a lower learning rate leads to an overloaded cost in the training. Dataset I and Dataset II

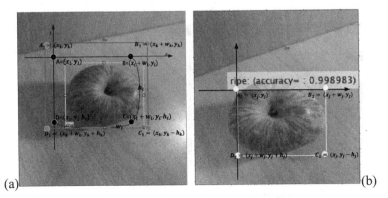

(a)   (b)

Fig. 5. The ground truth with labels, detected bounding boxes, and anchor boxes.

are selected as random datasets to test whether the number of training images will affect the results or not.

Ripe and overripe apple images in Dataset II have been applied to train ResNet-50 [36] and GoogLeNet. Due to the conditions (e.g., lighting and weather, etc.), the collection of training images have diversity.

The images in Dataset III were resized, no matter enlarged or shrunk. The dataset is scaled down, the image size is normalized to 224×224 from 512×512. Each image was rotated anticlockwise every 10 degrees as the interval. Additionally, Gaussian noises and salt-and-pepper noises are added to achieve the robustness of deep learning model through data augmentation [44, 45, 60].

Data augmentation is to primarily solve the problem of insufficient number of samples and uplift the quality of classification. We have imported a wealth of data for the model training, we avoid overfitting by focusing on general patterns rather than the specific ones. We use data augmentation to conduct various operations offline, including rotating, cropping, and resizing so as to adjust the amount of input data. Our data collection does not require excessive costs, the data augmentation caters for the demand of raising the volume of visual data.

The size of the neural network usually refers to the number of layers and weight parameters of the network. In this paper, we take use of ResNet model, which contains eighteen blocks, we choose ResNet-50 model with 50 blocks for our experiments.

The idea of average precision (mAP) is considered to find the region of interest (ROI) under precision-recall (PR) graph [57]. AP is computed as the average of maximum precision

$$AP = \frac{1}{N} \sum_{k}^{N} P(k) \tag{7}$$

where $P(k)$ is the probability of each ripeness class of an apple. If we need to average the classification accuracy of all the apples in the image, mAP (mean average precision) is calculated. For each class, we calculate AP and denote the average of all AP values as *mAP*, which is usually calculated based on one dataset, *mAP* is thought as a relatively objective and fair metric.

$$Accuracy = \frac{TP + TN}{TP + TN + FP + FN} \tag{8}$$

$$Precision = \frac{TP}{TP + FN} \tag{9}$$

$$Recall = \frac{TP}{TP + FN} \tag{10}$$

where *TP* (i.e., true positive) is the hit, *FP* (i.e., false positive) refers to the false alarm, *TN* (i.e., true negative) means correct rejection, *FN* (i.e., false negative) stands for miss.

Classification accuracy, no matter which category, as long as the prediction is correct, its number is placed on the numerator, the denominator is the total number of data, which shows that the accuracy is a judgment on all data. The accuracy corresponds to a class in the classification, the numerator is the number of correct prediction of the class, the denominator is the number of all data predicted to be classified.

In our experiments, we are use of both precision and accuracy method to evaluate the model no matter whether the model can accurately classify apple ripeness or not. From the accuracy, we judge whether a deep learning model is effective and qualifies as a classifier. Besides, precision and recall are offered to assess the performance of the models.

4 Our Experiments

Our three datasets were created with more than 10,000 images as shown in Table 1, where the apples gradually turn to overripe from unripe. The ripe and overripe apples were shot with a mobile phone camera. All of these three datasets are randomly split into training set and test set. Dataset I and Dataset II are mainly to compare the influence of data quantity for our experiments, Dataset III is used to compare the impact of data quality on the experiments after data augmentation.

Our experiment did not use a standard dataset, but manually collected pictures of apples under multiple environments like indoors and outdoors. In the real training, we used MATLAB 2020b as our experimental tool. During the experimentations, we used ordinary CPU computers for training. It takes over 48 h to train the Faster R-CNN model based on the datasets.

We have trained our models for multiple times, the results are listed in Tables 2, 3, 4 and 5. In the first round of training, a dataset was labelled into three classes. The parameters minibatch and epoch were firstly selected for training, the learning rate was set as 0.001.

In Table 3, we clearly see the classification performance of each model. For the class of overripe apples with obvious features, the model shows better performance, which means that the model performs better for this kind of apples.

Table 1. The number of samples of our datasets for this project

Datasets	Ripeness	Overripeness	Unripeness
(a) Number of apple images			
I	144	111	92
II	1325	1083	1040
III	4149	3713	–
(b) Corresponding numbers of labels			
I	552	452	409
II	5416	4475	3976
III	12564	10812	–

Table 2. The results of average precisions of our proposed models

Faster R-CNN		
Epochs	Deep learning models	mAP
10	ResNet-50 (ripe, overripe, Unripeness)	39.33%
10	ResNet-50 (ripe, overripe)	49%
30	ResNet-50 (ripe, overripe, Unripeness)	35.33%
10	GoogLeNet (ripe, overripe)	46.5%
30	GoogLeNet (ripe, overripe)	35.67%

Table 3. The results of precision rates using our datasets

Faster R-CNN model				
Epochs	Deep learning models	Ripeness	Overripeness	Unripeness
10	ResNet-50	13%	93%	12%
10	ResNet-50	50%	48%	–
30	ResNet-50	36%	53%	17%
10	GoogLeNet	40%	53%	–
30	GoogLeNet	32%	54%	21%

Given current mAP listed in Table 2, the results reveal that our model performs better for single class. We take use of 22 layers of GoogLeNet and 50 layers of ResNet-50 for model testing. In the current dataset, the number of network layers does not have a significant impact on the experimental results.

As we expected, by using larger datasets, more rounds of model training are required. But the total steps for convergence should be the same and independent on the size of

Table 4. The accuracy rates by using YOLOv3 model

YOLOv3 model			
Epochs	Deep learning models	Ripeness	Overripeness
10	YOLOv3(DarkNet)	99.96%	99.87%
30	YOLOv3(DarkNet)	84.58%	88.77%

Table 5. The precision rates by using YOLOv4 model

YOLOv4 model				
Epochs	Deep learning models	Ripeness	Overripeness	Unripeness
10	ResNet-50	100%	99.98%	99.93%

the dataset. If the model is further adjusted, early stopping method is demanded or the learning rate needs to be dipped.

The depth of the proposed neural network for apple classification is critical. Nevertheless, if the network gets deeper, the performance cannot be further enriched. The degradation problem occurs whilst the depth of the layers of the network increases. If the network model is sufficiently deep, the precision will get saturated and then degraded. This problem indicates that the depth of deep network does not satisfy the requirement of our experiments. Because the network is too deep, the accuracy of the model cannot be enhanced.

As shown in Table 4, the model is still with high performance. The precision ensures high accuracy. Accuracy is calculated based on all the predicted samples. Compared to the Faster R-CNN model, YOLOv3 and YOLOv4 outperform in apple classification in the binary classification. The YOLOv4 model reflects the overall advantages of the classifier with very high accuracy.

5   Conclusion

In this paper, multiple deep learning models have been applied to apple ripeness classification. We strongly recommend the state-of-the-art YOLO model because it achieves the best performance for the sake of tradeoff between computing speed and accuracy as well as precision and recall. Our future work is to probe the parameters of optimized models. We also need to compare both of the precision and accuracy to diminish the random errors [61, 63].

References

1. Amara, J., Bouaziz, B., Algergawy, A.: A deep learning-based approach for banana leaf diseases classification. In: BTW (Workshops), pp. 79–88 (2017)

2. Bodla, N., Singh, B., Chellappa, R., Davis, L.S.: Soft-NMS-Improving object detection with one line of code. In: IEEE International Conference on Computer Vision, pp. 5561–5569 (2017)

3. Buzzelli, M., Belotti, F., Schettini, R.: Recognition of edible vegetables and fruits for smart home appliances. In: International Conference on Consumer Electronics, Berlin, pp. 1–4 (2018)

4. Byeon, Y.H., Kwak, K.C.: A performance comparison of pedestrian detection using Faster RCNN and ACF. In: International Congress on Advanced Applied Informatics, pp. 858–863 (2017)

5. Cai, Z., Vasconcelos, N.: Cascade R-CNN: delving into high quality object detection. In: IEEE Conference on Computer Vision and Pattern Recognition, pp. 6154–6162 (2018)

6. Cao, C., et al.: An improved faster R-CNN for small object detection. IEEE Access **7**, 106838–106846 (2019)

7. Chen, D., Wang, H.: Application on intersection classification algorithm based on clustering analysis. In: Annual Computer Software and Applications Conference, pp. 290–297 (2018)

8. De Rita, N., Aimar, A., Delbruck, T.: CNN-based object detection on low precision hardware: racing car case study. In: IEEE Intelligent Vehicles Symposium (IV), pp. 647–652 (2019)

9. Dias, P.A., Tabb, A., Medeiros, H.: Multispecies fruit flower detection using a refined semantic segmentation network. IEEE Robot. Autom. Lett. **3**(4), 3003–3010 (2018)

10. Dong, E., Lu, Y., Du, S.: An improved SSD algorithm and its mobile terminal implementation. In: IEEE International Conference on Mechatronics and Automation, pp. 2319–2324 (2019)

11. Eaton, A. T.: Fruit injury types recognized in annual new hampshire apple harvest evaluations. Entomology, **13** (2017)

12. Fachrurrozi, M., Fiqih, A., Saputra, B. R., Algani, R., Primanita, A.: Content based image retrieval for multi-objects fruits recognition using K-means and K-nearest neighbor. In: International Conference on Data and Software Engineering (ICoDSE), pp. 1–6 (2017)

13. Fachantidis, A., Partalas, I., Taylor, M.E., Vlahavas, I.: Transfer learning with probabilistic mapping selection. Adapt. Behav. **23**(1), 3–19 (2015)

14. Feng, J., Zeng, L., He, L.: Apple fruit recognition algorithm based on multi-spectral dynamic image analysis. Sensors **19**(4), 949 (2019)

15. Gongal, A., Amatya, S., Karkee, M., Zhang, Q., Lewis, K.: Sensors and systems for fruit detection and localization: a review. Comput. Electron. Agric. **116**(C), 8–19 (2015)

16. Guo, L., Lei, Y., Xing, S., Yan, T., Li, N.: Deep convolutional transfer learning network: a new method for intelligent fault diagnosis of machines with unlabelled data. IEEE Trans. Industr. Electron. **66**(9), 7316–7325 (2018)

17. Huang, Z., Cao, Y., Wang, T.: Transfer learning with efficient convolutional neural networks for fruit recognition. In: IEEE Information Technology, Networking, Electronic and Automation Control Conference, pp. 358–362 (2019)

18. Hou, L., Wu, Q., Sun, Q., Yang, H., Li, P.: Fruit recognition based on convolution neural network. In: The International Conference on Natural Computation, Fuzzy Systems and Knowledge Discovery, pp.18–22 (2016)

19. Howlader, M.R., Habiba, U., Faisal, R.H., Rahman, M.M.: Automatic recognition of guava leaf diseases using deep convolution neural network. In: International Conference on Electrical, Computer and Communication Engineering, pp. 1–5 (2019)

20. Hsu, S.C., Huang, C.L., Chuang, C.H.: Vehicle detection using simplified Fast R-CNN. In: International Workshop on Advanced Image Technology, pp. 1–3 (2018)

21. Hsu, S.C., Wang, Y.W., Huang, C.L.: Human object identification for human-robot Interaction by using fast R-CNN. In: IEEE International Conference on Robotic Computing (IRC), pp. 201–204 (2018)

22. Jana, S., Basak, S., Parekh, R.: Automatic fruit recognition from natural images using color and texture features. In: The Conference on Devices for Integrated Circuit (DevIC), pp. 620–624 (2017)
23. Kendall, A.G.: Geometry and uncertainty in deep learning for computer vision (Ph.D. thesis), The University of Cambridge, UK (2019)
24. Kim, J.Y., Vogl, M., Kim, S.D.: A code-based fruit recognition method via image conversion using multiple features. In: International Conference on IT Convergence and Security, pp. 1–4 (2014)
25. Islam, M., Dinh, A., Wahid, K., Bhowmik, K.: Detection of potato diseases using image segmentation and multiclass support vector machine. In: Canadian Conference on Electrical and Computer Engineering, pp. 1–4 (2017)
26. Ji, W., Zhao, D., Cheng, F., Xu, B., Zhang, Y., Wang, J.: Automatic recognition vision system guided for apple harvesting robot. Comput. Electr. Eng. **38**(5), 1186–1195 (2012)
27. Juhnevica-Radenkova, K., Radenkovs, V., Seglina, D.: Microbiological changes and severity of decay in apples stored for a long-term under different storage conditions. Zemdirbyste Agric. **103**(4), 391–396 (2016)
28. Lal, S., Behera, S.K., Sethy, P.K., Rath, A.K.: Identification and counting of mature apple fruit based on BP feed forward neural network. In: International Conference on Sensing, Signal Processing and Security, pp. 361–368 (2017)
29. Li, G., Ma, Z., Wang, H.: Image recognition of grape downy mildew and grape powdery mildew based on support vector machine. In: Li, D., Chen, Y. (eds.) CCTA 2011. IAICT, vol. 370, pp. 151–162. Springer, Heidelberg (2012). https://doi.org/10.1007/978-3-642-27275-2_17
30. Liu, B., Zhang, Y., He, D., Li, Y.: Identification of apple leaf diseases based on deep convolutional neural networks. Symmetry **10**(1), 11 (2017)
31. Liu, B., Zhao, W., Sun, Q.: Study of object detection based on faster R-CNN. In: Chinese Automation Congress, pp. 6233–6236 (2017)
32. Liu, C., Tao, Y., Liang, J., Li, K., Chen, Y.: Object detection based on YOLO network. In: IEEE Information Technology and Mechatronics Engineering Conference (2018)
33. Lu, Y., Yi, S., Zeng, N., Liu, Y., Zhang, Y.: Identification of rice diseases using deep convolutional neural networks. Neurocomputing **267**, 378–384 (2017)
34. Manana, M., Tu, C., Owolawi, P.A.: Preprocessed faster RCNN for vehicle detection. In: International Conference on Intelligent and Innovative Computing Applications (ICONIC), pp. 1–4 (2018)
35. Marathe, A., et al.: Performance modeling under resource constraints using deep transfer learning. In: International Conference on High Performance Computing, Networking, Storage and Analysis, p. 31 (2017)
36. Mohamud, A.H., Gopalakrishnan, A.K.: Fruit feature recognition based on unsupervised competitive learning and backpropagation algorithms. In: International Conference on Engineering, Applied Sciences, and Technology, pp. 29–32 (2018)
37. Mohanty, S.P., Hughes, D.P., Salathe, M.: Using deep learning for image-based plant disease detection. Front. Plant Sci. **7**, 1419 (2016)
38. Murugan, V., Vijaykumar, V.R., Nidhila, A.: A deep learning RCNN approach for vehicle recognition in traffic surveillance system. In: International Conference on Communication and Signal Processing, pp. 0157–0160 (2019)
39. Nourmohammadi-Khiarak, J., Mazaheri, S., Moosavi-Tayebi, R., Noorbakhsh-Devlagh, H.: Object detection utilizing modified auto encoder and convolutional neural networks. In: Signal Processing: Algorithms, Architectures, Arrangements, and Applications (SPA), pp. 43–49 (2018)

40. Nyarko, E.K., Vidovic, I., Radocia, K., Cupec, R.: A nearest neighbor approach for fruit recognition in RGB-D images based on detection of convex surfaces. Expert Syst. Appl. **114**, 454–466 (2018)

41. Nguyen, D., Nguyen, T., Kim, H., Lee, H.-J.: A high-throughput and power-efficient FPGA implementation of YOLO CNN for object detection. IEEE Trans. Very Large Scale Integr. (VLSI) Syst. **27**(8), 1861–1873 (2019). https://doi.org/10.1109/TVLSI.2019.2905242

42. Rachmawati, E., Supriana, I., Khodra, M.L.: Toward a new approach in fruit recognition using hybrid RGBD features and fruit hierarchy property. In: International Conference on Electrical Engineering, Computer Science and Informatics, pp. 1–6 (2017)

43. Rochac, J.F., Zhang, N., Thompson, L., Oladunni, T.: A data augmentation-assisted deep learning model for high dimensional and highly imbalanced hyperspectral imaging data. In: IEEE International Conference on Information Science and Technology (2019)

44. Rochac, J.F., Zhang, N., Xiong, J., Zhong, J., Oladunni, T.: Data augmentation for mixed spectral signatures coupled with convolutional neural networks. In: IEEE International Conference on Information Science and Technology (2019)

45. Rzanny, M., Seeland, M., Waldchen, J., Mader, P.: Acquiring and preprocessing leaf images for automated plant identification: understanding the tradeoff between effort and information gain. In: BMC, vol. 7674 (2017)

46. Scheffler, O., Coetzee, C., Opara, U.: A discrete element model (DEM) for predicting apple damage during handling. Biosys. Eng. **172**, 29–48 (2018)

47. Song, W., Wang, H., Maguire, P., Nibouche, O.: Differentiation of organic and non-organic apples using near infrared reflectance spectroscopy—A pattern recognition approach. In: IEEE Sensors, pp. 1–3 (2016)

48. Sun, S., Wu, Q., Jiao, L., Long, Y., He, D., Song, H.: Recognition of green apples based on fuzzy set theory and manifold ranking algorithm. Optik **165**, 395–407 (2018)

49. Sun, W., He, Y.: Spatial-chromatic clustering for color image compression. In: IEEE World Congress on Computation Intelligence, pp. 1601–1604 (1998)

50. Shukla, D., Desai, A.: Recognition of fruits using hybrid features and machine learning. In: International Conference on Computing, Analytics and Security Trends (CAST), pp. 572–577 (2016)

51. Szegedy, S., et al.: Going deeper with convolutions. In: IEEE Conference on Computer Vision and Pattern Recognition, pp. 1–9 (2015)

52. Thilagavathi, M., Abirami, S.: Application of image processing in diagnosing guava leaf diseases. Int. J. Sci. Res. Manag. **5**(7), 5927–5933 (2017)

53. Tu, S., Xue, Y., Zheng, C., Qi, Y., Wan, H., Mao, L.: Detection of passion fruits and maturity classification using red-green-blue depth images. Biosys. Eng. **175**, 156–167 (2018)

54. Wang, S., Chen, Z., Ding, Z.: The unified object detection framework with arbitrary angle. In: International Conference on Big Data and Information Analytics (BigDIA), pp. 103–107 (2019)

55. Wang, X., Ma, H., Chen, X.: Salient object detection via fast R-CNN and low-level cues. In: IEEE International Conference on Image Processing (ICIP), pp. 1042–1046 (2016)

56. Yan, J., Wang, H., Yan, M., Diao, W., Sun, X., Li, H.: IOU-adaptive deformable R-CNN: make full use of IOU for multiclass object detection in remote sensing imagery. Remote Sens. **11**(3), 286 (2019)

57. Yang, C., Hu, Y., Lin, H., Sa, L., Liu, Y.: Overlapped fruit recognition for citrus harvesting robot in natural scenes. In: International Conference on Robotics and Automation Engineering (2017)

58. Zhang, X., Qiao, Y., Meng, F., Fan, C., Zhang, M.: Identification of maize leaf diseases using improved deep convolutional neural networks. IEEE Access **6**, 30370–30377 (2018)

59. Zhang, X., Wang, Z., Liu, D., Ling, Q.: DADA: deep adversarial data augmentation for extremely low data regime classification. In: International Conference on Acoustics, Speech and Signal Processing (ICASSP), pp. 2807–2811 (2019)

60. Zhou, X., Li, G., Gong, C., Liu, Z., Zhang, J.: Attention-guided RGBD saliency detection using appearance information. Image Vis. Comput. **95**, 103888 (2020)

61. Yan, W.Q.: Computational Methods for Deep Learning: Theoretic, Practice and Applications. Springer, Cham (2021). https://doi.org/10.1007/978-3-030-61081-4

62. Pan, C., Yan, W.Q.: Object detection based on saturation of visual perception. Multimed. Tools Appl. **79**(27–28), 19925–19944 (2020). https://doi.org/10.1007/s11042-020-08866-x

63. Yan, W.Q.: Introduction to Intelligent Surveillance: Surveillance Data Capture, Transmission, and Analytics. Springer, Cham (2019). https://doi.org/10.1007/978-3-030-10713-0

64. Pan, C., Li, X., Yan, W.: A learning-based positive feedback approach in salient object detection. In: IEEE IVCNZ (2018)

65. Al-Sarayreh, M., Reis, M., Yan, W., Klette, R.: Deep spectral-spatial features of snapshot hyperspectral images for red-meat classification. In: IEEE IVCNZ (2018)

66. Zhao, K., Yan, W.: Fruit detection from digital images using CenterNet. In: ISGV (2021)

67. Fu, Y.: Fruit freshness grading using deep learning. Master's Thesis, Auckland University of Technology, New Zealand (2020)

68. Liu, Z., Yan, W.Q., Yang, B.: Image denoising based on a CNN model. In: IEEE ICCAR, pp. 389–393 (2018)

A Hand-Held Sensor System for Exploration and Thermal Mapping of Volcanic Fumarole Fields

Patrick Irmisch[1]([✉]), Ines Ernst[1], Dirk Baumbach[1], Magdalena M. Linkiewicz[1], Vikram Unnithan[2], Frank Sohl[3], Jürgen Wohlfeil[1], and Denis Grießbach[1]

[1] Institute of Optical Sensor System, German Aerospace Center, Rutherfordstr. 2, 12489 Berlin, Germany
{Patrick.Irmisch,Ines.Ernst,Dirk.Baumbach,Magdalena.Linkiewicz, juergen.wohlfeil,Denis.Griessbach}@dlr.de
[2] Jacobs University, Department of Physics and Earth Sciences, Campus Ring 1, 28759 Bremen, Germany
v.unnithan@jacobs-university.de
[3] Institute of Planetary Research, German Aerospace Center, Rutherfordstr. 2, 12489 Berlin, Germany
Frank.Sohl@dlr.de

Abstract. Research from the field of planetary- and geoscience require investigation of geological features in harsh environments. Sampled data needs to be precisely localized spatially and in time, and to be prepared appropriately for further inspection and evaluation. In the case of thermal image data, the computer vision community has made enormous progress in the past years to combine thermal with spatial information in form of thermal 3D models. In this paper, we propose to use a camera-based hand-held sensor system to capture and georeference thermal images in rugged terrain and to prepare the data for further investigations by visualizing the thermal data in 3D. We use a global localization solution to gain fast 3D impressions of the environment and further Structure from Motion to generate detailed mid-scale models of selected interesting structures. We demonstrate our application based on a challenging dataset that we acquired in the active fumarole fields of Vulcano, Sicily.

Keywords: Thermal mapping · Volcanic fumaroles · Optical localization · Hand-held · Robotic exploration

1 Introduction

The exploration of planetary bodies requires the development of new and innovative mapping techniques. The large range of environmental conditions, such as extreme temperatures, harsh or low atmospheric conditions and broad terrain morphologies imposes many challenges in the development of methods and instruments for planetary mapping. One of the most challenging environments

© Springer Nature Switzerland AG 2021
M. Nguyen et al. (Eds.): ISGV 2021, CCIS 1386, pp. 68–84, 2021.
https://doi.org/10.1007/978-3-030-72073-5_6

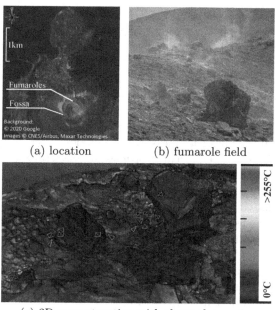

(a) location   (b) fumarole field

(c) 3D reconstruction with thermal mapping

Fig. 1. (a) shows the location of the fumarole field on Vulcano island that was investigated using IPS, equipped with an additional thermal camera. (b) shows a reconstructed example dataset with prominent boulders, (c) reconstructed using the panchromatic stereo camera (grey) and enriched with thermal information (color). The thermal camera poses are georeferenced and visualized in grey. (Color figure online)

is active volcanic fumarole fields, which are generally characterized by extreme ground temperatures and escaping corrosive gases.

Remote infrared sensing based on satellites, airborne or ground-based stations are widely used to monitor volcanic activity. Blackett [4] provides a comprehensive historical overview of thermal remote sensing of volcanoes. These methods provide accurate georeferenced data, but due to their limited spatial resolution, they potentially miss smaller structures and subsurface features such as covered fumaroles. To overcome this, *e.g.* Mannini *et al.* [25] used satellite- and stationary ground-based surveys in conjunction with measurements of a hand-held thermal camera that is used to directly sample vent temperatures. In this context, hand-held thermal cameras allow the investigation of structures in greater detail with georeferenced data using built-in GPS solutions. However, due to missing camera orientations and absence of depth information for the captured thermal image data, spatial relationships are difficult to derive. This severely limits its further usability and analysis.

In this paper, we aim to enrich thermal image data with detailed spatial information to allow in-depth inspection of active fumarole fields. Therefore, we deploy a multi-sensor hand-held localization system, the Integrated Positioning System (IPS) [5], that is equipped with an infrared imaging camera for thermal inspection. It fuses stereo camera based Visual Odometry (VO) with data from an Inertial Measurement Unit (IMU) and GPS for localization. The light weight of IPS allows fast inspection of interesting structures close-up and from different views. IPS is used in this work to estimate the global position and orientation of each thermal image and to visualize the thermal information using 3D reconstruction, exemplified in Fig. 1 (c).

Data for this paper was collected during the fifth Vulcano Summer School 2019, a two-week summer school at Vulcano, Sicily. The school is aimed at exposing young researchers and students to a broad background on planetary and terrestrial field studies. The study of terrestrial analogs is an important tool for planetary scientists, since geological processes on planetary bodies operate in comparable ways to those shaping the Earth's surface. As a consequence, the program of the summer school is built around topical lectures, experiments and sampling campaigns, covering geology, volcanology, geophysics, biology, oceanography and robotic environmental exploration [33].

Vulcano is the third largest and southernmost island of the Aeolian archipelago. It is also one of the most closely monitored, heavily researched and studied active volcanoes in the world. It hosts the largest unique assemblage of high and low temperature volcanic and hydrothermal minerals. The larger part of the island consists of two main edifices built by strombolian to phreatomagmatic eruptions in the last 200k years. The latest volcanic eruption took place in 1888 and since then the volcano has exhibited 2–3 phases of enhanced activity [2]. From a planetary perspective, the surface morphology of parts of the Fossa Crater on Vulcano are similar to lunar and Martian regions with extremely dry, arid conditions and little or no vegetation cover. Fumarolic activity presents strong temperature gradients, high spatial variability in the surface texture and morphology, and extreme environmental conditions (toxic SO_2 vapors), making this an excellent test case for the IPS.

Our contribution is the application of a hand-held system for inspection and large-scale 3D reconstruction, for recording, global localization and 3D visualization of thermal image data in harsh and dynamic environments. We therefore propose a pipeline for automatic rapid processing of large datasets and subsequent refinement of selected scenes to allow detailed analysis. We demonstrate this approach on data acquired on Vulcano's Fossa fields. With this contribution, we closer connect the computer vision field with geo- and planetary exploration.

In the following, we first summarize related work of ground-based mobile platforms for thermal 3D reconstruction and their applicability for our subject. Then we describe the used sensor system and introduce the method for localization and the two methods for 3D reconstruction. In the results section, we show excerpts from the georeferenced sensor data and corresponding 3D visualization. Finally, we discuss our results and the proposed approach and describe possible improvements and the future direction.

2 Related Work

Methods for 3D reconstruction based on ground-based mobile sensor platforms with superimposing of thermal information were frequently proposed in the last decade. A common method is to map thermal information onto previously generated point clouds using a calibrated sensor setup.

Light Detection And Ranging systems (LiDAR) allow accurate 3D reconstruction. Contextually, they have been applied by manually collecting several scans from different positions [11] or on mobile platforms to increase the degree of mobility and automation [7], and in large-scale vehicle-based applications [22]. However, this method is less suited in inaccessible and rugged terrain, such as fumarole fields, where the scene requires to be quickly viewed from different angles for detailed inspection.

A more light-weight sensor is the RGB-D sensor, which has been used for fast and accurate 3D reconstruction and thermal mapping in indoor scenarios. A hand-held system is presented by Vidas *et al.* [34], which operates in real-time. To avoid misregistration of the thermal data, they use a voxel-based occlusion algorithm and proposed a risk-averse neighborhood weighting mechanism. The latter selects one surface estimate from multiple thermal images based on a confidence value that is cautionary to object edges.

Using visual cameras, 3D reconstruction can also be effectively applied for outdoor scenarios using light-weight hand-held devices. In this context, Structure from Motion (SfM) is well suited for accurate 3D reconstruction, but relatively time consuming. For instance, Troung *et al.* [32] generated two models based on RGB and thermal images separately and aligned them afterwards with scale normalization. Based on the fixed camera transformation in the RGB-thermal stereo rig, they could estimate the metric scale of the model. For real-time applications, Visual Odometry (VO) and Simultaneous Localization and Mapping (vSLAM) is a widely used alternative to SfM. Contextually, Yamaguchi *et al.* [37] used a monocular RGB Visual Odometry approach for 3D reconstruction and superimposed the thermal image. They could also recover the scale using generated depth images from both domains using Multi-View-Stereo (MVS) and the known camera transformation in the RGB-thermal stereo rig. However, SfM and MVS from thermal images requires a high degree of image overlap, which is not guaranteed in our approach, due to our selective thermal imaging during inspection. Instead, to demonstrate our application, we use a stereo system for 3D reconstruction which has proven itself in similar environments [6] and for large-scale 3D reconstruction in similar configurations [3], and then map the thermal information.

3D reconstruction with thermal mapping has a wide range of applications, such as in energy-efficiency monitoring of buildings [12,19], Object Detection [21] or even fruit tree characterization [38], but also critical applications such as hotspot and fire detection [15,28] in buildings. Related to fumarole field monitoring, Lewis *et al.* [23,24] use SfM in the visible domain to generate a mid-scale digital elevation model to map and georeference pre-dawn thermal information from tripod-based stationary thermal cameras. This approach helps to minimize the impact of solar heating, though it is restricted to few thermal camera poses. In contrast, we concentrate on rapid large scale exploration and close-up inspection of numerous fumaroles, and use SfM as optional subsequent refinement. Related, a promising future application is in planetary robotic exploration, since rovers are often equipped with a thermal camera for inspection, such as in [36].

Description	Visual	Thermal
Camera	AVT GC1380H	Optris Pi 450
Sensitivity	0.4-0.9 μm	7.5-13 μm
Resolution	1360x1024 px	382x288 px
Pixel Size	6.45 μm	25 μm
Focal Length	4.8 mm	10.5 mm
Field of View	85 deg	53 deg

Fig. 2. IPS sensor system with protective gear (left) and camera parameters (right).

3   Data Acquisition

A hand-held IPS equipped with an additional thermal imaging camera and protective gear was used for data acquisition (see Fig. 2 (left)) during the campaign on Vulcano, Italy. In this section, we first describe the systems properties, calibration and synchronization. Then, the captured datasets are introduced along with the modification made to the system to protect it from the corrosive fumarolic gases.

3.1   Sensor System and Registration

The IPS demonstrator of [5] is used. The system consists of a stereo camera (AVT GC1380H) and a thermal imaging camera (Optris Pi 450), with parameters listed in Fig. 2 (right). Its relatively wide stereo baseline of 20 cm, high resolution and narrow field-of-view cameras allow detailed 3D reconstruction and inspection. For localization, IPS also has an IMU (ADIS-16488) and an optional low-cost GNSS receiver (u-blox LEA-6). The infrared data is automatically processed using the software Optris PI Connect [26] and the processed pixel-wise temperature values are logged. We selected an operating range of 0 to 250 °C, which covers most of the fumaroles with an estimated mean vent temperature of 185 °C in 2019 [25]. A Field Programmable Gate Array (FPGA) synchronously triggers both visual cameras and handles the timestamp assignment for all sensor data. The data is recorded and processed on an external laptop.

The thermal sensor data is registered geometrically and temporally to the basic IPS sensor data. For geometrical co-registration of the trifocal camera setup, the calibration provided by [9] is used. Here, a passive aluminum chessboard with alternating blank and matt-black-printed tiles is used, that leads to a clearly visible chessboard pattern in both visual cameras and the thermal camera image, if a low-temperature background is reflected by the blank tiles. For temporally registration, a hardware trigger is attached to the handle that triggers the thermal camera and a timestamp is logged by the FPGA. As the thermal camera uses its own internal frequency, this timestamp is not precise and is only used to assign the image to the nearest stereo frame. This can lead to inaccurate camera pose assignment during motion and therefore, we hold the system still

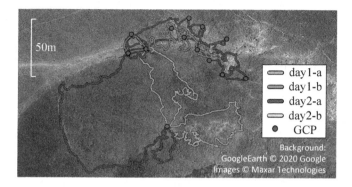

Fig. 3. IPS-Trajectories of the four datatsets.

while triggering the thermal camera. Further miss-alignment occur due to periodical Non-Uniformity Corrections of the Optris Pi 450 where the image stream is temporarily frozen during radiometric re-calibration. Corresponding thermal images are sorted out manually.

3.2   Datasets

During the two survey days (16th and 18th June 2019), four different datasets were acquired. The trajectories are shown in Fig. 3. The first two datasets (*day1*) aimed at the 3D reconstruction of a large-scale emissive structure within the rim zone. The different zones are characterized in [18]. The other two (*day2*) datasets focused on the exploration of potentially interesting small-scale structures, located in the middle zone. The datasets contain GCPs that were measured using GPS, where IPS is placed for a short time. They are intended to automatically register two different IPS trajectories and to introduce supervised loop closures. The first two recordings have a total length of 42 min and contain 240 thermal images. The other two have a length of 64 min and contain 560 thermal images.

3.3   Thermal Sensing Quality

Due the presence of corrosive gases in the fumarole field, the system had to be equipped with protective gear, which affected the sensing properties of the thermal camera. The used IPS has a solid aluminum frame with protective glasses in front of the visual cameras, see Fig. 2. The opening to the hardware on the back of the IPS needed to be closed using plastic utensils. The lens of the thermal camera was protected using a thin plastic foil, which requires an adjustment of the transmission factor. For this setup, a transmissivity of 0.9 was determined on site by comparison with a second thermal camera (Testo 875). For data acquisition in different locations of Vulcano island during the summer school, an emissivity of 0.93 was kept constant, which is in the broad range of the geological materials. [18] obtained an emissivity of 0.97 for surfaces within the Fossa field. Consequently, both fixed radiometric values introduce inaccuracies in the presented dataset. The error can be approximated using a validation set of 48 samples from 4 image pairs of both thermal cameras, in the range of 39 °C to 240 °C. For the (Testo 875), we process the data using the software IRsoft [31], while using an emissivity of 0.97. Based on this dataset, we approximate a mean absolute error of 3.4K to the reference measurement. We refer to [18] for further error consideration in thermal imaging within the Fossa field.

4 Methods

In this section we describe the localization and 3D reconstruction components. Figure 4 gives an overview of the individual components, which are explained in the following sections. To summarize, based on the different sensor information, IPS estimates a global trajectory T_{IPS}, that is used during Direct Reconstruction. Here, generated depth maps based on the stereo frames at each pose are used to generate the point cloud, where semantic segmentation is used to ignore specific objects during reconstruction and thermal values are directly mapped onto the point clouds. The result is PC_{Comb} that combines grey and thermal

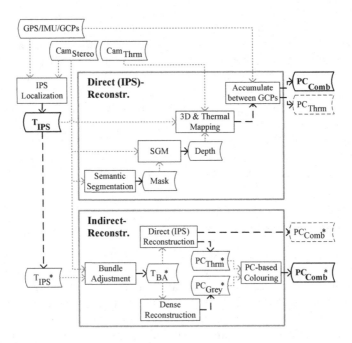

Fig. 4. Illustration of all components of the proposed pipeline with focus on 3D reconstruction. While during Direct Reconstruction the full trajectory is considered, for Indirect Reconstruction only a small part is considered and marked with (*). The method outputs are marked in bold.

color values, and is split into segments for easier investigation, which are constrained by GCPs or by user-defined temporal intervals. In Indirect Reconstruction, a trajectory segment is first selected T_{IPS}^* and refined using SfM with Bundle Adjustment. Here, Direct Reconstruction is used to reference the thermal values in 3D PC_{Thrm}^*, while the Dense Reconstruction PC_{Grey}^* is done separately by the used photogrammetry tool [27]. Finally, PC_{Comb}^* is generated by point cloud based color interpolation.

4.1 Localization

The IPS localization comprises 3 sub-modules, a local (a) and a global (b) navigation module, as well as a switchover module (c) from local to global navigation. The first two modules compute in Cartesian coordinates, whereby (a) refers to a local tangential plane and (b) to the earth-centered, earth-fixed (ECEF) coordinate system. The localization from (a) can be understood as an ad hoc solution, since it is generated purely with measurements of the IMU together with a camera based visual odometry in real time.

All four trajectories shown in Fig. 3 start with the same path section represented by a triangle of 3 GCPs. These GCPs are used to register the different runs. On the other hand, the presence of additional infrastructure based information such as GPS coordinates or GCPs the switchover from (a) to (b) can be done with the help of an estimated homogeneous transformation matrix including its associated covariance. This transformation depicts 3 parameters of rotation and translation as well as a scaling factor. In order to estimate these 7 unknowns, at least 3 or more pairs of 3D position vectors in local or global coordinates are required. With a closed form solution of the 7-parameter transformation, based on the well-known Helmert transformation (e.g. see [35]), the estimation vector of a non-linear system of equations is initialized. This means that only a few iterations are required to determine a solution in the subsequent Gauss-Newton algorithm. Since absolute measurements are not always available at run-time or only generated during the run (e.g. a loop closure due to repeated placement of IPS on an already known GCP), the switchover of the local navigation solution to a global coordinate system is regarded here as a subsequent optimization step.

The physical parameters of IPS localization include orientation described as a quaternion, position and speed, each in 3 dimensions. In addition, the axis-dependent offsets of the angular rates and acceleration sensors of the IMU are estimated and corrected. A detailed description of the equations of motion of (a) can be found in [16], that of (b) in [17]. The following sensors and their type of measurand are used in our localization pipeline:

- IMU: angular velocity and linear acceleration (6 DOF, 410 Hz)
- VO: stereo camera based visual odometer (change of position and orientation, 6 DOF, 10Hz)
- GPS: absolute position in global coordinates (3 DOF, 1–4 Hz)
- GCP: absolute position represented as synthetic loop closure (3 DOF, used on occurrence)

Fig. 5. Walking tourists and moving bicycles lead to disruptive artifacts during 3D modeling (left), that are eliminated using semantic information in our approach (right).

4.2 3D Reconstruction - Direct

The stereo-images of IPS can not only be used for reliable VO estimation (based on sparse 3D sets of points), but also for 3D point cloud generation. For the computationally expensive stereo matching that computes high-density depth maps, a semi-global matching (SGM) GPU-implementation [13] is used. It is implemented in OpenCL, includes preparatory image rectification, and uses a census cost function for the data term. From the depth maps, 3D points are generated for each recorded pair of images and fused with 3D points obtained at subsequent frames by incorporating the camera poses from the IPS trajectory T_{IPS}. The overall frame rate for point cloud generation is dynamically adapted as follows: if the calculated IPS navigation solution shows a substantial difference in pose or time to the previously used image pair, a new local 3D point cloud is extracted from the depth maps and transformed into the global navigation frame. Subsequently, the local point clouds are merged and accumulated into a high-density cloud and filtered into a 1.5 cm large voxel grid. This method builds on the Point Cloud Library [29].

The presence of moving objects, such as tourists in our dataset, can lead to disruptive artifacts during 3D reconstruction, as shown in Fig. 5 (left). Such artifacts can be removed by using semantic information during offline processing. For this step, we use a pre-trained MobileNetV2 [30] that was trained on the PASCAL 2012 dataset [14]. It has shown to give a good trade-off between accuracy and run-time for our datasets. The segmentation is computed in full resolution and is used to generate a mask for the object classes person and bicycle. The mask is additionally dilated by 10 pixel to cover inaccurate object boundaries and is applied directly on the depth map to exclude all depth values that belong to the forbidden object classes. In combination with statistical filters, almost all artifacts are removed without disturbing the static scene, as shown in Fig. 5 (right).

IPS can record additional sensor data synchronized with image and IMU data simultaneously. In the case of image data, they can be immediately mapped onto the 3D point cloud, which we use to map the thermal information in color rep-

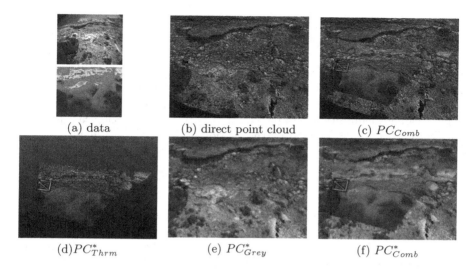

(a) data   (b) direct point cloud   (c) PC_{Comb}

(d)PC^*_{Thrm} (e) PC^*_{Grey} (f) PC^*_{Comb}

Fig. 6. Illustration of the thermal data mapping process with intermediate results for a single thermal image for Direct and Indirect Reconstruction. (b, c) show direct results before accumulation with neighboring point clouds. (Color figure online)

resentation from the additional thermal camera. Here, an exact registration of the thermal camera to the overall IPS is mandatory. By projecting the local 3D points into the valid IR camera image, considering the internal and relative orientations, the color or measured temperature values can be assigned directly to the respective surface points. For instance in Fig. 6, the points of (b) are mapped into the thermal image of (a) and colored accordingly, resulting in a combined model PC_{Comb} of (c) or only in a thermal point cloud (d). A voxel-based occlusion algorithm is used to prevent incorrect color assignment on occluded 3D points, building on the implementation of [1] in [29].

In a subsequent automatic filter process, voxels and their additional information are removed based on the frequency of the additional camera images, the number of 3D points found per voxel, the proportion of values with additional information and their reliability.

Local localization and Direct Reconstruction with thermal mapping can be done simultaneously in real-time using a capable laptop. In this work, we apply it as a post processing step on a global trajectory and add the module for semantic segmentation, which requires an additional GPU.

4.3   3D Reconstruction - Indirect

In Indirect Reconstruction we seek to exploit the potential of photogrammetry tools for detailed 3D reconstruction by using the SfM and Dense Reconstruction modules. We use the photogrammetry tool Pix4Dmapper [27], which we experienced to work generally well in combination with IPS. As SfM is highly time-consuming, we only concentrate on relatively small trajectory parts T^*_{IPS}

with around 800–1200 camera poses, for instance with 1200 greyscale images for the 3D model of Fig. 1 (c). These parts are defined by segments from Direct Reconstruction or custom time intervals. They are selected by a human operator due to the presence of interesting fumarole structures, found by investigating the direct 3D models and sensor data. To further shorten the processing time, we only use one visual camera and use camera poses from T_{IPS}^* as well as the intrinsic camera calibration parameters of IPS as a priori. The scale for T_{BA}^* and resulting PC_{Grey}^* is defined by the a priori T_{IPS}^*. Finally, a manual step is applied to remove occasional disruptive artifacts per hand.

For thermal mapping, we apply the Direct Reconstruction pipeline based on the optimized trajectory T_{BA}^*, which produces the thermal point cloud PC_{Thrm}^*, as shown in Fig. 6 (d). It is defined in the same coordinate system as PC_{Grey}^*. In a manual step, we interpolate color values of PC_{Thrm}^* onto PC_{Grey}^* in point cloud space using CloudCompare [10]. During thermal mapping on fine details, this method is relatively sensitive to smallest deviations of the surfaces of both point clouds, caused by scale- and calibration inaccuracies. To demonstrate the possibilities in our proposed application, we slightly correct the scale for PC_{Thrm}^* (via the stereo baseline) during Indirect Reconstruction to guarantee most detailed thermal mapping. All points that are not assigned a color value keep their grey value, resulting in PC_{Comb}^* and shown in Fig. 6 (f). For better visualization, we transform PC_{Comb}^* into polygonal meshes using Poisson Surface Reconstruction [20] in [10].

5   Results

The overall result is a global position and orientation for all sensory data with visualization in a georeferenced 3D model. In this chapter, we concentrate on excerpts of the results and interesting examples.

The global localization results of all four trajectories are illustrated in Fig. 3. Due to the used filter-based localization method, drifts occur in mid-term, but are limited in long-term by the GPS-aid. The magnitude of the mid-term drift can be exemplified using *day1-a*. It consists of 5 intermediate mid-scale loops that start and end at the same GCP. They can be used to approximate the

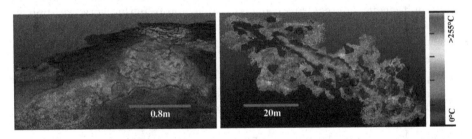

Fig. 7. Exemplary Direct Reconstruction (left), large-scale model after alignment refinement by a human operator (right).

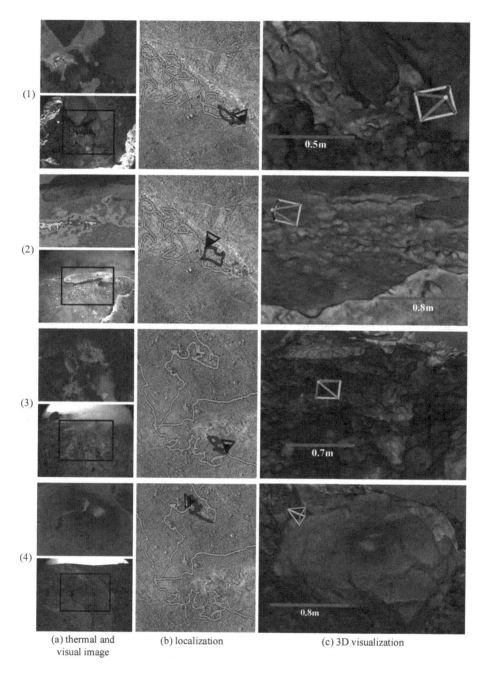

(a) thermal and   (b) localization   (c) 3D visualization
visual image

Fig. 8. Exemplary georeferenced sensory data: (a) camera images, where a black rectangle marks the view of the thermal camera, (b) global trajectory with reference to Fig. 3 and corresponding segment in blue, (c) thermal 3D visualization. (Color figure online)

trajectory drift for this session based on a closed loop error, before the position is corrected by the GCP. The closed loop errors show a mean of round 0.2 m or 0.5%, if normed by the traveled length.

Direct Reconstruction was applied on the full datasets and consists each of a large-scale model that was split into segments for simplified investigation. Figure 7 (left) gives an exemplary segment from Direct Reconstruction. It shows an excerpt of the elongated heat field. The heated area is clearly visible, while larger rocks and the surrounding area are at lower temperatures. In this way, the direct model provides a good qualitative 3D impression and scene understanding. Direct Reconstruction can also be used to generate coherent large scale models, as shown in Fig. 7 (right) for the entire two day1 sessions. Due to the applied GCPs, which introduced hard corrections in this dataset, the alignment quality of the segments is restricted by the accuracy of the used GPS and had to be refined manually.

Four generated 3D models based on Indirect Reconstruction are shown in Fig. 8. Each row shows (a) one exemplary thermal image in color representation that is assigned to one greyscale camera image. Based on IPS localization, the corresponding camera pose is referenced globally (b) and plotted in a global context. The trajectory segments, marked in blue, are used for reconstruction. The resulting 3D mesh and the corresponding thermal camera pose are shown in (c). In (3), the global position and scale of T^*_{BA} and PC^*_{Grey} could not be estimated automatically based on T^*_{IPS}. We recovered both by aligning T^*_{BA} with T^*_{IPS} manually.

Each of the examples in Figs. 8 show some distinctive and interesting fumarole structures: (1) a large bolder with hot fumaroles underneath, (2) a part of the large scale heat field structure with temperatures beyond the maximum measurable temperature of the used thermal camera configuration, (3) fumarole vents with a large amount of escaping steam, (4) a funnel with escaping steam trough a large cracked boulder.

6   Discussion

Using the presented hand-held camera system, we were able to record and prepare sensor data for detailed investigations of the fumaroles fields on Vulcano. Also, we mapped fumaroles and heated regions that would otherwise be hidden from above, such as shown in Fig. 8 (1). Data acquisition and processing in such harsh environments are often not straightforward. Corrosive gases, dense steam and high surface temperatures complicate data acquisition, damage the sensor system and affect the localization and reconstruction result. The hazards are not always visible, characterized by the many tourists that we encountered to walk on extremely hot areas ($>200°$) and through the steam without protection. Also, the dense steam often obscured large image areas, indicated in the upper part of the greyscale image in Fig. 8 (3a), and sometimes obscured the view completely.

Using IPS, we estimated a reliable global localization solution and detailed 3D models. Due to the absence of reference data for the presented datasets, a quantitative evaluation could not be conducted. In a relative manner, the localization results has shown to be of high quality in short-term, as it led to visibly appealing 3D models using the computational inexpensive Direct Reconstruction. In mid-term, they show small trajectory drifts, due to the temporary-relative nature of the chosen navigation solution. The trajectory drift and remaining statistical noise restrict quality and level of detail of the direct models. For the individual segments, Indirect Reconstruction mostly eliminated the trajectory drift using Bundle Adjustment and led to consistent and more detailed 3D models. Though, the details come at the expense of required computationally power and the proportion of manual steps in this method is relatively high. In an absolute manner, the global positioning accuracy is shaped by the quality and accuracy of the GPS sensor in the chosen filter-based implementation. The introduced GCPs helped well for registration of the different sessions, but due to their uncertain/inaccurate measurements, the coherent large-scale model could not be generated completely automatically. In future measurement campaigns, it would be beneficial to measure the GCP positions using differential GPS. Also, a vSLAM extension could help to reduce mid-term inconsistencies and to get closer to the qualitative results of the indirect method.

The presented 3D models show the overall well registered thermal data, that we mapped in color representation for demonstration, and give an appealing 3D visualization. Geometrically, inaccuracies can occur on object borders, where the thermal color values are not correctly mapped onto the point cloud. Possible sources of error are calibration inaccuracies and an inaccurate estimation of the thermal camera pose during motion, due to the rough temporary assignment of the thermal data. Radiometrically, the thermal properties changed due to the protective foil, which we reported in comparison with a second thermal camera. For future measurement campaigns, the system could benefit from a radiometric calibration for this setup. Also, the emissivity that was obtained in [18] for Vulcano's fumarole fields can be set. To prevent gross alignment errors on object borders, our method could benefit from the risk-averse neighborhood weighting mechanism of [34].

We may emphasize that this method can augment remote sensing methods, such as in [25]. Alternatively, airborne systems could be used to gain a broad large-scale model beforehand, which is then used to select interesting spots that are investigated in detail with the hand-held system.

Overall, the methods that we presented would be extremely well-suited for manned and robotic-based exploration and mapping of planetary bodies. Quick and accurate planetary exploration requires tools which are able to survive extremes in environmental conditions, working both on the surface and sub-surface. Sub-surface exploration is critical for example on Mars or the Moon, since signs of extant or extinct life is likely to be found in sub-surface caves [8]. With the recent drive towards space and planetary exploration, this work presents promising, innovative tools for mapping and exploration.

7   Conclusion

The Integrated Positioning System (IPS) was used for acquiring data in the harsh volcanic terrain of Vulcano. Based on the presented methods, we could reach fairly qualitative global localization and detailed mid-scale 3D-models with 3D visualization of the captured thermal data. Using the presented method for direct 3D reconstruction, quick and qualitative impressions of the complete scenes could be achieved. Then, indirect 3D reconstruction allowed to generate 3D models of high quality of selected parts in the expense of required computational power. In this work, we have made progress towards the development of a prototype for planetary exploration in the context of detailed inspection of geological features in extreme environments.

In future, an interesting direction will be to automatically detect and classify fumaroles based on the given imaging sensors. Generally, we seek to support geophysical, geochemical and planetary in-situ investigations.

Acknowledgements. The Vulcano Summer Schools have been generously supported by the Helmholtz Alliance Robotic Exploration of Extreme Environments (ROBEX) and the EU H2020 Europlanet program.

References

1. Amanatides, J., Woo, A.: A fast voxel traversal algorithm for ray tracing. Eurographics **87**, 3–10 (1987)
2. de Astis, G., et al.: Geology, volcanic history and petrology of Vulcano (central Aeolian archipelago). Geol. Soc. Lond. Mem. **37**(1), 281–349 (2013). https://doi.org/10.1144/M37.11
3. Benecke, N., et al.: Mobile solution for positioning, 3D-mapping and inspection in underground mining. In: (ISM) XVI International Congress for Mine Surveying (2016)
4. Blackett, M.: Review of the utility of infrared remote sensing for detecting and monitoring volcanic activity with the case study of shortwave infrared data for Lascar Volcano from 2001–2005. In: Geological Society of London Special Publications, London, vol. 380 (2013). https://doi.org/10.1144/SP380.10
5. Börner, A., et al.: IPS - a vision aided navigation system. Adv. Opt. Technol. **6**(2), 121–130 (2017). https://doi.org/10.1515/aot-2016-0067
6. Börner, A., Irmisch, P., Ernst, I., Baumbach, D.: Cameras for navigation and 3D modelling on planetary exploration missions. In: (IPM) International Workshop on Planetary Missions (2018)
7. Borrmann, D., Elseberg, J., Nüchter, A.: Thermal 3D mapping of building façades. In: Lee, S., Cho, H., Yoon, K.J., Lee, J. (eds.) Intelligent Autonomous Systems 12. Advances in Intelligent Systems and Computing, vol. 193, pp. 173–182. Springer, Heidelberg (2013). https://doi.org/10.1007/978-3-642-33926-4_16
8. Carrier, B.L., et al.: Mars extant life: what's next? Conference report. Astrobiology **20**(6), 785–814 (2020). https://doi.org/10.1089/ast.2020.2237
9. Choinowski, A., Dahlke, D., Ernst, I., Pless, S., Rettig, I.: Automatic calibration and co-registration for a stereo camera system and a thermal imaging sensor using a chessboard. In: (ISPRS) International Archives of the Photogrammetry, Remote Sensing and Spatial Information Sciences, vol. XLII-2/W13, pp. 1631–1635 (2019). https://doi.org/10.5194/isprs-archives-XLII-2-W13-1631-2019

10. CloudCompare: GPL Software (2019). http://www.cloudcompare.org/
11. Costanzo, A., Minasi, M., Casula, G., Musacchio, M., Buongiorno, M.F.: Combined use of terrestrial laser scanning and IR thermography applied to a historical building. Sensors **15**(1), 194–213 (2014). https://doi.org/10.3390/s150100194
12. Demisse, G., Borrmann, D., Nuchter, A.: Interpreting thermal 3D models of indoor environments for energy efficiency. In: (ICAR) International Conference on Advanced Robotics, pp. 1–8. IEEE (2013). https://doi.org/10.1109/ICAR.2013.6766550
13. Ernst, I., Hirschmüller, H.: Mutual information based semi-global stereo matching on the GPU. In: Bebis, G., et al. (eds.) ISVC 2008. LNCS, vol. 5358, pp. 228–239. Springer, Heidelberg (2008). https://doi.org/10.1007/978-3-540-89639-5_22
14. Everingham, M., Van Gool, L., Williams, C.K.I., Winn, J., Zisserman, A.: The PASCAL Visual Object Classes Challenge 2012 (VOC 2012) Results (2012)
15. Fritsche, P., Zeise, B., Hemme, P., Wagner, B.: Fusion of radar, LiDAR and thermal information for hazard detection in low visibility environments. In: (SSRR) International Symposium on Safety, Security and Rescue Robotics, pp. 96–101. IEEE (2017). https://doi.org/10.1109/SSRR.2017.8088146
16. Grießbach, D.: Stereo-vision-aided inertial navigation. Ph.D thesis, Freie Universität Berlin (2015). https://elib.dlr.de/97245/
17. Groves, P.D.: Principles of GNSS, Inertial, and Multisensor Integrated Navigation Systems, 2nd edn. Artech House, Norwood (2013)
18. Harris, A., Maciejewski, A.: Thermal surveys of the Vulcano Fossa fumarole field 1994–1999: evidence for fumarole migration and sealing. J. Volcanol. Geoth. Res. **102**(1–2), 119–147 (2000). https://doi.org/10.1016/S0377-0273(00)00184-0
19. Jarząbek-Rychard, M., Lin, D., Maas, H.G.: Supervised detection of façade openings in 3D point clouds with thermal attributes. Remote Sens. **12**(3), 543 (2020). https://doi.org/10.3390/rs12030543
20. Kazhdan, M., Hoppe, H.: Screened Poisson surface reconstruction. ACM Trans. Graph. **32**(3) (2013). https://doi.org/10.1145/2487228.2487237
21. Kim, P., Chen, J., Cho, Y.K.: Robotic sensing and object recognition from thermal-mapped point clouds. Int. J. Intell. Robot. Appl. **1**(3), 243–254 (2017). https://doi.org/10.1007/s41315-017-0023-9
22. Lagüela, S., Cereijo Garcia, J., Martínez-Sánchez, J., Bernárdez, D., Cimadevila, H.: Thermographic mobile mapping of urban environment for lighting and energy studies. J. Daylighting **1**, 8–15 (2014). https://doi.org/10.15627/jd.2014.2
23. Lewis, A., Hilley, G.E., Lewicki, J.L.: Integrated thermal infrared imaging and structure-from-motion photogrammetry to map apparent temperature and radiant hydrothermal heat flux at Mammoth Mountain, CA, USA. J. Volcanol. Geoth. Res. **303**, 16–24 (2015). https://doi.org/10.1016/j.jvolgeores.2015.07.025
24. Lewis, A., Sare, R., Lewicki, J.L., Hilley, G.E.: High-resolution imaging of hydrothermal heat flux using optical and thermal structure-from-motion photogrammetry. J. Volcanol. Geoth. Res. **393**, 106818 (2020). https://doi.org/10.1016/j.jvolgeores.2020.106818
25. Mannini, S., Harris, A.J.L., Jessop, D.E., Chevrel, M.O., Ramsey, M.S.: Combining ground- and ASTER-based thermal measurements to constrain fumarole field heat budgets: the case of Vulcano Fossa 2000–2019. Geophys. Res. Lett. **46**(21), 11868–11877 (2019). https://doi.org/10.1029/2019GL084013
26. Optris: Pi Connect: Process Imager Software (2018). www.optris.com
27. Pix4D: Pix4Dmapper (2020). Version 4.5.6. https://www.pix4d.com/

28. Rosu, R.A., Quenzel, J., Behnke, S.: Reconstruction of textured meshes for fire and heat source detection. In: (SSRR) International Symposium on Safety, Security, and Rescue Robotics, pp. 235–242. IEEE (2019). https://doi.org/10.1109/SSRR.2019.8848943

29. Rusu, R.B., Cousins, S.: 3D is here: point cloud library (PCL). In: (ICRA) International Conference on Robotics and Automation, pp. 1–4 (2011). https://doi.org/10.1109/ICRA.2011.5980567

30. Sandler, M., Howard, A., Zhu, M., Zhmoginov, A., Chen, L.C.: MobileNetV2: inverted residuals and linear bottlenecks. In: (CVPR) Conference on Computer Vision and Pattern Recognition, pp. 4510–4520. IEEE (2018). https://doi.org/10.1109/CVPR.2018.00474

31. Testo: IRSoft (2020). https://www.testo.com

32. Truong, T.P., Yamaguchi, M., Mori, S., Nozick, V., Saito, H.: Registration of RGB and thermal point clouds generated by structure from motion. In: (ICCVW) International Conference on Computer Vision Workshops, pp. 419–427. IEEE (2017). https://doi.org/10.1109/ICCVW.2017.57

33. Unnithan, V., et al.: Vulcano summer school 2019. In: EPSC-DPS Joint Meeting 2019. EPSC Abstracts, vol. 13, p. 2051 (2019)

34. Vidas, S., Moghadam, P., Sridharan, S.: Real-time mobile 3D temperature mapping. IEEE Sens. J. **15**(2), 1145–1152 (2015). https://doi.org/10.1109/JSEN.2014.2360709

35. Watson, G.A.: Computing Helmert transformations. J. Comput. Appl. Math. **197**(2), 387–394 (2006). https://doi.org/10.1016/j.cam.2005.06.047

36. Wedler, A., et al.: First results of the ROBEX analogue mission campaign: robotic deployment of seismic networks for future lunar missions. In: Proceedings of the International Astronautical Congress. IAF (2017)

37. Yamaguchi, M., et al.: Superimposing thermal-infrared data on 3D structure reconstructed by RGB visual odometry. IEICE Trans. Inf. Syst. **E101.D**(5), 1296–1307 (2018). https://doi.org/10.1587/transinf.2017MVP0023

38. Yandún Narváez, F.J., Salvo del Pedregal, J., Prieto, P.A., Torres-Torriti, M., Auat Cheein, F.A.: LiDAR and thermal images fusion for ground-based 3D characterisation of fruit trees. Biosyst. Eng. **151**, 479–494 (2016). https://doi.org/10.1016/j.biosystemseng.2016.10.012

Traffic Sign Recognition Using Guided Image Filtering

Jiawei Xing and Wei Qi Yan[✉]

Auckland University of Technology, Auckland, New Zealand
wyan@aut.ac.nz

Abstract. In challenging lighting conditions, such as haze, rain, and weak lighting condition, the accuracy of traffic sign recognition is not very high due to missed detection or incorrect positioning. In this paper, we propose a traffic sign recognition algorithm based on Faster R-CNN and YOLOv5. Firstly, we conduct image preprocessing by using guided image filtering for the input image to remove noises. The processed images are imported into the neural networks for training and testing. The outcomes of the traffic sign recognition are promising.

Keywords: Traffic sign recognition · Faster R-CNN · GTSDB dataset · FRIDA database

1 Introduction

Traffic signs are everywhere to assist our driving in real traffic scenes, a rich assortment of traffic signs have been set on roadside as shown in Fig. 1. But only using our human visual systems is tough to eye these signs due to fast moving or weather conditions. Therefore, advanced driver assistance systems have become the focus of our attention [1–3].

At present, traffic sign detection algorithms have emerged and achieved satisfactory results [4, 5], but these algorithms mainly aim at digital images of traffic signs acquired under ideal weather conditions. Owing to the rapid development of road construction and transportations in recent years, the smoggy weather has been increased year after year. The collected images of traffic signs are blurred, the colors are faded, which in turn slash the recognition accuracy of these algorithms. In response to this issue, an accurate locating and recognition algorithm for traffic signs in haze weather is proposed in this paper.

Traffic sign recognition (TSR) was developed in the early 1980s and has taken a great step in the field of autonomous vehicles in 1987 [6]. It mainly targets at speed limit signs and takes use of classic algorithms based on image segmentation and template matching. The recognition process takes around 0.5 s on average. Due to hardware being developed at that time, the systems are not working in real time, the images are relatively small and cannot be integrated into real applications.

© Springer Nature Switzerland AG 2021
M. Nguyen et al. (Eds.): ISGV 2021, CCIS 1386, pp. 85–99, 2021.
https://doi.org/10.1007/978-3-030-72073-5_7

Fig. 1. Foggy traffic signs in various scenarios.

After the 1990s, with the continuous improvement of the hardware and its computing capability, advanced technology in digital imaging and computer vision has been emerged to take effects on discovering the principle of TSR. A variety of solutions have been proposed, such as edge extraction, color segmentation, feature vector extraction, artificial neural network, etc. In recent years, with the successful applications of deep learning [7, 8], such as semantic segmentation, etc., deep learning methods have been gradually brought into TSR.

The existing TSR algorithms generally have two key steps: Positioning and recognition. Because of the swift development of deep learning, in this paper, we propose a method for traffic sign recognition based on Faster R-CNN model.

The remaining part of the paper is organized as follows: The existing work is critically reviewed in Sect. 2. The proposed methods of this paper will be detailed in Sect. 3. The experimental results will be showcased and analyzed in Sect. 4. Our conclusion and future work will be presented in Sect. 5.

2   Literature Review

Traffic sign recognition has become a hot topic of current research. With the gradual completion of hardware design and implementations, two types of methods are taken into consideration. One is to extract visual features in digital image for pattern classification by using deep learning methods, the other is to extract visual features of objects for classification by using CNNs and RNNs.

A comprehensive scheme [9] was proffered for traffic sign recognition. Firstly, a cascade of trained classifiers is employed to scan the background quickly so as to locate a region of interest (ROI), then Hough transform is applied to shape detection. This method is evaluated based on an image database including 135 traffic signs. The average recognition speed is 25 frames per second (FPS), the recognition accuracy is 93%. In [10], edge detection was accomplished by using a combination of color filtering and closed curves. Through a neural network, the extracted features are applied to classify the targets. The average recognition rate is up to 94.9%. The nearest neighbors are applied to classify and recognize traffic signs by calculating Euclidean distance between a traffic sign and its standard template, then the image is classified according to the minimum distance.

Girshick et al. [11] proposed a rich feature hierarchical structure for precise target detection and semantic segmentation, i.e., R-CNN, using selective search (SS) [12] instead of traditional. The sliding window method extracts 2,000 target candidate regions on the image, then takes use of a deep convolutional network to classify the target candidate regions. However, because it carries out convolution operations on each candidate area instead of sharing calculations, the detection speed is slow, but with 47.9% segmentation accuracy. He et al. [13] proposed the spatial pyramid pooling network (SPPnets), which improves speed by sharing convolutional feature maps. Fast R-CNN [14] extracts convolutional feature maps, the training improves the detection accuracy and speed [15].

SSD [16] was set forth to detect traffic signs by using Inception v3 network instead of VGG16. For SSD, a random center point with a prior designed strategy was proposed. Douville, et al. [17] firstly normalized the image of traffic signs, then extracted Gabor features, finally a three-layer perceptron was employed to classify and recognize the traffic sign. A perceptual confrontation network was put forwarded for highway traffic sign detection [18], which combined Faster R-CNN with a generative confrontation network. The residual network is applied to learn the differences between the feature maps of small visual objects and large target objects so as to uplift the rates of highway traffic sign detection and recognition. The detection results have been achieved based on the Tsinghua-Tencent 100K dataset.

3   Network Design

Our idea for traffic sign recognition in this paper is depicted in Fig. 2. We firstly employ image processing to cope with foggy images for artifacts removal [31, 32], then import the preprocessed images into a neural network for object detection and classification.

Fig. 2.   The pipeline for traffic sign detection and recognition

3.1   Guided Image Filtering

Image defogging is an important preprocess for haze removal, which enhances visual effects such as edges and contours. There are generally two types of image defogging algorithms, one is histogram equalization, which simply enhances the contrast of the image. The other is an image restoration-based defogging algorithm [19], which takes use of original images to compare with the foggy images so as to reconstruct the new image. The dehazing effect is salient, but it is difficult to achieve the quality of original image.

Image filtering can solve the drawbacks of the two dehazing algorithms. The algorithm adopts an image to guide and filter the target image so that the final output image roughly resembles to the target image, the texture is akin to the guiding image. The guiding or reference image can be either a different one or the same one as the input image. If the guiding image is equivalent to the input image, the filtering becomes an edge-preserving operation, which is able to be used for image reconstruction. By using visual features of the guided image filtering, haze image preprocessing for traffic signs achieved the results of image denoising, image smoothing, and fog removal. Therefore, we define the original image as p_i, l_i as the guiding image, and q_i as the output image. The relationship is linear as

$$q_i = a_k I_k + b_k \; i \in \omega_k \tag{1}$$

where a_k and b_k are specific factors, ω_k is a square window with a center point k, $i \in \omega_k$ guarantees that a_k is not too big. In order to ensure the guided image filtering has the best outcome, the difference between the original image and the output image needs to be minimized. Therefore, the cost function $E\,(a_k, b_k)$ is defined as

$$E(a_k, b_k) = \sum_{i, k \in \omega_k} \left(\left| (q_i - p_i)^2 - \varepsilon a_k^2 \right| \right) \tag{2}$$

The output is the best one if $E(a_k, b_k)$ is the smallest. We take use of the least square method to find a_k and b_k,

$$a_k = \frac{\frac{1}{|\omega|} \sum_{i \in \omega_k} I_i q_i - u_k \overline{p_k}}{\sigma_k^2 + \varepsilon}, \; b_{k=} \overline{p_k} - a_k u_k \tag{3}$$

where u is the mean of I in $\mathbf{W}$, σ is the variance of I in W, w is the number of pixels in the window. We input a_k and b_k into Eq. (1) and obtain,

$$q_i = \frac{1}{|\omega|} \sum_{i \in \omega_k} (a_k I_k + b_k) = \overline{a_i} I_i + \overline{b_i} \tag{4}$$

3.2 Improved Faster R-CNN

Convolutional networks usually include a convolutional layer and a pooling layer, where the convolutional layer is usually used to extract features from the target. The feature extraction network in Faster R-CNN is based on a convolutional neural network, which uses convolutional network and ReLU (Rectified Linear Unit) activation function to extract the features from the target image, then the extracted features are input into the RPN layer and ROI pooling layer, respectively.

Traditional methods may use sliding windows or selective search to generate detection windows. Faster R-CNN chooses RPN to generate the detection window. The network takes advantage of softmax function to determine the properties of anchor points (foreground or background). Then regression is employed to correct it. Finally, accurate proposals will be obtained.

(a) original picture   (b) after the guided filtering

Fig. 3. Fog removal from digital images, (a) is the original picture from FROSI databases, (b) is the picture obtained by removing the fog after the guided filtering method

In Fig. 3, the RPN structure is framed by dotted lines. After 3×3 convolution, the feature map flows into two different channels, respectively. The upper one is classified by using the softmax layer to obtain foreground and background, the detection target is foreground. In order to obtain a relatively accurate proposal, the feature passes through the channel to calculate the offset of the regression. Finally, while removing the proposal that exceeds the boundary and the value is too small, the previous information is integrated to obtain a new proposal. With the network structure, the RPN layer basically completes the operation of locating the object.

The input of the ROI pooling layer is the proposals with various sizes. However, the input and output sizes of a convolutional neural network after training are fixed, which resize the proposals to the same.

In Faster R-CNN, we have fine-tuned our parameters, set the learning rate as 0.01, the momentum as 0.9, the batch size as 24, and the epoch as 200. The input features contain the proposal of classification network which is composed of fully connected layer and softmax activation function so as to obtain the predicted probability of each class the traffic sign belongs to. Faster R-CNN is shown in Eq. (5).

$$L((f_i), (l_i)) = \lambda \frac{1}{N_{reg}} \sum_i f_i^* L_{reg}\left(l_i, l_i^*\right) + \frac{1}{N} \sum_i L_{cls}\left(f_i, f_i^*\right) \tag{5}$$

where i represents the anchor index, f_i stands for the output probability of the softmax layer of positive samples, f^* means the corresponding prediction probability, l refers to the predicted bounding box, l^* denotes the GT box corresponding to the positive anchor.

Taken into account the advantages of Faster R-CNN, this paper adopts Faster R-CNN model to detect traffic signs. Faster R-CNN is use of VGGNet [20] as the backbone of the net. However, as the performance of the basic network improves, in this paper, we use GoogLeNet [21] for the feature extraction in our experiments. The network parameters are shown in Table 1.

After experimental verification, GoogLeNet has achieved the best results in terms of time-consuming and model performance based on the given dataset. During convolution, the kernels with various sizes were taken for the convolutional operations, the output feature maps are connected together.

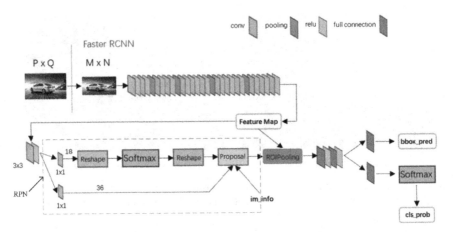

Fig. 4. The structure of faster R-CNN

Table 1. The parameters of GoogLeNet

Layer	Type	Size	Stride
1	Conv	(7, 7)	2
2	Max pooling	(3, 3)	2
3	Conv	(3, 3)	1
4	Max pooling	(3, 3)	2
5	Inception (a)		
6	Inception (b)		
7	Max pooling	(3, 3)	2
8	Inception (a)		
9	Inception (b)		
10	Inception (c)		
11	Inception (d)		
12	Inception (e)		
13	Max pooling	(3, 3)	2
14	Inception (a)		
15	Inception (b)		

Because the traffic sign will show multiple scales in the given image, after feature extraction, the signs with different scales are represented as features. We use cross-layer connection to improve the performance of multiscale target detection.

The detection net that we designed for the cross-layer connection is shown in Fig. 4. Pertaining to an image, CNN is accommodated to extract the features of the entire image. The RPN network is applied to extract a series of candidate regions based on the feature map. The change lies in the feature composition of the candidate region. This feature is no longer extracted by using only a single convolution layer, but is a fusion of features extracted from multiple convolution layers. The fused features contain not only semantic information but also local information.

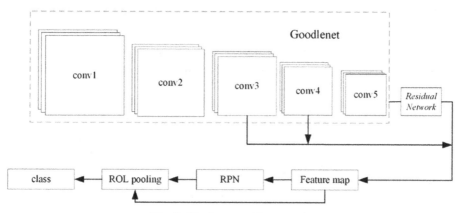

Fig. 5. The improved framework

In the given dataset, we often find a plethora of objects that resemble highway traffic signs. This will generate false detections. In order to achieve the purpose of reducing false detection, we use sample mining [22]. Firstly, the model is used to test on the training set. If there are negative samples with a score 0.8 or more in the obtained test results, they will be classified into a new sample class. In this way, the training set contains two classes: Traffic signs and traffic-like objects. The training set is used to obtain by mining negative samples so as to retrain a new detection model. Traffic signs are classified into the negative class and added to the training set, so that the model has increased the distinction between the two classes during the training time. This solves the problem that the model cannot classify background objects with minor differences between the positive class and the positive class if the amount of data is insufficient, thereby we obtain a satisfy outcome.

3.3 Improved YOLOv5

YOLO is a fast and compact open-source object detection model. Compared with other networks, it has stronger performance at the same size and has very good stability. The YOLO framework regards target detection as a regression problem, it is the first end-to-end neural network that predicts the class and bounding box of the object. At present, YOLOv5 has faster recognition speed and smaller network size than YOLOv4. For model training with different datasets, YOLOv3 and YOLOv4 need to calculate the initial anchor box, YOLOv5 embeds this function into the code to automatically calculate the best anchor box. However, in practice, it was found that the clustering is deviated from the statistical results of the samples. Therefore, in this paper, the anchor box clustering algorithm is optimized and random correction processing is added:

$$W_b = O_2^3(\text{random}[v1; v2] \times w_b) \qquad (6)$$

where O_2^3 (•) means that two of three cluster centers are randomly selected for correction, w_b is the width of the prior anchor box before correction, W_b is the width after correction. The numbers indicate the width and height of the anchor box respectively. It is observed that the minimum aspect ratio of the clustering results is 0.527 and the maximum is 0.714. For the data set in this paper, we find that 70% of the sample aspect ratios are between 0.72 and 1.00, 20% of the samples are between 0.6 and 0.7, 10% of the samples are between 0.6 and 0.7. From the analysis, we see that there is a deviation between the clustering results and the statistical results.

In traffic scenes, compared with pedestrians and vehicles, the physical size of traffic signs is smaller and there are at most three traffic signs in most samples. Because the ratio of foreground to background is severely unbalanced, most of the bounding boxes do not contain the target when the one-stage target detector is applied. Because the confidence error of these untargeted bounding boxes is relatively large, the loss of the foreground is submerged in the loss of the background. Therefore, in this paper, we optimize the original loss function. The main idea of optimization is to adaptively balance the loss of foreground and background. The loss function includes two parts, namely, regression loss and classification loss.

$$loss = \sum_{i=0}^{S}\sum_{j=0}^{S}\sum_{k=0}^{B} E_{ijk}^{obj} \{\omega_{coord}[(x_{gt} - x_p)^2 + (y_{gt} - y_p)^2 + (\sqrt{w_{gt}} - \sqrt{w_p})^2 + (\sqrt{h_{gt}} - \sqrt{h_p})^2]\}$$

$$+ \sum_{i=0}^{S}\sum_{j=0}^{S}\sum_{k=0}^{B} \{[\omega_{obj}E_{ijk}^{obj}(C_{gt} - C_p)^2] + [\omega_{noobj}E_{ijk}^{noobj}C_p(C_{gt} - C_p)^2]\} + \sum_{i=0}^{S}\sum_{j=0}^{S}\sum_{k=0}^{B}(P_{gt} - P_p)^2 \qquad (7)$$

where S is the width and height of the feature map. There are three sizes of the feature map in this paper: 52×52, 26×26, 13×13, B is the number of a priori boxes at each anchor box; E_{ijk}^{obj} represents the anchor point whether the box is responsible for predicting the target, E_{ijk}^{noobj} means it is irrelevant for predicting the target; x_{gt}, y_{gt}, w_{gt}, h_{gt} are ground truths, x_p, y_p, w_p, h_p are predicted values, indicating the coordinates of the target, width and height (in pixels); C_{gt} and C_p represent true confidence and prediction confidence, respectively; P_{gt} and P_p represent classification real probability and classification prediction probability, respectively; ω shows the weight coefficient of each loss part, for weight. The value is set in this paper as $\omega_{coord} = 5$, $\omega_{obj} = 1$, $\omega_{noobj} = 0.5$, the purpose of this setting is to reduce the loss of non-target regions and increase the loss of target ones in order to further avoid the loss of background values to confidence. In this paper, C_p is also used as a part of the weight to adjust the loss value of the background frame adaptively.

4 Results

4.1 Improved Faster R-CNN

In this paper, dataset GTSDB contains 900 images with a total of 1,206 traffic signs. There are four types of traffic signs: Mandatory, prohibitory, danger, and other. As there are not many foggy scenes in GTSDB, we also take use of FRIDA, FRIDA2, and FROSI databases. The dataset FRIDA consists of 90 composite images of 18 urban road scenes, meanwhile FRIDA2 consists of 330 composite images of 66 road scenes. They have the same driver's viewpoint, with different types of fogs added to each original image: Uniform fog, heterogeneous fog, cloudy fog, and cloudy heterogeneous fog, give way, watch out for pedestrians, etc. The FROSI dataset contains fog with the visibility ranging from 50 to 400 meters, including 1,620 traffic signs placed at various locations. By using these datasets, it is possible to train our YOLOv5 model comprehensively. In this paper, we combine two datasets for model training and testing. Among them, 60% samples are used for training, 20% for verification, and 20% for testing. In this paper, the evaluation index for traffic sign detection is measured by using mean average precision (mAP), which is popularly employed in object detection.

The test results include four categories: *TP*, *FP*, *FN*, *TN*. Precision is the probability that the positive sample is predicted correctly. Recall is for the primary positive samples, which indicates how many of the positive samples are predicted correctly. Therefore, the precision and recall are calculated as:

$$precision = \frac{TP}{TP + FP} \tag{8}$$

$$recall = \frac{TP}{TP + FN} \tag{9}$$

Firstly, we test various backbone networks. The performance of the network depends heavily on the ability of the network. Therefore, the part of feature extraction that directly affects network performance requires much effort. This paper offers classic networks as the feature extraction network of Faster R-CNN to compare the impact of different networks based on classification performance. Table 2 shows the experimental results of multiple networks. We see that the backbone networks have effects on the implementation. GoogLeNet and ResNet both have an improvement about 5.1% compared to VGGNET, whilst the running time of GoogLeNet is similar to that of VGG. Therefore, considered mAP and running time, Faster R-CNN as an object detector, GoogleNet is used as the backbone network.

Next, we tackle digital images with guided filtering and input the preprocessed image into the designed network to classify traffic signs. We compare the basic Faster R-CNN network. Table 3 shows the specific performance of our proposed method based on the given dataset. The PR curve of the experiments is shown in Fig. 5 (Fig. 6).

Table 2. The influence of feature extraction networks based on the detection results

Networks	Recall (%)	Precision (%)	mAP (%)	fps
VGGNet	88.2	89.1	90.2	16
GoogLeNet	88.7	93.2	95.3	17
ResNet	92.8	91.2	95.2	16

Table 3. Contrast experiments with the basic Faster R-CNN network

Methods	Recall (%)	Precision (%)	mAP (%)
Faster R-CNN	90.6	91.3	80.3
Our method	92.6	93.4	95.3

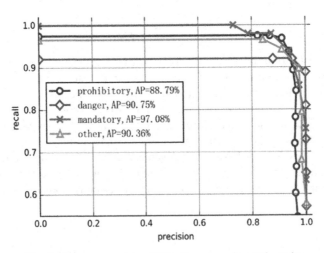

Fig. 6. Average precision (AP) of our experimental results

In Table 2, we compare the accuracy, recall and precision of the three feature extraction networks. We see that under the current scale of data training, the GoogLeNet is better than the VGG in recall and accuracy, but the running time will be relatively slower than the VGG network. Compared with ResNet, our recall rate is relatively low, other indicators are relatively better, but it takes a bit longer time.

In Table 3, the recall and accuracy of Faster R-CNN are relatively high. The reason is that there are a large number of traffic signs in reality. Accordingly, we took use of the guided image filtering for processing the image data. The feature fusion method based on the GoogLeNet is proposed in this paper for model training. Although the recall of target detection has not been changed too much, the accuracy has increased by 15%, which is explained as that by adding difficult negative samples, the net capability has been increased a lot owning to the data augmentation. Figure 5 shows the PR curves for four classifiers. In complex scenes, the general model usually cannot detect the traffic signs very well.

4.2   Improved YOLOv5

In this paper, we modify the YOLOv5 framework as the basis of the detection algorithm, and train two networks separately, one of which is the standard YOLOv5 network, which is used as a comparison method. The loss curve is shown in Fig. 7.

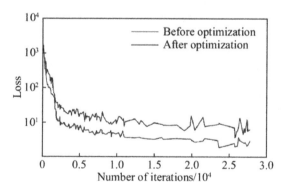

Fig. 7. The loss curves.

4.3   Comparsions of YOLOv5 and Faster R-CNN

These models are trained and evaluated based on a computer equipped with a Core i7-8th CPU, 16 GB of RAM, and NVIDIA RTX2060 GPU by using the same dataset. At first, we compare the training time. Faster R-CNN training took 14 h, while YOLOv5 training ran 11 h because YOLOv5 is a smaller size of network than Faster R-CNN. Secondly, the recognition speed of Faster R-CNN is 17 FPS, while the recognition speed of YOLOv5 is 60 FPS. YOLOv5 is much suitable for real-time traffic sign recognition. Finally, Fig. 8 and Fig. 9 show the results of the two classifications by using the FRIDA dataset.

Fig. 8. The results of traffic sign recognition based on FRIDA dataset by using YOLOv5

4.4 Guided Image Filtering

In this section, we use YOLOv5 as the basic framework to compare the results for dehazing. In Fig. 10(a), there is a traffic sign that is not able to be recognized.

Fig. 9. The results of traffic sign recognition based on FRIDA dataset by using faster R-CNN

(a) YOLOv5 without dehazing   (b) YOLOv5 with dehazing

Fig. 10. The results of traffic sign recognition without (a) and with (b) dehazing

5 Conclusion

Our proposed method is based on Faster R-CNN to achieve traffic sign detection and recognition, we compare the results of object detection and recognition with multiple networks. If the overall framework of our experiment is the same, we choose the excellent network as our base net.

We have effectively employed multiresolution feature maps through cross-layer connections to build up the feature maps of traffic signs with multiple scales. We take use of guided image filtering to eliminate the noises from the given images, and further improve the accuracy of our experiments.

There are two aspects in our future work [23–30]. One is to collect more traffic signs as the samples under complicated conditions to form our own dataset. The other is to further optimize the method to form an end-to-end TRS system.

References

1. Houben, S., Stallkamp, J., Salmen, J., Schlipsing, M., Igel, C.: Detection of traffic signs in real-world images: the German traffic sign detection benchmark. In: International Joint Conference on Neural Networks, pp. 1–8 (2013)
2. Yang, Y., Luo, H., Xu, H., Wu, F.: Towards real-time traffic sign detection and classification. IEEE Trans. Intell. Transp. Syst. 17(7), 2022–2031 (2016)
3. Berkaya, S.K., Gunduz, H., Ozsen, O., Akinlar, C., Gunal, S.: On circular traffic sign detection and recognition. Expert Syst. Appl. 48, 67–75 (2016)
4. Jie, Y., Xiaomin, C., Pengfei, G., Zhonglong, X.: A new traffic light detection and recognition algorithm for electronic travel aid. In: International Conference on Intelligent Control & Information Processing (2013)
5. Jin, J., Fu, K., Zhang, C.: Traffic sign recognition with hinge loss trained convolutional neural networks. IEEE Trans. Intell. Transp. Syst. 15(5), 1991–2000 (2014)
6. Priese, L., Klieber, J., Lakmann, R., Rehrmann, V., Schian, R.: New results on traffic sign recognition. In: IEEE Intelligent Vehicles Symposium (2002)
7. Sun, L., Chen, J., Xie, K., Gu, T.: Deep and shallow features fusion based on deep convolutional neural network for speech emotion recognition. Int. J. Speech Technol. 21(4), 931–940 (2018). https://doi.org/10.1007/s10772-018-9551-4
8. Ren, Y., Yang, J., Zhang, Q., Guo, Z.: Multi-feature fusion with convolutional neural network for ship classification in optical images. Appl. Sci. 9(20), 4209 (2019)
9. Ruta, A., Li, Y., Liu, X.: Detection, tracking and recognition of traffic signs from video input. In: Intelligent Transportation System, pp. 55–60 (2008)
10. Blancard, M.: Road sign recognition: a study of vision-based decision making for road environment recognition. In: Masaki, I. (ed.) Vision-Based Vehicle Guidance. Springer Series in Perception Engineering, pp. 162–172. Springer, New York (1992). https://doi.org/10.1007/978-1-4612-2778-6_7
11. Girshick, R., Donahue, J., Darrell, T.: Rich feature hierarchies for accurate object detection and semantic segmentation. In: IEEE CVPR (2014)
12. Uijlings, R., van de Sande, A., Gevers, T., Smeulders, M.: Selective search for object recognition. Int. J. Comput. Vision 104(2), 154–171 (2013)
13. He, K., Zhang, X., Ren, S., Sun, J.: Spatial pyramid pooling in deep convolutional networks for visual recognition. IEEE Trans. Pattern Anal. Mach. Intell. 37(9), 1904–1916 (2014)
14. Girshick, R.: Fast R-CNN. In: IEEE International Conference on Computer Vision (2015)

15. Inoue, Y., Kohashi, Y., Ishikawa, N., Nakajima, M.: Automatic recognition of road signs. In: International Symposium on Optical Science & Technology (2002)
16. Müller, J., Dietmayer, K.: Detecting traffic lights by single shot detection. In: International Conference on Intelligent Transportation Systems (2018)
17. Douville, P.: Real-time classification of traffic signs. Real-Time Imaging **6**(3), 185–193 (2000)
18. Barnes, N., Zelinsky, A.: Real-time speed sign detection using the radial symmetry detector. IEEE Trans. Intell. Transp. Syst. **9**(2), 322–332 (2016)
19. Illingworth, J., Kittler, J.: A survey of the Hough transform. Comput. Vis. Graph. Image Process. **43**(2), 280 (1988)
20. Simonyan, K., Zisserman, A.: Very deep convolutional networks for large-scale image recognition. Comput. Sci. (2014)
21. Szegedy, C., et al.: Going deeper with convolutions. In: IEEE Conference on Computer Vision and Pattern Recognition (2014)
22. Sung, K.: Learning and example selection for object and pattern detection. Ph.D. thesis, Massachusetts Institute of Technology, United States (1995)
23. Liu, X., Yan, W.: Traffic-light sign recognition using Capsule network. MTAP (2021)
24. Qin, Z., Yan, W.: Traffic-sign recognition using deep learning. In: International Symposium on Geometry and Vision (ISGV) (2021)
25. Liu, X., Yan, W.: Vehicle-related scene segmentation using CapsNets. In: IEEE IVCZN (2020)
26. Pan, C., Yan, W.: Salient object detection based on perception saturation. Multimed. Tools Appl. **79**(27–28), 19925–19944 (2020)
27. Liu, X., Nguyen, M., Yan, W.: Vehicle-related scene understanding using deep learning. In: ACPR Workshop (2019)
28. Pan, C., Yan, W.: A learning-based positive feedback in salient object detection. In: IEEE IVCNZ (2019)
29. Yan, W.: Computational Methods for Deep Learning. Springer, Heidelberg (2021). https://doi.org/10.1007/978-3-030-61081-4
30. Yan, W.: Introduction to Intelligent Surveillance: Surveillance Data Capture, Transmission, and Analytics. Springer, Heidelberg (2019). https://doi.org/10.1007/978-3-030-10713-0
31. Yan, W., Kankanhalli, M.: Detection and removal of lighting & shaking artifacts in home videos. In: ACM International Conference on Multimedia, pp. 107–116 (2002)
32. Yan, W., Kankanhalli, M., Wang, J.: Analogies-based video editing. Multimed. Syst. **11**(1), 3–18 (2005)

Towards a Generic Bicubic Hermite Mesh Template for Cow Udders

Harvey Ho[1](✉) and Øyind Nordbø[2,3]

[1] Auckland Bioengineering Institute, University of Auckland,
Auckland, New Zealand
`harvey.ho@auckland.ac.nz`
[2] Geno SA, Storhamargata 44, 2317 Hamar, Norway
[3] Norsvin SA, Storhamargata 44, 2317 Hamar, Norway

Abstract. The shape of cow udders represents an important trait for the functionality and longevity of dairy cows, yet traditional trait definitions cannot fully capture its complexity. In this work we propose a parametric cubic Hermite (CH) based mesh to model the shape of cow udders and teats. The workflow starts from selecting a subset of nodes from the data cloud captured by a depth scanner, and constructing a CH mesh from the nodes. Using a coherent point drifting (CPD) algorithm, the nodes on the mesh are registered from one cow to their counterparts of another cow while preserving the topological coherence of the mesh. This workflow works well for the udder surface when teats are excluded. However, when teats are included in the mesh, misaligned correspondences occur due to data point occlusion and insufficient sampling points. In summary, a first parametric mesh based 3D model has been constructed for the cow udder and teat. We have examined the efficacy of the morphing algorithm, and also the issues to be solved for a statistical cow udder and teat model.

Keywords: Udder · Coherent point drifting · Cubic hermite mesh

1 Introduction

The conformations of cow udders represent important traits for dairy cow breeders, because the shape of udders are important for the functionality [1], health [2] and longevity [3] of dairy cows. Traditionally, the conformation of udders is scored on a discrete scale by a technician, where several conformation traits are assessed. These traits include the attachment angle of the fore udder, the width, height, depth and balance of the rear udder [2]. However, this scoring system carries laborious work and is prone to subjective errors. In addition, the linear traits are not able to capture the curvature information of the udder surface, for which a more sophisticated criterion, and hence modelling methods are required. In recent years, the dairy industry has been using innovative technologies to measure the shapes of udders. For example, depth cameras/scanners are

© Springer Nature Switzerland AG 2021
M. Nguyen et al. (Eds.): ISGV 2021, CCIS 1386, pp. 100–107, 2021.
https://doi.org/10.1007/978-3-030-72073-5_8

used to obtain three dimensional (3D) data cloud of cow udders [4]. This kind of data cloud contains pixel-based, depth-encoded points in the number of thousands or more, from which a triangular mesh could be constructed to represent the 3D shape of a cow udder.

This method, however, is prone to noises and artifacts caused during the scanning process. Furthermore, the complex shape of cow udders require many mesh vertices to represent its full entirety, yet the vertices for teats are often occluded, as we will show later in the paper. Indeed, depth-point-based 3D udder models are rarely reported in literature. Here we suggest that a more succinct geometric representation of 3D geometries, such as a parametric mesh (e.g., of Hermite, splines) may serve the purpose better because a much smaller number of vertices are required [5]. The challenge for a parametric mesh, however, is to represent the udder shape in sufficient details than triangular meshes based upon a subset of available vertices.

Among parametric meshes, the cubic Hermite (CH) mesh has been previously used for statistical modelling of the liver [6,7], and for modelling the pig surface [5]. In work [7], a statistical liver model is morphed to subject-specific livers, and the landmark points on the template mesh are automatically fitted onto the target data cloud [6]. The weakness of this algorithm, however, is that the nodes on the CH mesh are not anchored onto feature points of the target data cloud. The correspondence problem could hamper the efficacy of this approach.

The aim of the work is twofold. Firstly, we aim to use a parametric mesh to represent the udder surface and the teat. Secondly, we aim to develop a workflow where the mesh vertices can cohesively morph from one udder to another. To that end we will apply a coherent point drifting (CPD) algorithm [8], which may be classified into a nonlinear registration method. In the following sections we will outline the workflow, and demonstrate its use in developing a generic cow udder template.

2   Methods

2.1   Data Cloud of Cow Udders

Cow udder data were retrieved using an Intel RealSense F200 camera, mounted on a selfie stick, and placed underneath cow udders. A colour-coded depth image and its binarised image are shown in Fig. 1(a) and (b), respectively. Since bovine structures outside cow udders, such as the legs and the background need to be removed, the udder area is manually segmented as a mask (Fig. 1c). With this mask, only the data points within the udder region are 3D re-constructed. Figure 1(d) shows the 3D point cloud of a udder in the cartesian coordinate system. The colour coding of the data points represents their distance from a baseline plane (in brown colour), e.g., the red coloured points are further away from the plane than blue coloured points.

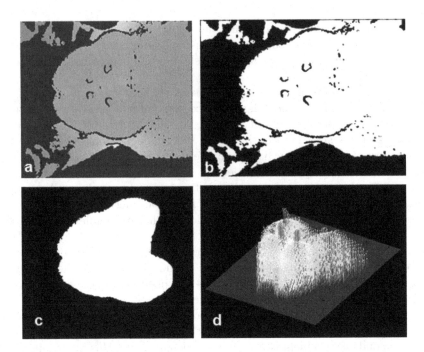

Fig. 1. Pre-processing of depth data image of cow udders: (a) and (b) Colour coded and binary images of cow udders; (b) The region containing cow udders is segmented and used as a mask for the 3D data cloud; (c) 3D reconstructed data cloud of the udders. (Color figure online)

2.2   Bicubic Hermite Mesh

A CH mesh uses a set of sparsely located nodes to represent a shape [9]. The basis functions for CHM have been introduced in many literatures, e.g., in [9], therefore are not repeated here. In a surface CH mesh, two material coordinates (ξ_1, ξ_2) define all nodes on the mesh. Figure 2 illustrates the process of constructing a CH mesh. In Fig. 2(a), from about two thousand data points of Fig. 1(d), some 12×9 nodes across the udder surface were selected. Then, a 11×8 mesh was constructed using an open source software CMGUI (https://www.cmiss.org/cmgui), as shown in Fig. 2(a). Note, in this mesh, the teats were excluded because their geometric representation requires a denser mesh. In Fig. 2(b), 44 nodes and 42 elements were used to represent a teat and a udder.

2.3   Coherent Point Drifting

We aim to morph a CH mesh such as the one shown in Fig. 2(a) to the data clouds of another cow udder. The key is to register the nodes on the mesh to their counterpart points in other udders. This is a non-rigid registration problem and is restated as below:

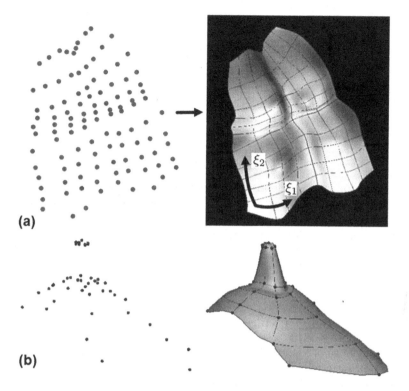

Fig. 2. Bi-cubic Hermite mesh for: (a) cow udders without teats that consists of 12×9 nodes and 11×8 elements; (b) a udder with teat that consists of 44 nodes and 42 elements.

- Given a set of nodes $Y_i(i = 1, 2, ..., M)$ of a CH mesh;
- Determine the corresponding M points from the target data cloud $X_i(i = 1, 2, ..., N)$;
- Determine the transformation matrix T.

Note, that the number of data points in X, Y need not to be the same. This is a desired feature in our case where Y contains a smaller number of nodes. For instance, the CH mesh of Fig. 2(a) contains 108 nodes, whereas the number of points in data cloud X can be hundreds or thousands. The core of the CPD algorithm is the Gaussian mixture model (GMM) algorithm [8], where the GMM probability density function is (we refer the interested reader to much more details of the following equations in literature [8]):

$$p(x) = \omega \frac{1}{N} + (1 - \omega) \sum_{m=1}^{M+1} P(m)p(x|m) \tag{1}$$

$$p(x|m) = \frac{1}{(2\pi\sigma^2)^{D/2}} e^{-\frac{|x - y_m|^2}{2\sigma^2}} \tag{2}$$

And a likelihood function E is minimised:

$$E(\theta, \sigma^2) = -\sum_{n=1}^{N} log \sum_{m=1}^{M+1} P(m)p(x_n|m) \tag{3}$$

where θ is used to parameterize the GMM centroids. The correspondence between two points y_m and x_n is obtained by using the posterior probabilities of the GMM centroids:

$$P(m|x_n) = P(m)p(x_n|m)/p(x_n) \tag{4}$$

The values for θ, σ^2 are determined from the expectation-maximization (EM) algorithm. The idea is to move the GMM centroids coherently as a group, and to preserve the topology of the mesh nodes. Concerning the implementation of the CPD algorithm, we made use of the source code in MATLAB (Mathworks, USA) provided from literature [10]. The postprocessing software was CMGUI.

3   Results

3.1   Morphing the CH Mesh of the Udder

Using the CH mesh of a udder (ID 0044), shown in Fig. 2(a) where the teats were excluded, we firstly morphed the mesh (ID 0044) as the GMM centroids to the 276 data points of another udder (ID 0055). Figure 3(a) shows the udder clouds of two cows before morphing, which are distinctly distributed in the cartesian coordinate system. Figure 3(b) shows the two data clouds after morphing mesh 0044. Figure 3(c) provides a detailed view of the nodes on the mesh pre- and post-morphing. It can be seen that the locations of teats, indicated by the red and blue arrows, were successfully tracked.

3.2   Geometric Modelling for the Teat

In Fig. 4(a), the data points of two udders and teats are shown in blue and purple points respectively. The data points of the two teats are of different orientations. After applying the CPD algorithm, as shown in Fig. 4(b), the data points on the udder surface fitted well. However, the eight points at the apex of the teat dropped to the wall of the teat (indicated by arrows) due to lack of corresponding points on the other teat. There were two reasons causing the problem: (1) the apex of teat is rather small, and thus is difficult to have sufficient data points to fit onto; (2) one side of the teat wall is often occluded, leading to missing data points.

4   Discussion

Udder conformations are important traits for dairy breeders, due to their importance for the functionality, animal health, and thus, the economy of dairy farmers. Traditional methods for scoring the shape of an udder relies on several linear traits, which are estimated by visual inspections, or measured by a customised meter for teats [11]. The aim of the work was to develop a generic udder template, and to morph such a generic template to data clouds of udders obtained from depth cameras. To serve the purpose, we used a CPD algorithm, where the nodes of the CH mesh are the centroids of GMM, and their corresponding nodes in the data cloud of another udder are selected via a density maximization algorithm. The current pilot work has shown the efficacy of this workflow in modelling the udder surface.

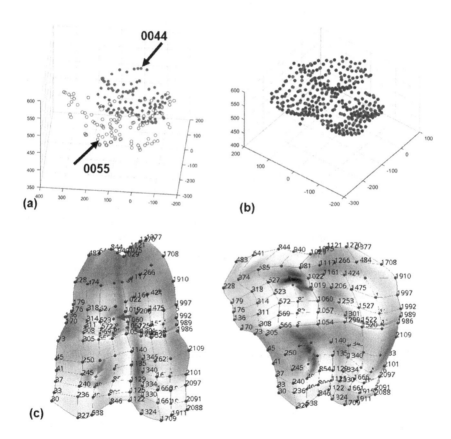

Fig. 3. The data clouds of the udders of two cows before and after applying the CPD algorithm, shown in (a) and (b) respectively; (c) feature points of udders, e.g. the locations of teats indicated by blue and red arrows, are consistent in the mesh template. (Color figure online)

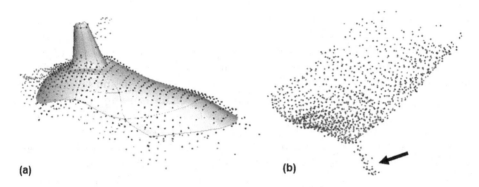

(a)   (b)

Fig. 4. (a) Data points of the teats of two cows, shown in blue and purple colours. The two teats are in different orientations; (b) after applying the CPD algorithm the data points of two udder surfaces are mapped, however the data point at the apex of teat incorrectly registered to the teat wall due to partial occlusion, indicated by the arrow. (Color figure online)

The novelty of the work is that it is the first time a parametric mesh has been used to model cow udders. Furthermore, a coupling of a CH mesh and the CPD algorithm captures the landmarkers better than the automatic fitting algorithm described in [7]. The workflow worked well for the udder surface, when teats were not included. To successfully model the teats, one depth camera may not be enough to retrieve the data points of a teat. Multiple cameras could help, e.g. the multiple Kinect system used in [4]. Alternatively, depth images may be taken from several complementary perspectives to complete the whole picture.

As mentioned in Introduction, our ultimate goal is to use a generic mesh as a statistical template for the cow udder, where genetic and health trait analysis could be made. Towards that end, the current model needs to be applied to a udder population. By a principal component analysis for the scattering pattern of the mesh, we may be able to identify novel traits for the udder shape [6].

5   Conclusion

We have developed the first parametric mesh based 3D model for cow udders and teats, and have shown the efficacy of coupling the parametric mesh with a coherent point drifting algorithm. Challenges remain due to eccentric teat shape and occlusion in developing a complete udder and teat model.

References

1. Jacobs, J.A., Siegford, J.M.: Lactating dairy cows adapt quickly to being milked by an automatic milking system. J. Dairy Sci. **95**(3), 1575–1584 (2012)
2. Van Dorp, T.E., Dekkers, J.C.M., Martin, S.W., Noordhuizen, J.P.T.M.: Genetic parameters of health disorders, and relationships with 305-day milk yield and conformation traits of registered Holstein cows. J. Dairy Sci. **81**(8), 2264–2270 (1998)

3. Vollema, A.R., Groen, A.F.: Genetic correlations between longevity and conformation traits in an upgrading dairy cattle population. J. Dairy Sci. **80**(11), 3006–3014 (1997)
4. Salau, J., Haas, J.H., Junge, W., Thaller, G.: Automated calculation of udder depth and rear leg angle in Holstein-Friesian cows using a multi-Kinect cow scanning system. Biosyst. Eng. **160**, 154–169 (2017)
5. Ho, H., Yu, H.B., Gangsei, L.E., Kongsro, J.: A CT-image based pig atlas model and its potential applications in the meat industry. Meat Sci. **148**, 1–4 (2019)
6. Yu, H.B., Nakagawa, Y., Ho, H., Saito, A., Shimizu, A.: Deformable cubic Hermite mesh templates for statistical liver shape analysis. In: Reuter, M., Wachinger, C., Lombaert, H., Paniagua, B., Lüthi, M., Egger, B. (eds.) ShapeMI 2018. LNCS, vol. 11167, pp. 93–101. Springer, Cham (2018). https://doi.org/10.1007/978-3-030-04747-4_9
7. Lu, Z., Shimizu, A., Ho, H.: Evaluation of a statistical shape model for the liver. In: 2018 International Conference on Image and Vision Computing New Zealand (IVCNZ), pp. 1–4 (2018)
8. Myronenko, A., Song, X.: Point set registration: coherent point drift. IEEE Trans. Pattern Anal. Mach. Intell. **32**(12), 2262–2275 (2010)
9. Bradley, C., Pullan, A., Hunter, P.: Geometric modeling of the human torso using cubic Hermite elements. Ann. Biomed. Eng. **25**(1), 96–111 (1997). https://doi.org/10.1007/BF02738542
10. Chui, H., Rangarajan, A.: A new point matching algorithm for non-rigid registration. Comput. Vis. Image Underst. **89**(2), 114–141 (2003)
11. Hamann, J., Mein, G.A.: Responses of the bovine teat to machine milking: measurement of changes in thickness of the teat apex. J. Dairy Res. **55**(3), 331–338 (1988)

Sign Language Recognition from Digital Videos Using Deep Learning Methods

Jia Lu[✉], Minh Nguyen[✉], and Wei Qi Yan[✉]

Auckland University of Technology, Auckland 1010, New Zealand
{jia.lu,minh.nguyen,weiqi.yan}@aut.ac.nz

Abstract. In this paper, we investigate the state-of-the-art deep learning methods for sign language recognition. In order to achieve this goal, Capsule Network (CapsNet) is proposed in this paper, which shows positive result. We also propose a Selective Kernel Network (SKNet) with attention mechanism in order to extract spatial information. Sign language as an important means of communications, the problems of recognizing sign language from digital videos in real time have become the new challenge of this research field. The contributions of this paper are: (1) The CapsNet attains the accuracy of overall recognition up to 98.72% based on our own dataset. (2) SKNet with attention mechanism is able to achieve the best recognition accuracy 98.88%.

Keywords: Sign language recognition · Deep learning · Selective Kernel Network (SKNet) · Attention mechanism · Capsule network (CapsNet) · Long short-term memory (LSTM)

1 Introduction

Gesture plays an important role in our daily conversation. Sign language is an organized form of gestures, including lip movements and gestures. Moreover, it uses symbols in visual space instead of oral communications and voice patterns.

Sign language recognition is regarded as a part of behavior recognition, it is a cooperative research field which is related to pattern recognition, computer vision, etc. The term of sign language recognition refers to the whole process of tracking human gestures, recognizing the representations, and converting them into semantically meaningful commands [1]. For the traditional approaches in sign language/gesture recognition, it includes three stages: Detection, tracking, and recognition to complete the most of hand talks [1–5]. Moreover, hand detection and segmentation of the corresponding image area is the primary task of the gesture recognition system. This segmentation is critical because it separates the task-related data from the image background and then passes it to the subsequent tracking and recognition stage. Therefore, the traditional approaches are time consuming, required multiple pre-processing steps.

In this paper, we implement and investigate multiple sign language recognition models, which are time efficiency and achieve high performance in model training and testing.

© Springer Nature Switzerland AG 2021
M. Nguyen et al. (Eds.): ISGV 2021, CCIS 1386, pp. 108–118, 2021.
https://doi.org/10.1007/978-3-030-72073-5_9

Moreover, the model has shown the capabilities to implement sign language recognition, how to make the model more stable and robust for sign language recognition has become a new challenge of this study. In summary, this paper aims to develop an accurate deep learning method to conduct sign language recognition without any interruptions. As the outcome of this paper, we hope to achieve over 90% accuracy for sign language recognition in real time.

Our contribution of this paper is to adopt the deep learning-based model to achieve sign language recognition by using capsule network (CapsNet). Moreover, an RTX 2080Ti GPU is used to accelerate the training process so as to achieve the efficiency.

The remaining parts of this paper are organized as follows: The related work will be described in Sect. 2. Our method will be explicated in Sect. 3. In Sect. 4, we showcase our experimental results. Finally, the conclusion and future work of this paper will be delineated and envisioned in Sect. 5.

2 Related Work

In the past decades, with the growth of computing capacity and computational speed, deep learning methods with its derived neural networks have attracted wide attention in visual object detection, which have opened up a new era of computer vision [6–9]. As the state-of-the-art technology, deep learning (DL) becomes more and more popular because of its superiority to conventional machine learning. Deep learning methods [10, 11] were implemented not only for vision-based object detection, but also for text-based natural language processing (NLP) as well as speech recognition. Moreover, deep learning as an end-to-end model normally does not require low-level processing which is able to cut off human labor and gain time efficiency though the training is costly.

The deep neural networks (DNNs) [11, 12] encapsulate hidden layers, the pretraining method is utilized to resolve the problems of optimal local solution. In the neural network model, the number of hidden layers increases with the "depth". The most advanced methods rely heavily on artificial neural networks, such as convolutional neural networks (CNNs), single shot multibox detector (SSD), you only look once (YOLO) etc. In addition, deep learning includes both supervised and unsupervised learning [13]. Apparently, the work clearly unfolds the differences between deep neural networks and shallow neural networks in various aspects [14].

CNN as a type of DNNs [15] is derived by combining digital image processing and artificial neural networks. The traditional CNN includes multiple convolutional layers and pooling operations, the outputs of convolutional layers are extracted as the feature maps which are flattened and fed to fully connected layer. As an active research area in computer vision, sign language recognition has successfully exploited by adopting CNN and achieved the outstanding results [7, 16].

2D CNN based on the single frame has been employed to extract feature maps and conduct temporal information to recognize gestures [17, 18]. Moreover, 2D CNN is expanded to 3D CNN [19–21] so as to learn the motion features by adopting 3D filters in the convolutional layers, which show the positive results for recognizing hand gestures. CNN model was proposed to detect and segment hands in both unlabeled and synthetic dataset, which achieved 82% accuracy based on segmentation and detection [22].

The CNN network has been well investigated to solve the image classification and recognition tasks. Moreover, it also has been investigated and implemented for sign language recognition in recent years. A CNN-based method was proposed with Gaussian skin color model and background subtraction to achieve gestures recognition from the camera images. The Gaussian skin color model controlled the influence of light on skin color, and the non-skin color of image is filtered out directly, which has 93.80% accuracy from a given dataset [23]. A two-stage CNN architecture (HGR-Net) was given, where the first stage was proposed to determine the region of interest by performing pixel-level semantic segmentation, the second stage is to recognize hand gesture [24]. Moreover, the combination of fully convolutional residual network with spatial pyramid pooling was adopted at the first stage, the result shows that proposed architecture improves 1.6% accuracy for recognition by using OUHands dataset.

A deep convolutional network was proposed with multidimensional feature learning approach (MultiD-CNN) to recognize the gestures from the RGB-D videos [25]. The method took use of 3D ResNet for training a model with both spatiotemporal features, the long short-term memory (LSTM) for processing temporal dependencies and the proposed method is outperformed compared with the previous methods based on different datasets. Chen et al. implemented the spatiotemporal attention with dynamic graph constructed (DG-STA) method to achieve hand gesture recognition. It took advantage of fully connected graph and self-attention mechanism to learn the node features and edges from the hand skeleton, a novel spatiotemporal mask is applied to reduce the computational cost. According to the experimental results, DG-STA method achieved the superior performance compared with others for recognizing hand gestures [26].

A deep-learning-based method was proposed by adopting two ResNet CNNs and soft attention with fully connected layer to recognize dynamic gestures. Moreover, a method was proposed to condense a digital video into a single RGB image and passed to the model for the final classification. The experimental result based on public datasets shows that the proposed method is able to improve the accuracy compared with other methods [27]. Three representations of depth sequences are constructed, which includes dynamic depth images (DDI), dynamic depth normal images (DDNI), and dynamic depth motion normal images (DDMNI) from the depth maps to capture the spatiotemporal information by adopting the bidirectional rank pooling, the CNNs-based model is considered to achieve gesture recognition. The proposed model was evaluated based on large-scale isolated gesture recognition at the ChaLearn LAP challenge 2016 and the model was achieved the growth of 16.34% accuracy on the IsoGD dataset [28].

Two different deep learning methods were fused to achieve gesture recognition. The convolutional two-stream consensus voting network (2SCVN) to explicitly simulate the short-term and long-term structures of RGB sequences, and 3D Depth-Saliency CNN stream (3DDSN) was used to present the motion features. The proposed methods have been evaluated based on ChaLearn IsoGD dataset with 4.47% growth of accuracy compared with other models in 2016 [29]. Molchanov et al. designed a dynamic hand gesture recognition method by adopting a recurrent 3D CNN model. Four kinds of visual data were fused to boost the recognition rate, which includes RGB, depth, optical flow and stereo IR. The proposed model achieved the positive accuracy rate based on ChaLearn dataset, which has 1% growth compared with other models [20]. A hand gesture recognition and identification model was proposed based on the two-stream CNNs, the depth map and optical flow as the inputs were utilized in this method. The proposed model has 18.91% accuracy improvement based on MSR Action3D dataset compared with the relevant models [18].

Rastgoo et al. set forth the model for hand sign language recognition by utilizing the restricted Boltzmann machine (RBM) for visual data. The model took use of RGB and depth as the input: Original image, cropped image, and noisy cropped image. The CNN is used to detect the hand in each image, three forms of the detected hand images are generated to the RGB and depth will be inputted to the RBM. The output of the RBM will be fused to recognize the sign label. As the result, the proposed model has been able to achieve significant improvement based on four different public datasets compared with the state-of-the-art models [30]. After the RBM model, Rastgoo et al. proposed a deep cascaded model for sign language recognition from the videos in 2020. The model employed three spatial features: Hand features, extra spatial hand relation (ESHR), and hand pose (HP) features which were fused in the model and feed into the LSTM for temporal feature extraction. The SSD model was also adopted for hand detection. The proposed model was evaluated based on IsoGD dataset, which achieved 4.25% accuracy improvement compared with others [31].

3   Our Method

CNN is good at capturing the existence of features, because the convolution structure was designed for this purpose. However, CNN is unable to explore the relationship between each feature attributes, such as relative positions, size, and direction of the feature etc. Thus, Sabour et al. firstly proposed a new deep learning network that is much effective for image processing, which called capsule network (CapsNet) [32]. It combines the advantages of CNN structure and takes into account the relative position, angle and other information that are missing from the CNN, thereby improving the recognition effect. The CapsNet structure contains two main components, which are primary capsule and digital capsule.

Capsule is a group of neurons whose input and output vectors represent the parameters of a specific type like the probability of occurrence of objects, conceptual entities, etc. It took use of the length of input and output vectors to represent the probability of the existence of the entity, the direction of a vector represents the instantiation parameters. Capsules of the same level predict the instantiation parameters of higher-level capsules through the transformation matrix. The higher-level capsules become active, if the multiple predictions are consistent. The activity of the neurons in an active capsule represents the various attributes of the specific entities that are appearing in the image, which contains the parameters, such as posture (position, size, direction), deformation, speed, reflectivity, color, texture, etc. The lengths of the output vectors represent the probability of an entity, its range is between [0, 1]. A nonlinear function called "squashing" was proposed to ensure that the length of the short vector is reduced to almost zero, while the length of the long vector is compressed. The following equation is the expression of the non-linear function:

$$V_j = \frac{\|S_j\|^2}{1 + \|S_j\|^2} \frac{S_j}{\|S_j\|} \tag{1}$$

where V_j represents the vector output of capsule j, S_j denotes the total input. Moreover, the total input S_j is a weighted sum over all predicted vectors from the capsules, which acquired by multiplying the vector output u_i from capsule in the layer below by the weight matrix W_{ij}.

$$S_j = \sum_i c_{ij} \hat{u}_{j|i} \tag{2}$$

where c_{ij} represents coupling coefficients, which are updated and determined iteratively by the dynamic routing process.

A spatial attention-based model SKNet is put forward [33] in this paper to recognize sign language, which explicates the positive results than previous deep learning models. Regarding the spatial attention, its focus is on where the information is. The Eq. (3) shows how to calculate the spatial attention:

$$M_s(F) = \sigma\left(f^{7 \times 7}\left([AvgPool(F); MaxPool(F)]\right)\right) \tag{3}$$

where $\sigma(\bullet)$ is the sigmoid function, $f^{7 \times 7}$ is a convolution operation with the filter size of 7×7. The spatial attention module utilizes average-pooling and max-pooling operations along the channel axis and concatenates them to generate an efficient feature descriptor. Consequently, a convolution operation with a 7×7 filter is applied to produce the feature maps, a sigmoid function for normalization is offered to yield the final feature maps.

A highly modularized deep learning network (ResNeXt) was recommended for image classification. It raises up accuracy without ramping up the complexity of the deep learning method, meanwhile it effectively cuts off the number of hyperparameters [34]. The ResNeXt was motivated from the idea of VGG stacking blocks of the same shape and the split-transform-merge idea of the Inception model, which holds robust scalability and is able to meliorate the accuracy without substantially altering the complexity of the model. ResNeXt is similar to Inception, the both follow the "split-transform-merge" paradigm. However, in ResNeXt, the outputs of the paths are combined by addition operations, in Inception module, they are deeply concatenated. Each path in Inception module has bias from each other, while in the ResNeXt module, all paths follow the same topology. It replaces the three-layer convolution block of original ResNet model by using a parallel stack of blocks with the same topology, which uplifts the accuracy without significantly raising the number of the parameters.

Simultaneously, the hyperparameters are reduced because of topological structure of ResNeXt model. Moreover, cardinality in ResNeXt is the size of the set of transformation and an essential factor to the dimensions of depth and width. By adopting ResNeXt model, the training error is much lower compared with the ResNet parameters. Moreover, by extending the cardinality, the model is much efficient compared with only extending the network depth or width on the ResNet model, thus dips 1.6% error rate.

In sign language recognition, most of researchers investigated both spatiotemporal information to extract the motion features in time sequences. Thus, LSTM is considered in this paper. We take use of LSTM to acquire the temporal information from video frames and predict sign language. Moreover, CapsNet and LSTM are combined together in the end by adopting the class score fusion to achieve sign language recognition in this paper.

4 Experimental Results

In this paper, we create our own sign language dataset for the purpose of model testing and validation in this project. Our dataset contains nine video footages of four classes with the tags: Hello, Nice, Meet, You, which includes the sign language data captured by ourself with the static camera. The resolution of this dataset is 960×564. The dataset contains 3,596 frames in total, there are 2,500 frames chosen for model training, 1,096 frames were selected for model testing. Figure 1 shows the example of our own dataset.

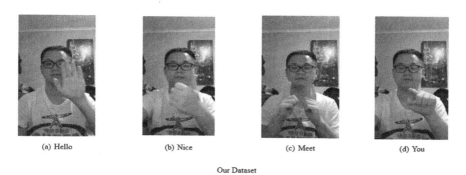

(a) Hello   (b) Nice   (c) Meet   (d) You

Our Dataset

Fig. 1. The example of our sign language dataset

Our focus of this paper is mainly on the proposed deep learning methods and its impact on our result outcomes. We chiefly took use of three different state-of-the-art deep learning methods to fulfil the sign language recognition. Moreover, an attention mechanism based on the SKNet and ResNeXt was verified in this paper. In Fig. 2, we demonstrate the result of sign language recognition from the video frames.

Figure 3 shows the training and validation losses by using adopted deep learning methods, especially SKNet, ResNeXt and its attention mechanism. From Fig. 3, we see that SKNet models are able to achieve 97.95% accuracy. Moreover, by combining the attention model with the SKNet net, the accuracy reaches to 98.88%. Compared with these two models, the accuracy grows 0.93%. ResNeXt individually achieved 97.82% accuracy with the assistance of our dataset; ResNeXt after combined with attention mechanism is able to earn 98.19% accuracy. In these experiments, it required large amount of computations, we chose the batch size 8 and learning rate 0.001. Moreover, the number of the epoch is set to 60. In Fig. 3, the green dots represent the training and validation accuracy, the red dots stand for the training and validation loss, and the x-axis denotes the number of epochs, the y-axis represents the accuracy/loss values.

(a) Hello   (b) Nice   (c) Meet   (d) You

Our Dataset

Fig. 2. The results of sign language recognition

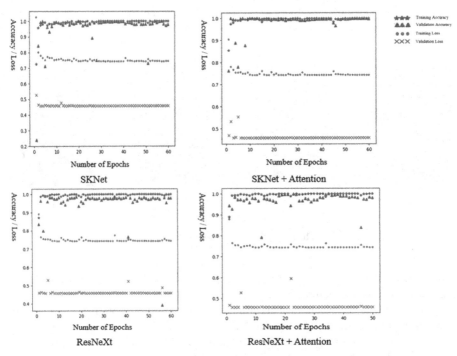

Fig. 3. The training and validation losses by using adopted deep learning methods

Figure 4 shows the training/testing accuracy and loss by using CapsNet for sign language recognition. The CapsNet individually achieved 98.72% accuracy with the assistance of our dataset. Compared with the previous SKNet method, the accuracy grows 0.77%. Moreover, the orange line represents the training set; the blue line stands for the testing set; where the x-axis represents the training/test steps, the y-axis represents the training/test values. In our experiment, the number of iterations is set to 10,000, the batch size is 8, and the learning rate is 0.001.

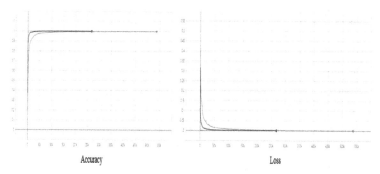

Fig. 4. The training/test accuracy and loss by using CapsNet

Throughout our experiments, we took use of various deep learning methods to compare our experimental results. The deep learning models with attention mechanism are much stable and robust in sign language recognition. Table 1. shows the comparison of our deep learning models on sign language recognition by adopting our own dataset.

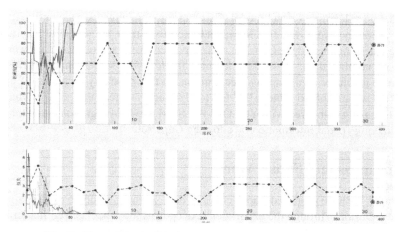

Fig. 5. The training/validation accuracy and loss by using LSTM

Figure 5 exhibits the sign language recognition of training/validation accuracy and loss by using LSTM, where the blue line denotes the training accuracy; the orange line denotes the training loss; the black dots denotes the training/validation accuracy and loss; the x-axis represents the number of iterations and the y-axis represents the values of the accuracy and loss. The LSTM attained 99.56% accuracy with the assistance of our dataset. In this experiment, due to the small dataset we use, the number of iterations is set to 380, the batch size is 4, and the learning rate is 0.001. We adopted CapsNet + LSTM model with class score fusion to fulfil this study.

In Table 1, SKNet net with attention mechanism shows positive results for sign language recognition. The network of SKNet with attention mechanism is able to get 98.88% accuracy which has 5.19% growth of the total accuracy compared with the

Table 1. The different deep learning methods on sign languagr recognition

Our dataset	Hello	Nice	Meet	You	Accuracy
DenseNet	95.23%	93.82%	95.28%	94.11%	94.61%
ResNet	94.77%	93.27%	94.89%	91.83%	93.69%
YOLOv3	94.35%	95.26%	96.71%	97.12%	95.86%
YOLOv4	96.37%	97.49%	97.55%	98.35%	97.44%
ResNeXt	96.87%	98.64%	98.25%	97.52%	97.82%
ResNext + Attention	97.63%	98.66%	98.36%	98.11%	98.19%
SKNet	97.89%	97.02%	97.93%	98.96%	97.95%
SKNet + Attention	98.91%	98.64%	98.93%	99.04%	98.88%
YOLOv3 + LSTM	97.28%	97.79%	95.33%	95.28%	96.42%
CapsNet	98.76%	98.96%	98.94%	98.22%	98.72%
CapsNet + LSTM	99.24%	98.53%	99.45%	98.62%	98.96%

traditional deep learning Resnet model. CapsNet for sign language recognition reaches 98.72% accuracy. Moreover, LSTM was adopted to extract the temporal information from the video frames and the CapsNet was employed to extract the spatial information. Finally, we combined these two deep learning models with score fusion which shows the positive result for sign language recognition. In this paper, by combining CapsNet with LSTM we are able to achieve 98.96% total accuracy of recognition rate, which has 2.54% increasing compared with YOLOv3 + LSTM and 0.24% growth compared with only extracting spatial information by adopting CapsNet.

5   Conclusion and Future Work

In this paper, we have proffered CapsNet-based deep learning model to achieve sign language recognition. Through the experiments, deep learning model is well implemented to achieve our goal. The CapsNet model shows positive results for sign language recognition, which has 0.77% growth of accuracy by using the SKNet. The SKNet with attention mechanism attains the highest recognition accuracy 98.88%.

From the outcomes, we see that most of the traditional deep learning models could be extended through either depth or width of the layers to improve the accuracy of the model and make the model more robust and stable. The convolution-based deep learning showcases that without increasing the complexity of the parameters, the model will be efficient and accurate. Moreover, by adopting the attention mechanism in the convolution-based deep learning methods, it shows the positive results in sign language recognition. Meanwhile, CapsNet model is also outperformed in this paper compared with other traditional deep learning methods.

In our future work, we will add the attention module into the proposed CapsNet model in order to get the temporal information, which achieves a better accuracy in sign language recognition.

References

1. Rautaray, S.S., Agrawal, A.: Vision based hand gesture recognition for human computer interaction: a survey. Artif. Intell. Rev. **43**(1), 1–54 (2012). https://doi.org/10.1007/s10462-012-9356-9
2. Dardas, N.H., Georganas, N.D.: Real-time hand gesture detection and recognition using bag-of-features and support vector machine techniques. IEEE Trans. Instrum. Meas. **60**(11), 3592–3607 (2011)
3. Tharwat, A., Gaber, T., Hassanien, A.E., Shahin, M.K., Refaat, B.: SIFT-based arabic sign language recognition system. In: Abraham, A., Krömer, P., Snasel, V. (eds.) Afro-European Conference for Industrial Advancement. AISC, vol. 334, pp. 359–370. Springer, Cham (2015). https://doi.org/10.1007/978-3-319-13572-4_30
4. Jasim, M., Hasanuzzaman, M.: Sign language interpretation using linear discriminant analysis and local binary patterns. In: International Conference on Informatics, Electronics & Vision, pp. 1–5 (2014)
5. Cote, M., Payeur, P., Comeau, G.: Comparative study of adaptive segmentation techniques for gesture analysis in unconstrained environments. In: IEEE International Workshop on Imagining Systems and Techniques, pp. 28–33 (2006)
6. Lu, J., Shen, J., Yan, W., Bacic, B.: An empirical study for human behavior analysis. Int. J. Digit. Crime Forensics **9**, 11–27 (2017)
7. Asadi-Aghbolaghi, M., et al.: A survey on deep learning based approaches for action and gesture recognition in image sequences. In: IEEE International Conference on Automatic Face & Gesture Recognition, pp. 476–483 (2017)
8. Herath, S., Harandi, M., Porikli, F.: Going deeper into action recognition: a survey. Image Vis. Comput. **60**, 4–21 (2017)
9. Girshick, R., Donahue, J., Darrell, T., Malik, J.: Rich feature hierarchies for accurate object detection and semantic segmentation. In: IEEE Conference on Computer Vision and Pattern Recognition, pp. 580–587 (2014)
10. LeCun, Y., Huang, F.J., Bottou, L.: Learning methods for generic object recognition with invariance to pose and lighting. In: IEEE Conference on Computer Vision and Pattern Recognition (2004)
11. Hinton, G.E., Osindero, S., Teh, Y.-W.: A fast learning algorithm for deep belief nets. Neural Comput. **18**, 1527–1554 (2006)
12. Szegedy, C., Ioffe, S., Vanhoucke, V., Alemi, A.A.: Inception-v4, Inception-ResNet and the impact of residual connections on learning. In: AAAI Conference on Artificial Intelligence (2017)
13. Ji, S., Xu, W., Yang, M., Yu, K.: 3D convolutional neural networks for human action recognition. IEEE Trans. Pattern Anal. Mach. Intell. **35**, 221–231 (2013)
14. Liu, W., et al.: SSD: single shot multibox detector. In: Leibe, B., Matas, J., Sebe, N., Welling, M. (eds.) ECCV 2016. LNCS, vol. 9905, pp. 21–37. Springer, Cham (2016). https://doi.org/10.1007/978-3-319-46448-0_2
15. LeCun, Y., Bottou, L., Bengio, Y., Haffner, P.: Gradient-based learning applied to document recognition. Proc. IEEE **86**(11), 2278–2324 (1998)
16. Rao, G.A., Syamala, K., Kishore, P.V.V., Sastry, A.S.C.S.: Deep convolutional neural networks for sign language recognition. In: The Conference on Signal Processing and Communication Engineering Systems, pp. 194–197 (2018)
17. Koller, O., Ney, H., Bowden, R.: Deep hand: how to train a CNN on 1 million hand images when your data is continuous and weakly labelled. In: IEEE Conference on Computer Vision and Pattern Recognition, pp. 3793–3802 (2016)

18. Wu, J., Ishwar, P., Konrad, J.: Two-stream CNNs for gesture-based verification and identification: Learning user style. In: IEEE Conference on Computer Vision and Pattern Recognition Workshops, pp. 42–50 (2016)
19. Liu, Z., Zhang, C., Tian, Y.: 3D-based deep convolutional neural network for action recognition with depth sequences. Image Vis. Comput. **55**, 93–100 (2016)
20. Molchanov, P., Yang, X., Gupta, S., Kim, K., Tyree, S., Kautz, J.: Online detection and classification of dynamic hand gestures with recurrent 3D convolutional neural network. In: IEEE Conference on Computer Vision and Pattern Recognition, pp. 4207–4215 (2016)
21. Huang, J., Zhou, W., Li, H., Li, W.: Sign language recognition using 3D convolutional neural networks. In: IEEE International Conference on Multimedia and Expo, pp. 1–6 (2015)
22. Neverova, N., Wolf, C., Taylor, G.W., Nebout, F.: Hand segmentation with structured convolutional learning. In: Cremers, D., Reid, I., Saito, H., Yang, M.-H. (eds.) ACCV 2014. LNCS, vol. 9005, pp. 687–702. Springer, Cham (2015). https://doi.org/10.1007/978-3-319-16811-1_45
23. Han, M., Chen, J., Li, L., Chang, Y.: Visual hand gesture recognition with convolution neural network. In: IEEE/ACIS International Conference on Software Engineering, Artificial Intelligence, Networking and Parallel/Distributed Computing, pp. 287–291 (2016)
24. Dadashzadeh, A., Targhi, A.T., Tahmasbi, M., Mirmehdi, M.: HGR-net: a fusion network for hand gesture segmentation and recognition. IET Comput. Vis. **13**(8), 700–707 (2019)
25. Elboushaki, A., Hannane, R., Afdel, K., Koutti, L.: MultiD-CNN: a multi-dimensional feature learning approach based on deep convolutional networks for gesture recognition in RGB-D image sequences. Expert Syst. Appl. **139**, 112829 (2020)
26. Chen, Y., Zhao, L., Peng, X., Yuan, J., Metaxas, D. N.: Construct dynamic graphs for hand gesture recognition via spatial-temporal attention. In: British Machine Vision Conference, pp. 1–13 (2019)
27. dos Santos, C.C., Samatelo, J.L.A., Vassallo, R.F.: Dynamic gesture recognition by using CNNs and star RGB: a temporal information condensation. Neurocomputing **400**, 238–254 (2020)
28. Wang, P., Li, W., Liu, S., Gao, Z., Tang, C., Ogunbona, P.: Large-scale isolated gesture recognition using convolutional neural networks. In: International Conference on Pattern Recognition, pp. 7–12 (2016)
29. Duan, J., Zhou, S., Wan, J., Guo, X., Li, S. Z.: Multi-modality fusion based on consensus-voting and 3D convolution for isolated gesture recognition. arXiv:1611.06689 (2016)
30. Rastgoo, R., Kiani, K., Escalera, S.: Multi-modal deep hand sign language recognition in still images using restricted Boltzmann machine. Entropy **20**(11), 809 (2018)
31. Rastgoo, R., Kiani, K., Escalera, S.: Video-based isolated hand sign language recognition using a deep cascaded model. Multimed. Tools Appl. **79**, 22965–22987 (2020). https://doi.org/10.1007/s11042-020-09048-5
32. Sabour, S., Frosst, N., Hinton, G. E.: Dynamic routing between capsules. In: Advances in Neural Information Processing Systems, pp. 3856–3866 (2017)
33. Lu, J., Nguyen, M., Yan, W.: Deep learning methods for human behavior recognition. In: IEEE IVCNZ (2020)
34. Xie, S., Girshick, R., Dollár, P., Tu, Z., He, K.: Aggregated residual transformations for deep neural networks. In: IEEE Conference on Computer Vision and Pattern Recognition, pp. 1492–1500 (2017)

New Zealand Shellfish Detection, Recognition and Counting: A Deep Learning Approach on Mobile Devices

Quan Nguyen, Minh Nguyen, Bowen Sun, and Huy Le(✉)

Auckland University of Technology, 55 Wellesley St E, Auckland 1010, New Zealand
minh.nguyen@aut.ac.nz, qyq0379@autuni.ac.nz

Abstract. New Zealand maintains excessive effort to organise the sustainable development of its marine resources, wildlife, and ecological environment. New Zealand has stringent rules to control fishing and to protect the continued growth of marine inhabitants. Fishing inspections, such as identifying and counting shellfish, are part of the daily routine of many New Zealand Fisheries officers. It is however considered labour-intensive and time-consuming work. This project, thus, develops a touch-less shellfish detection and counting web/mobile application on handheld devices using Mask R-CNN to assist New Zealand Fisheries officers in recognising and totalling shellfish automatically and accurately. New Zealand shellfish species are different from other places in the World. Thus, this study firstly investigates the best deep learning model to use for New Zealand shellfish recognition and detection. Selected shellfish dataset is collected from a local fish market in Auckland and trained by using the chosen artificial neural network. At last, a portable system is built to support Fisheries officers to count shellfish quickly and accurately. At this current stage, a web-based application has been successfully deployed at a local server (cvreact.aut.ac.nz) in which users can upload target objects to get results related to three major shellfish species including cockle, tuatua, and mussel. In the near future, this proposed model is scaled up to recognise more species to cover the popular shellfish species in New Zealand, thus benefiting the aquaculture as well.

Keywords: Object detection · Deep learning · Shellfish · Mask R-CNN · ResNet

1 Introduction and Backgrounds

New Zealand is well-known for its beautiful natural scenery and abundant natural resources. New Zealand has managed to organise the sustainable development of marine resources, wildlife and ecological environment. New Zealand, therefore, has legislated out for fishing different sea creatures such as finfish and shellfish in different regions and seasons. For instance, each fisherman can only gather 50 cockles per day in Auckland Coromandel area [1]. New Zealand Fisheries officers

M. Nguyen et al. (Eds.): ISGV 2021, CCIS 1386, pp. 119–133, 2021.
https://doi.org/10.1007/978-3-030-72073-5_10

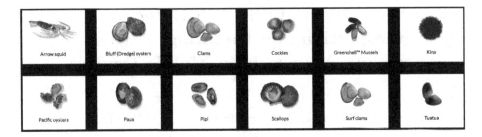

Fig. 1. New Zealand popular shellfish species

work hard to ensure the sustainability of New Zealand's fishery. Checking and counting shellfish manually is one of the daily work of New Zealand Fisheries officers; however, it is very time-consuming (Fig. 1).

Recently, actual applications using deep neural networks (DNNs) technologies have been widely applied and achieved remarkable successes in both of the research and industrial fields. Object detection, classification, and recognition are some of the most frequently used techniques that efficiently extract specific objects from images or video stream by pre-trained models. Artificial intelligence (AI) applications have taken over the roles of Fisheries officers in the time-consuming. It is useful to have a portable system to support Fisheries officers to recognise and count shellfish quickly, thereby reducing the workload of Fisheries officers. This research aims to develop an application to recognise and count shellfish based on input images or videos from a handheld camera. Its approach also figures out whether shellfish species being caught meet New Zealand different fishing rules [1].

Visual Object counting (VOC) as a useful application of object recognition has been widely applied in many areas in the real-world to measure the number of target objects with the input from images or videos. For instance, using cell counting system to count cells in microscopic images provides a faster and affordable disease diagnose solutions [11]. Image processing techniques, such as neural network, Hough transform, clustering, and shape matching, are adopted to recognise and detect patterns or objects [9]. However, big concerns when using VOC are the frequent overlap between objects, occlusion, and complex background environment. The object counting process in image processing can be performed by object detection, regression, and segmentation techniques. All of these approaches require a machine learning process on labelled data to build a detection model, thereby predicting the number of target objects in an image [13]. Global regression-based VOC (GR-VOC) and density estimation based VOC (DE-VOC) are two significant techniques using supervised approaches [17]. DE-VOC method counts object instances by a density function from dense local features of the image [5]. Both these two techniques can perform efficiently with sufficient training images. Convolutional neural networks (CNN) and hardware-accelerated optimisation can improve the performance of regression-based counting approach significantly [11]. An innovative framework to count objects without any preliminary training step was proposed and can count multiple object types [13]. To minimize the data preparation costs introduced by labelling training data of regression-based approaches, an unsupervised approach was introduced to count objects without object recognition [7].

Object detection has been a significant part of image processing and CV fields. It is a technique that localises and classifies an object in an input image by predicting the bounding box location that contains the object [4]. Geometry-based and appearance-based are two ways of object representation [14]. Object detection can be achieved using traditional machine vision approaches such as SVM (Support Vector Machines). The traditional method uses a sliding window to generate candidate regions on an input image, then extracts features and classifies the regions using a trained classifier [20]. Time-complexity is one of the main drawbacks of the traditional method. Compared to traditional methods, deep learning algorithms, such as CNN, are able to accept raw data as input and automatically learn features [10].

Object detection and counting techniques have been successfully implemented in agriculture fields. A model to detect and count plant seedling in the field using Faster R-CNN with Inception ResNet v2 was implemented [6]. Their model successfully achieved an F1 score of 0.969 at the IoU threshold of 0.5. Another model implemented a real-time corn kernel detection and counting to help farmers to estimate corn harvest and make marketing decisions [8]. The results indicated that the CNN model has higher accuracy (0.947) than HOG+SVM, since it can extract features automatically from an input. A fruit detection model was developed for strawberry harvesting check based on Mask R-CNN [18]. From their experiment results, the average precision rate is 95.78% out of 100 test images. A comparison of fruit detection and counting performance between Faster R-CNN with inception V2 and SSD with MobileNet on a fruit dataset was conducted [15]. Experiments have shown that Faster R-CNN has higher performance (94%) than SSD (90%). Furthermore, they pointed out that the detection performance of CNN architectures is relied on experimental dataset quality.

Apart from the agriculture fields, the use of deep learning methods for object detection and counting has been used in other areas in daily human life. A real-time vehicle counting system using SSD algorithm to monitor traffic was designed [2]. The SSD based network was replaced by ResNet-34, which is more accurate than the original based network (VGG-16). From the experiment results that the vehicle detection accuracy of the system can reach to 99.3% and the classification accuracy can achieve to 98.9%. A model to detect and count threatening objects from images using TensorFlow object detection API was built [12]. Their model was implemented by Faster R-CNN algorithm, and it is able to detect and classify two classes of threatening objects: knife and gun. The experiment results show relatively good accuracy and counting results.

This paper proposes the portable model based on Mask R-CNN, which recognises and counts target objects from an image or video to figure out a legal shellfish grabbing. The target objects are uploaded to a processing server, and then its results are popped up on the officer's handheld device. The notices or recommendations are also presented to make proper decisions.

2   Conceptualisation of Implementation Method

2.1   Overall System Design

A web application is easy to be used on a wide variety of operating systems of laptops and mobile devices. To facilitate the use of the detection system by New Zealand fisheries officers both in their offices and at beaches, this system is designed as a web application that allows users to upload images or videos to check the shellfish species and quantity. The entire recognition system with the shellfish detection model is hosted on a processing server. As shown in Fig. 2, the system is deployed on a processing server to detect and count the target shellfish objects from an uploaded image. The detection result that includes labelled shellfish and count numbers of each shellfish species is finally returned to the end-user.

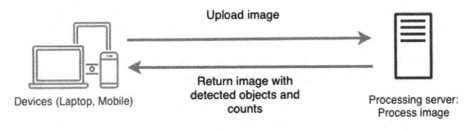

Fig. 2. Overall system design

2.2   Dataset Preparation

Cockle, tuatua are major shellfish species that New Zealanders can gather from beaches both in South Island and North Island. Cockles are plump, round shells with fine ridges, and they are widespread in New Zealand harbours. Tuatua is endemic to New Zealand which can be found when low tide and has a more irregular shell shape. Therefore, this study selects cockle and tuatua as target shellfish species to conduct the shellfish detection and counting task. To extend the application of this detection model, mussel, another common and popular shellfish, is included in this research.

The shellfish used in this study were collected randomly. The appearance of the same shellfish species varies among different regions. Therefore, the cockles used in this study are gathered initially from both South Island and North Island New Zealand, as shown in Fig. 3. Due to the resource constraints, the tuatua and mussel are originally gathered from North Island New Zealand.

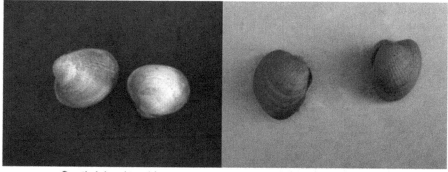

South Island cockle   **North Island cockle**

Fig. 3. Cockle from South Island and North Island

cockle   tuatua

mussel   shellfish combination

Fig. 4. Sample images of cockle, tuatua, mussel, and combined shellfish species

In this research study, 700 images that include 200 images of each shellfish species and 100 images of combined shellfish species are selected for the further detection experiment. The sample images of cockle, tuatua, and mussel are shown in Fig. 4. Figure 5 describes the data pre-processing process that includes data

annotation, data format conversion. Data augmentation is an essential technique
for expanding dataset in deep learning tasks.

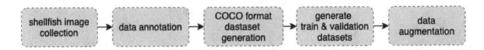

Fig. 5. Data pre-processing process

2.3 Detection Model Design

Since the purpose of this shellfish detection system is to accurately recognise
and count shellfish for New Zealand fishery control, this paper focuses more on
detection accuracy rather than detection speed. Faster R-CNN and Mask R-CNN
have better performance than YOLO and SSD [19]. Furthermore, the results of
general object detection experiments on the MS COCO dataset shows that Mask
R-CNN has higher AP than other deep learning object detection methods. Due
to the advantage in accuracy, Faster R-CNN and Mask R-CNN are considered
for this purpose.

Bearing in mind the model comparison and results of previous researches
above, this paper adopts Mask R-CNN to train the shellfish detection model.
Figure 6 demonstrates the structure design of the Mask R-CNN shellfish detection model that is used in this paper. This paper uses ResNet101 and FPN as
the backbone network to extract feature maps from an input image.

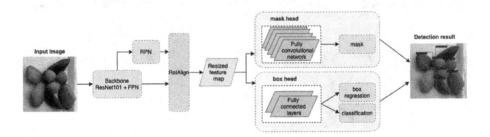

Fig. 6. Model structure of Mask R-CNN shellfish detector

2.4 Web Application Deployment Design

Once the detection model is trained, the final model and a user interface will be
deployed as a web application. This application is written in Python. The web
user interface is developed using Streamlit, which is an app framework designed
for data analysis and machine learning. Moreover, the application deployment
uses Docker which is a platform to help automatic software delivery using con-
tainers. Docker builds a lightweight image which can be deployed on various

cloud platforms such as AWS and Azure [3]. Figure 7 demonstrates the workflow of the system deployment. First, the system settings and package requirements are configured within a Docker file. Then the container image that contains the system libraries and application code is pushed and deployed on a cloud server. Finally, the cloud server will host the application and provide a website for users.

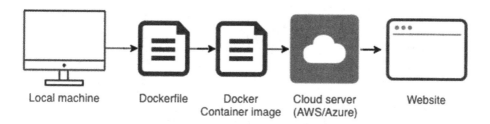

Local machine   Dockerfile   Docker   Cloud server   Website
                                        Container image   (AWS/Azure)

Fig. 7. Deployment workflow of the web application

The system provides the users with simple GUI application, to keep the page straightforward so that users with different knowledge backgrounds can easily use the application. Users can upload and preview an image by clicking 'browse files' on the main page. Once the image is uploaded, users can use this application to detect and view the predicted results by clicking 'Detect and Count' buttons on the web page.

3 Experiment

3.1 Data Pre-processing

Since this research aims to conduct the object detection task, the target objects on each image need to be labelled for training purpose. This project uses Labelme, which is an easy-to-use image annotation tool to label the shellfish objects on each image. As shown in Fig. 8, all target objects in the image are selected and labelled within a polygon that covers on each target object. Labelme generates a JSON file for each image to store the image information and annotations.

This project trains the detection model based on COCO pre-trained weight and uses COCO evaluation metrics. The shellfish data should be converted to COCO format dataset. A Python script randomly allocates 80% of images in the shellfish dataset to train dataset and the other 20% to the validation dataset. The detection model is trained with the training dataset and evaluated with the validation dataset. The size of training dataset for deep learning is critical for the performance of a model. The more data are involved, the more robust the model is, so data augmentation techniques that automatically enlarge the dataset with annotations are very crucial for dealing with small dataset in a CNN model training process. Data augmentation includes colour operations and

Fig. 8. Image annotation using Labelme

geometric operations. Flipping, cropping, and rotation are most used augmentation techniques in object detection tasks [16]. Data augmentation is able to increase detection accuracy over +3.2 mAP on COCO dataset [21] (Figs. 9 and 10).

Fig. 9. Data augmentation with rotations and horizontal flip

3.2   Model Implementation

Due to the limitation of hardware, the detection model training process is performed on Google Colaboratory. Additionally, this research uses TensorBoard to visualise the summary output of the model training process, such as AP and loss. Transfer learning is also adopted to train the detector. It is faster than training a model from scratch and can help the model achieve better performance in training on a small dataset.

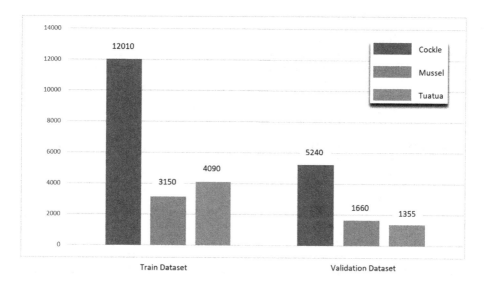

Fig. 10. Data distribution of instances among categories

In the experiment, the Mask R-CNN model is trained with a maximum of 10000 iterations. The values of other parameters are set to 0.9 momenta, 0.0001 weight decay, and batch size 2. The based model is trained with a learning rate of 0.02 on 8 GPUs. Since this research uses 1 GPU to train detection model, the learning rate should be 0.0025 in theory. As shown in Table 1, the inference results of Mask R-CNN ResNet101+FPN model with learning rate 0.001 has the highest bounding box prediction AP (86.826%) and segmentation AP (87.191%). The AP in the table is averaged over three categories on 10 IoU thresholds from 0.5 to 0.95. Additionally, the model with learning rate 0.001 has an acceptable inference speed which is around 0.1 s per image. Therefore, the learning rate is set to 0.001 to train the detection model.

Table 1. Mask R-CNN ResNet101+FPN with different learning rates

Learning rates	bbox AP(%)	segm AP(%)	Train time (s/iter)	Inference time
0.01	84.480	85.860	0.6579	0.1516
0.005	84.974	86.965	0.3783	0.1043
0.0025	85.151	86.200	0.3782	0.1043
0.001	86.826	87.191	0.3783	0.1038

The experiment evaluates the model on the validation dataset using COCO evaluation metrics during the training process. The evaluation performs every 500 iterations. Additionally, the experiment metrics like loss and average precision are visualised and monitored within TensorBoard during the training process. Finally, an inference is performed on the validation dataset using the final trained model. To evaluate the performance of the final detection model, models of Mask R-CNN with ResNet50+FPN, Mask R-CNN with ResNeXt101+FPN, and Faster R-CNN with ResNet101+FPN have experimented with the same settings as a comparison.

4   Analysis and Discussion

Since the main propose of this research is to recognize and locate the target shellfish objects. This research mainly analyses and discusses the results of the bounding box prediction accuracy. As Shown in the table, the average precision (AP) is averaged over 3 categories at 10 IoU thresholds which are 0.5, 0.55, 0.6, 0.65, 0.7, 0.75, 0.8, 0.85, 0.9, 0.95. The AP of the bounding box prediction is 87.414%, while the AP of segmentation prediction is 87.032%. Furthermore, AP50, which is similar to PASCAL VOC evaluation metrics, is calculated at 0.5 IoU threshold. The AP at 0.5 IoU threshold is 99.592% for both bounding box and segmentation prediction. The prediction results of AP50 show a good performance of the final prediction model. The detection results for each shellfish category that the model has better detection capabilities for mussel and tuatua, and the AP of bounding box prediction can reach 91.084% and 90.576% respectively.

Because the samples of cockle are collected from both South Island and North Island of New Zealand, their shapes and colors are different. Therefore, the average precision is a bit lower than that of mussel and tuatua, which is 80.584% for bounding box prediction and 81.142 for segmentation prediction. The training speed of the detection model is 0.3776 s for each iteration. The inference time is 0.1006 s for each image on one device. The testing results on random validation images show good detection performance, and the classification score for each object can reach over 95%.

Figure 11a shows the accuracy of classification during the training process. Accuracy indicates the percentage of the correctly predicted results in the total predictions. After around 500 steps, the accuracy of object classification remains at between 98% to 99%.

During the training process, a COCO model evaluation inferences on the validation dataset every 500 iterations over 1050 images. Figure 11b demonstrates the total loss of final Mask R-CNN model on training and validation dataset respectively. The total loss is obtained by the loss of classification, bounding box, and mask. As shown in Fig. 11b, the total loss stops dramatically decreasing and shows a smooth delay after 500 iterations. The total loss of both training and validation shows a slightly downward trend as expected.

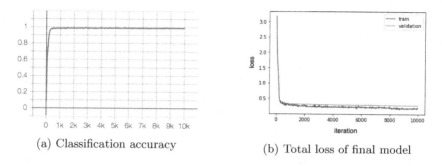

(a) Classification accuracy

(b) Total loss of final model

Fig. 11. Classification accuracy evaluation and total loss of final Mask R-CNN model

4.1 Model Comparison

Compared to the network with 101 layers, due to the smaller depth of ResNet50, the model training should be faster than the network with more layers. ResNet50 model is faster than other models both on train time and inference time. The training time of ResNet50 model can reach 0.289 s per iteration and the inference time is 0.073 s per image. In theory, a model with ResNeXt backbone should have better performance than ResNet. According to [19], ResNeXt is powerful and Mask R-CNN with ResNeXt101+FPN has slightly better prediction performance than ResNet101+FPN on MS COCO Test dataset. In this experiment, ResNeXt101 does not perform well on predicting the bounding box, the AP of IoU threshold from 0.5 to 0.95 is 87.417%, which is similar to ResNet101 (87.414%). This may be caused by the fact that shellfish dataset and training iterations are small.

Both the training time (0.8224 s/iter) and inference time (0.1916 1916 s/img) of ResNeXt101 are doubled compared to those of ResNet101 (train time: 0.3776 s/iter, inference time: 0.1006 s/img). When comparing with the results, ResNet101 is more suitable for shellfish detection than ResNeXt101. Because the prediction performance of ResNet101 model is similar to ResNeXt101, but the inference time, which is important for user experience, is twice as fast.

As shown in the detection results of the final Mask R-CNN model and Faster R-CNN model, the final Mask R-CNN model performs better than Faster R-CNN model. The AP of Faster R-CNN model is 86.273% which is lower than the final Mask R-CNN model (87.414%). The AP of Faster R-CNN model at 0.5 IoU threshold, which is 99.537%, is similar to Mask R-CNN model (99.592%). The results also point out that Faster R-CNN is slower both on train and inference speed than Mask R-CNN. The training speed and inference speed of Faster R-CNN are 0.6198 s per iteration and 0.1553 s per image respectively.

4.2 Results Demonstration

The evaluation results that are computed from the validation dataset is not enough to determine the model performance. Because the dataset used in the experiments is small, overfitting problem may be introduced by training. The final model should be tested using images that are not in the experimental dataset. Figure 12 shows the test result on a new image from the web interface. As can be seen, every tuatua is detected and counted from the test image.

Figure 13 demonstrates the detection results of an image that are downloaded from the Internet using the final model. The model can detect almost all shellfish objects even on the under layers of other objects. But the model classifies 2 cockles which are partly covered by other objects as tuatua. The object overlap makes the detection more difficult. Making the shellfish objects spread instead of overlapping with each other will increase the detection results. Additionally, the detection will be improved by increasing the dataset size and including tuatua and cockle from multiple locations both of the North Island and South Island of New Zealand.

Fig. 12. Shellfish detection and counting results

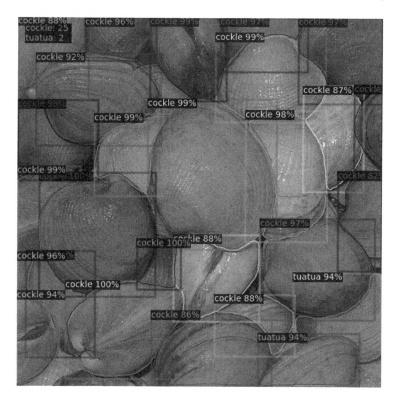

Fig. 13. Shellfish detection and counting results

5   Conclusion and Future Work

Recently, deep learning technology is developed strongly; it has been becoming beneficial for object detection techniques in order to reduce repetitive tasks. This study designs and develops a web/mobile application to recognize and count New Zealand shellfish from images or videos. This is a tool potentially built for helping New Zealand Fisheries officers to control shellfish gathering. At present, there are no studies that develop models to detect and count New Zealand shellfish species. This study can reduce not only the workload of New Zealand Fisheries officers but also fill the gap in the literature review of shellfish detection field. This research demonstrates a procedure of object detection implementation, which includes data pre-processing, model training, and evaluation. From the evaluation results of COCO evaluate metrics, the final Mask R-CNN detection model can recognize and count three major shellfish species, for example, cockle, tuatua, mussel. In terms of bounding box prediction, the average precision is 87.4% when the IoU threshold is calculated from 0.5 to 0.95. The AP at 0.5 IoU threshold can reach 99.6%. The proposed model has proven its potential application in fishery, and other fields to reduce the workload and improve the efficiency.

References

1. Ministry for Primary Industries: Auckland and Kermadec Fishing Rules (2019). https://www.fisheries.govt.nz/travel-and-recreation/fishing/fishing-rules/auckland-kermadec-fishing-rules/
2. Chen, L., Zhang, Z., Peng, L.: Fast single shot multibox detector and its application on vehicle counting system. IET Intell. Transp. Syst. **12**(10), 1406–1413 (2018)
3. Cochrane, K., Chelladhurai, J.S., Khare, N.K.: Docker Cookbook: Over 100 Practical and Insightful Recipes to Build Distributed Applications with Docker. Packt Publishing Ltd., Birmingham (2018)
4. Galeone, P.: Hands-on neural networks with TensorFlow 2.0: understand TensorFlow, from static graph to eager execution, and design neural networks. Packt (2019). http://ezproxy.aut.ac.nz/login?url=search.ebscohost.com/login.aspx?direct=true&db=cat05020a&AN=aut.b27409545&site=eds-live
5. Huang, X., Zou, Y., Wang, Y.: Example-based visual object counting for complex background with a local low-rank constraint. In: 2017 IEEE International Conference on Acoustics, Speech and Signal Processing (ICASSP), pp. 1672–1676. IEEE (2017)
6. Jiang, Y., Li, C., Paterson, A.H., Robertson, J.S.: DeepSeedling: deep convolutional network and Kalman filter for plant seedling detection and counting in the field. Plant Methods **15**(1), 141 (2019). https://doi.org/10.1186/s13007-019-0528-3
7. Katsuki, T., Morimura, T., Idé, T.: Unsupervised object counting without object recognition. In: 2016 23rd International Conference on Pattern Recognition (ICPR), pp. 3627–3632. IEEE (2016)
8. Khaki, S., Pham, H., Han, Y., Kuhl, A., Kent, W., Wang, L.: Convolutional neural networks for image-based corn kernel detection and counting. Sensors **20**(9), 2721 (2020)
9. Konam, S., Narni, N.R.: Statistical analysis of image processing techniques for object counting. In: 2014 International Conference on Advances in Computing, Communications and Informatics (ICACCI), pp. 2464–2469. IEEE (2014)
10. Manzoor, S., Joo, S.H., Kuc, T.Y.: Comparison of object recognition approaches using traditional machine vision and modern deep learning techniques for mobile robot. In: 2019 19th International Conference on Control, Automation and Systems (ICCAS), Control, Automation and Systems (ICCAS), pp. 1316–1321 (2019). http://ezproxy.aut.ac.nz/login?url=search.ebscohost.com/login.aspx?direct=true&db=edseee&AN=edseee.8971680&site=eds-live
11. Marsden, M., McGuinness, K., Little, S., Keogh, C.E., O'Connor, N.E.: People, penguins and petri dishes: adapting object counting models to new visual domains and object types without forgetting. In: Proceedings of the IEEE Conference on Computer Vision and Pattern Recognition, pp. 8070–8079 (2018)
12. Sai, B.K., Sasikala, T.: Object detection and count of objects in image using tensor flow object detection API. In: 2019 International Conference on Smart Systems and Inventive Technology (ICSSIT), pp. 542–546. IEEE (2019)
13. Setti, F., Conigliaro, D., Tobanelli, M., Cristani, M.: Count on me: learning to count on a single image. IEEE Trans. Circuits Syst. Video Technol. **28**(8), 1798–1806 (2018)
14. Treiber, M.A.: An Introduction to Object Recognition: Selected Algorithms for a Wide Variety of Applications. Springer, London (2010). https://doi.org/10.1007/978-1-84996-235-3

15. Vasconez, J., Delpiano, J., Vougioukas, S., Cheein, F.A.: Comparison of convolutional neural networks in fruit detection and counting: a comprehensive evaluation. Comput. Electron. Agric. **173**, 105348 (2020)
16. Wang, K., Fang, B., Qian, J., Yang, S., Zhou, X., Zhou, J.: Perspective transformation data augmentation for object detection. IEEE Access **8**, 4935–4943 (2019)
17. Wang, Y., Zou, Y., Chen, J., Huang, X., Cai, C.: Example-based visual object counting with a sparsity constraint. In: 2016 IEEE International Conference on Multimedia and Expo (ICME), pp. 1–6. IEEE (2016)
18. Yu, Y., Zhang, K., Yang, L., Zhang, D.: Fruit detection for strawberry harvesting robot in non-structural environment based on mask-RCNN. Comput. Electron. Agric. **163**, 104846 (2019)
19. Zhao, Z.Q., Zheng, P., Xu, S.T., Wu, X.: Object detection with deep learning: a review. IEEE Trans. Neural Netw. Learn. Syst. **30**(11), 3212–3232 (2019)
20. Zhiqiang, W., Jun, L.: A review of object detection based on convolutional neural network. In: 2017 36th Chinese Control Conference (CCC), pp. 11104–11109. IEEE (2017)
21. Zoph, B., Cubuk, E.D., Ghiasi, G., Lin, T.Y., Shlens, J., Le, Q.V.: Learning data augmentation strategies for object detection. arXiv preprint arXiv:1906.11172 (2019)

Coverless Video Steganography Based on Inter Frame Combination

Liming Zou[1], Wenbo Wan[1], Bin Wei[2], and Jiande Sun[1(✉)]

[1] School of Information Science and Engineering, Shandong Normal University,
Jinan, China
[2] Shandong Subcenter of National Computer Network and Information Security
Administrative Center, Jinan, China

Abstract. In most coverless image steganography methods, the number of images increases exponentially with the increase of hidden message bits, which is difficult to construct such a dataset. And several images in semantic irrelevance are usually needed to represent more secret message bits, which are easy to cause the attacker's attention and bring some insecurity. To solve these two problems, a coverless video steganography method based on inter frame combination is proposed in this manuscript. In the proposed method, the hash sequence of a frame is generated by the CNNs and hash generator. To hide more information bits in one video, a special mapping rule is proposed. Through this mapping rule, some key frames in one video are selected. In the selected frames, one or several frames are used to represent a piece of information with equal length. To quickly index out the corresponding frames, a three-level index structure is proposed in this manuscript. Since the proposed coverless video steganography method does not embed one bit in video, it can effectively resist steganalysis algorithms. The experimental results and analysis show that the proposed method has a large capacity, good robustness and high security.

Keywords: Coverless information hiding · Cover selection-based information hiding · Video steganography · Multimedia security

1 Introduction

In traditional image steganography methods [1–5], secret information is embedded in images to achieve convert communication. This process of embedding information results in the image being modified. It is possible that such marked image, which is modified by traditional image steganography methods, can be detected by the state-of-the-art steganalysis algorithm under a certain payload. Based on this, the idea of coverless information hiding is proposed. "Coverless"

This work was supported in part by Natural Science Foundation of China (U1736122), in part by Natural Science Foundation for Distinguished Young Scholars of Shandong Province (JQ201718).

M. Nguyen et al. (Eds.): ISGV 2021, CCIS 1386, pp. 134–141, 2021.
https://doi.org/10.1007/978-3-030-72073-5_11

does not mean that no carrier is needed when secret information transmission, but represent the secret information by the carrier itself without any modification [6].

The existing coverless image steganography methods based mapping rules can be roughly divided into two categories: spatial domain and frequency domain. Spatial domain-based methods usually extract features based on pixels, and then use these feature sequences to map secret information. For example, Zou et al. proposed a method based on the average value of sub image pixels [7]. In Zou's method, the image is first divided into several blocks and the average pixel value of each block is calculated. Then an 80-bit hash sequence is generated by comparing the average values of neighboring blocks. Finally, the 80-bit hash sequence is mapped to the secret information. This method is simple and effective, but its robustness needs to be further improved. Frequency domain-based methods usually transform pixel domain into frequency domain firstly, and then extract corresponding features of the frequency domain. Finally, these feature sequences are mapped with secret information. For example, the DCT based method of Zhang et al. [8] and the DWT based method of Liu et al. [9]. In Zhang's method, an 8×8 block discrete cosine transform of the image is performed. Then the hash sequence is generated by dc coefficients in these blocks. Finally, the dc coefficients based hash sequence is mapped to the secret information. In Liu's method, the image is divided into 4×4 blocks and discrete wavelet transform is performed in each block. Then the hash sequence is generated by these DWT coefficients of low-frequency. Finally, the DWT coefficients based hash sequence is mapped to the secret information. These frequency domain-based methods greatly improve the robustness. However, these mapping based coverless image steganography methods exist two problems need to be solved. The first problem is that the image database will increase exponentially when the secret information bits hidden in an image increase. This brings great difficulty to the construction of database. The second problem is that many semantically irrelevant images are usually selected when more secret information bits need to be hidden, which brings some security challenges.

Pan et al. [10] proposed a video coverless steganography algorithm based on semantic segmentation. Specifically, the hash sequence of a video frame was generated according to the semantic segmentation network based on deep learning and the statistical histogram. The video with the key frame corresponding to the secret information was transmitted as a marked carrier. Pan et al. used video as a carrier of coverless steganography scheme firstly, and brought a new idea to the field of coverless steganography. However, these problems existing in coverless image steganography were still unsolved in the method of Pan et al.

To solve these problems mentioned above, a coverless video steganography method based on inter frame combination is proposed in this manuscript. The contributions of this manuscript are summarized as follows.

1) It is easier to construct a video dataset to the coverless information hiding task by the proposed method.
2) The proposed method greatly increases the capacity that a carrier can represent.

3) The experimental results and analysis show that the proposed method has
   good robustness and high security.

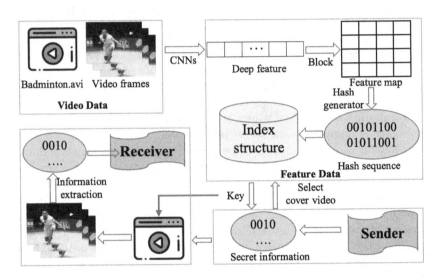

Fig. 1. The framework of the proposed method.

2   The Proposed Method

In this section, we discuss the proposed coverless video steganography method.
The framework of the proposed method is shown in Fig. 1. Firstly, we build
the video dataset constructed from short videos. Secondly, hash sequences of
video frames are obtained by CNNs and the hash generator. Finally, these hash
sequences and video frames are built the index structure to map secret information. For the sender, the secret information is divided into multiple pieces of
information with the same length. For each piece of secret information, it can
be mapped one or several key frames in one video according to the mapping
rule and index structure. To extract the secret information correctly, we record
the ID of key frames mapped with each piece of secret information as key information and send it to the receiver along with the cover video. On the receiving
end, the receiver can locate the key frames according to the key information and
extract the secret message correctly.

2.1   Generating Hash Sequence

In this manuscript, we use the CNNs provided in [11] to extract the 4096-
dimensional deep features of video frames. Then, each 4096-dimensional deep
feature is blocked and fused to a feature map with length of M, which direction
is the Zigzag-scan rule as shown in Fig. 2.

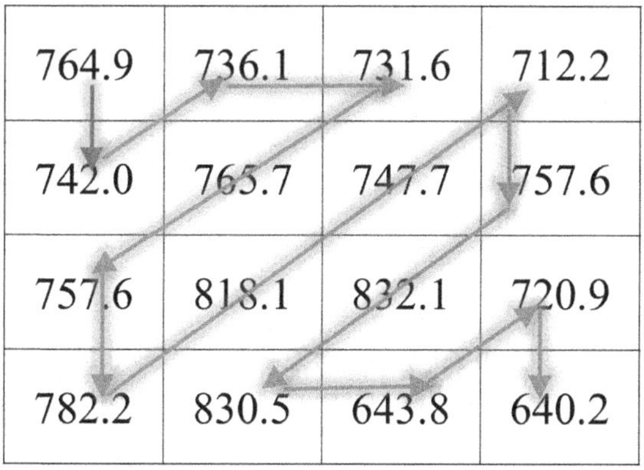

764.9	736.1	731.6	712.2
742.0	765.7	747.7	757.6
757.6	818.1	832.1	720.9
782.2	830.5	643.8	640.2

Fig. 2. The feature map and its Zigzag direction ($M = 16$).

After the feature map got, we can obtain the hash sequence H as shown in Eq. (1).

$$H = \{h_1, h_2, h_3, ..., h_M\} \tag{1}$$

Where, $h_i (1 \leq i \leq M)$ is calculated according to Eq. (2) and Eq. (3).

$$h_i = \begin{cases} 1, B_i > B_{i+1} \\ 0, B_i \leq B_{i+1} \end{cases} 1 \leq i \leq (M-1) \tag{2}$$

$$h_i = \begin{cases} 1, B_i > B_1 \\ 0, B_i \leq B_1 \end{cases} i = M \tag{3}$$

Where, B represent the block of feature map. And $B_i (1 \leq i \leq M)$ follows the direction of Zigzag-scan rule.

2.2 Mapping Rule

To hide more information bits in one cover video, we design a mapping rule based on inter frame combination. When M is defined, we know that a video frame can hide M-bit information. Under an ideal assumption, we hope that a video can represent 2^M information changes. We denote N_1 as the number of frames in a video. If each frame represents a M-bit information, then the video can represent at most N_1 information changes. If N_1 is less than 2^M, the video can not guarantee that any length of information can be hidden. In fact, there are only a few hundred frames in some short videos, which are much less than 2^M.

To improve the ability of a short video to hide information, we use a combination of two and three frames in the same video to represent a M-bit secret information. We denote N_2 and N_3 as the number of combinations of two and three frames, which are shown in Eq. (4) and Eq. (5).

$$N_2 = C_{N_1}^2 \tag{4}$$

$$N_3 = C_{N_1}^3 \tag{5}$$

The number of combinations that a video can hide M-bit information has expanded to N, as shown in Eq. (6)

$$N = N_1 + N_2 + N_3 \tag{6}$$

We denote H_{f_i} as the hash sequence of the frame with ID $= f_i$ $(1 \leq f_i \leq N_1)$. The hash sequence of two and three frames is calculated by Eq. (7) and Eq. (8), where $\oplus$ is the symbol for modular two plus.

$$H_{f_i \cdot f_j} = H_{f_i} \oplus H_{f_j}, \; 1 \leq f_i, f_j \leq N_1 \tag{7}$$

$$H_{f_i \cdot f_j \cdot f_k} = H_{f_i} \oplus H_{f_j} \oplus H_{f_k}, \; 1 \leq f_i, f_j, f_k \leq N_1 \tag{8}$$

Based on the inter frame combination, we establish a three-level index structure to improve the retrieval efficiency. The index structure is shown in Fig. 3. It is worth mentioning that the 1st level has the highest priority and the 3rd level has the lowest priority.

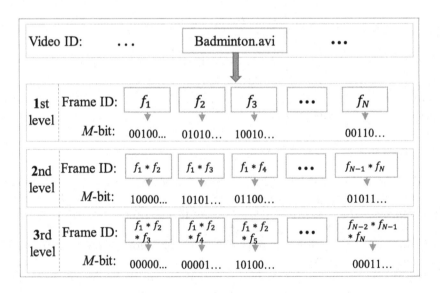

Fig. 3. Three-level index structure.

2.3   Information Hiding

On the sending end, suppose there is a L-bit secret information needs to be hidden. The process of information hiding is illustrated as follows.

1) Dividing L-bit secret information into n segments, which are denoted as $\{L_1, L_2, ..., L_n\}$. And the length of each segment L_t $(1 \leq t \leq n)$ is M. If L is not divisible by M, add 0 at the end. These 0 are recorded. n is the number of segments as shown in Eq. (9).

$$n = \begin{cases} \frac{L}{M}, & if\ L\ mod\ M = 0 \\ \frac{L}{M} + 1, & otherwise \end{cases} \qquad (9)$$

2) Indexing the frames corresponding with L_1 according to the three-level index structure. Selecting a video with the frame corresponding with L_1, and recording the frame ID as the key information.
3) Based on the video selected in step 2), indexing the frames corresponding with L_j $(2 \leq j \leq n)$. And recording frames ID as the key information.
4) If the video selected in step 2) can not hide all L-bit information, return to the step 2) to select another video that can hide all L-bit information.

2.4   Information Extraction

On the receiving end, the receiver can extract the secret information as follow steps.

1) The receiver locates the key frames in the cover video according to the key information.
2) For each key frame combination, the deep features are extracted by CNNs. And the hash sequences are calculated by hash generator. Finally, a M-bit secret information is obtained according to Eq. (7) and Eq. (8).
3) Connecting all the extracted M-bit information in order.
4) Cropping the excess zeros to get the final L-bit secret information according to the zero padding record.

3   Experiment Results and Analysis

In this manuscript, we select Hollywood dataset to verify the proposed method. The Hollywood dataset contains 937 short videos with 24fps (frame per second).

3.1   Capacity

In this section, we discuss the capacity of one video frame. The capacity of one video frame depends on M. The comparison results with some coverless information hiding methods are shown in Table 1.

Table 1. Hidden bit number comparison in one frame.

Methods	[10]	[12]	[13]	[14]	Proposed method ($M = 16$)
Capacity	8 bit	8 bit	8 bit	7–14 bit	16 bit

3.2 Robustness

In this section, we conduct the robustness experiments comparison with [10]. The attacks are shown in Table 2. In Table 2, the crf parameter is the constant rate factor of H.264 coding. The theoretical range of crf parameter is $[0, 51]$. Typically, $crf = 18$ is considered visually lossless and $crf = 23$ is the industry default. Therefore, we set $crf = 18$ and $crf = 23$ in this experiment.

Table 2. Kind of attacks used in the comparison experiment.

Attack	The special parameters
JPEG compression	The quality factors Q: 90
Gauss noise	The mean μ: 0, the variances σ: 0.001, 0.005
Speckle noise	The mean μ: 0, the variances σ: 0.01, 0.05
H.264	Constant rate factor crf: 18, 23

The results of robustness experiments are shown in Table 3. The robustness is represented by the accuracy of information bit recovery.

Table 3. The accuracy of information bit recovery.

Attack	Size	Literature [10]	Proposed
JPEG compression	$Q(90)$	0.8833	0.8589
Gauss noise	$\sigma(0.001)$	0.3055	**0.5089**
	$\sigma(0.005)$	0.2975	**0.5171**
Speckle noise	$\sigma(0.01)$	0.4959	**0.5250**
	$\sigma(0.05)$	0.3002	**0.5152**
H.264	$crf(18)$	–	**0.4986**
	$crf(23)$	–	**0.4990**

3.3 Security Analysis

In this manuscript, no one bit is embedded in the selected carrier by the proposed method. In other words, there is no modification in the selected carrier. Therefore, the proposed method can resist all steganalysis algorithms and has high security.

4   Conclusion

A novel coverless video steganography method is proposed in this manuscript. The proposed method solves two problems that the existing coverless image steganography and coverless video steganography have not settled, which are the difficulty of constructing a dataset and the large number of transmission carriers. Besides, large capacity, good robustness and high security are achieved by the proposed coverless video steganography method.

References

1. Tian, J.: Reversible data embedding using a difference expansion. IEEE Trans. Circuits Syst. Video Technol. **13**(8), 890–896 (2003)
2. Chan, C.K., Cheng, L.M.: Hiding data in images by simple LSB substitution. Pattern Recogn. **37**(3), 469–474 (2004)
3. Ni, Z., Shi, Y.Q., et al.: Reversible data hiding. IEEE Trans. Circuits Syst. Video Technol. **16**(3), 354–362 (2006)
4. Wang, K., Lu, Z.M., et al.: A high capacity lossless data hiding scheme for JPEG images. J. Syst. Softw. **86**(7), 1965–1975 (2013)
5. Hou, D., Zhang, W., et al.: Reversible data hiding in color image with grayscale invariance. IEEE Trans. Circuits Syst. Video Technol. **29**(2), 363–374 (2018)
6. Chen, X., Sun, H., Tobe, Y., Zhou, Z., Sun, X.: Coverless information hiding method based on the Chinese mathematical expression. In: Huang, Z., Sun, X., Luo, J., Wang, J. (eds.) ICCCS 2015. LNCS, vol. 9483, pp. 133–143. Springer, Cham (2015). https://doi.org/10.1007/978-3-319-27051-7_12
7. Zou, L., Sun, J., Gao, M., Wan, W., Gupta, B.B.: A novel coverless information hiding method based on the average pixel value of the sub-images. Multimed. Tools Appl. **78**(7), 7965–7980 (2018). https://doi.org/10.1007/s11042-018-6444-0
8. Zhang, X., Peng, F., et al.: Robust coverless image steganography based on DCT and LDA topic classification. IEEE Trans. Multimed. **20**(12), 3223–3238 (2018)
9. Liu, Q., Xiang, X., et al.: Coverless steganography based on image retrieval of DenseNet features and DWT sequence mapping. Knowl.-Based Syst. **192**, 105375 (2020)
10. Pan, N., Qin, J., Tan, Y., Xiang, X., Hou, G.: A video coverless information hiding algorithm based on semantic segmentation. EURASIP J. Image Video Process. **2020**(1), 1–18 (2020). https://doi.org/10.1186/s13640-020-00512-8
11. Jiang, Q.Y., Li, W.J.: Deep cross-modal hashing. In: Proceedings of the IEEE Conference on Computer Vision and Pattern Recognition, pp. 3232–3240 (2017)
12. Xia, Z., Wang, X., Sun, X., Liu, Q., Xiong, N.: Steganalysis of LSB matching using differences between nonadjacent pixels. Multimed. Tools Appl. **75**(4), 1947–1962 (2014). https://doi.org/10.1007/s11042-014-2381-8
13. Zheng, S., Wang, L., Ling, B., Hu, D.: Coverless information hiding based on robust image hashing. In: Huang, D.-S., Hussain, A., Han, K., Gromiha, M.M. (eds.) ICIC 2017. LNCS (LNAI), vol. 10363, pp. 536–547. Springer, Cham (2017). https://doi.org/10.1007/978-3-319-63315-2_47
14. Ruan, S., Qin, Z.: Coverless covert communication based on gif image. Commun. Technol. **50**(7), 1506–1510 (2017)

Character Photo Selection for Mobile Platform

Chuchu Xu[✉], Xinguo Yu, and Chao Sun

National Engineering Research Center for E-Learning,
Central China Normal University, Wuhan, China
ccxu@mails.ccnu.edu.cn, xgyu@mail.ccnu.edu.cn, csun@ccnu.edu.cn

Abstract. As the smartphones are widely used in daily life, people are habituated to take photos in anywhere at anytime. The character photos, which contain both people and landscapes, are the most extensive ones in all kinds of photos. However, it is usually time-consuming and laborious for people to select and manage desired character photos manually. Therefore, automatic photo selection became extremely significant. Most of the existing methods select best character photos by assigning a absolute score or binary label, regardless of the photo's content. The selected character photos are hence not satisfied. In this paper, we propose an effective automatic framework to select best character photos, which first automatically eliminates photos with unattractive character, then ranks photos and assists users to select the desired ones. Moreover, our framework is especially useful for mobile camera in practical application scenarios. To reduce the burden of photo selection and improve the efficiency of automatic selection from a large number of photos on mobile platform, we divide the photo selection into two stages: eliminating of unattractive photos based on designed efficient and effective features related to faces and human postures, and ranking the remaining photos using a two-stream convolution neural network. To ensure that informative features are selected and less useful ones are suppressed, we design and utilize the attention mechanism module in network. Experiments demonstrate the effectiveness of our method on the automatic selection of the satisfied photos from a large number of photos.

Keywords: Photo selection · Mobile camera · Convolution neural network

1 Introduction

To record the good life or other events, people often manually take a series of character photos in daily life. The widely use of mobile cameras enables people to easily take a series of character photos about the same object or scene from different angles in different positions [22]. However, such kind of character photos are usually too many to be easily selected and managed. When people want to select the most visually appealing character photos from the collection to share

© Springer Nature Switzerland AG 2021
M. Nguyen et al. (Eds.): ISGV 2021, CCIS 1386, pp. 142–156, 2021.
https://doi.org/10.1007/978-3-030-72073-5_12

on the social media or preserve in albums, it is usually time-consuming and laborious for people to browse the entire set of photos and then select desired ones, delete unwanted ones. Therefore, helping users to automatically select the desired character photos became extremely significant.

Automatically selecting a pleasing photo from a series of character photos is always a challenging problem, as the selection of the best photo is a subjective process. Previous researches on photo selection usually assign a absolute score (e.g., from zero to ten) or a label (e.g., high or low) to each photo by evaluating the quality of the photo based on the feature representation of the characters in the photo [10]. Such methods are independent evaluations for a series of photos, rather than comparative evaluations, which are easy to generate similar scores for similar photos, and difficult to select satisfactory character photos well. Inspired by the knowledge of praxiology, we notice that eliminating the unattractive photos is quite easier than selecting the satisfied ones, as the drawbacks are always conspicuous. Hence, we propose an automatic character photo selection method, which first automatically eliminates photos with unattractive character, then ranks photos and assists users to select the desired ones. Figure 1 displays some illustrations of photo selection results. Specifically, we divide our photo selection approach into two stages. At the first stage, we design a method to eliminate photos, which extracts efficient and effective features related to faces and human postures to gain character's quality scores in the photo. Based on the evaluation, we then eliminate photos with low-scoring or containing unattractive characters, so as to reduce the number of photos in the subsequent selection process. At the second stage, we utilize the Siamese network architecture [5] based on Resnet50 network [13] to gain a relative ranking of remaining photos. In addition, we notice that people can quickly choose high-value information from a large amount of information when reviewing a photo. The attention mechanism [28] in deep learning is essentially similar to this human visual attention mechanism. Therefore, we introduce the attention module combining the channel attention module and spatial attention module in the Siamese network, to improve the efficiency and accuracy of photo information process.

The main contributions are summarized as follows:

1. This paper proposes an effective automatic framework for selecting best photos from a large set of character photos, which first automatically eliminates photos with unattractive character and then lists higher-ranking photos. The method can assist users to select the desired photos without manual operations.
2. This paper designs a set of efficient features related to faces and human postures for photo elimination stage. The features are proved to be effective in experiments.
3. This paper redesigns a two-stream convolution neural network based on Resnet50 network using the photo pairs as its input. In order to obtain high-value information of salient areas, we introduce the attention

mechanism combining the channel attention module and spatial attention module in our method.

The paper is organized as follows. We introduce related works on feature extraction for person and photo selection in Sect. 2. The details of method are shown in Sect. 3. The details of experiments and analysis are introduced in Sect. 4. Finally concluding remarks are given in Sect. 5.

Fig. 1. Illustrations of photo selection results. The green boxes represent the best character photo in this series of photos. The numbers in the upper right indicate the ranking of this photo in this series of photos. Marking 'eliminated' in the photo means it is eliminated out during the elimination stage.

2 Related Work

2.1 Feature Extraction for Person

In character photos with people as the main subject, people regions are the most attractive regions in photos. Therefore, the information involving people, such as face, body posture, is very important for selecting character photo [3,8,15]. Previous researches mainly extract face-related features to represent the photo quality and then select best photos. Zhu et al. [29] used facial expressions to determine if a portrait photo is attractive, and described a method for providing feedback on portrait to select the most attractive portraits from large video/photo collections. Li et al. [19] focused on the characteristics related the face regions, such as facial blurring, face composition, face closeness, to evaluate photo quality. Newbury et al. [22] extracted nine descriptive features about face orientation, facial emotions, face exposure and blurriness by the face detection function in Google Cloud Vision for distinguishing good and bad quality face photos. Wang et al. [27] designed a set of high-level features about human face, and combine generic aesthetic features to predict the distinction of multiple group photos of diverse human states under the same scene. These methods only consider the factors of face quality in the photos and ignore the important information of the human postures. Actually, people's preference are often guided by more complex factors, in addition to face states, there are also people's posture states, such as the completeness of the human body area and the orientation of the human body [18]. Instead of selecting attractive photos based on quality of people, this paper designed both face and human posture features to evaluate the quality of people in photos, and eliminate photos with unattractive character.

2.2 Photo Selection

Photo selection has drawn the attention of both researchers and developers in recent years [12,16,21]. For example, Datta et al. [9] designed specific hand-crafted features and then made use of Support Vector Machine [24] and Decision Tree [23] to binary classification, and assign good or bad label to each photo. Tong et al. [26] adopt boosting to combine global low-level simple features (blurriness, contrast, colorfulness, and saliency) in order to classify professional photograph and ordinary snapshots. With the improvement of deep learning, convolution neural networks have shown superior performance in image understanding in recent years [11]. The RAPID model by Lu et al. [20] toke the entire photo and some parts of photo as input, and use an AlexNet-like architecture where the last fully-connected layer is set to output 2-dim probability for aesthetic binary classification. Talebi et al. [25] improved the loss function, and predicted the distribution of human opinion scores (from one to ten) using a convolution neural network. Several methods have recently been proposed to prove that selecting the best photo from a set of photos is a comparison-based process. Kong et al. [17] thought it is difficult to learn a common scoring mechanism for various photos, so they proposed to predict relative aesthetic rankings among images with similar visual content based on Siamese network. Chang et al. [7] collected the first large public dataset composed of series photos and established a relative ranking for "better" or "worse" photos from among a series of similar photos.

3 Method

3.1 Proposed Framework

The framework of the proposed automatic photo selection approach is shown in Fig. 2. A large number of series of character photos are used as input. In the photo elimination stage, the area of people in the photo is detected by extracting efficient and effective features related to human face and posture, and the quality of the characters in the photo is estimated. We then eliminate those photos with low quality of character. To gain a relative ranking of photos with high quality of character, we design a two-stream convolution neural network based on Resnet50 network which adopts the attention mechanism and combines the channel attention module and spatial attention module. In the following sections, we will elaborate the proposed method.

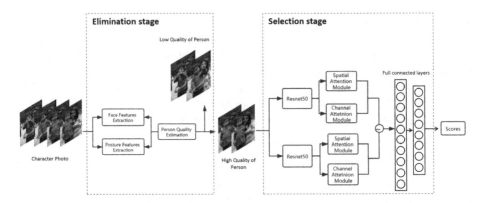

Fig. 2. The framework of our automatic photo selection approach.

3.2   Elimination Stage

Face Features Extraction. In character photos with people as the main subject, the human face is the most attractive area [6]. The quality of the face has a dominant impact on the quality of the entire photo. Face quality can be affected the illumination, blur, occlusion, and completeness of the face area. When people filter photos, they will not only consider the above factors, but also the states of the face in the photo, such as face orientation, closed eyes. If someone closes eyes, someone's face is occluded or someone is not facing the camera in a photo, we will naturally exclude this photo from the candidates of satisfied character photos.

Therefore, we first detect whether there is a human face in each photo or not, then eliminate those photos without any face in. Subsequently, we extract face-related information of each face per photo from three aspects(Eyes states, Face orientation, Quality metric) respectively.

(1) Eyes states. If someone's eyes are closed in a photo with people, the beauty of that will be greatly decreased. So we consider the left and right eye states(opening or closing) of each person in the photo. We obtain the confidence of left and right eye states of each person, marked as Cl and Cr respectively. Assuming N faces are detected in a character photo, we designed the features f1 and f2 of each face as follows:

$$f_1(i) = \begin{cases} 0 & if \ Cl^i < 0.3 \\ 1 & otherwise \end{cases} \quad i \in \{1, ..., N\}, \tag{1}$$

$$f_2(i) = \begin{cases} 0 & if \ Cr^i < 0.3 \\ 1 & otherwise \end{cases} \quad i \in \{1, 2, ..., N\}, \tag{2}$$

where $Cl^i(Cr^i)$ indicates that the degree of opening or closing about the left (right) eye of the ith person in the photo. We empirically set the threshold value to 0.3. When the confidence value of left(right) eye state is less than 0.3, it means the left(right) eye is closing, otherwise opening.

(2) Face orientation. If someone in a photo looks at the camera, but the head tilted, the photo is not a high-quality photo and is easily abandoned by people. Therefore, we get the roll, pitch, and yaw angle of each face as R, P, Y, where $R \in [-180, 180]$, $P \in [-90, 90]$, $Y \in [-90, 90]$. The recommended value range of R, P, Y is from -45 to 45 degree. It is considered that people is facing the camera. So we can eliminate only those face which is beyond of this range. The definitions of features f3, f4, f5 of each face are as follows:

$$f_3(i) = \begin{cases} 0 & if \ \ R^i \notin [-45, 45] \\ 1 & otherwise \end{cases} \quad i \in \{1, 2, ..., N\} \tag{3}$$

$$f_4(i) = \begin{cases} 0 & if \ \ P^i \notin [-45, 45] \\ 1 & otherwise \end{cases} \quad i \in \{1, 2, ..., N\} \tag{4}$$

$$f_5(i) = \begin{cases} 0 & if \ \ Y^i \notin [-45, 45] \\ 1 & otherwise \end{cases} \quad i \in \{1, 2, ..., N\} \tag{5}$$

(3) Face Quality metrics. In character photos, the most basic requirements are that the face area in the photo should be well illuminated, complete, clear and unoccluded [1]. Through simple quality metrics, We can easily eliminate photos that do not follow the basic requirements. Hence, we get four features attributes about illumination, occlusion, completeness, blur as I, O, C, B. I indicates the illumination level of the face area and its value ranges from 0 to 255. We empirically set the threshold value to 40. When the confidence value of illumination is less than 40, it means the illumination is poor. O represents the degree of occlusion of each face, and the range is from 0 to 1, where 0 means no occlusion, and 1 indicates complete occlusion. The confidence value of occlusion which is greater than 0.8 means severe occlusion. C represents the facial completeness in the photo, where the face area overflowing the image boundary is marked as 'False', otherwise 'True'. B indicates the degree of facial blur and its range is from 0 to 1, where 0 means the clearest face, 1 means the most blurry face. The threshold value is set to 0.7. The definitions of features f6, f7, f8, f9 of each face are as follows:

$$f_6(i) = \begin{cases} 0 & if \ \ I^i < 40 \\ 1 & otherwise \end{cases} \quad i \in \{1, 2, ..., N\} \tag{6}$$

$$f_7(i) = \begin{cases} 0 & if \ \ O^i > 0.8 \\ 1 & otherwise \end{cases} \quad i \in \{1, 2, ..., N\} \tag{7}$$

$$f_8(i) = \begin{cases} 0 & if \ \ C^i = \ 'False' \\ 1 & otherwise \end{cases} \quad i \in \{1, 2, ..., N\} \tag{8}$$

$$f_9(i) = \begin{cases} 0 & if \ \ B^i > 0.7 \\ 1 & otherwise \end{cases} \quad i \in \{1, 2, ..., N\} \tag{9}$$

(a)   (b)

Fig. 3. Compared to (a), (b) is obviously a less attractive photo. However, when only considering facial features, face quality evaluation will evaluate (b) to be better than (a). Because the face detector cannot detect the two objects bent over in (b), and detect one object with closed eyes in (a). Therefore, it eliminates (a) instead of (b).

Posture Features Extraction. Figure 3 shows the comparison of photos about different postures, illustrating the importance of extracting posture features. Therefore, we extract three important attributes related to the human body postures, and design features to eliminate photos with unattractive character based on these attributes information.

(1) Normal or abnormal human body. To tell whether the human body in the photo is normal is not to judge non-human creatures such as animals. We need to consider the completeness of people in character photo. A normal human body mainly refers to a human body in the photo with more than one-half of the body exposed, and generally the waist can be seen. An abnormal human body refers to a human body that has been severely cut off in the photo, such as only two heads or only two legs. We obtain 'is_human' attribute of each person in each photo. The 'is_human' attribute is marked as BH. If the human body in the photo is a abnormal human body, we mark BH as 'False', otherwise 'True'. Assuming M bodies are detected in a character photo, we design the features f10 as follows:

$$f_{10}(i) = \begin{cases} 0 & if \ BH^i = \ 'False' \\ 1 & otherwise \end{cases} \quad i \in \{1, 2, ..., M\} \quad (10)$$

(2) Body orientation. Similar to the face orientation attribute, the human body orientation is also a significant factor that we should consider when selecting character photos. For the front-facing and back-facing postures, people usually prefer the former. We obtain body orientation attribute of each person per photo

and mark it as BO. BO includes three possible values: 'front', 'side', 'back'. Therefore, feature f11 is formulated as follow:

$$f_{11}(i) = \begin{cases} 0 & if \ BO^i = \ 'back' \\ 0.5 & if \ BO^i = \ 'side' \\ 1 & if \ BO^i = \ 'front' \end{cases} \quad i \in \{1, 2, ..., M\} \quad (11)$$

(3) Body occlusion. When a large human body area appears in the character photo, we certainly hope that this body area is not occluded. We obtain body occlusion attribute of each person as BOC. BOC includes three possibilities of no occlusion, mild occlusion, and severe occlusion. Therefore, feature f12 is formulated as follow:

$$f_{12}(i) = \begin{cases} 0 & if \ BOC^i = \ 'severe' \\ 0.5 & if \ BOC^i = \ 'mild' \\ 1 & if \ BOC^i = \ 'no' \end{cases} \quad i \in \{1, 2, ..., M\} \quad (12)$$

Person Quality Estimation. Based on designed features above, they can be formalization as:

$$F_{k1} = \frac{1}{N} \sum_{i=1}^{N} f_{k1}(i) \quad k1 \in \{1, 2, ..., 9\}, \quad i \in \{1, 2, ..., N\} \quad (13)$$

$$F_{k2} = \frac{1}{M} \sum_{i=1}^{M} f_{k2}(i) \quad k2 \in \{10, 11, 12\}, \quad i \in \{1, 2, ..., M\} \quad (14)$$

where $F_{k1}(k1 \in 1, 2, ..., 9)$ represents the eight attributes of all faces in each photo and $F_{k2}(k2 \in 10, 11, 12)$ represents the three attributes of all bodies in each photo. We concatenate F_{k1} and F_{k2} as the 12 features of the person quality in this photo. Then we train a Artificial Neural Network to estimate the quality of detected people per photo. There are 5 hidden fully-connected layers in the network. Every layer uses ReLU activation. The input of the network is the 12 features, and the output layer is a scalar, reflecting the quality of person. Through the quality, we can first eliminate photos with unattractive character.

3.3 Selection Stage

In the previous elimination stage, we only consider the attributes of the person area in the photo. In this section, we will select best character photo according to the high-level semantic information of the entire photo. We explore using deep learning method to achieve automatic character photo selection.

Siamese Network. Automatic selecting the best photo from a set of character photos is a comparison-based process to a large extent [18]. For example, the quality of a particular photo seem low when viewed in an isolated manner, while in a group of photos, the same photo may be the best choice compared to other photos. In contrast to the previous methods that directly assign an absolute score for each photo, we consider to use Siamese network architecture to learn the difference of photo pairs and gain a relative ranking. In Siamese network architecture, two inputs are sent into two identical sub-networks independently, which share the same network parameters in both training and prediction phases. Inspired by [7], we utilized a Siamese network architecture which contains two identical streams of fine-tuned ResNet50 network with shared weight for extracting features. Photo pairs are taken as input.

Attention Module. We have noticed, when people observe a photo, they often firstly notice some important areas of the photo. These areas contain the information that most arouses the user's interest and best expresses the abundant content of the photo. Humans can use limited attention to quickly select high-value information from a large amount of information. The attention mechanism in deep learning is essentially similar to the human visual attention mechanism. Inspired by [28], we introduce attention mechanism to increase feature representation in Siamese network, which can effectively select important information and suppress less valuable information. The extracted features from the last layer of ResNet50 are respectively fed into a channel attention module and a spatial channel attention module.

(1) Channel attention module. The channel attention module is mainly to explore the relationship of feature maps between different channels. The channel attention module simultaneously uses average-pooling and max-pooling functions along the spatial dimension to calculate the context information of each channel, obtaining two channel attention vectors C_{avg} and C_{max} respectively. Then two vectors are fed into a two-layer fully connected network. Finally, the output obtained is the channel attention feature vector, denoted as F_c. In brief, the channel attention module is formulated as:

$$F_c = \sigma(W_{fc2}\delta(W_{fc1}(C_{avg} + C_{max}))) \tag{15}$$

where δ denotes the ReLU activation and σ denotes the sigmoid function. W_{fc1}, W_{fc2} are the weight parameters of fully connected network.

(2) Spatial attention module. The spatial attention module focuses on the spatial relationship between different feature maps, to make the network model focus on the feature spatial position of the feature maps. Similar to the channel attention module, the spatial attention module first uses average-pooling and max-pooling functions along the channel dimension to aggregate the context of each spatial position, yielding two spatial attention maps S_{avg} and S_{max} respectively. Then, two maps are concatenated and input into a 7*7 convolutional layer. Finally, the

output obtained is the spatial attention feature map, denoted as F_s. In brief, the spatial attention module is formulated as:

$$F_s = \sigma(Conv[S_{avg}, S_{max}]) \tag{16}$$

The features processing combining channel attention module and spatial attention module is shown in Fig. 4. We concatenate the features of the outputs from the two-stream networks respectively. Then, we calculate their distance and pass the distance to two hidden layers to classify the features of the photo pairs, each of which consists of a linear fully connected layer and a tanh activation layer. In addition, we use cross-entropy loss as the cost function. The final output of the network indicates which of the two input photos is better.

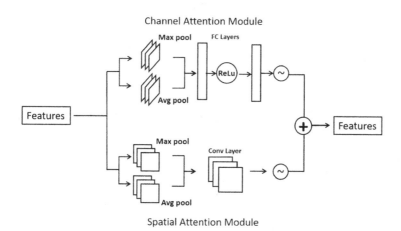

Fig. 4. Diagram of the features processing combining channel attention module and spatial attention module.

4 Experiments and Analysis

4.1 Dataset

The data used in this paper is from the photo series collected in [7] for series photo selection. The dataset includes 15,545 photos (5,953 series). The pairwise preference scores on two photos have been manually labeled. If the preference score in a photo pairs is greater than 0.5, it means that the first photo is better than the second one. Out of all 15,143 photo pairs, we sampled 4639 pairs photos with people for training, 585 pairs for validation, and the remaining 500 pairs for testing. In addition, in order to explain the stability and accuracy of our model better, we divided the sample dataset into single-person photos(2759 pairs for training, 361 pairs for validation and 308 pairs for testing) and group photos(1880 pairs for training, 224 pairs for validation and 192 pairs for testing) to evaluate our model. Figure 5 shows some illustrations of the dataset.

Fig. 5. Illustrations of the photo series dataset.

4.2   Features Importance Ranking

In elimination stage, we utilize the face detection method in BaiduAI [2], a recognition tool, to detect the presence of faces in each photo, and then combine the face attribute analysis method and human body attribute analysis method from BaiduAI to extract twelve person-related attributes in each photo. We empirically set different threshold values for these attributes and design efficient and effective features related to person.

We used the Random Forest [4] to rank the importance of features. The importance ranking of the top twelve features is shown in Fig. 6. It is observed that the importances of pitch feature and orientation of human body feature are much higher than other features, which indicates that the orientation of face and human body is the dominant feature when eliminating photos with unattractive characters in. The importance of roll, yaw, left and right eyes states, normal human body and facial illumination is also exceeded the average value, which means that these features also play an important role in the photo elimination stage. The reason for the lower ranking of facial blur is that the facial blur features in character photos are related to the resolution of the photo. If the photo is of low resolution, the face is also easily treated as blurred. Based on the above analysis of the features importance, we decide to choose these twelve human-related features in elimination stage.

4.3   Experimental Comparison and Analysis

Accuracy Comparison with Different Methods. We experimentally verified that our method enables achieve better character photo selection. We compared our method with baseline method proposed in [7] for character photo selection. ResNet50 [14] were also introduced as baselines. The performance of different methods were evaluated in terms of classification accuracy on photo

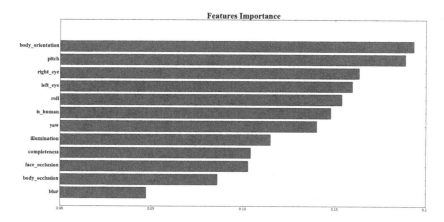

Fig. 6. The importance ranking of the top twelve features

pairs. Meanwhile, we perform experiments on single-person dataset and group dataset. Table 1 summarizes the comparison results. From the comparative analysis of Table 1, it is observed that our approach has a higher accuracy rate than the method presented in [7] and [14] on three datasets. In addition, our method with attention mechanism, is significantly better than [7] and [14] without attention mechanism, revealing the importance of applying the attention mechanism to our method.

Table 1. Accuracy comparison results of different methods on three datasets.

Method	Accuracy (sample dataset)	Accuracy (single-person)	Accuracy (group)
[7] (Alexnet)	61.61	62.94	59.71
[14] (Resnet50)	62.56	64.03	59.44
Ours	**66.03**	**66.67**	**62.24**

Accuracy Comparison with Different Attention Modules. We further perform experiments to compare three different ways of arranging attention modules: Siamese-Channel attention, Siamese-Spatial attention, and Siamese-Channel & Spatial attention(our method). The comparison results are shown in Table 2. On the sample dataset, it can be further observed that the accuracy rate of our method is higher than that of Siamese-channel attention and Siamese-spatial attention. This indicates that the performance of our method is better than other methods with single attention module, which verifies the necessity of effective combination of spatial attention module and channel attention module.

Table 2. Accuracy comparison of using different attention modules on three datasets.

Method	Accuracy (sample dataset)	Accuracy (single-person)	Accuracy (group)
Siamese-Channel attention [28]	61.16	64.91	58.46
Siamese-Spatial attention [28]	63.84	65.79	60.13
Ours	**66.03**	**66.67**	**62.24**

Stability Comparison with Different Models. We calculated F1-score to compare the stability of our model and models proposed in [7,14] on the sample data set. F1-score measures comprehensive performance as a harmonic mean value of precision and recall. Figure 7 shows the comparison of the F1-score curves of our method and other baselines on the validation set during the training process. It can be intuitively observed that our method leads to an relative improvement in the performance of the training process. The experimental results further verify the stability and effectiveness of our model.

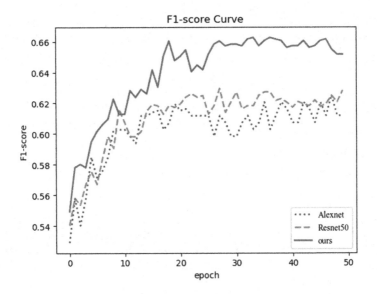

Fig. 7. F1-score curves on the validation set during training.

5   Conclusion

We have presented a novel method of automatic photo selection in this paper, which is able to automatically list higher-ranking photos and help users to select the desired ones. Our method first eliminates photos with unattractive character in elimination stage. Then it takes the remaining photos as input and utilizes the Siamese network architecture based on the Resnet50 network to gain the relative ranking of these photos. To improve the efficiency and accuracy of information processing, we have introduced attention mechanism in Siamese network. Experiments show that our method lead to promising results. Moreover, our method is especially useful for the mobile platform in practical application scenarios. In the future, we will further explore more discriminative features to capture the subtle differences between character photos.

Acknowledgement. We thank the anonymous reviewers for helpful suggestions. This work is supported by National Natural Science Foundation of China under Grant 61802142.

References

1. Abaza, A., Harrison, M.A., Bourlai, T., Ross, A.: Design and evaluation of photometric image quality measures for effective face recognition. IET Biom. **3**(4), 314–324 (2014)
2. BaiduAI: BaiduAI open platform. https://ai.baidu.com. Accessed 17 Oct 2020
3. Best-Rowden, L., Jain, A.K.: Learning face image quality from human assessments. IEEE Trans. Inf. Forensics Secur. **13**(12), 3064–3077 (2018)
4. Breiman, L., Friedman, J.H., Olshen, R.A., Stone, C.J.: Classification and regression trees (cart). Biometrics **40**(3), 358 (1984)
5. Bromley, J., et al.: Signature verification using a "Siamese" time delay neural network. Int. J. Pattern Recogn. Artif. Intell. **7**(04), 669–688 (1993)
6. Cavalcanti, C.S.V.C., Gomes, H.M., De Queiroz, J.E.R.: A survey on automatic techniques for enhancement and analysis of digital photography. J. Braz. Comput. Soc. **19**(3), 341–359 (2013). https://doi.org/10.1007/s13173-013-0102-1
7. Chang, H., Yu, F., Wang, J., Ashley, D., Finkelstein, A.: Automatic triage for a photo series. ACM Trans. Graph. (TOG) **35**(4), 1–10 (2016)
8. Choi, J., Lee, B.J., Zhang, B.T.: Human body orientation estimation using convolutional neural network. arXiv preprint arXiv:1609.01984 (2016)
9. Datta, R., Joshi, D., Li, J., Wang, J.Z.: Studying aesthetics in photographic images using a computational approach. In: Leonardis, A., Bischof, H., Pinz, A. (eds.) ECCV 2006. LNCS, vol. 3953, pp. 288–301. Springer, Heidelberg (2006). https://doi.org/10.1007/11744078_23
10. Deng, Y., Loy, C.C., Tang, X.: Image aesthetic assessment: an experimental survey. IEEE Signal Process. Mag. **34**(4), 80–106 (2017)
11. Dong, Z., Shen, X., Li, H., Tian, X.: Photo quality assessment with DCNN that understands image well. In: He, X., Luo, S., Tao, D., Xu, C., Yang, J., Hasan, M.A. (eds.) MMM 2015. LNCS, vol. 8936, pp. 524–535. Springer, Cham (2015). https://doi.org/10.1007/978-3-319-14442-9_57
12. Dong, Z., Tian, X.: Multi-level photo quality assessment with multi-view features. Neurocomputing **168**, 308–319 (2015)
13. He, K., Zhang, X., Ren, S., Sun, J.: Deep residual learning for image recognition. In: Proceedings of the IEEE Conference on Computer Vision and Pattern Recognition, pp. 770–778 (2016)

14. He, K., Zhang, X., Ren, S., Sun, J.: Deep residual learning for image recognition. In: IEEE Conference on Computer Vision & Pattern Recognition (2016)

15. Hernandez-Ortega, J., Galbally, J., Fierrez, J., Haraksim, R., Beslay, L.: FaceQnet: quality assessment for face recognition based on deep learning. In: 2019 International Conference on Biometrics (ICB), pp. 1–8. IEEE (2019)

16. Hosu, V., Goldlucke, B., Saupe, D.: Effective aesthetics prediction with multi-level spatially pooled features. In: Proceedings of the IEEE Conference on Computer Vision and Pattern Recognition, pp. 9375–9383 (2019)

17. Kong, S., Shen, X., Lin, Z., Mech, R., Fowlkes, C.: Photo aesthetics ranking network with attributes and content adaptation. In: Leibe, B., Matas, J., Sebe, N., Welling, M. (eds.) ECCV 2016. LNCS, vol. 9905, pp. 662–679. Springer, Cham (2016). https://doi.org/10.1007/978-3-319-46448-0_40

18. Kuzovkin, D., Pouli, T., Cozot, R., Le Meur, O., Kervec, J., Bouatouch, K.: Image selection in photo albums. In: Proceedings of the 2018 ACM on International Conference on Multimedia Retrieval, pp. 397–404 (2018)

19. Li, C., Gallagher, A., Loui, A.C., Chen, T.: Aesthetic quality assessment of consumer photos with faces. In: 2010 IEEE International Conference on Image Processing, pp. 3221–3224. IEEE (2010)

20. Lu, X., Lin, Z., Jin, H., Yang, J., Wang, J.Z.: Rapid: rating pictorial aesthetics using deep learning. In: Proceedings of the 22nd ACM International Conference on Multimedia, pp. 457–466 (2014)

21. Mohan, J., Philumon, J.: Automatic selection of better image from a series of same scene. Int. J. Adv. Res. Comput. Sci. **8**(5) (2017)

22. Newbury, R., Cosgun, A., Koseoglu, M., Drummond, T.: Learning to take good pictures of people with a robot photographer. arXiv preprint arXiv:1904.05688 (2019)

23. Quinlan, J.R.: Induction on decision tree. Mach. Learn. **1** (1986)

24. Sain, S.R.: The nature of statistical learning theory. Technometrics **38**(4), 409 (1997)

25. Talebi, H., Milanfar, P.: NIMA: neural image assessment. IEEE Trans. Image Process. **27**(8), 3998–4011 (2018)

26. Tong, H., Li, M., Zhang, H.-J., He, J., Zhang, C.: Classification of digital photos taken by photographers or home users. In: Aizawa, K., Nakamura, Y., Satoh, S. (eds.) PCM 2004. LNCS, vol. 3331, pp. 198–205. Springer, Heidelberg (2004). https://doi.org/10.1007/978-3-540-30541-5_25

27. Wang, Y., Ke, Y., Wang, K., Zhang, C., Qin, F.: Aesthetic quality assessment for group photograph. arXiv preprint arXiv:2002.01096 (2020)

28. Woo, S., Park, J., Lee, J.Y., So Kweon, I.: CBAM: convolutional block attention module. In: Proceedings of the European Conference on Computer Vision (ECCV), pp. 3–19 (2018)

29. Zhu, J.Y., Agarwala, A., Efros, A.A., Shechtman, E., Wang, J.: Mirror mirror: crowdsourcing better portraits. ACM Trans. Graph. (TOG) **33**(6), 1–12 (2014)

Close Euclidean Shortest Path Crossing an Ordered 3D Skew Segment Sequence

Nguyet Tran$^{(\boxtimes)}$ and Michael J. Dinneen

School of Computer Science, The University of Auckland, Auckland, New Zealand
ntra770@aucklanduni.ac.nz, mjd@cs.auckland.ac.nz

Abstract. Given k skew segments in an ordered sequence E and two points s and t in a three-dimensional environment, for any $\epsilon \in (0,1)$, we study a classical geometric problem of finding a $(1 + \epsilon)$-approximation Euclidean shortest path between s and t, crossing the segments in E in order. Let L be the maximum Euclidean length of the segments in E and h be the minimum distance between two consecutive segments in E. The running time of our algorithm is $O(k^3 \log(\frac{kL}{h\epsilon}))$. Currently, the running time of finding the exact shortest path for this problem is exponential. Thus, most practical algorithms of this problem are approximations. Among these practical algorithms, placing discrete points, named Steiner points, on every segment in E, then constructing a graph to find an approximate path between s and t, is most widely used in practice. However, using Steiner points will cause the running time of this approach to always depend on a polynomial function of the term $\frac{1}{\epsilon}$, which is not a close optimal solution. Differently, in this paper, we solve the problem directly in a continuous environment, without using Steiner points, in terms of the running time depending on a logarithmic function of the term $\frac{1}{\epsilon}$, which we call a close optimal solution.

Keywords: Euclidean shortest path · 3D path planning · Skew segment sequence

1 Introduction

Imagine that we are given two points s and t in a complex 3D space such that going straight between s and t is not allowed. For example, the space between s and t is intercepted by different screens (see Fig. 1). However, there is an ordered sequence of slits (on the screens, for example) where the path between s and t can only go through these slits. The problem in this paper is that how we can find the Euclidean shortest path between s and t, going through the slits in such an environment. Let $E = (e_1, \ldots, e_k)$ be an ordered sequence of slits between s and t, where $k \geq 1$. If the width of each slit e_i in E is extremely small, or negligible, e_i can be considered as a segment. In practice, this problem is important in a wide range of applications, such as in computer-assisted surgery, military, optics, manufacturing, and game industry. We formally define the problem as follows.

© Springer Nature Switzerland AG 2021
M. Nguyen et al. (Eds.): ISGV 2021, CCIS 1386, pp. 157–174, 2021.
https://doi.org/10.1007/978-3-030-72073-5_13

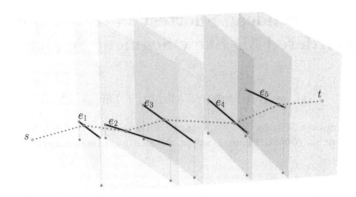

Fig. 1. An example of the problem.

Problem Statement: <u>E</u>uclidean <u>S</u>hortest <u>P</u>ath crossing a <u>3D</u> <u>s</u>kew <u>S</u>egment <u>S</u>equence (ESP-3D-3S). Let $E = (e_1, \ldots, e_k)$ be a sequence of $k \geq 1$ segments in 3D, where for every $i \in \{1, \ldots, k-1\}$, the lines through two consecutive segments e_i and e_{i+1} in E are skew lines. This means that the lines through e_i and e_{i+1} are not parallel and do not intersect with each other (see Fig. 2a). Given E and two points s and t in 3D, the ESP-3D-3S problem asks for the Euclidean shortest path $P^*(s,t) = (s = r_0, r_1, \ldots, r_k, r_{k+1} = t)$ such that $\sum_{i=0}^{k} d(r_i, r_{i+1})$ is minimum, where for every $i \in \{1, \ldots, k\}$, r_i, called a *crossing point*, is a point on the segment e_i in E, and $d(r_i, r_{i+1})$ is the Euclidean distance between r_i and r_{i+1}.

The main difficulty of the ESP-3D-3S problem is that because two consecutive segments e_i and e_{i+1} in E, $i \in \{1, \ldots, k-1\}$, are on two skew lines, the planar unfolding fails. This means that there exists no common plane containing both e_i and e_{i+1}.

Related Work of the ESP-3D-3S Problem. Let O be a set of disjoint polyhedral obstacles, and s and t be two points in 3D. The problem of finding the shortest path between s and t and avoiding intersecting the interior of any obstacle in O is classical and has been studied for decades. We call this problem ESP-3D. More specifically, the problem ESP-3D asks for a Euclidean shortest path $P^*(s,t) = (s = r_0, r_1, \ldots, r_l, r_{l+1} = t)$, where $l \geq 0$, and for every $i \in \{1, \ldots, l\}$, r_i is a point on an edge of an obstacle in O such that the segment between r_i and r_{i+1} does not intersect the interior of any obstacle, and $\sum_0^l d(r_i, r_{i+1})$ is minimum. It is proven that, to be an Euclidean shortest path, every crossing point r_i of $P^*(s,t)$, $i \in \{1, \ldots, l\}$, need to be on an edge of a polyhedral obstacle in O. Thus, the difficulty of the ESP-3D problem is raised by the following two questions: (1) which ordered sequence of edges (segments), namely E, of the obstacles in O does $P^*(s,t)$ cross, and (2) when E is determined, how can we find $P^*(s,t)$ crossing E? The ESP-3D problem is well-known to be NP-hard by Canny and Reif [1]. However, the reason that makes the ESP-3D problem NP-hard is due to question (1). This means that finding an ordered sequence of segments E in 3D that $P^*(s,t)$ needs to cross is NP-hard. Thus, in the case that E is given, how can we solve question (2)? Question (2) of the ESP-3D problem is exactly the ESP-3D-3S problem that we focus on in this paper.

For question (2), given E, the optimization criterion that makes $P^*(s,t)$ the Euclidean shortest path between s and t crossing E is that when $P^*(s,t)$ crosses a segment e_i in E, it must enter and leave e_i at the same angle (see Known Fact 2). Due to this, we can set up an algebraic system of equations to find the crossing points for $P^*(s,t)$. However, this method will result in a system of equations of degree four, which leads to an exponential running time [2]. Because of this algebraic difficulty, most existing solutions for the ESP-3D-3S problem are approximations. We briefly present some main approximation approaches for the problem as follows.

One solution to solve the ESP-3D-3S problem is initially taking any point on every segment e_i in E to initialize the first path between s and t crossing E. Then, an iterative scheme of sliding these crossing points is performed to shorten the path, such as the work by Bajaj and Moh [3] or Le et al. [4]. However, the problem of this approach is that we do not know how long the iterative procedure will converge, or how close to the optimal path a returned solution can be [5]. Another work by Polishchuk and Mitchell [6] uses a second order cone program (SOCP) to solve the ESP-3D-3S problem. However, as they stated in the paper, using SOCP to solve the ESP-3D-3S problem is considered as a "black box". This is also similar to the iterative approach mentioned above, in which we cannot predict or theoretically measure the result of the computed path.

Conversely, for the approximation methods that we can theoretically measure the result of the computed path, with an $\epsilon \in (0,1)$, let $P(s,t)$ be a $(1+\epsilon)$-approximation path between s and t crossing E, where the length of $P(s,t)$ is at most $(1+\epsilon)$ times of the length of $P^*(s,t)$. To find $P(s,t)$ in a polynomial running time of k and ϵ, we can basically use one of the existing approximation methods of the ESP-3D problem. That is, every segment in E is discretized by placing points, named Steiner points across the length of the segment. Then, these Steiner points will be interconnected together to create a weighted graph before a shortest path graph algorithm (e.g. Dijkstra) is used to find an approximate shortest path among the Steiner points. For example, one typical result of this group is from the work by Aleksandrov et al. [7], which can compute an $(1+\epsilon)$-approximation $P(s,t)$ in $O(\frac{n}{\epsilon^3} \log \frac{1}{\epsilon} \log n)$ time, where n is the number of vertices. For a comprehensive survey of different methods using Steiner points, we refer the interested readers to [8,9]. The drawback of this approach, however, is that the dependency on $\frac{1}{\epsilon}$ is always polynomial, which is not logarithmic [8]. This means that, when a close to optimal path is required, with ϵ being extremely small, then $\frac{1}{\epsilon}$ becomes extremely large. Thus, the algorithms using Steiner points can cause an impractical running time in comparison with the algorithms whose dependency on $\frac{1}{\epsilon}$ is logarithmic.

In terms of the dependency on $\frac{1}{\epsilon}$ being logarithmic, we notice the method by Burago et al. [10] whose dependency on $\frac{1}{\epsilon}$ is doubly logarithmic. Although they find an approximate shortest path $P(s,t)$ crossing a sequence of skew lines, not a sequence of skew segments, the problem does not change much. Let $L(E) = (l_1, \ldots, l_k)$ be the sequence of k lines with respect to E, where every line l_i, $i \in \{1, \ldots, k\}$, is the line containing the corresponding segment e_i in E. Let $P'(s, t) = (s, \sigma'_1, \ldots, \sigma'_k, t)$ be a $(1 + \epsilon)$-approximation shortest path between s and t crossing $L(E)$, where every crossing point σ'_i is a point on $l(e_i)$. Let $P(s, t) = (s, \sigma_1, \ldots, \sigma_k, t)$ be a $(1 + \epsilon)$-approximation shortest path between s and t crossing E, where every crossing point σ_i is a point on e_i. As mentioned in [3], $P(s, t)$ can be calculated from $P'(s, t)$ as follows. For every $i \in \{1, \ldots, k\}$, if σ'_i is on the segment e_i, σ_i is equal to σ'_i. Otherwise, if σ'_i is outside the segment e_i, σ_i will be one of the two endpoints of e_i. Let $\tilde{d}$ and $\tilde{\alpha}$ be the minimal distance and minimal sine of the angles between two consecutive lines in $L(E)$, respectively. The method of [10] can compute $P'(s, t)$ crossing $L(E)$ in time $O((\frac{Rk}{\tilde{d}\tilde{\alpha}})^{16} + k^2 \log \log \frac{1}{\epsilon})$, where R is defined as the radius of a ball in which the initial approximation can be placed. To our knowledge, this is the only method of computing a $(1 + \epsilon)$-approximation shortest path crossing E whose dependency on $\frac{1}{\epsilon}$ is doubly logarithmic.

Our Work Summary. To this end, we call a $(1+\epsilon)$-approximation algorithm as *close optimal* only if the dependency on $\frac{1}{\epsilon}$ of the running time of the algorithm is logarithmic.

1. Our solution for the ESP-3D-3S problem in this paper is a close optimal solution, finding a $(1 + \epsilon)$-approximation shortest path in $O(k^3 \log(\frac{kL}{h\epsilon}))$ time.
2. In comparison, while the running times of the approximation algorithms using Steiner points currently depend on $\frac{1}{\epsilon}$ polynomially, our method depends on $\frac{1}{\epsilon}$ logarithmically. This means that, when a close optimal path is required, where ϵ needs to be extremely small, our algorithm can run much faster than the algorithms using Steiner points.
3. As presented above, to our knowledge, currently, only the work by Burago et al. [10] is a close optimal algorithm for the ESP-3D-3S problem, with the running time being $O((\frac{Rk}{\tilde{d}\tilde{\alpha}})^{16} + k^2 \log \log \frac{1}{\epsilon})$. The dependency of this algorithm on $\frac{1}{\epsilon}$ is doubly logarithmic. However, its dependency on k is up to k^{16} while the dependency on k of our algorithm is only $k^3 \log k$.

The rest of the paper is organized as follows. Section 2 contains some definitions and preliminaries. Our proposed algorithm for solving the ESP-3D-3S problem is presented in Sect. 3. Finally, Section 4 concludes the paper.

2 Preliminaries

Let $P^*(s, t) = (s = r_0, r_1, \ldots, r_k, r_{k+1} = t)$ be the exact Euclidean shortest path between s and t crossing a sequence E of k skew segments in order, where for every $i \in \{1, \ldots, k\}$, r_i is a point on e_i in E. With any two points u and v, we denote (u, v) as the segment between u and v, and $\overrightarrow{uv}$ as the vector from u to v. We first consider the optimization criterion that makes $P^*(s, t)$ the Euclidean shortest path. For every segment e_i in E, $i \in \{1, \ldots, k\}$, let $l(e_i)$ be the line

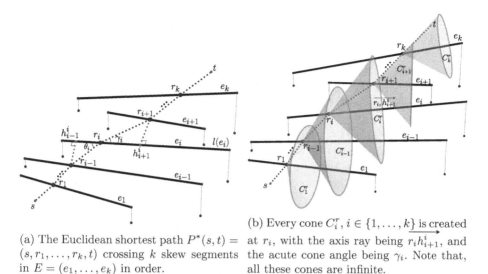

(a) The Euclidean shortest path $P^*(s,t) = (s, r_1, \ldots, r_k, t)$ crossing k skew segments in $E = (e_1, \ldots, e_k)$ in order.

(b) Every cone $C_i^r, i \in \{1, \ldots, k\}$ is created at r_i, with the axis ray being $\overrightarrow{r_i h_{i+1}^i}$, and the acute cone angle being γ_i. Note that, all these cones are infinite.

Fig. 2. The Euclidean shortest path $P^*(s,t)$ and its optimization criterion.

containing e_i (see Fig. 2a). Let h_{i-1}^i and h_{i+1}^i be two points on $l(e_i)$ such that the segments (r_{i-1}, h_{i-1}^i) and (r_{i+1}, h_{i+1}^i) are perpendicular to $l(e_i)$. Let θ_i and γ_i be two acute angles created by (r_i, r_{i-1}) and (r_i, h_{i-1}^i), and by (r_i, r_{i+1}) and (r_i, h_{i+1}^i), respectively. The two known facts below are due to [2].

Known Fact 1. $P^*(s,t)$ *is unique.*

Known Fact 2. *The path $P^*(s,t)$ is the exact Euclidean shortest path crossing k segments in E in order if and only if at every segment $e_i \in E$, $i \in \{1, \ldots, k\}$, for which r_i is not an endpoint of e_i, h_{i-1}^i and h_{i+1}^i are on the two different half lines of $l(e_i)$ induced by r_i and $\theta_i = \gamma_i$.*

Known Fact 2 suggests that, for every $i \in \{1, \ldots, k\}$, if an infinite, single-sided, right circular cone, named C_i^r, is created at r_i with the axis ray being the vector $\overrightarrow{r_i h_{i+1}^i}$, and the acute cone angle being γ_i, the point r_{i+1} will be the intersection point between the surface of the cone C_i^r and e_{i+1} (see Fig. 2b). We note that, all cones we use in this paper are infinite, single-sided, and right circular. Thus, to this end, to be simple, we call all of them as cones. Furthermore, to this end, when we mention cone, we mean the surface of the cone. That is, if we say a line or a segment intersects a cone, or two cones intersect with each other, we mean the line or segment intersects the surface of the cone, or the two surfaces of the cones intersect with each other. Additionally, a segment $e_i = (p_i, q_i)$ is denoted as being *inside* (resp. *outside*) a cone if both endpoints p_i and q_i are inside (resp. outside) the cone, or if p_i or q_i is on the surface of the cone, the remaining endpoint must be inside (resp. outside) the cone.

Definition 1. *Cone-Create-Rule.*

First, we consider the segment e_1 in E. Let a_1 be a point on e_1 (see Fig. 3). Let h_0^1 be the point on e_1 such that (s, h_0^1) is perpendicular to $l(e_1)$. Let θ_1 be the acute angle created by (a_1, s) and (a_1, h_0^1). Let C_1^a be the cone that is created on e_1, at a_1, with the axis ray being opposite to the vector $\overrightarrow{a_1 h_0^1}$, and the acute cone angle being $\gamma_1 = \theta_1$. We say that, C_1^a is created by s and a_1, based on the Cone-Create-Rule.

Similarly, for every $i \in \{2, \dots, k\}$, we consider the segment $e_i = (p_i, q_i)$ in E. Suppose that e_i intersects C_{i-1}^a at a_i. Let h_{i-1}^i be a point on e_i, where (a_{i-1}, h_{i-1}^i) is perpendicular to $l(e_i)$. Let θ_i be the acute angle created by (a_i, h_{i-1}^i) and (a_i, a_{i-1}). Let C_i^a be the cone that is created on e_i, at a_i, with the axis ray being opposite to the vector $\overrightarrow{a_i h_{i-1}^i}$, and the acute cone angle being $\gamma_i = \theta_i$. We say that, C_i^a is created by C_{i-1}^a, based on the Cone-Create-Rule.

Definition 2. *Euclidean-Ray with respect to a cone sequence.*

With a point a_1 on segment e_1, first, applying the Cone-Create-Rule, we can find the cone C_1^a on e_1. Suppose that e_2 intersects C_1^a at a_2. Then, using the Cone-Create-Rule, we can continue the calculations to obtain the path $R_a = (s, a_1, \dots, a_g)$, with respect to the cone sequence $C_a = (C_1^a, \dots, C_g^a)$, where $1 \leq g \leq k$ (see Fig. 3). This calculation stops at e_g when $g = k$, or if one of the following two conditions holds: (i) the segment e_{g+1} does not intersect the cone C_g^a, or (ii) e_{g+1} intersects the cone C_g^a at one of its two endpoints. We call R_a as a Euclidean-Ray with respect to the cone sequence C_a, from s, crossing E by starting at a_1 on e_1 to a_g on e_g.

From Definition 2, to find $P^*(s, t)$ crossing E, the following question remains. How can we find the point r_1 on e_1 such that, after calculating the Euclidean-Ray $R_r = (s, r_1, \dots, r_k)$ with respect to $C_r = (C_1^r, \dots, C_k^r)$, t is on C_k^r?

Proposition 1. *Let $R_u = (s, u_1, \dots, u_i)$ be a Euclidean-Ray with respect to $C_u = (C_1^u, \dots, C_i^u)$, crossing E from s, starting at u_1 on e_1 to u_i on e_i, where $i \leq k$. Let $R_v = (s, v_1, \dots, v_j)$ be another Euclidean-Ray with respect to $C_v = (C_1^v, \dots, C_j^v)$, crossing E from s, starting at v_1 on e_1 to v_j on e_j, where $j \leq k$. If $u_1 \neq v_1$, for every e_l, $l \in \{1, \dots, i\}$ if $i \leq j$, or $l \in \{1, \dots, j\}$ if $j \leq i$, then two cones C_l^u and C_l^v cannot intersect with each other.*

Proof. Without loss of generality, suppose that $i \leq j$. By contradiction, suppose that there exists a segment e_f, $1 \leq f \leq i$, that two cones C_f^u of C_u and C_f^v of C_v on e_f intersect with each other (see Fig. 4). Let O be the intersection circle between C_f^u and C_f^v. Let u_o and v_o be the intersection points between R_u and O and between R_v and O, respectively. Let $P_u(s, v_o) = (s, u_1, \dots, u_f, v_o)$ and $P_v(s, v_o) = (s, v_1, \dots, v_f, v_o)$ be two paths from s to v_o following R_u and R_v, respectively. Since v_o is also on C_f^u, the path $P_u(s, v_o)$ satisfies Known Fact 2. Thus, $P_u(s, v_o)$ is the Euclidean shortest path from s to v_o. However, the path $P_v(s, v_o)$ also satisfies Known Fact 2 to make $P_v(s, v_o)$ the Euclidean shortest path from s to v_o. Therefore, we have both $P_u(s, v_o)$ and $P_v(s, v_o)$ being two different Euclidean shortest paths from s to v_o. This is contrary to Known Fact 1. □

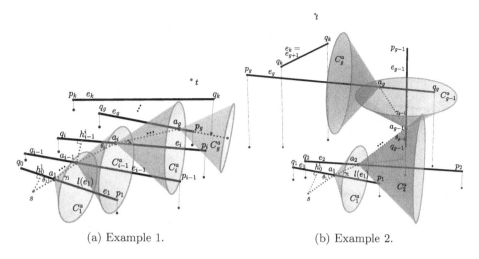

(a) Example 1.   (b) Example 2.

Fig. 3. Two examples of a Euclidean-Ray $R_a = (s, a_1, \ldots, a_g)$ with respect to $C_a = (C_1^a, \ldots, C_g^a)$, from s, crossing E by starting at a_1 on e_1 to a_g on e_g.

Due to Proposition 1, for any segment e_i in E, we now can see how all cones are distributed on e_i, as follows. On any segment $e_i = (p_i, q_i)$ in E, suppose that a Euclidean-Ray R_a, with respect to its cone sequence C_a, intersects e_i at a_i, and the cone C_i^a of C_a at a_i has the axis ray being $\overrightarrow{a_i p_i}$ and the acute cone angle being γ_i (see Fig. 5). Then, imaging that, if other cones are created on e_i gradually from a_i to p_i by different Euclidean-Rays from s, their acute cone angles must be gradually smaller in comparison with γ_i. This means that, for example, let u_i and v_i be two points on (a_i, p_i) with $d(a_i, u_i) < d(a_i, v_i)$ and C_i^u and C_i^v be two cones created at u_i and v_i from two different Euclidean-Rays from s, respectively. The acute cone angle of C_i^v must be smaller than the acute cone angle of C_i^u. It is easy to see that, if the acute cone angle of C_i^v is larger than the acute cone angle of C_i^u, C_i^u and C_i^v will intersect with each other, and this is contrary to Proposition 1. Otherwise, if other cones are created on e_i but gradually from a_i to q_i, first, their acute cone angles must be gradually larger than γ_i to 90°. From 90°, the axis rays of the remaining cones will be changed to $\overrightarrow{a_i q_i}$, then being gradually smaller.

Let S and S' be two sequences of segments. To this end, we use the notation $S \circ S'$ to denote the sequence of segments obtained from S and S' by appending S' to the end of S.

3 Euclidean Shortest Path Crossing a Sequence of 3D Skew Segments

We now consider a Euclidean-Ray $R_a = (s, a_1, \ldots, a_g)$ with respect to $C_a = (C_1^a, \ldots, C_g^a)$, $g \leq k$, where for every $i \in \{1, \ldots, g-1\}$, e_{i+1} intersects C_i^a at only one point. We will consider the case that e_{i+1} intersects C_i^a at two points (see

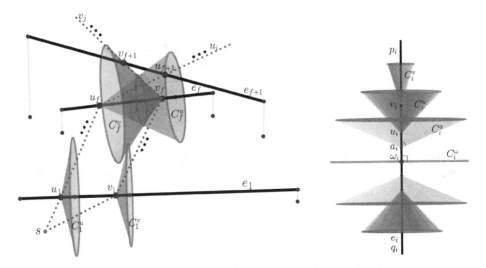

Fig. 4. Two Euclidean rays $R_u = (s, u_1, \ldots, u_i)$, with respect to $C_u = (C_1^u, \ldots, C_i^u)$, and $R_v = (s, v_1, \ldots, v_j)$, with respect to $C_v = (C_1^v, \ldots, C_j^v)$, have C_f^v and C_f^u intersect with each other on a segment e_f. This case cannot happen.

Fig. 5. Different cones are distributed on a segment e_i.

Fig. 6) later. For every $e_i = (p_i, q_i)$, $i \in \{1, \ldots, g\}$, we name the two endpoints p_i and q_i of e_i such that $\overrightarrow{a_i p_i}$ is the same direction with the axis ray of C_i^a (see Fig. 3).

Let $R_r = (s, r_1, \ldots, r_k)$ with respect to $C_r = (C_1^r, \ldots, C_k^r)$ be the Euclidean-Ray that hits t, where t is on the last cone C_k^r. Given a Euclidean-Ray $R_a = (s, a_1, \ldots, a_g)$ with respect to $C_a = (C_1^a, \ldots, C_g^a)$, $g \le k$, for every $i \in \{1, \ldots, g\}$, r_i on e_i of R_r can be determined on either (a_i, p_i) or (a_i, q_i), as follows. First, we see that if e_{g+1} is inside (resp. outside) C_g^a (see Fig. 3b), then r_g must be on (a_g, p_g) (resp. (a_g, q_g)). This observation is correct because if r_g is on (a_g, q_g), the cone C_g^r at r_g of R_r needs to intersect e_{g+1}, then C_g^r and C_g^a will intersect with each other, which is contrary to Proposition 1. Now, we know that r_g is on (a_g, p_g). As we constrained above, e_g intersects C_{g-1}^a at only one point a_g. Thus, between (a_g, p_g) and (a_g, q_g), one will be inside and the remaining one will be outside C_{g-1}^a. Suppose that (a_g, p_g) is outside C_{g-1}^a. Then, we can similarly determine that r_{g-1} on e_{g-1} of R_r must be on (a_{g-1}, q_{g-1}), which is outside C_{g-1}^a. By this way, if we continue tracing back from $g-1$ to 1, based on R_a, we can totally determine on every segment $e_i = (p_i, q_i)$ in E, which sub-segment, (a_i, p_i) or (a_i, q_i), of e_i that R_r crosses. Then, all the remaining sub-segments that R_r does not cross, called *unnecessary sub-segments*, will be trimmed or deleted. We present this idea in the function *Trim-Segments*.

Let $P(s, t)$ be a $(1 + \epsilon)$-approximation shortest path of $P^*(s, t)$. We now present the main idea of the function *Find-Approximate-Path* to find $P(s, t)$. Let δ be an extremely small value such that, if the Euclidean distance between two points, or between a point and a line is less than or equal to δ, then the two points are considered to be the same, or the point is considered to be on the line. Let m_1 be the middle point of e_1. From m_1, we use the function $Create\text{-}Euclidean\text{-}Ray$ (presented later) to find the Euclidean-Ray $R_m = (s, m_1, \ldots, m_g)$, $g \leq k$, with respect to its cone sequence $C_m = (C_1^m, \ldots, C_g^m)$. The function $Create\text{-}Euclidean\text{-}Ray$ helps find R_m, along with trimming the segments in E as needed, to guarantee that for every $i \in \{1, \ldots, g-1\}$, the segment e_{i+1}, after being trimmed, will intersect the cone C_i^m at only one point. We will present this trimming process later. After creating R_m, as presented above, we can totally determine on every segment e_i, $i \in \{1, \ldots, g\}$, which sub-segment, (m_i, p_i) or (m_i, q_i), that R_r crosses. Then, all the remaining unnecessary sub-segments of e_1 to e_g that R_r does not cross will be deleted. The function $Find\text{-}Approximate\text{-}Path$ iterates through this process until t is on C_k^m, or all segments $e_i = (p_i, q_i)$ in E are trimmed such that $d(p_i, q_i) \leq \delta$.

Find-Approximate-Path:
Input: $E = (e_1, \ldots, e_k)$, s and t
Output: An approximate shortest path $P(s,t)$, from s to t crossing E

1. Initialize: $P(s,t) = (\ )$, $root = s$, $l = 1$.
2. Let m_l be the middle point of $e_l = (p_l, q_l)$. If $d(p_l, q_l) \leq \delta$, go to Step 4. Otherwise, go to Step 3.
3. Set $R_m = (root, m_l)$ and $C_m = (\ )$. Run the function $Create\text{-}Euclidean\text{-}Ray(E, R_m, C_m)$ to get $R_m = (root, m_l, \ldots, m_g)$ and $C_m = (C_l^m, \ldots, C_g^m)$ (Note that, some segments in E can be trimmed in the function $Create\text{-}Euclidean\text{-}Ray$).
   3.1 If $g = k$ and t is on C_g^m, return $P(s,t) \circ R_m \circ (t)$.
   3.2 Otherwise, if $g = k$ and t is inside or outside C_g^m, or $g < k$, run the function $Trim\text{-}Segments(E, R_m, C_m, l, g, t)$ to delete all the unnecessary sub-segments of e_l to e_g that R_r does not cross. Go to Step 2.
4. $P(s,t) = P(s,t) \circ (root)$.
   4.1 If $l = k$, return $P(s,t) = P(s,t) \circ (m_l, t)$.
   4.2 Otherwise, if $l < k$, $root = m_l$, $l = l+1$, go to Step 2.

Trim-Segments:
Input: $E = (e_1, \ldots, e_k)$, $R_a = (root, a_l, \ldots, a_g)$, $C_a = (C_l^a, \ldots, C_g^a)$, l, g, t
Output: The segments from e_l to e_g in E will be trimmed such that for every segment $e_i = (p_i, q_i)$, $i \in \{l, \ldots, g\}$, only the sub-segment (a_i, p_i) or (a_i, q_i) that R_r crosses will be kept.

1. Initialize: $i = g$. If $g = k$, $e_{g+1} = (t, t)$.
2. If e_{i+1} is outside C_i^a, $e_i = (a_i, q_i)$, where (a_i, q_i) is outside C_i^a.
3. Otherwise, if e_{i+1} is inside C_i^a, $e_i = (a_i, p_i)$, where (a_i, p_i) is inside C_i^a.
4. $i = i - 1$. If $i = l - 1$, return. Otherwise, go to Step 2.

In the function $Find\text{-}Approximate\text{-}Path$, we use two variables l and $root$ such that when $l = 1$, $root = s$. Then, when $l \geq 2$ and $d(p_{l-1}, q_{l-1}) \leq \delta$, $root$ will be

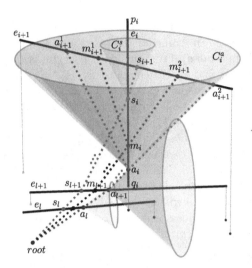

Fig. 6. Illustration of the Division-Ray between e_i and e_{i+1}.

the middle point of $e_{l-1} = (p_{l-1}, q_{l-1})$. Let $R_a = (root, a_l, \ldots, a_y)$, $l \le y < k$, with respect to the cone sequence $C_a = (C_l^a, \ldots, C_y^a)$, be an existing Euclidean-Ray from $root$, starting at a_l on e_l to a_y on e_y. The function $Create\text{-}Euclidean\text{-}Ray(E, R_a, C_a)$ will receive R_a and C_a, then continue constructing R_a, from a_y on e_y, to a_g on e_g, $g \le k$, to output $R_a = (root, a_l, \ldots, a_y, \ldots, a_g)$, with respect to $C_a = (C_l^a, \ldots, C_y^a, \ldots, C_g^a)$, where $g \le k$. In the function $Create\text{-}Euclidean\text{-}Ray$, we also solve the special case that a segment e_{i+1} in E, $i \in \{1, \ldots, g-1\}$, intersects C_i^a at two points, named a_{i+1}^1 and a_{i+1}^2 (see Fig. 6), as follows.

We see that, from a_i, if we create two Euclidean-Rays following both a_{i+1}^1 and a_{i+1}^2, and continue the calculations by this way for all of the next segments, it will cause the number of the Euclidean-Rays to increase exponentially. However, observe that, there exists a Euclidean-Ray $R_s = (root, s_l, \ldots, s_i, s_{i+1}, \ldots, s_j)$, $j \le k$, with respect to $C_s = (C_l^s, \ldots, C_i^s, C_{i+1}^s, \ldots, C_j^s)$, such that e_{i+1} intersects C_i^s at only one point s_{i+1} on (a_{i+1}^1, a_{i+1}^2), or e_{i+1} is a tangent to C_i^s (see Fig. 6). Thus, we first find the Euclidean-Ray R_s, then use the function $Trim\text{-}Segments$ to delete all the unnecessary sub-segments in E that R_r does not cross based on R_s. As presented above, after this trimming, the segment $e_{i+1} = (p_{i+1}, q_{i+1})$ will remains either (s_{i+1}, p_{i+1}) or (s_{i+1}, q_{i+1}). Thus, e_{i+1} will intersect C_i^a at only on point, which is either a_{i+1}^1 or a_{i+1}^2.

We call a part of the Euclidean-Ray R_s, from $root$ to s_{i+1}, $DR_s(e_i, e_{i+1}) = (root, s_l, \ldots, s_i, s_{i+1})$, with its cone sequence $DC_s(e_i, e_{i+1}) = (C_l^s, \ldots, C_i^s, C_{i+1}^s)$, as *Division-Ray* between e_i and e_{i+1}. The Division-Ray $DR_s(e_i, e_{i+1})$ between two consecutive segments e_i and e_{i+1} helps divide $e_{i+1} = (p_{i+1}, q_{i+1})$ into two sub-segments (s_{i+1}, p_{i+1}) and (s_{i+1}, q_{i+1}) such that one sub-segment will be kept and the remaining one will be deleted. We note that, in the function $Create\text{-}Euclidean\text{-}Ray$ below, we use a global array A to store all Division-Rays between two consecutive segments in E when they are found. The reason for using this array will be explained later.

Create-Euclidean-Ray:

Input: $E = (e_1, \ldots, e_k)$, $R_a = (root = a_{l-1}, a_l, \ldots, a_y)$, $C_a = (C_l^a, \ldots, C_y^a)$

Output: $R_a = (root, a_l, \ldots, a_y, \ldots, a_g)$, $C_a = (C_l^a, \ldots, C_y^a, \ldots, C_g^a)$

1. Initialize: $i = y$, $a_i = a_y$
   1.1 If $C_a = (\ )$, let C_i^a be the cone created by $root$ and a_i, based on the
   • Cone-Create-Rule. $C_a = (C_i^a)$.
   1.2 Otherwise, if $C_a \neq (\ )$, $C_i^a = C_y^a$.
2. If $i = k$, return R_a and C_a.
3. Otherwise, if $i < k$,
   3.1 If e_{i+1} intersects C_i^a at one point a_{i+1}, create the cone C_{i+1}^a by C_i^a, based on the Cone-Create-Rule. $R_a = R_a \circ (a_{i+1})$, $C_a = C_a \circ (C_{i+1}^a)$, $i = i + 1$, go to Step 2.
   3.2 If e_{i+1} does not intersect C_i^a, return R_a and C_a.
   3.3 If e_{i+1} intersects C_i^a at two points a_{i+1}^1 and a_{i+1}^2 (see Fig. 6),
      – If the global array A contains the Division-Ray $DR_s(e_i, e_{i+1}) = (root, s_l, \ldots, s_i, s_{i+1})$, with respect to $DC_s(e_i, e_{i+1})$, between e_i and e_{i+1}, get $DR_s(e_i, e_{i+1})$ from A.
      Otherwise, if $DR_s(e_i, e_{i+1})$ does not exist in A, run the function *Find-Division-Ray(E', R_a, C_a, a_{i+1}^1, a_{i+1}^2)* to find $DR_s(e_i, e_{i+1})$, where $E' = (e_l, \ldots, e_{i+1})$ is a copy of the segments from e_l to e_{i+1} in E. Then, store $DR_s(e_i, e_{i+1})$ into A.
      – Set $R_s = DR_s(e_i, e_{i+1})$ and $C_s = DC_s(e_i, e_{i+1})$.
      – Run the function *Create-Euclidean-Ray(E, R_s, C_s)* to continue calculating the Euclidean-Ray R_s from e_{i+1} to have
      $R_s = (root, s_l, \ldots, s_i, s_{i+1}, \ldots, s_j)$, $i + 1 \leq j \leq k$, with respect to $C_s = (C_l^s, \ldots, C_i^s, C_{i+1}^s, \ldots, C_j^s)$.
      – Run the function *Trim-Segments(E, R_s, C_s, l, j, t)* (In this function, $e_{i+1} = (p_{i+1}, q_{i+1})$ will be trimmed, which remains either (s_{i+1}, p_{i+1}) or (s_{i+1}, q_{i+1})).
      – Let a_{i+1}' be the point that e_{i+1}, after being trimmed, intersects C_i^a. Now, a_{i+1}' is coincide with either a_{i+1}^1 or a_{i+1}^2. Create the cone C_{i+1}^a by C_i^a, based on the Cone-Create-Rule, at the intersection point a_{i+1}'. $R_a = R_a \circ (a_{i+1}')$, $C_a = C_a \circ (C_{i+1}^a)$, $i = i + 1$, go to Step 2.

We use the function *Find-Division-Ray* to find the Division-Ray $DR_s(e_i, e_{i+1})$ between e_i and e_{i+1}. The idea of this function is also similar to the idea of the function *Find-Approximate-Path*. First, we trim e_{i+1} to be (a_{i+1}^1, a_{i+1}^2). Then, based on the input Euclidean-Ray R_a, we can determine which sub-segments from e_l to e_i that $DR_s(e_i, e_{i+1})$ crosses to intersect (a_{i+1}^1, a_{i+1}^2), then using the function *Trim-Segments* to delete all the unnecessary sub-segments from e_l to e_i that $DR_s(e_i, e_{i+1})$ does not cross. After that, similar to the function *Find-Approximate-Path*, we create the Euclidean-Ray R_m from $root$, starting at the middle point m_l of e_l to e_i. When R_m can come to e_i

at m_i and create the cone C_i^m, one of the following three conditions holds: (i) e_{i+1} intersects C_i^m at two points, named m_{i+1}^1 and m_{i+1}^2, or (ii) e_{i+1} intersects C_i^m at only one point m_{i+1}, or (iii) e_{i+1} does not intersect C_i^m. For (i), e_{i+1} will only need to keep the sub-segment (m_{i+1}^1, m_{i+1}^2). Then, we use the function *Trim-Segments* to delete all the unnecessary sub-segments from e_l to e_i that $DR_s(e_i, e_{i+1})$ does not cross, based on R_m. For (ii), R_m is the Division-Ray that we need to find. For (iii), since the cone C_i^s at e_i of $DR_s(e_i, e_{i+1})$ must cross e_i, then s_i must be on (m_i, q_i), where (m_i, q_i) is outside the cone C_i^m. Thus, e_i only needs to keep the sub-segment (m_i, q_i). Then, we use the function *Trim-Segments* to delete all the unnecessary sub-segments from e_l to e_{i-1}, based on R_m. The function *Find-Division-Ray* below iterates through this process until e_{i+1} intersects C_i^m at only one point, or all the segments $e_j = (p_j, q_j)$ from e_l to e_i are trimmed until $d(p_j, q_j) \leq \delta$.

An important note is that trimming segments from e_l to e_{i+1} in the function *Find-Division-Ray* is just to supply finding $DR_s(e_i, e_{i+1})$, which should not affect the process of finding R_r. Thus, in the function *Create-Euclidean-Ray*, we use a copy of the segments in E, named E', to put into the function *Find-Division-Ray*. This is to notice that E will not be affected when E' is trimmed in the function *Find-Division-Ray*.

Find-Division-Ray:
Input: $E = (e_l, \ldots, e_i, e_{i+1})$, $R_a = (root, a_l, \ldots, a_i)$, $C_a = (C_l^a, \ldots, C_i^a)$, a_{i+1}^1, a_{i+1}^2 (where e_{i+1} intersects C_i^a at a_{i+1}^1 and a_{i+1}^2)
Output: $DR_s(e_i, e_{i+1}) = (root, s_l, \ldots, s_i, s_{i+1})$, with respect to $DC_s(e_i, e_{i+1}) = (C_l^s, \ldots, C_i^s, C_{i+1}^s)$ (where e_{i+1} intersects C_i^s at only one point s_{i+1}).

1. Initialize: $DR_s(e_i, e_{i+1}) = (\ )$, $DC_s(e_i, e_{i+1}) = (\ )$, $e_{i+1} = (a_{i+1}^1, a_{i+1}^2)$, $f = l$, $rootS = root$, run the function *Trim-Segments*$(E, R_a, C_a, l, i, null)$.
2. Let m_f be the middle point of $e_f = (p_f, q_f)$. If $d(p_f, q_f) \leq \delta$, go to Step 4. Otherwise, go to Step 3.
3. Set $R_m = (rootS, m_f)$, $C_m = (\ )$. Run the function *Create-Euclidean-Ray*$(E - \{e_{i+1}\}, R_m, C_m)$ to get $R_m = (rootS, m_f, \ldots, m_g)$ and $C_m = (C_f^m, \ldots, C_g^m)$, where $E - \{e_{i+1}\}$ is the segment sequence E without e_{i+1}.
   3.1 If $g = i$,
      – If e_{i+1} intersects C_i^m at two points m_{i+1}^1 and m_{i+1}^2, $e_{i+1} = (m_{i+1}^1, m_{i+1}^2)$, *Trim-Segments*$(E, R_m, C_m, f, i, null)$. Go to Step 2.
      – If e_{i+1} intersects C_i^m at one point m_{i+1}, $DR_s(e_i, e_{i+1}) = DR_s(e_i, e_{i+1}) \circ R_m \circ (m_{i+1})$, $DC_s(e_i, e_{i+1}) = DC_s(e_i, e_{i+1}) \circ C_m \circ (C_{i+1}^m)$, where C_{i+1}^m is the cone created at m_{i+1} by C_i^m, based on the Cone-Create-Rule. Return $DR_s(e_i, e_{i+1})$ and $DC_s(e_i, e_{i+1})$.
      – Otherwise, if e_{i+1} does not intersects C_i^m, $e_i = (m_i, q_i)$, where (m_i, q_i) is outside C_i^m, *Trim-Segments*$(E, R_m, C_m, f, i-1, null)$. Go to Step 2.
   3.2 Otherwise, if $g < i$, *Trim-Segments*$(E, R_m, C_m, f, g, null)$. Go to Step 2.
4. $DR_s(e_i, e_{i+1}) = DR_s(e_i, e_{i+1}) \circ (rootS)$, $DC_s(e_i, e_{i+1}) = DC_s(e_i, e_{i+1}) \circ (C_f^m)$, where C_f^m is the cone created on e_f by $rootS$ and m_f, based on the Cone-Create-Rule.

4.1 If $f = i$, $DR_s(e_i, e_{i+1}) = DR_s(e_i, e_{i+1}) \circ (m_i, m_{i+1})$, where m_{i+1} is the middle point of (m_{i+1}^1, m_{i+1}^2), and $DC_s(e_i, e_{i+1}) = DC_s(e_i, e_{i+1}) \circ (C_{i+1}^m)$, where C_{i+1}^m is the cone created at m_{i+1} by C_i^m, based on the Cone-Create-Rule. Return $DR_s(e_i, e_{i+1})$ and $DC_s(e_i, e_{i+1})$.

4.2 Otherwise, if $f < i$, $rootS = m_f$, $f = f + 1$, go to Step 2.

We first note that, $DR_s(e_i, e_{i+1}) = (root, s_l, \ldots, s_i, s_{i+1})$, which is found by the function *Find-Division-Ray* is a $(1 + \epsilon)$-approximation Division-Ray (proved later), not the exact one. Suppose that $root = s$. The function *Find-Division-Ray* found $DR_s(e_i, e_{i+1}) = (s, s_1, \ldots, s_{l-1}, s_l, \ldots, s_i, s_{i+1})$. Let $DR_s^*(e_i, e_{i+1}) = (s, s_1^*, \ldots, s_{l-1}^*, s_l^*, \ldots, s_i^*, s_{i+1}^*)$ be the exact Division-Ray between e_i and e_{i+1}. For every $j \in \{1, \ldots, i+1\}$, $d(s_j, s_j^*) \le \delta$.

Another note is that, suppose that when the function *Create-Euclidean-Ray* calls the function *Find-Division-Ray*, the approximate path $P(s, t)$ has been found a part $(s, \sigma_1, \ldots, \sigma_{l-1} = root)$. The function *Find-Division-Ray* then only finds the Division-Ray between e_i and e_{i+1} from $root$. Observe that if the Division-Ray between e_i and e_{i+1} is found from s, we also have $s_j = \sigma_j$, for every $j \in \{1, \ldots, l-1\}$. Thus, to be simple, we only need to keep $DR_s(e_i, e_{i+1})$ from $root$.

Next, we prove in Proposition 2 that, $DR_s^*(e_i, e_{i+1})$ is unique. Thus, when $DR_s(e_i, e_{i+1})$ is found and $e_{i+1} = (p_{i+1}, q_{i+1})$ is trimmed to remain either (s_{i+1}, p_{i+1}) or (s_{i+1}, q_{i+1}), any Euclidean-Ray R_m that is created after that will have the cone C_i^m on e_i intersecting e_{i+1} at only one point.

We also see that, due to the recursion used in the function *Create-Euclidean-Ray*, finding a Division-Ray $DR(e_i, e_{i+1})$ between any two consecutive segments e_i and e_{i+1}, $i \in \{1, \ldots, k-1\}$, can be repeated many times. This might cause an exponential running time in the worst case. As deduced from Proposition 2 that if the Division-Ray $DR(e_i, e_{i+1})$ between two consecutive segments e_i and e_{i+1} exists, it is unique, we use a global array A to store all of the Division-Rays between two consecutive segments that appear in the calculation to avoid finding any Division-Ray for the second time.

Proposition 2. *Let $DR_s^*(e_i, e_{i+1}) = (s, s_1^*, \ldots, s_i^*, s_{i+1}^*)$ be the exact Division-Ray between two consecutive segments e_i and e_{i+1} in E. For every $i \in \{1, \ldots, k-1\}$, if $DR_s^*(e_i, e_{i+1})$ exists, it is unique.*

Proof. Let R_a be a Euclidean-Ray from s crossing E by starting at a point a_1 on e_1 such that e_{i+1} intersects the cone C_i^a of R_a at two points a_{i+1}^1 and a_{i+1}^2. Suppose that the axis ray of C_i^a is $\overrightarrow{a_i p_i}$ (see Fig. 7a). Let R_b be a Euclidean-Ray from s crossing E by starting at a point b_1 on e_1 such that $a_1 \ne b_1$ and R_b intersects e_i at b_i on (a_i, q_i). We first prove the fact that, for any b_i on (a_i, q_i), if e_{i+1} intersects the cone C_i^b of R_b at two points, named b_{i+1}^1 and b_{i+1}^2, then the segment (b_{i+1}^1, b_{i+1}^2) always contains the segment (a_{i+1}^1, a_{i+1}^2) (see Figure 7a). If this fact is correct, then $DR_s(e_i, e_{i+1})$ is unique.

To see that the fact is correct, by contradiction, we suppose that there exists a place on (a_i, q_i) for b_i such that e_{i+1} intersects the cone C_i^b of R_b at b_{i+1}^1 and b_{i+1}^2, but (b_{i+1}^1, b_{i+1}^2) does not contain (a_{i+1}^1, a_{i+1}^2) (see Fig. 7b). We next prove

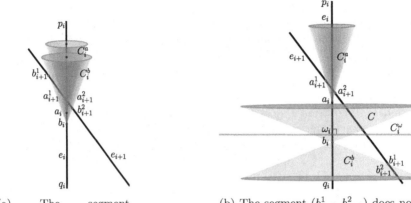

(a) The segment (b^1_{i+1}, b^2_{i+1}) contains the segment (a^1_{i+1}, a^2_{i+1}).

(b) The segment (b^1_{i+1}, b^2_{i+1}) does not contain the segment (a^1_{i+1}, a^2_{i+1}). This case cannot happen.

Fig. 7. Segment e_{i+1} intersects C^a_i at a^1_{i+1} and a^2_{i+1}, and intersects C^b_i at b^1_{i+1} and b^2_{i+1}.

that this case cannot exist. Let R_ω be a Euclidean-Ray from s that intersects e_i at ω_i such that the cone C^ω_i created at ω_i has the acute cone angle $90°$. One of the following two conditions holds: (i) b_i is on (a_i, ω_i), or (ii) b_i is on (ω_i, q_i). First, for (i), if b_i is on (a_i, ω_i), as presented previously, C^b_i will have the same axis ray $\overrightarrow{a_i p_i}$ with C^a_i and the acute cone angle of C^b_i will be larger than the acute cone angle of C^a_i. Thus, if e_{i+1} intersects C^b_i at two points b^1_{i+1} and b^2_{i+1}, the segment (b^1_{i+1}, b^2_{i+1}) always contains the segment (a^1_{i+1}, a^2_{i+1}). Next, for (ii), suppose that b_i is on (ω_i, q_i) and e_{i+1} intersects C^b_i at two points b^1_{i+1} and b^2_{i+1}. Because b_i is on (ω_i, q_i), C^b_i must have the axis ray being $\overrightarrow{b_i q_i}$. Let C be a cone created at b_i such that C is opposite to C^b_i with the axis ray being $\overrightarrow{b_i p_i}$ and the acute cone angle being equal to the acute cone angle of C^b_i. Because e_{i+1} intersects C^a_i and C^b_i each at two points, e_{i+1} must intersect C. Thus, e_{i+1} intersects C^b_i at two points and C at one point at least. This case cannot happen because a line can only intersect two opposite but equal cones at two points at most.   □

Let $P(s,t) = (s = \sigma_1, \sigma_1, \ldots, \sigma_k, \sigma_{k+1} = t)$ be the approximate shortest path between s and t crossing E that is found by the function *Find-Approximate-Path*, where every σ_i, $i \in \{1, \ldots, k\}$, is a point on e_i in E. With $P^*(s,t) = (s = r_0, r_1, \ldots, r_k, r_{k+1} = t)$ being the exact shortest path between s and t crossing E, for every $i \in \{1, \ldots, k\}$, we have $d(r_i, \sigma_i) \le \delta$.

Lemma 1. *Let $\epsilon \in (0,1)$ be an error tolerance and $\delta = \frac{h\epsilon}{6k}$, where h is the minimum distance between two consecutive segments in E. The Euclidean length of $P(s,t)$ found by the function Find-Approximate-Path is at most $(1 + \epsilon)$ times the Euclidean length of $P^*(s,t)$.*

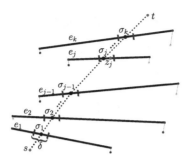

Fig. 8. An approximate path $P(s,t)$ from the function *Find-Approximate-Path*.

Proof. We need to prove $d(P(s,t)) \leq (1+\epsilon)d(P^*(s,t))$. The following proof is deduced from the proof of Lemma 8.1 in [5]. First, we prove, by induction, that (1) holds for every $i \in \{0, \ldots, k\}$.

$$d\left(P\left(\sigma_i, t\right)\right) \leq \left(1 + \frac{\epsilon}{2}\right) d\left(P^*\left(\sigma_i, t\right)\right) + 3\left(k - i\right)\delta \tag{1}$$

When $i = k$, (1) becomes $d\left(P\left(\sigma_k, t\right)\right) \leq \left(1 + \frac{\epsilon}{2}\right) d\left(P^*\left(\sigma_k, t\right)\right)$. We have $P(\sigma_k, t) = P^*(\sigma_k, t) = (\sigma_k, t)$ (see Fig. 8). Thus, (1) holds for $i = k$. Assume that (1) holds for $i = j$, we have,

$$d\left(P\left(\sigma_j, t\right)\right) \leq \left(1 + \frac{\epsilon}{2}\right) d\left(P^*\left(\sigma_j, t\right)\right) + 3\left(k - j\right)\delta \tag{2}$$

We need to prove that (1) also holds for $i = j - 1$, which is

$$d\left(P\left(\sigma_{j-1}, t\right)\right) \leq \left(1 + \frac{\epsilon}{2}\right) d\left(P^*\left(\sigma_{j-1}, t\right)\right) + 3\left(k - j + 1\right)\delta \tag{3}$$

Then based on (2), we have,

$$\begin{aligned}
d\left(P\left(\sigma_{j-1}, t\right)\right) &= d\left(\sigma_{j-1}, \sigma_j\right) + d\left(P\left(\sigma_j, t\right)\right) \\
&\leq d\left(\sigma_{j-1}, \sigma_j\right) + \left(1 + \frac{\epsilon}{2}\right) d\left(P^*\left(\sigma_j, t\right)\right) + 3\left(k - j\right)\delta
\end{aligned} \tag{4}$$

Suppose that $P^*(\sigma_{j-1}, t)$, which is the exact shortest path from σ_{j-1} to t, crosses e_j at z_j. We have,

$$d(P^*(\sigma_j, t)) \leq d(\sigma_j, z_j) + d(P^*(z_j, t)) \tag{5}$$

From (4) and (5), we have,

$$\begin{aligned}
d(P(\sigma_{j-1}, t)) &\leq d(\sigma_{j-1}, \sigma_j) + \left(1 + \frac{\epsilon}{2}\right)(d(\sigma_j, z_j) + d(P^*(z_j, t))) + 3(k - j)\delta \\
&= \underbrace{d(\sigma_{j-1}, \sigma_j) + \left(1 + \frac{\epsilon}{2}\right) d(\sigma_j, z_j) + 3(k - j)\delta}_{B} + \left(1 + \frac{\epsilon}{2}\right) d(P^*(z_j, t))
\end{aligned}$$

$$\tag{6}$$

In the triangle created by σ_{j-1}, σ_j, z_j, we have, $d(\sigma_{j-1}, \sigma_j) \leq d(\sigma_j, z_j) + d(\sigma_{j-1}, z_j)$. Thus, the part B of (6) becomes

$$B \leq d(\sigma_j, z_j) + d(\sigma_{j-1}, z_j) + \left(1 + \frac{\epsilon}{2}\right) d(\sigma_j, z_j) + 3(k - j)\delta$$
$$= d(\sigma_{j-1}, z_j) + \left(2 + \frac{\epsilon}{2}\right) d(\sigma_j, z_j) + 3(k - j)\delta \tag{7}$$

Because $d(\sigma_j, z_j) \leq \delta$, we have $\left(2 + \frac{\epsilon}{2}\right) d(\sigma_j, z_j) < 3d(\sigma_j, z_j) \leq 3\delta$. Thus, (7) becomes

$$B \leq d(\sigma_{j-1}, z_j) + 3(k - j + 1)\delta \tag{8}$$

From (6) and (8), we have,

$$d(P(\sigma_{j-1}, t)) \leq d(\sigma_{j-1}, z_j) + 3(k - j + 1)\delta + \left(1 + \frac{\epsilon}{2}\right) d(P^*(z_j, t))$$
$$\leq \left(1 + \frac{\epsilon}{2}\right) (d(\sigma_{j-1}, z_j) + d(P^*(z_j, t))) + 3(k - j + 1)\delta \tag{9}$$
$$= \left(1 + \frac{\epsilon}{2}\right) d(P^*(\sigma_{j-1}, t)) + 3(k - j + 1)\delta$$

Thus, (3) is correct, which means that (1) holds for every $i \in \{0, \ldots, k\}$. Now, with $i = 0$, (1) becomes

$$d(P(\sigma_0, t)) \leq \left(1 + \frac{\epsilon}{2}\right) d(P^*(\sigma_0, t)) + 3k\delta$$
$$d(P(s, t)) \leq \left(1 + \frac{\epsilon}{2}\right) d(P^*(s, t)) + \frac{h\epsilon}{2}, \text{ because } \delta = \frac{h\epsilon}{6k} \tag{10}$$

Since $h \leq d(P^*(s, t))$, (10) becomes

$$d(P(s, t)) \leq \left(1 + \frac{\epsilon}{2}\right) d(P^*(s, t)) + \frac{\epsilon}{2} d(P^*(s, t))$$
$$= (1 + \epsilon) d(P^*(s, t)) \tag{11}$$

□

Lemma 2. *The function Find-Approximate-Path runs in $O(k^3 \log(\frac{kL}{h\epsilon}))$ time, where L is the maximum Euclidean length of the segments in E and h is the minimum distance between two consecutive segments in E.*

Proof. We first consider the case that in the function *Create-Euclidean-Ray*, when creating any Euclidean-Ray, finding Division-Rays is not required. The case that finding Division-Rays is required will be considered later. Initially, the function *Find-Approximate-Path* sets $l = 1$ and $root = s$. Then a Euclidean-Ray R_m from $root$, starting at m_l on e_l is created. Based on R_m, the segments in E are trimmed by the function *Trim-Segments*. After every trimming, the length of e_l is reduced by a half. Thus, to make the length of e_l less than or equal to δ, we need to create $O(\log \frac{L}{\delta})$ Euclidean-Rays. Since E has k segments, in the worst case, we need to create $O(k \log(\frac{L}{\delta}))$ Euclidean-Rays along with trimming.

Creating a Euclidean-Ray and then trimming the segments in E based on the Euclidean-Ray take $O(k)$ time. Thus, the total running time, in the worst case, of the function *Find-Approximate-Path* when finding Division-Rays is not required is $O(k^2 \log(\frac{L}{\delta}))$.

The idea of the function *Find-Division-Ray* is similar to the idea of the function *Find-Approximate-Path*. Thus, the running time of the function *Find-Division-Ray* when finding the Division-Ray between two consecutive segments e_i and e_{i+1}, $i \in \{1, \ldots, k-1\}$, in the case that no other Division-Ray between e_j and e_{j+1}, $j < i$, is required, is $O(i^2 \log(\frac{L}{\delta}))$.

We now consider the case that in the function *Create-Euclidean-Ray*, when creating a Euclidean-Ray, finding Division-Rays is required. Let $TER(l)$ be the running time of creating a Euclidean-Ray R_m from *root*, crossing the segments from e_l. Let $TDR(i, i+1)$ be the running time of finding the Division-Ray $DR_s(e_i, e_{i+1})$ between two consecutive segments e_i and e_{i+1} in E, which is run by the function *Find-Division-Ray*. As we mentioned above, $TER(l) = O(k)$ when finding the Division-Ray between any two consecutive segments in E is not required. However, if a $DR_s(e_i, e_{i+1})$ is required, we have $TER(l) = O(k) + TDR(i, i+1) + TER(i+1)^* + O(k) + TER(i+1)$, which is explained as follows. The Euclidean-Ray R_m is created from e_l to e_i, taking $O(k)$ time in the worst case, then will be stopped to wait for finding the Division-Ray $DR_s(e_i, e_{i+1})$. Finding $DR_s(e_i, e_{i+1})$ takes $TDR(i, i+1)$ time. If $DR_s(e_i, e_{i+1})$ is calculated previously and stored in the global array A, $TDR(i, i+1) = O(1)$. Then, continuing finding the Euclidean-Ray R_s for $DR_s(e_i, e_{i+1})$ takes $TER(i+1)^*$ time. Trimming the segments in E based on R_s takes $O(k)$ time, in the worst case. After this trimming, R_m, which is stopped at e_i, now can continue being calculated, takes $TER(i+1)$ time. We use $TER(i+1)^*$ and $TER(i+1)$ just to distinguish between the running times of creating Euclidean-Rays from e_{i+1} for R_s, and from e_{i+1} for R_m, respectively. Observe that, finding another Division-Ray $DR_s(e_j, e_{j+1})$, $i \neq j$, can be required in the processes of $TDR(i, i+1)$, or $TER(i+1)^*$ of R_s, or $TER(i+1)$ of R_m. Thus, we consider the worst case that all the Division-Rays between every two consecutive segments, from $DR_s(e_1, e_2)$ to $DR_s(e_{k-1}, e_k)$, are required. Let f be the number of the Euclidean-Rays that related to the appearance of $DR_s(e_1, e_2)$ to $DR_s(e_{k-1}, e_k)$. We have $f \leq k-1$. Let T_f be the running time for calculating these f Euclidean-Rays. We have $T_f = O(fk) + TDR(e_1, e_2) + \cdots + TDR(e_{k-1}, e_k)$. Every $TDR(e_i, e_{i+1})$, $i \in \{1, \ldots, k-1\}$, in T_f, at this time, is the running time of the function *Find-Division-Ray*, where no other Division-Ray $DR_s(e_j, e_{j+1})$, $j < i$, is required to find. As presented above, in this case, $TDR(e_i, e_{i+1}) = O(i^2 \log(\frac{L}{\delta}))$. Therefore, $T_f = O(fk + (1^2 + 2^2 + \cdots + (k-1)^2) \log(\frac{L}{\delta})) = O(fk + \frac{(k-1)k(2k-1)}{6} \log(\frac{L}{\delta})) = O(k^3 \log(\frac{L}{\delta}))$.

Also as presented above, the function *Find-Approximate-Path* needs to create total $O(k \log(\frac{L}{\delta}))$ Euclidean-Rays, where the segments in E will be trimmed right after every of these Euclidean-Rays is created. Thus, excluding the f Euclidean-Rays that take T_f time above, the function *Find-Approximate-Path* needs $O(k \log(\frac{L}{\delta}) - f)$ Euclidean-Rays where finding any Division-Ray is not required, or it can be required, but it is stored in the global array A already. Let T_r be the running time for creating these $O(k \log(\frac{L}{\delta}) - f)$ Euclidean-Rays. We have, $T_r = O(k(k \log(\frac{L}{\delta}) - f)) = O(k^2 \log(\frac{L}{\delta}))$. Let T_t be the total time of trimming the segments in E after every Euclidean-Ray is created. We have $T_t = O(k^2 log(\frac{L}{\delta}))$. In total, the function *Find-Approximate-Path* takes $T_f + T_r + T_t = O(k^3 \log(\frac{L}{\delta})) = O(k^3 \log(\frac{kL}{h\epsilon}))$, where $\delta = \frac{h\epsilon}{6k}$.   □

4   Conclusion

We have presented a $(1 + \epsilon)$-approximation algorithm, running in $O(k^3 \log(\frac{kL}{h\epsilon}))$ time for the ESP-3D-3S problem. We first propose in Proposition 1 that two Euclidean-Rays cannot intersect with each other. Based on this geometrical characteristic, the algorithm is created. The most difficult problem that we need to process in the algorithm is that, in some cases, a segment e_{i+1} can intersect a cone C_i^a at two points, which can lead the number of the possible optimal paths to increase exponentially. We then use the idea of the Division-Rays to deal with this difficulty. For future work, we will measure the running times of the algorithm by using practical experiments.

References

1. Canny, J., Reif, J.: New lower bound techniques for robot motion planning problems. In: 28th Annual Symposium on Foundations of Computer Science, pp. 49–60 (1987)
2. Akman, V.: Solution of the general instance of FINDPATH. In: Akman, V. (ed.) Unobstructed Shortest Paths in Polyhedral Environments. LNCS, vol. 251, pp. 19–33. Springer, Heidelberg (1987). https://doi.org/10.1007/3-540-17629-2_8
3. Bajaj, C., Moh, T.T.: Generalized unfoldings for shortest paths. Int. J. Robot. Res. **7**(1), 71–76 (1988)
4. Trang, L.H., Truong, Q.C., Dang, T.K.: An iterative algorithm for computing shortest paths through line segments in 3D. In: Dang, T.K., Wagner, R., Küng, J., Thoai, N., Takizawa, M., Neuhold, E.J. (eds.) FDSE 2017. LNCS, vol. 10646, pp. 73–84. Springer, Cham (2017). https://doi.org/10.1007/978-3-319-70004-5_5
5. Mitchell, J.S.B., Papadimitriou, C.H.: The weighted region problem: finding shortest paths through a weighted planar subdivision. J. ACM **38**(1), 18–73 (1991)
6. Polishchuk, V., Mitchell, J.S.: Touring convex bodies - a conic programming solution. In: Canadian Conference on Computational Geometry, pp. 290–293 (2005)
7. Aleksandrov, L., Maheshwari, A., Sack, J.R.: Approximation algorithms for geometric shortest path problems. In: Proceedings of the Thirty-Second Annual ACM Symposium on Theory of Computing, pp. 286–295 (2000)
8. Mitchell, J.S.B.: Chapter 31: shortest paths and network. In: Toth, C.D., O'Rourke, J., Goodman, J.E. (eds.) Handbook of Discrete and Computational Geometry. Chapman and Hall/CRC (2017)
9. Bose, P., Maheshwari, A., Shu, C., Wuhrer, S.: A survey of geodesic paths on 3D surfaces. Comput. Geom. **44**(9), 486–498 (2011)
10. Burago, D., Grigoriev, D., Slissenko, A.: Approximating shortest path for the skew lines problem in time doubly logarithmic in 1/epsilon. Theoret. Comput. Sci. **315**(2–3), 371–404 (2004)

A Lane Line Detection Algorithm Based on Convolutional Neural Network

Ling Ding[1,3], Zhuoran Xu[2], JiaFei Zong[1], Jinshen Xiao[3], Chen Shu[3], and Bin Xu[1(✉)]

[1] School of Computer Science and Technology, Hubei University of Science and Technology, Xianning 437100, China
jwcxb@hbust.edu.cn
[2] School of Educational Information Technology, Central China Normal University, Wuhan 430072, China
[3] School of Electronic Information, Wuhan University, Wuhan 430072, China

Abstract. This paper presents an algorithm for lane line detection based on convolutional neural network. The algorithm adopts the structural mode of encoder and decoder, in which the encoder part uses VGG16 combined with cavity convolution as the basic network to extract the features of lane lines, and the cavity convolution can expand the receptive field. Through experimental comparison, the full connection layer of the network is discarded, the last maximum pooling layer of the VGG16 network is removed, and the processing of the last three convolutional layers is replaced by empty convolution, which can better balance the detection rate and accuracy. The decoder part USES the index function of the maximum pooling layer to carry out up-sampling of the encoder in an anti-pooling way to achieve semantic segmentation, and combines with the instance segmentation, and finally realizes the detection of lane lines through fitting. The test results show that the algorithm has a good balance in speed and accuracy and good robustness.

Keywords: Convolutional neural network · The lane line · Detection · Dotted line · The solid line

1 Introduction

With regard to lane line detection, the traditional detection methods mainly use image processing technology to carry out edge detection, threshold processing and curve fitting of road images. The main steps are to preprocess the image first, select the Region of Interest (ROI), and detect its edges. After Hough Transformation, threshold processing is carried out, and then straight line or curve fitting is performed on the result. Common fitting methods mainly include least square method, polynomial fitting and Random Sample Consensus (RANSAC) algorithm.

Traditional lane line detection methods [1] rely on highly specialized, hand-made features and heuristic constraints, and usually require optimization of various post-processing techniques, which are extremely unstable due to changes in road scenes. In recent years, deep learning has developed rapidly in the field of computer vision. With the improvement of hardware, especially the computing power of GPU, a breakthrough

© Springer Nature Switzerland AG 2021
M. Nguyen et al. (Eds.): ISGV 2021, CCIS 1386, pp. 175–189, 2021.
https://doi.org/10.1007/978-3-030-72073-5_14

has been made in deep learning schemes. More and more scholars use deep learning to conduct lane line detection.

In 2014 literature [2], a Convolutional Neural network (CNN) combined with RANSAC's lane line detection method is proposed. Firstly, the edge detection and lane information enhancement of the original image were carried out. Then, it was judged that in simple road scenes, the literature author believed that the RANSAC method could be used to complete the detection, while for complex road conditions, such as shadow, fence and other interference, the RANSAC method could be used after CNN processing. The CNN network structure consists of three convolutional layers, two lower sampling layers, multi-layer perceptron and three full connection layers. The edge image of the region of interest is input, and the image containing only white lane lines and black background is output through the CNN network. The judgment of scene complexity depends on the setting of conditional threshold, and different scenes have different requirements on conditions. Meanwhile, the CNN network structure is very simple, so the robustness of the whole algorithm is not high.

The 2016 literature [3] obtained the corresponding top view from the image front view by inverse perspective transformation method, and obtained the candidate region and the candidate lane line by the cap weighted filter. Double View Convolutional Neural Network (DVCNN) is designed to input the original front view image and top view image corresponding to the candidate region into the dvcnn network simultaneously. The final optimal lane line output is obtained by using the global optimization function considering the information including lane length, number, probability, direction and width. Combining different views improves the accuracy of detection, but also increases the running speed of the algorithm. In terms of speed, Jang et al. [4] proposed a convolutional neural network fast Learning algorithm based on Extreme Learning Machine (ELM) in 2017 and applied it to lane line detection. The convolutional neural network can enhance the input image before lane detection by eliminating noises and obstacles irrelevant to edge detection results. ELM is a fast learning method for calculating the network weight between the output and hidden layers in one iteration. This method reduces the learning time of the network, but the role of the network focuses on the enhancement of the image.

In 2018, Liu X et al. [5] proposed an RPP model based on single convolution visual road detection. Specifically, Robust Planar Pose(RPP) algorithm is a deep complete convolution residual segmentation network with pyramid pools. In order to greatly improve the predictive accuracy of kitti-Road detection tasks, Liu proposed the new strategy by adding road edge tags and introducing appropriate data enhancements. It is an effective way to use semantic segmentation in deep learning to complete the detection of road or lane.

2   Method

The algorithm in this paper is an improvement on the road segmentation and lane detection algorithm [6], and the application of discriminant loss function [7] in LaneNet [8] algorithm and the application of cavity convolution in DeepLabv1 [9] and Local Mean Decomposition(LMD) [10] algorithm are used for reference. The cavity convolution is a replacement of the ordinary convolutional layer to extract the feature to enlarge the receptive field, while the discriminant loss function is easy to be integrated into different network structures and realize instance segmentation through post-processing. The algorithm in this paper combines these two advantages to complete the fast and correct detection of lane lines.

In the lane line detection algorithm based on convolutional neural network in this paper, Encoder and Decoder structure modes are adopted to improve Encoder and Decoder parts respectively on the basis of existing algorithms. Encoder drops the full connection layer of VGG16 network and the last 2×2 maximum pooling layer. Encoder ends the convolutional layer with three layers are set as empty convolution. Decoder has two branches, one of which is an up-sampling of Encoder to achieve semantic segmentation. Using the index function of the pooling layer, the upsampling was carried out in the way of unpool. After each upsampling, multiple convolutional layers were immediately followed and the standard cross entropy loss function was used to train the segmentation network. The other branch is the instance segmentation branch. The network generates the pixel vector feature map in the high-dimensional feature space, USES the discriminant loss function combined with the semantic segmentation results to realize the instance segmentation, and finally realizes the instance detection of lane lines through fitting.

2.1 Algorithm Framework

2.1.1 Introduction to Network Structure

Algorithm in this paper the Encoder - Decoder structure model, in which the Encoder part adopts VGG16 network based model to extract the lane line features, discarded VGG16 network connection layer, and only keep VGG16 in the first four biggest pooling layer, 2×2 empty convolution can be used to expand the characteristics of the receptive field, the 11th, 12th and 13th convolution layer set to empty, empty rate was 2. Decoder has two branches, one is the Encoder on sampling, realize the semantic segmentation, mainly using the largest pooling layer index function, sampling, on the basis of Upsampling by four Upsampling layer and ten convolution, after each Upsampling layer activation function ReLU to better deal with gradient disappeared, using the standard cross entropy loss function training network segmentation. The other branch is the instance segmentation branch, which USES the discriminant loss function based on distance metric learning to realize the instance segmentation on the generated pixel vector feature graph, and finally completes the instance detection of lane lines through clustering fitting.

2.1.2 Computational Flow Chart

The algorithm flow chart of this paper is shown in Fig. 1. The specific network structure is introduced in Sect. 3.1, and the specific parameter distribution is introduced in each module in the following chapters. The sample data to be input during network training include the original graph containing lane lines, the semantic segmentation real labels of the original graph and the instance segmentation real labels of the original graph. The network model is obtained after the training convergence, and then the lane line detection

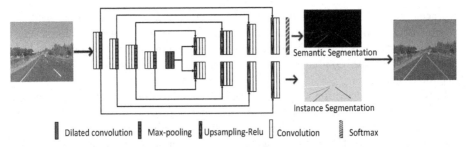

Fig. 1. Algorithm flow chart in this paper.

is carried out on the test data using the model, which is useful for post-processing of clustering fitting in the test process.

2.2 The Encoder

Encoder is the part of algorithm network structure to extract image features. Based on VGG16, Encoder is mainly composed of convolutional layer and pooling layer.

The resolution of the input training samples was adjusted to 512×256, a set of feature graphs were generated by convolution operation with the filter bank, and then they were batch standardized, followed by the activation function linear rectifier function. Then, the maximum pooling is used to perform a two-fold subsampling, and before the subsampling, the location of the maximum eigenvalue in each pooled window is stored for each feature map. In the last three convolution layer, to not continue with the largest pool of operations, but use, is the hole at a rate of 2 empty convolution instead of the ordinary convolution operation, therefore, the resolution of the encoder network at the end of the feature mapping tripled, hollow convolution can expand the receptive field and does not require any additional parameters and calculate the cost.

2.3 The Decoder

The semantic segmentation part mainly realizes the segmentation of lane line and background, and achieves the same resolution of output and input data by up-sampling the encoder. In computer vision, up-sampling generally includes three methods, namely bilinear interpolation, de-pooling and deconvolution. The main idea of bilinear interpolation is to perform a linear interpolation in two directions. Deconvolution is the inverse process of convolution operation. Compared with the former two, the parameters in the deconvolution process need to be trained and learned. Theoretically, deconvolution can realize anti-pooling operation if the parameters of convolution kernel are set reasonably. Anti-pooling operations tend to be more efficient in terms of memory usage because they require fewer indexes to be stored. The schematic diagram of de-pooling and deconvolution is shown in Fig. 2, where Figure (a) represents maximum pooling and corresponding de-pooling operation, and figure (b) represents convolution and corresponding deconvolution operation.

The function of semantic segmentation is mainly to provide masks for instance segmentation. Instance segmentation involves the post-processing of clustering. If the

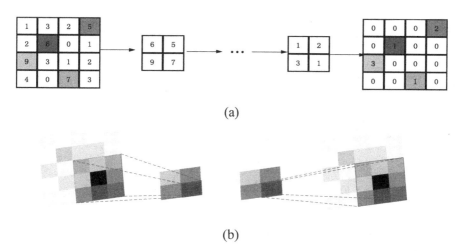

(a)

(b)

Fig. 2. Schematic diagram of contrast between deconcentration and deconvolution.

clustering effect consumes a lot of time in the whole image, the mask provided according to semantic segmentation can ignore the background information which accounts for a large proportion, which can accelerate the speed of clustering.

In order to prevent the occurrence of overfitting, Dropout emerges at the right moment, which reduces the risk of network structure by randomly setting part weight or output to zero during the learning process. The zeroing of some weights will reduce the interdependence among nodes, which is conducive to the regularization of network structure, reduce the incidence of overfitting, and improve the generalization ability of the model. The main working principle of Dropout is shown in Fig. 3, in which Figure (a) represents the standard neural network structure and figure (b) represents the neural network structure after the use of Dropout, and it can be seen that some weights are randomly zeroed.

The Dropout layer usually exists in networks with many parameters such as full connection, and is rarely used in the ordinary convolutional network hidden layer, mainly because of the sparseness of convolution itself and the use of many sparse activation functions, such as ReLU. At the same time, the probability P value of Dropout layer is a super parameter, and different networks need different probability values. However, there is no specific and effective method to determine the P value, so it is necessary to keep trying the P value, which will undoubtedly consume a lot of training time.

After removing the full connection layer, the number of parameters in this paper is greatly reduced. Compared with the Dropout layer with different P values, the training effect of Dropout layer with different P values is not good. However, the training effect of Dropout layer with different P values is normal, and the model performs well in different test data.

The semantic segmentation of one of the decoder branches USES the cross entropy loss function. Its main purpose is to segment the two categories of lane line and image background. However, the proportion of lane line and image background is extremely unbalanced, and the background information seriously interferes the segmentation effect.

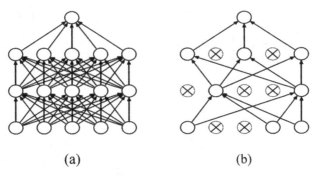

Fig. 3. Use the Dropout neural network model.

Data imbalance means that the proportion of each category varies greatly. If the data is unbalanced, such as the proportion of category 1 is 1% and the proportion of category 2 is 99%, the network model will get the highest accuracy if the prediction result is biased to category 2, but the effect is not good in practical application.

There are mainly two kinds of strategies to solve the problem of data imbalance: one is to consider the data set used for training and achieve the relative category data balance by increasing the training sample with a low data proportion or reducing the training sample with a large data proportion; The other is based on the structural algorithm. For example, the weighted loss value of different categories can be approximated by imposing penalty costs with different weights on different categories.

For this reason, category weights should be added to weight the cross entropy, as shown in formula (1)

$$w_{class} = \frac{1}{ln(c + p_{class})} \tag{1}$$

Where, is the probability of the occurrence of the corresponding category in the population sample, is the super parameter, which is set as 1.03 in this paper.

3   The Implementation Process

3.1   Remove the Full Connection Layer

In many common algorithms, Fully Connected Layers generally follow several convolutional Layers and pooling Layers, acting as a "classifier". The convolutional layer and pooling layer map the input original data to the hidden layer feature space for feature extraction, while the full connection layer maps the learned features to the sample marker space. As shown in Fig. 4, nodes a,b and c of the full connection layer are connected with nodes X, Y and Z of the previous layer respectively, which play a role in integrating the previously extracted features. But at the same time, due to the feature that all nodes are connected, the parameters of the whole connection layer generally take the largest proportion in the network structure. For example, in the familiar VGG16, for the input of 224 × 224 × 3, the first full connection layer FC6 has a total of 4096 nodes, and the upper layer of FC6 is the fifth largest pooling layer, with $7 \times 7 \times 512$, a total of 25088 nodes, which means that 4096×25088 weights are needed, which consumes a huge amount of memory.

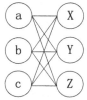

Fig. 4. Schematic diagram of full connection layer.

Full connection layer is used in both semantic segmentation FCN network and literature [6] network. Literature [6] reduces the number of filters in full connection layer from 4096 to 1024. However, even so, parameters of full connection layer are still very redundant. In order to maintain the resolution of the feature map and consider the running speed of the algorithm, this paper chose to directly discard the operation of the full connection layer, thus greatly reducing the number of parameters. Finally, the comparison experiment also confirmed the acceleration of the speed.

3.2 Increase the Cavity Convolution

In the current semantic segmentation algorithms, it is almost inevitable to apply down-sampling [11]. The existence of down-sampling makes the operating filter have a larger receptive field, which is conducive to collecting more context information and improving the segmentation accuracy. However, the output of the final result of semantic segmentation requires the same resolution as the input, which means that the strong down-sampling will require the same strong up-sampling; On the other hand, down-sampling not only reduces the resolution of features, but also loses important spatial information such as edge shape, and it is much less operable to restore the lost information to its original state. In this regard, the proposal and application of void convolution can well avoid these problems. Void convolution provides an effective mechanism to control the visual field, and can expand the filter's receptive field to contain greater context information without using down-sampling.

Figure 5 (a) The size of the convolution kernel is 3×3, and the cavity rate is 1, which is not different from common convolution operations. Figure 5 (b) The size of the convolution kernel is 3×3, and the cavity rate is 2. Only the nine red points and the 3×3 convolution kernel are convolved, while the remaining points are not convolved. It can also be considered that the size of the convolution kernel is 7×7, and only the red points have non-0 weight, while the weight of the remaining points is 0. Therefore, it can be understood that although the size of the convolution kernel is only 3×3, the receptive field of convolution operation has reached 7×7. Similarly, in Fig. 8 (c), the convolution kernel size is 3×3 and the cavity rate is 4, but the receptive field of convolution operation increases to 15×15.

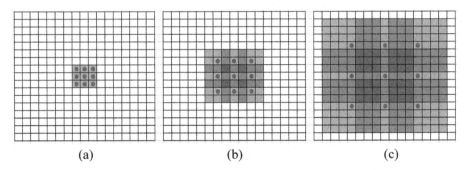

(a)   (b)   (c)

Fig. 5. Schematic diagram of empty convolution.

If the size of the convolution kernel is 3 × 3 and the cavity rate is 1, 2 and 4 respectively in the three successive convolutional layers, as shown in Fig. 5 (a), Fig. 5 (b) and Fig. 5 (c), then the nine red points in Fig. 5 (b) are the output of Fig. 5 (a) and the nine red points in Fig. 5 (c) are the output of Fig. 5 (b), and the receptive field of the entire three-layer convolution reaches 15 × 15. Compared with the ordinary convolution operation, the convolution operation with the size of the continuous three-layer convolution kernel is 3 × 3. In the case of the same step size of 1, the perceptron with only 7 × 7 can be calculated according to the formula (Kernel-1 × layer + 1). Thus, it can be seen that the receptive field of ordinary convolution operation has a linear relationship with the number of layers, while the receptive field of empty convolution has an exponential relationship with the number of layers.

This article will last three convolution encoder layer using hollow convolution instead of, not only expand the receptive field, at the same time do not need any additional parameters and calculate the cost, combined with discarding the largest pool of different number of layers, the last experiment just remove the last one of the biggest pooling layer for the lane line detection effect is best, especially to reduce the residual.

3.3 Instance Segmentation

Instance segmentation branch network is mainly realized by discriminant loss function.

A differentiable function is used to map each pixel in the image to a point in the high-dimensional feature space. N is used to represent the N-dimensional feature space, and its size is related to the samples used for training. The more samples there are, the larger n will be. In the high-dimensional feature space, the pixel embedded vectors with the same label will end up close to each other after training, while the pixel embedded vectors with different labels will move away from each other [12]. Discriminant loss function is developed on the basis of literature, which proposes a loss function to implement pixel embedding, including two terms: one is used to punish embedded pixels with the same label but with a large distance; the other is used to punish embedded pixels with different labels but with a small distance. The discriminant loss function improves the second item [13]. For a frame of image, the number of instances in the image is less than the pixels in the image [14]. Therefore, for the object with different labels but small distance, the average embedding of different labels will be changed from each pair of embedded pixels, which will be much faster in calculation.

3.4 Afterprocessing

Discriminant loss function used by Decoder instance segmentation branch involves clustering operation, which is only needed when lane detection is carried out but does not participate in the training process, and clustering is completed through iteration [8]. First, mean shift clustering was used to make the cluster center move along the direction with high density. Then, threshold processing was carried out. With the cluster center as the center of the circle and $2\delta_v$ as the radius, all embedded pixel vectors in the circle were selected to be grouped into the same lane line. Repeat this step until all lane lines embedded pixel vectors are assigned to the corresponding instance lane. Finally, the output instance lane line is obtained by fitting.

Common fitting methods include voting method based on Hough Transform, Bessel curve fitting, polynomial fitting based on least square and random sampling consistent algorithm [15]. The voting method converts the coordinate space into parameter space, and then performs traversal after obtaining the lane edge points. The method is simple, but if there are too many data, the traversal speed will be affected. Moreover, it cannot handle the curve well, so it is suitable for the straight road with simple environment. Bessel curve, also known as Baez curve, is composed of line segments and nodes with accurate fitting, but the calculation is complex and cannot be modified locally. Changing the position of a control point has an impact on the whole curve. RANSAC iteratively estimates the parameters of the mathematical model, which is an uncertain algorithm with only a certain probability to get the appropriate model. In addition, relevant thresholds need to be set. Polynomial fitting based on least square is the most simple lane line fitting method with a small amount of computation. However, the lane segmentation clustering algorithm in this paper has a relatively high accuracy, and the least square method can also be used to fit lane lines well for sections with curvature.

Fig. 6. Cluster fitting result diagram.

As shown in Fig. 11, Fig. 6 (a) and Fig. 6 (b) are renderings after clustering, and Fig. 6 (c) and Fig. 6 (d) are result graphs after corresponding fitting. It can be clearly seen from the figure that clustering has completed the detection of lane lines, but it contains a lot of background information. After fitting, the specific location of lane lines can be more accurately represented.

4   Experimental Results and Analysis

4.1   Lane Line Detection Results

The algorithm presented in this paper to test a variety of environment under the scenario of video sequences, including day, high-speed, night, rain, such as scene, the scene also includes the corners, vehicle interference, shade, strong light, the complex road conditions, such as a bar line interference, a total of 8 groups of video, algorithm running speed and accuracy as the evaluation standard for statistics. In addition, various open source lane-line data sets are tested in this paper to verify the robustness of the algorithm. Finally, the experimental results prove the effectiveness of the proposed algorithm.

4.1.1   Test Results of Homemade Data Set

Detection results in each scene of the self-made data set: different colors represent different lane instances; solid line represents solid line; dashed line represents dashed line.

Fig. 7. Multi-lane section detection results.

In Fig. 7 (a), Fig. 7 (b) and Fig. 7 (c), there are lane double lines. Since the algorithm in this paper does not distinguish the category of double lines, it is regarded as the detection conducted by different lane instances.

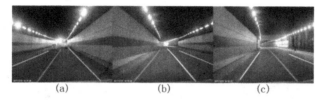

Fig. 8. Tunnel section detection results.

Fig. 9. Test results of bend section.

Fig. 10. Environmental test results on rainy days.

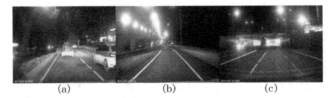

Fig. 11. Night environment test results.

Above shows a good traffic lane line recognition effect under different environment, as shown in Fig. 7 shows a multi lane road lane line test results correctly, as shown in Fig. 8 shows the tunnel section lane line identification results, Fig. 9 shows the bend lane line basic accurate test results, Fig. 10 for rainy days under the environment of the lane line detection effect, Fig. 11 shows the night environment lane line identification results.

The missing and false detection results in the experimental test are shown in Fig. 12.

Fig. 12. Schematic diagram of false detection and omission.

Figure 12 (a) shows the false detection caused by the similarity of road tooth characteristics, and Fig. 12 (b) shows the missing detection caused by different lane line widths.

Missing detection analysis: considering the running speed of the algorithm, the network structure is relatively simple; The diversity of data sets is not reflected in the fact that lane lines of different widths are not considered.

Mistakenly identified analysis: data sets production not precise enough, especially longer dotted line is easy to cause error checking, and the solid line is wear block, and so on and so forth will be mistakenly identified as a dotted line, the other tags form when using the coordinates, then get the split samples set width of real labels, inevitably contains background information. When network clustering, the setting of super parameters does not meet all the circumstances of the lane. In addition, similar features are also easy to cause false detection.

4.1.2 Open Source Dataset Test Results

Open source data set detection results: Where different colors represent different lane instances, solid lines represent solid lane lines, and dashed lines represent dashed lane lines.

Fig. 13. Test results of the data set of the 2018 Smart Car Future Challenge.

Figure 13 (a) The interference of vehicle occlusion can be accurately detected; Fig. 13 (b) Interference with strong light; Fig. 13 (c) Interference with colored bar lines on the ground.

Fig. 14. Tucson dataset detection results.

The materials of Tucson data set are all taken from the highway, but it is not easy to detect. The difficulty lies in that the lane lines are badly worn and the characteristics of the lane lines are not obvious. However, the detection results of this algorithm are relatively good (Fig. 14).

Fig. 15. CULane dataset detection results.

The CULane data set has a relatively large resolution and contains more interference information of its own vehicle head. In the case of good road conditions, the algorithm proposed in this paper can still accurately identify lane lines (Fig. 15).

Fig. 16. KITTI dataset detection.

The KITTI data set provides two types of markings, road and current lane, which are mainly used for the study of the division of the drivable area of vehicles, with lane lines mainly existing in the middle of the road, and the method in this paper has basically accurately identified the lane lines.

5   Conclusion

In the experiment of this algorithm, lane lines under different data sets and different weather conditions were tested respectively, and the accuracy and robustness were verified by experimental results. In the algorithm comparison experiment, the detection speed of this algorithm is 30.38% faster than that of the algorithm in reference [6], and the corresponding accuracy is almost the same, only 1.39% lower. When comparing the traditional methods based on voting, the algorithm in this paper is much slower in detection speed, but much higher in detection accuracy. Especially for the virtual and real detection of lane lines and curve detection, it is difficult for traditional methods to achieve effective detection. By contrast, the algorithm in this paper can basically achieve accurate detection.

Acknowledgement. This work was supported by the industry-university-research innovation fund of science and technology development center of Ministry of Education: 2020QT02.

References

1. Narote, S.P., Bhujbal, P.N., Narote, A.S., et al.: A review of recent advances in lane detection and departure warning system. Pattern Recogn. **73**, 216–234 (2018)
2. Kim, J., Lee, M.: Robust lane detection based on convolutional neural network and random sample consensus. In: Loo, C.K., Yap, K.S., Wong, K.W., Teoh, A., Huang, K. (eds.) ICONIP 2014. LNCS, vol. 8834, pp. 454–461. Springer, Cham (2014). https://doi.org/10.1007/978-3-319-12637-1_57

3. He, B., Ai, R., Yan, Y., et al.: Accurate and robust lane detection based on Dual-View Convolutional Neutral Network. In: Intelligent Vehicles Symposium, pp. 1041–1046 (2016)
4. Kim, J., Kim, J., Jang, G.J., et al.: Fast learning method for convolutional neural networks using extreme learning machine and its application to lane detection. Neural Netw. **87**, 109–121 (2017)
5. Liu, X., Deng, Z.: Segmentation of drivable road using deep fully convolutional residual network with pyramid pooling. Cogn. Comput. **10**(2), 272–281 (2017). https://doi.org/10.1007/s12559-017-9524-y
6. Oliveira, G.L., Burgard, W., Brox, T., et al.: Efficient deep models for monocular road segmentation. In: Intelligent Robots and Systems, pp. 4885–4891 (2016)
7. De Brabandere, B., Neven, D., Van Gool, L.: Semantic instance segmentation with a discriminative loss function. arXiv:1708.02551 (2017)
8. Neven, D., De Brabandere, B., Georgoulis, S., et al.: Towards end-to-end lane detection: an instance segmentation approach. In: IEEE Intelligent Vehicles Symposium, pp. 286–291 (2018)
9. Chen, L.C., Papandreou, G., Kokkinos, I., et al.: Semantic image segmentation with deep convolutional nets and fully connected CRFs. arXiv preprint arXiv:1412.7062 (2014)
10. Chen, P., Lo, S., Hang, H., et al.: Efficient road lane marking detection with deep learning. In: International Conference on Digital Signal Processing, pp. 1–5 (2018)
11. Peng, C., Zhang, X., Yu, G., et al.: Large kernel matters - improve semantic segmentation by global convolutional network. In: Computer Vision and Pattern Recognition, pp. 1743–1751 (2017)
12. Pinheiro, P.H., Collobert, R., Dollar, P., et al.: Learning to segment object candidates. In: Neural Information Processing Systems, pp. 1990–1998 (2015)
13. He, K., Gkioxari, G., Dollar, P., et al.: Mask R-CNN. In: International Conference on Computer Vision, pp. 2961–2969 (2017)
14. Kim, J., Park, C.: End-to-end ego lane estimation based on sequential transfer learning for self-driving cars. In: Computer Vision and Pattern Recognition, pp. 1194–1202 (2017)
15. Paszke, A., Chaurasia, A., Kim, S., Culurciello, E.: ENet: a deep neural network architecture for real-time semantic segmentation. arXiv preprint arXiv:1606.02147 (2016)

Segment- and Arc-Based Vectorizations by Multi-scale/Irregular Tangential Covering

Antoine Vacavant[1]($\boxtimes$)(ID), Bertrand Kerautret[2](ID), and Fabien Feschet[3](ID)

[1] Université Clermont Auvergne, CNRS, SIGMA Clermont, Institut Pascal,
63000 Clermont-Ferrand, France
`antoine.vacavant@uca.fr`
[2] Univ Lyon, Lyon 2, LIRIS, 69676 Lyon, France
`bertrand.kerautret@univ-lyon2.fr`
[3] Université Clermont Auvergne, CNRS, ENSMSE, LIMOS,
63000 Clermont-Ferrand, France
`fabien.feschet@u-auvergne.fr`

Abstract. In this paper, we propose an original manner to employ a tangential cover algorithm - minDSS - in order to vectorize noisy digital contours. To do so, we exploit the representation of graphical objects by maximal primitives we have introduced in previous work. By calculating multi-scale and irregular isothetic representations of the contour, we obtained 1-D (one-dimensional) intervals, and achieved afterwards a decomposition into maximal line segments or circular arcs. By adapting minDSS to this sparse and irregular data of 1-D intervals supporting the maximal primitives, we are now able to reconstruct the input noisy objects into cyclic contours made of lines or arcs with a minimal number of primitives. We explain our novel complete pipeline in this work, and present its experimental evaluation by considering both synthetic and real image data.

Keywords: Vectorization · Noisy contours · Multi-scale analysis · Irregular grids · Tangential cover

1 Introduction

Image vectorization (or raster-to-vector) process has been a scientific and technical challenge since the 60's [14] and still stimulates the development of modern approaches with focus on different points like drawing vectorization [1,6], Deep learning based method [4,12], perception based clip-art vectorization [3], from geometric analysis [11], or with real time constraint [27]. Image noise is a central problem in this complex task. We can employ denoising algorithms to reduce this alteration as a pre-processing step [13]. Furthermore, segmentation methods can integrate smoothing terms, to control the behavior of active contours for instance [8,26]. Even if we can reach to smooth contours by such approaches, a

© Springer Nature Switzerland AG 2021
M. Nguyen et al. (Eds.): ISGV 2021, CCIS 1386, pp. 190–202, 2021.
https://doi.org/10.1007/978-3-030-72073-5_15

lot of parameters must be tuned finely, depending on the input noise, and execution times can be very long. Modern deep learning approaches requires large datasets to be tuned finely, for a specific application (sometimes, like for pixel art vectorization, the reference does not exist).

As a consequence, another strategy consists in calculating geometrical representations of noisy image objects, even if simple pre-processing and segmentation methods are employed first. Researches employing digital geometry notions and algorithms have mainly dealt with the reconstruction of graphical objects into line segments or circular arcs, originally by considering noise-free contours [2,19], later by processing noisy data [15,17,18].

Following this literature of digital geometrical-based approaches, in this article, we propose a complete pipeline based on our previous contribution [22] in order to vectorize noisy digital contours into line segments or circular arcs. This related work aimed at representing such contours with maximal primitives, by processing 1-D (one-dimensional) intervals obtained by a multi-scale and irregular approach, summarized in Fig. 1.

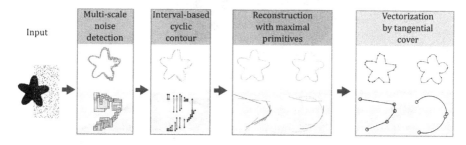

Fig. 1. Global work-flow of our vectorization approach in relation to previous work [22] (in red) and new reconstruction, highlighted on the right (green). (Color figure online)

From this representation, we now propose to use the tangential cover algorithm minDSS introduced in [7] to build a representative vectorization composed of either lines or arcs. Originally, minDSS problem is the determination of the minimal length polygonalization (in term of input intervals) of a maximal primitive representation of a given regular eight-connected curve [7]. In this article, we adapt this approach by using sparse irregular 1-D intervals as inputs.

The article is organized as follows. Section 2 relates synthetically on our previous contribution devoted to represent noisy digital contours into maximal primitives (lines or arcs) [22]. Then, Sect. 3 is dedicated to our novel approach that consists in adapting tangential cover algorithm for our specific contour representation, in order to vectorize input objects into cyclic geometrical structures. Section 4 presents the experimental results we have obtained for synthetic and real images, and a comparison with related works by considering robustness against contour noise. Finally, Sect. 5 concludes the paper with different axes of progress.

2   Reconstructions into Maximal Primitives

2.1   Multi-scale Noise Detection

We automatically detect the amount of noise present on a digital structure by the algorithm detailed in [9]. From such a multi-scale analysis, the proposed algorithm consists in constructing, for each contour point, a multi-scale profile defined by the segment length of all segments covering the point for larger and larger grid sizes. From each profile, the noise level is determined by the first scale for which the slope of the profile is decreasing. This noise level can be represented as boxes and as exposed in Fig. 2, a high noise in the contour will lead to a large box, and *vice-versa*. The algorithm can be tested on-line from any digital contour given by a netizen [10].

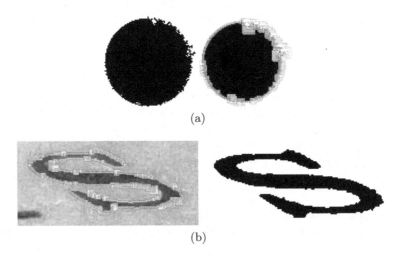

(a)

(b)

Fig. 2. Examples of multi-scale noise detection upon a synthetic binary image (a) and a segmentation obtained from a real image (b).

Also, Fig. 2 illustrates the possible noise altering image objects. In (a), a synthetic circle is generating for testing our approach, while in (b) the segmentation by a thresholding process leads to a noisy contour.

2.2   Irregular Isothetic Cyclic Representation

The multi-scale contour representation calculated earlier is converted into irregular isothetic objects, defined on the following generalized grid model [21] restricted to the 2-D case:

Definition 1 (*d*-D I-grid). *Let P be a hyper-rectangular subset of $\mathbb{R}^d$. A d-D I-grid denoted by G is a tiling of P with rectangular hyper-parallelepipeds (or* *cells), which do not overlap, and whose faces of dimension $d-1$ are parallel to successive axes of the chosen space. A cell R of G is defined by a central point (position)* $\mathbf{p}_R = (p_R^1, p_R^2, \ldots, p_R^d) \in \mathbb{R}^d$ *and a size along each axis* $\mathbf{l}_R = (l_R^1, l_R^2, \ldots, l_R^d) \in \mathbb{R}_+^{*\,d}$.

As illustrated in Fig. 3, the input meaningful boxes are converted into k-curves, formalized as:

Definition 2 (k-curve). *Let $A = (R_i)_{1 \leq i \leq n}$ be a path from R_1 to R_n. A is a k-curve iff each cell R_i of A has exactly two k-adjacent cells in A.*

In this definition, k-adjacency in 2-D is given by:

Definition 3 (k-adjacency in 2-D). *Let R_1 and R_2 be two cells of a 2-D $\mathbb{I}$-grid G. R_1 and R_2 are ve$-$adjacent ("vertex and edge" adjacent) if :*

$$or \begin{cases} |x_{R_1} - x_{R_2}| = \frac{l_{R_1}^x + l_{R_2}^x}{2} \text{ and } |y_{R_1} - y_{R_2}| \leq \frac{l_{R_1}^y + l_{R_2}^y}{2} \\ |y_{R_1} - y_{R_2}| = \frac{l_{R_1}^y + l_{R_2}^y}{2} \text{ and } |x_{R_1} - x_{R_2}| \leq \frac{l_{R_1}^x + l_{R_2}^x}{2} \end{cases} \quad (1)$$

R_1 and R_2 are e-adjacent ("edge" adjacent) if we consider an exclusive "or" and strict inequalities in this definition.

In this article, we consider $k = ve$ wlog. Adjacency is defined as the spatial relationship between edges and vertices of two cells and may be compared to classic 4- and 8-adjacencies of regular square grids [21].

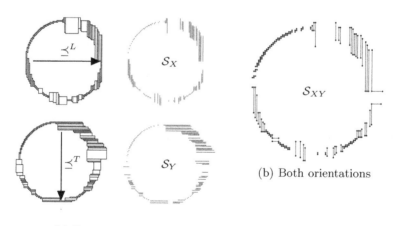

(a) Separate orientations

(b) Both orientations

Fig. 3. Encoding of irregular isothetic cells into k-curves, following 2 order relations ($\preceq^L$ and $\preceq^T$), with interfaces stored inside the lists $\mathcal{S}_X$ and $\mathcal{S}_Y$. We then obtain a set of horizontal and vertical segments representing the input shape. In $\mathcal{S}_{XY}$, internal vertices are white, external ones are black.

Moreover, as presented in Fig. 3, we have proposed to calculate two k-curves, one for each axis, following the order relations $\preceq^L$ (X axis) and $\preceq^T$ (Y axis) [21].

Then, both curves are combined to obtain 1-D X- and Y- aligned intervals stored inside the $\mathcal{S}_X$ and $\mathcal{S}_Y$ lists respectively. Finally, a single set $\mathcal{S}_{XY}$ is constructed by merging them, with a special care to respect the curvilinear abscissa of the input contour when ordering the intervals in this list (see Fig. 3 (b)).

2.3   Recognition of Line Segments and Circular Arcs

From this 1-D interval representation, we then obtain maximal segments or arcs by employing a GLP (Generalized Linear Programming) approach. In this step, we consider the internal and external points of the segments into two different sets P° and $P^\bullet$. This algorithm has been adapted from the works [20,25], which aim to solve the problem of minimal enclosing circle. In our case, its purpose is to obtain primitives enclosing a set of points (*e.g.* P°) but not the other ($P^\bullet$). Figure 4 depicts the results obtained for two noisy digital contours, using maximal segments or arcs. More details can be found in [22].

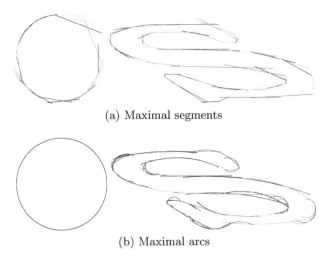

(a) Maximal segments

(b) Maximal arcs

Fig. 4. Reconstruction of digital shapes presented in Fig. 2 by maximal segments (a) and arcs (b). Each primitive is presented with a random color.

3   Adapted Tangential Covering

Using the results from the previous sections, at this step we have a collection of geometric primitives, either segments or circular arcs. This collection can be ordered according to the initial ordering of the constraints in $\mathcal{S}_{XY}$. The ordered set of primitives is induced by the constraints in $\mathcal{S}_{XY}$ such that its density is dependent on the density of the constraints. Hence, there is no reason to have a uniform density. So the density is not linked to the underlying curve of the constraints. This is different from the usual tangential cover. However, the tangential cover can be viewed as a proper circular arcs graph. In other word, the main structure of the tangential cover is an ordered set of overlapping primitives corresponding to different portions of the underlying digital curve. This is what we got from previous sections. More precisely, for two primitives, we can build the overlapping predicate from the underlying intervals bounding each recognized primitive by considering that the predicate is true when the two primitives share constraints. The predicate is false otherwise. Hence for two primitives, they overlap if and only if they share a set of constraints. As a result, our structure can be embedded as a proper circular arcs graph. With this structure, we can adapt the minDSS algorithm [7] to obtain the minimal length cycle of the set of primitives since it is solely based on the graph structure of the tangential cover. Length must be understood as the number of primitives in a cycle. We now recall the minDSS algorithm in Sect. 3.1 and provides its adaptation in Sect. 3.2.

3.1   The minDSS Algorithm

Let us recall the initial purpose of the minDSS algorithm by exposing its input/output, following a question of A. Rosenfeld:

Input: An ordered list of geometric primitives, DSS (digital straight segments) in [7] and an underlying curve.

Output: Shortest length cycle, in number of primitives, with worst case time complexity $\mathcal{O}(n)$.

The shortest length cycle problem could be trivially solved in quadratic time complexity but remained a challenge in linear time complexity. The original minDSS algorithm has two phases. In the first phase, for a DSS D, it defines the residue of D as the set of points of the underlying curve that only belongs to D. The main property proved in this phase is the following [7]. If there exists a primitive D with non empty residue then the shortest cycle can be constructed from any point inside the residue. This result is of practical importance since digital curves having not all empty residues are easily encountered in practice. The first phase of minDSS is totally parallel. However, there exists digital curves whose residues are all empty. Hence, the first phase is not sufficient to solve the problem.

In a second phase, a propagation of marks is done in the tangential cover to detect a decision case. The goal is to detect locally two cycles having different lengths. Since the length of any cycle is either the minimum length or the minimum length plus one, detecting such cycles is sufficient to solve minDSS. The propagation of marks is done in the connectivity graph of the primitives using only an overlapping predicate. Let us denote the primitives by $\{T_k\}_{k=0,n-1}$ with an arbitrary first element T_0. A cyclic ordering is used that is the *next* primitives following T_k is $T_{(k+1) \mod n}$ and the *previous* primitive is $T_{(k-1) \mod n}$. By iterations using *next* and *previous*, we can move along the set of primitives by using iterates as $next^{(k)} = next(next^{(k-1)})$ and $next^{(0)} =$ Id and obviously the same for *previous*.

For a primitive T_k, we can define the *forward* function $f(T_k)$ such that $f(T_k) = next^{(j)}(T_k)$ with T_k and $f(T_k)$ overlapping and j maximal. It is a farthest forward move with overlapping. Since T_k overlaps itself, this is well defined. By convention, we define $f^{-1}()$ similarly but using *previous* instead of *next*.

By construction $f^{-1}(f(T_k))$ is a primitive that overlaps $f(T_k)$. In a wide sense, it is a primitive before T_k in the cyclic ordering, that is using *previous* starting at $f(T_k)$. We can remark that the interval $[f^{-1}(f(T_k)); f(T_k)]$ is a separator of all cycles in the graph. Indeed, each cycle must contain a primitive in this interval. As a consequence, propagation of marks in minDSS can be done only for primitives inside a separator so to decide locally the shortest length cycle problem. The complexity of the marking is proved to be $\mathcal{O}(n)$ [7].

3.2   Adaptation of minDSS

In our approach, there is no underlying curve, that is, even if $\mathcal{S}_{XY}$ is a support set, it is not a curve. For instance, its density is not constant and is different from one as in the regular grid. Furthermore, this density can vary on different parts of the curve. However, it has a global ordering obtained from the isothetic cyclic representation. The indices of the constraints in $\mathcal{S}_{XY}$ permit to define any primitive as a succession of intervals in $\mathcal{S}_{XY}$. Hence, we can define a connectivity graph on the set of recognized primitives using the index of any element in $\mathcal{S}_{XY}$. Connectivity is well defined and so we can calculate $f()$ and $f^{-1}()$. Moreover, the propagations calculated in minDSS can be done on the new connectivity graph. To do so, it is sufficient to recreate the connectivity graph by using our new overlapping predicate. Two successive primitives in $\mathcal{S}_{XY}$ that overlap with respect to the vertical or horizontal intervals are connected in the graph. The *forward* function only uses this connectivity and *next* and *previous* to compute the separator. Moreover, the propagation of marks is done according to the connectivity graph only and can be thus applied with no modifications. We refer to the original paper [7] for details about propagation of marks.

Of course, minimizing the number of primitives, while having variable density, should be analyzed carefully. Indeed, minimizing the number of primitives led to different length steps in the underlying curve because length is directly linked with primitives' density. Hence, at the portions of the underlying curve with high density, using the primitives induced small movements while in the portions with low density changing from one primitive to the next one, can produce large movements in the curve. The fact that minDSS is actually a graph-based algorithm makes it independent of the embedding of the graph onto the underlying curve.

The output of the minDSS algorithm is a cycle in the set of intervals using the link between intervals made by the existence of a geometric primitive intersecting all of them. Hence, the output of minDSS is a list of intervals and not a set of primitives. As seen in Fig. 5, for segments as well as for arcs, from a list of intervals, there exists an infinite number of primitives corresponding to the given intervals. So, after the computation of the solution of minDSS, a geometric

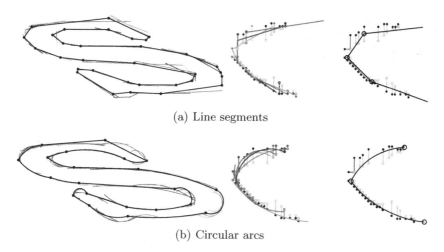

(a) Line segments

(b) Circular arcs

Fig. 5. From the collection of maximal primitives obtained by GLP (random colors), minDSS leads to a set of potential reconstructions, for both kinds of primitives; in this figure one of them is depicted in black. By considering the starting and ending intervals of these primitives (see bottom), minDSS produces cycles by minimizing the number of intervals. The intervals represented in red are examples of not intersected intervals. (Color figure online)

solution must be reconstructed by choosing primitives for all edges in the graph solution given by minDSS. There are several ways to do that and a fast and simple solution is obtained by using the middle points of the intervals (see Fig. 5). Of course, the consequence of such a choice is that some intervals might not be intersected by the primitives and this happens when the extremal points of an interval is a must use points for defining the original solution of compatibility between intervals (see for instance the red intervals of Fig. 5). Since there are several solutions for minDSS, each graph solution leads to a different geometric solution.

4 Experimental Results

4.1 Global Overview of the Method

We first propose to expose the different steps of our pipeline for a low resolution *fish* binary image leading to a noisy shape (Fig. 6-a), from the binary shape data sets[1]. We depict the meaningful scales (b), the set of intervals $\mathcal{S}_{XY}$ (c), the collections of maximal segments and arcs and the associated tangential cover outcomes (d,e).

Thanks to our system, we can obtain faithful vectorizations of such digital contours, with a low number of primitives.

---

[1] http://vision.lems.brown.edu/content/available-software-and-databases.

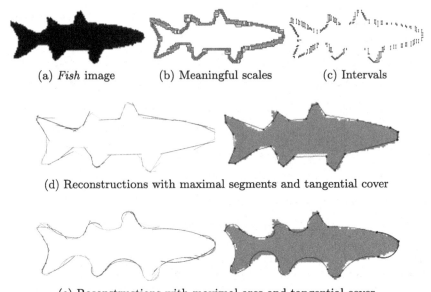

(a) *Fish* image   (b) Meaningful scales   (c) Intervals

(d) Reconstructions with maximal segments and tangential cover

(e) Reconstructions with maximal arcs and tangential cover

Fig. 6. Overview of our pipeline

More precisely, when we consider segments, we can observe that straight parts of the shape are represented with line segments (*e.g.* see the bottom part), since meaningful scales have a very fine resolution, and few intervals are thus required. More complex parts have been simplified faithfully (as triangular shapes for fish fins).

When we select arcs instead, roundy parts of the shape are individually represented by circular primitives. Even if some regions are more smoothed (*e.g.* see fish fins at top-left), these are relevant approximations for such a low resolution image (with no visual aberrant inverted arcs). Furthermore, it should be recalled that tangential cover computes one solution, and other options could be of better interest, depending on the final application.

4.2   Visual Inspection of Results with Synthetic Images

In Fig. 7, two synthetic noisy objects, with polygonal and curved shapes, are respectively vectorized with segments and arcs.

In (a), a polygon image has been corrupted with different noises, to study the impact of variable perturbations into a single sample. We can notice that the final segment-based reconstruction is very stable and represents faithfully the underlying object.

In (b), a curved shape is corrupted with local noises. Our algorithm can produce a relevant arc-based reconstruction, with a low number of primitives. As a whole, even in the presence of severe (possibly only local) perturbation, we can calculate reconstructions geometrically close to the underlying contours.

4.3   Visual Inspection of Results with a Real Image

Finally, in Fig. 8, we have selected a large image composed of two contours, processed independently by our approach. The external elliptical contour is vectorized with arcs, while the internal one is reconstructed with segments.

We can see from the meaningful scales computed (a) that some parts of the contours are very finely represented (*e.g.* see top-left part of the external part), which leads to small maximal primitives in (b) and in the tangential cover (c). On the contrary, noisy regions are reconstructed with longer primitives (*e.g.* see straight lines of the internal part).

Even if the input contours are long (in term of number of pixels) tangential cover leads to reconstruction with few primitives.

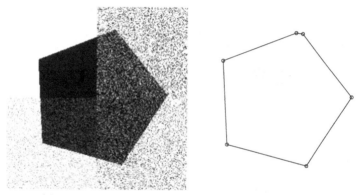

(a) Segment-based reconstruction of a polygonal shape

(b) Arc-based reconstruction of a curved shape

Fig. 7. The reconstructions obtained for 2 synthetic images

5   Conclusion and Future Works

We have proposed a novel framework to vectorize possibly noisy digital contours by line segments or circular arcs, by combining our previous work devoted to reconstruct maximal primitives [22] and the tangential cover algorithm minDSS [7]. By means of the experiments we have exposed, that this method achieves faithful vectorization according to the underlying object contour. Moreover, by employing minDSS, we ensure that the number of primitives is low.

Our first research lead is to compare our method with other classic and modern vectorization approaches, by considering various quality measures as we did in [23] (Hausdorff distance, error of tangents' orientation, Euclidean distance between points). We would like to show that our pipeline permits to obtain robust reconstructions (according to the input contour noise), with respect to the state-of-the-art.

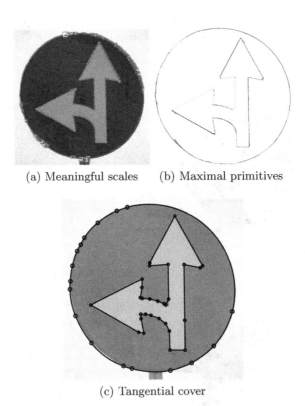

(a) Meaningful scales   (b) Maximal primitives

(c) Tangential cover

Fig. 8. Visual evaluation of our pipeline with a large image

Another important concern is to calculate a single reconstruction combining segments and arcs. To do so, we would like to propose a combinatorial optimization process as developed in [5]. Such scheme would select the best primitive to be integrated in the final solution, depending on a given predicate, *e.g.* the geometrical length of the primitive. An alternative option is to first compute a set of maximal primitives containing both types, by considering the straight and curved part of the input noisy shape, as we employed already in [23].

Finally, we plan to compare the future reconstructions with other approaches able to choose the primitive automatically like the method proposed by Nguyen and Debled [16] and to explore other applications like the one related to 3-D printing [24].

References

1. Bessmeltsev, M., Solomon, J.: Vectorization of line drawings via polyvector fields. ACM Trans. Graph. **38**(1), 12 p. (2019). https://doi.org/10.1145/3202661
2. Damaschke, P.: The linear time recognition of digital arcs. Pattern Recogn. Lett. **16**, 543–548 (1995)
3. Dominici, E.A., Schertler, N., Griffin, J., Hoshyari, S., Sigal, L., Sheffer, A.: Poly-Fit: perception-aligned vectorization of raster clip-art via intermediate polygonal fitting. ACM Trans. Graph. (TOG) **39**(4), 77-1 (2020)
4. Egiazarian, V., et al.: Deep vectorization of technical drawings. In: Vedaldi, A., Bischof, H., Brox, T., Frahm, J.-M. (eds.) ECCV 2020. LNCS, vol. 12358, pp. 582–598. Springer, Cham (2020). https://doi.org/10.1007/978-3-030-58601-0_35
5. Faure, A., Feschet, F.: Multi-primitive analysis of digital curves. In: Wiederhold, P., Barneva, R.P. (eds.) IWCIA 2009. LNCS, vol. 5852, pp. 30–42. Springer, Heidelberg (2009). https://doi.org/10.1007/978-3-642-10210-3_3
6. Favreau, J.D., Lafarge, F., Bousseau, A.: Fidelity vs. simplicity: a global approach to line drawing vectorization. ACM Trans. Graph. **35**(4), 120:1–120:10 (2016)
7. Feschet, F., Tougne, L.: On the min DSS problem of closed discrete curves. Discret. Appl. Math. **151**(1), 138–153 (2005)
8. Kass, M., Witkin, A., Terzopoulos, D.: Snakes: active contour models. Int. J. Comput. Vision **1**(4), 321–331 (1988). https://doi.org/10.1007/BF00133570
9. Kerautret, B., Lachaud, J.: Meaningful scales detection along digital contours for unsupervised local noise estimation. IEEE Trans. Pattern Anal. Mach. Intell. **34**(12), 2379–2392 (2012)
10. Kerautret, B., Lachaud, J.: Meaningful scales detection: an unsupervised noise detection algorithm for digital contours. Image Process. On Line **4**, 98–115 (2014)
11. Kerautret, B., Ngo, P., Kenmochi, Y., Vacavant, A.: Greyscale image vectorization from geometric digital contour representations. In: Kropatsch, W.G., Artner, N.M., Janusch, I. (eds.) DGCI 2017. LNCS, vol. 10502, pp. 319–331. Springer, Cham (2017). https://doi.org/10.1007/978-3-319-66272-5_26
12. Kim, B., Wang, O., Öztireli, A., Gross, M.: Semantic segmentation for line drawing vectorization using neural networks. In: Computer Graphics Forum, vol. 37, no. 2, pp. 329–338. Wiley Online Library (2018)
13. Lebrun, M., Colom, M., Buades, A., Morel, J.: Secrets of image denoising cuisine. Acta Numerica **21**, 475–576 (2012)
14. Montanari, U.: Continuous skeletons from digitized images. J. ACM **16**(4), 534–549 (1969)
15. Nguyen, T.P., Debled-Rennesson, I.: Arc segmentation in linear time. In: Real, P., Diaz-Pernil, D., Molina-Abril, H., Berciano, A., Kropatsch, W. (eds.) CAIP 2011. LNCS, vol. 6854, pp. 84–92. Springer, Heidelberg (2011). https://doi.org/10.1007/978-3-642-23672-3_11
16. Nguyen, T.P., Debled-Rennesson, I.: Decomposition of a curve into arcs and line segments based on dominant point detection. In: Heyden, A., Kahl, F. (eds.) SCIA 2011. LNCS, vol. 6688, pp. 794–805. Springer, Heidelberg (2011). https://doi.org/10.1007/978-3-642-21227-7_74

17. Nguyen, T.P., Kerautret, B., Debled-Rennesson, I., Lachaud, J.-O.: Unsupervised, fast and precise recognition of digital arcs in noisy images. In: Bolc, L., Tadeusiewicz, R., Chmielewski, L.J., Wojciechowski, K. (eds.) ICCVG 2010. LNCS, vol. 6374, pp. 59–68. Springer, Heidelberg (2010). https://doi.org/10.1007/978-3-642-15910-7_7

18. Rodríguez, M., Largeteau-Skapin, G., Andres, E.: Adaptive pixel resizing for multiscale recognition and reconstruction. In: Wiederhold, P., Barneva, R.P. (eds.) IWCIA 2009. LNCS, vol. 5852, pp. 252–265. Springer, Heidelberg (2009). https://doi.org/10.1007/978-3-642-10210-3_20

19. Rosin, P., West, G.: Nonparametric segmentation of curves into various representations. IEEE Trans. Pattern Anal. Mach. Intell. **17**(12), 1140–1153 (1995)

20. Sharir, M., Welzl, E.: A combinatorial bound for linear programming and related problems. In: Finkel, A., Jantzen, M. (eds.) STACS 1992. LNCS, vol. 577, pp. 567–579. Springer, Heidelberg (1992). https://doi.org/10.1007/3-540-55210-3_213

21. Vacavant, A.: Robust image processing: definition, algorithms and evaluation. Habilitation, Université Clermont Auvergne (2018)

22. Vacavant, A., Kerautret, B., Roussillon, T., Feschet, F.: Reconstructions of noisy digital contours with maximal primitives based on multi-scale/irregular geometric representation and generalized linear programming. In: Kropatsch, W.G., Artner, N.M., Janusch, I. (eds.) DGCI 2017. LNCS, vol. 10502, pp. 291–303. Springer, Cham (2017). https://doi.org/10.1007/978-3-319-66272-5_24

23. Vacavant, A., Roussillon, T., Kerautret, B., Lachaud, J.: A combined multiscale/irregular algorithm for the vectorization of noisy digital contours. Comput. Vis. Image Underst. **117**(4), 438–450 (2013)

24. Valdivieso, H.: Polyline defined NC trajectories parametrization. A compact analysis and solution focused on 3D printing. arXiv preprint arXiv:1808.01831 (2018)

25. Welzl, E.: Smallest enclosing disks (balls and ellipsoids). In: Maurer, H. (ed.) New Results and New Trends in Computer Science. LNCS, vol. 555, pp. 359–370. Springer, Heidelberg (1991). https://doi.org/10.1007/BFb0038202

26. Wirjadi, O.: Survey of 3D image segmentation methods. Technical report, Berichte des Fraunhofer ITWM (2007)

27. Xiong, X., Feng, J., Zhou, B.: Real-time contour image vectorization on GPU. In: Braz, J., et al. (eds.) VISIGRAPP 2016. CCIS, vol. 693, pp. 35–50. Springer, Cham (2017). https://doi.org/10.1007/978-3-319-64870-5_2

Algorithms for Computing Topological Invariants in Digital Spaces

Li Chen[(✉)]

University of the District of Columbia, Washington, D.C., USA
`lchen@udc.edu`

Abstract. Based on previous results in digital topology, this paper focuses on algorithms related to topological invariants of objects in 2D and 3D Digital Spaces. Specifically, we are interested in hole counting objects in 2D and closed surface genus calculation in 3D. We also present a proof of the hole counting formula in 2D. This paper includes fast algorithms and implementations for topological invariants such as connected components, hole counting in 2D, and boundary surface genus for 3D. For 2D images, we designed a linear time algorithm to solve the hole counting problem. In 3D, we also designed a $O(n)$ time algorithm to obtain the genus of a closed surface. These two algorithms are both in $O(\log n)$ space complexity.

Keywords: Digital space · Images · Number of holes · Genus of surfaces · Algorithm · Time and space complexity

1 Introduction

Gathering topological properties for objects in 2D and 3D space is an important task in image processing. An interesting problem, called hole counting, involves summarizing the number of holes found in 2D images. In 3D, people in computer graphics or computational geometry usually uses triangulation to represent a 3D object. It uses the marching-cube algorithm to transfer a digital object into the representation of simplicial complexes, which requires a very large amount of computer memory.

This paper introduces fast algorithms for these calculations based on digital topology. This paper provides a complete process to deal with simulated and real data in order to obtain the topological invariants for 2D and 3D images. The algorithms are: (1) 2D hole counting, and (2) 3D boundary surface genus calculation.

One of the most difficult parts of real-world image processing is dealing with noise or pathological cases. This paper also gives detailed procedures for detecting such cases and will provide reasons for modifying the original image into an image where the mathematical formula could be applied.

The results of this paper have considerable potential to be used in big data processing, especially topological data processing [8,10,19].

© Springer Nature Switzerland AG 2021
M. Nguyen et al. (Eds.): ISGV 2021, CCIS 1386, pp. 203–218, 2021.
https://doi.org/10.1007/978-3-030-72073-5_16

2   Background Concepts of Digital Spaces

Digital topology was developed for image analysis in digital space, which is a discrete space where each point can be defined as an integer vector [13]. Some definitions of digital connectedness can also be found in [1,13]. The following figure provides some examples of digital space (Fig. 1).

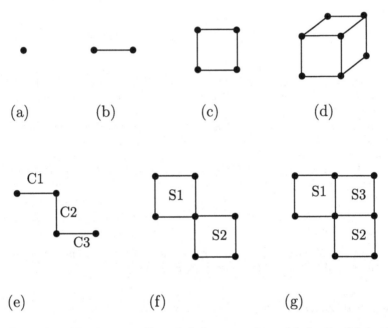

Fig. 1. Examples of basic unit cells and their connections: (a) 0-cells, (b) 1-cells, (c) 2-cells, (d) 3-cells, (e) Point-connected 1-cells, (f) Point-connected 2-cells, and (f) Line-connected 2-cells.

Certain related theorems using Euler characteristics and the Gauss-Bonnet theorem have already been proven. The first is about simple closed digital curves.

C is a simple closed curve in direct (4-) adjacency where each element in C is a point in Σ_2.

We use IN_C to represent the internal portion of C. Since direct adjacency has the Jordan separation property, $\Sigma_2 - C$ will be disconnected.

We also call a point p on C a CP_i point if p has i adjacent points in $IN_C \cup C$. In fact, $|CP_1| = 0$ and $|CP_i| = 0$ if $i > 4$ in C.

CP_2 contains outward corner points, CP_3 contains straight-line points, and CP_4 contains inward corner points.

For example, the following center point is an outward corner point in an array (see Fig. 2):

$$0\ 0\ 0$$
$$0\ 1\ 1$$
$$0\ 1\ x$$

However, in the next array, the center point is an inward corner point:

$$0\ 1\ x$$
$$1\ 1\ x$$
$$x\ x\ x$$

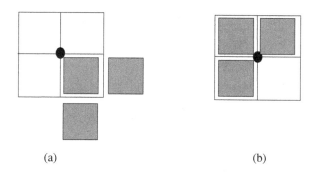

(a)   (b)

Fig. 2. Outward corner points and inward corner points

In [2], we used the Euler theorem to show these results for a simple closed curve C:

Lemma 1.
$$CP_2 = CP_4 + 4. \tag{1}$$

In 3D, let M be a closed (orientable) digital surface in 3D grid space with direct adjacency. We know that there are exactly 6 types of digital surface points (see Fig. 3), which was discovered by Chen and Zhang in [6]. Related definitions involving digital surfaces can be found in [6].

Assume M_i (M_3, M_4, M_5, M_6) is the set of digital points with i neighbors in the surface. M_4 and M_6 have two different types, respectively.

As we know, the Gauss-Bonnet theorem states if M is a closed manifold, then

$$\int_M K_G dA = 2\pi\chi(M) \tag{2}$$

where dA is a small element representing area and K_G is the Gaussian curvature.

Its discrete form is

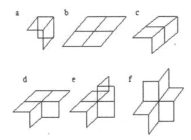

Fig. 3. Six types of digital surface points in 3D

$$\Sigma_{\{p \text{ is a point in } M\}} K(p) = 2\pi \cdot (2 - 2\,g) \tag{3}$$

where g is the genus of M. Chen and Rong obtained the following [7]:

$$g = 1 + (|M_5| + 2 \cdot |M_6| - |M_3|)/8. \tag{4}$$

For a k-manifold, homology group H_i, $i = 0, ..., k$ provides information on the number of holes in each i-skeleton of the manifold. When the genus of a closed surface is obtained, we can then calculate the homology groups corresponding to its 3D manifold [9,11].

3   Hole Counting Algorithms in 2D

Hole counting in 2D describes the number of holes in a 2D image. Previous research can be found in [12,17]. In this paper, we use a simple method to solve the hole counting problem.

A line or curve in the real world, for human interpretation, always has a degree of thickness regardless of how thin the structure is. However, a digital line may be interpreted differently. For example, Fig. 4 shows how similar digital objects can produce different results.

However, images in the digital world have a great deal of differentiability than humans shown in Fig. 4. The difference between (1) and (2) is not the same as the difference between (2) and (3). This is because Fig. 4(1) can be interpreted as a (square-)dotted line for one of its legs in terms of direct adjacency or 4-adjacency. A dotted line is a collection of several disconnected objects in 4-adjacency. Figure 4(4) may have no hole, one hole, or two holes. In 8-adjacency, there is no hole, and in 4-adjacency, the points are not connected. The best way in image processing would be to use 8-adjacency for "1"s (foreground) and 4-adjacency for "0"s (background). Only Fig. 4(6) will give a result most similar to the human interpretation in that there are two holes.

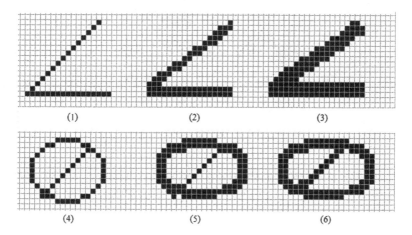

Fig. 4. Similar 2D digital objects with topological differences: (1) an angle with *thickness* = 1 using MS Paint Software, (2) an angle with *thickness* = 2, (3) an angle with *thickness* = 3, (4) an ellipse and a line with *thickness* = 1, (5) an ellipse and a line with varying thickness, and (6) an ellipse and a line with *thickness* = 2.

If we use 8-adjacency for "1"s and 4-adjacency for "0"s, this type of adjacency is called (8,4)-adjacency. This may cause other problems. For instance, let us assume we have two parallel "1" lines with one "0" line between them at a 45-degree angle. Each "0" point will be reviewed as a separated component, and they do not form a connected "0" line. This is also against human interpretation.

Our method assumes C does not contain the following cases (if there is any, we will modify the original image to remove these scenarios, which is discussed later):

$$
\begin{matrix} 1 & 0 \\ 0 & 1 \end{matrix}
$$

and

$$
\begin{matrix} 0 & 1 \\ 1 & 0 \end{matrix}
$$

These two cases are called pathological cases (see Fig. 5).

It is obvious that the solution we present does not solve all problems or cover all cases and is strict in its use. However, the advantage with our method is to obtain a simple treatment.

Our algorithm fills or deletes certain points in the original image to avoid pathological cases. We also want to remove single points, whether they are black or white, and treat them as noise.

Topological invariants should maintain the Jordan property. We only allow direct adjacency in order to deal with topological invariants, at least in most cases.

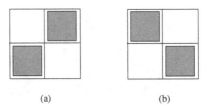

(a)   (b)

Fig. 5. Two pathological cases in 2D

Note that the number of holes in a connected component in 2D images is a basic invariant. With this, a simple formula can be proven using our previous results in digital topology [2].

3.1 The Simple Formula for the Number of Holes in S

An image segmentation method can extract a connected component. A connected component S in a 2D digital image is often used to represent a real object. The identification of the object can be done first by determining how many holes are in the component. For example, letter "A" has one hole and "B" has two holes. In other words, if S has h holes, then the complement of S has $h + 1$ connected components (if S does not reach the boundary of the image).

Theorem 1. *Let $S \subset \Sigma_2$ be a connected component and its boundary B be a collection of simple closed curves without pathological cases. Then, the number of holes in S is*

$$h = 1 + (CP_4 - CP_2)/4 \qquad (5)$$

$CP_4, CP_2 \subset B$.

In this section, we provide a proof using the 3D formula to get the theorem for holes.

Proof: Let $S \subset \Sigma_2$ be a connected component where its boundary does not have any pathological cases, something we can actually detect in linear time.

We can embed S into Σ_3 to make a double S in Σ_3. On the $z = 1$ plane, we have an S, denoted by S_1. We also have the exact same S on the $z = 2$ plane, denoted by S_2.

Without loss generality, $S_1 \cup S_2$ is a solid object. (For simplicity, we omit some technical details for the strict definition of digital surfaces here.) Its boundary consists of closed digital surfaces with genus $g = h$. We know

$$g = 1 + (|M_5| + 2 \cdot |M_6| - |M_3|)/8$$

It is easy to see that there will be no points in M_6 on the boundary of the 3D object bounded by $S_1 \cup S_2$. We might as well just using $S_1 \cup S_2$ to represent the solid object.

For each point x in CP_2 of $C \subset S$ where C is the boundary of S, we will have two points in M_3 in the solid $S_1 \cup S_2$. In the same way, if a point y is inward in $CP_4 \in C$, then we will get two points in M_5 in the solid $S_1 \cup S_2$. Since there is no point in M_6, i.e., $|M_6| = 0$. Therefore, $2|C_2| = |M_3|$ and $2|C_4| = |M_5|$. We have

$$h = g = 1 + (|M_5| + 2 \cdot |M_6| - |M_3|)/8 = 1 + (2|C_4| - 2|C_2|)/8$$

Thus,

$$h = 1 + (|C_4| - |C_2|)/4.$$

$\square$

We can also prove this theorem using Lemma 1 for digital curves: $CP_2 = CP_4 + 4$ for a simple closed curve. This theorem can also be proven intuitively [6].

We can see that this is a very simple formula for obtaining the number of holes (genus) for a 2D object and does not require any additional sophisticated algorithms. It only counts if the point is a corner point, inward point, or outward point.

However, we could not get a similar simple formula for triangulated representation of 2D objects since some of these special properties only hold in digital space.

3.2   Algorithms for Hole Counting

The key of the algorithm is to avoid all pathological cases. There are two types of such cases, and it may be difficult to decide whether we need to add or delete a point in order to avoid having a pathological case.

The first method is based on the original grid space. Sometimes, deleting a pixel to change a pathological case may result in another pathological case. In such scenarios, we add a pixel instead to change the original pathological case and vice versa.

In other scenarios where adding or deleting pixels will not eliminate the pathological case, we use delete since eventually it will complete the job. This is the example shown in Fig. 6.

The second method applies to the many instances of the image shown in Fig. 6. We need to consider a refinement method, e.g. using half-grid space to avoid the deletion and addition of a cell that will result in another pathological case. This method increases the amount of space needed. We use a half-size cell to fill the space or delete a half-size cell in order to remove the pathological case.

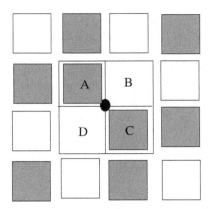

Fig. 6. Any deletion or addition of a pixel may add a new pathological case

Algorithm 3.1. Algorithm for calculating the number of holes in 2D images.

Step 1. Get connected components using direct-adjacency (4-adjacency).

Step 2. Extract every component using the following: Fill all single "0" pixels (unit-square or 2-cell) in as "1" if all their indirect neighbors (8-adjacency) are "1". Delete all single "1" pixels if all their indirect neighbors (8-adjacency) are "0".

Step 3. Find all pathological cases. Delete or add a pixel if this action does not create a new pathological case. If both actions create a new pathological case, then use delete. Repeat this step until all pathological cases are removed.

Step 4. Count all inward edge points CP_4 and outward points CP_2.

Step 5. $h = 1 + (CP_4 - CP_2)/4$.

Note that if deleting a pixel means changing the single "0" pixel (unit-square or 2-cell) to a "1" pixel. This may delete a hole or reduce a noise pixel. Do a refinement may be better for this case. The above calculation is to obtain holes for each component. Algorithm 3.1 is an $O(\log n)$ space algorithm without Step 1 since it is only counting the number of point types. If we assume the number of pathological cases is constant, this algorithm will have linear time complexity.

4   Algorithms and Implementations for the Genus of Digital Surfaces in 3D

Basically, the topological properties of an object in 3D contains connected components, genus of its boundary surfaces, and other homologic and homotopic properties. In 3D, the problem of obtaining fundamental groups is decidable, but no practical algorithm has yet been found. Therefore, homology groups have played the most significant role [6,9].

Theoretical results show that there exist linear time algorithms for calculating genus and homology groups for 3D Objects in 3D space [9]. However, the implementation of these algorithms is not simple due to the complexity of real data sampling. Most of the algorithms require triangulation of the input data since it is collected discretely. However, for most medical images, the data was sampled consecutively, meaning that every voxel in 3D space will contain data. In such cases, researchers use the marching-cubes algorithm to obtain the triangulation since it is a linear time algorithm [15]. In addition, the spatial requirements for such a treatment will be at least doubled by adding the surface-elements (sometimes called faces). Another defect of the marching-cubes algorithm is that it may generate a 3D object that is not a strict mathematical manifold even though the original triangulation is. Chen suggested using the so called convex-hull boundary method to complete such a task in digital geometry [5,6].

The theoretical work of calculating genus based on simple decomposition will turn into two different procedures: (1) finding the boundary of a 3D object and then using polygon mapping, also called polygonal schema, and (2) cell complex reductions where a special data structure will be needed.

In this paper, we look at a set of points in 3D digital space, and our purpose is to find the homology groups of the data set. The direct algorithm without utilizing triangulation was proposed by Chen and Rong in year 2008 [7]. However, this algorithm is based on the strict definition of digital surfaces. Many real 3D data sets may not satisfy this definition. In other words, a set of connected points may not be able to undergo such a process without further considerations using theoretical or practical methods.

In [7], we discuss the geometric and algebraic properties of manifolds in 3D digital spaces and the optimal algorithms for calculating these properties. We consider *digital manifolds* as defined in [6]. We presented a theoretical optimal algorithm with time complexity $O(n)$ to compute the genus and homology groups in 3D digital space, where n is the size of the input data [7]. More information related to digital geometry and topology can be found in [13,14]. Now we present the theoretical algorithm in [7] below.

Algorithm 4.1. Let us assume we have a connected M that is a 3D digital manifold in 3D.

Step 1. Track the boundary of M and ∂M, which is a union of several closed surfaces. This algorithm only needs to scan though all the points in M to see if the point is linked to any point outside of M, which will be a point on the boundary.

Step 2. Calculate the genus of each closed surface in ∂M using the method described in Sect. 2. We just need to count the number of neighbors on a surface. and put them in M_i using formula (4) to obtain g.

Step 3. Using theorem [7,9], we can get H_0, H_1, H_2, and H_3, where H_0 is Z. For H_1, we need to get $b_1(\partial M)$, which is the summation of the genus in all connected components of ∂M. (See [11] and [9].) H_2 is the number of components in ∂M, and H_3 is trivial.

Lemma 2. *Algorithm 4.1 is a linear time algorithm.*

Therefore, we can use linear time algorithms to calculate g and all homology groups for digital manifolds in 3D based on Lemma 2 and formula (4). We also have:

Theorem 2. *There is a linear time algorithm to calculate all homology groups for each type of manifold in 3D.*

However, this algorithm could not be directly used for real data set. We will explain next.

4.1 Practical Algorithms and Implementations

Above algorithm 4.1 is based on the condition that the a closed surface separates a 3D solid object into to connected components. It is related to Jordan manifolds, meaning that a closed $(n-1)$-manifold will separate the n-manifold into two or more components. For such a case, only direct adjacency will be allowed since indirect adjacency will not generate Jordan cases. The following figure shows four cases that must be deleted before performing the algorithm. These cases are called pathological cases in 3D.

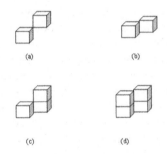

Fig. 7. Four pathological cases in 3D

We can see that when a data set contains indirect adjacent voxels, we need a procedure to detect the situation and delete some voxels in order to preserve the homology groups.

Assuming we only have a set of points in 3D. We can digitize this set into 3D digital spaces. There are two ways of doing so: (1) by treating each point as a cube-unit, called the raster space, (2) by treating each point as a grid point, called the point space. These two are dual spaces. Using the algorithm described in [2], we can determine whether the digitized set forms a 3D manifold in 3D space in direct adjacency for connectivity. The algorithm can be completed in linear time.

In terms of algorithms for connected component search, Pavlidis realized that one can use Tarjan's breadth-first-search (BFS) or depth-first-search (DFS) for images. The complexity of the algorithm is $O(n)$ [16]. In 3D, we have 6-, 18-,

26- connectivity. Since real data contains noise, it is better to consider all of these connectivities. Therefore, we use 26-connectivity to get the connected components. Since such connected component of real processing is not strictly 6-connected. The topological theorem generated previously in [7] is no longer applicable. Therefore we want to transform a 26-connected component to a 6-connected component.

In theory, this type of transformation should be done using the careful adding or deleting process since optimization of the minimum number of changes could be an NP-hard problem. A similar problem was considered in [18] where a decision problem using adding voxels was proposed.

Now we present the practical algorithms as follows:

Algorithm 4.2. Assume the Input is 3D points or voxels in 3D. We can treat 3D points to voxels. Let B be the boundary of the 3D object M.

Step 1: Separate the set of voxels to connected components using BST or DFS algorithm in 3D. We have a set of connected 3D objects. Let's working on a connected 3D object M.

Step 2: Delete pathological cases:

The following rules (observations) are reasonable: In a neighborhood $N_{27}(p)$ that contains 8 cubes and 27 grid points, use following prcedure:

a) If a voxel only shares a 0-cell with another voxel, then this voxel can be deleted.

b) If a voxel only shares a 1-cell with another voxel, then this voxel can be deleted.

c) If a boundary voxel v shares a 0,1-cell with another voxel, assume v also shares a 2-cell with a voxel u on the boundary, then u must share a 0,1-cell with a voxel that is not in the object M. Deleting v will not change the topological properties.

d) If, in a $2 \times 2 \times 2$ cube, there are 6 boundary voxels and their complement (two zero-valued voxels) are the case in Fig. 7(a). Add a voxel to this $2 \times 2 \times 2$ cube such that the new voxel shares as many 2-cells in the set as possible. This means that we want the added voxel to be inside the object where possible. (Record if more 3D objects are created by this step and put them in different sets/memory locations).

Step 3: Track the boundary M, said B, which is a union of several closed surfaces. This algorithm only needs to scan though all the points in M to see if the point is linked to a point outside of M. That point will be on boundary.

Step 4: Calculate the genus of each closed surface (e.g., B(1) . . . , B(k)) in the boundary B. The method is the following: since there are six different types of boundary points (on the boundary surface), two of them has 4 neighbors, and two of them has 6 neighbors in the surface (Fig. 3). We can use M_3, M_4, M_5, M_6 to denote the numbers of different types. M_i represents the number of points each of which has i-neighbors. The genus $g = 1 + (|M_5| + 2 \cdot |M_6| - |M_3|)/8$.

Step 5: Get homology groups H_0, H_1, H_2, and H_3. H_0 is Z. For $H1$, we need to get $b_1(B)$ that is just the summation of the genus in all connected components in B. H_2 is the number of components in B. H_3 is trivial. These are based on the Theorem in [7,9].

Therefore, we can use linear time algorithms to calculate g and all homology groups for digital manifolds in 3D.

Theorem 3. *There is a linear time algorithm to calculate all homology groups for each type of manifold in 3D when using Algorithm 4.2.*

Since this algorithm going through each point to test whether or not the neighborhood is on the boundary, it is a linear time and $O(log(n))$ space algorithm.

We add the following details to give more explanation to Step 2 of Algorithm 4.2: (1) There are only two cases in cubical or digital space [2] where two voxels (3-cells) share a 0-cell or 1-cell. Therefore, the algorithm needs to modify the voxel set so two voxels share exactly a 2-cell (or are not adjacent), or there is a local path (in the neighborhood) where two adjacent voxels share a 2-cell [2,6]. A case was mentioned in [18], which is the complement of the case where two voxels share a 0-cell (see Fig. 7(a)). Such a case may create a tunnel or it could be filled. Here, the algorithm simplifies the problem by adding a voxel in a $2 \times 2 \times 2$ cube. The similar case in point-space can also refer to the case in Fig. 7(a). We would like to point out that detection is easy but deleting certain points (and deleting the minimum number of points) to preserve homology groups seems to be a bigger issue.

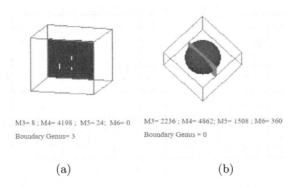

M3= 8 ; M4= 4198 ; M5= 24; M6= 0   M3= 2236 ; M4= 4862; M5= 1508 ; M6= 360

Boundary Genus= 3   Boundary Genus = 0

(a)   (b)

Fig. 8. Genus calculation for lab data.

4.2   Implementations and Data Samples

We implemented Algorithm 4.2 in C++ where the program modifies the date to fit the theoretical definition of 3D manifolds and their boundary surfaces that are supposed to be digital surfaces defined in [2]. We have tested many cases using lab data. The results for the genus were correct. It means that detection processing (plus adding or deleting some data points) preserves the topology of the objects. Two examples are shown in Fig. 8. We also applied the program to real data samples. From our observations, the results were also correct, see Fig. 9.

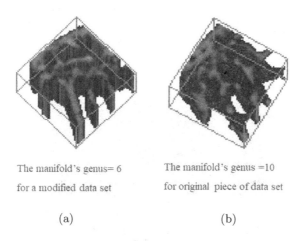

The manifold's genus= 6   The manifold's genus =10

for a modified data set   for original piece of data set

(a)   (b)

Fig. 9. Genus calculation for 3D real bone images.

Note that when the object becomes more complex, it is possible for pathological situations to arise (Fig. 10).

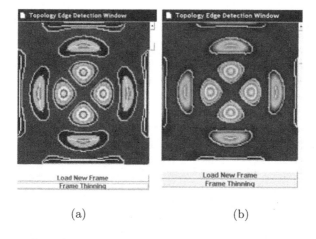

(a)   (b)

Fig. 10. Topological edge detection with different thresholds for 2D images.

5   Remarks on Programming

Programming and image display differ from theoretical or conceptual drawing. For different purposes, we sometimes need to use raster space, meaning that we treat a 3D point (a voxel) as a 3-cell. In other cases, we need to treat a 3D point as a 0-cell. The refinement can be used to reduce some conflicts but will enlarge the memory space needed. For 2D cases, we also need a similar consideration. The following figure shows the 2D topological edge detection with different thresholds. The software was made by the author.

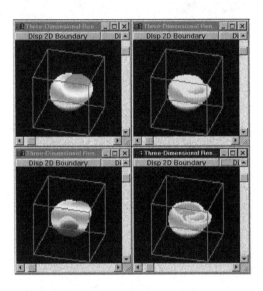

Fig. 11. Boundary tracking and display for different thresholds of 2D images.

In general, if the input data is in raster space, the boundary surface would be in point space. We must first make the translation from raster space to point space. Then, for each point on the surface, we count how many neighbors exist in order to determine its configuration category. The following figure shows the boundary tracking and display. The original data contains two holes inside. We track the boundary and display using thin-voxels as shown by the last image in Fig. 11.

6   Summary and Discussion

In this paper, we use digital topology to get a formula for calculating the number of holes in a connected component in 2D digital space. The formula is simple and can easily be implemented. The author does not know whether this formula has already been studied or obtained by other researchers. For 3D images, we developed a practical way of calculating the genus by extracting boundary surfaces and removing pathological cases. Both algorithms are optimal in terms of time and space complexity (assuming the number of pathological cases are constant). In the future, we will make Python programming code to use the methods described in this paper to topological big data analysis.

This paper is modified based on a previously unpublished note [4] and an informally published conference paper [3]. The original version of this paper was posted in 2013 on arxiv.org at https://arxiv.org/abs/1309.4109. We did some modification in this version.

References

1. Brimkov, V.E., Klette, R.: Border and surface tracing. IEEE Trans. Pattern Anal. Mach. Intell. **30**(4), 577–590 (2008)
2. Chen, L.: Discrete Surfaces and Manifolds. SP Computing, Rockville (2004)
3. Chen, L.: Genus computing for 3D digital objects: algorithm and implementations. In: Proceedings of the Workshop on Computational Topology in Image Context 2009, Austria, pp. 29–40 (2009)
4. Chen, L.: Determining the number of holes of a 2D digital component is easy, November 2012. http://arxiv.org/abs/1211.3812
5. Chen, L.: Digital Functions and Data Reconstruction. Springer, New York (2013). https://doi.org/10.1007/978-1-4614-5638-4
6. Chen, L.: Digital and Discrete Geometry. Springer, Heidelberg (2014). https://doi.org/10.1007/978-3-319-12099-7
7. Chen, L., Rong, Y.: Linear time recognition algorithms for topological invariants in 3D. In: Proceedings of International Conference on Pattern Recognition (ICPR08) (2008)
8. Chen, L., Biswas, S.: Digital curvatures applied to 3D object analysis and recognition: a case study. In: Barneva, R.P., Brimkov, V.E., Aggarwal, J.K. (eds.) IWCIA 2012. LNCS, vol. 7655, pp. 45–58. Springer, Heidelberg (2012). https://doi.org/10.1007/978-3-642-34732-0_4
9. Dey, T.K., Guha, S.: Computing homology groups of simplicial complexes in R^3. J. ACM **45**, 266–287 (1998)
10. Gholizadeh, S.: Topological data analysis in text processing. Doctoral Dissertation, The University of North Carolina at Charlotte (2020)
11. Hatcher, A.: Algebraic Topology. Cambridge University Press, Cambridge (2002)
12. Lin, X., Yang, J., Summers, W.: Hold holes countable in binary images. Technicial report, School of Computer Science, Colubus State University (2010). http://cs.columbusstate.edu/about_us/HolesCounting-Technical-Report.pdf
13. Klette, R., Rosenfeld, A.: Digital Geometry: Geometric Methods for Digital Image Analysis. Morgan Kaufmann, Burlington (2004)
14. Kong, T.Y., Rosenfeld, A. (eds.): Topological Algorithms for Digital Image Processing. Elsevier, Amsterdam (2006)
15. Lorensen, W.E., Cline, H.E.: Marching cubes: a high resolution 3D surface construction algorithm. Comput. Graph. **21**(4), 163–169 (1987)
16. Pavlidis, T.: Theodosios Algorithms for Graphics and Image Processing. Computer Science Press (1982)
17. Qian, K., Bhattacharya, P.: Determining holes and connectivity in binary images. Comput. Graph. **16**(3), 283–288 (1992)

18. Siqueira, M., Latecki, L.J., Tustison, N., Gallier, J., Gee, J.: Topological repairing of 3D digital images. J. Math. Imaging Vis. **30**(3), 249–274 (2008)
19. Snášel, V., Nowaková, J., Xhafa, F., Barolli, L.: Geometrical and topological approaches to big data. Future Gener. Comput. Syst. **67**, 286–296 (2017)

Discrete Linear Geometry on Non-square Grid

Troung Kieu Linh[1] and Atsushi Imiya[2]([⊠])

[1] School of Science and Technology, Chiba University,
Yayoi-cho 1-33, Inage-ku, Chiba 263-8522, Japan
[2] Institute of Management and Information Technologies, Chiba University,
Yayoi-cho 1-33, Inage-ku, Chiba 263-8522, Japan
`imiya@faculty.chiba-u.jp`

Abstract. We define the algebraic discrete geometry to hexagonal grid system on a plane. Since a hexagon is an element for tiling on a plane, hexagons are suitable as elements of discrete objects. For the description of linear objects in a discrete space, algebraic discrete geometry provides a unified treatment employing double Diophantus equations. Furthermore, we develop an algorithm for the polygonalisation of discrete objects on the hexagonal grid system.

1 Introduction

This paper deals with algebraic discrete geometry on hexagonal grid systems [1–8]. In the following, we first derive a set of inequalities for the parameters of a Euclidean linear manifold from sample points in the hexagonal grid system and an optimisation criterion with respect to this set of constraints for the recognition of the Euclidean line on the hexagonal grid system. Second, using this optimisation problem, we prove uniqueness and ambiguity theorems for the reconstruction of a Euclidean line on the hexagonal grid system. Finally, we develop a polygonalisation algorithm for the boundary of a discrete shape from a sequence of hexagonal grids.

Algebraic discrete geometry [9–13] allows us to describe linear manifolds, which are collections of unit elements, in two-dimensional discrete space as double Diophantus inequalities. For the reconstruction of a smooth boundary from sample points, polygonalisation on a plane is the first step. Following polygonalisation, we estimate the geometric features of a figure, such as the normal vector at each point on the boundary, and the length and area of planar shapes. There are basically three types of model for the expression of a linear manifold in the grid space, supercover, standard, and naive models [13]. We deal with the supercover model for the hexgonal grid system on a plane.

A hexagon on a plane has both advantages and disadvantages as an elemental cell of discrete objects [1–6]. The area encircled by a hexagon is closer to the area encircled by a circle than is the area encircled by a square. Although the dual lattice of a square grid is a square grid, the dual grid of a hexagonal grid

M. Nguyen et al. (Eds.): ISGV 2021, CCIS 1386, pp. 219–232, 2021.
https://doi.org/10.1007/978-3-030-72073-5_17

is a trianglar grid [14]. Therefore, for multi-resolution analysis, we are required to prepare two types of grid. From the application in omni-directional imaging systems in computer vision and robot vision [15,16], the spherical camera model has recently been of wide concern. Although the square grid yields uniform tiling on a plane, it is not suitable as a grid element on the sphere. The hexagonal grid system provides a uniform grid on both a sphere [15,17–19] and a plane [1–6].

In refs. [20–22] a linear-programming-based method for the recognition of linear manifolds for the square grid system has been proposed. This method is based on the mathematical property that a point set determines a system of linear inequalities for the parameters of a linear manifold, and the recognition process for a linear manifold is converted to the computation of the feasible region for this system of inequalities. The other class for the recognition of a linear manifold is based on the binary relation among local configurations in 3×3 pixel regions, since the geometrical properties of the discrete linear manifold are characterised by a sequence of 3×3 pixel regions [7,8,14]. Our method proposed in this paper is based on the former method for the derivation of constraints on parameters of the Euclidean line that passes through hexagonal grids.

2   Hexagonal Grid System on a Plane

We first define hexagonal grids on a two-dimensional Euclidean plane (x, y).

Definition 1. *We call the region*

$$\begin{cases} y_0 - 1 \leq y \leq y_0 + 1, \\ 2x_0 + y_0 - 2 \leq 2x + y \leq 2x_0 + y_0 + 2, \\ 2x_0 - y_0 - 2 \leq 2x - y \leq 2x_0 - y_0 + 2, \\ x_0 = 3\alpha, y_0 = 2\beta \ or \ x_0 = 3(\alpha + \frac{1}{2}), y_0 = 2\beta + 1, \\ \alpha, \beta \in \mathbf{Z} \end{cases} \tag{1}$$

the hexagonal grid centred at $x_0 = (x_0, y_0)^\top$. *Simply, we call it the hexel at* x_0.

The supercover [12,13] in the hexagonal grid is defined as follows.

Definition 2. *The supercover in the hexagonal grid system is a collection of all hexagons that cross a certain line.*

Figure 1(a) shows an example of the supercover in the hexagonal grid. Since the vertices of a hexagon are $(x_0 - 1, y_0)^\top$, $(x_0 + 1, y_0)^\top$, $(x_0 - \frac{1}{2}, y_0 + 1)^\top$, $(x_0 + \frac{1}{2}, y_0 + 1)^\top$, $(x_0 - \frac{1}{2}, y_0 - 1)^\top$, and $(x_0 + \frac{1}{2}, y_0 - 1)^\top$, the distances from these vertices to the centre of the hexagon are

$$D = \{d_i\}_{i=1}^6$$
$$= \{\frac{x_0 a + y_0 b + \mu - a}{\sqrt{a^2 + b^2}}, \ \frac{x_0 a + y_0 b + \mu + a}{\sqrt{a^2 + b^2}}, \ \frac{x_0 a + y_0 b + \mu + b - \frac{1}{2}a}{\sqrt{a^2 + b^2}},$$
$$\frac{x_0 a + y_0 b + \mu + b + \frac{1}{2}a}{\sqrt{a^2 + b^2}}, \ \frac{x_0 a + y_0 b + \mu - b - \frac{1}{2}a}{\sqrt{a^2 + b^2}}, \ \frac{x_0 a + y_0 b + \mu - b + \frac{1}{2}a}{\sqrt{a^2 + b^2}}\}.$$
$$\tag{2}$$

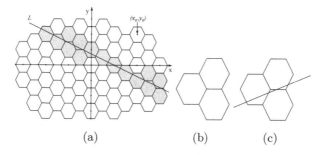

Fig. 1. Line on the hexagonal grid system. (a) Supercover in the hexagonal grids. (b) Bubble in the hexagonal grids. (c) Local relation between a line and a bubble on hexagonal grid system.

Therefore, if a line crosses a hexagon, we have the relations

$$\min\{d_i\} \leq 0 \leq \max\{d_i\}$$

$$\Longleftrightarrow -\max\{|a|, \frac{1}{2}|a| + |b|\} \leq x_0 a + y_0 b + \mu \leq \max\{|a|, \frac{1}{2}|a| + |b|\}$$

$$\Longleftrightarrow \quad 0 \leq |x_0 a + y_0 b + \mu| \leq \max\{|a|, \frac{1}{2}|a| + |b|\}. \tag{3}$$

These relations lead to the next theorem.

Theorem 1. *Setting a and b to be integers, the supercover of a line $L : ax + by + \mu = 0$ on the hexagonal grid is a collection of hexagons that satisfy the relations*

$$\mathcal{L} = \{(x, y)^\top \mid x = 3\alpha, y = 2\beta, \ |ax + by + \mu| \leq \max\{|a|, \frac{1}{2}|a| + |b|\}\}$$

$$\cup\{(x, y)^\top \mid x = 3(\alpha + \frac{1}{2}), y = 2\beta + 1, \ |ax + by + \mu| \leq \max\{|a|, \frac{1}{2}|a| + |b|\}\} \tag{4}$$

for integers α and β.

The following is a geometric definition of the bubble [10–13] in the hexagonal grid system.

Definition 3. *A bubble in the hexagonal grid system is three connecting hexagons that share a vertex, as shown in Fig. 1(b).*

Figure 1(c) shows that a supercover in the hexagonal grid system contains bubbles if a line crosses a pair of edges that share a vertex. Considering this geometric property of a bubble, we derive mathematical conditions of a line whose supercover contains bubbles.

First, we sort the elements of $D = \{d_i\}_{i=1}^{6}$, which are defined by (2), as

$$d_1 \leq d_2 \leq d_3 \leq d_4 \leq d_5 \leq d_6.$$

If a line crosses a pair of edges that share a vertex, the relations

$$d_1 \leq 0 \leq d_2 \leq d_3 \leq d_4 \leq d_5 \leq d_6 \tag{5}$$

or

$$d_1 \leq d_2 \leq d_3 \leq d_4 \leq d_5 \leq 0 \leq d_6 \tag{6}$$

are satisfied. These conditions are equivalent to

$$d_1 \leq 0 \leq d_2, \tag{7}$$
$$d_5 \leq 0 \leq d_6. \tag{8}$$

Therefore, setting

$$C = \{-a, a, b - \frac{1}{2}a, b + \frac{1}{2}a, -b - \frac{1}{2}a, -b + \frac{1}{2}a\}$$
$$= \{c_i \mid i = 1, \cdots, 6, c_1 \leq c_2 \leq c_3 \leq c_4 \leq c_5 \leq c_6\}, \tag{9}$$

Equations (7) and (8) are expressed as

$$c_1 \leq ax + by + \mu \leq c_2, \tag{10}$$
$$c_5 \leq ax + by + \mu \leq c_6. \tag{11}$$

Furthermore, Definition 3 implies that the centre of a hexagonal grid $(x, y)^\top$ satisfies the conditions

$$x = 3\alpha, y = 2\beta, \tag{12}$$

or

$$x = 3(\alpha + \frac{1}{2}), y = 2\beta + 1, \tag{13}$$

for integers α and β. This algebraic relation implies the following system of inequalities:

$$c_1 \leq 3a\alpha + 2b\beta + \mu \leq c_2, \tag{14}$$
$$c_5 \leq 3a\alpha + 2b\beta + \mu \leq c_6, \tag{15}$$
$$c_1 \leq 3a(\alpha + \frac{1}{2}) + b(2\beta + 1) + \mu \leq c_2, \tag{16}$$
$$c_5 \leq 3a(\alpha + \frac{1}{2}) + b(2\beta + 1) + \mu \leq c_6. \tag{17}$$

These relations lead to the conclusion that the supercover of line $ax + by + \mu = 0$ contains bubbles in the hexagonal grid system if a pair of integers (α, β) satisfies Eq. (14), (15), (16), or (17). The analysis above leads to the next theorem.

Theorem 2. *If the relations*

$$\frac{\mu - c_1 - m}{\gcd(3|a|, 2|b|)} \in \mathbf{Z} \quad \vee \quad \frac{\mu + b + \frac{3}{2}a - c_1 - n}{\gcd(3|a|, 2|b|)} \in \mathbf{Z}$$

$$\vee \quad \frac{\mu - c_5 - n}{\gcd(3|a|, 2|b|)} \in \mathbf{Z} \quad \vee \quad \frac{\mu + b + \frac{3}{2}a - c_5 - n}{\gcd(3|a|, 2|b|)} \in \mathbf{Z} \tag{18}$$

are satisfied, the supercover of line $ax + by + \mu = 0$ *contains bubbles, where*

$$0 \le m + c_1 \le c_2, \ \ 0 \le n + c_5 \le c_6, \ \ m + c_1 \in \mathbf{Z}, \ \ n + c_5 \in \mathbf{Z},$$

$$C = \{-a, a, b - \frac{1}{2}a, b + \frac{1}{2}a, -b - \frac{1}{2}a, \ -b + \frac{1}{2}a\}$$

$$= \{c_i \mid i = 1, \cdots, 6, c_1 \le c_2 \le c_3 \le c_4 \le c_5 \le c_6\}.$$

Now, we show two examples for the supercover in the hexagonal grid system.

Example 1. *For line* $2x + 7y - 1 = 0$, *we have*

$$C = \{-2, 2, 6, 8, -8, -6\}$$

$$= \{-8, -6, -2, 2, 6, 8\}$$

$$= \{c_i \mid i = 1, \cdots, 6, c_1 \le c_2 \le c_3 \le c_4 \le c_5 \le c_6\}, \tag{19}$$

$$\gcd(3|a|, 2|b|) = \gcd(6, 14) = 2. \tag{20}$$

From this relation, we can select m *and* n *from* $m = 0, 1, 2$, *and* $n = 0, 1, 2$, *respectively. If we select* $m = 1$, *we have the relation*

$$\frac{\mu - c_1 - m}{\gcd(3|a|, 2|b|)} = 3 \in \mathbf{Z}. \tag{21}$$

Therefore, the supercover of line $2x + 7y - 1$ *contains bubbles, as shown in Fig. 2(a)*

Example 2. *For line* $2x - 3y + 1 = 0$, *we have*

$$C = \{-2, 2, -4, -2, 2, 4\}$$

$$= \{-4, -2, -2, 2, 2, 4\}$$

$$= \{c_i \mid i = 1, \cdots, 6, c_1 \le c_2 \le c_3 \le c_4 \le c_5 \le c_6\}, \tag{22}$$

$$\gcd(3|a|, 2|b|) = \gcd(6, 6) = 6.$$

From this relation, we can select m *and* n *from* $m = 0, 1, 2$ *and* $n = 0, 1, 2$, *respectively. Here, plugging all combinations of* m *and* n *to Eq. (18) of theorem 2, we have the relations*

$$\frac{\mu - c_1 - m}{\gcd(3|a|, 2|b|)} = \frac{5}{6}, \frac{2}{3}, \frac{1}{2},$$

$$\frac{\mu + b + \frac{3}{2}a - c_1 - n}{\gcd(3|a|, 2|b|)} = \frac{5}{6}, \frac{2}{3}, \frac{1}{2},$$

$$\frac{\mu - c_5 - n}{\gcd(3|a|, 2|b|)} = -\frac{1}{6}, -\frac{1}{3}, -\frac{1}{2},$$

$$\frac{\mu + b + \frac{3}{2}a - c_5 - n}{\gcd(3|a|, 2|b|)} = -\frac{1}{6}, -\frac{1}{3}, -\frac{1}{2}.$$

Since all combinations of m *and* n *yield noninteger, the supercover of line* $2x - 3y + 1$ *does not contain any bubbles, as shown in Fig. 2(b).*

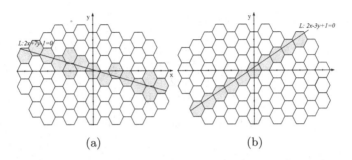

Fig. 2. Line on hexagonal grid and bubbles of dual hexels. (a) Supercover of $2x + 7y - 1 = 0$ on the hexagonal grid system. (b) Supercover of $2x - 3y + 1 = 0$ on the hexagonal grid system.

3   Reconstruction of Euclidean Line

In this section, we develop an algorithm for the reconstruction of the Euclidean line [12, 20–22] from sample hexels. For integers α_i and β_i, setting

$$P = \{(x_i, y_i)^\top \,|\, x_i = 3\alpha_i,\, y_i = 2\beta_i,\, i = 1, 2, \cdots, N\} \tag{23}$$

or

$$P = \{(x_i, y_i)^\top \,|\, x_i = 3(\alpha_i + \tfrac{1}{2}),\, y_i = 2\beta_i + 1,\, i = 1, 2, \cdots, N\} \tag{24}$$

to be the centroids of the hexels, for a pair of positive integers a and b, we have four cases:

$$\text{case1}: a \geq 2b > 0, 0 \leq |ax_i + by_i + \mu| \leq a, \tag{25}$$

$$\text{case2}: a \geq 2b > 0, 0 \leq |ax_i - by_i + \mu| \leq a, \tag{26}$$

$$\text{case3}: 0 < a < 2b, 0 \leq |ax_i + by_i + \mu| \leq \frac{1}{2}a + b, \tag{27}$$

$$\text{case4}: 0 < a < 2b, 0 \leq |ax_i - by_i + \mu| \leq \frac{1}{2}a + b. \tag{28}$$

Equations (23) and (24) are derived from Eqs. (12) and (13), respectively.

Here, we show the reconstruction algorithm for case 1. Assuming that all sample hexels are elements of the supercover of line $ax + by + \mu = 0$ for $a \geq 0$ and $b \geq 0$, we have the relations

$$\begin{cases} -a \leq ax_i + by_i + \mu \leq a, \\ a - 2b \geq 0, \\ a, b > 0, \\ i = 1, 2, \cdots, N, \end{cases}$$

$$\Longleftrightarrow \begin{cases} (x_i + 1)a + y_ib + \mu \geq 0 \\ -(x_j - 1)a - y_jb - \mu \geq 0 \\ a - 2b \leq 0 \\ a, b > 0 \\ i \neq j, \ i, j = 1, 2, \cdots, N, \end{cases}$$

$$\Longleftrightarrow \begin{cases} -(x_i + 1)a - y_ib \leq \mu \leq -(x_j - 1)a - y_jb, \\ (x_i - x_j + 2)a + (y_i - y_j)b \geq 0, \\ a - 2b \geq 0, \\ a, b > 0 \\ i \neq j, \ i, j = 1, 2, \cdots, N, \end{cases} \tag{29}$$

for

$$X_{ij} = x_i - x_j + 2, \quad Y_{ij} = y_i - y_j. \tag{30}$$

Then, Eq. (29) becomes

$$\begin{cases} -(x_i + 1)a - y_ib \leq \mu \leq -(x_j - 1)a - y_jb \\ X_{ij}a + Y_{ij}b \geq 0 \\ a - 2b \geq 0 \\ a, b > 0 \\ i \neq j, \ i, j = 1, 2, \cdots, N. \end{cases} \tag{31}$$

This expression allows us to use the algorithm derived in the ref. [23].

4   Polygonalisation from Hexels

Using the optimisation procedure for the recognition of a Euclidean line from a collection of hexels, in this section, we develop an algorithm for the polygonalisation of the discrete boundary of a binary shape [12].

Setting **P** to be a digital curve which is described a sequence of hexels, our problem is described as follows.

Problem 1. *Let* **P** *be the digital boundary curve of an object on the hexagonal grid system. Compute a partition of* **P**, *such that* $\mathbf{P} = \cup_{i=1}^{n} \mathbf{P}_i$, $\mathbf{P}_i = \{\mathbf{p}_{ij}\}_{j=1}^{n(i)}$ *for* $\mathbf{p}_{ij} = (x_{ij}, y_{ij})^{\top}$ *and* $|\mathbf{P}_i \cap \mathbf{P}_{i+1}| = \varepsilon$ *for an appropriate small integer* ε.

We solve the problem using the minimisation problem.

Problem 2. *Compute the number of polygonal edges* n *and triplets of parameters* $\{(a_i, b_i, \mu_i)\}_{i=1}^{n}$ *for edges that minimise the criterion*

$$z = \sum_{i=1}^{n} (|a_i| + |b_i| + \mu_i) \tag{32}$$

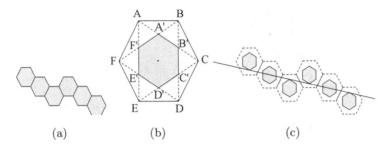

Fig. 3. Configuration of hexels and dual hexels. (a) Sequence of hexels, (b) Sequence of dual hexels in hexels, and (c) Local configuration of a line, hexels and dual hexels.

with respect to the system of inequalities,

$$|a_i x_{ij} + b_i y_{ij} + \mu_i| \leq \max\{|a_i|, \frac{1}{2}|a_i| + |b_i|\}, \quad x_{ij} = 3\alpha_{ij}, y_{ij} = 2\beta_{ij} \qquad (33)$$

or

$$|a_i x_{ij} + b_i y_{ij} + \mu_i| \leq \max\{|a_i|, \frac{1}{2}|a_i| + |b_i|\}, \quad x_{ij} = 3(\alpha_i + \frac{1}{2}), y_{ij} = 2\beta_{ij} + 1, \quad (34)$$

where $\alpha_{ij}, \beta_{ij} \in \mathbf{Z}$.

The following is an incremental algorithm for this minimisation problem.

---

step 1: Input the centroids of hexels, say, $\mathbf{P} = \{\mathbf{p}_i \,|i = 0, 1, 2, \cdots, n\}$.
step 2: Set $head = 0, j = 0$.
step 3: Set $tail = head + 3$.
step 4: Set $\mathcal{L}_j = \{\mathbf{p}_i\}_{tail}^{head}$.
step 5: If a line l_j which passes through $\mathcal{L}_j = \{\mathbf{p}_i\}_{tail}^{head}$,
         then set $tail = tail + 1$ and go to step 3.
step 6: If $j = 0$, then set $j = j + 1, head = tail$ and go to step 2.
step 7: If $j > 0$, then compute the common point of l_{j-1} and l_j,
         and set it as A_{j-1}.
step 8: If A_{j-1} exists and it is included in $\mathcal{L}_j$ or $\mathcal{L}_{j-1}$, then go to step 10.
step 9: Set $head = head - 1$ and go to step 3.
step 10: Output $\mathcal{L}_{j-1}$ and l_{j-1}.
step 11: If $tail < n$, then set $head = tail$ and $j = j + 1$, and go to step 3.
step 12: If $tail = n$, then stop.

To remove the bubbles from the supercover of a line, we introduce a dual hexel. For hexel ABCDEF in Fig. 3(b), we define the dual hexel A'B'C'D'E'F', as shown in Fig. 3(b). As shown in Fig. 3(c), if line L passes through points A'B'C'D'E'F' without crossing with vertices A, B, C, D, E, and F, the supercover of L is bubble-free.

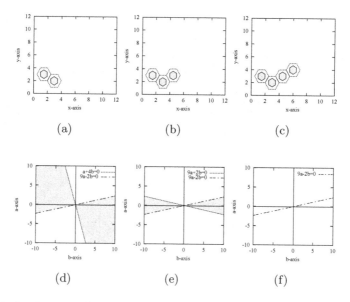

Fig. 4. Relation between the feasible regions and the number of dual hexels. (a), (b), and (c) are configurations of dual hexels in the connected hexels. (d), (e), and (f) are feasible regions of parameters that define Euclidean lines for the hexel configurations of (a), (b), and (c), respectively.

Setting $(x_i, y_i)^\top$ to be the centroid of a hexel, the vertices of the dual hexel are $(x_i - \frac{1}{2}, y_i)^\top$, $(x_i - \frac{1}{2}, y_i + \frac{1}{3})^\top$, $(x_i, y_i + \frac{2}{3})^\top$, $(x_i + \frac{1}{2}, y_i + \frac{1}{3})^\top$, $(x_i + \frac{1}{2}, y_i - \frac{1}{3})^\top$, $(x_i, y_i - \frac{2}{3})^\top$, and $(x_i - \frac{1}{2}, y_i - \frac{1}{3})^\top$. Therefore, the bubble-free supercover defined by hexels whose centroids are $\{p_i = (x_i, y_i)^\top\}_{i=1}^{n-1}$ is

$$0 \le |ax_i + by_i + \mu_i| \le \max\{\frac{2|b|}{3}, \frac{|a| + |b|}{2}\}, \quad i = 0, 1, 2, ..., n - 1. \tag{35}$$

Figures 4 and 5 show the transition of the feasible regions of the parameters of lines for the dual hexel and hexels, respectively. In Fig. 4, (a), (b), and (c) are configurations of dual hexels in the connected hexels. (d), (e), and (f) are feasible regions of parameters that define Euclidean lines for the hexel configurations of (a), (b), and (c), respectively. Furthermore, In Fig. 5, (a), (b), and (c) are configurations of dual hexels in the connected hexels. (d), (e), and (f) are feasible regions of parameters that define Euclidean lines for the hexel configurations of (a), (b), and (c), respectively.

5 Numerical Examples

For error analysis, we have evaluated the total areas encircled by the reconstructed curves and the total lengths of reconstructed curves for the circles whose radius are from 10 to 1000.

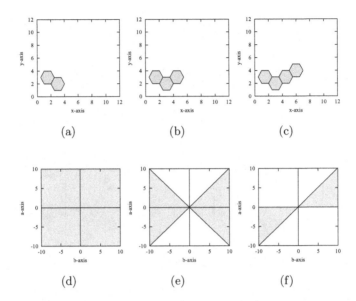

Fig. 5. Relation between the feasible regions and the number of hexels. (a), (b), and (c) are configurations of dual hexels in the connected hexels. (d), (e), and (f) are feasible regions of parameters that define Euclidean lines for the hexel configurations of (a), (b), and (c), respectively.

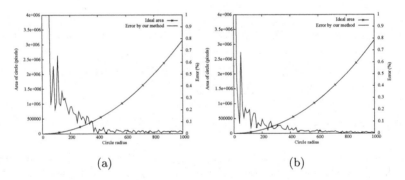

Fig. 6. Error analysis of polygonalisation from hexels. (a) Error analysis for the polygons reconstructed from hexels (b) Error analysis for the polygons reconstructed from dual hexels.

Figure 6(a) and 6(b) show the results of error analysis for the polygons reconstructed from hexels and dual hexels, respectively. These results show that by increasing the resolution, the reconstructed curves converge to the original curves.

Figures 7 and 8 show the results of polygonalisation from digital curves of hexels and dual hexels, respectively. The order of the dual-hexel sequence is the same as that of the original hexels on the curve. The numbers of edges of the

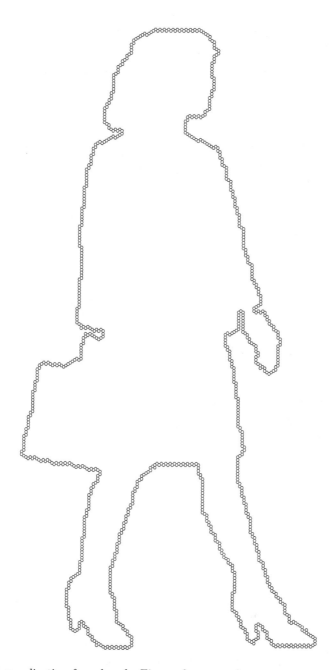

Fig. 7. Polygonalisation from hexels. Figure shows a polygon reconstructed from hexels. The number of edges of the polygon is 130.

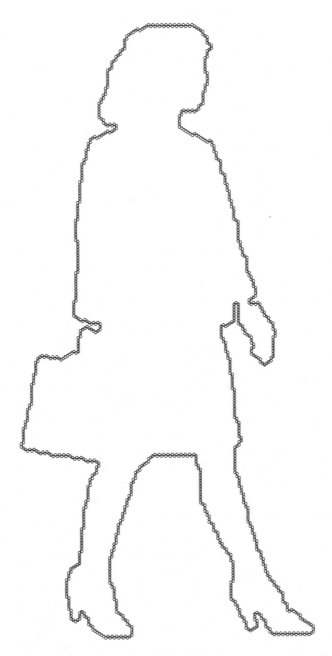

Fig. 8. Polygonalisation from hexels. Figure shows a polygon reconstructed form dual hexels. The number of edges of the polygon is 260. This polygon is bubble-free. Furthermore, edges of this polygon pass through the inner areas of hexels.

polygon in Figs. 7 and 8 are 130 and 260, respectively. Furthermore, the edges of the polygon in Fig. 8 pass through the inner areas of the original hexel and there is no bubble of three hexels. These results show the validity of our bubble removal strategy introduced in the previous section.

6   Conclusions

We defined algebraic discrete geometry to hexagonal grids on a plane. Using algebraic discrete geometry, we developed an algorithm for the polygonalisation of discrete objects on a hexagonal-grid plane.

In this paper, we aimed to formulate the recognition of a linear manifold from a discrete point set as a nonlinear optimisation problem. We dealt with a supercover model on a plane and in a space. We first derived a set of inequalities for the parameters of a Euclidean linear manifold from sample points and an optimisation criterion with respect to this set of constraints for the recognition of the Euclidean linear manifold. Second, using this optimisation problem, we develop an algorithm for the computation of parameters of the Euclidean linear manifold from hexels on a plane.

Liu [2,3] introduced algorithms for the generation of sequences of connected hexagons from a line and a circle, respectively. In this paper, we dealt with three problems

1. Generation of a sequence of hexels from piecewise linear curves.
2. Generation of a sequence of hexels that contain given hexels.
3. Reconstruction of a piecewise linear curve from a sequence of connected hexels.

Therefore, our algorithm generally resolves the problems dealt wiht by Liu [2,3].

Most of this paper is based on the research conducted by Troung Kieu Linh while she was at the School of Science and Technology, Chiba University.

References

1. Her, I.: Geometric transformations on the hexagonal grid. IEEE Trans. Image Process. **4**, 1213–1222 (1995)
2. Liu, Y.-K.: The generation of straight lines on hexagonal grids. Comput. Graph. Forum **12**, 27–31 (1993)
3. Liu, Y.-K.: The generation of circle arcs on hexagonal grids. Comput. Graph. Forum **12**, 21–26 (1993)
4. Stauton, R.C.: An analysis on hexagonal thinning algorithms and skeletal shape representation. Pattern Recogn. **29**, 1131–1146 (1996)
5. Middleton, L., Sivaswamy, J.: Edge detection in a hexagonal-image processing framework. Image Vis. Comput. **19**, 1071–1081 (2001)
6. Middleton, L., Sivaswamy, J.: Hexagonal Image Processing. Springer, Heidelberg (2005). https://doi.org/10.1007/1-84628-203-9
7. McAndrew, A., Osborn, C.: The Euler characteristic on the face-centerd cubic lattice. Pattern Recogn. Lett. **18**, 229–237 (1997)

8. Saha, P.K., Rosenfeld, A.: Strongly normal set of convex polygons or polyhedra. Pattern Recogn. Lett. **19**, 1119–1124 (1998)
9. Schramm, J.-M.: Coplanar tricubes. In: Ahronovitz, E., Fiorio, C. (eds.) DGCI 1997. LNCS, vol. 1347, pp. 87–98. Springer, Heidelberg (1997). https://doi.org/10.1007/BFb0024832
10. Vittone, J., Chassery, J.M.: Digital naive planes understanding. In: Proceedings of SPIE, vol. 3811, pp. 22–32 (1999)
11. Reveilles, J.-P.: Combinatorial pieces in digital lines and planes. In: Proceedings of SPIE, vol. 2573, pp. 23–34 (1995)
12. Coeurjolly, D., Zerarga, L.: Supercover model, digital straight line recognition and curve reconstruction on the irregular isothetic grids. Comput. Graph. **30**, 46–53 (2006)
13. Andres, E., Nehlig, P., Françon, J.: Supercover of straight lines, planes and triangles. In: Ahronovitz, E., Fiorio, C. (eds.) DGCI 1997. LNCS, vol. 1347, pp. 243–254. Springer, Heidelberg (1997). https://doi.org/10.1007/BFb0024845
14. Barneva, R.P., Brimkov, V.E., Nehlig, P.: Thin discrete triangular meshes. Theoret. Comput. Sci. **246**, 73–105 (2000)
15. Kimuro, K., Nagata, T.: Image processing on an omni-directional view using a hexagonal pyramid. In: Proceedings of JAPAN-USA Symposium on Flexible Automation, vol. 2, pp. 1215–1218 (1992)
16. Benosman, R., Kang, S.-B. (eds.): Panoramic Vision, Sensor, Theory, and Applications. Springer, Heidelberg (2001). https://doi.org/10.1007/978-1-4757-3482-9
17. Shar, K., White, D., Kimerling, A.J.: Geodesic discrete global grid systems. Cartogr. Geogr. Inf. Syst. **30**, 121–134 (2003)
18. Randall, D.A., Ringler, T.D., Heikes, R.P., Jones, P., Baumgardner, J.: Climate modeling with sperical geodesic grids. IEEE Comput. Sci. Eng. **4**, 32–41 (2002)
19. Morgan, F.: Riemannian Geometry: A Beginner's Guide. Jones and Bartlett Publishers (1993)
20. Françon, J., Schramm, J.-M., Tajine, M.: Recognizing arithmetic straight lines and planes. In: Miguet, S., Montanvert, A., Ubéda, S. (eds.) DGCI 1996. LNCS, vol. 1176, pp. 139–150. Springer, Heidelberg (1996). https://doi.org/10.1007/3-540-62005-2_12
21. Buzer, L.: A linear incremental algorithm for naive and standard digital lines and planes recognition. Graph. Models **65**, 61–76 (2003)
22. Buzer, L.: A simple algorithm for digital line recognition in the general case. Pattern Recogn. **40**, 1675–1684 (2007)
23. Linh, T.K., Imiya, A.: Nonlinear optimization for polygonalization. In: Nyström, I., Sanniti di Baja, G., Svensson, S. (eds.) DGCI 2003. LNCS, vol. 2886, pp. 444–453. Springer, Heidelberg (2003). https://doi.org/10.1007/978-3-540-39966-7_42

Electric Scooter and Its Rider Detection Framework Based on Deep Learning for Supporting Scooter-Related Injury Emergency Services

Hoa Nguyen$^{(\boxtimes)}$, Minh Nguyen$^{(\boxtimes)}$, and Qian Sun$^{(\boxtimes)}$

Auckland University of Technology, Auckland, New Zealand
{h.nguyen,minh.nguyen}@aut.ac.nz

Abstract. Electric scooters (e-scooters) have been considered as a "last mile" solution to existing public transportation systems in many cities all over the world due to their convenience at a highly affordable price. E-scooters enable users to travel distances which are too long to walk but too short to drive, so they help to reduce the number of cars on the roads. Along with its increasing popularity, accidents involving e-scooters have become a growing public concern, especially in large cities with heavy traffic.

It is useful to detect and include e-scooters in traffic control. However, there is no available pre-built-model for detecting an electric scooter. Therefore, in this paper, we proposed a scooter and its rider detection framework that supports emergency management for scooter-related injuries. The framework helps to identify scooter and its rider in livestream videos and can be applied in traffic incidents detection applications. Our model was developed based on deep learning object detection models. Using ImageAI API, we trained and deployed our own model based on 200 images acquired on the internet. The preliminary results appeared to be robust and fast; however, the accuracy of our proposed model could be improved if using a larger dataset for training and evaluating.

Keywords: Object detection · Deep learning · Electric scooter · Emergency services

1 Introduction

1.1 Motivation

Electric scooters (e-scooters), promoted by sharing companies, first launched in San Francisco in 2017, and then expanded as a "last mile" solution to existing public transportation systems in many cities all around the world [1,2]. Reports from the two most popular companies, Lime and Bird, showed that each has more than 10 million rides since their first operation in July and September

© Springer Nature Switzerland AG 2021
M. Nguyen et al. (Eds.): ISGV 2021, CCIS 1386, pp. 233–246, 2021.
https://doi.org/10.1007/978-3-030-72073-5_18

2017, respectively [3]. Not only offering an attractive travelling method for too long distances to walk but too short to drive, e-scooters may help to reduce the number of cars on the roads as well. However, the increasing popularity of e-scooters has raised public safety concerns to riders and pedestrians [4].

There have been numerous reports of e-scooter-related injuries involving its riders, pedestrians and other road vehicles. In Singapore, around 90 crashes related electric devices including e-scooters have been reported in the first half of 2017, resulting in about 90 injuries and 4 deaths [5]. A study conducted by Trivedi et al. [6] reported that 249 patients presented to 2 urban emergency departments in Southern California with injuries associated with standing electric scooter use during the study period from September 2017 to August 2018. In Australian countries, an increased burden on healthcare services for e-scooter related injuries has been seen [1]. A study performed at a single emergency department in Brisbane showed that 78% of e-scooter patients required X-rays and 24% required CT scans [7]. While over 200 plain films and 47 CT scans were requested for e-scooter related injuries at Auckland City Hospital in the first 2 months after e-scooters have been launched [8]. Unsafe riding behaviours, such as going into unauthorized traffic lanes, not wearing helmet, or overloading the scooter with multiple riders, etc., may be associated with the presentations for e-scooter related injuries [9].

Thanks for the development and progress of science and technology, object detection based on deep learning has been widely applied in various applications, such as driver-less car, robotics, video surveillance and pedestrian detection [10]. The technology is capable of assisting people to efficiently solve traffic problems by detecting vehicles in the traffic.

1.2   Proposed Idea

In this paper, we propose an e-scooter and its rider detection framework based on deep learning as illustrated in Fig. 1. There are four loosely connected components: camera system, YouTube server, processing computer, and control centre. The camera system captures activities from real-life and then broadcasts the stream to YouTube server. Processing computer downloads data from YouTube server and sends the broadcast results back to server. Afterwards, the detection result of the traffic flow including e-scooters, riders, vehicles as well as pedestrians will be displayed on the computer. Finally, the computer sends the results and notification to the control centre which provides the analysis and statistics for supporting decision making, or generates alarm in case the system detects a rider falling from scooter. The system helps detect incidents when e-scooters are used in the traffic. For example, from the auto-detection, we can detect the number of people riding on the e-scooter, whether the scooter goes into unauthorized traffic lanes or not, or even whether there is any falling from the e-scooter or not. Risk situations are reported and alarms will be sent to emergency services if an incident is detected. The custom model that can achieve scooter and its rider detection was trained by 200 images of scooters and its rider dataset which was collected from the internet. It has the ability to detect both scooter and its rider with background noise.

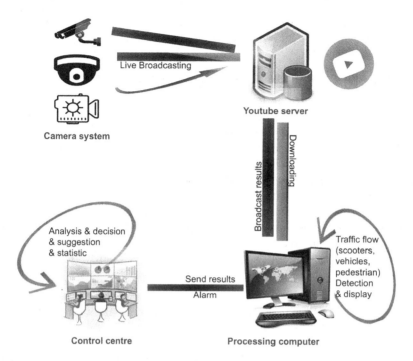

Fig. 1. Overall diagram of our proposed intelligent video-surveillance framework

2   Background

With the development and progress of science and technology, repetitive and time-consuming work have been taken over by the computer. Computer vision, as an inter-discipline based on image processing, machine learning and pattern recognition, is a rapidly developing research field in recent years. Object detection is a significant task in computer vision and it is used in detecting an object from certain scenes via some specific approach and algorithm [11]. One of the common application of object detection for public problem is to detect vehicles in the traffic. This section summarized traditional object detection methods as well as deep learning-based algorithms of object detection which is the background for building our deep learning model.

2.1   Traditional Object Detection Algorithms

In earlier studies, various artificially extracted features were employed for object detection. The three most commonly used features were Haar [12], HOG [13], and LBP [14]. The classifiers matched by these three features which mainly include the support vector machine (SVM), Adaboost, and the Haar feature set combined with the Adaboost. For many years, they have been widely used in the computer vision methods, initially intended for face detection [15]. The

HOG feature combined with the SVM classifier, has been widely used in image recognition, and it has achieved great success in pedestrian detection.

2.2 Deep Learning-Based Object Detection Algorithms

In recent years, deep learning methods has been becoming a hot research topic for many researchers, and a large number of deep learning target detection algorithms have been developed. Compared with traditional methods, deep learning method requires a massive amount of data, and automatic learning can reflect the characteristics of data differences, hence, makes it more representative. In the meantime, in visual recognition, the process of a Convolutional Neural Network (CNN) layer feature extraction is similar to the human visual mechanism, which represents the process from the edge to a part to the whole [16]. Recently, the deep learning target detection algorithms have obtained competitive real-time performance compared with the traditional methods due to the continuous expansion in data volume and rapid update of devices hardware. Thus, it has begun to gain recognition from the industry worldwide.

R-CNN: The first R-CNN algorithm was proposed by Ross Girshick in 2014, he combined region proposals with CNNs to achieve scale object detection [18]. The R-CNN algorithm performs the region search first, and then classifies the candidate regions. The Selective Search Method of R-CNN is used to generate candidate regions [18]. Its outstanding feature is to reduce information redundancy and increase detection speed.

Fast R-CNN: Fast R-CNN, an upgraded network structure based on both of R-CNN and SPP-Net, was proposed by Girshick in 2015 [19]. It applied Softmax classifier instead of SVM classifier so that achieving end-to-end training with a multi-task loss rather than single-stage. Training is able to update all network layers, in order to get higher detection accuracy, which is the most advantage of the algorithm. The RoI pooling is the core algorithm module. Max pooling is being used in the RoI pooling layer to transfer the features inside all valid area where is related into a smaller feature map along with a static spatial range of H × W. The H and W are the layer hyper-parameters which are isolated from any specific RoI [19].

Faster R-CNN: Faster R-CNN, such a kind of optimization Fast R-CNN, has saved more the running time of detection networks than Fast R-CNN [20]. Moreover, it is a single, unified network for object detection. Because it introduces a concept of the Region Proposal Network (RPN), which will generate region proposals from neural network used to learn by itself. RPN is a fully-convolutional network that is naturally implemented, which support being trained end-to-end by back-propagation as well as stochastic gradient descent. Any size of the image will be taken as input by the RPN. Then the RPN outputs a set of rectangular object proposals which has an objectness score [20].

YOLO: YOLO, an abbreviation for You Look Only Once, is a new algorithm for object detection. Compared to previous work in the related fields, YOLO mount object detection as a spatial regression problem to isolated bounding boxes and related class probabilities. It is a single neural network which can predict bounding boxes and class probabilities directly from full images in one single evaluation process [21]. This algorithm is capable of predicting what type of objects are included and where they are in the frame. It has three significant advantages than other object detection algorithms. Firstly, it performs very fast due to its instinct for the regression problem without a complex pipeline. Secondly, it executes the reasoning via the global approach when performing prediction in which leads to less background errors. Finally, YOLO learns the data from a more generic representation which helps to learn easily in another domain [21]. Whereas, YOLO still have some limitations of object detection. YOLO limits the number of adjacent objects that our model can predict due to the spatial restriction. The spatial restriction is due to each grid cell can only predict two boxes with only one class [21]. Therefore, the issue will occur with small objects coming up as groups.

YOLOv3: YOLOv3 is a better solution compared to YOLO as it takes the anchor box idea from Faster R-CNN. YOLOv3 makes it better to detect small objects due to using the Darknet53 network which is based on the residual network as a feature extractor, and thus multi-scale detection and multi-label classification are the improvements of YOLOv3 [22]. Furthermore, YOLOv3 gets rid of the manually selected anchor box and execute k means clustering based on the dimension of the bounding boxes to achieve a better prior [23]. Especially in the aspect of handling the issue of the same target having two labels, Sigmoid function as the activation function for class prediction has better performance than softmax function [23]. As a result, YOLOv3 enable to perform multi-tag classification of a specific target via binary cross-entropy loss and logistic regression during the training process [22].

3 Design and Implementation

Figure 1 illustrates the overall diagram of our proposed framework. In this paper, we mainly focus on training a deep learning model for detecting electric scooter and its rider.

3.1 E-Scooter and Its Rider Detection Framework

Our proposed framework for detecting e-scooter and its rider is illustrated in Fig. 2. By default, the camera system captures images from real-life and sends the stream to Youtube server. The processing computer downloads the data from YouTube server and runs custom object detection algorithm. Here YOLOv3 object detection model is applied to detect the object. However, using the official object detection model (YOLOv3), our system can only recognize a number of

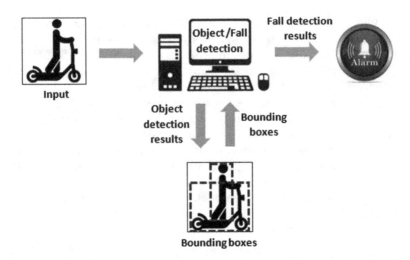

Fig. 2. Proposed e-scooter and its rider detection framework

pre-defined classes of objects. A new model was trained by transfer learning to achieve recognition for e-scooter and its rider. Object detection application provides bounding boxes of the objects including scooters, riders (person with scooter) and pedestrians. Bounding boxes of riders are considered as input of fall detection application. If it detects a fall, it generates an alarm and sends to control centre. Algorithm 1 summarizes object detection process and Algorithm 2 defines fall detection process. The pseudocode for Algorithm 1 and Algorithm 2 are below.

Algorithm 1. Pseudo code for custom object detection

Input: Data (video stream) from YouTube.
Output: Bounding boxes.
Method:

1: Receive data (video stream) from YouTube.
2: Run custom object detection model.
3: Save bounding boxes into xml file.
4: When End of data ⇒ **Exit**.

Figure 3 shows how the model works based on YOLOv3 algorithm. Our custom model forms the model of detection as a regression perspective. It separates the image into an even grid and parallel calculates bounding boxes with its confidence and class probabilities.

Algorithm 2. Pseudocode code for fall detection

Input: Bounding boxes (scooters, riders) from xml file.
Output: Fall detection results (1: Fall, 0: Not fall).
Method:

    Receive data (bounding boxes) from xml file.
2: Run custom fall detection model.
    Save fall detection results into xml file.
4: If Fall then send alarm to control centre.
    When End of data ⇒ **Exit**.

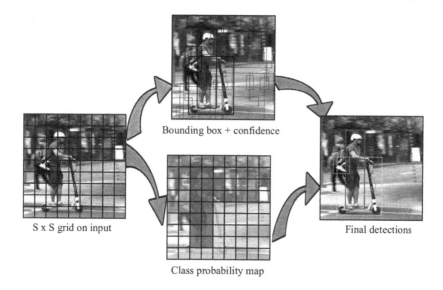

Fig. 3. E-scooter and its rider detection model based on YOLO

3.2 E-Scooter and Its Rider Detection Model Training and Deploying

The task of e-scooter and its rider detection model training and deploying includes the following parts.

Prepare Dataset: 200 images are collected from Google Image and Baidu Image using keyword "rider and scooter". We take the first 140 (70%) images as the training set and take the rest 60 (30%) images as the validation set. We use the labelling tool to select the person area and the scooter area at the image respectively and then save it to the annotation xml file. We repeat this process 200 times. After labelling the images, the folder structure of the dataset folder includes training dataset and validation dataset.

Install ImageAI and Dependencies: The processing computer used in this work is a non-GPU machine - a MacBook Air machine with Intel Core i5 processor @ 1.6 GHz and 4.00 GB of RAM, running macOS Mojave operating. Since our local Mac Book does not have GPU, Google colab is the best way to run the training for the new model. ImageAI is used for high-level training the new deep learning network and it can be installed via *"!pip3 install imageai –upgrade"*. Tensorflow is installed via *"!pip3 install tensorflow-gpu==1.13.1"* as the lower level dependency of ImageAI.

Train Custom Model: For achieving the goal, Google Colab, a free cloud service, is utilized to train the model. The custom model training uses the ImageAI *DetectionModelTrainer* API. This API is based on YOLOv3 algorithm, which is for unified, real-time object detection. Processing images via YOLOv3 is simple and straightforward to shorten detection time. In order to achieve a better detection accuracy, transfer learning from a pre-trained YOLOv3 model will be applied in the training.

Evaluate Model: In evaluation step, we import the DetectionModelTrainer class and create an instance of it. Then we set the model type to YOLOv3 and set the data directory as well as pass the path of files including h5 file, json file as the *"model_path"* and the *"json_path"*.

Test Model: We use the *CustomVideoObjectDetection* API from ImageAI to test our custom scooter and its rider detection model. Firstly, we import the *CustomVideoObjectDetection* class from ImageAI and the os. Then we instantiate a new instance from the *CustomVideoObjectDetection* class and set the model type to YOLOv3 (pre-trained transfer model). After that, we load the trained model and pass the path of the input video and the path of the output video created by ImageAI.

3.3   Fall Detection Implementation

Fall detection process is illustrated in Fig. 4. From the person bounding box detected by object detection model, we identify the centre point of the box and track this point. We draw the movement of the centre point in continuous detected bounding boxes. Standing and lying states are defined based on the aspect ratio of a bounding box (HW ratio), which is the ratio of the box's height to the box's width [28]. If height is larger than width, it is standing state. If height is smaller than width, it is lying state. The distance between centres of points of bounding boxes after each fall is used to verify real falls away from all other actions (include false positive). Fall event notification is only activated when the detected human does not show to be able to stand up after the fall.

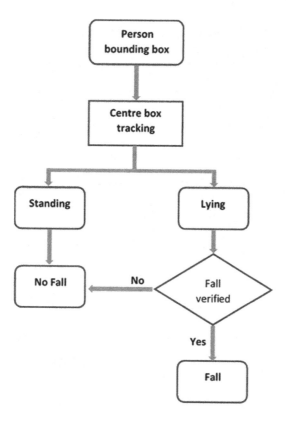

Fig. 4. Fall detection process

4 Results and Evaluations

4.1 Training Model Process

Once the object is detected, the generated output video will contain boxes with percentage probabilities numbers on the object detected from ImageAI. A screenshot of e-scooter and its rider detection is shown by Fig. 5

During the custom scooter and its rider detection training process, the value of both *"batch_size"* and *"epoch"* are the significant factors to determined the detection accuracy, due to the loss value will be influenced.

The result of the Fig. 6 shows that the overall trend is that as numbers of epoch increases, the loss decreases. The significant drop of the loss is after the first two epoch. Comparing the batch size 4 and batch size 8, the batch size 4 has less loss than size 8 overall.

The result of this accuracy vs epoch chart shows demonstrates the difference between running the training against batch size 8 and 4 in Fig. 7. As shown in the Y axis, the accuracy increases slowly after the 3rd epoch. Consequently, the figure shows that the size of batch 4 achieves better accuracy than the size 8.

Fig. 5. E-scooter and its rider detection results

4.2 Evaluation Model Process

We mainly use three threshold values to control the process of the evaluation during the implementation stage of scooter and its rider detection. Those three thresholds are *"iou_threshold"*, *"object_threshold"* and *"nms_threshold"*.

- **"iou_threshold":**
  "iou_threshold", is the value of minimum Intersection over Union (IoU). It can set from 0.0 to 1.0. The IoU score is a common benchmark score for semantic segmentation [25]. It is being used widely in the area of computer vision due to the PASCAL VOC segmentation challenges which is a benchmark for visual object category detection and recognition. It supplies a standard dataset of images with their annotation as well as the standard evaluation processes for machine learning [26].

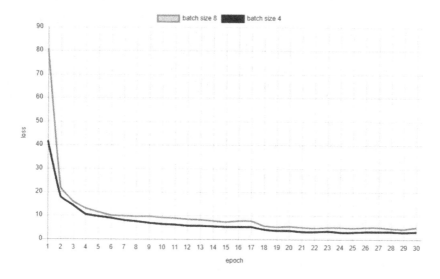

Fig. 6. The loss of batch size 4 and 8

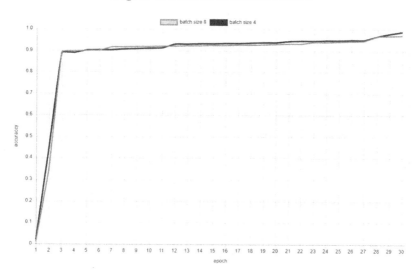

Fig. 7. The accuracy of batch size 4 and 8

– **"Object_threshold":**
  "Object_threshold" is another parameter of minimum class score for the mAP computation.
– **"nms_threshold":**
  "nms_threshold", is the Non-maximum suppression(NMS) for the mAP computation. NMS is a post-processing algorithm accountable for combining all detections which all belong to the same object [27].

In the context of this experiment, both the *iou* and *nms* set to 0.5, while the *object threshold* is set to 0.3. After succesffully running the evaluation code, the evaluation results of the model is shown in Fig. 8. From the evaluation results, taking mAP and loss value into accounts, it obviously shows that in most cases, the accuracy of the model increases when mAP increases or the loss decreases.

Model File: dataset/models/detection_model-ex-07--loss-4.44.h5
Using IoU : 0.5
Using Object Threshold : 0.3
Using Non-Maximum Suppression : 0.5
scooter: 0.9321
mAP: 0.9321

Model File: dataset/models/detection_model-ex-10--loss-3.25.h5
Using IoU : 0.5
Using Object Threshold : 0.3
Using Non-Maximum Suppression : 0.5
scooter: 0.9625
mAP: 0.9625

Model File: dataset/models/detection_model-ex-05--loss-5.21.h5
Using IoU : 0.5
Using Object Threshold : 0.3
Using Non-Maximum Suppression : 0.5
scooter: 0.9104
mAP: 0.9104

Model File: dataset/models/detection_model-ex-03--loss-6.24.h5
Using IoU : 0.5
Using Object Threshold : 0.3
Using Non-Maximum Suppression : 0.5
scooter: 0.8020
mAP: 0.8020

Fig. 8. Evaluation results

5   Conclusion and Future Work

With the rapid development and progress of science and technology, especially in the area of computer vision research, object detection is the main hot topic via deep learning. This technology can apply to different scenarios to make our life becoming more intelligent. One of the common applications of object detection is to detect vehicles in the traffic via deep learning model. It is widely applied in assisting people to efficiently solve traffic problems.

As e-scooters have become more and more popularity in many large cities all around the world, detecting and including e-scooters in traffic control are useful. These applications may help to support safe e-scooter riding behaviours as well as provide timely emergency intervention if incidents related to e-scooters happen, and then may eliminate bad affect of e-scooter related injuries.

This paper focused on applying deep learning models to detect e-scooter and its rider in the traffic. The aim of this research is to support risk situations awareness and timely emergency management if incidents happen. Due to the limitation of the hardware, we only used 200 images for training and evaluating the scooter and its rider detection model. Results from running with maximum 30 epochs shows that the accuracy is acceptable to detect objects in images and videos.

The future work involves developing fall detection model, training and testing our proposed framework with a larger dataset to improve the accuracy of our model. Furthermore, we will test our proposed system on live streaming videos to evaluate its capability of applying in real applications.

References

1. Beck, S., Barker, L., Chan, A., Stanbridge, S.: Emergency department impact following the introduction of an electric scooter sharing service. Emerg. Med. Australas. **32**(3), 409–415 (2020)
2. Sipe, N., Pojani, D.: Can e-scooters solve the 'last mile' problem? They'll need to avoid the fate of dockless bikes (2018)
3. Aizpuru, M., Farley, K.X., Rojas, J.C., Crawford, R.S., Moore Jr., T.J., Wagner, E.R.: Motorized scooter injuries in the era of scooter-shares: a review of the national electronic surveillance system. Am. J. Emerg. Med. **37**(6), 1133–1138 (2019)
4. DiMaggio, C.J., Bukur, M., Wall, S.P., Frangos, S.G., Wen, A.Y.: Injuries associated with electric-powered bikes and scooters: analysis of US consumer product data. Injury Prev. **26**(6), 524–528 (2019)
5. Che, M., Lum, K.M., Wong, Y.D.: Users' attitudes on electric scooter riding speed on shared footpath: a virtual reality study. Int. J. Sustain. Transp. **15**, 1–10 (2020)
6. Trivedi, T.K., et al.: Injuries associated with standing electric scooter use. JAMA Netw. Open **2**(1), e187381–e187381 (2019)
7. Mitchell, G., Tsao, H., Randell, T., Marks, J., Mackay, P.: Impact of electric scooters to a tertiary emergency department: 8-week review after implementation of a scooter share scheme. Emerg. Med. Australas. **31**(6), 930–934 (2019)
8. Mayhew, L.J., Bergin, C.: Impact of e-scooter injuries on emergency department imaging. J. Med. Imaging Radiat. Oncol. **63**(4), 461–466 (2019)
9. Terrell, G.C.: Characterizing electric scooter riding behavior to detect unsafe and non-compliant use (2019)
10. Tang, C., Feng, Y., Yang, X., Zheng, C., Zhou, Y.: The object detection based on deep learning. In: 4th International Conference on Information Science and Control Engineering (ICISCE), pp. 723–728. IEEE, China (2017)
11. Chen, Z., Khemmar, R., Decoux, B., Atahouet, A., Ertaud, J.Y.: Real time object detection, tracking, and distance and motion estimation based on deep learning: application to smart mobility. In: Eighth International Conference on Emerging Security Technologies (EST), pp. 1–6. IEEE, UK (2019)

12. Kozakaya, T., Shibata, T., Yuasa, M., Yamaguchi, O.: Facial feature localization using weighted vector concentration approach. Image Vision Comput. **28**(5), 772–780 (2010)
13. Dalal, N., Triggs, B.: Histograms of oriented gradients for human detection. In: 2005 IEEE Computer Society Conference on Computer Vision and Pattern Recognition (CVPR 2005), vol. 1, pp. 886–893. IEEE, USA (2005)
14. Zhang, G., Huang, X., Li, S.Z., Wang, Y., Wu, X.: Boosting local binary pattern (LBP)-based face recognition. In: Li, S.Z., Lai, J., Tan, T., Feng, G., Wang, Y. (eds.) SINOBIOMETRICS 2004. LNCS, vol. 3338, pp. 179–186. Springer, Heidelberg (2004). https://doi.org/10.1007/978-3-540-30548-4_21
15. Leistner, C., Roth, P.M., Grabner, H., Bischof, H., Starzacher, A., Rinner, B.: Visual on-line learning in distributed camera networks. In: 2008 Second ACM/IEEE International Conference on Distributed Smart Cameras, pp. 1–10. IEEE, USA (2008)
16. LeCun, Y., Bengio, Y., Hinton, G.: Deep learning. Nature **521**(7553), 436–444 (2015)
17. Dhande, M.: What is the difference between AI, machine learning and deep learning. Geospatial World (2017)
18. Girshick, R., Donahue, J., Darrell, T., Malik, J.: Rich feature hierarchies for accurate object detection and semantic segmentation. In: Proceedings of the IEEE Conference on Computer Vision and Pattern Recognition, pp. 580–587. IEEE, USA (2014)
19. Girshick, R.: Fast R-CNN. In: Proceedings of the IEEE International Conference on Computer Vision, pp. 1440–1448. IEEE, Chile (2015)
20. Ren, S., He, K., Girshick, R., Sun, J.: Faster R-CNN: towards real-time object detection with region proposal networks. In: Advances in Neural Information Processing Systems, pp. 91–99 (2015)
21. Redmon, J., Divvala, S., Girshick, R., Farhadi, A.: You only look once: unified, real-time object detection. In: Proceedings of the IEEE Conference on Computer Vision and Pattern Recognition, pp. 779–788. IEEE, USA (2016)
22. Wang, H., Zhang, Z.: Text detection algorithm based on improved YOLOv3. In: 9th International Conference on Electronics Information and Emergency Communication (ICEIEC), pp. 147–150. IEEE, China (2019)
23. Wu, F., Jin, G., Gao, M., Zhiwei, H.E., Yang, Y.: Helmet detection based on improved yolo v3 deep model. In: 16th International Conference on Networking. Sensing and Control (ICNSC), pp. 363–368. IEEE, Canada (2019)
24. Yajai, A., Rodtook, A., Chinnasarn, K., Rasmequan, S.: Fall detection using directional bounding box. In: 12th International Joint Conference on Computer Science and Software Engineering (JCSSE), pp. 52–57. IEEE, USA (2015)
25. Nowozin, S.: Optimal decisions from probabilistic models: the intersection-over-union case. In: Proceedings of the IEEE Conference on Computer Vision and Pattern Recognition, pp. 548–555. IEEE, USA (2014)
26. Everingham, M., Van Gool, L., Williams, C.K., Winn, J., Zisserman, A.: The pascal visual object classes (voc) challenge. Int. J. Comput. Vision **88**(2), 303–338 (2010)
27. Hosang, J., Benenson, R., Schiele, B.: Learning non-maximum suppression. In: Proceedings of the IEEE Conference on Computer Vision and Pattern Recognition, pp. 4507–4515. IEEE, USA (2017)
28. Yajai, A., Rodtook, A., Chinnasarn, K., Rasmequan, S.: Fall detection using directional bounding box. In: 2015 12th International Joint Conference on Computer Science and Software Engineering (JCSSE), pp. 52–57. IEEE, July 2015

Tracking Livestock Using a Fully Connected Network and Kalman Filter

Farah Sarwar[1] , Anthony Griffin[1(✉)] , and Timotius Pasang[2]

[1] Electrical and Electronic Engineering Department,
Auckland University of Technology, Auckland 1142, New Zealand
{farah.sarwar,anthony.griffin}@aut.ac.nz
[2] Mechanical Engineering Department,
Auckland University of Technology, Auckland 1142, New Zealand
timotius.pasang@aut.ac.nz

Abstract. Multiple object tracking (MOT) consists of following the trajectories of different objects in a video with either fixed or moving background. In recent years, the use of deep learning for MOT in the videos recorded by unmanned aerial vehicles (UAVs) has introduced more challenges and hence has a lot of room for extensive research. For the tracking-by-detection method, the three main components, object detector, tracker and data associator, play an equally important role and each part should be tuned to the highest efficiency to increase the overall performance. In this paper, the parameter selection of the Kalman filter and Hungarian algorithm for sheep tracking in paddock videos is discussed. An experimental comparison is presented to show that if the detector is already providing good results, a small change in the system can degrade or improve the tracking capabilities of remaining components. The encouraging results provide an important step in an automated UAV-based sheep tracking system.

Keywords: Livestock · UAV · Tracking · CNN · Kalman filter

1 Introduction

Research in the field of object tracking—especially multiple object tracking (MOT)—is gaining more and more attention with the increase in demand to automate the systems for crowd estimation, facial recognition, wildlife monitoring, autonomous driving, vehicle detection and surveillance, to name a few. Some applications, like tracking eye movement of drivers for fatigue detection, require the detection and tracking of a single object, while many others like autonomous driving, pedestrians detection, and livestock tracking have to simultaneously track multiple objects in the consecutive video frames. Irrespective of single object tracking, an important step in MOT is to associate the track identities (IDs) with detection, known as data association. This step is needed to keep a track of all those objects that enter or leave any frames and also to keep the IDs associated with respective objects only, especially in occlusion [8].

© Springer Nature Switzerland AG 2021
M. Nguyen et al. (Eds.): ISGV 2021, CCIS 1386, pp. 247–261, 2021.
https://doi.org/10.1007/978-3-030-72073-5_19

MOT can be performed as an online or offline task; online tracking [6] is usually done for real-time applications where future frames are not available and information from the previous frames is used to predict objects' motion, while offline tracking [15] is usually performed for recorded videos that can utilise the information from past and future frames. However, in both cases, the main challenges are the presence of noise in a video recorded from a low-resolution camera, complex object contour, object occlusion, variation in object scale and blurriness. The use of an unmanned aerial vehicle (UAV) adds more challenges, like a sudden change in the movement pattern of an object due to the fluctuations in the UAV flight in a windy environment and increase in scene complexity due to moving background along with objects. The object size also varies with changes in UAV altitude and results in the loss of most of the distinguishing features. As images and videos from different perspectives are needed for object detection and tracking—rather than using fixed position cameras—the use of UAVs is gaining similar interest in various research areas of computer vision and artificial intelligence.

In this research article, we propose a tracking-by-detection method for livestock detection, tracking and counting using a UAV. The data was collected at different heights using DJI Phantom 3 Pro in sheep farms near Pirinoa, New Zealand. In this article, the results of videos recorded from a height of 80 m are reported. The task of sheep detection was performed using a U-Net model [13,14]. For livestock tracking, a Kalman filter [17] as a motion predictor and Hungarian algorithm [9] as a detection-to-track linker were used. It was observed that as all sheep look tiny and similar from this height, a careful parameter selection is needed for the Kalman filter and Hungarian algorithm to predict the next state close to the actual location. Although the object detector has the main impact on such systems, the adjustment of the tracker and data associator parameters is equally important and a small change can increase the overall efficiency.

2   Related Work

Tracking algorithms are broadly classified in two main categories; (i) detection-based tracking [4] and (ii) detection-free tracking [10]. The detection-based tracking—also known as tracking-by-detection—has a pre-trained object detector to locate objects in each frame as a preliminary step. These values—either as a bounding box or centroid—are used by the tracker to initialize the tracking process. If an object detector fails in its task at any intermediate frame, due to occlusion or any reason, the tracker keeps predicting the object's state for a few more frames. It is the task of data associator to link the same track with a respective object once it reappears in the video. However, if the object stays undetected for many frames then the track is deleted and a new track is assigned to it later, if needed. Detection-free tracking, on the other hand, requires initialization of the object locations in the first frame and tracks them throughout the video using the objects' features. It works best for videos recorded by fixed position cameras, which have distinctive objects in the foreground with a non-moving background. It is not a very useful approach for those videos where objects can enter or leave in the middle of the video.

Siqi Ren, Yue Zhou and Liming He [12] performed MOT by initially dividing detection results into false, high uncertain, and low uncertain categories, and delayed the results of low uncertain detections until the end of the video. They penalized the false detections and constructed a tracking tree for less uncertain detections. This helped them to improve the overall performance of the system. Tubelets with convolutional neural networks (T-CNN) was proposed by Kai Kang et al. [7] as an end-to-end deep learning framework for detection and tracking by incorporating temporal and contextual information. Gaoang Wang et al. [15] also combined temporal and appearance information to generate tracklets by associating detection results in consecutive frames, known as TrackletNet Tracker (TNT). Similarly, Zhongdao Wang et al. [16] proposed a shared MOT model that combined a target detection and appearance model into a single-shot detector in a way that it can simultaneously output detection and update location. Shivani et al. [8] used the Deep Simple Online Real Tracking (Deep SORT) algorithm as a baseline to build their algorithm and used a combination of YOLOv3 and RetinaNet for generating detection results in a video recorded by a drone-mounted camera. Kwangjin Yoon et al. [18] proposed a data association method for MOT using deep neural networks and highlighted the importance of the data association method in tracking-by-detection methods. They used bounding boxes and a track-history as input for long short term memory (LSTM) networks. The final output is an association matrix to show correspondence between tracks and detection. Similarly, a multiple hypothesis tracker (MHT) [3,21] and particle filter [4] can be used with good efficiency but with a comparatively high computational cost. Recent survey papers [5,20] gave a systematic literature review of various MOT algorithms in their four main stages: feature extraction, detection, motion prediction and data association. They highlighted the issues related to MOT and how the complex background and occlusion problems can decrease the performance of any algorithm.

MOT using Kalman filter and different data association methods have been used by many researchers [6,10,19]. To the authors' knowledge, the literature has revealed that the adjustment of its parameters taking into account the physical context of the objects have not been discussed in detail. Kalman filters have been previously used for tracking large objects in different scenarios. This research article focuses on the parameter adjustment to observe the impact on its performance for tracking many small and similar objects, in videos recorded by a UAV-mounted camera. Instead of using the bounding boxes, the centroid values of the respective sheep are used.

3   Methodology

In the tracking-by-detection method, the object detector plays a vital role in keeping up the overall efficiency of the system. By improving the performance of the detector, it becomes easier for the tracker and data associator to estimate

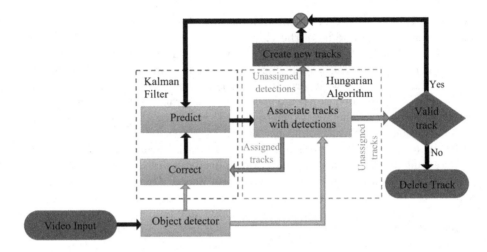

Fig. 1. A system diagram of livestock detection, tracking and data association, starting from the second frame of the video. A Kalman filter provides the predicted states of the tracks and Hungarian algorithm use these predicted state values and object detector's estimations to link tracks with detected objects. Correction of tracks is the last step of this system and all tracks are predicted for the upcoming frame in the next time step.

motion and associate detections with existing tracks, respectively. The detector used in this research is a U-Net model to detect sheep in videos recorded by a UAV, which can detect sheep with a very high recall [14] and gives the centroid values of all the detected objects. Offline tracking is performed and Fig. 1 shows the flowchart of our object tracking methodology. It is further explained in the following subsections.

3.1   Object Tracker

Some pre-processing steps were performed to reduce the overall tracking time. It was assumed that the fenced area was pre-defined in video frames and no objects were detected outside the paddock fence. The recorded videos—as well as video frames—were downsampled by a factor of two, and every second frame was fed to the tracker and object detector. The original dimension of each RGB frame was 4096 × 2160 pixels and was reduced to 2048 × 1080 pixels. After these pre-processing steps, the first frame was only used by the object detector to estimate the centroid of each object in the first frame and initialize the Kalman filter accordingly. Figure 1 shows the process from the second frame onward.

The trained U-Net model [14] was used to detect sheep in each frame of the video, and provides two outputs: a probability map and an object count. The mean shift clustering algorithm is applied to the probability map to compute the centroids of the detected sheep in the respective frame. These centroid values, and the object's velocity in x and y directions, were provided to the Kalman filter [17] as the initial value of the object's state. Although, the coordinates are directly provided by the detector, the velocity can be provided in two ways. Either by setting the initial velocity to zero and using higher covariance values for the filter, or using the average velocity of livestock obtained from the information in previous frames. The second option is only valid where all objects are moving with the same velocity, and the same value can be used for all objects. To observe how the tracker adjusts the states in a noisy environment, the results are presented by setting initial velocity to zero. So, for the m-th object in the i-th frame, the state vector is provided as

$$\mathbf{s}_i^m = [c_{\mathrm{x},i}^m,\ v_{\mathrm{x},i}^m,\ c_{\mathrm{y},i}^m,\ v_{\mathrm{y},i}^m]^T, \tag{1}$$

where $c_{\mathrm{x},i}^m$ and $c_{\mathrm{y},i}^m$ are the x- and y-coordinates of the true centroid of the m-th object, and $v_{\mathrm{x},i}^m$, $v_{\mathrm{y},i}^m$ are its velocities in the respective directions. For each object, the state in the i-th frame can be modelled using the value of the state of the respective objects in the $(i-1)$-th frame as follows

$$\mathbf{s}_i = \mathbf{F}\mathbf{s}_{i-1} + \mathbf{w}_i, \tag{2}$$

where $\mathbf{F}$ is the state transition matrix and $\mathbf{w}_i$ is the process noise, which is zero mean normal distribution with covariance $\mathbf{Q}$. The state transition model is the core of the filter and needs to be designed carefully according to the physical context and motion properties of the tracked object. This is a very crucial step and is a main factor in predicting the next state from the current state. $\mathbf{Q}$ accounts for the unexpected noise in the whole system. For example, in the case of a UAV, a smooth flight can experience disturbances due to gusty wind or the UAV speed may need adjustments repeatedly, hence causing unexpected variations in object motion. This value can be adjusted according to the quality of recorded video and how much variation appeared in the object's motion.

For each frame, a measurement related to each state can be modelled as

$$\mathbf{z}_i = \mathbf{H}\mathbf{s}_i + \mathbf{v}_i, \tag{3}$$

where $\mathbf{H}$ is the measurement model matrix and covers the difference between the detector's measurement and the corresponding state of the Kalman filter. $\mathbf{H}$ remains constant throughout the process and simply maps an object's measurement to the respective state. Here, $\mathbf{v}_i$ is the observation noise and is also assumed to be zero mean normal distribution with covariance $\mathbf{R}$. Like $\mathbf{Q}$, $\mathbf{R}$ should be adjusted as per the uncertainty of the detector's output and small values should be used if the detector's estimations are very accurate. The Kalman filter is a recursive algorithm, that predicts the optimal states before reading the observation, and updates the states using the values provided by the detector for the current frame.

3.2   Data Association

The assignment problem was solved using the Hungarian algorithm [9] to link the predicted states of the tracker with the detector's estimations for the current frame. It uses a cost matrix that is computed between each value provided by the detector and the existing tracks. A cost of non-association (CNA) needs to be provided to adjust the leniency of this assignment task and was adjusted experimentally. This helped to assign the existing track IDs to the same detected object, and identify unassigned detections and tracks. The assigned tracks were sent to the correction step of the filter to correct and update trackers' states. New tracks were created for the unassigned detections, while unassigned tracks were checked against a few conditions to decide whether they should be deleted or kept in the loop.

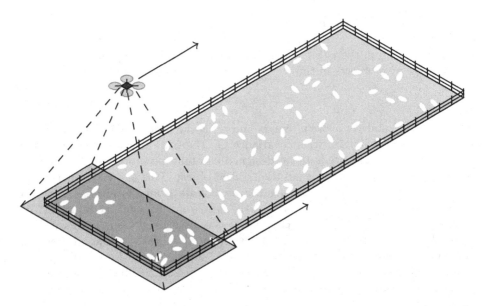

Fig. 2. A visual overview of how a video of paddock is recorded using a UAV, with white ellipses representing sheep. As the UAV moves forward, sheep exit at the bottom of the current frame, and new sheep enter at the top.

3.3   New and Old Tracks

As the UAV flies over the paddock, many objects leave the frame from the bottom and many enter the frame through the top, as illustrated in Fig. 2. As this happens, new tracks need to be created with unique IDs and a few need to be deleted accordingly. Tracks were terminated using one of the following three conditions:

1. The visibility of the track was less than 60% and it was visible for less than two frames,
2. The predicted state of the track was outside the frame dimension,

3. The object linked with the track was not detected consecutively in more than F_{lost} frames.

The first condition was used to terminate false positive (FP) detections as they appear only a few times in the video, and the second condition was for all those objects which left the frame from the bottom of the video. Such tracks should be deleted as early as possible to avoid an unbounded growth of tracks and reduce computational resources. However, there were some cases where a sheep, standing in a group, was detected in a frame and then the detector was unable to locate it in some consecutive frames. In such situations, the track was kept in the loop for at least F_{lost} frames and was then deleted afterwards. The third condition was for these kinds of objects and was very crucial.

4   Experimental Evaluation

4.1   Parameter Selection

The height of 80 m for the UAV flight was chosen to keep the paddock fences within a frame from the left and right sides. The UAV moved in one direction only so the objects—sheep—exhibit linear motion of constant velocity. A few sheep showed random non-linear motion in some frames, and the parameters of the Kalman filter and Hungarian algorithm were tuned to cover such issues. The values of the variables used in the prediction step were as follows:

$$\mathbf{F} = \begin{bmatrix} 1 & T_x & 0 & 0 \\ 0 & 1 & 0 & 0 \\ 0 & 0 & 1 & T_y \\ 0 & 0 & 0 & 1 \end{bmatrix}, \quad \mathbf{Q} = q\,I_{4\times4}, \quad \mathbf{R} = r\,I_{4\times4}, \tag{4}$$

where $I_{4\times4}$ is the 4×4 identity matrix, and T_* is the sampling interval which was set to 1, and is used to keep the velocity of the object in the respective direction constant. The values of q and r were varied from $[1, 2, 3, 4, 5, 10]$, to see their impact on object tracking. Usually larger values of these covariances ensure that each track is always linked with some detection but this can worsen the condition of ID switching and, hence can degrade the tracking performance. As one of the goals was to count all the sheep in a paddock, a trade-off point needed to be selected between the creation of multiple tracks for a missed object within frame boundaries, or keeping the track until the object appeared again. If a track is deleted and created for such objects this increases the number of false negatives (FNs) in the system. However, the opposite case increases the number of false positives (FP), especially if the predicted location by the tracker is not close to the actual object. To observe this, F_{lost} was tested for values of $[2, 4, 6, 8, 10]$ frames and the impact of variation among these values is discussed shortly.

4.2   Metrics

There are many metrics defined to evaluate the performance of multiple object tracking [1,2,11], and each one of them covers different aspects of the overall efficiency. The standard MOT evaluation metrics were used to report results in this article. However, it was difficult to compare results with any other researchers' work, as there are no publicly available datasets of livestock that can be used by others working in our field.

MOT precision (MOTP), MOT accuracy (MOTA) and FP rate (FPR) were used as the main metrics. MOTP measures the tracker's precision as a motion predictor and is defined as

$$\text{MOTP} = 1 - \frac{\sum_i d(\hat{c}_i, c_i)}{\sum_i \text{M}(i)}, \tag{5}$$

where $\hat{c}_i$ and c_i are 2 × 1 vectors containing the x- and y-coordinates of the predicted and ground truth centroids of the objects, respectively. $d(a, b)$ is the Euclidean distance between a and b, and $\text{M}(i)$ is the number of the matches between $\hat{c}_i$ and c_i. The closer the predicted and true centroids of the sheep, the lower the Euclidean distance between them, and hence the higher the MOTP.

The MOTA gives a measure of all the errors that occurred during the whole tracking process, and is computed as

$$\text{MOTA} = 1 - \frac{\sum_i [\text{FP}(i) + \text{FN}(i)]}{\sum_i \text{GT}(i)}, \tag{6}$$

where $\text{FP}(i)$, $\text{FN}(i)$ and $\text{GT}(i)$ represent the number of false positives, false negatives, and ground truth values in the i-th frame, respectively. The FPR measures the number of FPs as a fraction of the total objects in all the frames, defined as

$$\text{FPR} = \frac{\sum_i \text{FP}(i)}{\sum_i \text{GT}(i)}. \tag{7}$$

To count the total livestock in a paddock, the sheep that leave the frame from lower boundary are counted and then the sheep count from the last frame are added.

4.3   Results

Videos were recorded from the same paddock in sunny and cloudy weather, and Fig. 3 shows the first frame from each video. The respective paddock had a total of 352 sheep in it and the recorded videos had between 100 to 250 sheep in each frame. Although the actual sheep count was the same in both videos, the livestock spread was different—as the recording was done on different days—and so there is a difference in the total ground truth values for the respective videos. Thus the cumulative ground truth was 15045 and 19798 in the overcast and sunny videos, respectively.

Fig. 3. First frames of videos recorded by the UAV at 80 m altitude in (a) sunny and (b) cloudy weather.

Table 1. Tracking performance metrics for various values of the process and measurement noise covariances, q and r. CNA and F_{lost} were set at 20 and 10, respectively. For both weather conditions the total sheep in the paddock were 352.

(a) Cloudy Conditions – Ground truth matches are 15045							
Noise covariances	Metrics						
q and r	Sheep count	Total FP	Total FN	Total M	FPR	MOTP	MOTA
1	865	26571	56	14989	176.61%	97.61%	−76.98%
2	786	21564	54	14991	143.33%	97.66%	−43.69%
3	753	16492	52	14993	109.62%	97.63%	−9.96%
4	704	14055	49	14996	93.42%	97.59%	6.25%
5	690	12065	49	14996	80.19%	97.58%	19.48%
10	528	5224	50	14995	34.72%	97.62%	64.95%
(b) Sunny Conditions – Ground truth matches are 19798							
Noise Covariances	Metrics						
q and r	Sheep count	Total FP	Total FN	Total M	FPR	MOTP	MOTA
1	384	660	611	19187	3.33%	92.92%	93.58%
2	353	322	599	19199	1.63%	92.70%	95.70%
3	352	249	601	19197	1.26%	92.73%	95.70%
4	352	250	602	19196	1.27%	92.74%	95.70%
5	351	252	608	19190	1.27%	92.89%	95.65%
10	350	235	616	19182	1.19%	93.02%	95.70%

The effect of selecting values for parameters such as process and observation noise covariance, CNA and F_{lost} was observed experimentally. Here, we will refer to q and r both as noise covariance because both values were changed simultaneously. In the first case, values of F_{lost} and CNA were kept constant at 10 and 20, respectively, and the covariance was varied through $[1, 2, 3, 4, 5, 10]$. Values of F_{lost} and CNA were selected to keep the system a bit relaxed in terms of deleting the invalid tracks, and data assignment task respectively. The variation in the performance of system during this process is shown in Table 1. For the video recorded in cloudy weather the value of MOTA was negative for lower values of the covariance. New track IDs were created repeatedly for the existing tracks, and this kept on increasing the cumulative values of FP and FN with each new frame and resulted in a higher value of the numerator in Eq. 6. Hence,

MOTA was negative for lower values of noise covariance, but this was not the case for the other video. One of the reasons behind higher rate of new tracks creation for the first video is that the Kalman filter was unable to predict the next location of the sheep properly and the lower CNA was letting the filter create new tracks instead of linking them with existing ones. We were observing multiple ID switches in both videos for higher values of covariance, and a value of 2 was used while observing the effect of variation in other parameters on the system.

Table 2. Tracking performance metrics for various values of CNA. Values of q, r and F_{lost} were set at 2, 2 and 10, respectively. For both weather conditions the total sheep in the paddock were 352.

(a) Cloudy Conditions – Ground truth matches are 15045							
CNA	Metrics						
	Sheep count	Total FP	Total FN	Total M	FPR	MOTP	MOTA
20	786	21564	54	14991	143.33%	97.66%	−43.69%
40	361	105	47	14998	0.70%	97.60%	98.99%
60	353	46	43	15002	0.31%	97.48%	99.41%
80	353	37	42	15003	0.25%	97.41%	99.47%
100	353	37	42	15003	0.25%	97.41%	99.47%
(b) Sunny Conditions – Ground truth matches are 19798							
CNA	Metrics						
	Sheep count	Total FP	Total FN	Total M	FPR	MOTP	MOTA
20	353	322	599	19199	1.63%	92.70%	95.35%
40	350	191	595	19203	0.96%	92.74%	96.03%
60	350	191	595	19203	0.96%	92.74%	96.03%
80	350	190	595	19203	0.96%	92.74%	96.03%
100	350	193	601	19197	0.97%	92.80%	95.99%

Next the values of noise covariance and F_{lost} were fixed at 2 and 10 respectively, while CNA was varied between $[20, 40, 60, 80, 100]$. The higher values of CNA improved the system's efficiency, shown in Table 2, as new tracks were only created for those sheep that enter the frame from the top or those which were not detected by the object locator in the previous few frames. For both videos, little variation was observed above the value of 60 for CNA, and as per the presented results, the value of 80 was considered to be a good option for both cases. However, as tracks for the undetected objects were still allowed to stay for at least 10 frames, a reduction in this value can reduce the number of FPs and FNs.

The next observations were made using the noise covariance value of 2, CNA equal to 80 and F_{lost} varied on $[2, 4, 6, 8, 10]$. The results with these settings for both videos are shown in Table 3. The system's response is slightly different for both videos and the MOTA decreased if tracks were kept for more than 4 and 2 frames in the video recorded in cloudy and sunny weather, respectively. The best values of MOTA were observed to be 99.55% and 96.26%. For the second video, as the detector was not detecting a few sheep in some consecutive frames, it caused higher a cumulative FN for all the cases. Still, 96.26% shows a good performance of the overall system. The experimental evaluation shows that the best selection of the covariance values in the Kalman filter for tracking small objects should be close to the radius of tracked objects. Higher values may lead to an ID switch or mismatch error. Also, even if the Kalman filter is at its best performance, the data linker can degrade the performance by not linking the tracks with corresponding detected objects when the value of CNA is less. The main parameter of our concern is MOTA as it covers the different types of errors made by the tracking system, and it was improved by reducing the F_{lost} value, as shown in Table 3.

Table 3. Tracking performance metrics for various values of F_{lost}. The process and measurement noise covariances, q and r, and CNA were set at 2, 2 and 80, respectively. For both weather conditions the total sheep in the paddock were 352.

(a) Cloudy Conditions – Ground truth matches are 15045							
Threshold F_{lost}	Metrics						
(frames)	Sheep count	Total FP	Total FN	Total M	FPR	MOTP	MOTA
2	350	19	53	14992	0.12%	97.76%	99.52%
4	352	25	43	15002	0.17%	97.53%	99.55%
6	352	31	43	15002	0.21%	97.52%	99.51%
8	353	35	42	15003	0.23%	97.45%	99.49%
10	353	37	42	15003	0.25%	97.41%	99.47%
(b) Sunny Conditions – Ground truth matches are 19798							
Threshold F_{lost}	Metrics						
(frames)	Sheep count	Total FP	Total FN	Total M	FPR	MOTP	MOTA
2	344	75	666	19132	0.38%	93.77%	96.26%
4	346	116	628	19170	0.59%	93.42%	96.24%
6	346	145	611	19187	0.73%	93.08%	96.18%
8	348	172	601	19197	0.87%	92.77%	96.09%
10	350	190	595	19203	0.96%	92.74%	96.03%

Figure 4 shows a case of FN and FP from one of the intermediate frames. The blue color shows an FN instance, and the Kalman filter has predicted the location of this sheep at a different location which is shown in cyan color. In this case the system gives one FN and one FP instance. The red color shows that the detector was unable to detect the object, however, the Kalman filter predicted the location correctly in this frame. It is neither an FP nor an FN case and still counted as a matched track. Figure 5 shows that if the sheep is not detected for any less than F_{lost} frames, the same track ID is assigned to it later. These are the sub-images cropped from four consecutive frames and show two such cases

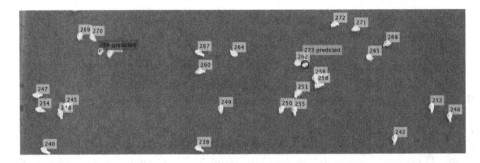

Fig. 4. The cyan color shows an FP detection, the blue shows an FN instance and red shows that the detector does not estimate this object but tracker estimated the object location perfectly. (Color figure online)

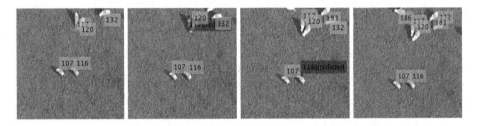

Fig. 5. Cropped sub-images from four successive frames (left to right). In the second frame the sheep with track ID 117 was not detected by the object detector but was tracked successfully by the Kalman filter. In the third frame it was detected again and same track ID was assigned to it. The same issue occurred for the sheep with track ID 116 in the third and fourth frames.

of sheep with IDs 116 and 117. Both of these figures were captured when the values of q, r, F_{lost} and CNA were set to 2, 2, 4 and 80 respectively.

Finally, Figs. 7 and 6 show the overlaying graphs of ground truth and matched object counts, which are referred as true count and matched count, respectively. The difference of these values was higher in the case of sunny video as the detector was missing a few sheep in each frame. However, a maximum per frame difference of one and ten was observed in the cloudy and sunny videos, respectively.

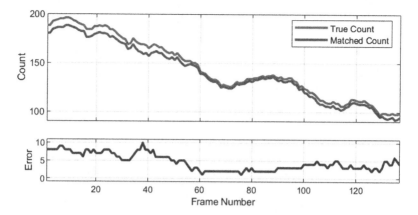

Fig. 6. True and matched counts in respective frames for the video recorded in sunny weather, the lower plot highlights the per frame difference between these two values. In this video the object detector failed to detect a few sheep in multiple frames which degraded the performance of the overall system too. A maximum difference of 10 sheep was recorded in 39-th frame of this video.

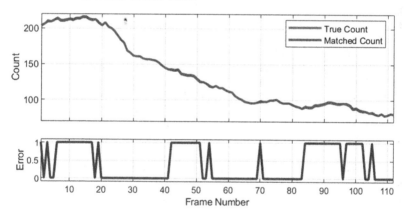

Fig. 7. True and matched counts in respective frames for the video recorded in cloudy weather, the lower plot highlights the per frame difference between these two values. The object detector used performs better in cloudy weather, and this is illustrated in the maximum tracking error of one being recorded.

5   Conclusion

In this paper, we presented an offline, tracking-by-detection method for livestock tracking in videos recorded by a UAV-mounted camera. We used our previous object detector whose high accuracy made tuning the tracking parameters an achievable task. Parameters of the Kalman filter and Hungarian algorithm were tuned to improve the performance of the overall system. With the best combinations of these parameters, MOTAs of 99% and 96% were achieved in different weather conditions. However, such performance may not be possible if the object detector failure rate increases beyond a certain limit.

Future work will include capturing and labelling more videos including ones at higher altitudes.

References

1. Bernardin, K., Elbs, A., Stiefelhagen, R.: Multiple object tracking performance metrics and evaluation in a smart room environment. In: 6th IEEE International Workshop on Visual Surveillance, in Conjunction with ECCV, vol. 90, pp. 91–99 (2006)
2. Bernardin, K., Stiefelhagen, R.: Evaluating multiple object tracking performance: the CLEAR MOT metrics. EURASIP J. Image Video Process. **2008**, 1–10 (2008). https://doi.org/10.1155/2008/246309
3. Blackman, S.S.: Multiple hypothesis tracking for multiple target tracking. IEEE Aerosp. Electron. Syst. Mag. **19**(1), 5–18 (2004). https://doi.org/10.1109/MAES.2004.1263228
4. Breitenstein, M.D., Reichlin, F., Leibe, B., Koller-Meier, E., Van Gool, L.: Robust tracking-by-detection using a detector confidence particle filter. In: IEEE 12th International Conference on Computer Vision, pp. 1515–1522. IEEE (2009)
5. Ciaparrone, G., Sánchez, F.L., Tabik, S., Troiano, L., Tagliaferri, R., Herrera, F.: Deep learning in video multi-object tracking: a survey. Neurocomputing **381** 61–88 (2020). https://doi.org/10.1016/j.neucom.2019.11.023
6. Iraei, I., Faez, K.: Object tracking with occlusion handling using mean shift, Kalman filter and edge histogram. In: 2nd IEEE International Conference on Pattern Recognition and Image Analysis (IPRIA), pp. 1–6. IEEE (2015). https://doi.org/10.1109/PRIA.2015.7161637
7. Kang, K., et al.: T-CNN: tubelets with convolutional neural networks for object detection from videos. IEEE Trans. Circ. Syst. Video Technol. **28**(10), 2896–2907 (2017)
8. Kapania, S., Saini, D., Goyal, S., Thakur, N., Jain, R., Nagrath, P.: Multi object tracking with UAVs using Deep SORT and YOLOv3 RetinaNet detection framework. In: Proceedings of the 1st ACM Workshop on Autonomous and Intelligent Mobile Systems, pp. 1–6 (2020). https://doi.org/10.1145/3377283.3377284
9. Kuhn, H.W.: The Hungarian method for the assignment problem. Naval Res. Logistics Q. **2**(1–2), 83–97 (1955). https://doi.org/10.1002/nav.3800020109
10. Li, X., Wang, K., Wang, W., Li, Y.: A multiple object tracking method using Kalman filter. In: The 2010 IEEE International Conference on Information and Automation, pp. 1862–1866. IEEE (2010). https://doi.org/10.1109/ICINFA.2010.5512258
11. Milan, A., Schindler, K., Roth, S.: Challenges of ground truth evaluation of multi-target tracking. In: IEEE Conference on Computer Vision and Pattern Recognition Workshops, pp. 735–742 (2013)
12. Ren, S., Zhou, Y., He, L.: Multi-object tracking with pre-classified detection. In: Kim, J.-H., et al. (eds.) RiTA 2017. AISC, vol. 751, pp. 503–513. Springer, Cham (2019). https://doi.org/10.1007/978-3-319-78452-6_40
13. Sarwar, F., Griffin, A., Periasamy, P., Portas, K., Law, J.: Detecting and counting sheep with a convolutional neural network. In: 15th IEEE International Conference on Advanced Video and Signal Based Surveillance (AVSS), pp. 1–6. IEEE (2018). https://doi.org/10.1109/AVSS.2018.8639306

14. Sarwar, F., Griffin, A., Rehman, S.U., Pasang, T.: Towards detection of sheep onboard a UAV. arXiv preprint arXiv:2004.02758 (2020)
15. Wang, G., Wang, Y., Zhang, H., Gu, R., Hwang, J.N.: Exploit the connectivity: multi-object tracking with TrackletNet. In: Proceedings of the 27th ACM International Conference on Multimedia, pp. 482–490 (2019). https://doi.org/10.1145/3343031.3350853
16. Wang, Z., Zheng, L., Liu, Y., Wang, S.: Towards real-time multi-object tracking. arXiv preprint arXiv:1909.12605 (2019)
17. Welch, G., Bishop, G., et al.: An Introduction to the Kalman Filter (1995)
18. Yoon, K., Kim, D.Y., Yoon, Y.C., Jeon, M.: Data association for multi-object tracking via deep neural networks. Sensors 19(3), 559–673 (2019). https://doi.org/10.3390/s19030559
19. Zhang, Y., Wang, J., Yang, X.: Real-time vehicle detection and tracking in video based on faster R-CNN. J. Phys.: Conf. Ser. 887, 012068 (2017). https://doi.org/10.1088/1742-6596/887/1/012068
20. Zhou, S., Ke, M., Qiu, J., Wang, J.: A survey of multi-object video tracking algorithms. In: Abawajy, J., Choo, K.-K.R., Islam, R., Xu, Z., Atiquzzaman, M. (eds.) ATCI 2018. AISC, vol. 842, pp. 351–369. Springer, Cham (2019). https://doi.org/10.1007/978-3-319-98776-7_38
21. Zulkifley, M.A., Moran, B.: Robust hierarchical multiple hypothesis tracker for multiple-object tracking. Exp. Syst. Appl. 39(16), 12319–12331 (2012). https://doi.org/10.1016/j.eswa.2012.03.004

A Comparison of Approaches for Synchronizing Events in Video Streams Using Audio

Mohammad Norouzifard[1]([⊠])(iD), Ali Nemati[2], Saeed Mollaee[1],
Hamid GholamHosseini[3](iD), Joanna Black[4], Benjamin Thompson[4,5,6],
Jason Turuwhenua[1,4], and on behalf of the hPOD Study Team

[1] Auckland Bioengineering Institute, University of Auckland, Auckland, New Zealand
m.norouzifard@auckland.ac.nz
[2] Institute for Health & Equity, Medical College of Wisconsin, Milwaukee, USA
[3] School of Engineering, Computer, and Mathematical Sciences,
Auckland University of Technology (AUT), Auckland, New Zealand
[4] School of Optometry and Vision Science, University of Auckland,
Auckland, New Zealand
[5] School of Optometry and Vision Science, University of Waterloo, Waterloo, Canada
[6] Centre for Eye and Vision Research, Hong Kong, China

Abstract. A common scenario found in experimentation is to synchronize events, such as breaks between visual stimulus, with the video record taken of an experiment made of participants as they undertake the task. In our case, we recently synchronized a protocol of stimulus presentations shown on a laptop display, with webcam video made of participants' (who were two year old children) facial and eye movements as they were shown trials of stimulus containing moving dots (a random dot kinematogram or RDK). The purpose was to assess eye movements in response to these RDK stimulus as a part of a potential neurological assessment for children. The video contained audio signals such as "beeps" and musical interludes that indicated the start and end of trials, thereby providing a convenient opportunity to align these audio events with the timing of known events in the video record.

The process of alignment can be performed manually, but this is a tedious and time consuming task when considering, for example, large databases of videos. In this paper, we tested two alternate methods for synchronizing known audio events using: 1) a deep learning based model, and a 2) standard template matching algorithm. These methods were used to synchronize the known protocol of stimulus events in videos by processing the audio contents of the recording. The deep learning approach utilized simple mel-spectrum audio signal feature extraction, whilst we adopted a cross-correlation algorithm that detected an audio template in the time domain. We found that whilst correlation was not effective as a means of beep detection; but our machine learning-based technique was robust with 90% accuracy in the testing dataset and did not the same amount of remediation required of the correlation approach.

© Springer Nature Switzerland AG 2021
M. Nguyen et al. (Eds.): ISGV 2021, CCIS 1386, pp. 262–272, 2021.
https://doi.org/10.1007/978-3-030-72073-5_20

Keywords: Video synchronization · Audio signal processing · Deep learning · Template matching · Eye tracking

1   Introduction

Audio or visual cues can be used to indicate salient parts of a video record taken of an experiment. Recently, we used this approach in a visual assessment experiment that occurred as part of a larger study, called the hypoglycaemia Prevention with Oral Dextrose (hPOD) study [5,17]. In this study, babies at risk of hypoglycaemia who had been administered a dextrose gel at birth participated in a follow-up test of visual function at two years old. The primary aim of that assessment was to measure global motion coherence threshold (MCT), the ability to see overall (or global) motion as measured by a visual stimulus [11] called a random dot kinematogram (RDK).

The reader is directed elsewhere for details of the visual assessment procedure [18]. However, in brief, the participants (2-year-old children) viewed a laptop screen whilst they were shown trials of moving dots (including community and home settings). At the same time, video of their facial area and eyes were recorded using a webcam or in-built camera of a laptop. The video records were analysed post-hoc by experienced observers trained to assess the presence or absence of eye movements induced by the visual stimuli; a highly challenging and time intensive process. Furthermore, key events, such as the start or end of a trial in the experiment were only signalled by audible "beeps" in the video record, thereby presenting a difficulty: how to align the known stimulus on the display with the corresponding position in the video? This is a problem common to experiments of this kind, and arises when time stamping of video recordings cannot be performed during data collection.

Manual alignment is a particularly demanding and time consuming task when considering studies with large numbers of participants. The purpose of this paper is to present a comparison of two methods for determining the occurrence of key audio events or audio events in uncontrolled environments (i.e., in-the-wild): 1) a method based on deep learning of frequency space features (specifically, the mel spectrum features) and 2) a standard template matching approach. This paper is organized as follows: firstly, we describe the two major approaches that were used to detect beeps within the audio signal. Secondly, we describe the experimental methods that were used on a private database of videos, and finally, we discuss how the audio signal was synchronized to the timestamp data. We find that overall, the deep learning method is a robust solution that does not suffer from event-detection sensitivity to the same extent as template matching. However, we make recommendations here toward both improved template matching and ML (machine learning) model based trial event detection.

2   Background

In this study, we were concerned with two approaches to identifying key events from video using audio: 1) a deep learning model and 2) a standard template-matching algorithm. In the first approach, we employed a deep neural network to detect and classify audio beep features in the frequency domain. We recognized audible "beep" patterns using audio specific features (mel- spectrogram coefficients) which identified the start and end times of trials in the video footage. The second approach employed template matching with a cross-correlation algorithm to match times using the audio track of video streams. We have described both approaches in Sect. 3. The rest of this section briefly explain algorithms which were employed in our proposed pipeline. In both cases, the detected signals are used to reconstruct the intervals in which visual stimulus was explained, and we compare the two methods also from this perspective.

2.1 The Mel Spectrogram

The mel spectrogram is a representation of the audio content of a signal as it varies over time. Whereas a typical spectrogram, determined using the Fourier transform [2,8,10], is represented by a linear frequency scaling where each frequency is spaced an equal number of Hertz apart, the Mel-frequency spectrogram is found by averaging the Fourier spectrogram values over mel-frequency bands [1]. These bands are spaced according to a perceptual scale of pitches judged by listeners to be equal in distance from one another [3].

2.2 Template Matching with Cross-Correlation

We utilized for comparison purposes a common template matching approach for detecting the time of audio events from the soundtrack of the video: cross-correlation in the time domain [16].

The approach depends on having a fixed kernel or template of sound data, which slides along the incoming audio signal producing a correlation value at each point along the signal. By sliding the kernel along the test signal we aim to generate a time series of correlation values, and from it we locate point(s) of maximum correlation. The cross-correlation, G which is defined by equality (Eq. 1) which is specified by measuring the similarity between two waveforms, a fixed kernel h and 1D/ 2D input signal data F. The cross-correlation equation for 1D signal input data is as follows:

$$G\left[i\right] = \sum_{u=-k}^{k} h\left[u\right] F\left[i+u\right] \tag{1}$$

$G\left[i\right]$ represents the output 1D array at index value I, as the correlation of kernel h (template) and F, the input signal array.

3   Data Collection

The collection of these eye-tracking videos followed the tenets of the Declaration of Helsinki. Written informed consent was obtained from all study participants. Participants were young children who had been measured by laptop or computer by an experienced assessor.

3.1   Database of Videos

Videos were collected as part of the hPOD study [5]. Experienced assessors performed the protocol which occurred either in assessments in an office environment at the University of Auckland, or in a home-based assessment in which a laptop and in-built camera/webcam were used to perform recording.

Videos contained the facial and eye areas of the participants as they viewed a sequence of 50 presentations. These presentations were shown in groups of five trials of RDK stimulus (6 s duration), followed by an animated movie. Before and after each trial were a potentially variable number of computer-generated beeps, with the trial start beep being different from the trial end beep. A short children's animated movie (10 to 20 s) occurred after every five trials to encourage children to concentrate on the experimental test. We worked with a subset of five different participants' videos (total of 32 min, 200 trials during which time a stimulus was shown to the participant). The recorded videos were roughly 6 min in duration, but the time length of each video varied according to factors such as attention of child and setup time. Two of the videos were employed for training and self validation of the deep learning model, and three unseen videos were utilized for testing purposes.

3.2   Manual Annotation for Training

We extracted mono audio of videos with Python scripting, and using Audacity(R) version 2.4.1 (https://www.audacityteam.org) recording and editing software to visualize the audio signal and beep annotation [13]. We manually labelled training data including beep events, and the time duration of trials using the "label" tool in the Audacity software application. This is referred to as manual annotation.

4   Methods

In this paper, we used two algorithms including deep learning and template matching which are described in this section.

4.1   Deep Learning Model

We utilized a pipeline for deep learning method shown by Fig. 1. Audio extracted mel-spectrum features were fed to the input layer in a deep MNN (*multilayer neural network*) [9,12]. We extracted mel-spectrum features in the frequency domain using a 4096 window size (of samples) and 512 hop length (the distance between two subsequent windows).

The MNN consisted of four fully-connected (dense) layers, 256 neurons in the first layer, 128 neurons in the second layer, then a layer with 32 neurons, and finally two neurons in the last fully connected layer. We employed a ReLU activation function on the first three layers and the Softmax activation function

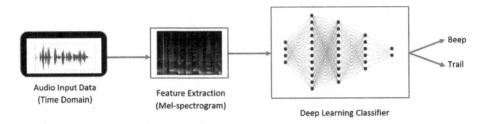

Fig. 1. Schematic diagram with deep neural network approach and mel-spectrum feature extraction in the frequency domain [7].

on the last layer (see Table 1). The task of the activation function was to express a final output for given inputs. The proposed model used the Adam optimizer and categorical cross-entropy as a loss function [4,6].

We extracted ~ 10,000 feature vectors from the mel-spectrogram data, which were assigned to either a beep class (1456 feature vectors), or a trial class (8654 features). The labelled features were used for training (two videos used to fit and tune the parameters of a classifier model) and validation (three new videos used). Because of the unbalance of data toward the trial class, we needed to tune the deep MNN model to achieve high-performance synchronization. The test dataset was used only to assess the performance of the final model fit on the training dataset [14]. The training feature dataset was divided into two parts, 80% for the training set, 20% for validation.

Training was performed by cycling through the total training dataset (or an epoch - which is one cycle). The training set was divided into batches of

Table 1. The configuration of the deep learning model for audio pattern recognition to synchronize unseen videos.

Layer	Input-size	Output-size	Comment
Input	32	32	–
Dense	32	256	–
Activation	–	–	relu
Dropout	–	–	0.5
Dense	256	128	–
Activation	–	–	relu
Dropout	–	–	0.2
Dense	128	32	–
Activation	–	–	relu
Dropout	–	–	0.1
Dense	32	2	–
Activation	–	–	softmax

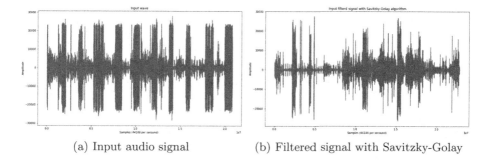

(a) Input audio signal   (b) Filtered signal with Savitzky-Golay

Fig. 2. (a): Input audio signal with ~eight minutes length. (b): Result of preprocessed signal based on Savitzky-Golay algorithm with window kernel size:41, and the order of polynomial is two.

samples, and an iteration was the number of batches. For example, we had 9984 sample data in the training dataset, the batch size was 32 sample, yielding 312 iterations. Therefore, batch is the number of training samples in one iteration.

We used 10-fold cross-validation technique to determine the reliability of the result. We dealt with the over-fitting and unbalanced dataset problems using a dropout technique without data augmentation [6,15].

4.2   Template Matching Model

Template matching was applied to the audio input signal in the time domain. We used an example of a beep extracted from the data. The cross-correlation with the signal was determined in the time domain using a kernel of 0.5 s duration. The choice of this kernel was based primarily on time efficiency considerations. Template matching was slowed (in its present form) considerably by the choice of window length. In any instance, prior to correlation we applied a filtering using the Savitzky-Golay algorithm (Fig. 2.b) to reduce the effect of noise. The polynomials order was 2 and the window size was 41 samples.

We applied a very simple proportional thresholding for indicating beep times in the correlation time series signal to determine the correlation peaks corresponding to beeps. We detected maxima in the signal, and then applied a proportional threshold which was 85% of the peak with maximum amplitude. An example of an input audio signal is illustrated in Fig. 2.a indicating the presence of beeps pattern with peaks in the time domain. It is noted that this process resulted in "clusters" of peaks around each beep event.

4.3   Re-creation of Trial and Evaluation Metric

We recreated trial times, the times when visual stimulus was shown to the participant, from the detected beep events. As mentioned, the experimental protocol consisted of five trials in which the participant concentrated on the experimental test, followed by a movie. A variable number of beeps often occurred between each trial, because they occurred during a waiting period that was user controlled and depended on the inattention of participants.

We evaluated our results' accuracy by determining the average overlap between trial intervals using both manual annotation and machine learning results. In Fig. 7, we present an example of an annotation showing in green, the times in which visual stimulus was shown to the participant, versus, in red, times when it was not. The thicker red bars shown after every fifth green stripe corresponds to times when the movie was shown.

We employed an overlap threshold to evaluate machine learning (ML) and template matching (TM) results. An overall overlap threshold was calculated as the average of trial times differentiating between manual labelling and our results as a proportion.

5 Results and Discussions

We ran the deep learning and template matching algorithms to align two videos (stimulus and eye displacement videos) based on beep event detection. Both models were deployed on the hPOD private dataset and results were compared with manual annotation by an expert.

5.1 Deep Learning Outcome

The proposed deep learning pipeline was applied based on Mel spectrum features. The training-loss value was 0.12, and training accuracy was 93.98%. The model validation loss function value was 0.16. Figure 3 illustrates accuracy versus loss in the training and validation stages of the Deep MNN model. Figure 3.b illustrates the reduction in loss of training and validation with increasing numbers of epochs. Figure 3.a describes the accuracy trend on training and validation with increasing numbers of epochs. Training the deep learning model took about 10 s

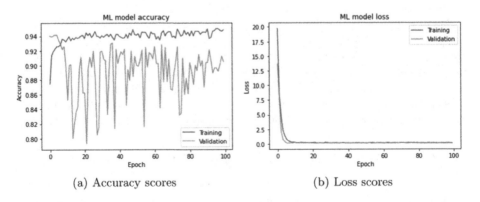

(a) Accuracy scores   (b) Loss scores

Fig. 3. Scores of accuracy and loss function for training and validation stages on deep neural network.

with TPU and 20 s on the training dataset with a GPU processor based on the Google cloud and we only needed to do it one time.

The trained model was tested with test data on the hPOD dataset for checking the model. The result was 90.24% accuracy with test dataset in comparison with manual labelled dataset using the average overlap measure.

5.2   Template Matching Outcome

An example template matching approach results for a beep template is illustrated in Fig. 4.

The method was found to be very sensitive and reduced signal to noise segregation (see in Fig. 5 and Fig. 6) compared with the ML based method. The template matching was sensitive with mixed noise and value of the threshold. Our experience was that the cross-correlation algorithm was simpler to implement, but more difficult to generalize on all audio within the large dataset with a long recording time. We assessed an average overlap of 86% and 78% with the template matching model in corresponding trials using overlap thresholds of 80% and 90% respectively.

Even though, template-matching algorithm was simple to run. The template matching algorithm was time consuming for a long video stream; as an example: processing time was about 148 s with TPU and 272 s with a GPU processor based on the Google cloud to calculate the cross-collaboration module with an input audio signal consisting of 22899366 samples (8 min) and the kernel with 20505 samples (0.5 s).

As mentioned, in order to have a time efficient model we employed 0.5 s for both beep and movie kernels. This could have resulted in reduced discriminative performance. One of the solutions may use down-sampling to optimise processing time to avoid mis-classification of movie and beep kernels. It was also found that events such as a child's laughter could be mistakenly identified as a beep, it is illustrated in Fig. 6, and there is another false detection in Fig. 5, which is related to movie start time.

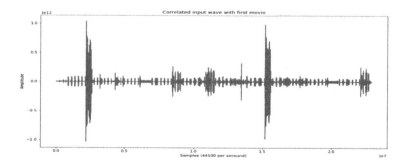

Fig. 4. Result of using template-matching algorithm with beep kernel.

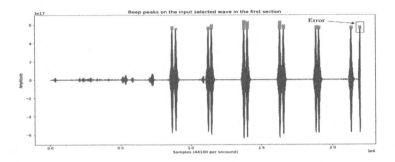

Fig. 5. The first five trials with movie false detection (shown as error). Beep detection (orange points) using a proportional threshold applied to the cross-correlation with false detection. (Color figure online)

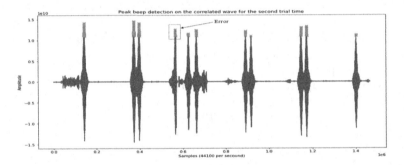

Fig. 6. The second five trials containing a child's laugh as a false detection (shown as error).

5.3 Reconstruction of Trial Times from Detected Events

In Fig. 7, we show reconstructions of the complete trials for machine learning, template matching, and manual annotation results. The results indicate a good reconstruction of the experimental record using deep learning in particular, over the simple template matching algorithm.

The results indicate many inaccuracies for the template-matching model in the long video stream. This appears to be due to poor detection of beep peaks. We determined an average overlap of 94% and 84% with the machine-learning model using overlap thresholds of 80% and 90% respectively.

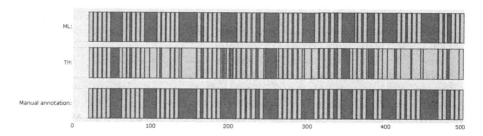

Fig. 7. The reconstruction of trail times from detected events with both machine learning (ML) and template matching (TM) algorithms. Red one is noise including beep or movie, Green one is a period of visual stimulus (trial time). (Color figure online)

6   Conclusion

We studied an audio event pattern recognition technique to synchronize unseen video streams in frequency and time domains using a deep neural network and template matching algorithms. Mel-spectrum audio signal feature extraction and cross-correlation algorithms were employed to detect particular audio patterns in-the-wild.

We utilized roughly 10,000 training and validation feature vectors with optimization and tuning in the function of each layer of the deep neural network model to achieve accurate results. The machine-learning model we applied was more robust than the cross-correlation model to detect beep events.

In this paper, the application of deep neural networks in audio signal processing and pattern recognition was studied, in comparison to a standard template matching approach. Template matching has the benefit of conceptual simplicity, but in our work, we found that it can suffer when the input signal is degraded by noise and in long video streams. However, in comparison the deep learning approach had good performance and can detect trial time accurately to synchronize audio signal in-the-wild with an unseen video stream. Contributions of this paper are as follows:

– We employed feature extraction with a template matching and a deep neural network model. The template matching was not effective over the dataset we tested, and could not be generalized, at least in its present form.
– The indicate that mel-spectrum features employed in a machine learning algorithm enables a consistent and generalized model. At least in this small dataset.

Overall, this research points toward an appropriate path for two video alignment using a deep learning algorithm.

References

1. Anden, J., Mallat, S.: Deep scattering spectrum. IEEE Trans. Signal Process. **62**(16), 4114–4128 (2014). https://doi.org/10.1109/TSP.2014.2326991

2. Bailey, D.H., Swarztrauber, P.N.: A fast method for the numerical evaluation of continuous Fourier and Laplace transforms. SIAM J. Sci. Comput. **15**(5), 1105–1110 (1994). https://doi.org/10.1137/0915067

3. Byrne, C.L.: Signal Processing: A Mathematical Approach. CRC Press, Boca Raton (2014). https://doi.org/10.1201/b17672

4. Golovin, D., Solnik, B., Moitra, S., Kochanski, G., Karro, J., Sculley, D.: Google vizier: a service for black-box optimization. In: Proceedings of the 23rd ACM SIGKDD International Conference on Knowledge Discovery and Data Mining, pp. 1487–1495 (2017). https://doi.org/10.1145/3097983.3098043

5. Griffith, R., et al.: Two-year outcomes after dextrose gel prophylaxis for neonatal hypoglycaemia. Arch. Dis. Child.-Fetal Neonatal Ed. (2020). https://doi.org/10.1136/archdischild-2020-320305

6. Hamad, R.A., Kimura, M., Lundström, J.: Efficacy of imbalanced data handling methods on deep learning for smart homes environments. SN Comput. Sci. **1**(4), 1–10 (2020). https://doi.org/10.1007/s42979-020-00211-1

7. LeNail, A.: NN-SVG: publication-ready neural network architecture schematics. J. Open Source Softw. **4**(33), 747 (2019). https://doi.org/10.21105/joss.00747

8. Lenssen, N.: Applications of Fourier analysis to audio signal processing: an investigation of chord detection algorithms (2013)

9. Liu, W., Wang, Z., Liu, X., Zeng, N., Liu, Y., Alsaadi, F.E.: A survey of deep neural network architectures and their applications. Neurocomputing **234**, 11–26 (2017). https://doi.org/10.1016/j.neucom.2016.12.038

10. Madisetti, V.: Video, Speech, and Audio Signal Processing and Associated Standards. CRC Press, Boca Raton (2018). https://doi.org/10.1201/9781315216065

11. USPTO. report, Head and eye tracking patent application. https://uspto.report/patent/app/20200069179. Accessed 10 Jan 2021

12. Norouzifard, M., Nemati, A., Abdul-Rahman, A., GholamHosseini, H., Klette, R.: A comparison of transfer learning techniques, deep convolutional neural network and multilayer neural network methods for the diagnosis of glaucomatous optic neuropathy. In: Chang, C.-Y., Lin, C.-C., Lin, H.-H. (eds.) ICS 2018. CCIS, vol. 1013, pp. 627–635. Springer, Singapore (2019). https://doi.org/10.1007/978-981-13-9190-3_69

13. Release Notes 2.4.2. Audacity Wiki, 26 June 2020. https://wiki.audacityteam.org/wiki/Release_Notes_2.4.2. Accessed 20 Nov 2020

14. Ripley, B.D.: Pattern Recognition and Neural Networks. Cambridge University Press, Cambridge (2007)

15. Srivastava, N., Hinton, G., Krizhevsky, A., Sutskever, I., Salakhutdinov, R.: Dropout: a simple way to prevent neural networks from overfitting. J. Mach. Learn. Res. **15**(1), 1929–1958 (2014)

16. Zahid, S., Hussain, F., Rashid, M., Yousaf, M.H., Habib, H.A.: Optimized audio classification and segmentation algorithm by using ensemble methods. Math. Probl. Eng.(2015). https://doi.org/10.1155/2015/209814

17. McKinlay, C.J., et al.: Neonatal glycemia and neurodevelopmental outcomes at 2 years. N. Engl. J. Med. **373**(16), 1507–1518 (2015)

18. Yu, T.Y., Jacobs, R.J., Anstice, N.S., Paudel, N., Harding, J.E., Thompson, B.: Global motion perception in 2-year-old children: a method for psychophysical assessment and relationships with clinical measures of visual function. Invest. Ophthalmol. Vis. Sci. **54**(13), 8408–8419 (2013)

Union-Retire: A New Paradigm for Single-Pass Connected Component Analysis

Donald G. Bailey[1]([✉])[iD] and Michael J. Klaiber[2][iD]

[1] Centre for Research in Image and Signal Processing, Massey University,
Palmerston North 4442, New Zealand
D.G.Bailey@massey.ac.nz
[2] Computer Science, Baden-Wuerttemberg Cooperative State University (DHBW),
70178 Stuttgart, Germany
michael.klaiber@lehre.dhbw-stuttgart.de

Abstract. Most connected component labelling and analysis algorithms are based on some variant of *Union-Find*. In this paper, it is shown the *Find* operation is unnecessary for single-pass algorithms, leading to the *Union-Retire* approach where the focus is on connectivity rather than labelling. The computational complexity of the resulting algorithm is linear with the number of pixels within an image. It is shown that the resulting algorithm requires significantly less memory than existing algorithms, making it ideal for embedded image processing.

Keywords: Union-Find · Connected components · Feature extraction

1 Introduction

Connected component analysis (CCA) is a fundamental operation in many image analysis and machine vision tasks. The purpose of CCA is to derive the feature vector of each set of connected object pixels within a binary image.

Prior to CCA, an input image must be preprocessed to detect the objects of interest and to segment the objects from the background. This results in a binary image, with each connected set of detected pixels corresponding to an object. Then a connected component labelling (CCL) algorithm is commonly used to assign a unique label to each connected component. Finally, a feature vector is extracted for each object, using the component labels to distinguish pixels associated with different objects.

Direct CCA algorithms combine the labelling and feature extraction steps, directly producing the set of feature vectors from a binary image. Consequently, the labelled image is not actually required, but is only used as an intermediate data structure to aid in calculating the feature vector for a completed component.

Most CCL and CCA algorithms are based on some form of *Union-Find* data structure and algorithm [11,19]. Typical CCL algorithms require two raster-scan

© Springer Nature Switzerland AG 2021
M. Nguyen et al. (Eds.): ISGV 2021, CCIS 1386, pp. 273–287, 2021.
https://doi.org/10.1007/978-3-030-72073-5_21

passes through the image. During the first pass, preliminary labels are assigned to each pixel by propagating labels from adjacent already processed object pixels. If an object pixel has no labels within its processed neighbourhood then a new label is assigned. If an object pixel has two different preliminary labels within its neighbourhood, for example where sub-components join at the bottom of a "U" shaped object, then these labels represent the same object and the labels, or sets of labels, from the two branches are then combined. This is a *Union* operation, with the resultant set containing all of the preliminary labels that represent a single connected component. To obtain a consistently labelled image, a second pass is necessary to relabel each pixel with the representative label from the set associated with a connected component. The *Find* operation returns the representative label from the set containing a given preliminary label.

In contrast, single-pass CCA only processes each pixel once. This requires extracting the feature vector during the labelling process [1,2]. When regions merge (during a *Union*) it is necessary to also combine the associated feature vectors. This limits the components of feature vectors to those that can be accumulated and combined associatively, for example: area, bounding box, centre of gravity, best-fit ellipse, perimeter, average pixel value, average colour [5]. Single-pass CCA also requires a *Find* operation for each object pixel to ensure that the data for each pixel is accumulated into the correct feature vector. *Union* and *Find* operations are therefore intermixed depending on the particular arrangement of object pixels within the image being processed.

1.1   *Union-Find* Algorithms

The data structures which represent equivalences (as a result of a *Union*) between preliminary labels are often mapped to arrays, where the label is the index into one or more arrays. These arrays are used to represent a directed acyclic graph (DAG), with the nodes within a connected graph representing the preliminary labels assigned to a single connected component. With a single array, commonly each node has only a single arc leaving it. Example graphs and their corresponding array representations are shown in Fig. 1.

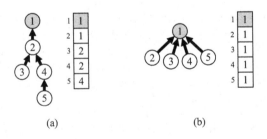

(a)   (b)

Fig. 1. Graphs of preliminary labels associated with a connected component and their array representation. The shaded node corresponds to the representative label. (a) General case. (b) *Quick-Find*.

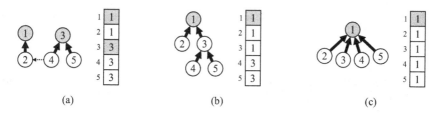

Fig. 2. A *Union* operation between nodes ② and ④: (a) Input graphs. (b) *Quick-Union*. (c) *Quick-Find*.

A *Find* operation follows the arcs to determine the current representative label for a component. This may require several look-ups within the associated table, in the general case (Fig. 1(a)). The *Quick-Find* variant of *Union-Find* [6] arranges the graph so that all nodes point directly to the representative label (Fig. 1(b)), enabling the representative label to be found with a single lookup.

For a *Union* operation, it is necessary to first *Find* the representative label of each set, and then link the trees if these are different. Consider a *Union* between nodes ② and ④ in Fig. 2; the representative labels are nodes ① and ③ respectively. The *Quick-Union* algorithm [6] directly links node ③ to ① (Fig. 2(b)) requiring only one additional operation. However, within *Quick-Union* a *Find* may require multiple lookups. To enable *Quick-Find*, when performing a *Union* operation it is necessary to find all the nodes linked to the old representative label (③) and link these directly to the new representative label (① in Fig. 2(c)). Both *Quick-Union* and *Quick-Find* have quadratic computation complexity in the worst case [15].

This may be partially overcome by using *Quick-Union* with path compression. Whenever a *Find* operation is performed, all of the nodes visited in the search from the initial node to the representative node are linked directly to the representative node so that subsequent searches on that path are faster. The complexity of *Quick-Union* with path compression grows with the inverse Ackermann function [19], which is only slightly worse than linear.

With CCL, the focus is the algorithms is on the labelling process, as the goal is to provide a labelled image. This also carries over to CCA algorithms, which have as CCL as their root, even though a labelled image is not actually required. This stems from the underlying *Union-Find* algorithm, where the goal of the *Find* operation is to determine the representative label of the set. To overcome this, we propose a new approach which focuses on connectivity between sub-components, rather than the labels. *Union-Retire* does not need the *Find* operation, and this is replaced with *Retire* when a node is no longer required.

1.2   Contributions

The key contributions of this paper are the algorithmic description and analysis of the novel *Union-Retire* algorithm.

The remainder of the paper is structured as follows: Sect. 2 explores earlier work on single-pass CCA algorithms in terms of the underlying *Union-Find* algorithms used. Then a complete algorithmic description of *Union-Retire* is provided in Sect. 3. The correctness of the new algorithm is analysed in Sect. 4, and the complexity is compared with other single-pass CCA algorithms, before giving the conclusions in Sect. 5.

2   Prior Work

Klaiber et al. [11] analysed several CCL and CCA algorithms in relation to their underlying merging methods in terms of *Union-Find*. Here, we build on and extend this work in the context of single-pass CCA algorithms. A recent review investigated the history and development of single-pass CCA algorithms [5]. Here, the focus will be on the underlying variation of *Union-Find* that is used by each single-pass CCA algorithm.

Early work by Selkow [16] and Veillon [23] used a set of finite state automata, one per column, to process the image one line at a time. The representative label of each component was the column of the leftmost pixel within the component on the current row, which is unique for each component. This definition results in the representative label changing with each row in the image. The image was processed one row at a time, with Selkow considering single pixels and Veillon runs of consecutive pixels. Overlaps between successive rows caused the propagation of labels from the previous row along the current row. There is no explicit *Union*, although overlapping runs from one row to the next are used to determine which component a pixel or run belongs to. The label propagation along the row is effectively performing a *Find* for each pixel on a row.

The early work by Bailey [1], although more region growing than CCA, did extract feature vectors in a single pass. This clearly used *Quick-Find*, with all of the old links immediately updated to the new representative label. Consequently, a *Union* was relatively expensive (quadratic complexity), especially when there was a chain of mergers, which require the same labels to be updated multiple times.

Trein et al. [21] used run-length encoding, and then processed a run of consecutive object pixels at a time, propagating the representative label from adjacent runs in the previous row. A single pointer from the old label to the representative label is added for a *Union* operation (*Quick-Union*). The *Find* is not explicitly described, but would require multiple lookups to determine the representative label.

Most of the remaining algorithms process a pixel at a time (rather than runs) and are based on the early work by Bailey and Johnston [2,8]. These use a *Quick-Union* algorithm with path compression deferred to the end of the row, enabling a single lookup to be used to determine the representative label. Chains of mergers (a sequence of *Union* operations) do not affect the processing of the remainder of the current row, since the old labels are not accessible again until the following row. Affected pairs of labels are pushed onto a stack, enabling them to be quickly revisited in the reverse order at the end of the row to relink them to their respective representative label (context-based path compression). The overhead of performing this path compression is typically 1–2%, although could be 20% of the image width in the worst case.

Klaiber et al.'s [9,10] refinements to Bailey and Johnston's algorithm mainly improved memory efficiency by recycling labels that were no longer used within the processing. The underlying *Union-Find* algorithm is the same. Klaiber et al. [11] also showed that it was only necessary to perform a double lookup of the first pixel in a run, and use that label for all pixels in the run. This is a minor variation on *Quick-Union* with context-sensitive path compression.

By processing rows in zig-zag order [4], path compression is handled automatically when processing the following line. This enables *Quick-Union* with a single lookup to be used for the *Find* operation without any end of row overhead.

Spagnolo et al. [17] used *Quick-Union*, with a triple lookup for *Find*. While this is successful for many practical images, three lookups may not necessarily reach the representative label. Such cases must be resolved at the end of the frame. Similarly, Thornberg and Lawal [20] and Malik et al. [13] perform a simple *Union* and defer merger resolution until the end of the frame.

Aggressive relabelling by Ma et al. [3,12] reassigns labels for each row processed. This effectively requires two lookups: the first to determine the representative label in the previous row, and the second to translate that to the corresponding representative label used in the current row. The algorithm uses *Quick-Union* with context-based path compression at the end of each row. However, since some mergers are implicitly managed through the translation from one row to the next, the worst case overhead reduced to 6.3% [11,12].

A modification by Zhao et al. [26] defers assigning a label until the end of a run of successive object pixels. This can reduce the number of trivial mergers, and reduce the depth of the resulting tree. Zhao incorrectly claimed that this eliminates the need for path compression at the end of each row, however a single lookup is not sufficient to give the correct representative label. Therefore, this *Quick-Union* without path compression is insufficient, and consequently, the feature vectors are likely to be incorrect for some patterns.

Jeong et al. [7] took a different approach. For the *Union* operation, they replaced all of the old labels directly with the representative label in parallel using hardware. Thus only one label us used for a connected component at any time, effectively a form of *Quick-Find*.

The next two papers reviewed perform run-based labelling, but check for mergers using a 2×2 pixel window. Zhao et al. [25] assign a sequential index for each run within a row, and a serial number of the run within the image. The image-based serial number is used as the representative label, whereas the row-based index is used to address the feature vector and the mapping to the serial number. When runs in successive rows overlap, a form of *Quick-Union* is used to identify equivalences from one row to the next, with the process of merging feature vectors and resolving equivalences deferred until the end of each row. The merger resolution process has quadratic computational complexity.

Tang et al. [18] represent the *Union-Find* data structure using a linked-list. This is implemented using 3 tables: *head, next,* and *tail.* The *head* is the current representative label, and changes dynamically as labels expire. Data is accumulated in the representative label. When runs in successive rows overlap, the *Union* operation combines the lists, and provides translation of labels between rows. The *head* and *tail* tables also enable the *Find* operation in constant time.

The focus of all of these algorithms is primarily on the labelling of pixels or runs, with the feature vector accumulation almost a by-product of the processing. This is perhaps a little less so in Tang et al. [18], which is the most similar to our proposed approach. *Union-Retire* removes the focus on any particular node as being the representative node, and in so doing relaxes the required representation.

3 *Union-Retire* Algorithm

Like Zhao et al. [25] and Tang et al. [18], each run of consecutive object pixels along a row is sequentially assigned a unique index. The basic principle is to represent each run as a node within a DAG where each connected graph corresponds to a single connected component. Within this description, the terms node, run, and index are used interchangeably.

When runs overlap between successive rows, a *Union* operation links the associated nodes. This link is represented by an arc within the DAG from the earlier index to the later index.

Since the focus is shifted from labelling, a *Find* operation is unnecessary, since there is no representative label or node. Linking is therefore simplified, with the graph no longer constrained to be a tree structure. As long as the set of nodes within a component are connected, the underlying DAG may have several roots and leaves.

When a run of pixels is no longer accessible (due to the raster scan), a *Retire* operation removes the corresponding node from the DAG, simplifying the graph's structure. Any feature data associated with a retired node is then accumulated into one of its children, and the graph adjusted to maintain connectivity. Finally, when the last node within a component is *Retired*, the connected component is completed, and the associated feature vector is output.

Thus, the primary attention of *Union-Retire* is on adding (*Union*) and removing (*Retire*) nodes from a graph, rather than on the incidental task of finding the representative node or label. Throughout this process, the focus is on maintaining the overall connectivity between the constituent runs within the component.

3.1 Data Structures

The DAG is represented as an array, indexed by the node index. Each node can have up to two outgoing arcs, with the destination node for each arc are stored in one of two link arrays, $L1[\ ]$ and $L2[\ ]$.

Each node also has associated feature vector data, stored in the data array, $D[\ ]$. This includes the feature vector derived from the run of pixels, plus any data passed from retired nodes.

Algorithm 1 *Union-Retire* CCA algorithm

Input: Binary image I of width W and height H
Output: A feature vector for each connected component in I

  1: $R_p := R_c := 0$ ▷ Initialise run indices
  2: **for** $y := 0$ **to** H **do**
  3:   **for** $x := 0$ **to** W **do**   ▷ Scan
  4:     Window $:= I[x-1:x; y-1:y]$ ▷ Form 2×2 window
  5:     **if** Window $=$ ▧ **then**   ▷ Start of run in previous row
  6:       $R_p += 1$
  7:     **end if**
  8:     **if** Window $=$ ▧ **then**   ▷ Start of run in current row
  9:       $R_c += 1$
10:       $L1[R_c] := L2[R_c] := 0$ ▷ No links yet
11:       $D[R_c] := FV(x,y)$ ▷ Feature vector for pixel
12:     **else if** Window $=$ ▧ **then**   ▷ Continuing current run
13:       $D[R_c] += FV(x,y)$ ▷ Accumulate feature vector
14:     **end if**
15:     **if** Window **in** {▧▧▧▧} **then**   ▷ *Union*, link nodes
16:       **if** $L1[R_p] = 0$ **then**   ▷ No links yet
17:         $L1[R_p] := R_c$
18:       **else if** $L2[R_p] = 0$ **and** $L1[R_p] \neq R_c$ **then**   ▷ Only one link
19:         LINK$(L1[R_p] \rightarrow R_c)$
20:         $L1[R_p] := R_c$
21:       **else if** $L1[R_p] \neq R_c$ **and** $L2[R_p] \neq R_c$ **then**   ▷ Two links
22:         LINK$(L2[R_p] \rightarrow R_c)$
23:         $L2[R_p] := R_c$
24:       **end if**
25:     **end if**
26:     **if** Window $=$ ▧ **then**   ▷ *Retire*, unlink node
27:       **if** $L1[R_p] = 0$ **then**   ▷ No links
28:         **Output:** $D[R_p]$ ▷ Object completed
29:       **else if** $L2[R_p] = 0$ **then**   ▷ Only one link
30:         $D[L1[R_p]] += D[R_p]$ ▷ Accumulate data
31:       **else**   ▷ Two links
32:         $D[L2[R_p]] += D[R_p]$ ▷ Accumulate data
33:         LINK$(L1[R_p] \rightarrow L2[R_p])$ ▷ Maintain linkages
34:       **end if**
35:     **end if**
36:   **end for**
37: **end for**
38: **procedure** LINK$(R_a \rightarrow R_b)$ ▷ Link two nodes
39:   **if** $L1[R_a] = 0$ **then**   ▷ No links
40:     $L1[R_a] := R_b$ ▷ Add link
41:   **else if** $L2[R_a] = 0$ **and** $L1[R_a] \neq R_b$ **then**   ▷ Only one link
42:     $L2[R_a] := R_b$ ▷ Add second link
43:   **else if** $L1[R_a] \neq R_b$ **and** $L2[R_a] \neq R_b$ **then**   ▷ Two links
44:     LINK$(L2[R_a] \rightarrow R_b)$ ▷ Pass link on
45:   **end if**
46: **end procedure**

Within the algorithm description below, the indices are simply sequential. However, for a given image width, W, there can be at most $\lfloor \frac{W}{2} \rfloor + 2$ indices in use at any one time. In practise, the run index is provided by a counter that can wrap around, and this limits size of the memory arrays required.

3.2   Algorithm Description

The processing steps for *Union-Retire* are listed in Algorithm 1.

The image is scanned in raster fashion, using a 2×2 local window to determine connectivity (8-connectivity is assumed here, but can be trivially changed for 4-connectivity). For simplicity, the handling of the edge of the image is ignored here by processing one extra pixel in each row, and one extra row of the image, with the assumption that pixel values outside the image are background pixels. In practise, by handling the border cases appropriately, it is only necessary to process each pixel without adding extra rows or columns. The bottom right corner of the 2×2 window corresponds to the current pixel. Within the algorithm, the window is represented by a 2×2 graphic, where white represents background, black represents an object pixel, and grey is a "don't care" (either object or background).

While the run indices are shown as unique in Algorithm 1 (the index is incremented for each successive run), in practise, the indices wrap, with the corresponding entries within the memory arrays reused. Since these are both assigned and retired sequentially, it is unnecessary to maintain a queue of recycled indices. Let R_p and R_c be the most recently used indices on the previous and current rows respectively. These are updated (incremented) when a new object pixel is found in the corresponding row (previous row: ▨, line 5; current row: ▨, line 8).

The feature vector (stored in $D[\,]$) for the node on the current row is initialised at the start of a run (▨, line 8), and updated for each object pixel within a run on the current row (▨, line 12).

When a run in the previous row is connected to a run in the current row, a *Union* operation is invoked, which adds a link between the corresponding nodes to connect the two sub-components. This is detected either at the end of the run on the current row when there is an object pixel in the previous row, or at the end of a run on the previous row when there is an object pixel in the current row (▨▨▨▨▨, line 15). This link is always added from an earlier node to a later node to facilitate the *Retire* operation. If the node on the previous row already has link, then the link is added to its successor, so that several successive nodes are linked in a chain (see *Union*(1,4) and *Union*(1,5) in the following example). If the successor node already has two links, then the link is propagated to the successor's most recent successor (see *Union*(6,11) and *Union*(7,12) in the following example).

At the end of a run on the previous row (▨, line 26), the associated index is never accessed again. Therefore, a *Retire* operation is performed, removing the corresponding node from the graph. The feature vector associated with the retired node is accumulated into a linked node (if any). If there are no linked nodes, then the object is detected as completed, and the feature vector of the connected component is output. If there are two linked nodes, then it is necessary to insert a link from the earlier node to the later node to maintain overall connectivity within the DAG.

3.3 Example

The sequence of *Union* and *Retire* operations for an example image is shown in Fig. 3, with the associated directed graphs after each operation. The key features of the algorithm will be highlighted using this example.

At pixel (6,2) the first *Union* operation links nodes ① and ③. The link is always from an earlier node to a later node.

At (9,2) when nodes ① and ④ are linked, a link is inserted between nodes ③ (the current child of ①) and ④, and the node on the previous row is updated so that it points to the node just inserted. This is so that a sequence of *Unions* from the same source run can be efficiently processed without requiring a large number of links from the source node. Note that although there is no longer a direct link between nodes ① and ③, they are still implicitly connected via ④.

Then, when node ⑤ is linked at (10,2), it can simply be added at the end of the chain. Note that the *Union* operation is performed before node ① is *Retired*. When ① is *Retired*, its data is combined into ⑤, and it is removed from the graph. ① is no longer accessible and plays no further part in the operations. However, the effects of its connectivity with each of nodes ③, ④ and ⑤ are represented in the links between those nodes.

At pixel (4,3), the connection between ③ and ⑦ links the two constituent sub-components. The child of ③ is ④, so the link to ⑦ is added to ④. It does not matter that ④ is not the end of the chain; node ④ now has 2 links.

Similarly, when ④ is linked to ⑨, ⑨ is added as a second link to ⑦. Node ⑤ remains connected to ④. When ④ is *Retired* at (9,3), it has two child nodes: ⑤ and ⑨. To maintain connectivity, it is necessary to link from ⑤ to ⑨.

At (2,4) when ⑥ is linked to ⑪, ⑥'s child ⑦ already has 2 children, so the link table for ⑦ is full. Therefore the link is propagated to ⑦'s most recent child, and is added to ⑨. Similarly at (4,4) when ⑦ is linked to ⑫.

At the bottom of the loop, at pixel (8,5) with *Union*(13,14), nodes ⑬ and ⑭ are already linked, so no update is required to the DAG.

Finally, when ⑭ is *Retired* at (8,6) it has no children. Therefore the connected component is complete, and the associated feature vector can be output. Note that this is the earliest possible time that completion could be detected.

4 Analysis

4.1 Correctness

There are two aspects to the correctness of the algorithm that need to be demonstrated. The first is that each pixel in a connected component is assigned to the

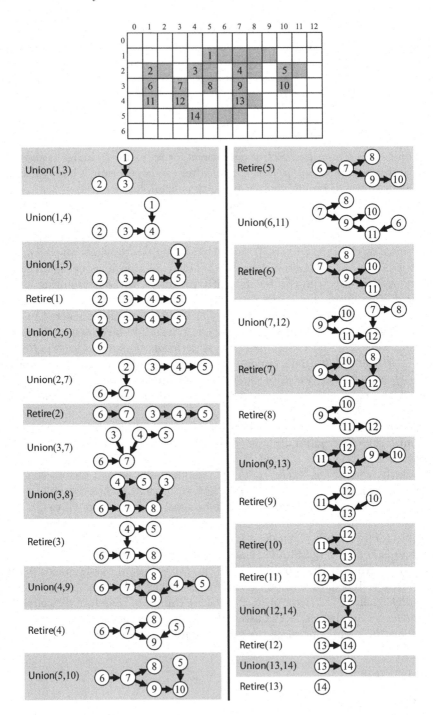

Fig. 3. Example image showing linkages between runs after each *Union* and *Retire* step. Node numbers correspond to run indices.

correct component, and the second (related to the first) is that the correct feature is calculated for each connected component.

Each node in the DAG is associated with an index. Each pixel is assigned an index with all consecutive object pixels within a run assigned the same node. Incrementing the index on the first pixel of a run is sufficient to guarantee that each node has a unique index. When recycling indices, it is essential that the index is retired before it is assigned to another run. This is satisfied by having at least $\lfloor \frac{W}{2} \rfloor + 2$ indices.

Since successive runs of object pixels must have at least one background pixel between them, it is clear that there cannot be a direct connection between different runs of pixels on the same row. The only direct connections that can be made are between runs on adjacent rows, where the runs overlap (or there is a diagonal connection for 8-connectivity). With a raster scanned 2×2 window, any such overlap will continue until the end of the run on either the previous row or the current row, which provides a condition for their unique detection. This is the condition for the *Union* operation, which is used to link the nodes representing the connected indices. The linking always maintains the connectivity by adding the node on the current row into the graph, and maintaining a link from the node on the previous row to the added node.

After the end of a run on the previous row, the associated node can never be accessed again (although with index recycling, the same index can later be used for another run). This invokes the *Retire* operation, which removes the node from the network. Just as nodes are created in a sequential order, they are also retired in the exact same order, and the associated links disappear as well.

Since arcs are always from an earlier node to a later node, any node being retired can have no incoming links, because any such links would have to come from earlier nodes, which would have already been retired. Removing a retired node with only one outgoing link will not affect the connectivity of the graph. A node with two outgoing links may connect two sub-graphs. Therefore, to maintain connectivity it is necessary to link these, which is achieved by adding a link from the earlier node to the later node. At any one time the remaining graph of connected nodes correspond to all of the runs of pixels that can currently extend the object further. Finally, a node being retired with no outgoing links has no further connections within the image, and is therefore the last node of a completed object.

The second aspect is that the final calculated feature vector represents the complete connected component. Each pixel within a run contributes to the run's feature vector as it is being scanned. When a run is retired, its feature vector (plus any others that have been merged into it) is accumulated into that of another run within the component, so the data is not lost when the node is *Retired*. Therefore, each run will contribute to the final feature vector. When the final node of the connected component is *Retired*, its accumulated feature vector will therefore have contributions from each pixel within the connected component.

4.2 Validation

To validate the *Union-Retire* CCA, the output feature vectors were compared
with those produced by using a conventional two-pass CCL and analysis algorithm [24]. The algorithms were compared on over 10,000 randomly generated
binary images, plus also the approximately 300 images from the USC-SIPI image
database [22], binarised using a global threshold using Otsu's algorithm [14].

All of the images gave identical sets of feature vectors from both algorithms.
While this does not guarantee correctness, this regression test provides validation
of the algorithm.

4.3 Memory Requirements

Within an embedded system, two factors of primary importance are the memory requirements and computational efficiency. The memory requirements of
the proposed *Union-Retire* algorithm are compared with several state-of-the-art
single-pass CCA algorithms in Table 1. Note that the memory requirements for
the feature vector depend on the particular features being extracted. However,
these are the same as for all of the compared algorithms (those which require
two copies of the data table, e.g. [12,25], or those that had large tables because
they deferred processing until the end of the frame, e.g. [2,13,17,20], were not
considered) so are not included in the table.

Table 1. Comparison of memory required for *Union-Find* (*U-F*) data structures and
computational complexity of state-of-the-art single-pass CCA algorithms.

Algorithm	Row buffer	*U-F* Memory	Complexity
Double-lookup, [11]	Label	Augmented label + chain stack + recycle queue	Linear +20% overhead
Zig-zag scan, [4]	Label +1 bpp zig-zag	Augmented label + recycle queue	Linear
Linked-list based, [18]	2 bpp	3 link tables	Linear
Union-Retire	1 bpp	2 link tables	Linear

There are two areas where memory is required (assuming a streamed image
input). The first is the row buffer required to cache labels for the previous row of
the scan window; this is of the width of the image. The second is for the *Union-
Find* (or equivalent) data structures required to manage the connectivity, which
have size proportional to the number of labels.

Both the double-lookup method of Klaiber et al. [11] and the zig-zag scan
method [4] propagate the labels. Therefore, the row buffer needs to hold the
labels assigned in the current row. In addition to this, the zig-zag scan method

requires an additional 1 bit per pixel buffer for zig-zag reordering. In contrast, the linked-list method of Tang et al. [18] and the proposed *Union-Retire* only need to buffer the original binary image because the labels or indices are assigned deterministically. Therefore the latter two methods require significantly less memory for the row buffer.

The linked-list method assumes 4-connectivity. Tang et al. proposed a filter to convert an 8-connected image to a 4-connected one, and this requires an extra bit per pixel to be buffered to correctly calculate the feature vector. Since the proposed method can be applied with either 4- or 8-connectivity, for 8-connected images, the proposed method uses half of the row buffer memory.

Both the double-lookup and zig-zag scan store augmented labels in their merger table. These comprise the label, and the row number in which the label was first allocated. Both methods also require a recycle queue for label allocation and recycling. In addition, the double-lookup method requires a stack for efficiently implementing path compression. The linked-list method [18] requires 3 tables to represent the links between labels, whereas *Union-Retire* only requires 2 tables for representing connectivity. Therefore, the proposed *Union-Retire* approach requires 33% less memory for the *Union-Find* data structures than the previous best design.

4.4   Computational Complexity

Although the algorithm is quite simple, the computational complexity is not as simple to determine. Feature vector accumulation takes constant processing time per pixel, as accumulating the initial feature vector for each run takes one operation per pixel. As each run is *Retired*, a single operation is used to accumulate the data into the remaining graph.

The complicating factor is the linking, which is required for both *Union* and *Retire* operations. If the node being linked already has two arcs from it, the link is passed onto the next node. A single such deferral is constant time per operation, implying linear computational complexity with the number of pixels. However, if the source node after deferral also has two arcs already, then the computational complexity potentially becomes non-linear.

A formal proof that subsequent deferred links never occur is very complex (see for example [11]). Therefore we have focussed on the analysis of a subset of images, rather than worst case analysis. In processing 10,000+ random images, and the 300 natural SIPI images, a second deferral never occurred. Therefore, for this domain of images, there is at most one deferred link per run of pixels, implying linear computational complexity. If a second deferral ever occurs, it is likely to be very rare, and does not substantially alter this conclusion.

5   Summary and Conclusion

We have proposed a new approach to CCA, which moves away from the conventional *Union-Find* algorithm. Instead of focussing on the labelling of each connected component, more attention is given to connectivity, which is represented by a directed acyclic graph. A single pass is made through the image, with runs of consecutive object pixels treated as a single unit. A *Union* operation links runs connected on adjacent rows by adding an arc to the graph. Whenever a run falls out of the processing window, a *Retire* operation removes the corresponding node from the graph, and adjusts the links to maintain connectedness. A feature vector of each connected component is built incrementally by accumulating feature vectors of each pixel in a run. When a node is *Retired*, the associated feature vector is merged with that of a remaining node. When the last node of a connected component is *Retired*, the associated feature vector is output.

We have shown that this new approach to CCA is correct both through informal proof and regression testing against a standard 2-pass algorithm. Testing has also shown that the algorithm has linear computational complexity, although this is more difficult to prove formally. The *Union-Find* memory requirements of the algorithm are shown to be 33% lower than the best state-of-the-art CCA algorithm. These make the *Union-Retire* approach attractive for embedded image processing.

Future work is to explore a hardware implementation of the *Union-Retire* algorithm using a field programmable gate array (FPGA).

References

1. Bailey, D.G.: Raster based region growing. In: 6th New Zealand Image Processing Workshop, Lower Hutt, NZ, 29–30 August 1991, pp. 21–26 (1991)
2. Bailey, D., Johnston, C.: Single pass connected components analysis. In: Image and Vision Computing New Zealand, Hamilton, NZ, 5–7 December 2007, pp. 282–287 (2007)
3. Bailey, D.G., Johnston, C.T., Ma, N.: Connected components analysis of streamed images. In: International Conference on Field Programmable Logic and Applications, Heidelberg, Germany, 8–10 September 2008, pp. 679–682 (2008). https://doi.org/10.1109/FPL.2008.4630038
4. Bailey, D.G., Klaiber, M.J.: Zig-zag based single pass connected components analysis. J. Imaging 5(4), article 45, 26 p. (2019). https://doi.org/10.3390/jimaging5040045
5. Bailey, D.G.: History and evolution of single pass connected component analysis. In: 35th International Conference on Image and Vision Computing New Zealand, Wellington, NZ, 25–27 November 2020, pp. 317–322 (2020). https://doi.org/10.1109/IVCNZ51579.2020.9290585
6. Hopcroft, J.E., Ullman, J.D.: Set merging algorithms. SIAM J. Comput. 2(4), 294–303 (1973). https://doi.org/10.1137/0202024
7. Jeong, J., Lee, G., Lee, M., Kim, J.-G.: A single-pass connected component labeler without label merging period. J. Sign. Process. Syst. 84(2), 211–223 (2015). https://doi.org/10.1007/s11265-015-1048-7
8. Johnston, C.T., Bailey, D.G.: FPGA implementation of a single pass connected components algorithm. In: IEEE International Symposium on Electronic Design, Test and Applications, Hong Kong, 23–25 January 2008, pp. 228–231 (2008). https://doi.org/10.1109/DELTA.2008.21

9. Klaiber, M.J., Bailey, D.G., Baroud, Y.O., Simon, S.: A resource-efficient hardware architecture for connected component analysis. IEEE Trans. Circuits Syst. Video Technol. **26**(7), 1334–1349 (2016). https://doi.org/10.1109/TCSVT.2015.2450371

10. Klaiber, M.J.: A parallel and resource-efficient single lookup connected components analysis architecture for reconfigurable hardware. Ph.D. thesis, Stuttgart University (2017)

11. Klaiber, M.J., Bailey, D.G., Simon, S.: Comparative study and proof of single-pass connected components algorithms. J. Math. Imaging Vis. **61**(8), 1112–1134 (2019). https://doi.org/10.1007/s10851-019-00891-2

12. Ma, N., Bailey, D., Johnston, C.: Optimised single pass connected components analysis. In: International Conference on Field Programmable Technology, Taipei, Taiwan, 8–10 December 2008, pp. 185–192 (2008). https://doi.org/10.1109/FPT.2008.4762382

13. Malik, A.W., Thornberg, B., Imran, M., Lawal, N.: Hardware architecture for real-time computation of image component feature descriptors on a FPGA. Int. J. Distrib. Sens. Netw. **10**(1), 815378 (2014). https://doi.org/10.1155/2014/815378

14. Otsu, N.: A threshold selection method from gray-level histograms. IEEE Trans. Syst. Man Cybern. **9**(1), 62–66 (1979). https://doi.org/10.1109/TSMC.1979.4310076

15. Sedgewick, R., Wayne, K.: Algorithms, 4th edn. Addison-Wesley Professional, Boston (2011)

16. Selkow, S.M.: One-pass complexity of digital picture properties. J. ACM **19**(2), 283–295 (1972). https://doi.org/10.1145/321694.321701

17. Spagnolo, F., Perri, S., Corsonello, P.: An efficient hardware-oriented single-pass approach for connected component analysis. Sensors **19**(14), 3055 (2019). https://doi.org/10.3390/s19143055

18. Tang, J.W., Shaikh-Husin, N., Sheikh, U.U., Marsono, M.N.: A linked list run-length-based single-pass connected component analysis for real-time embedded hardware. J. Real-Time Image Process. **15**(1), 197–215 (2016). https://doi.org/10.1007/s11554-016-0590-2

19. Tarjan, R.E.: Efficiency of a good but not linear set union algorithm. J. ACM **22**(2), 215–225 (1975). https://doi.org/10.1145/321879.321884

20. Thornberg, B., Lawal, N.: Real-time component labelling and feature extraction on FPGA. In: International Symposium on Signals, Circuits and Systems, Iasi, Romania, 9–10 July 2009, pp. 1–4 (2009). https://doi.org/10.1109/ISSCS.2009.5206100

21. Trein, J., Schwarzbacher, A.T., Hoppe, B., Noffz, K.H., Trenschel, T.: Development of a FPGA based real-time blob analysis circuit. In: Irish Signals and Systems Conference, Derry, Northern Ireland, 13–14 September 2007, pp. 121–126 (2007)

22. USC-SIPI: USC-SIPI image database. http://sipi.usc.edu/database/

23. Veillon, F.: One pass computation of morphological and geometrical properties of objects in digital pictures. Sign. Process. **1**(3), 175–189 (1979). https://doi.org/10.1016/0165-1684(79)90018-5

24. Wu, K., Otoo, E., Suzuki, K.: Optimizing two-pass connected-component labeling algorithms. Pattern Anal. Appl. **12**(2), 117–135 (2009). https://doi.org/10.1007/s10044-008-0109-y

25. Zhao, C., Duan, G., Zheng, N.: A hardware-efficient method for extracting statistic information of connected component. J. Sign. Process. Syst. **88**(1), 55–65 (2016). https://doi.org/10.1007/s11265-016-1126-5

26. Zhao, F., Lu, H.Z., Zhang, Z.Y.: Real-time single-pass connected components analysis algorithm. EURASIP J. Image Video Process. **2013:21**, 10 (2013). https://doi.org/10.1186/1687-5281-2013-21

Improving Object Detection in Real-World Traffic Scenes

Waqar Khan[1]([⊠]), Fang Liu[1], and Marta Vos[2]

[1] Wellington Institute of Technology Ltd., Wellington, New Zealand
wkha011@aucklanduni.ac.nz
[2] Whitireia Community Polytechnic Ltd., Wellington, New Zealand

Abstract. *Single Shot Multi-Box Detector* (SSD) is a well-known object detection algorithm. It can detect 20 different types of objects making it suitable for an object detector for traffic scenes. In a real-world traffic scene, objects can appear in different sizes and pose different details. This can potentially lead to false detections made by an SSD. Depending on how input information (image) is provided to SSD (leading to a proposed SSD model), the accuracy of the proposed model can vary. The overall objective of this study is to evaluate different SSD models while examining accuracy of object detection where the object type is only a vehicle.

This study is derived from human vision. Where, an object is easily identifiable in a sharper image with brightness than a blurry one with darkness. Based on these assumptions hypotheses were created, based on which SSD based models were proposed. Comparison based on true positives and false positives was performed and the winner was identified by using the *Enpeda. Image Sequence Analysis Test Site* (EISATS) stereo image barriers dataset set 9.

Keywords: Object detection · Ground truth · True/false positive · Precision · Recall · Win count

1 Introduction

According to the *World Health Organization* (WHO), the road accident casualties were more than 1.35 million in year 2016 [1]. To avoid such scenarios, computer vision based safety systems can assist in identifying hazards and either apply brakes or warn the driver about imminent collision, so that he/she could apply brakes [2]. These safety systems have to track an object of interest with time to estimate their trajectory, and after they are confident, can issue the warning to the driver. Apart from the stereo measurement inaccuracies [3], there are also object tracking inaccuracies, particularly in scenarios where objects keep on crossing each other. And, drift could occur.

In such a challenging scenario, a hybrid approach is often adopted, where object is detected in every frame, and each detection is compared with previously tracked object, to identify if it is the same object or a different one. This process is also known as data association [4]. Data association is particularly important when the visual tracker fails

© Springer Nature Switzerland AG 2021
M. Nguyen et al. (Eds.): ISGV 2021, CCIS 1386, pp. 288–299, 2021.
https://doi.org/10.1007/978-3-030-72073-5_22

due to different factors like occlusion, etc. So, in other words, object detection is not only important to detect an object in the first frame, however, continuous detections are also essential.

In other words, this implies that when the vehicles in the traffic scene are always moving (like in EISATS set 9 [5]). Then, the accuracy of detector is determined by its performance in every frame/image. A moving camera in particular depicts a different scene for the same object. It is because the pose of the object of interest relative to the camera capturing the scene is always changing with time. It is true, provided that both the object of interest and the ego-vehicle (with camera mounted on it) are moving at a different velocity in world co-ordinates.

In the context of object detection, only left camera images are sufficient from EISATS set 9 which consists of 400 greyscale images. An object detector identifies the type of object and its location. Therefore, the performance of a detector is based on how accurately it classifies an object's type as well as its location in the 2D image. To evaluate the performance, data with *ground truth* (GT) is used.

The evaluation output could be *true positive* (TP), where detected object (type and location) matches with the actual (type and location) of object as indicated by GT. It could be *false positive* (FP), where the detection type or location do not match with GT. It could be *false negative* (FN), where there is no detection, however, an object exists in GT. And, finally it could be *true negative* (TN), where no object is detected and no object exists at that location in GT either.

FNs often occur when objects are smaller in size as they are farther from the camera, or when the objects of interest are occluded. Because EISATS set 9 dataset consists of a sequence of images captured over time, this allows for TPs, FPs and FNs to be critically evaluated.

2 Literature Review

Before the introduction of *convolutional neural networks* (CNN), object detection relied on basic features as they were supported by limited processing powered devices. For example, Viola and Jones developed a detector called VJ detector which could detect faces in real-time [7]. They used sliding window operations to compute features in all locations and at different scales.

In 2005, N. Dalal and B. Triggs built a pedestrian detector based on *Histogram of Oriented Gradients Feature Descriptor* (HOG descriptor) [8]. HOG was generalized and was able to detect various objects of different sizes. It was able to achieve that because, it resized the input window to match with the fixed filter window size and used it to compute the feature descriptor. This approach has been adopted by several later algorithms including *Deformable Part-based Model* (DPM). DPM was first proposed by P. Felzenszwalb et al. in 2008 [9], which was further improved by R. Girshick in 2010 [10]. DPM won series of detection challenges from year 2007 to 2009. In the training phase, DPM breaks down an object into its parts, while in the testing phase it tries to assemble detections to those parts. The development of DPM also involved development of multi-instance learning as well as bounding box regression.

In 2012, a revolutionary deep learning method: CNN was proposed by A. Krizhevsky, I. Sutskever, and G. E. Hinton [11]. It was able to classify more than 1 million images in an ImageNet training set, consisting of 1000 different classes. Its error rate of 39.7 percent was significantly lesser than others proposed at the same time.

Typically, in a CNN, all pixel values of an input image are processed via multiple hidden layers. These layers consists of several convolutional layers, which allows for the extraction of features like edges or corners etc. These layers also consist of max pooling, which is a process adopted to reduce the dimensions of data, leading to reduction in processing time.

In 2014, Girshick et al. proposed the *Regions with CNN features* (R-CNN) which is a two-stage detector [12]. Other, two stage detectors followed including Fast R-CNN [13], and Faster R-CNN [14].

In 2016, W. Liu et al. proposed one-stage detector named SSD [15]. SSD needs only a single shot to detect multiple objects in an input image. Due to this, SSD is much faster than two stage detectors. For example, SSD300 achieved an mAP of 74.3 percent, with 59 *frames per second* (FPS) while SSD500 achieved 76.9 percent mAP at 22 FPS. Both of these outperform Faster R-CNN which had 73.2 percent mAP and 7 FPS. While YOLOv1 had 63.4 percent mAP at 45 FPS.

3   Methodology

Although we chose to use the EISATS set 9 dataset, which is ideal for evaluating the effect of size of any object as well as brightness conditions, it does not come with GT. Our first step was to create a GT dataset for the object type vehicle/car for all 400 frames. For the purpose of evaluation, GT data had to capture the bounding box co-ordinates for each object in each frame. This was a completely manual exercise at least without any object tracking to identify the object location in subsequent frames. Nevertheless Python scripting was used to capture the ground truth into a text file.

Algorithm 1 describes the steps taken for capturing GT for 400 images of EISATS set 9.

Algorithm 1: GT collection from raw images of dataset

```
Set car_ground-truth_list
Set truck_ground-truth_list
for i in range (1,401):
    Read image i
    WHILE user inputs 'n' to log in new object's box
        IF user indicates to capture a car by pressing 'c'
            Write to file mouse_coordinates_car
        ELSEIF user indicates to capture a truck by pressing 't'
            Write to file mouse_coordinates_truck
        ELSEIF user indicates to go to next image by pressing 'n'
            BREAK
        ENDIF
```

Write top-left corner as (x1, y1) and bottom-right corner as (x2, y2).

The evaluations were based on the performance of SSD based models on the given dataset. Each model was proposed on top of the previous one. So, overall this research was an iterative process, as illustrated in Fig. 1.

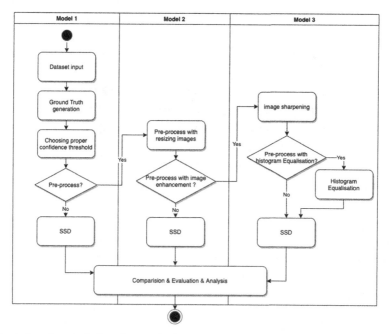

Fig. 1. A flowchart including three swim lanes demonstrates three models of SSD detection.

Model 1: Raw greyscale images were processed by SSD, the SSD detection accuracy was measured against the GT using the FPs, TPs and FNs for each image of the dataset. Several experiments were conducted to create a hypothesis for proposing an appropriate model for stage 2. The detection accuracy for each image constitutes result 1.

Model 2: SSD processed resized greyscale images using the hypothesis from stage 1. Experiments similar to stage 1 were repeated to create a further hypothesis and an appropriate model was proposed for stage 3. The detection accuracy lead to result 2.

Model 3: SSD used previous hypothesis. This model also used pre-processed images with image sharpening and histogram equalisation respectively.

A new model iSSD (with two variance iSSDv1 and iSSDv2) was proposed based on the iterations above.

Since the detection bounding box location could be anywhere for a given object and it potentially would not occupy the same region as GT bounding box. So, *intersection over union* (IoU) ratio is computed to identify if the detection (of the same object type) is TP or FP. The IoU process is further illustrated in Fig. 2.

Because GT is labelled manually, without any correlation from one image to the following with time. Therefore, a loose IoU measure of 0.5 is chosen to complement the tightness of GT production. Usually only when IoU ≥ 0.5, can a detection be considered as TP. If IoU < 0.5, then that detection is considered as a FP. Furthermore, all the detections, where the categories do not belong to GT categories, are considered as FPs as well. For example, if a detection is categorised as a bus or a horse, but there are no such categories in GT, they will be deemed as FPs.

Fig. 2. IoU presents the level of similarity between SSD detection and GT.

Furthermore, when two or more detections overlapping with each other, and, both have an IoU greater or equal 0.5 with the same object. Then, the one with larger IoU is considered as TP, and other/s is/are deemed as FP for the given object.

3.1 Precision and Recall

In computer vision, precision (also known as positive detection value) equals the fraction of TPs from all the retrieved object instances [16]. It is a metric to show precision of detecting instances. The standard formula of precision is

$$P_{old}^{CT} = \frac{TP}{TP + FP}$$

Where CT stands for *confidence threshold*.

On the other hand, recall which is also known as sensitivity, or TP rate, is the fraction of the total amount of correct detections compare to the actual total instances. This also results in computing a percentage. The standard formula of recall:

$$R_{old}^{CT} = \frac{TP}{TP + FN}$$

Precision and Recall together are a common pair of metrics used to evaluate the performance of object detection algorithms.

However, a new precision and new recall were proposed for this study.

New Precision and New Recall

To avoid 0-division error, when there are no detections in the given image, the formula was slightly modified to

$$P_{new}^{CT} = \frac{TP}{TP + FP + 0.00001}$$

Similarly, to avoid undefined recall values due to no TPs in the given image. The formula was slightly modified to

$$R_{new}^{CT} = \frac{TP + 1}{TP + FN + 1}$$

To be specific, when comparing different models against each other, R_{old}^{CT} does not appropriately serve in distinguishing between them. This is further described in the following example scenario:

Image A has one car in GT, while image B has ten cars in GT. If TP = 0 for both images, then based on the examples, the performance evaluator should indicate that a detector performed far more poorly on image B with FN = 10 than on image A with FN = 1. However, R_{old}^{CT} for both image A and B is equal and zero. Therefore, a slightly modified version is proposed from R_{old}^{CT} to R_{new}^{CT}. Based on this, with R_{new}^{CT} it gives 0.5 and 0.0909 for images A and B respectively. Such difference becomes critical to cross evaluate several models against each other for each image.

Furthermore, in vision-based driver safety systems, every FN means a hazard is missed by the system, which is costly. More FN are more costly than fewer FN. So, it is better to distinguish this situation using R_{new}^{CT}.

3.2 Score System

Due to the complexity of image inputs and result outputs, it is difficult to compare the performance of different models independently. In [17], W. Khan et al. proposed a win count system to compare models. Based on their method, in this research, a slightly different score system was designed, named "scorePR", for precision and recall. Where, for each image one model may or may not be scored in terms of recall and precision. After the winning score for precision or recall for each image has been collated, a total score is computed to find out which candidate/model gets higher score for the entire dataset in relation to either precision or recall.

For example, three situations described based on three example images and for each three candidates are evaluated, where each candidate is just an SSD model:

- In image 1, no candidates win because all candidates are equal due to zero precision. All candidates get zero mark.
- In image 2, only candidate 1 wins because only candidate 1 has the highest precision value. Candidate 1 gets one mark; the others get zero mark.
- In image 3, both candidate 1 and candidate 2 win, because they both have the equal highest precision value of 1. Candidate 1 and candidate 2 get one mark, while others get zero mark.

After applying the same approach on each image, scores can be summed for each candidate. The total in the example becomes, two, one and zero for candidates 1, 2, and 3 respectively. So, based on this candidate 1 is the winner based on score precision or scoreP. Similarly, score recall is computed and together they are called scorePR.

The same system was applied to recall. Based on this, the overall performance could be evaluated and compared quantitatively, rather than qualitatively.

3.3 SSD Based Models

Three models are evaluated. SSD is evaluated against improved SSD which adopts pre-processing to images in the form of histogram equalization. This model is called iSSDv1. Whereas, the iSSDv2 incorporates histogram equalization as well as image sharpening. Figure 3 illustrates histogram equalization on one of the images from EISATS set 9.

The histograms in Fig. 3 describe the grey scale intensity frequencies i.e. from 0 (dark) up to 255 (white). In Fig. 3 (A), it is clear that by default the image has more dark pixels than white. Whereas, after histogram equalization, when the pixel intensities are relatively equally distributed, the dark regions became brighter (see Fig. 3 (B)).

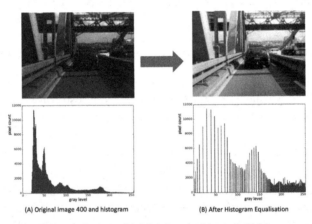

(A) Original image 400 and histogram   (B) After Histogram Equalisation

Fig. 3. Image 400 of EISATS set 9 with (right) and without (left) histogram equalisation.

4 Results and Discussion

The evaluation is also a three stage process. In the first stage, the goal is to identify the best CT for the given dataset. Once this is identified, in the later experiments the chosen CT is kept as constant, and suitable image resolution is identified. In the final experiment, both CT and resolutions are kept constant, and the performance of image sharpening and histogram equalization is evaluated.

4.1 Model 1: Suitable CT Identification Using Default SSD

SSD can have a good TP for a given CT on a given image. However, for the same image, it can also have FP. Therefore, there is a need to identify a suitable CT by analysing both precision (representing the detection performance of a detector) and recall (representing the accuracy in regards to number of candidate objects in GT).

To compare and evaluate how CT affects the recall rate on the dataset, scoreR is computed one each image using different CTs. The winner CT is identified based on best scoreR.

The number shown on the curve in the Fig. 4, is the sum of marks each CT gets for entire dataset. The horizontal axis indicates different CT (from 0.1 to 0.9), while the vertical axis represents the scoreR CTs get.

The SSD detector starts detecting objects more often when they become larger in size, i.e. from image 282 onwards. Therefore, there is no winner for images from 0 to 281, so for the further analysis based on recall these images were ignored based on the experiment.

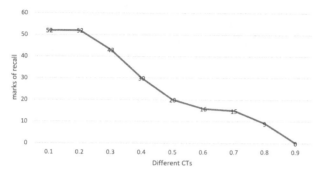

Fig. 4. Scores of Recall comparison for different CTs.

For images 282 onwards, CT $= (0.1 \| 0.2)$ has the best recall-based winner. To further analyse this, let's consider an image 293 in EISATS set 9 where CT $= (0.1 \| 0.2)$ is a winning combination. To be more specific, $R_{new}^{0.1} = R_{new}^{0.2} = 0.5$, $R_{new}^{0.4} = R_{new}^{0.5} = \ldots = R_{new}^{0.9} = 0.25$ according to our experiments.

Figure 5 shows an example of image 293 from EISATS set 9 with different SSD detections due to various CTs.

(A) Ground Truth. There are three cars as ground truth.

(B) When CT=0.1, one car in the center is detected.

(C) When CT=0.2, one car in the center is detected.

(D) By CT=0.3 and more, no object can be detected.

Fig. 5. Image 293 is processed by SSD at different CT, with various outcomes.

The lower CT chosen, the better is the recall rate demonstrated. This is reasonable, because some cars are detected with a lower confidence. If a lower confidence threshold is chosen it will pass the filter and be shown as a detection in the output. However, for a higher CT than the confidence, it will not pass the filter of CT and consequently cannot be shown in the detection result. That will lead to a lower TP, as well as lower recall.

(2) All the detected cars come with confidence more than 20 percent, therefore CT = 0.1 and CT = 0.2 win in all the images, or at least perform as well as other CT (when no detection is produced).

To compare precision between different CTs scoreP was used. However, unlike scoreR, the scoreP curve is nonlinear (see Fig. 6A). Instead of a highest CT or lowest CT, CT of 0.7 using $P^{0.7}_{new}$ has best performance.

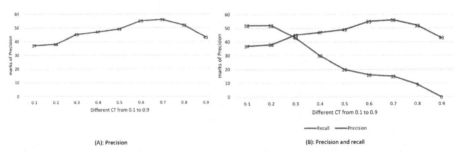

(A): Precision   (B): Precision and recall

Fig. 6. Comparison for different CTs on EISATS set 9 using scorePR as marks. (A).Precision only. (B). Precision and recall.

From our previous experiment we know that lower CT can produce more detections. However, most of the detections at lower CT are FPs. These are due to the detections of buses, boats, aeroplanes, chairs and trains. Neither of these are present in GT, hence they are FP detections. P^{CT}_{new} determines how many of detections out of total detections were TP. This explains the lower score of P^{CT}_{new} for lower CTs.

The reason that $P^{0.7}_{new}$ gets higher score in scoreP system than $P^{0.8}_{new}$ and $P^{0.9}_{new}$ is mainly because some detections come with a medium confidence. For example, in image 381, only one detection with confidence 79.4 percent is produced, no false detections. In such a situation, CT = 0.1 ~ 0.7 lead to precision of 100 percent, but CT = 0.8 ~ 0.9 lead to 0 percent. This is not a common scene among the whole dataset, so the value of CT = 0.8 and 0.9 are lower but relatively near to CT = 0.7.

To find the best fit for both recall and precision, both are plotted together (see Fig. 6B). Based on it, both the curves meet at CT = 0.3. This initially indicates CT = 0.3 as a candidate for a trade-off of recall and precision. This concludes hypothesis 1 and is used in following models.

4.2 Model 2: Suitable Resolution Using Default SSD and CT = 0.3

Each greyscale image in the EISATS set 9 dataset is of resolution [W × H] = [640 × 480] pixels. Where, W indicates horizontal count of pixels, while H stands indicates vertical count. The default SSD model resizes input image to [W × H] = [300 × 300] pixels.

We scale up the image up to 1.25 times i.e. [800 × 600] pixels, and then down to 0.75 times i.e. [480 × 360] pixels, and 0.5 times i.e. [320 × 240] pixels.

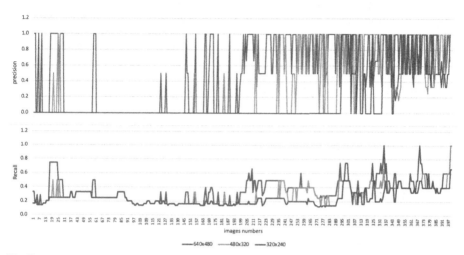

Fig. 7. ScorePR values for different input image resolutions and CT = 0.3 on EISATS set 9. Top: Precision score. Bottom: Recall score.

Based on Fig. 7 where comparison is only about original or scaled down resolution, the resolution [W × H] = [640 × 480] pixels gains highest number of peaks most frequently, therefore it is a clear winner. Similarly, when the resolution is reduced, SSD recall's performance degrades accordingly. Additionally, we found that the method used to change the scale of image can also impact the performance of SSD. In our analysis, we compared *nearest neighbour interpolation* (NNI) with bilinear interpolation, NNI with area, bi-cubic interpolation and with Lanczos interpolation. We found that the method used for scaling up, can positively improve SSD's performance. Based on which we were able to identify that with NNI method, resolution [800 × 600] pixels outperformed the image's default resolution i.e. [640 × 480] pixels.

4.3 Model 3: Preprocessing Comparison on SSD Models with CT = 0.3 and Resolution = [800 × 600] Pixels

Figure 8 illustrates a comparison based on scorePR on complete dataset without pre-processing, with image sharpening only, with histogram equalisation only, with image sharpening as well as histogram equalisation. Based on this, it is clear that the default model without any pre-processing relatively has the worst performance. With pre- histogram equalisation only, SSD gives the best recall score. With both image sharpening and histogram equalisation as pre-processing, SSD gives the best result for precision. Based on this it can be concluded that there is not a single winner. However, pre-processing does improve the overall outcome of SSD. And, same can be expected for other more recent object detectors.

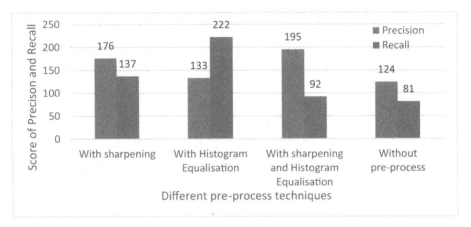

Fig. 8. Different score of various pre-processing techniques.

5 Conclusions

CT is a basic factor which could impact the result of SSD detection. In our experiments on EISATS set 9, we found that CT = 0.3 outperformed others when evaluations was performed using the novel scorePR system. Furthermore, based on further experiments we deduced that the resolution of images is crucial to the SSD. Scaling up or scaling down the resolution of images could change the performance of SSD detection results.

We further explored the impact of visual image quality upon the accuracy of SSD using scorePR. Specifically, improving image quality by histogram equalisation and image sharpening could effectively improve the SSD accuracy. Based on these findings, a few new models of SSD were proposed, including iSSDv1 and iSSDv2.

We also believe that accuracy of more recent detectors can be improved by improving image quality as well as image resolution. Furthermore, it is important to maintain the scale of object in both directions when scaling up or down. The performance of proposed models can be evaluated with scorePR as well.

References

1. 'WHO—Global status report on road safety 2018. WHO (2018). https://www.who.int/vio lence_injury_prevention/road_safety_status/2018/en/. Accessed 18 Aug 2019
2. Khan, W., Morris, J.: Safety of stereo driver assistance systems. In: 2012 IEEE Intelligent Vehicles Symposium, Alcala de Henares, pp. 469–475 (2012). https://doi.org/10.1109/IVS. 2012.6232188
3. Khan, W., Morris, J., Klette, R.: Stereo accuracy for collision avoidance. In: 2009 24th International Conference Image and Vision Computing New Zealand, Wellington, pp. 67–72 (2009). https://doi.org/10.1109/IVCNZ.2009.5378358
4. Wu, Z., Thangali, A., Sclaroff, S., Betke, M.: Coupling detection and data association for multiple object tracking. In: 2012 IEEE Conference on Computer Vision and Pattern Recognition (CVPR), Providence, RI, pp. 1948–1955 (2012). https://doi.org/10.1109/CVPR.2012. 6247896

5. Hermann, S., Morales, S., Klette, R.: Half-resolution semi-global stereo matching. In: 2011 IEEE Intelligent Vehicles Symposium (IV), pp. 201–206, June 2011. https://doi.org/10.1109/IVS.2011.5940427

6. Geiger, A., Lenz, P., Urtasun, R.: Are we ready for autonomous driving? The KITTI vision benchmark suite. In: 2012 IEEE CVPR, Providence, RI, pp. 3354–3361, June 2012. https://doi.org/10.1109/CVPR.2012.6248074

7. Viola, P., Jones, M.: Rapid object detection using a boosted cascade of simple features. In: Proceedings of the 2001 IEEE CVPR 2001, vol. 1, p. I–I, December 2001. https://doi.org/10.1109/CVPR.2001.990517

8. Dalal, N., Triggs, B.: Histograms of oriented gradients for human detection. In: 2005 IEEE CVPR 2005, San Diego, CA, USA, vol. 1, pp. 886–893 (2005). https://doi.org/10.1109/CVPR.2005.177

9. Felzenszwalb, P., McAllester, D., Ramanan, D.: A discriminatively trained, multiscale, deformable part model. In: 2008 IEEE CVPR 2008, pp. 1–8 (2008). https://doi.org/10.1109/CVPR.2008.4587597

10. Felzenszwalb, P.F., Girshick, R.B., McAllester, D., Ramanan, D.: Object detection with discriminatively trained part-based models. IEEE Trans. Pattern Anal. Mach. Intell. **32**(9), 1627–1645 (2010). https://doi.org/10.1109/TPAMI.2009.167

11. Krizhevsky, A., Sutskever, I., Hinton, G.E.: ImageNet classification with deep convolutional neural networks. In: Pereira, F., Burges, C.J.C., Bottou, L., Weinberger, K.Q. (eds.) Advances in Neural Information Processing Systems 25, pp. 1097–1105. Curran Associates, Inc. (2012)

12. Girshick, R., Donahue, J., Darrell, T., Malik, J.: Rich feature hierarchies for accurate object detection and semantic segmentation. In: 2014 IEEE CVPR, Columbus, OH, USA, pp. 580–587, June 2014. https://doi.org/10.1109/CVPR.2014.81

13. Girshick, R.: Fast R-CNN, pp. 1440–1448 (2015). Accessed 30 July 2019

14. Ren, S., He, K., Girshick, R., Sun, J.: Faster R-CNN: towards real-time object detection with region proposal networks. In: Cortes, C., Lawrence, N.D., Lee, D.D., Sugiyama, M., Garnett, R. (eds.) Advances in Neural Information Processing Systems 28, pp. 91–99. Curran Associates, Inc. (2015)

15. Liu, W., et al.: SSD: single shot multibox detector. In: Leibe, B., Matas, J., Sebe, N., Welling, M. (eds.) ECCV 2016. LNCS, vol. 9905, pp. 21–37. Springer, Cham (2016). https://doi.org/10.1007/978-3-319-46448-0_2

16. Olson, D.L., Delen, D.: Advanced Data Mining Techniques. Springer, Berlin (2008)

17. Khan, W., Suaste, V., Caudillo, D., Klette, R.: Belief propagation stereo matching compared to iSGM on binocular or trinocular video data. In: 2013 IEEE Intelligent Vehicles Symposium (IV), pp. 791–796, June 2013. https://doi.org/10.1109/IVS.2013.6629563

Comparison of Red versus Blue Laser Light for Accurate 3D Measurement of Highly Specular Surfaces in Ambient Lighting Conditions

Arpita Dawda[1,2]([✉]) and Minh Nguyen[1]

[1] Auckland University of Technology, Auckland 1010, New Zealand
[2] Facteon Intelligent Technology Ltd., Auckland 2013, New Zealand
https://www.aut.ac.nz/
https://facteon.global/

Abstract. Inspection or Quality Control is an essential stage of the production line. For some products, their accurate three-dimensional (3D) reconstructions are necessary for inspection [1]. The type of surface of the product plays a critical part in choosing a suitable 3D reconstruction method. The inspection of highly specular surfaces is still a limitation of most of the state-of-art 3D measurement techniques. Most of the available commercial solutions cannot inspect specular surfaces in ambient lighting conditions. This research paper focuses on a simple and accurate 3D measurement technique using laser and stereo cameras for the inspection of reflective surface objects. In this technique, a single laser line is projected onto the surface, and its stereo images are captured and processed for 3D reconstruction. The method overcomes the limitation of traditional methods and works robustly in ambient lighting conditions. As our experiments are performed in ambient lighting conditions, it is essential to project the right type of laser light on the object. Two different colours (Red and Blue) of laser lights are considered. Here, we reconstructed 3D profiles of three different shapes and estimated sizes of these objects using these two lights. This research article compares the output 3D profiles obtained using red laser light with which achieved using blue laser light. The results are quantitatively evaluated in terms of accuracy with the ground truth 3D model of the acquitted objects for accuracy evaluation. We also discuss the dependency on the specularity of the surface.

Keywords: 3D measurements · Reflective surface · Red and Blue laser line projection · Stereo vision · Inspection · Ambient lighting conditions

1 Introduction

For customer satisfaction, reliable inspection and quality control of the product is necessary. It also assures confidence to the manufacturer and reduces manu-

Facteon Intelligent Technology Ltd.

© Springer Nature Switzerland AG 2021
M. Nguyen et al. (Eds.): ISGV 2021, CCIS 1386, pp. 300–312, 2021.
https://doi.org/10.1007/978-3-030-72073-5_23

facturing cost by eliminating scrap losses. The quality results help to simulate failure modes and verify strength criteria to validate functional product design [4]. Same as the manufacturing process, the quality checking process also needs to be fast, accurate, simple, cost-effective and automatic. "Machine vision is the technology and methods used to provide imaging-based automatic inspection and analysis [3]." This research has been carried out in collaboration with Facteon Intelligent Technology Limited. Facteon manufactures different parts of consumer appliances such as drums, doors and panels, cabinets and cases, water heater cases and refrigeration foaming lines [5]. The base material of most of the products is stainless steel which makes the surface highly specular in the presence of light.

As seen in Fig. 1, any slight variations in the viewing plane, the angle of view, and camera position; they can significantly affect the appearing colour. In general, the more direct the reflection, the brighter the colour and vice versa. Also, the ambient lighting conditions of the working environment cause significant difficulty for quality inspection.

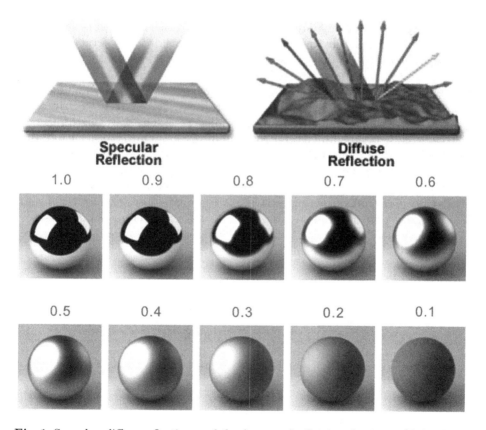

Fig. 1. Specular, diffuse reflection, and the degrees of reflection glossiness. (Color figure online)

A significant number of 3D shape measurement techniques have been proposed in the last few decades. Time-of-flight, stereo vision, laser range scanning and structured lighting are some example of the surface non-contact techniques used for high-speed inspection of objects [6]. These techniques provide accurate results for non-reflective surfaces. Structured lighting and stereo vision are considered as the most effective techniques for specular surfaces. However, the shape or curvature of the specular surface will cause reflection in ambient lighting conditions. Even by using structured lighting or stereo vision techniques, it is challenging to observe every small feature of the object in the region of reflection [7]. Therefore, we use the method which combines the concepts of sheet-of-light and stereo vision for the inspection of highly specular surface.

Here, a narrow band of light is projected onto a 3D surface. "The projection produces a distorted line of illumination, which represents the profile of an object [2]." Stereo cameras capture the image of the distorted laser line in a calibrated environment. An algorithm is developed to detect the laser line accurately in both photos. After accurately detecting the laser line in both images, stereo matching is performed for 3D reconstruction of the laser profile in World Coordinate System (WCS).

The output accuracy mainly depends on the detection of projected laser line. To get accurate results in ambient lighting conditions, it is important that the projected narrow band of laser line is sharp and it should resemble the shape of the product. Here, we have used red and blue light lasers as a source of light. A laser emits coherent light. As a result, the laser beam stays narrow and focused over a great distance [8]. The effect of the projected narrow band of light onto the accuracy of the output 3D profile is studied here. The wavelength of Red-light laser diode is generally 638 nm, 650 nm or 670 nm. On the other hand, the wavelength of Blue-light laser diode is normally 450 nm, 473 nm or 488 nm [12]. All these wavelengths come under the visible light region of the electromagnetic radiation spectrum [13]. The visible-beam lasers are classified into four classes based on its maximum output power: Class 2, Class 3R, Class 3B and Class 4 [14]. Figure 2 shows that the eye injury hazard increases as the laser's power increases [15]. As the experiments are performed in an open working environment, we have used class 2 lasers for this research.

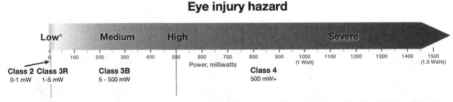

Fig. 2. Laser classes and eye injury hazard [15].

In this paper, we projected a narrow band of red and blue laser line onto three different shapes of objects. The first object is the drum of washing machine manufactured by Facteon. The drum is made of stainless steel which makes its surface highly specular. The other two items are a cube and a prism. They are wrapped in an aluminium foil to create the effect of reflective surfaces. The 3D profiles of each object are created for red and blue laser lights using the above-specified technique. For each object, the output 3D profile obtained using red laser light is compared with the output 3D profile obtained using blue laser light. Later, they are also compared with the ground truth three-dimensional model of the acquired objects for accuracy evaluation.

The remainder of this paper is structured as follows: Sect. 2 briefly describes the reviewed literature and shows a comparison of commercial solutions for Red vs Blue laser light. Section 3 explains our 3D measurement technique in detail and illustrates the dependency of the type of laser light on the specularity of the surface. All steps of our approach with experimental results are shown in Sect. 4. Section 5 concludes the paper.

2 Commercial Solutions

In this section, the commercial solutions which use Red-light laser are compared with the commercial solutions which use Blue-light laser.

Table 1 compares products which are based on the concept of sheet-of-light.

A trade-off between the accuracy of the output and the field of view (FOV) covered by the system is seen in all these solutions. Also, the FOV covered by these products is very small for higher resolution. Therefore, multiple laser profilers are required to inspect large objects. This increases the cost of the

Table 1. Comparision of laser profilers.

Laser Profiler	Laser	Field of View (mm)	Resolution z (mm)	Resolution x (mm)	Measurement Distance (mm)	Clearance Distance (mm)
Gocator 2510 [9]	Blue	13.0 - 14.5	-	0.008	6	17.0
Gocator 2512 [9]	Blue	13.0 - 14.5	-	0.008	6	17.0
Gocator 2520 [9]	Blue	25.0 - 32.5	-	0.013 – 0.017	25	47.5
Gocator 2880[9]	Red	390-1260	0.092-0.488	0.375-1.1	800	350
Cognex In-Sight Laser Profiler DS910B [10]	Blue	9.4 – 10.7	0.001	0.0073-0.0084	8	52.5
Cognex In-Sight Laser Profiler DS910B [10]	Blue	23.4 – 29.1	0.002	0.0183 – 0.0227	25	53.5
Cognex In-Sight Laser Profiler DS1101 [10]	Red	64-162	0.010-0.052	0.063-0.158	220	135
Cognex In-Sight Laser Profiler DS1300 [10]	Red	90-410	0.016-0.265	0.088-0.410	725	180
Micro-Epsilon 29xx-100 [11]	Red	83.1-120.8	0.012	1280 points/profile	100	-

inspection process. Another disadvantage is that most of the solutions do not work in the ambient lighting conditions of the working environment. Moreover, the resolution of the red-light laser is low compared to the blue-light laser. Also, some of the red-light laser profilers do not work for highly specular surfaces. Therefore, blue-light laser profilers are considered as a better choice for the inspection of small specular objects.

3   Methodology

The flow chart in Fig. 3, represents our suggested approach for the inspection of reflective surfaces. A narrow band of light is projected on the surface of the object. The stereo cameras capture the images of the product in the calibrated environment. These captured images are first rectified using calibration parameters. To generate the Region of Interest (ROI) automatically, we have used the concept of two-dimensional (2D) shape matching.

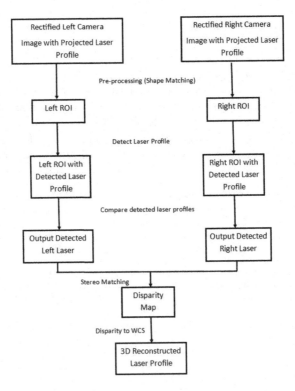

Fig. 3. Overall approach for 3D inspection.

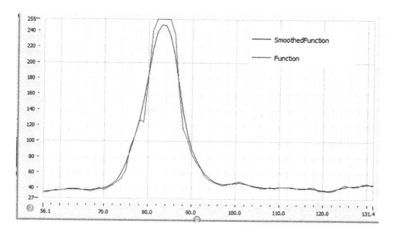

Fig. 4. Intensity distribution for region without highlights. (Color figure online)

In Fig. 4, the Red curve depicts the intensity distribution of the projected laser line for the first row. As we can see, the intensity distribution for the projected laser profile resembles a bell-shaped curve. The first step of the detection algorithm is to smooth the curve using a Gauss function [17]. The blue curve shows the smoothed function. The next step is to find local maximums for the blue curve [18]. Also, we find the location of the pixel with the highest grey value intensity for the red curve. Now, we compare the pixel location of each local maximum with the location of the highest grey value pixel. We try to find the area which is nearest to the location of the highest grey value pixel. The nearest local maximum would be considered as the detected point of the laser line. In the case of multiple values, an algorithm is developed to choose the best suitable amount. This algorithm also considers the grey value intensity at each local maximum point for the accurate decision-making process.

However, we can not repeat the same process for each row. If the ROI contains highlights caused by ambient light, the distribution of intensity would be affected [2]. As we can see in Fig. 5, there are two possible circumstances. In the first case, the highlight is separate from the projected laser line. The second case is where the highlight is merged with the laser line by making the intensity distribution a wide bell-shaped curve. In Fig. 5a, the first peak is the peak of the highlight. The same method will assume the highest intensity of highlight as a projected laser profile. Therefore, the location of the detected laser point in the previous row is taken as a reference for the next row. "If the location of the detected laser profile is (x, y), then in the next row, we search pixel locations $(x+1, y-10)$ to $(x+1, y+10)$ for finding the pixel with the highest grey value [2]." Now, we repeat the process used for the first line to detect the laser line.

The problem of detecting the laser line when it is merged with the highlight is solved in the next stage of the experiment. Here, we compare the detected laser line in both images. Typically, the highlights caused by ambient lighting

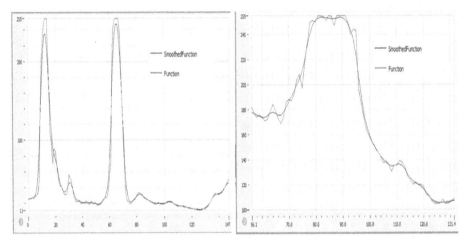

(a) Case 1: The laser line is separate from the highlight.

(b) Case 2: The laser line is merged with the highlight.

Fig. 5. Intensity distribution for region with highlights.

conditions will not be visible in both photos. Therefore, the highlights which are present in the left image will not be present in the right image and vice versa. For the case where the laser line is merged with the highlight in one shot, we would still be able to detect the laser line accurately in the other image. By comparing, we can specify the region which has inaccurate output because of the reflection.

Another critical factor of the detection process is that the reflected region should not be considered as a part of the projected laser profile because of its high intensities. The red-light laser penetrates deeper into the target surface compared to the blue-light laser. Therefore, the red-light laser light looks blurry and diffused and merges with the reflected region. On the other hand, the blue-light laser generates a much more focused laser band when projected on to the surface [19]. Figure 6 show the images of the projected red-light and blue-light lasers on the washing machine drum in ambient lighting conditions. Here, both the lasers have the same maximum output power. As seen in Fig. 6, the red-light laser has low intensities compared to the blue-light laser. Therefore, while trying to detect the red-light laser in the highlighted region, the reflected region is detected as a part of the laser line. In contrast, the projected blue-light laser is detected accurately, even in the presence of the reflected area. This is one of the advantages of using blue-light laser instead of red-light laser for 3D reconstruction of highly specular surfaces.

4 Experiments and Results

The setup of the experiment is shown in Fig. 7. In this experiment, we are using red and blue light lasers of class 2M. The maximum output power of both lasers

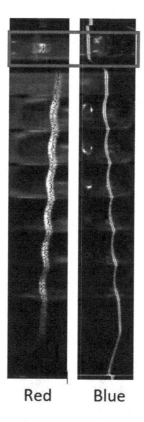

Red   Blue

Fig. 6. Detection of laser light in the presence of highlight.

is 20 mW. Both single-line lasers have the same fan angle of 45 degrees. Now, the position of the laser is one of the most critical parameters of this technique. To understand the concept, we projected a narrow band of a horizontal laser line on to a flat surface. Figure 8 shows the captured image of the projected laser line. As seen in Fig. 8, the intensity of the laser decreases as the distance from the centre of the image increases. Also, the laser line diffuses and causes reflection when it is projected directly in the centre of the image. However, if the laser line is projected too far from the centre of the image, then the intensity of the laser line is low, and it merges with the background. Therefore, we need to choose the position of the laser in such a way that it does not cause any reflection and does not get merged with the background in both images.

For the cameras, we are using two Genie Nano M4020 monochrome camera, which has 4112×3008 resolution. The focal lengths of both cameras are identical. Also, the stereo cameras are placed in Canonical Stereo Geometry, which means their optic axes are parallel. The baseline distance, which is the distance between the optical axes of two cameras is 130 mm for this experiment [16]. The setup is the same for both lasers. The experiment is first performed using red-light laser

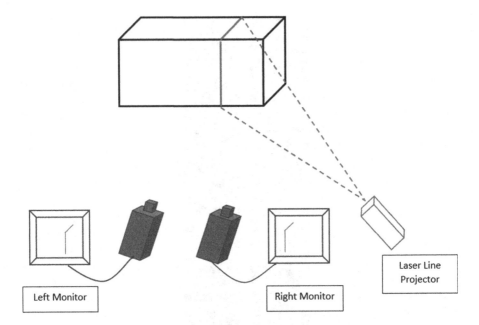

Fig. 7. Setup of experiment.

Fig. 8. Change in the intensity of laser.

and afterwards using blue-light laser. Moreover, HALCON software is used to perform image processing tasks.

The stereo cameras are calibrated using Halcon calibration plate, which has a pattern of hexagonally arranged black marks printed on white background. A narrow band of the red-light laser line is projected on the object after calibrating stereo cameras. Figure 9 show images of different shaped objects with a projected laser band. Stereo cameras capture the images of the object with a projected laser line. The next step is to rectify the captured stereo images. After rectification, we use the fundamentals of 2D shape matching to get the Region of Interest (ROI) automatically. Now, we apply the algorithm to detect the projected laser line in both images. The left and right ROI images with detected laser profiles are shown in Fig. 10. Stereo matching is performed only on the detected laser profiles to calculate its disparity. We can reconstruct the projected laser line in the World Coordinate System (WCS) using the calculated disparity value and calibration parameters. "For a full 3D reconstruction of the object, the object is rotated at specific intervals. At each interval, the projected laser profile is reconstructed. By merging these reconstructed laser profiles, we can reconstruct the shape of the object in 3D for accurate measurements [2]."

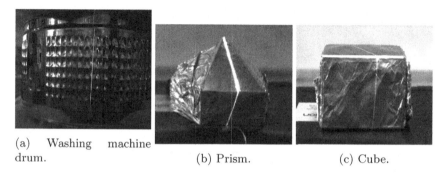

(a)   Washing   machine drum.   (b) Prism.   (c) Cube.

Fig. 9. Objects with projected laser profile.

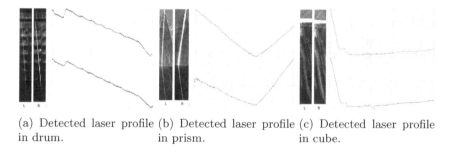

(a) Detected laser profile (b) Detected laser profile (c) Detected laser profile in drum.   in prism.   in cube.

Fig. 10. ROIs with detected laser profiles using Red-light laser. (Color figure online)

For each object, we repeat the whole process by replacing the red-light laser with the blue-light laser. No changes have been made in the setup for blue-light laser. Figure 11 shows the left and right ROI images with detected laser profiles for blue-light laser. In Fig. 12, we compare the output reconstructed 3D profiles by red-light laser with the output reconstructed 3D profiles by blue-light laser. The accuracy of the output mainly depends on the detection of the laser profile. The Table 2 shows the number of scan required to reconstruct each object

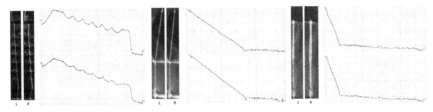

(a) Detected laser profile (b) Detected laser profile (c) Detected laser profile
in drum.   in prism.   in cube.

Fig. 11. ROIs with detected laser profiles using Blue-light laser. (Color figure online)

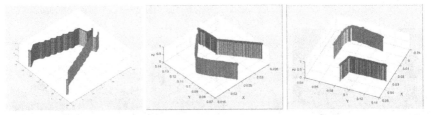

(a) Reconstructed laser (b) Reconstructed laser (c) Reconstructed laser
profiles for drum.   profiles for prism.   profiles for cube.

Fig. 12. 3D reconstructed laser profiles.

Table 2. Output accuracy for red and blue light laser.

Parameters	Object 1: Drum		Object 2: Prism		Object 3: Cube	
	Red	Blue	Red	Blue	Red	Blue
Total no. of scans	3768	7536	1130	2260	100	200
Accuracy (mm)	0.7	0.03	0.4	0.02	0.4	0.02
No. of False Positives	26	10	12	0	6	0
Max. Deviation(Pixels)	± 3	± 1	± 3	± 1	± 3	± 1

using red and blue light laser. Here, false positive specifies how many times the
reflection is falsely detected as a part of a laser line. From the deviation results,
we can tell that the detected red-light laser is quite noisy. On the other hand,
the detected blue-light laser is quite sharp, and it detects all small features of
the object accurately.

5   Conclusion

To conclude, blue-light laser is proven to be more accurate compared to red-light laser for the 3D shape measurement of highly specular surfaces in identical conditions. Also, the projected beam of red-light laser diffuses and merges with the reflection caused by ambient light. On the other hand, the blue-light laser does not penetrate the surface. It provides a sharp narrow beam when projected onto a highly specular surface. Therefore, we can accurately detect the blue-light laser even in the presence of reflection. The accuracy of the output is improved by using the blue-light laser. Moreover, the proposed method is proven to be a simple, fast, feasible, accurate and cost-effective solution for the inspection of reflective objects even in ambient lighting conditions. Unlike commercial laser profilers, there is no trade-off between the field of view and the accuracy of the output.

Acknowledgment. Supported by Facteon Intelligent Technology Ltd.

References

1. Asoudegi, E., Pan, Z.: Computer vision for quality control in automated manufacturing systems. Comput. Ind. Eng. **21**(1–4), 141–145 (1991)
2. Dawda, A., Nguyen, M., Klette, R.: Accurate 3D measurement of highly specular surface using laser and stereo reconstruction. In: 2019 International Conference on Image and Vision Computing New Zealand (IVCNZ), pp. 1–6. IEEE, December 2019
3. Machine Vision (2019). https://en.wikipedia.org/wiki/Machine_vision
4. Inspection Production and Operations Management (2019). Wisdom IT Services India Pvt. Ltd. https://www.wisdomjobs.com/e-university/production-and-operations-management-tutorial-295/inspection-9633.html
5. Flexible & Intelligent manufacturing solutions (2019). Facteon Intelligent technology Ltd. https://facteon.global/products-and-services/equipment/
6. Lin, H., Gao, J., Zhang, G., Chen, X., He, Y., Liu, Y.: Review and comparison of high-dynamic range three-dimensional shape measurement techniques. J. Sens. (2017)
7. Chen, F., Brown, G.M., Song, M.: Overview of three-dimensional shape measurement using optical methods. Opt. Eng. **39**(1), 10–22 (2000)
8. Laser (2020). https://en.wikipedia.org/wiki/Laser
9. Gocator 2500 Series (2019). LMI Technologies Inc. https://lmi3d.com/products/gocator-3d-laser-sensors/gocator-2500-series
10. In-sight Laser Profiler (2019). Cognex Corporation https://www.cognex.com/en-nz/products/machine-vision/3d-laser-profilers/in-sight-laser-profiler
11. Laser scanners for 2D/3D profile measurements (2019). Micro-Epsilon https://www.micro-epsilon.com/2D_3D/laser-scanner/
12. Laser pointer (2020). https://en.wikipedia.org/wiki/Laser_pointerColors_and_wavelengths
13. Visible spectrum (2020). https://en.wikipedia.org/wiki/Visible_spectrum
14. Laser classes chart (2020). https://www.laserpointersafety.com/laserclasses.html

15. Eye injury hazard (2020). www.laserpointersafety.com/resources/Diagrams/Arrow---eye-injury-hazard-for-laser-classes-0800-v2.png
16. Klette, R.: Concise Computer Vision. Springer, London (2014)
17. smooth_funct_1d_gauss (2020). MVTec Software GmbH. https://www.mvtec.com/doc/halcon/12/en/smooth_funct_1d_gauss.html
18. local_min_max_funct_1d (2020). MVTec Software GmbH https://www.mvtec.com/doc/halcon/13/en/local_min_max_funct_1d.html
19. Displacement (2020). Bestech Australia https://www.bestech.com.au/blogs/displacement/3-reasons-to-use-blue-over-red-lasers-in-displacement-measurement/

Fruit Detection from Digital Images Using CenterNet

Kun Zhao$^{(\boxtimes)}$ and Wei Qi Yan$^{(\boxtimes)}$

Auckland University of Technology, Auckland 1010, New Zealand
{kvz5449,weiqi.yan}@aut.ac.nz

Abstract. In this paper, CenterNet is chosen as the model to settle fruit detection problem from digital images. Three CenterNet models with various backbones were implemented, namely, ResNet-18, DLA-34, and Hourglass. A fruit dataset with four classes and 1,690 images was established for this research project. By comparing those models, followed the experimental results, the deep learning-based model with DLA-34 was selected as the final model to detect fruits from digital images, the performance is excellent. In this paper, the contribution is that we deploy a model based on CenterNet for visual object detection to resolve the problem of fruit detection. Meanwhile, there are 1,690 images distributed in four classes. Throughout evaluating the performance of the model, we eventually affirm the CenterNet based on DLA-34 to detect multiclass fruits from our images. The performance of this method is better than the existing ones in fruit detection.

Keywords: CenterNet · ResNet-18 · DLA-34 · Hourglass net · Fruit detection

1 Introduction

Fruit industry, as a typical one with high economic value, has an intensive requirement for automation [1]. In the fruit industry, the cost spent on picking holds the dominant percentage of the whole cost. A large amount of electric power, fuel, irrigation, and chemical fertilizer are demanded in agriculture development. The speed, cost, and safety of picking directly affect the final output and quality of fruit production. Hence, more and more harvesting robots are being deployed in the fruit industry to reduce the cost of picking and improve the quality of fruit [1]. For harvesting robots, a rich assortment of tasks needs to be handled, such as detection, picking, localization, classification, selection, and grading.

Among these missions, visual object detection is the most critical one [33, 34], hence, we should settle this problem firstly [2]. The follows show how to detect visual objects from an image, which is thought as an answer to object detection in computer vision [2]. The methods to handle this research problems mainly have been categorized into two groups: Machine learning-based (ML-based) method and deep learning-based (DL-based) method [3, 31, 32].

Owing to those methods, in this paper, we expect to design a new model to resolve this fruit detection problem. What the ML-based methods as the base of visual object

© Springer Nature Switzerland AG 2021
M. Nguyen et al. (Eds.): ISGV 2021, CCIS 1386, pp. 313–326, 2021.
https://doi.org/10.1007/978-3-030-72073-5_24

detection are the main process of how to deploy a model for object detection. However, those methods are not working well as they used to be due to the development of the theory and hardware in the past decades. Therefore, we design a DL-based model that could settle fruit detection fast and accurately.

The main purpose of this project is to find a practical model that could resolve this problem with object detection for fruits. Therefore, we will analyze those existing ML-based methods. Consequently, we detail the advantages and disadvantages. Finally, we choose the most appropriate method for this project and create a new model. Furthermore, we need to test and evaluate this model and confirm that this model is robust and accurate by using our own dataset. At last, CenterNet is treated as an effective method for this paper. Moreover, it will be tested based on three backbone models and the most suitable one will be picked up. In this paper, we also collect a new dataset for four classes of fruits. Besides, we train and test the model by using our dataset.

The contributions of this paper are: (1) We design a model to handle fruit detection problems based on CenterNet; (2) A dataset with four classes of fruits for this research project has been created; (3) Training and testing this model by using our dataset, as well as, evaluating the performance of this model are delineated in this paper.

The remaining parts of this paper are organized as follows. We review literature in Sect. 2, our method is presented in Sect. 3, the results are showcased in Sect. 4, our conclusion and future work will be addressed in Sect. 5.

2 Literature Review

A vast majority of research work has been conducted in visual object detection. Many methods have been designed and implemented. The methods are grouped into twofold depending on a theoretical basis. The first one is the machine learning-based (ML-based) methods, the second one is the deep learning-based (DL-based) methods [4].

ML inspires us in multiple ways, especially for pattern classification from huge amounts of high dimensional images, which also brings in the development of computer vision [5]. After obtained an image, the sliding window method will be applied to generate candidate bounding boxes. This process is named as region selection, which means the region we expect to detect has been selected into these boxes. After this step, feature extraction will be commenced for each candidate bounding box. The feature inside each box will be extracted from the image by using specific methods. Finally, a classifier will be employed to classify each box based on its features [6].

In 2004, Viola and Jones put forward a method to detect visual object by using Haar feature [7], which takes use of AdaBoost as the classifier to classify each box based on already extracted Harr feature. In 2005, a method was proposed based on SVM and HOG [8]. A method DPM was put forward in 2008 [9]. Similarly, the classifier of DPM is SVM which enhances the HOG by using a combing signed gradient with an unsigned gradient to make it richer so as to express a broad spectrum of visual objects. Meanwhile, it utilizes PCA (i.e., principal component analysis) to work for dimension reduction so as to reduce complexity and accelerate the computational speed. Hence, it could get a balance between the complexity and the speed of classification.

Regarding ML-based methods, the features generally are extracted for a class of specific objects [10]. Thus, the visual features for object detection generally are various.

In another word, those features are not transportable, the designer needs to specify other features for a different object [10]. Besides, the sliding window method will generate a pretty rich number of bounding boxes to detect the visual object, which will waste considerable computational resources [11].

We know that the ML-based methods are applied to resolve the object detection problem. The conception of deep learning (DL) comes from artificial neural networks (ANNs), which essentially means a kind of specific structure with a depth of hidden layers. The ANNs were inspired by research outcomes of our human brain, which deals with various tasks by simulating the mechanism of human neurons. The first and the most basic model was named as the MP (i.e., McCulloch and Pitts) model, which is based on a class of artificial neural cells [12].

The base of current deep neural networks was regarded as perceptron in 1958 [12]. The original purpose was to handle binary classification problems. In 1970, automatic differentiation was put forward, which is based on BP (i.e., Backpropagation) algorithm, it is a crucial method for improving the speed of ANN training [13]. Combing BP and ANNs together inspired the subsequent MLP (Multilayer Perception) [14] in 1986.

Furthermore, the activation function was replaced by a sigmoid function. This nonlinear map function could enhance the performance of MLP, which could effectively tackle the nonlinear classification problem. According to the structure of our human brain, the idea is to imitate the multilayer stacked human brain. But how to train a deep network confuses researchers for a long time. The problems of vanishing gradients and exploding gradients are the reasons why deep nets could not be trained well. The attenuation of error for BP in the deep net will exponentially be increased with the growth of the network layers [15].

In 2006, deep belief net (DBN) was designed in 2006. This network solved the problem that a DNN is hard to be trained by using layer by layer pretraining [16]. Convolutional neural networks (CNNs) as a kind of ANNs, were inspired by the visual system. The original conception was enlightened by using the visual layer of cats, as named as the receptive field [17]. In 1979, neocognitron was put forward by being combined with ANNs and receptive field, which was thought as the first CNN structure [18]. In 1989, weight sharing was brought up by LeCun [19], each convolutional kernel was used to detect a particular feature and greatly decrease the parametric quantity of CNNs so as to make the complex computations to be possible.

In 1998, LeCun combines convolutional layers and downsampling layers to design a model named LeNet, AlexNet was put forward in 2012 [20]. AlexNet has considerable progress in various improvement. Firstly, it replaces sigmoid function with another activation function, ReLU function, which tackles the gradient vanishing problem and decreases the amount of computations. Another improvement of AlexNet is to decrease overfitting by using the dropout method, which could make the whole network having a better generalization ability that does not depend on local features [20]. VGGNet as the offspring network of AlexNet has great improvements to obtain a better performance in 2014 [21]. The most important change is that VGGNet takes use of multiple convolutional kernels with a size of 3×3 to replace a big size kernel. In 2014, GoogLeNet by using the inception module parallelly executes multiple size convolutional operations [22].

A DL-based method R-CNN [22] was implemented to overcome those problems of ML-based methods. The feature extraction of R-CNN takes use of CNN instead of the HOG feature. AlexNet was chosen to extract visual feature of each box automatically. Based on this, DL-based method overcomes the disadvantage of the ML-based method in the feature extraction. For the classification, R-CNN still selects SVM as its classifier. Because of its complex calculations, the speed of R-CNN is very slow. Fast R-CNN [23] conducts visual feature extraction based on the whole image, instead of abundant region proposals. This could save the time of computations as well as memory for the CNN nodes. Faster R-CNN has a better performance than Fast R-CNN by using region proposal net (RPN) to generate region proposals. But the method to generate region proposals still spends a huge amount of time. Therefore, how to overcome this bottleneck is the improvement of Faster R-CNN [24].

A one-stage method YOLO was designed to make the network very fast [25]. YOLO directly predicts the class and location of the visual object without anchor and RPN. Hence, its speed is very fast, but its accuracy has been dipped. It does not have a prior box, the detection problem is thought as a regression problem, its structure is very simple, the speed is very fast. In order to have a similar speed of YOLO and accuracy of Faster R-CNN in object detection, SSD was designed as a new model that combines both advantages of them [26]. Furthermore, it makes use of multiscale feature maps to detect the visual object with various sizes. SSD does achieve better performance based on speed and accuracy. However, the semantic information is not enough by using the feature map as shown in Fig. 2, which leads to the difficulty for detecting a small object.

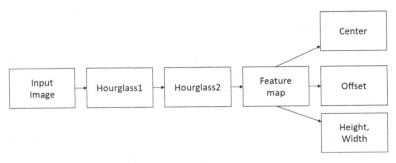

Fig. 1. The structure of CenterNet

In order to overcome the shortcoming of anchors, multiple models were designed without an anchor. Inspired by the first anchor-free model, a one-stage and anchor-free model CenterNet was proposed [27] as shown in Fig. 1. CenterNet makes use of three heads to detect an object, which conducts center pooling for the feature map to get the center. Meanwhile, it works for cascade corner pooling to obtain the offset and size. The center gets from the feature map as shown in Fig. 2, which will be transformed to a heatmap, the location of the object which has the highest value is the center. The center should be surrounded, the offset is used to assess the deviation of centers between the feature map and the original image. Hence, this model used size, center, and offset to detect the object. As an anchor-free model, it could handle with our fruit detection problem. In this paper, we choose CenterNet as our net to accomplish the fruit detection problem from digital images.

0.0164482	0.0271186	0.0397485	0.0517942	0.0599995	0.0617904	0.0565719	0.0460455	0.0333181	0.0214328
0.0348209	0.05741	0.0841475	0.109648	0.127019	0.13081	0.119763	0.0974783	0.0705344	0.0453733
0.0655542	0.108048	0.158368	0.206362	0.239054	0.246189	0.225398	0.183458	0.132748	0.0853941
0.109648	0.180779	0.264974	0.345273	0.399972	0.411911	0.377123	0.306951	0.222107	0.142877
0.163096	0.268899	0.394133	0.513574	0.594936	0.612694	0.560949	0.456573	0.330372	0.212521
0.21567	0.355579	0.521183	0.679126	0.786715	0.810197	0.741772	0.60375	0.436868	0.281028
0.253538	0.418013	0.612694	0.798369	0.924849	0.952454	0.872015	0.709758	0.513574	0.330372
0.264974	0.436868	0.64033	0.83438	0.966564	0.995415	0.911348	0.741772	0.536739	0.345273
0.246189	0.405898	0.594936	0.77523	0.898044	0.924849	0.846741	0.689187	0.498689	0.320796
0.203349	0.335266	0.491409	0.64033	0.741772	0.763915	0.699397	0.569259	0.411911	0.264974
0.149321	0.246189	0.360847	0.470201	0.544691	0.560949	0.513574	0.418013	0.30247	0.194573
0.0974783	0.160715	0.235564	0.306951	0.355579	0.366193	0.335266	0.272883	0.197455	0.127019
0.0565719	0.0932713	0.136711	0.17814	0.206362	0.212521	0.194573	0.158368	0.114594	0.0737159
0.0291877	0.0481224	0.0705344	0.0919097	0.10647	0.109648	0.100388	0.0817086	0.0591236	0.038033
0.0133877	0.0220726	0.0323524	0.0421568	0.0488353	0.050293	0.0460455	0.0374778	0.0271186	0.0174448

Fig. 2. A sample of heatmap

3   Our Method

The method of how CenterNet seeks the center point is that it only finds the local peak point in the heat map. Each peak point is a center of an object. Without NMS processing and anchor, it could save our running time.

Firstly, the input image was denoted as $I \in R^{W \times H \times 3}$, W is the width of our image, the height is H. The channel number of our image is 3, which means that the input image is a color one. The feature map is transformed into a keypoint heatmap through Gaussian Kernel.

For the keypoint heatmap, given $\hat{Y} \in [0, 1]^{\frac{W}{R} \times \frac{H}{R} \times C}$, R is the downsampling rate, which equals four in our project, C is the number of classes. In our dataset, we only have four kinds of fruits, hence C equals to 4. Given $\hat{Y}_{xyc} = 1$, for class c, it was detected in the (x, y) of the heatmap. On the contrary, $\hat{Y}_{xyc} = 0$ means it was not detected.

As shown in Fig. 2, the middle one is the most approximately near 1.0, that means there is an object at this location. For net training, the center point p of the ground truth needs to be calculated, $p = \left(\frac{x_1+x_2}{2}, \frac{y_1+y_2}{2} \right)$, where x and y are the coordinates in the ground truth. But the feature map was downsampled, p is also downsampled by using R, $\tilde{p} = \left[\frac{p}{R} \right]$. Thus, $\tilde{p}$ is the center point of truth data in the feature map. Then $Y_{xyc} = \exp\left(-\frac{(x-\tilde{p}_x)^2+(y-\tilde{p}_y)^2}{2\sigma_p^2} \right)$ as a Gaussian kernel was used to find the distribution of the keypoints in the feature map. In order to train this network, a loss function is needed to be implemented to assess its result.

$$L_{det} = L_c + \lambda_{size}L_{size} + \lambda_{off}L_{off} \tag{1}$$

where L_{det} is the total loss. In Eq. (1), the total loss contains three losses, each of which corresponds to a head of CenterNet, L_c is the loss of center, L_{size} is the loss of bounding box size, or the loss of width and height, L_{off} is the loss of offset, λ_{size} and λ_{off} are hyperparameter to modify the influence of off loss and size loss.

This model is assessed by combining these three different losses. Among them, the center loss is the most important one.

$$L_c = -\frac{1}{N} \sum_{xyz} \begin{cases} \left(1 - \widehat{Y_{xyc}}\right)^a \log\left(\widehat{Y_{xyc}}\right) & \text{if } Y_{xyc} = 1 \\ \left(1 - Y_{xyc}\right)^\beta \left(\widehat{Y_{xyc}}\right)^a \log\left(1 - \widehat{Y_{xyc}}\right) & \text{otherwise} \end{cases} \tag{2}$$

where $\alpha = 2$, $\beta = 4$. This refers to focal loss, which avoids weights having a dominant control and deals with the unbalance of the positive and negative samples. It makes use of the training process focusing on hard examples, instead of easy samples. In this way, it could tremendously decrease the weight of easy negatives.

Inspired by focal loss, the center loss is also designed to make this model focusing on useful information. The hyperparameters α, β are used to adjust the relationship between the loss of center and non-center points. Apart from the hyperparameters α, β, N is the number of keypoints of the input image, which is used to normalize the positive focal loss within the interval [0,1]. Besides, Y_{xyc} corrects the training process, $\widehat{Y_{xyc}}$ means that whether it is detected as a class or not.

During training, given $\widehat{Y_{xyc}} = 1$, $Y_{xyc} = 1$, it is a point that is easy to be detected after training. For this point, $\left(1 - \widehat{Y_{xyc}}\right)^a$ will be used to minimize the L_c to let our net learn other information from different parts, to train the net better. It is a method to avoid easy samples and focus on the hard samples. In another word, it has obtained enough information for model training from these features. If trained too much, the deep learning model will be overfitting because these features will have excessive weights. Hence, this model needs to use $\left(1 - \widehat{Y_{xyc}}\right)^a$ and decrease the contribution of the weights.

It is a very important idea of how this model to learn without the anchor. In order to achieve this purpose, our model will only focus on the center of each object. We need to increase the weight of the center point whilst reducing the weight of its neighbors by synthesizing $\left(1 - Y_{xyc}\right)^\beta$ and $\left(\widehat{Y_{xyc}}\right)^a$. Hence, we combine the two parts of values depending on the distance between them and the center point. This will make our model learn the critical features from those points which are far from the center. In this way, it enhances the center point while undermining the neighbor points. It is a useful method to tackle the unbalance of positive and negative samples.

After trained our model by using the center loss function, the offset loss for each center point will be performed. If the feature map is remapped to the original image, it will lead to a location offset. In order to assess this offset, L_{off} will be applied.

$$L_{off} = \frac{1}{N} \sum_p \left| \widehat{O_{\tilde{p}}} - \left(\frac{p}{R} - \tilde{p}\right) \right| \tag{3}$$

After mapped the image to feature map for four times, the location of the center point will have a precision loss, which is called offset loss. To evaluate this offset loss, we use the predicted offset $\widehat{O_{\tilde{p}}}$ to minus the truth offset $\left(\frac{p}{R} - \tilde{p}\right)$. Then, the sum of the absolute value will be averaged by using the L_1 loss method.

$$L_{size} = \frac{1}{N} \sum_{k=1}^{N} \left| \widehat{S_{p_k}} - S_k \right| \tag{4}$$

where $\widehat{S_{p_k}}$ is the size that our model predicts, $S_k = \left(x_2^{(k)} - x_1^{(k)}, y_2^{(k)} - y_1^{(k)} \right)$ is a truth size calculated by using the value after downsampling the location of the top-left and bottom-right of the dataset. Finally, the sum of all the differences will be averaged by using the L_1 norm method. As a result, the size loss will be obtained.

Thus, we see that the CenterNet combines three loss values: Center loss, size loss, and offset loss to evaluate the performance of this model. The CenterNet takes use of the center loss method, which is inspired by the focal loss to handle the hard and easy samples problem. Hence, it could make this model adaptively learn those samples and features with various weights.

The performance of CNN networks does not obtain an improvement with deepening depth. The reason is the degeneration generated by deepening the network, the SGD optimizer could not achieve a satisfactory result. ResNet was designed to overcome this problem by using shortcut structure [28]. An 18-layer residual network is chosen as the backbone of our model.

The second backbone of our model is DLA [29], which merges the feature from multiple depths. In Fig. 5, we see that DLA makes use of iterative deep aggregation (IDA) and hierarchical deep aggregation (HDA) to conduct the upsampling. The IDA part merges the feature extracted from each subnetwork grade by grade. Each red box labels that the hierarchical deep aggregation, whose block only receives the feature from the previous block. By combing IDA and HDA together, DLA is able to improve the utilization ratio of features between the layers or blocks (Fig. 3).

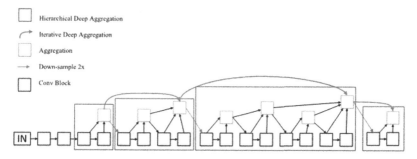

Fig. 3. The structure of DLA-34

Our last method is Hourglass network [30]. The structure is shown in Fig. 4. The original purpose of Hourglass was used to catch the information on each scale to avoid missing small local features. On the left part, from c_1 to c_4, in this bottom-up process, the image is downsampled from high resolution to low one. Meanwhile, it will extract features based on multiple scales and transport them to CNN in the up part from c_{1a} to

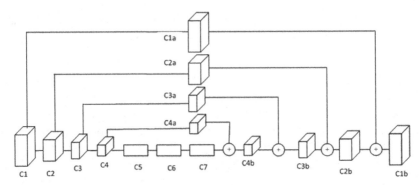

Fig. 4. The structure of Hourglass

c_{41}. On the right part, it will conduct upsampling to restore the feature map. Meanwhile, the right part will merge the feature from up and left finally to c_{1b}. Hence, Hourglass utilizes the hourglass model to extract as many features as it can. It was used as our third backbone model.

4   Our Results

4.1   Data Collection

In this paper, our task is to design a model and detect fruits from digital images. Therefore, we collect our visual data by taking photos for fruits firstly. Then, we label the fruits in each image to get the class and location of each bounding box. The dataset we collect consists of four classes of fruits: Apple, banana, orange, pear. We have 1,690 images in total, the sample number of each class is 400. This dataset was categorized into three groups for training, validation, and testing. Table 1 shows the proportion of our dataset.

Table 1. The numbers of digital images in the dataset

Description	Total	Training	Validation	Testing
Quantity	1,690	1,352	169	169

This dataset for fruit detection was collected by using the camera of a mobile phone with the resolution of 1920 × 1080, nearly 3,000 images. Finally, we selected 1,690 images from those photos. In our dataset, there is a single fruit in each image or multiple ones in the same image. That could test the ability of our model for conducting single object detection and multiobject detection.

4.2   Experimental Results

From our experiments, the performance of CenterNet with different backbone nets is desirable by using our dataset, we make use of loss functions to observe the convergence

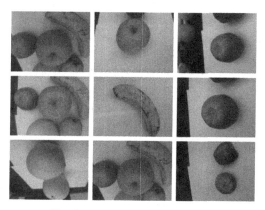

Fig. 5. The samples of our dataset

of model training. The loss function of CenterNet includes three parts: Heatmap loss or center loss, offset loss, and size loss.

Both DLA-34 and Hourglass have a good performance at the speed of convergences. From observation of the structure, DLA-34 not only has the IDA to connect the different layers to transform the feature information from bottom to top like what the ResNet does, but also merges the feature from multiple branches and scale. In this way, it immensely enhances the ability to combine various features to reduce redundant computation. After compared to the convergency of our models based on different backbones, the time costs of each model are listed in Table 2.

Table 2. The time cost of each model (seconds)

	Loading	Preprocessing	Object detection	Post-processing	Total
DLA-34	0.001	0.006	0.047	0.001	0.055
ResNet-18	0.001	0.008	0.017	0.001	0.028
Hourglass	0.001	0.008	0.046	0.001	0.056

All these three models have a similar distribution of time costs. The time spent on loading, preprocessing and postprocessing does not reach half of the whole time. The most consuming part is object detection, there are lots of convolutional neural operations in the step. Thus, we conclude that the model based on ResNet-18 is thought of as the fastest model.

Compared to these three methods, the result of DLA-34 is outperformed than other ResNet and Hourglass as shown in Table 3. It has the highest mAP 0.9, which is evidently higher than ResNet-18, a little bit better than Hourglass. The performance of DLA-34 in precision and recall is better than ResNet and Hourglass.

The reason why DLA-34 and Hourglass converge very fast is the well-designed network structure. Both of them have a much complex structure to deal with the information which got from various branches, not only limited by the depth.

Table 3. The average accuracy analysis

	DLA-34		ResNet-18		Hourglass	
	Precisions	Recalls	Precisions	Recalls	Precisions	Recalls
1	0.870	0.744	0.781	0.665	0.845	0.722
2	0.995	0.898	0.953	0.816	0.996	0.878
3	0.987	0.899	0.914	0.818	0.975	0.877
4	0.801	0.845	0.655	0.697	0.717	0.765
5	0.878	0.906	0.793	0.827	0.855	0.887
mean	0.906	0.858	0.8194	0.765	0.878	0.826
mAP	0.9		0.786		0.88	

DLA-34 takes use of the aggregation module to combine the feature from different depth layers, at the same time, DLA-34 also uses the HDA module to combine the feature from other scales by using upsampling. In this way, it reuses and integrates the feature information from various layers, just like the method of ResNet.

As a typical encoder to decoder structure, Hourglass merges the information from multiple scales like DLA-34. In the downsampling part, it extracts visual feature from input images in multiple scales. Then, the features are merged in the upsampling part. Hence, it efficiently merges and reuses the feature information, which is alike to the DLA-34. In a word, DLA-34 and Hourglass have a better performance in the convergency than the ResNet-18 due to the advanced structure.

After the analysis of the performance in convergency, we know the structures of DLA-34 and Hourglass are more complex than that of ResNet. Throughout the complex structures, DLA-34 and Hourglass could have better results of accuracy than ResNet.

For object detection, we make a tradeoff between speed and accuracy. Therefore, by comprehensively analyzing the experimental results, in this project, we chose DLA-34 as the backbone of our CenterNet model to settle this fruit detection problem.

Figure 6 shows the image samples for CenterNet based on DLA-34. From Fig. 6, we see that those full-view fruits should be detected from an image perfectly. Even if there are several fruits at the corner, our model is still able to detect them easily.

Figure 7 shows the examples of object detection from digital images. Those samples reveal that our model is able to detect both single object and multiobject with high accuracy. Our model still is able to detect them from the given images. From this work, we find the performance of our network is quite well. It is able to not only detect the class of our fruit correctly but also mark those fruits appropriately.

As a one-stage detector without anchor, the accuracy of the anchor-free detector is rather high based on our dataset. We detect a single fruit or multiple fruits together. For those occluded objects, our model still is able to detect the fruits which are overlapped.

Fig. 6. The successful examples for fruit detection based on DLA-34

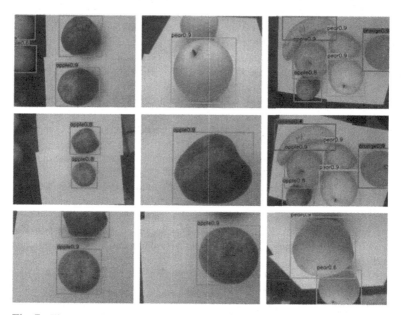

Fig. 7. The examples of object detection result of CenterNet based on DLA-34

5 Conclusion

In this paper, we set forth fruit detection from digital images. We prob the object detection problem based on computer vision, which is mainly comprised of two branches: ML-based methods and DL-based methods. We briefly introduce the ML-based methods. Then, we reviewed the DL-based methods. We concisely present the innovation and shortcoming. Finally, CenterNet is used as our proposed model. After designed the algorithm to conquer the problem of easy sample dominant and collecting dataset, we choose three networks: DLA-34, ResNet-18, and Hourglass as our backbone to train our model. Based on the results of our experiments, by taking into consideration of convergency, speed, and accuracy, the DLA-34 method is finally chosen as our backbone to tackle this fruit detection problem. In a nutshell, the CenterNet based on DLA-34 is the best method that is able to successfully handle our fruit detection problem.

In future, a more powerful backbone and training platform should be accommodated to design a better model [31, 32]. This will assist us to design and compare those models more quickly and easily for fruits and food science [35–40]. In future, we will apply a newer model to achieve a better result for this fruit objection problem [33, 34, 41].

References

1. Edan, Y., Han, S., Kondo, N.: Automation in agriculture. In: Springer Handbook of Automation, pp. 1095–1128 (2009). https://doi.org/10.1007/978-3-540-78831-7_63
2. Moltó, E., Pla, F., Juste, F.: Vision systems for the location of citrus fruit in a tree canopy. J. Agric. Eng. Res. **52**, 101–110 (1992)
3. Voulodimos, A., Doulamis, N., Doulamis, A., Protopapadakis, E.: Deep learning for computer vision: a brief review. Comput. Intell. Neurosci. **2018**, article ID 7068349 (2018). https://doi.org/10.1155/2018/7068349
4. Prince, S.J.: Computer Vision: Models, Learning, and Inference. Cambridge University Press, Cambridge (2012)
5. Nixon, M., Aguado, A.: Feature Extraction and Image Processing for Computer Vision. Academic Press (2019)
6. Gould, S.: DARWIN: a framework for machine learning and computer vision research and development. J. Mach. Learn. Res. **13**(1), 3533–3537 (2012)
7. Viola, P., Jones, M.: Robust real-time object detection. Int. J. Comput. Vision **4**, 34–47 (2014)
8. Dalal, N., Triggs, B.: Histograms of oriented gradients for human detection. In: IEEE CVPR 2005, pp. 886–893 (2005)
9. Felzenszwalb, P.F., Girshick, R.B., McAllester, D.: Cascade object detection with deformable part models. In: IEEE Conference on Computer Vision and Pattern Recognition, pp. 2241–2248 (2010)
10. Rosenfield, M.: Computer vision syndrome: a review of ocular causes and potential treatments. Ophthalmic Physiol. Opt. **31**(5), 502–515 (2011)
11. Patrício, D.I., Rieder, R.: Computer vision and artificial intelligence in precision agriculture for grain crops: a systematic review. Comput. Electron. Agric. **153**, 69–81 (2018)
12. Rosenblatt, F.: The perceptron: a probabilistic model for information storage and organization in the brain. Psychol. Rev. **65**(6), 386 (1958)
13. Gomolka, Z.: Backpropagation algorithm with fractional derivatives. In: ITM Web of Conferences, vol. 21, p. 00004 (2018)
14. Werbos, P.J.: Backpropagation through time: what it does and how to do it. Proc. IEEE **78**(10), 1550–1560 (1990)

15. Hochreiter, S., Schmidhuber, J.: Long short-term memory. Neural Comput. **9**(8), 1735–1780 (1997)
16. Krizhevsky, A., Sutskever, I., Hinton, G.E.: ImageNet classification with deep convolutional neural networks. Commun. ACM **60**(6), 84–90 (2017)
17. Hubel, D.H., Wiesel, T.N.: Receptive fields, binocular interaction and functional architecture in the cat's visual cortex. J. Physiol. **160**(1), 106 (1962)
18. Fukushima, K.: Artificial vision by multi-layered neural networks: neocognitron and its advances. Neural Netw. **37**, 103–119 (2013)
19. LeCun, Y., et al.: Backpropagation applied to handwritten zip code recognition. Neural Comput. **1**(4), 541–551 (1989)
20. Srivastava, N., Hinton, G., Krizhevsky, A., Sutskever, I., Salakhutdinov, R.: DropOut: a simple way to prevent neural networks from overfitting. J. Mach. Learn. Res. **15**(1), 1929–1958 (2014)
21. Simonyan, K., Zisserman, A.: Very deep convolutional networks for large-scale image recognition. arXiv preprint arXiv:1409.1556 (2014)
22. Szegedy, C., Vanhoucke, V., Ioffe, S., Shlens, J., Wojna, Z.: Rethinking the Inception architecture for computer vision. In: IEEE Conference on Computer Vision and Pattern Recognition, pp. 2818–2826 (2016)
23. Girshick, R.: Fast R-CNN. In: IEEE International Conference on Computer Vision, pp.1440–1448 (2015)
24. Ren, S., He, K., Girshick, R., Sun, J.: Faster R-CNN: towards real-time object detection with region proposal networks. In: Advances in Neural Information Processing Systems, pp. 91–99 (2015)
25. Redmon, J., Divvala, S., Girshick, R., Farhadi, A.: You only look once: unified, real-time object detection. In: IEEE Conference on Computer Vision and Pattern Recognition, pp. 779–788 (2016)
26. Liu, W., et al.: SSD: single shot multibox detector. In: Leibe, B., Matas, J., Sebe, N., Welling, M. (eds.) ECCV 2016. LNCS, vol. 9905, pp. 21–37. Springer, Cham (2016). https://doi.org/10.1007/978-3-319-46448-0_2
27. Zhou, X., Wang, D., Krähenbühl, P.: Objects as points. arXiv:1904.07850 (2019)
28. He, K., Zhang, X., Ren, S., Sun, J.: Deep residual learning for image recognition. In: IEEE Conference on Computer Vision and Pattern Recognition, pp. 770–778 (2016)
29. Yu, F., Wang, D., Shelhamer, E., Darrell, T.: Deep layer aggregation. In: IEEE Conference on Computer Vision and Pattern Recognition, pp. 2403–2412 (2018)
30. Newell, A., Yang, K., Deng, J.: Stacked hourglass networks for human pose estimation. In: Leibe, B., Matas, J., Sebe, N., Welling, M. (eds.) ECCV 2016. LNCS, vol. 9912, pp. 483–499. Springer, Cham (2016). https://doi.org/10.1007/978-3-319-46484-8_29
31. Yan, W.: Introduction to Intelligent Surveillance - Surveillance Data Capture, Transmission, and Analytics (Third Edition), Springer (2019). https://doi.org/10.1007/978-3-030-107 13-0_1
32. Yan, W.: Computational Methods for Deep Learning - Theoretic, Practice and Applications. Springer (2021). https://doi.org/10.1007/978-3-030-61081-4_1
33. Pan, C., Yan, W.Q.: Object detection based on saturation of visual perception. Multimed. Tools Appl. **79**(27–28), 19925–19944 (2020). https://doi.org/10.1007/s11042-020-08866-x
34. Pan, C., Yan, W.: A learning-based positive feedback in salient object detection. In: IVCNZ (2019)
35. Al-Sarayreh, M., Reis, M.M., Yan, W.Q., Klette, R.: Detection of adulteration in red meat species using hyperspectral imaging. In: Paul, M., Hitoshi, C., Huang, Q. (eds.) PSIVT 2017. LNCS, vol. 10749, pp. 182–196. Springer, Cham (2018). https://doi.org/10.1007/978-3-319-75786-5_16

36. Al-Sarayreh, M., Reis, M., Yan, W., Klette, R.: Detection of red-meat adulteration by deep spectral-spatial features in hyperspectral images. J. Imaging **4**(5), 63 (2018)
37. Al-Sarayreh, M., Reis, M., Yan, W., Klette, R.: Chemometrics and hyperspectral imaging applied to assessment of chemical, textural and structural characteristics of meat. Meat Sci. **144**, 100–109 (2018)
38. Al-Sarayreh, M., Reis, M.M., Yan, W.Q., Klette, R.: A Sequential CNN approach for foreign object detection in hyperspectral images. In: Vento, M., Percannella, G. (eds.) CAIP 2019. LNCS, vol. 11678, pp. 271–283. Springer, Cham (2019). https://doi.org/10.1007/978-3-030-29888-3_22
39. Al-Sarayreh, M., Reis, M., Yan, W., Klette, R.: Deep spectral-spatial features of snapshot hyperspectral images for red-meat classification. In: IEEE IVCNZ (2019)
40. Al-Sarayreh, M., Reis, M., Yan, W., Klette, R.: Potential of deep learning and snapshot hyperspectral imaging for classification of species in meat. Food Control **117**, 107332 (2020)
41. Liu, Z., Yan, W., Yang, B.: Image denoising based on a CNN model. IEEE ICCAR **1**(1), 389–393 (2018)

A Graph-Regularized Non-local Hyperspectral Image Denoising Method

Ling Lei[1], Binqian Huang[1], Minchao Ye[1(✉)], Hong Chen[1], and Yuntao Qian[2]

[1] Key Laboratory of Electromagnetic Wave Information Technology and Metrology of Zhejiang Province, College of Information Engineering, China Jiliang University, Hangzhou 310018, China
yeminchao@cjlu.edu.cn
[2] College of Computer Science, Zhejiang University, Hangzhou 310027, China

Abstract. A lot of hyperspectral images (HSIs) are corrupted by noises when they are captured. Noise removal is an essential pre-processing for the noisy HSIs. Though denoising algorithms for common (grayscale or RGB) images have been studied for decades, HSIs have their inherent characteristics, so denoising algorithms for HSIs need to be specially designed. In this work, we have developed a non-local denoising algorithm for HSIs based on multi-task graph-regularized sparse nonnegative matrix factorization (MTGSNMF). MTGSNMF delivers noise removal in both spatial and spectral views. In spatial view, patch-based sparse recovery is performed by sparse nonnegative matrix factorization (SNMF), which conducts noise suppression and local pattern preservation. Graph regularization is imposed on the SNMF model for maintaining the non-local similarities between patches. In spectral view, spectral structure is extracted by multi-task learning, i.e., denoising tasks of different bands are bound by sharing the same coefficient matrix. By exploiting the non-local similarity in spatial view and spectral structure in spectral view, MTGSNMF achieves superior denoising performance on HSI datasets.

Keywords: Hyperspectral image denoising · Non-local denoising · Graph regularization · Nonnegative matrix factorization · Multi-task learning

1 Introduction

Hyperspectral images (HSIs), more or less, are corrupted by noises. The noises in HSIs can greatly affect the applications on HSIs, e.g., pixel classification, target detection, etc. As a necessary pre-processing, noise reduction plays an important role in applications of HSIs. In earlier researches, heavily noisy bands were

Supported partly by the National Natural Science Foundation of China (grant numbers 61701468 and 62071421), and partly by the National Key Research and Development Program of China (grant number 2018YFB0505000).

directly removed. For example, most noisy bands in Indian Pines data were typically dropped before classification [5]. However, some researches suggested that noisy bands still contain useful information that may contribute to the subsequent applications and thus should not be removed [11]. Therefore, HSI denoising has become a hot topic in recent years. Different from a common color image, a HSI contains hundreds of spectral bands, forming a data cube that spanned by two spatial dimensions and one spectral dimension. The spectral-spatial structure is desired to be preserved when denoising algorithm is performed on a HSI. Various algorithms have been proposed for HSI denoising in recent years. For examples, structured sparse representation on three-dimensional blocks [16], spatio-spectral total variation [1], tensor factorization [17], block-matching and 4D filtering (BM4D) [18], etc. Aforementioned methods have achieved inspiring results. Nevertheless, we believe there is still space for improvements.

In our previous research work, we proposed a nonnegative matrix factorization (NMF)-based algorithm HSI denoising, namely multi-task sparse NMF (MTSNMF) [19]. MTSNMF is a patch-based denoising algorithm. Each band image is divided into overlapping patches. The patches are denoised by sparse recovery using sparse NMF (SNMF). By incorporating multi-task learning, MTSNMF binds together denoising tasks of all bands. The multi-task learning scheme contributes to full utilization of cross-band correlations embedded in HSIs. It showed great success and surpassed most of existing HSI denoising algorithms. However, MTSNMF can still be improved by taking the intrinsic properties of HSIs into consideration.

Non-local similarity is a commonly used property in image denoising. It implies that image patches in different positions of an image may share similar patterns. The related works include 2D/3D non-local means filtering (NLMF) [3,15], block-matching and 3D/4D filtering (BM3D/BM4D) [8,13], non-local sparse recovery [14,16], etc. A latest research combined global low-rank denoising and non-local denoising [10].

In this work, we add the non-local similarity information into our previous work of MTSNMF [19]. During denoising, the non-local similarities between patches are represented by a graph. Then a graph regularization is imposed on MTSNMF, forming a new denoising model named multi-task graph-regularized sparse NMF (MTGSNMF). The proposed MTGSNMF has following advantages: 1) local structures and patterns are maintained by the sparse approximation of SNMF; 2) non-local similarities are kept by the graph regularization between patches; 3) spectral correlation is represented by sharing a common coefficient matrix among all bands. Shown by the experimental results, MTGSNMF achieves superior results when compared to other noise removal algorithms.

2   Related Work

The proposed MTGSNMF is a combination of MTSNMF [19] and graph-regularized NMF (GNMF) [4]. The basics MTSNMF and GNMF are introduced in this section.

2.1   MTSNMF

MTSNMF is a multi-task denoising algorithm, where noise elimination in each band image is seen as a single task. In each 2D band image, overlapping image patches are extracted via a sliding window. Each patch sized $\sqrt{N} \times \sqrt{N}$ is reshaped to a column vector $\mathbf{x} \in \mathbb{R}_+^{N \times 1}$ and thus can be recovered by a low-dimensional and sparse approximation:

$$\min_{\mathbf{v}} \|\mathbf{x} - \mathbf{U}\mathbf{v}\|_2^2 + \lambda \|\mathbf{v}\|_1 \quad \text{s.t.} \quad \mathbf{U} \geq 0, \mathbf{v} \geq 0, \tag{1}$$

where $\mathbf{U} \in \mathbb{R}_+^{N \times R}$ is a trained basis matrix, or alternatively called a dictionary, R is the dictionary size (number of basis atoms in $\mathbf{U}$), $\mathbf{v} \in \mathbb{R}_+^{R \times 1}$ is the sparse representation (coefficient vector) of $\mathbf{x}$ based on the dictionary $\mathbf{U}$, and $\|\mathbf{v}\|_1 = \sum_{i=1}^{R} |v_i|$ is the ℓ_1-norm regularization for sparsity, with λ controlling the sparseness. It is worth noting that if nonnegative constant is imposed on $\mathbf{v}$, ℓ_1-norm can be simplified to $\|\mathbf{v}\|_1 = \sum_{i=1}^{R} v_i$. Assume that there are M patches within each band image, we can merge their denoising models into a unified one:

$$\min_{\mathbf{U}, \mathbf{V}} \|\mathbf{X} - \mathbf{U}\mathbf{V}\|_F^2 + \lambda \|\mathbf{V}\|_1 \quad \text{s.t.} \quad \mathbf{U} \geq 0, \mathbf{V} \geq 0, \tag{2}$$

where $\mathbf{X} = [\mathbf{x}_1, \mathbf{x}_2, \ldots, \mathbf{x}_M]$ is the input data matrix containing all patches within a band image, $\mathbf{V} = [\mathbf{v}_1, \mathbf{v}_2, \ldots, \mathbf{v}_M]$ is the coefficient matrix, and $\| \cdot \|_F$ is the Frobenius norm. This comes to a SNMF model on each band.

Considering the spectral correlation among different bands, it is proposed in MTSNMF that different band-wize noise removal tasks can be bound by sharing a common coefficient matrix $\mathbf{V}$ across all band images. Thus the MTSNMF model can be mathematically represented by

$$\min_{\mathbf{U}_1, \ldots, \mathbf{U}_K, \mathbf{V}} \sum_{k=1}^{K} \left(\|\mathbf{X}_k - \mathbf{U}_k \mathbf{V}\|_F^2 + \lambda_k \|\mathbf{V}\|_1 \right)$$
$$\text{s.t.} \quad \mathbf{U}_k \geq 0 (k = 1, \ldots, K), \mathbf{V} \geq 0, \tag{3}$$

where $\mathbf{X}_k$ is the patch sample matrix of kth band image, $\mathbf{U}_k$ is the basis matrix of the kth band image, $\mathbf{V}$ is the common coefficient matrix shared across all the band images, which maintains the spectral correlation. MTSNMF has shown inspiring signal-to-noise ratio (SNR) in our previous work [19].

2.2   GNMF

GNMF model was originally proposed by Cai et al. in [4]. The motivation of GNMF is to maintain the relationship between samples (or so called the structure of data manifold) during the factorization. Suppose we have a nonnegative input matrix $\mathbf{X} = [\mathbf{x}_1, \mathbf{x}_2, \ldots, \mathbf{x}_M] \in \mathbb{R}_+^{N \times M}$ containing M samples with N dimensions. An adjacent matrix $\mathbf{W} \in \mathbb{R}^{M \times M}$ is defined to represent the similarity graph, where w_{ij} stands for the similarity between $\mathbf{x}_i$ and $\mathbf{x}_j$. Then the objective function of GNMF can be defined as

$$\min_{\mathbf{U},\mathbf{V}} \|\mathbf{X} - \mathbf{U}\mathbf{V}\|_F^2 + \frac{\mu}{2} \sum_{i=1}^{M} \sum_{j=1}^{M} w_{ij} \|\mathbf{v}_{:i} - \mathbf{v}_{:j}\|_2^2 \tag{4}$$

$$\text{s.t.} \quad \mathbf{U} \geq 0, \mathbf{V} \geq 0,$$

where $\mathbf{U} \in \mathbb{R}_+^{N \times R}$ is the basis matrix, $\mathbf{V} = [\mathbf{v}_{:1}, \mathbf{v}_{:2}, \dots, \mathbf{v}_{:M}] \in \mathbb{R}_+^{R \times M}$ is the coefficient matrix, $\mathbf{v}_{:i}$ and $\mathbf{v}_{:j}$ stand for the ith and the jth columns of matrix $\mathbf{V}$. In GNMF, if $\mathbf{x}_i$ and $\mathbf{x}_j$ are similar, w_{ij} and w_{ji} will be large, and then $\mathbf{v}_{:i}$ and $\mathbf{v}_{:j}$ are forced to be close to each other under the graph regularization. μ is the regularization parameter controlling the strength of graph regularization. GNMF and its variants have been successfully applied to HSIs for preserving the similarities between pixels [6,21].

3   Non-local Denoising for HSIs with MTGSNMF

3.1   Non-local Denoising

The idea of non-local denoising was firstly proposed in non-local means filtering (NLMF) [3]. In NLMF, non-local similarity of two pixels is measured by Gaussian weighted Euclidean distance:

$$w(i, j) = \frac{1}{Z(i)} \exp\left(-\frac{\|\mathcal{N}_i - \mathcal{N}_j\|_{2,\mathcal{G}}^2}{h^2}\right), \tag{5}$$

where $\|\mathcal{N}_i - \mathcal{N}_j\|_{2,\mathcal{G}}$ is Gaussian weighted distance, h controls the degree of filtering, and $Z(i) = \sum_j \exp\left(-\frac{\|\mathcal{N}_i - \mathcal{N}_j\|_{2,\mathcal{G}}^2}{h^2}\right)$ is a normalization factor. NLMF calculates the denoised pixel by weighted average of all pixels using the weights calculated by Eq. (5).

After NMLF, Block Matching 3D (BM3D) algorithm was proposed for non-local denoising, where similar patches are stacked into a 3D signal block, and 3D filtering is performed for collaborative denoising [7]. Then non-local similarity was adopted in non-local sparse denoising, where similar patches are put together and a joint sparse representation is adopted to achieve similar sparse pattern between them [14].

Following aforementioned researches, we propose a new non-local denoising approach based on graph modeling in this work.

3.2   Modeling the Non-local Similarity by Graph

Non-local similarity is an inherent property of natural images. It has been widely utilized in the applications of HSIs, e.g., denoising [12,15], classification [22], super-resolution [9], etc. In this work, we adopt the patch-based modeling for non-local similarity in a remotely sensed HSI, which is illustrated by Fig. 1. Similar patches may cover the same type of land cover object or contain the same material. It is worth noting that patches in a HSI are 3D volumetric patches (i.e., 3rd-order tensors) rather than 2D patches in grayscale images. The similarity measurement between volumetric patches takes both spatial and spectral similarities into account.

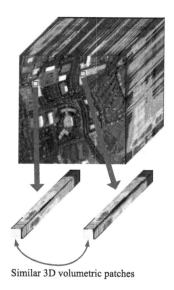

Similar 3D volumetric patches

Fig. 1. The non-local similarity in a HSI.

Graph is a powerful tool to represent pairwise similarities between samples (i.e., volumetric patches here). Moreover, graph is easy to be embedded into recovery/denoising models. Supposed that we have M volumetric patches inside a HSI, each sized $\sqrt{N} \times \sqrt{N} \times K$, where $\sqrt{N} \times \sqrt{N}$ is the spatial size (number of pixels), while K is the spectral size (number of bands). Then an adjacent matrix $\mathbf{W} \in \mathbb{R}^{M \times M}$ is defined on the non-local similarity graph, where w_{ij} represents the similarity between the ith volumetric patch $\mathcal{X}_i$ and the jth volumetric patch $\mathcal{X}_j$. To calculate w_{ij}, a spectral-spatial Euclidean distance is adopted

$$d(\mathcal{X}_i, \mathcal{X}_j) = \|\mathcal{X}_i - \mathcal{X}_j\|_F, \tag{6}$$

where $\|\cdot\|_F$ is the Frobenius norm. With the distance defined, we propose a fast method to build a sparse graph. First, a k-means clustering is performed on all patches using the spectral-spatial Euclidean distance defined in Eq. (6). Then a 0-1 weighting is performed to build the graph:

$$w_{ij} = \begin{cases} 1, & \mathcal{X}_i \text{ and } \mathcal{X}_j \text{ are in the same cluster,} \\ 0, & \text{otherwise.} \end{cases} \tag{7}$$

It needs to be mentioned that a direct clustering on a noisy HSI may lead to an incorrect non-local similarity graph: two originally dissimilar patches may look similar after being corrupted by noises. So it is recommended to conduct a coarse signal-noise separation first, and then build the non-local similarity graph on the "clean" signal component. In this work, the coarse signal-noise separation is accomplished with the algorithm proposed in [20].

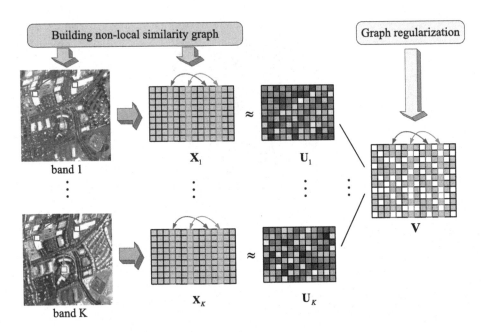

Fig. 2. The model framework of MTGSNMF.

3.3   Noise Removal Based on MTGSNMF

With the non-local similarity graph defined in the previous sub-section, we present our MTGSNMF model here. The model framework is displayed in Fig. 2. By adding the non-local similarity graph regularization to Eq. (3), we can get the proposed MTGSNMF model

$$\min \mathcal{C}(\mathbf{U}_1, \ldots, \mathbf{U}_K, \mathbf{V}) =$$

$$\sum_{k=1}^{K} \|\mathbf{X}_k - \mathbf{U}_k \mathbf{V}\|_F^2 + \left(\sum_{k=1}^{K} \lambda_k \right) \|\mathbf{V}\|_1 + \frac{\mu}{2} \sum_{i=1}^{M} \sum_{j=1}^{M} w_{ij} \|\mathbf{v}_{:i} - \mathbf{v}_{:j}\|_2^2 \quad (8)$$

$$\text{s.t.}\quad \mathbf{U}_k \geq 0 (k = 1, \ldots, K), \mathbf{V} > 0.$$

The symbols in Eq. (8) have the same meanings as that in Eqs. (3) and (4). There are three terms in the cost function $\mathcal{C}$ of Eq. (8):

1. $\sum_{k=1}^{K} \|\mathbf{X}_k - \mathbf{U}_k\mathbf{V}\|_F^2$ is the recovery error to ensure an approximation of the original noisy image;

2. $\left(\sum_{k=1}^{K} \lambda_k\right) \|\mathbf{V}\|_1$ is the sparse regularization to accomplish noise reduction;

3. $\frac{\mu}{2} \sum_{i=1}^{M} \sum_{j=1}^{M} w_{ij} \|\mathbf{v}_{:i} - \mathbf{v}_{:j}\|_2^2$ is the graph regularization to maintain non-local similarity during the recovery. If μ is set to zero, MTGSNMF degenerates to MTSNMF.

By combining these three terms, a non-local similarity preserving denoising model is developed.

3.4   Optimization Algorithm for MTGSNMF

To minimize Eq. (8), we first define the following matrices and variables

$$\mathbf{X} = [\mathbf{X}_1^\mathrm{T}, \mathbf{X}_2^\mathrm{T}, \ldots, \mathbf{X}_K^\mathrm{T}]^\mathrm{T}, \tag{9}$$

$$\mathbf{U} = [\mathbf{U}_1^\mathrm{T}, \mathbf{U}_2^\mathrm{T}, \ldots, \mathbf{U}_K^\mathrm{T}]^\mathrm{T}, \tag{10}$$

$$\lambda = \sum_{k=1}^{K} \lambda_k, \tag{11}$$

$$\mathbf{D} = \mathrm{diag}(\sum_{j=1}^{M} w_{1j}, \sum_{j=1}^{M} w_{2j}, \ldots, \sum_{j=1}^{M} w_{Mj}), \tag{12}$$

$$\mathbf{L} = \mathbf{D} - \mathbf{W}. \tag{13}$$

Then Eq. (8) can be simplified to

$$\min \mathcal{C}(\mathbf{U}, \mathbf{V}) = \|\mathbf{X} - \mathbf{U}\mathbf{V}\|_F^2 + \lambda\|\mathbf{V}\|_1 + \mu\,\mathrm{Tr}(\mathbf{V}\mathbf{L}\mathbf{V}^\mathrm{T})$$
$$\text{s.t.}\quad \mathbf{U} \geq 0, \mathbf{V} \geq 0. \tag{14}$$

The partial derivatives are:

$$\nabla_\mathbf{U}\mathcal{C} = -2\mathbf{X}\mathbf{V}^\mathrm{T} + 2\mathbf{U}\mathbf{V}\mathbf{V}^\mathrm{T}, \tag{15}$$

$$\nabla_\mathbf{V}\mathcal{C} = -2\mathbf{U}^\mathrm{T}\mathbf{X} + 2\mathbf{U}^\mathrm{T}\mathbf{U}\mathbf{V} + \lambda + 2\mu\mathbf{V}\mathbf{L}^\mathrm{T}. \tag{16}$$

Considering the KKT conditions $\mathbf{U} \odot \nabla_\mathbf{U}\mathcal{C} = 0$ and $\mathbf{V} \odot \nabla_\mathbf{V}\mathcal{C} = 0$ ($\odot$ is the element-wise multiplication of two matrices), we can obtain the updating rules

$$\mathbf{U} = \mathbf{U} \odot \frac{\mathbf{X}\mathbf{V}^\mathrm{T}}{\mathbf{U}\mathbf{V}\mathbf{V}^\mathrm{T}}, \tag{17}$$

$$\mathbf{V} = \mathbf{V} \odot \frac{\mathbf{U}^\mathrm{T}\mathbf{X} + \mu\mathbf{V}\mathbf{W}^\mathrm{T}}{\mathbf{U}^\mathrm{T}\mathbf{U}\mathbf{V} + \frac{\lambda}{2} + \mu\mathbf{V}\mathbf{D}^\mathrm{T}}. \tag{18}$$

By initializing $\mathbf{U}$ and $\mathbf{V}$ with nonnegative random values and applying Eqs. (17) and (18) iteratively, the minimization of Eq. (14) can be achieved.

4 Experiments

To evaluate the denoising performance of MTGSNMF, experiments are carried out on synthetic dataset and Indian Pines dataset.

4.1 Compared Algorithms and Parameter Settings

The following algorithms are compared:

1. BM4D[1]: block-matching and 4D filtering (BM4D) is a denoising algorithm for volumetric data based on non-local similarity [13]. In BM4D, Gaussian noise model is assumed and noise standard deviation is automatically estimated.
2. NLMF[2]: non-local means filtering was initially proposed for 2D image denoising [3]. It was then extended to a 3D version for HSI denoising [15], which is selected for comparison in this work. NLMF has a parameter h controlling the strength of filtering, which is set as $h \in \{0.01, 0.02, \ldots, 0.05\}$ in the experiments.
3. NGmeet[3]: NGmeet is a state-of-the-art algorithm for HSI denoising brought out in CVPR 2019 [10]. NGmeet needs the noise variance σ_0^2 to be the input. Since the true noise variance is actually unknown, a noise estimation is performed with the algorithm in [2].
4. MTGSNMF[4]: MTGSNMF is the algorithm proposed in this work. It is an extension of MTSNMF [19] with non-local similarity graph embedding. The parameters of MTGSNMF include

    (a) patch size $N = 7 \times 7 = 49$,
    (b) dictionary size $R \in \{100, 200\}$,
    (c) sparse regularization parameter $\lambda_k = \hat{\sigma}_k \sqrt{2 \log(R)}$, where $\hat{\sigma}_k$ is the estimated noise standard deviation of the kth band image using the algorithm in [2],
    (d) graph regularization parameter $\mu \in \{0, 50, \ldots, 200\}$ for synthetic data and $\mu \in \{0, 1, 10, 100\}$ for Indian Pines data.

It should be clarified that some algorithms will be tested with a series of parameter settings as listed above. In the comparisons between different algorithms, we take the best result (with optimal parameter setting) of each algorithm.

---

[1] The code of BM4D is available at https://www.cs.tut.fi/~foi/GCF-BM3D/BM4D_v3p2.zip.

[2] The code of NLMF is available at https://www.mathworks.com/matlabcentral/fileexchange/27395-fast-non-local-means-1d-2d-color-and-3d.

[3] The code of NGmeet is available at https://github.com/quanmingyao/NGMeet.

[4] The code of the proposed MTGSNMF is available at https://github.com/yeminchao/MTGSNMF.

4.2   Experimental Results on Synthetic Data

Since the quantitative criteria of denoising need a clean image for reference, a noiseless HSI named Reno is adopted for generating the synthetic data. A subset sized $200 \times 200 \times 356$ is selected for experiments. The clean band images can be found in Figs. 4a and 5a. Gaussian noise is added to each band image, where noise standard deviation varies from band to band. We set the noise standard deviation of the kth band image as $\sigma_k = 0.2\bar{x}_k$, where $\bar{x}_k$ is the mean value of the kth band image. Noisy band images can be found in Figs. 4b and 5b.

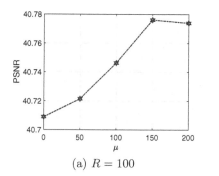 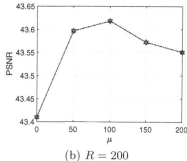

(a) $R = 100$ (b) $R = 200$

Fig. 3. The PSNR of MTGSNMF with respect to parameter μ in synthetic data.

Table 1. PSNR achieved by different algorithms

	BM4D	NLMF	NGmeet	MTGSNMF
PSNR	39.9571	37.3884	42.6819	**43.6181**

Peak signal-to-noise ratio (PSNR) is the most commonly adopted quantitative criterion of denoising and thus is adopted in this work for performance evaluation. To show the influence of graph regularization, the PSNR of MTGSNMF with respect to graph regularization parameter μ is plotted in Fig. 3. It can be found in Fig. 3 that 1) the optimal setting of μ is related to dictionary size R; 2) a more redundant dictionary with $R = 200$ leads to better results. The PSNR achieved by different algorithms are listed in Table 1. It can be recognized that MTGSNMF wins the comparison by about 1dB higher PSNR than the state-of-the-art algorithm NGmeet. The visual denoising results on band 2 and band 340 are shown in Figs. 4 and 5. It can be seen that BM4D and NLMF cause over-blurring in a heavily noisy band (e.g. band 2), and NGmeet and MTGSNMF generate comparable visual results.

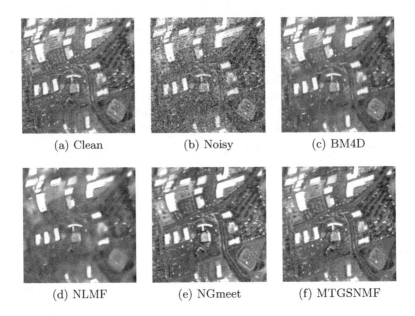

(a) Clean   (b) Noisy   (c) BM4D

(d) NLMF   (e) NGmeet   (f) MTGSNMF

Fig. 4. Band 2 of synthetic data before and after denoising.

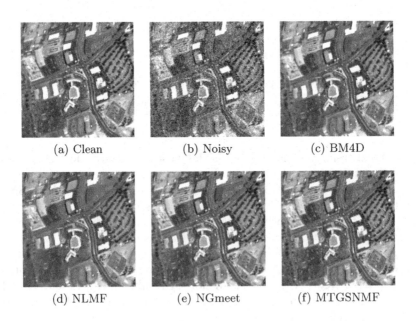

(a) Clean   (b) Noisy   (c) BM4D

(d) NLMF   (e) NGmeet   (f) MTGSNMF

Fig. 5. Band 340 of synthetic data before and after denoising.

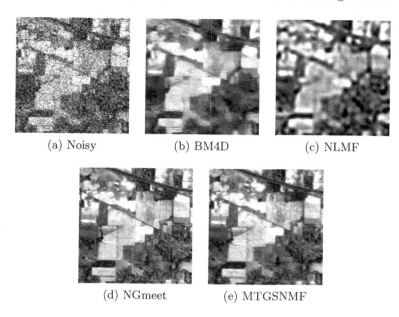

(a) Noisy   (b) BM4D   (c) NLMF

(d) NGmeet   (e) MTGSNMF

Fig. 6. Band 103 of Indian Pines data before and after denoising.

Table 2. Classification accuracies with different denoising algorithm on Indian Pines data

	BM4D	NLMF	NGmeet	MTGSNMF
OA	0.7879	**0.8874**	0.7446	0.7923
AA	0.8800	**0.9338**	0.8456	0.8810
κ	0.7606	**0.8718**	0.7133	0.7650

4.3 Experimental Results on Indian Pines Data

We select Indian Pines image as the real-world data, since it is a severely noisy HSI. Since Indian Pines image does not have a clean version for reference, PSNR is no longer available. Hence the visual results and classification accuracies are provided. Visual results of the compared algorithms on two representative bands are displayed in Figs. 6 and 7. In Indian Pines image, BM4D produces noticeable artifacts, especially on the heavily noisy band 220. NLMF gets blurred results, making small objects unrecognizable. Both NGmeet and MTGSNMF produce clean and clear results, but less stripes remain in the results of MTGSNMF (comparing Figs. 7d and 7e). Classification experiments with SVM are conducted on the denoised data cubes. In each land cover class, 50 samples are randomly selected as training samples, expert for small classes, where 15 samples are selected for training. Remaining labeled samples are all regarded as test simples. The overall accuracy (OA), average accuracy (AA) and kappa coefficient (κ) are reported in Table 2. The results show that classification accuracy is not

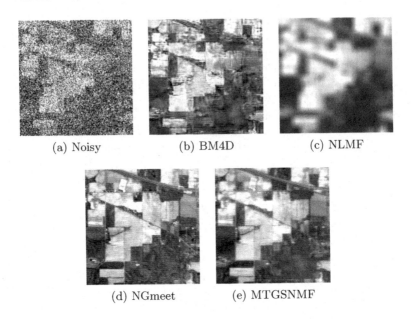

(a) Noisy   (b) BM4D   (c) NLMF

(d) NGmeet   (e) MTGSNMF

Fig. 7. Band 220 of Indian Pines data before and after denoising.

always positively related to denoising performance, i.e., the best accuracies are obtained with the over-blurring denoising result with NLMF (see Figs. 6c and 7c). The proposed MTGSNMF yields a compromise between visual effect and classification accuracy.

5   Conclusion

In this research, we have proposed a multi-task graph-regularized sparse non-negative matrix factorization (MTGSNMF) model for noise reduction of HSIs. The non-local similarity is modeled with a graph through a clustering on volumetric patches. Then a graph regularization is imposed on the MTSNMF-based denoising model, forming the proposed MTGSNMF model. The advantages of MTGSNMF include: 1) patch-based modeling preserves local patterns; 2) sparse recovery delivers noise removal; 3) binding denoising tasks on different bands can keep the spectral structures; 4) graph regulation maintains non-local similarity of the HSI. Experimental results on both synthetic and real-world datasets prove the effectiveness of MTGSNMF.

References

1. Aggarwal, H.K., Majumdar, A.: Hyperspectral image denoising using spatio-spectral total variation. IEEE Geosci. Remote Sens. Lett. **13**(3), 442–446 (2016)
2. Bioucas-Dias, J.M., Nascimento, J.M.P.: Hyperspectral subspace identification. IEEE Trans. Geosci. Remote Sens. **46**(8), 2435–2445 (2008)

3. Buades, A., Coll, B., Morel, J.: A non-local algorithm for image denoising. In: Proceedings of IEEE/CVF Conference on Computer Vision and Pattern Recognition, vol. 2, pp. 60–65 (2005)
4. Cai, D., He, X., Han, J., Huang, T.S.: Graph regularized nonnegative matrix factorization for data representation. IEEE Trans. Pattern Anal. Mach. Intell. **33**(8), 1548–1560 (2011)
5. Camps-Valls, G., Bruzzone, L.: Kernel-based methods for hyperspectral image classification. IEEE Trans. Geosci. Remote Sens. **43**(6), 1351–1362 (2005)
6. Chen, H., Ye, M., Lu, H., Lei, L., Qian, Y.: Dual dictionary learning for mining a unified feature subspace between different hyperspectral image scenes. In: Proceedings of IEEE International Geoscience and Remote Sensing Symposium, pp. 1096–1099 (2019)
7. Dabov, K., Foi, A., Katkovnik, V., Egiazarian, K.: Image denoising by sparse 3-D transform-domain collaborative filtering. IEEE Trans. Image Process. **16**(8), 2080–2095 (2007)
8. Dabov, K., Foi, A., Katkovnik, V., Egiazarian, K.: Image denoising with block-matching and 3D filtering. In: Proceedings of SPIE, Image Processing: Algorithms and Systems, Neural Networks, and Machine Learning, pp. 354–365 (2006)
9. Dian, R., Fang, L., Li, S.: Hyperspectral image super-resolution via non-local sparse tensor factorization. In: Proceedings of IEEE/CVF Conference on Computer Vision and Pattern Recognition (2017)
10. He, W., Yao, Q., Li, C., Yokoya, N., Zhao, Q.: Non-local meets global: an integrated paradigm for hyperspectral denoising. In: Proceedings of IEEE/CVF Conference on Computer Vision and Pattern Recognition, pp. 6861–6870 (2019)
11. Jia, S., Ji, Z., Qian, Y., Shen, L.: Unsupervised band selection for hyperspectral imagery classification without manual band removal. IEEE J. Sel. Topics Appl. Earth Observ. Remote Sens. **5**(2), 531–543 (2012)
12. Li, J., Yuan, Q., Shen, H., Zhang, L.: Hyperspectral image recovery employing a multidimensional nonlocal total variation model. Signal Process **111**, 230–248 (2015)
13. Maggioni, M., Katkovnik, V., Egiazarian, K., Foi, A.: Nonlocal transform-domain filter for volumetric data denoising and reconstruction. IEEE Trans. Image Process. **22**(1), 119–133 (2013)
14. Mairal, J., Bach, F., Ponce, J., Sapiro, G., Zisserman, A.: Non-local sparse models for image restoration. In: Proceedings of IEEE International Conference On Computer Vision, pp. 2272–2279 (2009)
15. Qian, Y., Shen, Y., Ye, M., Wang, Q.: 3-D nonlocal means filter with noise estimation for hyperspectral imagery denoising. In: Proceedings of IEEE International Geoscience and Remote Sensing Symposium, pp. 1345–1348 (2012)
16. Qian, Y., Ye, M.: Hyperspectral imagery restoration using nonlocal spectral-spatial structured sparse representation with noise estimation. IEEE J. Sel. Topics Appl. Earth Observ. Remote Sens. **6**(2), 499–515 (2013)
17. Xiong, F., Zhou, J., Qian, Y.: Hyperspectral restoration via l_0 gradient regularized low-rank tensor factorization. IEEE Trans. Geosci. Remote Sens. **57**(12), 10410–10425 (2019)
18. Xu, P., Chen, B., Xue, L., Zhang, J., Zhu, L., Duan, H.: A new MNF-BM4D denoising algorithm based on guided filtering for hyperspectral images. ISA Trans. **92**, 315–324 (2019)
19. Ye, M., Qian, Y., Zhou, J.: Multitask sparse nonnegative matrix factorization for joint spectral-spatial hyperspectral imagery denoising. IEEE Trans. Geosci. Remote Sens. **53**(5), 2621–2639 (2015)

20. Ye, M., Chen, H., Ji, C., Lei, L., Qian, Y.: Spectral-spatial joint noise estimation for hyperspectral images. In: Proceedings of International Geoscience and Remote Sensing Symposium, pp. 230–233 (2019)
21. Ye, M., Zheng, W., Lu, H., Zeng, X., Qian, Y.: Cross-scene hyperspectral image classification based on DWT and manifold-constrained subspace learning. Int. J. Wavelets Multiresolut. Inf. Process. 15(06), 1750062 (2017)
22. Zhang, H., Li, J., Huang, Y., Zhang, L.: A nonlocal weighted joint sparse representation classification method for hyperspectral imagery. IEEE J. Sel. Topics Appl. Earth Observ. Remote Sens. 7(6), 2056–2065 (2014)

Random Convolutional Network for Hyperspectral Image Classification

Jiongye Zhu[1], Xiaohan Wang[1], Ling Lei[1], Minchao Ye[1(✉)], and Yuntao Qian[2]

[1] Key Laboratory of Electromagnetic Wave Information Technology and Metrology of Zhejiang Province, College of Information Engineering, China Jiliang University, Hangzhou 310018, China
yeminchao@cjlu.edu.cn
[2] College of Computer Science, Zhejiang University, Hangzhou 310027, China

Abstract. Convolutional neural network (CNN) has proved remarkable performance in the field of hyperspectral image (HSI) classification for it has excellent feature extraction ability. However, HSI classification is a small-sample-size problem due to the labour cost of labeling. CNN may perform poorly on HSI data due to the ill-conditioned and overfitting problems caused by the lack of enough training samples. Extreme learning machine (ELM) is a kind of single-layer feedforward neural network (FNN) with high training efficiency, which simplifies the learning of parameters. Therefore, in this paper, we try to combine the convolutional feature extraction method of CNN and the parameter randomization idea of ELM, and then propose a random convolutional network (RCN) model. The proposed RCN randomly generates the parameters of three-dimensional (3D) convolution kernels in convolutional layer used for the joint spectral-spatial feature extraction. RCN avoids ill-conditioned and overfitting problems in the case of small samples by significantly reducing the number of parameters to be trained. At the same time, further analyses on the convolution kernel sizes and the number of convolution kernels have been carried out. Experiments on two real-world HSI datasets have demonstrated that the proposed RCN algorithm has excellent generalization ability.

Keywords: Hyperspectral image · Spectral-spatial feature extraction · Convolutional neural network · Extreme learning machine

1 Introduction

It is generally known that hyperspectral image (HSI) classification has long been a hot research topic. Over the past decades, various methods have been

---

Supported partly by the National Natural Science Foundation of China (grant numbers 61701468 and 62071421), and partly by the National Key Research and Development Program of China (grant number 2018YFB0505000).

M. Nguyen et al. (Eds.): ISGV 2021, CCIS 1386, pp. 341–353, 2021.
https://doi.org/10.1007/978-3-030-72073-5_26

adopted for higher accuracy, including support vector machine (SVM) [13], random forest [5], sparse logistic regression (SLR) [15], convolutional neural network (CNN) [4], extreme learning machine (ELM) [8,9], etc.

Feature extraction is a method to extract the representative features of the data, which is one of the most important parts in the process of HSI classification [1]. Extracting prominent features has a great influence on the generalization performance of classifiers. A series of feature extraction methods have been used, such as deep stacked autoencoders [3], manifold learning [17] and minimum noise fraction (MNF) [6]. However, the above methods with insufficient ability of feature extraction are unable to acquire satisfactory classification accuracy. Meanwhile, CNN has outstanding performance of feature extraction on HSIs. CNN uses convolution kernels to extract features from data with convolutional layers, and the parameters of convolution kernels are updated in the training process so that it avoids the complex and unreliable explicit feature extraction process.

Generally, the labeling work of HSI data costs a lot of manpower which puts forward higher requirements for the generalization ability of the classifiers in the case of small samples. However, there are a large number of parameters in CNN, which means a lot of training samples are required. When the number of available samples is limited, the overfitting and ill-conditioned problems are more likely to occur, which will reduce the classification accuracy of CNN. Besides, time consuming is one of the disadvantages of CNN for it has to update all the parameters in the training process through back propagation (BP) [12] algorithm which is executed iteratively. Compared with CNN, ELM randomly generates its parameters of hidden neurons, which reduces the number of parameters to be trained. Therefore, ELM tends to have good performance in small-sample-size classification tasks for it averts ill-conditioned problems. Meanwhile, the straightforward solution idea of ELM makes it have fast computation capability.

To deal with the problem of imbalance between the number of parameters and available training samples, we propose a new network in this paper, namely random convolutional network (RCN), which combines spectral-spatial convolutional feature extraction of CNN and the parameter randomization of ELM. The proposed approach greatly reduces the number of the parameters in the model by randomly generating the parameters of three-dimensional (3D) convolution kernels. Therefore, RCN not only works efficiently but also has high generalization ability. The rest of this paper is organized as follows. Section 2 introduces CNN and ELM. Section 3 presents the proposed RCN model. The experimental results on HSI data are analyzed in Sect. 4, followed by conclusions in Sect. 5.

2   Related Work

2.1   Convolutional Neural Network (CNN)

CNN is a variation development of Multilayer Perceptron (MLP) [11]. In recent years, it has demonstrated remarkable performance in the field of image classification and attracted considerable attentions. CNN consists of input layer, hidden layers and output layer. The hidden layers of CNN include convolutional layer, pooling layer and fully-connected layer [7]. The feature extraction of CNN is realized via several convolution kernels [10] in convolutional layers. Sliding on the input image, each convolution kernel obtains a corresponding feature map, then a series of feature maps are transferred to pooling layer which downsamples the image to reduce the number of parameters and retain useful information. The fully-connected layer summarizes all previous operations and combines the extracted features. Finally, what the output layer does is to output the classification labels through logic function or softmax function. As a kind of deep neural network (DNN) [16], CNN trains the parameters by constructing a loss function, and then it calculates the input and output values of each layer by parameter initialization and forward propagation to obtain the output layer error. Afterwards, parameters will be iteratively updated through BP algorithm until loss function minimizes.

The weight-sharing network structure of CNN reduces the number of parameters and complexity of the network calculation scale. However, there are still plenty of parameters which need to be trained so that numerous available training samples are generally required for enabling CNN to have higher classification accuracy. Furthermore, using BP algorithm to update parameters increases time complexity of the algorithm.

2.2   Extreme Learning Machine (ELM)

In the traditional artificial neural networks, the parameters of hidden layer nodes are optimized by iterative algorithm [2]. These iterative steps often make the training process of parameters take up a lot of time, so that the efficiency of the training process can not be guaranteed. In order to overcome this drawback of BP algorithm, ELM was proposed by Huang [9]. The parameters of hidden layer nodes are generated randomly, and the output weights of the network are obtained by minimizing the loss function, which can be solved in an explicit form, so that no iterative steps are required.

For a single hidden layer neural network, suppose there are N training samples as $\mathbf{X} = [\mathbf{x}_1^T, \mathbf{x}_2^T, \ldots, \mathbf{x}_N^T]^T \in \mathbb{R}^{N \times m}$, where each row $\mathbf{x}_i$ represents the input feature vector of a sample, and m is the input feature dimension. The labels are represented by one-hot encoding $\mathbf{T} = [\mathbf{t}_1^T, \mathbf{t}_2^T, \ldots, \mathbf{t}_N^T]^T \in \mathbb{R}^{N \times P}$, where P is the number of classes. The output of hidden layer with L hidden neurons can be expressed as

$$\mathbf{t}_i = \sum_{j=1}^{L} \beta_j g(\mathbf{w}_j \cdot \mathbf{x}_i + b_j), \quad i = 1, 2, \ldots, N, \tag{1}$$

where $g(x)$ is the activation function (e.g., sigmoid), $\mathbf{w}_j \in \mathbb{R}^m$ denotes the weight vector connecting input layer to hidden layer, $\beta_j \in \mathbb{R}^P$ denotes the weight vector from hidden layer to output layer, b_j is the bias of jth hidden neuron.

Note that Eq. (1) can be rewritten as

$$\mathbf{H}\beta = \mathbf{T}, \tag{2}$$

where

$$\mathbf{H} = \begin{bmatrix} g(\mathbf{w}_1 \cdot \mathbf{x}_1 + b_1) & \cdots & g(\mathbf{w}_L \cdot \mathbf{x}_1 + b_L) \\ \vdots & \cdots & \vdots \\ g(\mathbf{w}_1 \cdot \mathbf{x}_N + b_1) & \cdots & g(\mathbf{w}_L \cdot \mathbf{x}_N + b_L) \end{bmatrix}_{N \times L} , \quad \boldsymbol{\beta} = \begin{bmatrix} \beta_1 \\ \vdots \\ \beta_L \end{bmatrix}_{L \times P} . \quad (3)$$

$\mathbf{H}$ is the output of hidden layer, $\boldsymbol{\beta}$ is the weight matrix in the output layer, and $\mathbf{T}$ is the expected output matrix. In ELM, $\mathbf{w}_j$ and b_j $(j = 1, 2, \ldots, L)$ are assigned with random numbers, so $\mathbf{H}$ can be directly calculated. Then $\boldsymbol{\beta}$ can be directly solved via

$$\hat{\boldsymbol{\beta}} = \mathbf{H}^\dagger \mathbf{T}, \qquad (4)$$

where $\mathbf{H}^\dagger$ is the Moore-Penrose generalized inverse of matrix $\mathbf{H}$.

Due to the good generalization ability, ELM has recently drawn increasing attentions in the pattern recognition and machine learning fields. However, for the lack of feature extraction ability, ELM is difficult to provide satisfactory accuracy in the field of HSI classification. In addition, the number of hidden neurons demands manual adjustment.

3   Random Convolutional Network

In this paper, in order to solve ill-conditioned problems in the absence of samples and improve the training efficiency, we propose the RCN with combination of convolutional feature extraction method of CNN and the parameter randomization of ELM. The proposed RCN algorithm adopts a random convolutional layer with 3D convolution kernels as the feature extraction layer. Specially designed for HSIs, RCN has joint spectral-spatial feature extraction ability by adopting 3D convolution kernels. Besides, the convolution kernels in RCN are randomly generated so that the number of network parameters which need to be trained is greatly reduced. Therefore, even in the case of small samples, RCN has high generalization ability for it averts ill-conditioned problems and can extract spectral-spatial features. Also, for the reason that the time-consuming BP algorithm is no longer used, the speed of the training process is increased.

Figure 1 shows the architecture of RCN. The proposed RCN extracts features through several 3D convolution kernels. More specifically, a HSI data cube $\mathcal{D} \in \mathbb{R}^{A \times B \times C}$ is convoluted with multiple convolution kernels $\mathcal{K}_i \in \mathbb{R}^{I \times J \times K}$ $(i = 1, 2, \ldots, U$, where U denotes the number of kernels) to get the ith feature cube $\mathcal{D}_i^F \in \mathbb{R}^{A \times B \times C}$. All feature cubes are stacked along the spectral dimension to form the final feature cube $\mathcal{D}^F \in \mathbb{R}^{A \times B \times UC}$ (see Fig. 2), and features of the pixels can be extracted from $\mathcal{D}^F$. In the output layer, RCN adopts SVM with radial basis function kernel (SVM-RBF) as classifier. The algorithm framework of RCN is listed in Algorithm 1.

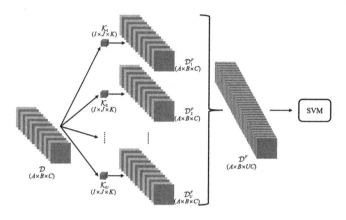

Fig. 1. The architecture of the proposed RCN.

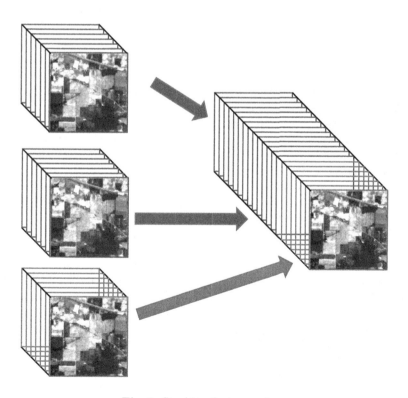

Fig. 2. Stacking feature cubes.

Algorithm 1. RCN

Input:

    HSI data cube $\mathcal{D}$.

    Size of convolution kernels I, J, K.

    Number of convolution kernels U.

Output:

    Feature cube $\mathcal{D}^F$.

 1: **for** $i = 1, 2, \ldots, U$ **do**

 2:    Generate the convolution kernel $\mathcal{K}_i$ with random numbers in $[0, 1]$.

 3:    Obtain the ith feature cube by 3D convolution: $\mathcal{D}_i^F = \mathcal{D} \otimes \mathcal{K}_i$.

 4: **end for**

 5: Obtain feature cube $\mathcal{D}^F = [\mathcal{D}_1^F, \mathcal{D}_2^F, \ldots, \mathcal{D}_U^F]_3$, which is the concatenation of $\mathcal{D}_i^F$ $(i = 1, 2, \ldots, U)$ on the third dimension.

---

4   Experimental Results

After the introduction of proposed RCN algorithm in previous sections, we conduct experiments on two real-world HSI datasets to evaluate the performance of the RCN here. The experimental process of this article is shown in Fig. 3.

4.1   HSI Datasets

Two well-known HSI datasets are adopted for experiments, namely Indian Pines and Pavia University, respectively.

    The Indian Pines was obtained by Airborne Visible/Infrared Imaging Spectrometer (AVIRIS) sensor over the Indian Pine Test Site of Northwestern Indiana on June 12, 1992. The spatial size of the raw image is 145×145, and the spectral size is 220. The noisy bands (bands 104–108, 150–163, and 220) are discarded, so the dataset used for experiments only has 200 bands remained. Indian Pines includes 16 kinds of land-cover classes and 10249 labeled pixels. Table 1 lists the number of labeled samples for each class.

    The second HSI dataset is the Pavia University, which was captured by the ROSIS sensor over the city of Pavia, Italy. After removing 12 noisy bands, the image has the size of $610 \times 340 \times 103$. The Pavia University consists of 9 kinds of land-cover classes and 42776 labeled pixels in total, which are listed in Table 2.

    The numbers of training samples and testing samples are the same as in Ref. [14]. In Indian Pines dataset, the required training set and testing set are listed in Table 1. In Pavia University dataset, we take 50 samples per class as training set, which are listed in Table 2.

4.2   Experimental Design

In order to test the performance of proposed RCN algorithm, following four classification algorithms are compared:

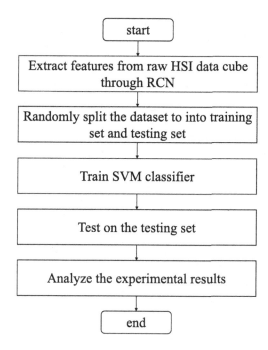

Fig. 3. The experimental process.

Table 1. Indian Pines: the total number of labeled samples and the number of samples in the training set and testing set.

#	Class name	Labled samples	Training set	Testing set
C1	Alfalfa	46	33	13
C2	Corn-notill	1428	50	1378
C3	Corn-min	830	50	780
C4	Corn	237	50	187
C5	Grass/Pasture	483	50	433
C6	Grass/Trees	730	50	680
C7	Grass/Pasture-mowed	28	20	8
C8	Hay-windrowed	478	50	428
C9	Oats	20	14	6
C10	Soybeans-notill	972	50	922
C12	Soybeans-min	2455	50	2405
C12	Soybeans-clean	593	50	543
C13	Wheat	205	50	155
C14	Woods	1265	50	1215
C15	Bldg-Grass-Tree-Drives	386	50	336
C16	Stone-steel towers	93	50	43
	Total	10249	717	9532

– **CNN** [14]: CNN is a kind of feedforward neural network (FNN) with convolution computation and depth structure. It is one of the representative

Table 2. Pavia University: the total number of labeled samples and the number of samples in the training set and testing set.

#	Class name	Labled samples	Training set	Testing set
C1	Asphalt	6631	50	6581
C2	Meadows	18649	50	18599
C3	Gravel	2099	50	2049
C4	Trees	3064	50	3014
C5	Painted metal sheets	1345	50	1295
C6	Bare Soil	5029	50	4979
C7	Bitumen	1330	50	1280
C8	Self-Blocking Bricks	3682	50	3632
C9	Shadows	947	50	897
	Total	42776	450	42326

Fig. 4. The architecture of compared CNN.

algorithms of deep learning, which is widely used in HSI classification. In this paper, the compared CNN consists of an input layer, three convolutional layers with ReLU activation function, two maxpool layers, four fully-connected layers and one output layer. The architecture of compared CNN is shown in Fig. 4. The detailed parameter settings can be found in [14]. It should be noted that the feature extraction process in [14] is quite different from proposed RCN in this paper, we do not re-conduct experiments in [14], and only directly take the accuracies from [14] for comparison.

- **MLP** [14]: Multi-layer perceptron (MLP) compared here has three layers: an input layer, a hidden layer with ReLU as activation function and an output layer with softmax function. The number of nodes in the input layer is equal to the number of bands in the specific HSI dataset, and the output layer contains the same number of nodes as the number of classes. The number of nodes in the hidden layer is calculated by the formula $(n_b + n_c) \cdot \frac{2}{3}$, where n_b and n_c denote the number of bands and classes respectively. Specifically, for the Indian Pines dataset, MLP topology is set to $200 - 144 - 16$, and $103 - 75 - 9$ for the Pavia University dataset. The experimental results are directly taken from [14].

- **ELM** [8]: ELM is a single-layer FNN, the hidden node parameters of which are generated rondomly without using any iterative algorithm. The compared ELM in this paper uses sigmoidal function as activation function and the number of hidden nodes is set to 1000.

- **SPEC-SVM**: As a supervised classification algorithm, SVM is a frequently adopted as a benchmark. Here SVM is applied to raw spectrums. Misclassification penalty parameter is set to $C \in \{2^{-10}, 2^{-9}, \ldots, 2^{10}\}$, and RBF kernel is utilized with parameter $\gamma \in \{2^{-10}, 2^{-9}, \ldots, 2^{10}\}$.

Table 3. Experimental design for testing the size of convolution kernels.

#	1	2	3	4	5	6	7	8
Size of kernels	$(3 \times 3 \times 3) \times 1$	$(3 \times 3 \times 5) \times 1$	$(3 \times 3 \times 7) \times 1$	$(3 \times 3 \times 9) \times 1$	$(5 \times 5 \times 3) \times 1$	$(5 \times 5 \times 5) \times 1$	$(5 \times 5 \times 7) \times 1$	$(5 \times 5 \times 9) \times 1$
#	9	10	11	12	13	14	15	16
Size of kernels	$(7 \times 7 \times 3) \times 1$	$(7 \times 7 \times 5) \times 1$	$(7 \times 7 \times 7) \times 1$	$(7 \times 7 \times 9) \times 1$	$(9 \times 9 \times 3) \times 1$	$(9 \times 9 \times 5) \times 1$	$(9 \times 9 \times 7) \times 1$	$(9 \times 9 \times 9) \times 1$

Table 4. Experimental design for testing the number of convolution kernels.

#	1	2	3	4	5	6
Number of kernels	$(3 \times 3 \times 3) \times 1$	$(3 \times 3 \times 3) \times 2$	$(3 \times 3 \times 3) \times 3$	$(5 \times 5 \times 5) \times 1$	$(5 \times 5 \times 5) \times 2$	$(5 \times 5 \times 5) \times 3$
#	7	8	9	10	11	12
Number of kernels	$(7 \times 7 \times 7) \times 1$	$(7 \times 7 \times 7) \times 2$	$(7 \times 7 \times 7) \times 3$	$(9 \times 9 \times 9) \times 1$	$(9 \times 9 \times 9) \times 2$	$(9 \times 9 \times 9) \times 3$

- **RCN**: The algorithm proposed in this work. Feature cubes are extracted from raw HSI data cube in the convolutional layer of RCN. SVM with RBF kernel is used as the classifier with the same parameters range as that adopted in SPEC-SVM.

In this paper, we design experiments to analyze the effect of convolution kernel sizes and the number of convolution kernels on the accuracies. In all the experiments of RCN, $(I \times J \times K) \times U$ means that RCN adopts U convolution kernels sized $(I \times J \times K)$.

Testing the Size of Kernels: We randomly generate the parameters of 16 convolution kernels with different sizes to analyze the influence of kernel's spatial and spectral sizes on accuracies. The sizes of these 16 convolution kernels are shown in Table 3.

Testing the Number of Kernels: We choose four kinds of basic convolution kernel sizes and set up experiments for analyzing the number of convolution kernels' influence on accuracies. The experimental settings are listed in Table 4.

In order to make the results reliable, we repeat the experiments for 10 times, the training samples and testing samples are randomly selected in each run. The accuracies are averaged over 10 times of experiments.

4.3   Experimental Results and Analysis

Overall accuracy (OA), average accuracy (AA) and kappa coefficient (κ) are adopted as evaluation criteria.

For Indian Pines dataset, the experimental results are shown in Table 5. As we can see in Table 5, the proposed RCN has better performance than CNN, MLP, ELM and SPEC-SVM. For instance, RCN with $(3 \times 3 \times 3) \times 1$ convolution kernel reaches 85.60% OA while MLP obtains 75.24%, ELM obtains 54.12%, and SPEC-SVM obtains 72.91%. Compared with CNN, the accuracies of RCN are approximately 6% higher in OA and AA, 3% higher in κ.

Testing the Size of Kernels: In Table 5, we can see that when spatial size of kernel is fixed, with the increase of spectral size from 3 to 9, the accuracies

Table 5. Indian Pines: accuracies achieved by RCN with different convolution kernel sizes and RCN with different number of convolution kernels and comparisons with other algorithms.

#	C1	C2	C3	C4	C5	C6	C7	C8	C9	C10	C11	C12	C13	C14	C15	C16	OA	AA	κ
CNN	98.70	70.76	78.92	96.54	89.86	97.40	100.00	99.29	100.00	80.39	65.82	80.84	99.61	91.21	91.14	100.00	80.85	90.03	78.44
MLP	98.26	63.40	66.00	86.16	90.52	93.45	97.14	96.32	99.00	75.12	62.81	79.39	98.54	83.65	74.46	98.49	75.24	85.17	72.18
ELM	53.08	42.95	44.26	47.11	73.69	75.72	56.25	57.48	70.00	56.57	42.90	47.59	96.26	71.01	53.90	76.28	54.12	60.32	48.04
SPEC-SVM	93.85	64.61	64.68	84.54	90.42	93.22	88.75	94.21	98.33	74.62	57.24	74.83	98.32	86.59	67.44	96.28	72.91	83.00	69.36
RCN (3 × 3 × 3) × 1	100.00	82.64	83.14	92.94	92.70	97.06	100.00	97.55	95.00	87.45	73.34	89.78	99.35	94.18	87.77	98.37	85.60	91.95	83.61
RCN (3 × 3 × 5) × 1	98.46	82.55	83.73	91.60	93.19	96.72	97.50	98.32	100.00	86.26	73.91	88.73	99.42	94.84	85.06	100.00	85.61	91.89	83.62
RCN (3 × 3 × 7) × 1	92.31	83.89	81.67	93.85	93.90	97.41	98.75	98.06	98.33	86.59	73.08	86.32	99.09	94.34	85.27	99.53	85.36	91.40	83.34
RCN (3 × 3 × 9) × 1	97.69	80.64	80.73	92.67	93.97	96.21	100.00	97.45	96.67	85.08	73.62	89.32	99.22	94.80	84.64	99.07	84.89	91.36	82.79
RCN (5 × 5 × 3) × 1	98.46	86.29	86.65	96.37	91.15	96.43	100.00	99.02	98.33	87.06	78.02	88.68	99.68	94.39	93.69	99.30	87.77	93.34	86.06
RCN (5 × 5 × 5) × 1	99.23	85.71	87.39	96.26	94.16	95.74	98.75	99.25	100.00	86.98	79.61	89.91	99.10	94.40	93.13	99.07	88.27	93.67	86.62
RCN (5 × 5 × 7) × 1	99.23	81.64	85.47	95.56	94.32	97.19	100.00	98.99	98.33	86.62	77.13	90.09	99.10	94.61	92.05	98.84	86.95	93.07	85.13
RCN (5 × 5 × 9) × 1	99.23	84.89	84.03	94.60	92.40	96.69	97.50	98.46	95.00	90.00	75.87	88.45	99.42	93.89	89.85	99.07	86.88	92.46	85.06
RCN (7 × 7 × 3) × 1	100.00	84.10	87.21	96.15	93.03	97.81	100.00	99.86	100.00	86.69	80.23	92.05	99.61	94.45	94.43	99.77	88.46	94.09	86.84
RCN (7 × 7 × 5) × 1	100.00	85.14	87.46	95.56	93.53	97.13	100.00	99.56	98.33	85.37	78.72	89.41	99.16	95.33	93.15	99.77	87.98	93.60	86.30
RCN (7 × 7 × 7) × 1	99.23	85.09	85.56	95.94	91.29	96.50	100.00	99.53	100.00	87.12	80.14	87.61	99.35	93.83	94.79	99.30	87.97	93.46	86.28
RCN (7 × 7 × 9) × 1	99.23	83.50	81.96	94.33	92.49	96.04	100.00	99.58	98.33	87.26	73.12	88.18	99.10	94.45	92.95	99.53	85.72	92.50	83.78
RCN (9 × 9 × 3) × 1	100.00	84.32	85.58	97.01	92.03	97.78	100.00	99.56	100.00	88.20	78.83	89.14	99.81	94.10	95.77	99.54	87.95	93.85	86.27
RCN (9 × 9 × 5) × 1	100.00	84.08	85.03	95.51	93.37	95.47	100.00	99.46	100.00	86.53	78.81	89.39	99.87	94.19	93.39	98.60	87.50	93.36	85.76
RCN (9 × 9 × 7) × 1	100.00	84.22	84.91	96.95	90.62	97.12	100.00	99.25	98.33	86.41	76.87	89.32	99.74	95.30	93.22	98.60	87.15	93.18	85.38
RCN (9 × 9 × 9) × 1	99.23	84.80	81.91	96.37	91.39	96.38	100.00	99.53	98.33	85.10	75.14	85.06	98.84	93.80	94.14	99.30	85.99	92.46	84.06
RCN (3 × 3 × 3) × 2	97.69	82.14	84.99	93.21	93.58	96.65	98.75	98.13	100.00	88.54	75.70	87.57	99.55	93.87	87.29	98.84	86.25	92.28	84.33
RCN (5 × 5 × 5) × 2	97.69	86.37	87.10	95.78	92.38	96.46	98.75	98.37	100.00	87.55	78.97	88.18	99.22	94.11	94.17	99.77	88.06	93.43	86.39
RCN (7 × 7 × 7) × 2	100.00	84.51	84.46	95.40	95.04	96.66	100.00	99.58	95.00	88.17	74.55	89.28	99.35	95.57	94.11	99.77	86.95	93.22	85.17
RCN (9 × 9 × 9) × 2	100.00	83.91	84.37	97.43	91.22	97.06	100.00	99.21	100.00	86.98	75.17	87.20	99.35	94.25	93.33	98.60	86.46	93.01	84.61
RCN (3 × 3 × 3) × 3	98.46	82.37	85.72	94.44	94.00	97.47	100.00	98.13	96.67	86.70	75.22	87.40	99.35	93.63	88.40	99.77	86.14	92.36	84.22
RCN (5 × 5 × 5) × 3	100.00	85.85	86.78	95.03	94.27	97.15	97.50	98.09	100.00	89.88	79.74	90.75	99.35	95.43	92.74	98.84	**88.75**	93.84	**87.17**
RCN (7 × 7 × 7) × 3	99.23	84.71	85.31	95.35	90.74	96.69	100.00	99.74	100.00	87.55	77.17	89.67	99.03	93.43	93.84	100.00	87.20	93.28	85.43
RCN (9 × 9 × 9) × 3	100.00	82.82	84.05	95.19	90.39	97.07	100.00	99.09	96.67	86.78	74.12	87.18	99.42	93.45	95.30	99.07	85.87	92.54	83.94

present a downward trend. RCN obtains maximum accuracies (OA: 88.46%, AA: 94.09%, κ: 86.84%) when the size of convolution kernel is $(7 \times 7 \times 3) \times 1$ in this part.

Testing the Number of Kernels: From Table 5, it can be seen that RCN with two or three convolution kernels is much easier to obtain better accuracies than that with only one kernel. That is to say, multiple convolution kernels may enable RCN to have better recognition ability easily. RCN with $(5 \times 5 \times 5) \times 3$ convolution kernels obtains maximum accuracies (OA: 88.75%, AA: 93.84%, κ: 87.17%).

We can see that best OA (88.75%) and κ (87.17%) are obtained by RCN with $(5 \times 5 \times 5) \times 3$ convolution kernels and RCN with $(7 \times 7 \times 3) \times 1$ convolution kernel reaches best AA (94.09%) in Table 5.

For Pavia University dataset, RCN also reaches higher accuracies than MLP, ELM and SPEC-SVM (see Table 6). When it comes to be compared with CNN, the proposed RCN generally has better performance.

Testing the Size of Kernels: Table 6 shows us that when kernel size is $(5 \times 5 \times 5) \times 1$, RCN reaches best OA (92.48%) and best κ (90.06%) while the maximum AA (92.83%) is obtained by RCN with $(3 \times 3 \times 3) \times 1$ convolution kernel. In general, with the increase of spectral size, the accuracies decrease a little gradually.

Table 6. Pavia University: accuracies achieved by RCN with different convolution kernel sizes and RCN with different number of convolution kernels and comparisons with other algorithms.

#	C1	C2	C3	C4	C5	C6	C7	C8	C9	OA	AA	κ
CNN	79.86	88.97	83.52	**96.31**	99.83	90.72	91.88	82.91	99.65	88.17	90.40	84.63
MLP	81.29	82.83	84.71	91.64	99.18	84.87	89.35	79.57	99.79	84.37	88.14	79.87
ELM	70.20	80.05	72.12	89.56	98.20	78.62	88.14	74.12	99.74	79.35	83.42	73.52
SPEC-SVM	79.35	84.38	78.80	93.12	99.44	84.35	91.78	81.27	**99.86**	84.69	88.04	80.17
RCN (3 × 3 × 3) × 1	88.38	90.74	87.96	92.79	99.94	91.13	96.07	88.80	99.64	90.90	92.83	88.07
RCN (3 × 3 × 5) × 1	90.91	88.09	89.29	91.35	**99.96**	90.71	96.38	86.17	99.63	89.82	92.50	86.73
RCN (3 × 3 × 7) × 1	86.81	89.69	87.45	90.32	99.75	88.68	**97.89**	88.32	99.72	89.71	92.07	86.53
RCN (3 × 3 × 9) × 1	84.96	85.34	88.32	93.54	99.72	89.38	97.17	88.77	99.77	87.88	91.88	84.31
RCN (5 × 5 × 3) × 1	86.08	87.65	86.36	92.22	99.76	88.85	95.86	86.67	99.72	88.60	91.46	85.16
RCN (5 × 5 × 5) × 1	90.97	91.61	84.72	89.08	99.85	95.09	96.25	88.30	99.11	91.67	92.77	89.07
RCN (5 × 5 × 7) × 1	87.95	88.47	87.23	91.30	99.81	90.54	96.71	87.64	99.59	89.54	92.14	86.36
RCN (5 × 5 × 9) × 1	87.35	88.55	86.82	91.29	99.78	90.51	96.77	87.94	99.58	89.48	92.07	86.29
RCN (7 × 7 × 3) × 1	87.46	88.32	86.69	91.49	99.78	90.87	96.55	87.86	99.56	89.43	92.06	86.24
RCN (7 × 7 × 5) × 1	87.96	88.92	86.36	91.08	99.80	91.17	96.43	87.68	99.51	89.74	92.10	86.62
RCN (7 × 7 × 7) × 1	86.09	89.55	84.37	92.22	99.61	90.78	93.41	86.17	96.43	89.38	90.96	86.11
RCN (7 × 7 × 9) × 1	84.22	87.12	80.71	93.91	99.80	90.91	90.47	88.05	95.76	88.04	90.11	84.45
RCN (9 × 9 × 3) × 1	86.10	**95.92**	81.95	92.26	99.75	96.73	94.39	83.88	90.50	**92.48**	91.28	**90.06**
RCN (9 × 9 × 5) × 1	86.75	93.08	81.42	93.53	99.49	**96.90**	94.75	81.23	91.64	91.21	90.98	88.47
RCN (9 × 9 × 7) × 1	85.24	90.27	79.99	91.77	99.49	93.01	93.87	81.73	92.06	89.11	89.71	85.77
RCN (9 × 9 × 9) × 1	82.52	90.57	79.13	91.51	99.86	92.38	92.55	80.87	88.14	88.51	88.61	84.95
RCN (3 × 3 × 3) × 2	**91.02**	86.54	**89.54**	92.27	99.83	92.53	96.20	88.13	99.71	89.61	92.87	86.50
RCN (5 × 5 × 5) × 2	90.37	91.76	86.53	91.67	99.88	95.97	95.75	89.66	99.20	92.12	**93.42**	89.67
RCN (7 × 7 × 7) × 2	87.82	91.23	85.52	91.76	99.75	91.90	94.36	87.01	96.21	90.64	91.73	87.72
RCN (9 × 9 × 9) × 2	82.18	88.98	77.63	92.52	99.37	93.12	94.80	85.56	90.77	88.35	89.43	84.80
RCN (3 × 3 × 3) × 3	87.14	90.63	87.12	94.25	99.83	92.18	96.78	**92.56**	99.76	91.18	93.36	88.46
RCN (5 × 5 × 5) × 3	89.65	91.36	87.54	92.66	99.49	91.26	95.45	89.88	98.95	91.40	92.92	88.70
RCN (7 × 7 × 7) × 3	86.84	91.60	84.67	91.92	99.88	89.85	94.70	87.70	96.28	90.46	91.49	87.47
RCN (9 × 9 × 9) × 3	84.77	92.04	83.73	92.48	99.72	95.13	94.16	83.63	92.38	90.49	90.89	87.53

Testing the Number of Kernels: When the number of convolution kernels increases, to some extent, the accuracies are better than that with a single kernel (see Table 6). In this part, RCN with $(5 \times 5 \times 5) \times 2$ convolution kernels reaches maximum accuracies (OA: 92.12%, AA: 93.42%, κ: 89.67%).

In Table 6, when the size of convolution kernel is $(9 \times 9 \times 3) \times 1$, RCN achieves best OA (92.48%) and κ (90.06%) while RCN with $(5 \times 5 \times 5) \times 2$ convolution kernels reaches best AA (93.42%).

To sum up, the performance of RCN is much better than that of ELM and SPEC-SVM. Also, RCN performs better than CNN in general for it solves the overfitting and ill-conditioned problems in the case of small samples. For RCN itself, increasing the spectral size of convolution kernel may have a negative effect on the accuracies. For a specific HSI dataset, when only one convolution kernel is used, it is meaningful to select the appropriate kernel size to get better generalization ability. When the number of convolution kernels increases, RCN will get better performance in general. In other words, if higher precision is demanded, using multiple convolution kernels is worth trying.

5 Conclusion

In this paper, we have proposed a new network named RCN for joint spectral-spatial feature extraction in HSIs. The proposed algorithm applys the straight-forward solution idea of ELM on the CNN model which has remarkable feature extraction performance. Similar to ELM, the parameters of convolution kernels are randomly generated without any iterative tuning. These 3D convolution kernels form a random convolutional layer of RCN, which is used for feature extraction. After extracting features from raw HSI data, SVM-RBF is used for classification in the output layer. Compared with CNN, it can be seen that RCN greatly reduces the number of parameters which need to be trained so that RCN is easier to obtain more accurate solutions for it avoids overfitting and ill-conditioned problems in the case of small samples. Through the experiments on two HSI datasets in this paper, it can be concluded that the proposed RCN outperforms CNN, MLP, ELM and SPEC-SVM in classification tasks, which proves that RCN is an algorithm with excellent generalization ability and high training efficiency.

References

1. Amin, H.U., et al.: Feature extraction and classification for EEG signals using wavelet transform and machine learning techniques. Aust. Phys. Eng. Sci. Med. **38**(1), 139–149 (2015). https://doi.org/10.1007/s13246-015-0333-x
2. Beck, A., Teboulle, M.: A fast iterative shrinkage-thresholding algorithm for linear inverse problems. SIAM J. Imag. Sci. **2**(1), 183–202 (2009)
3. Chen, Y., Lin, Z., Zhao, X., Wang, G., Gu, Y.: Deep learning-based classification of hyperspectral data. IEEE J. Sel. Top. Appl. Earth Observ. Remote Sens. **7**(6), 2094–2107 (2014)
4. Chen, Y., Jiang, H., Li, C., Jia, X., Ghamisi, P.: Deep feature extraction and classification of hyperspectral images based on convolutional neural networks. IEEE Trans. Geosci. Remote Sens. **54**(10), 6232–6251 (2016)
5. Ham, J., Chen, Y., Crawford, M.M., Ghosh, J.: Investigation of the random forest framework for classification of hyperspectral data. IEEE Trans. Geosci. Remote Sens. **43**(3), 492–501 (2005)
6. Harris, J.R., Rogge, D., Hitchcock, R., Ijewliw, O., Wright, D.: Mapping lithology in canada's arctic: application of hyperspectral data using the minimum noise fraction transformation and matched filtering. Can. J. Earth Sci. **42**(12), 2173–2193 (2005)
7. Hu, B., Lu, Z., Li, H., Chen, Q.: Convolutional neural network architectures for matching natural language sentences. In: Ghahramani, Z., Welling, M., Cortes, C., Lawrence, N.D., Weinberger, K.Q. (eds.) Proceedings of Advance Neural Information Processing Systems, pp. 2042–2050. Curran Associates, Inc. (2014)
8. Huang, G.B., Zhou, H., Ding, X., Zhang, R.: Extreme learning machine for regression and multiclass classification. IEEE Trans. Syst. Man Cybern. **42**(2), 513–529 (2012)
9. Huang, G.B., Zhou, Q.Y., Siew, C.K.: Extreme learning machine: theory and applications. Neurocomputing **70**(1), 489–501 (2006)

10. Huang, S.G., Lyu, I., Qiu, A., Chung, M.K.: Fast polynomial approximation of heat kernel convolution on manifolds and its application to brain sulcal and gyral graph pattern analysis. IEEE Trans. Med. Imag. 1 (2020)
11. Lawrence, S., Giles, C.L., Tsoi, A.C., Back, A.D.: Face recognition: a convolutional neural-network approach. IEEE Trans. Neural Netw. 8(1), 98–113 (1997)
12. Malathi, M., Sinthia, P.: MRI brain tumour segmentation using hybrid clustering and classification by back propagation algorithm. Asian Pac. J. Cancer Prev. 19(11), 3257–3263 (2018)
13. Melgani, F., Bruzzone, L.: Classification of hyperspectral remote sensing images with support vector machines. IEEE Trans. Geosci. Remote Sens. 42(8), 1778–1790 (2004)
14. Paoletti, M., Haut, J., Plaza, J., Plaza, A.: A new deep convolutional neural network for fast hyperspectral image classification. ISPRS J. Photogramm. Remote. Sens. 145, 120–147 (2018)
15. Qian, Y., Ye, M., Zhou, J.: Hyperspectral image classification based on structured sparse logistic regression and three-dimensional wavelet texture features. IEEE Trans. Geosci. Remote Sens. 51(4), 2276–2291 (2013)
16. Schmidhuber, J.: Deep learning in neural networks: an overview. Neural Netw. 61, 85–117 (2015)
17. Xu, C., Lu, C., Gao, J., Zheng, W., Wang, T., Yan, S.: Discriminative analysis for symmetric positive definite matrices on lie groups. IEEE Trans. Circuits Syst. Video Technol. 25(10), 1576–1585 (2015)

MamboNet: Adversarial Semantic Segmentation for Autonomous Driving

Jheng-Lun Liu[2], Augustine Tsai[1,3(✉)], Chiou-Shann Fuh[2], and Fay Huang[3]

[1] The Institute for Information Industry, Taipei, Taiwan
`atsai@iii.org.tw`
[2] Department of CSIE, National Taiwan University, Taipei, Taiwan
`fuh@csie.ntu.edu.tw`
[3] Department of CSIE, National Ilan University, Yilan, Taiwan
`fay@niu.edu.tw`

Abstract. Environment semantic maps provide essential information for autonomous vehicles to navigate in complex road scenarios. In this paper, an adversarial network to complement the conventional encoder-decoder semantic segmentation network is introduced. A newly proposed adversarial discriminator is piggybacked to the segmentation network, which is used to improve the spatial continuity and label consistency in a scene without explicitly specifying the contextual relationships. The segmentation network itself serves as a generator to produce an initial segmentation map (pixel-wise labels). The discriminator then takes the labels and compare them with the ground truth data to further update the generator in order to enhance the accuracy of the labeling result. Quantitative evaluations were conducted which show significant improvement on spatial continuity.

Keywords: Generative Adversarial Network (GAN) · Semantic segmentation · Autonomous driving

1 Introduction

Surrounding understanding is critical to the safety of autonomous vehicles. The ability to recognize the drivable areas and dynamic objects on the road enables the safe navigation. Conventionally, camera frames are used to detect pedestrians, cars, motorcycles, roads, and sidewalks in pixel-level. The goal of this task is to produce semantic segmentations by assigning each input data point, namely a pixel, a unique class label. With the advancements of LiDAR sensor technology in recent years, many commercial products can detect points beyond 200 m. In this paper, we tackled the semantic segmentation task using a rotating LiDAR scanners. Comparing to solely using camera frames, 3D point clouds obtained by LiDAR provide a richer spatial and geometry information. However, the unstructured and sparse nature of the 3D data presents another level of challenges.

The major contribution of this paper is a novel method which can efficiently improve 3D LiDAR point cloud segmentation. We complemented an end-to-end encoder decoder

M. Nguyen et al. (Eds.): ISGV 2021, CCIS 1386, pp. 354–362, 2021.
https://doi.org/10.1007/978-3-030-72073-5_27

segmentation pipeline with an adversarial network which is derived from Generative Adversarial Network (GAN) [1]. The network improves the spatial continuity and label consistency without explicitly specifying the contextual information. The adversarial network was only applied during model training, and was removed during the online inference stage. The complexity of the overall architecture is kept in minimum.

2 Related Work

Semantic segmentation is one of the most important deep learning applications. In 2D image segmentation, U-Net [2] pioneered the encoder-decoder CNN architecture adoption, they transferred the entire feature map from encoders to the corresponding decoders and concatenates them to up-sampled (via deconvolution) decoder feature maps. In order to reduce memory requirements, Kendall [3] proposed to store the max pooling indices instead of concatenation with fewer parameters for decoder reconstruction.

Nowadays, 360° revolving LiDAR is the most common laser scanner for autonomous driving. In order to address 3D point cloud segmentation using aforementioned 2D segmentation paradigm, common approach is to spherically project the 3D point cloud data onto 2D range image plane. Leading the online frame-rate processing for practical applications, Wu [4] proposed a light weighted model derived from SqueezeNet to process data in 2D image plane. SqueezeSegV2 [5] extended V1 with Contextual Aggregation Module (CAM) [6] to mitigate LiDAR sensor data drop out issues.

A synthetic point cloud generation using GTA-V game engine with intensity rendering was also proposed to augment the training data. Due to nonhomogeneous spatial distribution of point cloud, SqeeuzeSegV3 [7] proposed Spatial-Adaptive Convolutions (SAC) which may change the weights according to the input data location. Miliotos [8] extended Wu [4] 3 label classes to 19 classes and replace extended the label classes from three to nineteen, and replaced the 2D CRF to 3D GPU-based nearest neighbor search acting directly on the full, un-ordered point cloud. This last step helps the retrieval of labels for all points in the cloud, even if they are occluded in the range image.

Cortinhal [9] transformed the deep network with Bayesian treatment by introducing uncertainty measures, epistemic and aleatoric noises. Luc [10] introduced an adversarial network to discriminate the predicted segmentation maps either from the ground truth or segmentation network to mitigate the higher order label inconsistencies. Souly [11] introduced a semi-supervised segmentation using weakly labelled data for the generator. In this paper, the proposed MamboNet was inspired by many of these approaches and mostly by Luc's adversarial network.

3 Method

A. *3D to 2D Projection*

The projection method as mentioned in [4, 5, 7–9] has been applied for data pre-processing. Each raw 3D point cloud in 360° surrounding is spherical projected onto a 2D grid point on a range image as illustrated in Fig. 1. A 3D point (x, y, z) with respect to the world coordinate system originated at the sphere center is projected to the image with coordinates of $(\theta_{loc}, \varphi_{loc})$, which is calculated as follows:

$$\theta = \arcsin \frac{z}{\sqrt{x^2 + y^2 + z^2}}, \theta_{loc} = \lfloor \theta / \Delta\theta \rfloor$$
$$\phi = \arcsin \frac{y}{\sqrt{x^2 + y^2}}, \phi_{loc} = \lfloor \phi / \Delta\phi \rfloor \tag{1}$$

Here, $\Delta\theta$ and $\Delta\phi$ are quantization steps. Each grid point represents a five-dimensional feature vector: three for its associated 3D location (x, y, z), one for the intensity value, and the other for the range value.

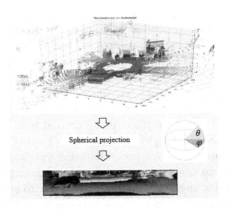

Fig. 1. Spherical projection

B. *Architecture*

The main objective of applying adversarial network is to enforce the spatial continuity and label consistency. Conventional encoder-decoder network [3] creates a segmentation map (pixel-wise labeling), and then follows up with conditional random field (CRF) to impose pixel grouping constraints. We replaced CRF with a discriminator which is only used during the training and can be dropped in inference to maintain minimum network complexity and it is similar to bag of freebies in [11]. Our adversarial network (shown in Fig. 2) is similar to [10], the discriminator takes two inputs, namely, predicted and ground truth maps. Both maps are concatenated with the same 2D input data. The predicted map is generated by the encoder-decoder semantic segmentation network.

A detailed version of the generator is shown in Fig. 3, each yellow block of the encoder is an Inception [13] like module with a group of mixed kernel sizes and dilation rates. Each block has three parallel convolution layers, the outputs are concatenated and then summed up with forth convolution layer. Between encoder and decoder, an Astrous Spatial Pyramid Pooling (ASPP) [2] module is inserted for exploiting multi-scale features and enlarging the receptive field. ASSP is employed to capture small street objects, such as pedestrian and cyclists. In decoder, the conventional transpose convolution layer

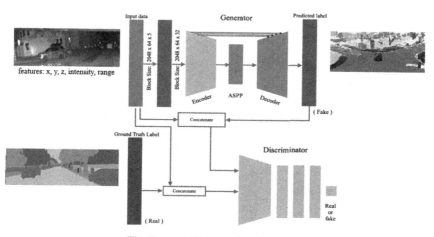

Fig. 2. Overall network architecture

is replaced with the low computation pixel-shuffle layer, similar to super resolution [14]. It can leverage low resolution feature map to generate up-sampled feature maps by converting information of the channel dimension to the spatial dimension. The operation is to convert a feature map of $(H \times W \times Cr^2)$ to $(Hr \times Wr \times C)$, where H, W, C and r are the height, width, number of channel, and up-sampling factor.

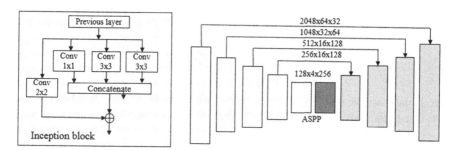

Fig. 3. Details of the generator

The discriminator is a VGG based convolutional network shown in Fig. 4. The data size is $2048 \times 64 \times 6$. The first two dimensions are the image width and height, and the third dimension includes $x, y, z,$ intensity, range, and class label. Each layer uses 3×3 convolution kernel and is followed by a 2×2 max pooling except for the 1st layer. The sizes of the last three fully connected layers are 2048, 512, and 512, respectively.

C. *Loss Function and Training*

The training, shown in Fig. 5, is based on conditional *GAN (cGAN)* [15] architecture. The discriminator, D, learns to classify fake (predicted semantic map) and real (ground truth map). Both generator and discriminator observe the same 2D range imagery input.

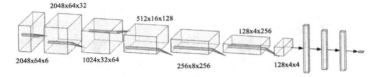

Fig. 4. Discriminator: VGG based convolutional network

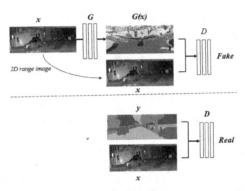

Fig. 5. Conditional GAN training: map 2D range imagery to segmentation map.

There are three lost terms, the first term is the general cross-entropy term for segmentation network (generator), $S(\cdot)$, to predict each location (pixel-wise) of the output map with independent class label. It is a weighted cross-entropy loss as is expressed as.

$$L_{wce} = -\sum_{c\in C} \frac{1}{\sqrt{f_c}} Y_c log(S_c) \qquad (2)$$

where Y and S are the one-hot vector maps for ground truth and predicted label, respectively. Due to the imbalance data nature of the street scene, pedestrians and cyclists are less seen compared to other cars, the way to mitigate the network biases toward to the classes with higher frequency of occurrence is to add a weighted factor f. The second term is the *Lovász -Softmax* loss [16]. The loss is used to improve the intersection-of-union (IoU) or *Jaccard index*. The convex *Lovász* extension of submodular losses relaxes the IoU hypercube constraint where each vertex is a plausible combination of the class labels. Therefore, IoU score can be defined anywhere inside the hypercube. This term is expressed as

$$L_{ls} = \frac{1}{|C|} \sum_{c\in C} \Delta J_C(m(c)) \qquad (3)$$

$$m_i(c) = 1 - x_i(c) \; if \; c = y_i(c)$$
$$= x_i(c), \; otherwise$$

where $x_i(c) \in [0,1]$ is the pixel-wise predicted probability, $y_i(c)$ is the predicted label. The loss will penalize the wrong prediction.

The third term is the adversarial loss which can be expressed as.

$$L_{adv}(G, D) = E_{x,P_{gt}}[log D(x, y)] + E_{x,P_p}[log(1 - D(x, G(x, z)))], \qquad (4)$$

where D is the discriminator which produces *Real* and *Fake* binary outputs, and G generates the predicted label, x is the 2D range image, z is the optional random noise input, P_{gt} is the distribution of ground truth label, y, and P_p is the distribution of the predicted label.

D tries to maximize the *Jensen-Shannon* divergence [1] between P_{gt} and P_p. On the contrary, G tries to minimize the same distribution divergence in order to make P_p. Indistinguishable from P_{gt}. The final objective is a mix-max optimization of the loss summation of cross entropy, *Lovász -Softmax* and adversarial terms as shown in Eq. (5)

$$G^* = arg \min_G \max_D L_{adv} + L_{ls} + L_{ce} \qquad (5)$$

4 Experiments

Semantic KITTI data set [17] was used for algorithm evaluation. The dataset contains 28 classes including classes of non-moving and moving objects. The scanned sequences of 0–10 except 8 were used for training, and sequence 8 was used for validation. Sequences 11–21 was used for testing, however, the annotations for the testing sequence are not available to the general public. In order to evaluate the performance, the labeled data were submitted to Semantic KITTI official server for test results. The evaluation metric is based on *Jaccard Index* or mean Intersection-over-Union (IoU) metric as shown in the Eq. (6).

$$mIoU = \frac{1}{C} \sum_{c=1}^{C} \frac{TP_c}{TP_c + FP_c + FN_c} \qquad (6)$$

where *TP, FP,* and *FN* correspond to the number of true positive, false positive, and false negative predictions for class c, and C is the number of classes.

A. *Quantitative Results*

In Table 1, our method not only out performs most of the 3D point-wise methods [18–21], but also is superior to other projection based methods, especially in small object segmentation, such as person, bicyclist, and motor-cyclist categories. We compare our method with two other networks, the first one is the SalsaNext baseline [9], and the second one is the SalsaNext augmented with a discriminator. The discriminator is a VGG-based convolutional network. In the beginning, we trained the SalsaNext baseline using their open source Github repository, and the test result of mIOU is 57.2, which is a little lower than the published result (59.5) [9]. The discrepancy can be due to the limited batch size [15] in our single board training configuration. In Table 1, SalsaNext with discriminator outperforms baseline in 15 out of 19 categories, and the mIOU of 57.9 is slightly improved. Our method, MamboNet, achieves over one percent mOUT improvement of 58.5.

Table 1. Quantitative results comparison on SemanticKITTI testing set (Sequence 11–21).

	Approach	car	bicycle	motor-cycle	truck	other-vehicle	person	bicyclist	motor-cyclist	road	parking	sidewalk	Other-ground	building	fence	vege-tation	trunk	terrain	Pole	Traffic-sign	mean-IOU
Point-wise	Pointnet	46.3	1.3	0.3	0.1	0.8	0.2	0.2	0.0	61.6	15.8	35.7	1.4	41.4	12.9	31.0	4.6	17.6	2.4	3.7	14.4
	Pointnet++	53.7	1.9	0.2	0.9	0.2	0.9	1.0	0.0	72.0	18.7	41.8	5.6	62.3	16.9	46.5	13.8	30.0	6.0	8.9	20.1
	RandLA-Net	94.2	26.0	25.8	40.1	38.9	49.2	48.2	7.2	90.7	60.3	73.7	20.4	86.9	56.3	81.4	61.3	66.8	49.2	47.1	53.9
	LatticeNet	88.6	12.0	20.8	43.3	24.8	34.2	39.9	60.9	88.8	64.6	73.8	25.5	86.9	55.2	76.4	67.9	54.7	41.5	42.7	52.2
Projection-based	SqueezeSegV2	81.8	18.5	17.9	13.4	14.0	20.1	25.1	3.9	88.6	45.8	67.6	17.7	73.7	41.1	71.8	35.8	60.2	20.2	36.3	39.7
	SqueezeSegV2-CRF	82.7	21.0	22.6	14.5	15.9	20.2	24.3	2.9	88.5	42.4	65.5	18.7	73.8	41.0	68.5	36.9	58.9	12.9	41.0	39.6
	RangeNet++	91.4	25.7	34.4	25.7	23.0	38.3	38.8	4.8	91.8	65.0	75.2	27.8	87.4	58.6	80.5	55.1	64.6	47.9	55.9	52.2
	SqueezeSegV3	92.5	38.7	36.5	29.6	33.0	45.6	46.2	20.1	91.7	63.4	74.8	26.4	89.0	59.4	82.0	58.7	65.4	49.6	58.9	55.9
	SalsaNext (train by ourself)	91.1	43.7	34.3	37.5	29.9	59.1	53.6	30.4	90.9	60.4	73.2	23.6	87.6	56.6	79.5	58.6	63.9	51.3	62.0	57.2
	SalsaNext +Discriminator	91.1	46.6	32.0	37.1	31.8	57.5	55.0	26.2	91.0	61.8	74.7	25.7	87.9	57.6	80.1	61.1	66.2	54.7	62.6	57.9
	MamboNet	92.0	47.4	39.0	25.6	34.6	59.0	57.6	27.8	91.8	64.9	75.0	21.3	88.8	60.5	81.3	64.7	64.7	54.6	61.2	58.5

B. *Qualitative Results*

In Fig. 6, four blocks of segmented map results are shown for visual examination. Each block has three maps, the top is the SalsaNext baseline, the middle one is our method with adversarial discriminator, and the bottom one is the ground true for comparison.

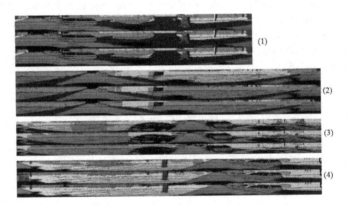

(1)

(2)

(3)

(4)

Fig. 6. Qualitative evaluation with four examples: the top strip of each example is the result without adversary training, the middle strip is with adversary training, and the bottom strip is the ground-truth label.

In the top strip of the first example, there is a small mis-classified pink circle inside the dark purple region (road). The middle strip of the same example, the circle disappears due to the discriminator power of enforcing regional consistency. The same rectification can be observed in the second and third examples, all middle strips correctly identify the fence region (brown), while the top strip mis-classify part of the fence to be the building regions (yellow). Finally in the fourth example, the top strip also misclassifies portion of light green (terrain) to be dark green (vegetation), however, the middle strip correctly identifies the terrain area.

5   Conclusion

We augmented an encoder-decoder segmentation network with an adversarial network to improve the semantic segmentation performance. Adversarial network can implicitly enforce the regional contextual continuity. Unlike conventional CRF and KNN post processing techniques, the adversarial is learnt only during the offline training and is not active during the test. Therefore, the online computation is greatly reduced and yet the comparable results are still attainable.

References

1. Goodfellow, I.J., et al.: Generative adversarial networks. In: NIPS (2014)
2. Ronneberger, O., Fischer, P., Brox, T.: U-net: convolutional networks for biomedical image segmentation. In: Medical Image Computing and Computer-Assisted Intervention (2015)
3. Kendall, A., Badrinarayanan, V., Cipolla, R.: Bayesian SegNet: model uncertainty in deep convolutional encoder-decoder architectures for scene understanding. In: Proceedings of the British Machine Vision Conference (BMVC), pp. 57.1–57.12. BMVA Press (2017)
4. Wu, B., Wan, A., Yue, X., Keutzer, K.: Squeezeseg: convolutional neural nets with recurrent CRF for real-time road-object segmentation from 3D lidar point cloud. In: ICRA (2018)
5. Wu, B., Zhou, X., Zhao, S., Yue, X., Keutzer, K.: Squeezesegv2: improved model structure and unsupervised domain adaptation for road-object segmentation from a lidar point cloud. In: ICRA (2019)
6. Yu, F., Koltun, V.: Multi-scale context aggregation by dilated convolutions. In: ICLR (2016)
7. Xu, C., et al.: Squeezesegv3: spatially-adaptive convolution for efficient point-cloud segmentation, arXiv:2004.01803 (2020)
8. Milioto, A., Vizzo, I., Behley, J., Stachniss, C.: RangeNet++: fast and accurate LiDAR semantic segmentation. In: IROS (2019)
9. Cortinhal, T., Tzelepis, G., Aksoy, E.E., SalsaNext: fast, uncertainty-aware semantic segmentation of LiDAR point clouds for autonomous driving, arXiv:2003.03653 (2020)
10. Luc, P., Couprie, C., Chintala, S., Verbeek, J.: Semantic segmentation using adversarial network. In: 2016, Workshop on Adversarial Training, in NIPS (2016)
11. Souly, N., Spampinato, C., Shah, M.: Semi supervised semantic segmentation using generative adversarial network. In: ICCV (2017)
12. Bochkovskiy, A., Wang, C.Y., Liao, H.Y.M.: YOLOv4: Optimal Speed and Accuracy of Object Detection, arXiv:2004:10934 (2020)
13. Szegedy, C., et al.: Going deeper with convolutions. In: CVPR (2015)
14. Shi, W., et al.: Real-time single image and video super-resolution using an efficient sub-pixel convolutional neural network. In: CVPR (2016)
15. Isola, P., Zhu, J.Y., Zhou, T., Efros, A.A.: Image-to-Image translation with conditional adversarial networks. In CVPR (2017)
16. Berman, M., Triki, A.R., Blaschko, M.B.: The Lovász-softmax loss: a tractable surrogate for the optimization of the intersection-over-union measure in neural networks. In: CVPR (2018)
17. Behley, J., et al.: SemanticKITTI: a dataset for semantic scene understanding of LiDAR sequences. In: Proceedings of International Conference on Computer Vision, Seoul, Korea, p. 17 (2019)
18. Hu, Q., et al.: Randla-net: efficient semantic segmentation of largescale point clouds. In: CVPR (2020)
19. Qi, C.R., Su, H., Mo, K., Guibas, L.J.: Pointnet: deep learning on point sets for 3D classification and segmentation. In: CVPR (2017)

20. Qi, C.R., Yi, L., Su, H., Guibas, L.J.: Pointnet++: deep hierarchical feature learning on point sets in a metric space. In: NIPS (2017)
21. Rosu, R.A., Schütt, P., Quenzel, J., Behnke, S.: LatticeNet: Fast Point Cloud Segmentation Using Permutohedral Lattices, arXiv:1912.05905 (2019)

Effective Pavement Crack Delineation Using a Cascaded Dilation Module and Fully Convolutional Networks

Yasmina Benkhoui[1]([✉]), Tahar El-Korchi[2], and Ludwig Reinhold[1]

[1] Department of Electrical and Computer Engineering, WPI, Worcester, USA
ybenkhoui@wpi.edu
[2] Department of Civil and Environmental Engineering, WPI, Worcester, USA

Abstract. Crack detection in concrete surfaces is a critical structural health monitoring task. In fact, cracks are an early indication of the decaying of the structure that can lead to severe consequences. Manual inspection is time-consuming, costly, and contingent on the subjective judgment of inspectors. To address these challenges, we propose to use state-of-the-art techniques in computer vision to approach the crack delineation problem as a semantic segmentation task where pixels of the same class (background or crack) are clustered together. Our proposed method uses dilated convolution to enlarge the receptive field and preserve the spatial resolution. In this work, we present a fully convolutional network that consists of an encoder, a cascaded dilation module, and a decoder. While the encoder extracts the feature maps from input images, the cascaded dilation module aggregates multi-scale contextual information and finally, the decoder fuses low-level features, performs pixel-wise classification, restores the initial resolution of the images and subsequently outputs the segmentation results. Based on the same meta-architecture, we compare three different dilated encoder-decoder (DED) models: DED-VGG16, DED-ResNet18, and DED-InceptionV3. The three models have been trained and validated using a dataset comprised of 40000 images. For evaluation purposes, we used common performance metrics for semantic segmentation tasks: Precision, Recall, F1-score, IoU, and ROC curves. Our results show that DED-VGG16 achieved the highest accuracy (91.78%) and generated precise visual semantic segmentation results.

Keywords: Semantic segmentation · Deep convolutional neural networks · Dilated convolution · Fully convolutional networks · Crack detection · Critical infrastructure

1   Introduction

According to the U.S. Department of Transportation 2018 National Bridge Inventory (NBI) database [1], 47,052 bridges are classified as structurally deficient or functionally obsolete. More often than not, concrete is used for bridge

© Springer Nature Switzerland AG 2021
M. Nguyen et al. (Eds.): ISGV 2021, CCIS 1386, pp. 363–377, 2021.
https://doi.org/10.1007/978-3-030-72073-5_28

superstructure components such as decks, curbs, sidewalks and pre-stressed concrete beams. Consequently, crack identification in concrete is a crucial aspect of structural health monitoring and serviceability evaluation. However, bridge inspection in the United States is not only complicated but also costly. In fact, this process relies primarily on visual inspection which cannot guarantee accuracy nor reliability and might result in inadequate structural integrity assessment since it is error-prone and dependent on the human judgement. Early research efforts [2] on detecting cracks are mainly built upon image processing techniques (IPTs) such as edge detection (Sobel, Canny, fast Fourier transform, fast Haar transform etc.), image filtering [3] and histogram analysis [4]. While these methods are able to identify cracks, their orientation and width, they are still significantly affected by lighting conditions and image noise; they tend to perform poorly in real-life inspection scenarios. To overcome the aforementioned drawbacks, researchers used IPTs as feature extractors and combined them with machine learning algorithms to identify specific crack characteristics such as depth, width and location within the image. Examples include but are not limited to regionally enhanced multi-phase segmentation technique for damaged surfaces [5], spatially tuned robust multi-feature [6], textural pattern recognition [7] and local directional pattern features [8]. In [9], support-vector machine (SVM) was utilized to identify images with or without cracks from concrete by extracting hand engineered features. The issue in these scenarios is that cracks are idealized and simplified which does not lead to robust crack detection. Other techniques include using unsupervised learning such as k-nearest neighbor [10] where extracted crack pixels are clustered. The advantage of unsupervised learning is that the model does not call for manually annotated data, however, performance is compromised especially under adverse lighting and shading conditions. To address these limitations, Computer Vision and specifically Convolutional Neural Networks (referred to as CNN or ConvNet) are widely used in image classification [11], semantic segmentation [12] and object recognition [13]. The recent surge of interest in deep learning methods is due to its proven ability to outperform previous state-of-the-art techniques [14,15]. Deep convolutional neural networks [16] automatically learn a set of network weights to extract features that are needed to achieve a certain task. In fact, in recent years, state-of-the-art DCNN have outperformed traditional methods and humans in tasks such as edge detection [17] where DCNN successfully labeled crack images at a rate of 99% compared to edge detection techniques which accurately detected 79% of cracked pixels. This outperformance is due to the fact that in DCNNs [18], the features automatically learned during the supervised learning process are more representative of the textural characteristics of the images compared to the features extracted using traditional IPTs.

Semantic segmentation consists of labelling each pixel in an image which leads to a better localization of cracks without using bounding boxes. It can be regarded as classification at the pixel level. Long et al. [19] utilized the classification capabilities of the modern DCNN architectures (AlexNet, VGG-16, GoogLeNet, ResNet) and modified them to get the output granularity required for such a task. This was done by converting the fully connected layers into fully convolutional networks; it consisted of casting the fully connected layers to convolutions with kernels that are equal to their fixed input regions.

Efforts have recently focused on crack detection based on pixel-wise classification. Fully Convolutional Networks (FCNs) [20] and Auto-Encoders [21] are the most popular methods to solve this problem. In [20], the authors proved that the combination of dilated convolution and FCN improves the accuracy of semantic segmentation. The network used ResNet18 and ResNet50 as a backbone and compared their results. The generated feature maps output to five branches where different dilation rates are applied and then concatenated. In our work, we present a cascaded dilation module that works sequentially on the feature maps generated instead of following a parallel process. We show further in this paper the logic behind this reasoning and how it improves the fine details of the crack pixels. In [21], a two-stage algorithm is proposed where the first stage uses two-cascaded auto-encoders to segment the defects while the second stage focuses on classifying the cropped defect regions using a CNN classifier. Furthermore, in [22], the authors present an Encoder-Decoder based method, DeepCrack which is a deep hierarchical network that performs semantic segmentation to detect pavement crack. This architecture is based on SegNet [23] encoder-decoder model. The features generated are fused in pairs at the same scale and concatenated to generate a final fused output. While DeepCrack performs well in extracting thinner cracks, some width information is lost. Similarly, SegNet uses classification networks directly for pixel-wise segmentation. This results in a low resolution output mainly due to max-pooling and subsampling which reduces the feature map quality.

Our work presented in this paper falls into this same context: our aim is to accurately delineate the crack in concrete while preserving high resolution information. To serve this purpose, we propose a dilated convolutional FCN encoder-decoder network based architecture. The contributions of this paper can be summarized as follows:

- We developed an end-to-end trainable crack segmentation network. The designed model is an FCN encoder-decoder equipped with a dilated module that controls the receptive field. The changes of dilation rates effectively enlarge the kernel size without extra computation. As a result, the proposed network is able to obtain more abundant and high spatial resolution features.
- We present three different models based on the same meta-architecture by adopting three different encoder backbones: ResNet, VGG16 and InceptionV3.
- We improve the loss function to offset the highly unbalanced class problem related to the presence of a larger portion of positive pixels compared to negative ones. Positive pixels refer to crack pixels detected whereas negative pixels refer to non-crack pixels.
- We evaluate the crack delineation proposed framework by leading a complete study based on relevant metrics such as Precision, Recall, F-score, ROC curves and IoU.

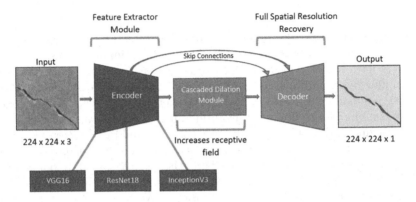

Fig. 1. An illustration of the different modules of the proposed encoder-decoder meta-architecture. This FCN overview shows the three backbone encoders explored in this work (VGG16, ResNet18 and InceptionV3), the cascaded dilation module and the Decoder . We modified the encoder backbone so that we can execute dense prediction tasks by omitting the down-sampling operation in the last two layers. The feature maps generated are then forwarded to the cascaded dilation module which captures information at different spatial scales. Finally, the low-level features obtained by the skip connections are fused with the captured information and the decoder recovers the initial dimensions of the input images.

The remainder of this paper is structured as follows: Sect. 2 provides an overview of the models and methods used for the design of the system. Section 3 describes the implementation details, evaluation metrics used and discusses the results obtained. Finally, we conclude our findings in Sect. 4.

2   Models and Methods

2.1   Overview

In this section, we present the architecture of the FCN proposed for the task of crack delineation. The processing pipeline is illustrated in Figure 1. The encoders used are modified versions of VGG16, Resnet18, and InceptionV3 where the final layers are replaced by the cascaded dilation module. This is needed since the original DCNNs used as encoders will produce a low dimensionality dense representation of the input image; however, they lack fine details which are crucial in our case for crack detection. As illustrated in Sect. 3, there is a high imbalance between the background and the crack pixels in the dataset samples, which results in a biased classifier to the background class during the training process and consequently, generates poor segmentation results. To resolve this problem, we take into account the frequency of each class and use it to improve the softmax cross entropy loss function. Let us assume that the frequency of a given class l in the training data is f_l and that the sum of frequency of all classes (background and crack) is 1, i.e.: $\sum_l f_l = 1$. We add the inverse frequency of each class to the cross entropy loss function which accounts for the pixels with less frequency classes. The cross entropy loss function is given by:

$$loss_{ce} = \frac{-1}{N} \sum_{i=1}^{n} \frac{1}{f_{y_i}} y_i log(p_i)$$ (1)

where N is the total number of pixels in an image, y_i is the class associated with pixel i and pi the predicted probability of a pixel with the correct class label.

2.2 Encoder-Decoder

A crucial step of designing an architecture is the choice of the encoder backbone since it converts the inputs to feature maps. Choosing the right neural network will result in an acceptable convergence rate. Deeper networks with smaller kernels tend to be more performant than shallower networks with larger kernels given a similar number of parameters. Although the pretrained networks VGG16, InceptionV3 and ResNet18 were initially designed for classification tasks, they can be used for segmentation purposes by serving as encoders. Moreover, transfer learning can be leveraged to significantly reduce the training time and would require fewer labeled training data. The earlier layers of a network can be fixed to help extract the main features of the new data and the rest of the layers can be retrained when dealing with a relatively small dataset. In semantic segmentation tasks, the encoder generates a tensor containing the main features such as shape and size illustrated in Fig. 2, whereas the decoder takes this information and produces the segmentation masks. Therefore, to process the generated feature maps, a decoder module is implemented. It proceeds by concatenating low level features from the early blocks of the encoder backbone with convolutional layers, dropout layers, and bilinear interpolations responsible of restoring the initial resolution of the inputs and generating the output maps. Finally, the generated dense filter maps are sent to a softmax classifier which performs pixel-wise classification.

2.3 Dilated Convolutions

Deep Convolutional Neural Networks (DCNNs) integrate context assimilation through continuous pooling and down-sampling layers, resulting in a loss of detail information about the object edges and degradation of the image resolution. One of the main issues of using a basic FCN architecture to perform semantic segmentation tasks is restoring the original image from a low resolution one. Thus, to perform pixel-wise labelling, the output resolution has to be increased which can be done using one of the three following methods:

– Deconvolutions: are based on creating the inverse layer of a convolutional layer. Since these deconvolution layers need to be trained, the network becomes deeper and more expensive.

Fig. 2. Visualization of the Feature Maps Extracted From the First Convolutional Layer in Encoder (In this case VGG16)

- Unpooling: This operation is the opposite of pooling, it consists of storing the winning activations in the different pooling layers. To restore the original input resolution, each pixel is set to the corresponding winning activation whereas its neighboring are set to 0.
- Dilated convolutions: Proposed by Yu et al. [24], this approach exponentially enlarges the receptive field which results in a denser feature map. This method uses kernels of the same size as a basic convolutional layer but captures a larger field of view through the insertion of "holes" which are zero values as shown in Fig. 3. As a result, the resolution is preserved while the receptive field of the kernel is exponentially increased.

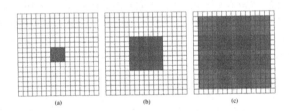

Fig. 3. Dilation leads to an exponential increase in the field of view without losing resolution. (a) 1 Dilated Convolution, (b) 2 Dilated Convolution, (c) 4 Dilated Convolution. The receptive field grows in an exponential fashion while the number of parameters increases linearly.

A 2D dilated convolution can be defined as follow:

$$y(m,n) = \sum_{i=1}^{M} \sum_{j=1}^{N} x(m+r, n+n+r \times j) w(i,j) \tag{2}$$

Where y(m, n) is the output of the dilated convolution from input x(m, n) and a filter w(i, j) with the length and the width of M and N respectively. The parameter r is the dilation rate. If r = 1, a dilated convolution turns into a normal convolution. As the dilation rate r increases, the receptive field exponentially enlarges as shown in Fig. 4:

Let $F : \mathbb{Z}^2 \rightarrow \mathbb{R}$ be a discrete function. Let $\Omega_r = [-r, r]^2 \cap \mathbb{R}$ be a discrete filter of size $(2r + 1)^2$. Here the discrete convolution operator $*$ is defined as:

$$(F * k)(p) = \sum_{s+t=p} F(s)k(t) \tag{3}$$

We now generalize this operator. Let l be a dilation factor and let $*_l$ be defined as:

$$(F *_l k)(p) = \sum_{s+lt=p} F(s)k(t) \tag{4}$$

We will refer to $*_l$ as a dilated convolution or an l-dilated convolution. The familiar discrete convolution $*$ is simply the 1-dilated convolution. Let $F_0, F_1, ..., F_n - 1 : \mathbb{Z}^2 \rightarrow \mathbb{R}$ be discrete functions and let $k_0, k_1, ..., k_{n-2} : \Omega_1 \rightarrow \mathbb{R}$ be discrete 3 × 3 filters. Let's consider that we are applying a dilated filter with an exponential increase where: $F_i + 1 = F_{i*2^i}k_i$ for $i = 0, 1, ..., n - 2$ The receptive field of the element p in F_{i+1} is defined as a set of elements in F_0 that modify the value of $F_{i+1}(p)$. Assume that the size of each element in F_{i+1} is $(2^{i+2} - 1) \times (2^{i+2} - 1)$. We implement a cascaded dilation module with geometrically increasing dilation scale (i.e. 1, 2, 4, 8) . Figure 4 illustrates the cascaded module used in this work. It efficiently expands receptive field without increasing the number of parameters of the network.

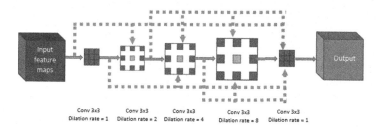

Fig. 4. Illustration of the proposed cascaded dilation module with geometrically increasing dilation scale. The final layer is a 1-dilation convolution to fuse all the former outputs.

3   Experimental Study and Evaluation

3.1   Implementation Details

The experimental platform of this study is Keras [25] with Tensorflow [26] backend, Intel Quad-Core i7-6700HQ CPU and NVIDIA GeForce GTX1060 GPU.

We used the training and validation set to estimate our hyper-parameters and avoid the adjustment of the model to the test set. For each hyper-parameter, we train the network on the training set then test it on the validation set. Subsequently, the best setup was selected to train the final model. Our network was trained for 40 epochs and a batch size of 16. The initial learning rate was set to 0.001, we used cross entropy as a loss function and Adam [27] as an optimization algorithm. Given the relatively small dataset used, over-fitting is likely to happen, therefore, to avoid over-fitting, we used a dropout rate of 50% during the training process.

3.2 Dataset

The data used in this work are 2D-RGB annotated images collected from various METU Campus building [28]. The dataset is comprised of 40000 images, 20000 for each class (Positive: images with cracks, negative: images with no cracks.) Fig. 5 shows sample images from the dataset.

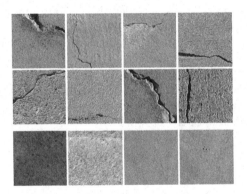

Fig. 5. Sample images from the dataset used in this work. The top two rows illustrate images with defects whereas the bottom row has distress free images.

The resolution of the images is $227 \times 227 \times 3$. VGG16 and ResNet18 require 224×224 input images whereas InceptionV3 need 299×299 data input, therefore, we had to pre-process the images by re-scaling them in order to be accepted as inputs to the three different encoders used in this work. We split the dataset into 3 parts: 60% of the images are used for training, 20% for validation and 20% for testing. The training set was used to train the model and the verification set to observe the performance of the model during the training process. The parameters were then saved and the model was evaluated using the test set. The images included in the dataset are diversified, they are captured in different lighting conditions, have different surface roughness, color, scaling and edges.

3.3   Performance Metrics and Evaluation

In this section, we describe performance metrics used to evaluate and analyze the semantic image segmentation results. While Overall accuracy assesses the proportion of correctly labeled pixels, Per-Class accuracy represents the percent of correctly classified pixels of each individual class. When we consider Per-Class accuracy, we are essentially evaluating a binary mask; a pixel that is correctly attributed to a given class is a true positive whereas a pixel incorrectly attributed to a class is a true negative. The overall accuracy is given by:

$$Acc_{overall} = \frac{T_P + T_N}{T_P + T_N + F_P + F_N} \tag{5}$$

where F_P and F_N represent false positives and false negatives respectively. However, this metric might lead to ambiguous results in the presence of very imbalanced class pixels in a segmented image. Therefore, we adopt the following metrics:

- Precision: also called positive predictive value is the fraction of relevant instances among all retrieved ones. In other words, out of all detected cracks how many are actually matching the ground truth. Precision is computed as follows:

$$Precision = \frac{T_P}{T_P + F_P} \tag{6}$$

- Recall: also known as sensitivity answers the following question: of all the crack annotated in the ground truth, how many were effectively captured as positive predictions in the segmented images. It is calculated as follows:

$$Recall = \frac{T_P}{T_P + F_N} \tag{7}$$

- F-score: measures a test's accuracy. It is the weighted harmonic mean of the test's precision and recall.

$$F_{score} = \left(\frac{Precision^{-1} + Recall^{-1}}{2} \right)^{-1} \tag{8}$$

$$F_{score} = 2 \left(\frac{Precision.Recall}{Precision + Recall} \right) \tag{9}$$

- IoU: also known as Jaccard index, it is used to determine how accurate is the segmentation of a given image when compared to ground truth segmentation. It is defined as follows:

$$IoU = \frac{T_P}{T_P + F_P + F_N}. \tag{10}$$

- ROC curve: receiver operating characteristic curve is a plot that summarizes the performance of a given network at correctly classifying an object into the positive class, in our case, a crack. While the x-axis indicates the

False Positive Rate (specificity), the y-axis indicates the True Positive Rate (sensitivity). Therefore, ROC curve enables us to plot the fraction of correct predictions for the positive class versus the fraction of errors of the negative one. The best classifier has its ROC curve towards the top-left of the plot where the fraction of correct predictions is close to 1 and the fraction of incorrect negative predictions are close to 0. Specificity and sensitivity are defined as follows:

$$Specificity = FPR = \frac{FP}{FP + TN}. \tag{11}$$

$$Sensitivity = TPR = \frac{TP}{TP + FN}. \tag{12}$$

- AUC: the Area under ROC curve is usually calculated to give a single score to a model across all threshold values. It can be transcribed as the probability that the scores of a classifier will rank randomly chosen positive occurrences higher than randomly chosen negative ones.

We used VGG-16, ResNet18, and InceptionV3 as encoders in the experimental study of this work. The input resolution of VGG-16 and ResNet18 is $224 \times 224 \times 3$ whereas the input size of InceptionV3 is $299 \times 299 \times 3$. To experiment with these networks, we resize the images before feeding the data into the three models for training and testing.

Figures 6 shows that DED-InceptionV3 has a higher loss than both suggested networks: DED-VGG16 in Fig. 7 and DED-ResNet18 in Fig. 8.

We also observe that the loss of DED-VGG16 is higher than that of DED-ResNet18, but this trend becomes inverted during the test process. Moreover, the VGG-based network computation time is 2348.60 s whereas the ResNet-based network and InceptionV3-based network achieve a computation time of 3152.70 s and 8137.30 s respectively. Therefore, DED-VGG16 is faster, which can be explained by less numbers of parameters. Moreover, DED-VGG16 performed the most with an IoU of 91.78% whereas DED-ResNet18 achieved 89.36% IoU and DED-InceptionV3 78.26% IoU. This also means that our proposed networks are effective at detecting fine details of the cracks since it exploits the cascaded dilation module to detect multi-scale features from multi-scale information in image inputs.

Table 1 shows the performance of the 4 semantic segmentation networks: DED-VGG16, DED-ResNet18, DED-InceptionV3 and U-Net [29]. DED-VGG16 performed the most in terms of Precision, Recall and F1-score.

Figure 9 shows the ROC curves of the different tested models and compares them to state-of-the-art model U-Net. The ROC curves of DED-VGG16, DED-ResNet 18 and U-Net on the METU dataset are comparable and the AUC of these two networks are 0.98, 0.96 and 0.92 respectively contrary to the AUC of DED-InceptionV3 that achieved 0.79. We notice that DED-VGG16 has a 2% improvement over U-Net, in fact, DED-VGG16 has a larger receptive field which enables it to capture more details especially the thin cracks as it can be seen in the qualitative results obtained.

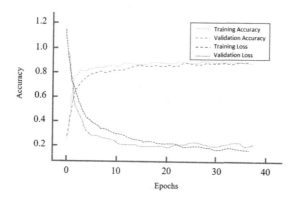

Fig. 6. Accuracy and loss of Training/Validation of DED-VGG16

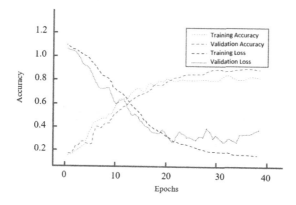

Fig. 7. Accuracy and loss of Training/Validation of DED-InceptionV3

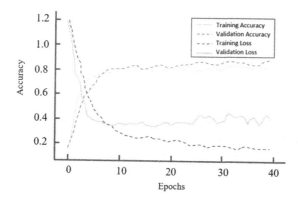

Fig. 8. Accuracy and loss of Training/Validation of DED-ResNet18

Table 1. Comparison of the three proposed networks and U–Net based on Precision, Recall and F1-score.

Network	Precision	Recall	F1-score
DED-VGG16	0.9367	0.9216	0.9290
U-Net	0.9135	0.8973	0.9053
DED-ResNet18	0.8804	0.7958	0.8359
DED-InceptionV3	0.8674	0.7349	0.7956

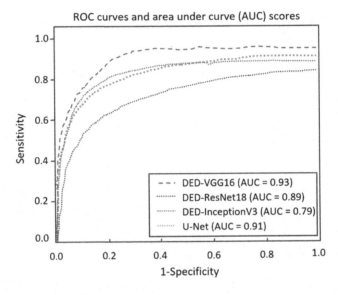

Fig. 9. ROC curves of the four compared networks: DED-VGG16, DED-ResNet18, DED-InceptionV3 and U-Net

Our results indicate that the proposed framework is efficient at performing an end-to-end crack delineation by differentiating between the background (non-cracked concrete, shadows, stains etc.) and the crack pixels. The use of CNNs encoders resulted in a robust feature extraction compared to traditional methods that consist of designing feature extractors manually. In fact, they require tuning to adapt to more complex samples, additional storage and are not suited for real-time applications. The cascaded module proposed has different dilation rates which increases the robustness of features extraction and integrate multi-scale context without reducing the resolution of the feature maps. This results in an overall improvement of the accuracy of crack delineation. The qualitative results obtained are shown in Fig. 10.

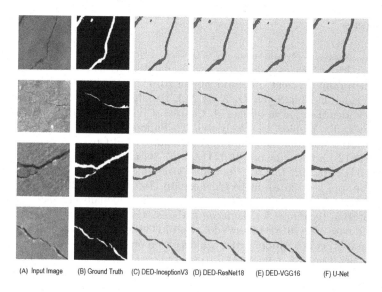

(A) Input Image   (B) Ground Truth   (C) DED-InceptionV3   (D) DED-ResNet18   (E) DED-VGG16   (F) U-Net

Fig. 10. Qualitative results for the proposed networks based on encoder-decoder architecture combined with a cascaded dilation module on the cracks dataset.

4   Conclusions

In this work, we present an end-to-end crack delineation framework based on an encoder-decoder meta-architecture. The model is equipped with a cascaded dilation module to enlarge the receptive fields and skip connections to fuse low-level information. First, the image samples are fed to the encoder that extracts high-level features; then, the cascaded dilation module captures context information at different scales which finally go through upsampling where they are fused with low-level features. The combination of different levels of information leads to a detailed delineation of the cracks. Although all three networks show satisfactory experimental results, DED-VGG16 achieved the best performance with a precision of 93%, recall of 92%, F1-score of 92%, and IoU of 91.78% which are higher compared to DED-InceptionV3 and DED-ResNet18. Also, the semantic segmentation qualitative results show that the framework presented is not only accurate but also robust enough to overcome interferences present in the image samples. Finally, deep Learning technics have known a tremendous amount of attention over the last few years in applications from all fields. Similarly, the civil and transportation field can benefit from these advances especially in monitoring and inspecting civil infrastructures such as bridges. As a result condition and health assessment of structures can become truly automated, cost-effective and, safe.

References

1. ARTBA analysis reveals over 47,000 U.S. bridges are structurally deficient (2019). https://roadsbridges.com/artba-analysis-reveals-over-47000-us-bridges-are-structurally-deficient. Accessed 24 Jan 2019
2. Abdel-Qader, I., Abudayyeh, O., Kelly, M.E.: Analysis of edge-detection techniques for crack identification in bridges. J. Comput. Civil Eng. **17**(4), 255–263 (2003)
3. Nishikawa, T., Yoshida, J., Sugiyama, T., Fujino, Y.: Concrete crack detection by multiple sequential image filtering. Comput. Aided Civil Infrastruct. Eng. **27**, 29–47 (2012). https://doi.org/10.1111/j.1467-8667.2011.00716.x
4. Dinh, T.H., Ha, Q., La, H.: Computer vision-based method for concrete crack detection, pp. 1–6 (2016). https://doi.org/10.1109/ICARCV.2016.7838682
5. O'Byrne, M., Ghosh, B., Schoefs, F., Pakrashi, V.: Regionally enhanced multiphase segmentation technique for damaged surfaces. Comput. Aided Civil Infrastruct. Eng. **29**, 644–658 (2014). https://doi.org/10.1111/mice.12098
6. Prasanna, P., et al.: Automated crack detection on concrete bridges. IEEE Trans. Autom. Sci. Eng. **13**, 1–9 (2014). https://doi.org/10.1109/TASE.2014.2354314
7. Cord, A., Chambon, S.: Automatic road defect detection by textural pattern recognition based on AdaBoost. Comput. Aided Civil Infrastruct. Eng. **27**, 244–259 (2012). https://doi.org/10.1111/j.1467-8667.2011.00736.x
8. Chen, J.H., Su, M., Cao, R., Hsu, S., Lu, J.: A self organizing map optimization based image recognition and processing model for bridge crack inspection. Autom. Constr. **73**, 58–66 (2017). https://doi.org/10.1016/j.autcon.2016.08.033
9. Sharma, M., Sharma, M., Leeprechanon, N., Anotaipaiboon, W., Chaiyasarn, K.: PCA Based SVM Classification Approach for Crack Detection in Concrete Structures (2016)
10. Zhang, A., Wang, K., Ji, R., Li, Q.: Efficient system of cracking-detection algorithms with 1-mm 3D-surface models and performance measures. J. Comput. Civil Eng. **30**, 04016020 (2016). https://doi.org/10.1061/(ASCE)CP.1943-5487.0000581
11. Convolutional Neural Network Model Innovations for Image Classification (2019). https://machinelearningmastery.com/. Accessed 28 Feb 2020
12. Yuan, Y., Chen, X., Wang, J.: Object-Contextual Representations for Semantic Segmentation. ArXiv 2019, arXiv:1909.11065
13. Zhao, Z., Zheng, P., Xu, S., Wu, X.: Object Detection with Deep Learning: A Review. ArXiv 2019, arXiv:1807.05511v2
14. Cha, Y.J., Choi, W., Buyukozturk, O.: Deep learning-based crack damage detection using convolutional neural networks. Comput. Aided Civil Infrastruct. Eng. **32**, 361–378 (2017). https://doi.org/10.1111/mice.12263
15. Fan, Z., Wu, Y., Lu, J., Li, W.: Automatic Pavement Crack Detection Based on Structured Prediction with the Convolutional Neural Network (2018)
16. Krizhevsky, A., Sutskever, I., Hinton, G.: ImageNet classification with deep convolutional neural networks. Neural Inf. Process. Syst. **25**, 1097–1105 (2012). https://doi.org/10.1145/3065386
17. Dorafshan, S., Thomas, R., Maguire, M.: Comparison of deep convolutional neural networks and edge detectors for image-based crack detection in concrete. Constr. Build. Mater. **186**, 1031–1045 (2018). https://doi.org/10.1016/j.conbuildmat.2018.08.011
18. LeCun, Y., Bengio, Y., Hinton, G.: Deep Learn. Nature **521**, 436–44 (2015). https://doi.org/10.1038/nature14539

19. Long, J., Shelhamer, E., Darrell, T.: Fully Convolutional Networks for Semantic Segmentation. Arxiv. 2014
20. Zhang, J., Lu, C., Wang, J., Wang, L., Yue, X.: Concrete cracks detection based on FCN with dilated convolution. Appl. Sci. **9**, 2686 (2019). https://doi.org/10. 3390/app9132686
21. Yusiong, J.P., Naval, P.: Multi-scale Autoencoders in Autoencoder for Semantic Image Segmentation (2019). https://doi.org/10.1007/978-3-030-14799-0_51
22. Zou, Q., Zhang, Z., Li, Q., Qi, X., Wang, Q., Wang, S.: DeepCrack: learning hierarchical convolutional features for crack detection. IEEE Trans. Image Process. **28**, 1 (2018). https://doi.org/10.1109/TIP.2018.2878966
23. Badrinarayanan, V., Kendall, A., Cipoll, R.: SegNet: a deep convolutional encoder-decoder architecture for image segmentation. IEEE Trans. Pattern Anal. Mach. Intell **39**, 2481–2495 (2015). https://doi.org/10.1109/TPAMI.2016.2644615
24. Yu, F., Koltun, V.: Multi-scale Context Aggregation by Dilated Convolutions (2015)
25. Keras (2015). https://keras.io
26. Abadi, M., et al.: TensorFlow: A system for large-scale machine learning (2016)
27. Kingma, D., Ba, J.: Adam: A Method for Stochastic Optimization. International Conference on Learning Representations (2014)
28. Çağlar F.Ö.: Concrete Crack Images for Classification (2018). https://doi.org/10. 17632/5y9wdsg2zt.1
29. Ronneberger, O., Fischer, P., Brox, T.: U-Net: convolutional networks for biomedical image segmentation. In: Navab, N., Hornegger, J., Wells, W.M., Frangi, A.F. (eds.) MICCAI 2015, Part III. LNCS, vol. 9351, pp. 234–241. Springer, Cham (2015). https://doi.org/10.1007/978-3-319-24574-4_28

D-GaussianNet: Adaptive Distorted Gaussian Matched Filter with Convolutional Neural Network for Retinal Vessel Segmentation

Dora E. Alvarado-Carrillo[1]([⊠]) [iD], Emmanuel Ovalle-Magallanes[2] [iD],
and Oscar S. Dalmau-Cedeño[1] [iD]

[1] Center for Research in Mathematics (CIMAT), 36000 Guanajuato, GTO, Mexico
{dora.alvarado,dalmau}@cimat.mx
[2] University of Guanajuato, 36885 Salamanca, GTO, Mexico
e.ovallemagallanes@ugto.mx

Abstract. Automating retinal vessel segmentation is a primary element of computer-aided diagnostic systems for many retinal diseases. It facilitates the inspection of shape, width, tortuosity, and other blood vessel characteristics. In this paper, a new method that incorporates Distorted Gaussian Matched Filters (D-GMFs) with adaptive parameters as part of a Deep Convolutional Architecture is proposed. The D-GaussianNet includes D-GMF units, a variant of the Gaussian Matched Filter that considers curvature, placed at the beginning and end of the network to implicitly indicate that spatial attention should focus on curvilinear structures in the image. Experimental results on datasets DRIVE, STARE, and CHASE show state-of-the-art performance with an accuracy of 0.9565, 0.9647, and 0.9609 and a F1-score of 0.8233, 0.8141, and 0.8077, respectively.

Keywords: Retinal blood vessel segmentation · Gaussian matched filter · Convolutional neural network

1 Introduction

Fundus retinal imaging is a popular non-invasive technique for monitoring the retinal structure, which consists of obtaining a two-dimensional projection of the retinal semitransparent tissues, using specialized cameras with reflective light [1,5]. Fundus images are highly important for the early diagnosis and tracking of various diseases related to vascular changes, such as diabetic retinopathy, age-related macular degeneration, and glaucoma, since the retina is the only structure that allows direct imaging of blood circulation [3,22,37].

This work is partially supported by CONACyT, Mexico (Doctoral Studies Grants no. 626155 and 626154).

M. Nguyen et al. (Eds.): ISGV 2021, CCIS 1386, pp. 378–392, 2021.
https://doi.org/10.1007/978-3-030-72073-5_29

The retinal vascular tree is a major structure to be studied in the analysis of fundus images. Inspection of shape, width, tortuosity, and other blood vessel characteristics contributes to identify many retinal diseases [4,18]. Moreover, the detection and subtraction of the vascular tree facilitate the recognition of other lesions that appear in the retina, so a precise delineation of the vessels is required. However, fundus images are characterized by low contrast and notable illumination changes [32,41]. In addition, blood vessels consist of a varied morphology: vessels are bifurcated, tortuous, and their width is reduced to extremely thin sections. Hence, blood vessel detection is a time-consuming task, its manual fulfillment is usually limited by the availability of ophthalmologists in the healthcare system, resulting in diagnosis delays and elevated treatment costs [5,19].

As an alternative to contribute to the early diagnosis of eye diseases, several methods for automating blood vessel segmentation have been presented in recent years. Nevertheless, the task is considered a challenging problem up to date, since there are conditions—for instance, the similarity in color between vessels and microaneurysms, the central reflex in some vessels, the presence of multiple branching points and neovascularization, among others—where the state-of-the-art algorithms have difficulties to perform an accurate result. Furthermore, many recent deep learning methods use generic architectures for feature extraction, whose performance is strongly tied to the quantity and quality of the examples available in the training phase. Since in the area of biomedical image processing, it is common to work with a limited number of examples, different training strategies are required. Frequently, this issue is overcome by applying transferred learning [18,25,29] or using patches rather than full images for training [9,11,19,23], while a few papers have proposed hybrid techniques for feature extraction [12,34]. In this paper, a new method that incorporates distorted Gaussian Matched Filters with adaptive parameters as part of a Deep Convolutional Architecture is proposed. The strategy aims to alleviate the traditional neural convolutional models' dependence on large datasets, by aggregating robustness through a hybrid design that considers both *a priori* information about the curvilinear shape of the vessels, as well as deep learning techniques. The contributions of this paper are as follows: first, a new technique for incorporating curvature into Gaussian Matched Filters, Distorted GMF (D-GMF), is presented. The approach intends to relax the strong assumption that blood vessels are piecewise linear; second, a preprocessing method based on random quantum circuits is integrated into a deep learning strategy for blood vessel segmentation. To the best of the authors' knowledge, this is the first time a quantum preprocessing has been applied for fundus images, although there are few related works in the area of biomedical imaging [2,14]; third, a novel neural convolutional architecture with adaptive units of distorted Gaussian Matched Filters is presented, the units are placed at the beginning and end of the network to implicitly indicate that spatial attention should focus on elongated structures in the image.

The rest of the paper is organized as follows. In Sect. 2, a brief review of the related work is presented. In Sect. 3, the key elements of the proposed method—quantum preprocessing, distorted Gaussian Matched Filters, and the Convolutional Neural architecture—are explained in detail. In Sect. 4, experimental results and comparison with state-of-the-art approaches are presented. In Sect. 5, a discussion on the proposed method is carried out.

2   Related Work

Based on the type of information applied in the process, automatic blood vessel segmentation methods can be classified into two large groups: unsupervised and supervised methods. For both approaches, a brief review of related work is presented below.

2.1   Unsupervised Methods

Unsupervised methods purely use prior knowledge about vascular structure—such as length, width, and grayscale intensity—to design strategies that highlight the vessels.

Template filtering methods use predefined templates to model the elongated shape of the vessels. Khan *et al.* [20] present generalized multiscale line detectors, by proposing adjustable window size in filters: the window and line sizes grow proportionally, instead of fixing one or both of them. Filter orientations are estimated locally. Line detectors perform well for detecting thin vessels, as the line template always maintains a width of one pixel. However, the resulting images often contain artifacts and require post-processing.

Morphological methods use operations such as dilation and erosion to discard round structures and highlight curvilinear vessel alike elements. Sazak *et al.* [28] propose a method based on two banks of structuring elements at different scales. The first bank contains disks with varied diameters, the second bank contains lines of different thickness and orientation. For both banks, opening operations are performed with the input image. Then, difference images are computed between disk and line results, the maximum response is preserved. This combination of structuring elements produces better segmentation results in vessel bifurcations. Pal *et al.* [26] use morphological operations to improve image contrast and segment the vascular structure. First, a Top-Hat Transform is combined with the wavelet Transform to highlight the vessels, improve contrast, and eliminate the optic disc; then, the Hit-or-Miss Transform is applied with two structuring elements, one to highlight the background and the other to highlight vessels at different scales. For each scale, the difference between the two outputs is obtained, the final image is computed as the maximum of these differences.

Tracking methods use vessel connectivity to distinguish the vascular region. Given an initial point and direction, the vessels' edges and their bifurcations are determined by exhaustive search using tracking strategies. Zhao *et al.* [40] propose an algorithm based on multiscale SLIC superpixels to reduce the number of possible paths to be traced. The multiscale is built by varying the superpixel size, then a filtering process is implemented to select the correct scale, considering intensity and variance.

The methods reviewed in this section do not need additional information to perform the segmentation task. However, their performance is moderate, as their ability to model the intricate vascular structure is limited, noise artifacts are created in the output image, and require meticulous selection of their parameters.

2.2   Supervised Methods

Supervised methods require manually labeled data. The segmentation task is approached as a classification problem: a classifier is trained—using labeled examples—to assign a class to each pixel in the input image, so that the pixels with the same label share certain features. In the case of blood vessel segmentation, the classification is binary, since the goal is to differentiate the region with blood vessels, *i.e.*, class 1, from the rest of the image, *i.e.*, class 0. Condurache *et al.* [7] propose to use different filters (Bothat transform, Hessian Matrix, Laplacian Pyramid) to obtain vascular maps that emphasize pixels belonging to elongated structures of a certain width. From these maps, feature vectors are created for each pixel, which feeds a classifier based on hysteresis. Wang et al. [36] present a different method with a divide and conquer strategy, which consists of clustering pixels according to the width of the blood vessel and its position in it (whether it is in the center or on the edge). The clusters are obtained using 2-D Gabor wavelet kernels, then a funnel architecture composed of SVM classifiers is used to classify the pixels, initially in three classes (vessel, no vessel, uncertain) and in a final stage in two classes. Liskowski *et al.* [23] propose a neural network for automatic blood vessel segmentation. The architecture consists of four convolutional layers with an increasing number of filters (64, 64, 128, and 128 filters, respectively) and three fully connected layers (521, 512, and 2 neurons, respectively). Feng et al. [9], inspired by the design of the UNet [27], propose a cross-architecture in which the most superficial layers are densely connected to the deepest layers of the network. The model does not use an encoder-decoder design, instead each block outputs an activation map of the same dimensions, which simplifies the fusion between maps from different levels in the network. Jin *et al.* [19] propose to replace traditional convolutions with deformable convolutions to overcome some of the limitations of the UNet model. Adaptive receptive fields are included in the network's design to capture the complicated structure of blood vessels. The architecture shows the ability to extract thin vessels, but the computational time increases considerably, compared to models on which it is based, UNet and Deformable-ConvNet. Li *et al.* [21] propose to take as a starting point an initial prediction obtained with a UNet architecture and to refine the result iteratively, using a simplified version of the UNet, called mini-unet. This approach allows the model to make corrections on the initial prediction, *e.g.*, disconnected vessel segments that should be connected. The number of iterations of the mini-unet is a parameter that must be adjusted carefully, as a bad selection may cause overfitting.

Manual feature extraction methods have a direct interpretation of the criteria used for segmentation and their performance is good when trained with a database of moderate size. However, in recent years these techniques have been surpassed by the ability of Deep Neural Networks for automatic feature extraction and model generalization. This last approach also has its limitations, it requires a greater number of examples in the training step, and like its hand-crafted counterpart has difficulties detecting thin vessels, bifurcations, and central vessel regions with reflexes, among other cases.

In this paper, a new method that considers both *a priori* information on the vessels' geometry and automatic extraction of features is presented. The following section describes the algorithm in detail.

3   Methods/Methodology

The proposed method consists of a Residual Network where Distorted Gaussian Matched Filters have been incorporated. In this section, we briefly cover the topics of Quantum Convolutional Layers for Image Preprocessing, Residual Networks, and Gaussian Matched Filters, since these elements are a fundamental part of the algorithm. Subsequently, the proposed strategy to incorporate a curvature component to GMFs and their incorporation into the neuronal architecture are described in detail.

3.1   Quantum Preprocessing

Fundus images are affected by illumination, producing variations in background intensity. Some preprocessing techniques can be applied to improve the contrast of medical images, such as Contrast Limited Adaptive Histogram Equalization (CLAHE). In this work, a new type of preprocessing by leveraging certain promising quantum computation aspects was investigated. A so-called Quantum Convolutional Layer (QCL) [15] was applied to generate a multi-channel fundus image. Given a neighborhood Ω_x of size $n \times n$ where $n > 1$, around a pixel position (u, v), an encoding function e, quantum circuit parameters $\mathbf{q}$ (*e.g.*, a set of Pauli Gates), and a decoding measurement d, a Quantum Convolutional Layer transform the input data into different output channel pixel values at position (u, v), such as:

$$f_x = \mathbf{Q}(\Omega_x, e, \mathbf{q}, d), \quad f_x : \mathbb{R}^{n \times n \times 1} \to \mathbb{R}^{1 \times 1 \times (n \cdot n)}. \tag{1}$$

Furthermore, unlike the classical convolution, which convolves a filter through the image, a QCL transforms input data employing a quantum circuit. Figure 1 shows and example of a quantum circuit applied for each neighborhood Ω_x.

3.2   The Distorted Gaussian Matched Filter (D-GMF)

For this part, a new technique to incorporate curvature to the classic Gaussian Matched Filter (GMF) is presented.

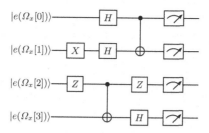

Fig. 1. An example of a quantum circuit for a neighborhood of size $n = 2$. The quantum circuit gates are randomly generated. Finally, a Pauli-Z operation is performed to obtain the decoding measurements.

The Gaussian Matched Filter (GMF). The GMF is a method for highlighting tubular structures in two-dimensional images [6]. It is motivated by the observation that a blood vessel's grayscale intensity profile resembles a one-dimensional Gaussian distribution. Under the assumption that vessels are piecewise linear structures, the GMF can be used to simultaneously identify vessel sections with the same amplitude. It is defined as follows:

$$k(x, y) = -\frac{1}{\sqrt{2\pi\sigma^2}} \exp\left(-\frac{x^2}{2\sigma^2}\right), \ \forall |x| \leq 3\sigma, \ \forall |y| \leq \frac{L}{2}, \tag{2}$$

where σ is a parameter that controls the amplitude of the Gaussian profile, and its value is selected according to the width in pixels of the structures to be highlighted. L represents the length for which said structures are assumed to be linear, *i.e.*, it corresponds to the filter's size.

Multiple variants of the original GMF have been proposed, not only in the medical area, but in any field where the detection of curvilinear objects is required [8,24,35,38]. However, GMF and its variants are based on a strong assumption about curvature, claiming that for an appropriate value of L curvilinear objects do not present a significant level of curvature and can be considered linear. Thus, parameters L and σ become fundamental for the method's good performance.

The Distorted Gaussian Matched Filter (D-GMF). The D-GMF is inspired by techniques used to generate additional data in handwriting recognition: besides the distortions that can be applied to any image (such as translations, rotations, zooming and skewing), handwritten characters can also have variations related to physical factors such as hand movement, and which can be modeled through elastic deformations [30]. Analogously, blood vessels and other curvilinear structures are not completely straight but can have a degree of curvature that makes them difficult to detect with the original GMFs. To model this curvature, an elastic deformation transformation is applied to the original GMF filter.

Elastic deformations [30] can be modeled by generating random displacement fields, Δx and Δy for horizontal and vertical directions, respectively. First, random fields Rand_x and Rand_y are generated with uniform distribution in the interval $[-1, 1]$. Then, a two-dimensional Gaussian filter with a standard deviation of β, $G(\beta)$, is convolved with said fields to ensure similar displacements around a neighborhood. Finally, a scale factor α is applied to obtain the final displacement fields, as shown in Eq. (3) and (4).

$$\Delta x = \alpha \cdot \left(\text{Rand}_x(m, n) * G(\beta) \right), \tag{3}$$

$$\Delta y = \alpha \cdot \left(\text{Rand}_y(m, n) * G(\beta) \right), \tag{4}$$

where $*$ denotes the operand of discrete convolution, and m and n are the displacement field's height and width, respectively. Then, each pixel with position (x, y) in the GMF filter, i.e., $k(x, y)$, is mapped to a new position (u, v), determined by its displacement components $\Delta x(x, y)$ and $\Delta y(x, y)$, as specified in the following equation:

$$\widetilde{k}(u, v) = k\big(x + \Delta x(x, y), y + \Delta y(x, y)\big) \tag{5}$$

The Gaussian filter $G(\beta)$ locally averages the uniform random fields: if β is very small, then Rand_x and Rand_y are practically not affected by the filter and keep their random appearance; In contrast, if β is very large, the displacements are very small (their average being close to zero), and the deformations are imperceptible; Intermediate values in the range $[4, 8]$ are recommended to obtain the appearance of elastic deformation. The value of α determines the intensity of the distortion, i.e., the curvature level in the Gaussian Matched Filter.

Figure 2 illustrates a GMF filter and its distorted versions using uniform random displacements and elastic deformations.

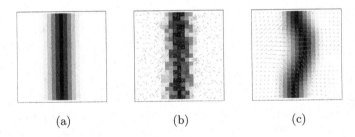

(a)   (b)   (c)

Fig. 2. (a) Original GMF filter with parameters ($\sigma = 1$, $L = 21$), (b) Distorted GMF filter using uniform random displacements in the interval $(-1, 1)$, (c) Distorted GMF filter using elastic deformations with parameters ($\beta = 4, \alpha = 30$). The green arrows represent the pixel displacement vectors.

By integrating a curvature level, the Distorted Gaussian Matched Filter (D-GMF) aims to overcome some limitations that classical GMFs have in modeling complicated shapes. In the following sections, an end-to-end convolutional neural network incorporating D-GMF filters is presented, so that amplitude and curvature can be automatically adjusted in the training phase while guiding the network's spatial attention to highlight blood vessels –or curvilinear elements in general– of the input images.

3.3   Adaptive Distorted Gaussian Matched Filters with Convolutional Neural Network

The overall D-GaussianNet architecture is presented in Fig. 3. The structure is based on the UNet [27], formed by three main parts—encoder, bottleneck, and decoder—and skip-connections between feature maps from the encoder path to the decoder path. The model proposed in this study differs from the original UNet in various aspects. First, stem blocks—formed by a D-GMF layer and two convolutional layers—have been added at the beginning and end of the network, in order to implicitly indicate that the spatial attention of the network must be focus on the curvilinear structures of the image. The D-GMFs have not been placed in levels with less dimensionality than the original image to maintain the interpretation, so the input map has the same dimensions of the original image and its spatial characteristics are mostly preserved, therefore it seems reasonable to apply the proposed filters.

Besides, the conventional convolutional blocks of each level have been replaced with residual convolutional blocks, similarly to previous works presented for segmentation of curvilinear objects in [17,39].

This modification is motivated by the nature of the model, which incorporates D-GMF blocks to perform adaptive curvilinear structures enhancement on the same neuronal architecture. This could lead to problems such as premature convergence or degradation of training accuracy. However, residual models alleviate this problem by proposing a mechanism that includes a reformulation of the convolutional block mapping function, so that they also learn a residual component between the desired transformation and the input of the block. Residual networks are concisely explained in the following paragraphs.

The Residual Model. A Residual Neural Network [13], or ResNet, is an architecture that simulates identity mapping functions inside its blocks of convolutional layers, by using shortcut connections that skip intermediate layers and directly add the input feature map of each block to its last layer.

A difficulty encountered by Deep Neural Networks is the degradation of training accuracy, which occurs when—by increasing the depth of a network—accuracy becomes saturated and degrades rapidly.

The ResNet focuses on solving this problem by explicitly posing a residual mapping layer. For a certain block of layers in the network, let x be the input feature map, $\{W_i\}$ the weights of the i-th layer and $\mathcal{H}(x)$ the desired mapping to learn, the residual between both is given by the expression:

$$\mathcal{F}(x, \{W_i\}) = \mathcal{H}(x) - x. \tag{6}$$

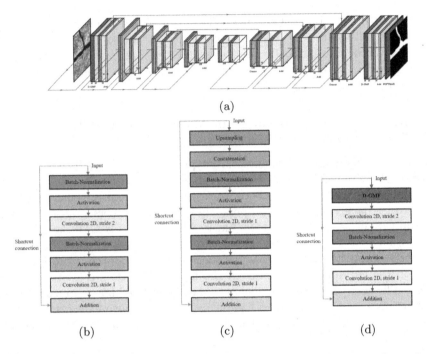

Fig. 3. D-GaussianNet overall architecture: (a) The proposed architecture with D-GMF Blocks at the beginning and end of the network; (b) Encoder Block; (c) Decoder Block; (d) Residual D-GMF block used in the proposed architecture

Assuming that it is easier to optimize the residual mapping $\mathcal{F}(x)$ than the original $\mathcal{H}(x)$—since intuitively it is simpler for a layer to learn a mapping to zero than to learn the identity function, it is proposed to reorder the above equation as:

$$\mathcal{H}(x) = \mathcal{F}(x, \{W_i\}) + x. \tag{7}$$

This change preserves the main objective of learning the desired mapping $\mathcal{H}(x)$, with the difference that at the same time, the network also learns the residual $\mathcal{F}(x, \{W_i\})$.

The residual Eq. (7) is achieved by incorporating shortcut connections that link the input feature map of a block with its output, so that both can be added. Taking advantage of this design, a Residual Architecture with adaptive D-GMFs is proposed in this study. The residual mechanism proposed for the adaptive incorporation of D-GMFs over a Deep Neural Network is described.

The Adaptive D-GMF Unit. The D-GMF Adaptive Unit consists of a convolutional layer of D-GMF filters, followed by two conventional convolutional layers, between which Batch-Normalization and ReLu-Activation are applied. The block incorporates a residual connection that connects the input of the block with the second convolution output in an Addition layer, where both feature maps are merged.

The D-GMF convolutional layer only requires the configuration of a number of filters N, while the amplitudes and curvature levels of each filter are automatically adjusted in the training phase of the neural network. The behavior of the layer is as follows, let $\{\sigma_j\}$ and $\{\alpha_j\}$ be two parameters sets that specify amplitude and curvature level of N filters in a D-GMF layer, with $1 \leq j \leq N$.S

1. Filter parameters $\{\sigma_j\}$ and $\{\alpha_j\}$ are randomly initialized,
   a. Values in $\{\sigma_j\}$ are initialized using a continuous uniform distribution in the interval (a, b), i.e., $\sigma_j \sim \mathcal{U}(a, b)$,
   b. Values in $\{\alpha_j\}$ are initialized using a continuous uniform distribution in the interval (c, d), i.e., $\alpha_j \sim \mathcal{U}(c, d)$.
   where tuple (a, b) corresponds to the lower and upper boundaries for the initial amplitude values, and tuple (c, d) corresponds to the lower and upper values for the initial curvature values.
2. For each filter f_j ,
   a. a set $\{f_j^{(\theta)}\}$ composed of rotated versions of f_j is constructed, where θ is the rotation angle, which takes evenly spaced values in the interval $[0, 2\pi)$;
   b. the filters in set $\{f_j^{(\theta)}\}$ are applied to the layer's input feature map I, obtaining responses $\{R_j^{(\theta)}\}$;
   c. the filter's output O_j is computed by keeping the maximum response at element level among the set of responses $\{R_j^{(\theta)}\}$, i.e., :

$$O_j(x, y) = \max\{R_j^{(\theta)}(x, y)\} \tag{8}$$

   where (x,y) is a position in the input feature map domain.
   d. The set of filter outputs $\{O_j\}$ constitutes the output feature map of the layer.

3.4   Datasets

The proposed model was evaluated with three public datasets: DRIVE, STARE and CHASE. The dataset DRIVE [33] consists of 40 images of 565×584 pixels, which are divided into a training set and a test set, of 20 images each; There are two sets of manually segmented images available, created by observers instructed by an expert. The dataset STARE [16] consist of 20 images of 700×605 pixels, which were manually labeled to produce ground-truth vessel segmentation images; The set contains 10 images without pathologies and 10 images with pathologies that obscure the image. The dataset CHASE [10] consist of 28 images of 999×960 pixels, acquired from 14 children from multi-ethnic schools in England; the images were manually labeled by two different observers. For STARE and CHASE datasets, training and test partitions are not provided, therefore sets of 10 and 14 images were used for training, and sets of 10 and 14 images for testing, respectively.

3.5   Performance Evaluation Metrics

The metrics considered for the evaluation of the method are Sensitivity (TPR), Specificity (TNR), Precision (PPV), Accuracy (ACC) and F1-Score (F1).

TPR refers to the proportion of pixels that are correctly classified as positive, among the total number of positive pixels. TNR measures the proportion of pixels that are correctly classified as negative, among the total number of negative pixels. PPV refers to the proportion of pixels that are correctly classified as positive, among the total number of pixels examined. ACC indicates the proportion of pixels correctly classified, both positives and negatives, among the total number of pixels examined. The F1 score is the harmonic average of the PPV and the TPR. These metrics have the following expressions.

$$\text{TPR} = \frac{\text{TP}}{\text{TP} + \text{FN}} \tag{9}$$

$$\text{TNR} = \frac{\text{TP}}{\text{TP} + \text{FN}} \tag{10}$$

$$\text{PPV} = \frac{\text{TP}}{\text{TP} + \text{FP}} \tag{11}$$

$$\text{ACC} = \frac{\text{TP} + \text{TN}}{\text{TP} + \text{FP} + \text{TN} + \text{FN}} \tag{12}$$

$$\text{F1} = 2 \cdot \frac{\text{PPV} \cdot \text{TPR}}{\text{PPV} + \text{TPR}} \tag{13}$$

Where TP represents the number of true positive pixels, TN represents the number of true negative pixels, FP represents the number false positive pixels and FN represents the number of false positive pixels.

Additionally, the performance was evaluated with the Area Under the ROC Curve (AUC), which refers to the area under a curve that allows evaluating the quality of a result by calculating the rate of change of Sensitivity (TPR) versus Specificity (TNR).

4   Experimental Results

The model was trained from scratch on random patches, extracted from the pre-processed images. As described in Sect. 3.4, each dataset was divided in training and test sets. Additionally, a 10% percentage of the training set was used as a validation set for the parameter selection. Only pixels within the Field of View (FOV) were considered in the evaluation. For the STARE and CHASE datasets, which do not provide a binary mask to identify the FOV, they were created using a manually chosen global threshold.

The patch size was modified during the training process, using a progressive resizing strategy as follows. For a total of 90 epochs, the training process was divided into three parts of 30 epoch each: first, a patch size of 24 × 24 pixels was used; then, a patch size of 32 × 32 pixels was used; finally, a patch size of 48 × 48 pixels was used. As the patch size changed, the best weights from the previous part were used to initialize the model weights. For the evaluation, ordered patches extracted from the preprocessed images, of size 48 × 48 with an overlapping of 10 pixels were used. The optimization configuration consist of the Adam optimizer with a cyclical learning rate strategy as described in [31] with an initial learning rate set to 0.005. Binary cross-entropy was used as loss function. All experiments were implemented using the Pytorch framework and an NVIDIA Tesla K80 GPU.

The proposed method was compared with various state-of-the-art methods, including methods based on complete image prediction, patch-based prediction, and pixel-based prediction (from a patch neighborhood). The evaluation was performed using the metrics presented in Sect. 3.5. From the Table 1, it is shown that the proposed method is competitive with state-of-the-art methods: for CHASEDB and DRIVE databases, it obtains the highest and second highest score in the F1 metric, respectively; for STARE and DRIVE databases, it obtains the highest and second highest value in TPR, respectively, and the second-best value in ACC for both cases.

Table 1. Performance comparison against state-of-the-art methods on DRIVE, STARE and CHASE datasets.

Dataset	Method/Author	TPR	TNR	AUC	ACC	F1
DRIVE	DNN/Liskowski et al. [23]	0.7811	0.9807	0.9790	0.9535	–
	CcNet/Feng et al. [9]	0.7625	*0.9809*	0.9678	0.9528	–
	DUNet/Jin et al. [19]	**0.7963**	0.9800	*0.9802*	0.9566	**0.8237**
	IterNet/Li et al. [21]	0.7791	**0.9831**	**0.9813**	**0.9574**	*0.8218*
	Proposed method	*0.7960*	0.9799	0.9772	*0.9565*	*0.8233*
STARE	DNN/Liskowski et al. [23]	0.7448	0.9828	0.9720	0.9525	–
	CcNet/Feng et al. [9]	0.7709	0.9848	0.9700	0.9633	–
	DUNet/Jin et al. [19]	0.7595	*0.9878*	0.9832	0.9641	*0.8143*
	IterNet/Li et al. [21]	*0.7715*	**0.9886**	**0.9881**	**0.9701**	**0.8146**
	Proposed method	**0.7904**	0.9843	*0.9837*	*0.9647*	0.8141
CHASEDB	DUNet/Jin et al. [19]	**0.8155**	0.9752	*0.9804*	*0.9610*	0.7883
	IterNet/Li et al. [21]	*0.7970*	**0.9823**	**0.9851**	**0.9655**	*0.8073*
	Proposed method	0.7530	**0.9863**	0.9798	0.9609	**0.8077**

5   Conclusions

In this paper, a novel end-to-end convolutional neural network for the automatic retinal vessel segmentation was proposed. Herein, a new variant of the Gaussian Matched Filters that incorporates curvature to the filter was presented. It improves the modeling of curvilinear structures, detecting tortuosity and other intricate shapes in vessels. The incorporation of distorted Gaussian Matched filters on a residual convolutional architecture allowed the amplitude and curvature parameters to be adjusted automatically, based on the input images. Additionally, a Quantum Convolutional Layer was incorporated as a new type of preprocessing. The experimental results show that the proposed method has a competitive performance with the state-of-the-art methods, and even surpasses in terms of sensitivity to the state-of-the-art methods for the STARE database, and in terms of F1-score for the CHASE database.

References

1. Abramoff, M.D., Garvin, M.K., Sonka, M.: Retinal imaging and image analysis. IEEE Rev. Biomed. Eng. **3**, 169–208 (2010)
2. Acar, E., Yilmaz, I.: Covid-19 detection on IBM quantum computer with classical-quantum transfer learning. medRxiv (2020)
3. Amil, P., Reyes-Manzano, C.F., Guzmán-Vargas, L., Sendiña-Nadal, I., Masoller, C.: Network-based features for retinal fundus vessel structure analysis. PloS one **14**(7), e0220132 (2019)
4. Badawi, S.A., Fraz, M.M.: Optimizing the trainable B-COSFIRE filter for retinal blood vessel segmentation. PeerJ **6**, e5855 (2018)
5. Chalakkala, R.J., Abdullaa, W.H., Hongb, S.C.: Fundus retinal image analyses for screening and diagnosing diabetic retinopathy, macular edema, and glaucoma disorders. Diabetes and Fundus OCT, p. 59 (2020)
6. Chaudhuri, S., Chatterjee, S., Katz, N., Nelson, M., Goldbaum, M.: Detection of blood vessels in retinal images using two-dimensional matched filters. IEEE Transactions on medical imaging **8**(3), 263–269 (1989)
7. Condurache, A.P., Mertins, A.: Segmentation of retinal vessels with a hysteresis binary-classification paradigm. Comput. Medi. Imaging Graph. **36**(4), 325–335 (2012)
8. Cruz-Aceves, I., Cervantes-Sanchez, F., Avila-Garcia, M.S.: A novel multiscale gaussian-matched filter using neural networks for the segmentation of x-ray coronary angiograms. J. Healthcare Eng. **2018** (2018). https://doi.org/10.1155/2018/5812059
9. Feng, S., Zhuo, Z., Pan, D., Tian, Q.: CcNet: a cross-connected convolutional network for segmenting retinal vessels using multi-scale features. Neurocomputing **392**, 268–276 (2020)
10. Fraz, M.M., et al.: Ensemble classification system applied for retinal vessel segmentation on child images containing various vessel profiles. In: Campilho, A., Kamel, M. (eds.) Image Analysis and Recognition, pp. 380–389. Springer, Heidelberg (2012)
11. Fu, Q., Li, S., Wang, X.: MSCNN-AM:: a multi-scale convolutional neural network with attention mechanisms for retinal vessel segmentation. IEEE Access **8**, 163926–163936 (2020)
12. Geng, L., Li, P., Zhu, W., Chen, X.: M2E-Net: multiscale morphological enhancement network for retinal vessel segmentation. In: Pen, Y., et al. (eds.) PRCV 2020, Part. LNCS, vol. 12305, pp. 493–502. Springer, Cham (2020). https://doi.org/10.1007/978-3-030-60633-6_41
13. He, K., Zhang, X., Ren, S., Sun, J.: Deep residual learning for image recognition. In: Proceedings of the IEEE Conference on Computer Vision and Pattern Recognition, pp. 770–778 (2016)

14. Heidari, S., Naseri, M., Nagata, K.: Quantum selective encryption for medical images. Int. J. Theor. Phys. **58**(11), 3908–3926 (2019)

15. Henderson, M., Shakya, S., Pradhan, S., Cook, T.: Quanvolutional neural networks: powering image recognition with quantum circuits. Quant. Mach. Intell. **2**(1), 1–9 (2020). https://doi.org/10.1007/s42484-020-00012-y

16. Hoover, A., Kouznetsova, V., Goldbaum, M.: Locating blood vessels in retinal images by piecewise threshold probing of a matched filter response. IEEE Trans. Med. Imaging **19**(3), 203–210 (2000)

17. Huang, G., Liu, Z., Van Der Maaten, L., Weinberger, K.Q.: Densely connected convolutional networks. In: Proceedings of the IEEE Conference on Computer Vision and Pattern Recognition, pp. 4700–4708 (2017)

18. Jiang, Z., Zhang, H., Wang, Y., Ko, S.B.: Retinal blood vessel segmentation using fully convolutional network with transfer learning. Comput. Med. Imaging Graph. **68**, 1–15 (2018)

19. Jin, Q., Meng, Z., Pham, T.D., Chen, Q., Wei, L., Su, R.: DUNet: a deformable network for retinal vessel segmentation. Knowl.-Based Syst. **178**, 149–162 (2019)

20. Khan, M.A.U., Khan, T.M., Bailey, D.G., Soomro, T.A.: A generalized multi-scale line-detection method to boost retinal vessel segmentation sensitivity. Pattern Anal. Appl. **22**(3), 1177–1196 (2018). https://doi.org/10.1007/s10044-018-0696-1

21. Li, L., Verma, M., Nakashima, Y., Nagahara, H., Kawasaki, R.: Iternet: retinal image segmentation utilizing structural redundancy in vessel networks. In: The IEEE Winter Conference on Applications of Computer Vision, pp. 3656–3665 (2020)

22. Liew, G., Wang, J.J.: Retinal vascular signs: a window to the heart? Revista Española de Cardiologia **64**(6), 515–521 (2011)

23. Liskowski, P., Krawiec, K.: Segmenting retinal blood vessels with deep neural networks. IEEE Trans. Med. Imaging **35**(11), 2369–2380 (2016)

24. Maharana, D.K., Das, P.: Automatic extraction of vessels from newly accessible dataset. In: Soft Computing: Theories and Applications, pp. 1139–1150. Springer (2020). https://doi.org/10.1007/978-981-15-0751-9_105

25. Mo, J., Zhang, L.: Multi-level deep supervised networks for retinal vessel segmentation. Int. J. Comput. Assist. Radiol. Surg. **12**(12), 2181–2193 (2017). https://doi.org/10.1007/s11548-017-1619-0

26. Pal, S., Chatterjee, S., Dey, D., Munshi, S.: Morphological operations with iterative rotation of structuring elements for segmentation of retinal vessel structures. Multidimens. Syst. Signal Process. **30**(1), 373–389 (2018). https://doi.org/10.1007/s11045-018-0561-9

27. Ronneberger, O., Fischer, P., Brox, T.: U-Net: convolutional networks for biomedical image segmentation. In: Navab, N., Hornegger, J., Wells, W.M., Frangi, A.F. (eds.) MICCAI 2015 Part III. LNCS, vol. 9351, pp. 234–241. Springer, Cham (2015). https://doi.org/10.1007/978-3-319-24574-4_28

28. Sazak, Ç., Nelson, C.J., Obara, B.: The multiscale bowler-hat transform for blood vessel enhancement in retinal images. Pattern Recognit. **88**, 739–750 (2019)

29. Birgui Sekou, T., Hidane, M., Olivier, J., Cardot, H.: Retinal blood vessel segmentation using a fully convolutional network – transfer learning from patch- to image-level. In: Shi, Y., Suk, H.-I., Liu, M. (eds.) MLMI 2018. LNCS, vol. 11046, pp. 170–178. Springer, Cham (2018). https://doi.org/10.1007/978-3-030-00919-9_20

30. Simard, P.Y., Steinkraus, D., Platt, J.C., et al.: Best practices for convolutional neural networks applied to visual document analysis. In: ICDAR, vol. 3 (2003)

31. Smith, L.N.: Cyclical learning rates for training neural networks. In: 2017 IEEE Winter Conference on Applications of Computer Vision (WACV), pp. 464–472. IEEE (2017)

32. Soomro, T.A., Khan, T.M., Khan, M.A., Gao, J., Paul, M., Zheng, L.: Impact of ICA-based image enhancement technique on retinal blood vessels segmentation. IEEE Access **6**, 3524–3538 (2018)

33. Staal, J., Abramoff, M., Niemeijer, M., Viergever, M., van Ginneken, B.: Ridge based vessel segmentation in color images of the retina. IEEE Trans. Med. Imaging **23**(4), 501–509 (2004)

34. Tamim, N., Elshrkawey, M., Abdel Azim, G., Nassar, H.: Retinal blood vessel segmentation using hybrid features and multi-layer perceptron neural networks. Symmetry **12**(6), 894 (2020)

35. Trujillo, M.C.R., Alarcón, T.E., Dalmau, O.S., Ojeda, A.Z.: Segmentation of carbon nanotube images through an artificial neural network. Soft Comput. **21**(3), 611–625 (2017)

36. Wang, X., Jiang, X.: Retinal vessel segmentation by a divide-and-conquer funnel-structured classification framework. Signal Process. **165**, 104–114 (2019)

37. Zapata, M.A., et al.: Artificial intelligence to identify retinal fundus images, quality validation, laterality evaluation, macular degeneration, and suspected glaucoma. Clin. Ophthalmol. **14**, 419 (2020). (Auckland, NZ)

38. Zhang, A., Wang, K.C., Yang, E., Li, J.Q., Chen, C., Qiu, Y.: Pavement lane marking detection using matched filter. Measurement **130**, 105–117 (2018)

39. Zhang, Z., Liu, Q., Wang, Y.: Road extraction by deep residual u-net. IEEE Geosci. Remote Sens. Lett. **15**(5), 749–753 (2018)

40. ZhaoZhao, J., et al.: Automatic retinal vessel segmentation using multi-scale super-pixel chain tracking. Digit. Signal Process. **81**, 26–42 (2018)

41. Zhou, M., Jin, K., Wang, S., Ye, J., Qian, D.: Color retinal image enhancement based on luminosity and contrast adjustment. IEEE Trans. Biomed. Eng. **65**(3), 521–527 (2017)

Author Index

Printed in the United States
by Baker & Taylor Publisher Services